GW00372003

CART OFFICIAL GUIDE TO ISRAEL

and Complete Gazetteer to all Sites in the Holy Land

The State of Israel
Ministry of Defence Publishing House

Carta, The Israel Map & Publishing Co. Ltd.

NOTE
Great care has been taken to ensure that the information contained in this Guide is accurate and up-to-date. However, the publishers cannot be responsible for any consequences arising from errors, omissions or misleading information.

We shall be grateful for corrections of errors and inaccuracies sent to:
Carta, P.O. Box 2500,
Jerusalem 91024, Israel.

Second English edition

ISBN 965–220–089–1

Printed in Israel

FOREWORD

Carta's Official Guide to Israel, a comprehensive handbook, has two sections: the gazetteer — which is a complete alphabetical listing of every named site in areas under Israel's jursidiction, and a concise survey of historical and modern Israel.

Facts included in the gazetteer have been compiled from scholarly and other official sources and augmented by firsthand information obtained from municipalities, local councils and local residents. The information thus collected should satisfy varied interests.

Alongside the name of each entry is a grid reference made up of six digits whereby its location can be found on Israel maps: the first three digits are read on the map from west to east and the last three from south to north. Biblical place names carry a reference denoting one significant passage where this name appears in the Old or New Testament.

Transcription of proper names presents a variety of choices. First are the many English translations of the Bible. There is the official transliteration system, sponsored by the Hebrew language academy, of rendering Hebrew and Arabic letters into Latin characters. There are various scientific methods, as well as everyday usage of newspapers and magazines. Variations, though, are in the main minor and names are generally easily recognizable in any of these versions. We have rendered Hebrew and Arabic names according to the official transliteration system. Biblical names appear as they are written in the Bible published by the American Bible Society. Names with an accepted and familiar form in English appear thus: Acre, Galilee, Tiberias, Nazareth, Bethlehem etc. For the maps a simplified system of transcription has been used.

We are deeply indebted to the editors of the original editions of the Hebrew *Kol Maqom* which was first published in the early 50's. The original slim book was compiled by the Chief Education Officer of the Israel Defence Forces. The last printing of the original took place in 1967. A new expanded and revised edition for which Adam Druks, Ze'ev Yeivin, Baruch Sarel, Dan Schleyer and many others did yeoman's service, is published jointly by Carta and the Ministry of Defence.

For this English edition we would like to express gratitude to Moshe Shalvi who shouldered the great task of translating the gazetteer into English; also to Robert Kaplan who adapted and expanded articles on favoured tourist sites. The Historical Survey was written by Beverly Cayford, Benjamin Jaffe, and Moshe Aumann. Similarly we would like to thank all those who are listed in the original Hebrew work and others to whom we have expressed our thanks verbally.

The Publishers.

CONTENTS

LIST OF MAPS

KEY TO SYMBOLS

Type of Settlement

- Jewish city
- Arab city
- Jewish local council
- Arab local council
- Jewish farm
- Arab farm
- Moshav
- Arab village
- Kibbutz
- Naḥal outpost
- Educational institute
- Bedouin encampment
- Abandoned Arab settlement
- Regional rural centre

Economic Branches

- Industry
- Transport
- Petrol station
- Garage
- Fishing
- Dairy
- Poultry
- Sheep
- Grains, cereals
- Orchards
- Vegetables
- Vineyards
- Tobacco
- Olives
- Nursery

Sites and Institutions

- National park
- Nature reserve
- Scenic spot
- Parking
- Youth hostel
- Hotel
- Rest-house
- Field school
- Yeshiva
- University
- Archaeological site
- Museum
- Memorial
- Amphitheatre
- Stadium
- Picnic site
- Campsite
- Synagogue
- Mosque
- Church, monastery
- Druze place of worship
- Holy site

KEY TO WORDS OFTEN APPEARING IN PLACE NAMES:

Hebrew

Bat — daughter
Be'er — well
Ben — son
Berekha — pool
Bet — house
Biq'a — valley
Derekh — way
'Emeq — valley
'En — spring
Even — stone
Gan — garden
Giv'a — hill
Har — mount
Ḥawwa — farm
Ḥurba — ruin
Ḥursha — wood
Kefar — village
Ma'ale — ascent
Mappal — waterfall
Ma'yan — spring
Me'ara — cave
Meẓad — fort
Migdal — tower
Mishmar — guardpost
Miẓpe — look-out point
Naḥal — river, stream
Naḥal — agricultural, military settlement
Newe — fertile dwelling place
Nir — field
Or — light
Qirya — town, suburb
Rama — hill
Rosh — summit
Sede — field
Sha'ar — gate
Shemura — reserve
Tel — mound
Ya'ar — forest
Yad — memorial

Arabic

Abu — father
Bab — gate
Balad — city, town
Bani — sons of
Beit — house
Bilad — country, state
Bint — daughter
Bir — well
Birke — pool
Burj — fort
Deir — courtyard, monastery, church
Dur, dar — house with courtyard
'Ein — spring
Ḥamma — hot springs
Ḥammam — hot baths
Jabal — mount
Jazira — island
Kafr — village
Khirbe — ruin
Maghara — cave
Majdal — tower
Mar — Christian saint
Nabi — prophet
Naqb — mountain pass
Qabr — tomb
Qal'a — fort
Qaṣr — palace
Ras — summit
Rujm — stone mound
Sabkha — salt pan
Sheikh — elder, tribe chief
Tal'a — ascent
Tariq — road, way
Tell — mound

GLOSSARY

Abandoned village
Arab village abandoned as a result of one of the wars between Israel and the Arab states.

Acropolis
Elevated part of the city, usually fortified and housing government buildings, temples and major storehouses.

'Alawites
Sect of Shi'ite Moslems inhabiting N Syria.

'Aliyah
Immigration of Jews to Israel

First Aliyah	1882-1903
Second Aliyah	1904-1918
Third Aliyah	1919-1923

Amoraim
Jewish sages of the Talmudic Period (3rd-5th c.)

Betar
Zionist youth movement founded 1923; abbreviated name for Berit Trumpeldor.

Bilu
Acronym for *Bet Ya'aqov Lekhu WeNelkha* (Isa. 2:5); pioneers of the First Aliyah.

Columbarium
Structure or cave with tiers of niches, used for burial in Roman Period.

Development town
Settlement established to develop new areas and to promote immigrant absorption.

Dolmen
Megalithic monument associated with burial rites.

Dunam
A unit of land equal to about ¼ acre.

Dressed stone
Hewn building stone. First used during period of the Monarchy.

Glacis
Embankment sloping down from fort, used to heighten defensive walls and expose attackers to fire.

Haganah
Underground Jewish defence organization founded before establishment of the State.

HaKibbutz HaMeuḥad
Union of *kibbutzim* founded by Third Aliyah pioneers in 1927.

HaPo'el HaMizraḥi
Religious Zionist movement founded 1922; later formed the National Religious Party.

HaPo'el HaẒa'ir
Labour party founded by pioneers of Second Aliyah in 1905.

HaShomer
Watchmen organization of Jewish settlers established during Ottoman Period.

HaShomer HaẒa'ir
Socialist-Zionist pioneering movement founded in Poland before WWI.

HeḤaluẓ
Federation of Socialist-Zionist pioneer youth movement until WWII.

Ḥibbat Ẓion
"Love of Zion" movement formulated in Russia and which produced the First Aliyah (1882).

ICA
Jewish Colonization Association — land society founded by Baron de Hirsch to promote settlement (1900-1924).

Khan
Caravanserai used from Arab Period onwards.

Kibbutz
Sizable commune constituting a settlement based mainly on agriculture but engaging also in industry.

Ma'bara
Immigrant transit camp set up in early 1950's.

Maqam
Holy Arab shrine.

Mishnah
Legal codification of basic Jewish law.

Moshav
Cooperative small holder's agricultural village combining features of both cooperative and private farming.

Moshava (Agricultural village)
Jewish village set up in Turkish Period in which farming was conducted on individual farms, mostly on privately-owned lands.

Moshav shittufi
Agricultural village whose members possess individual homesteads but where the agriculture and economy are conducted as a collective unit.

Naḥal outpost
Agricultural-military settlement usually located near the border or some other strategic location and operated by a regular unit of the Israel Defence Forces.

Onomasticon of Eusebius
A classification of Bible places and gospels, written ca. 324, arranged alphabetically and identified according to contemporary sites.

Ostracon
Ink-inscribed sherd.

Palmaḥ
Striking arm of the Haganah.

PICA
Palestine Jewish Colonization Association — land society, founded by Baron Edmond de Rothschild to promote colonization (1924-1957).

Po'alei Ẓion
Socialist-Zionist movement founded by Ber Borochov in 1907.

Sarcophagus
Stone coffin, often inscribed with sculptural reliefs.

"Stockade and watch-tower" settlement
Type of settlement established during Disturbances of 1936-1939 (mainly in areas of Bet She'an Valley and the Galilee) to provide immediate security against Arab attacks. Surrounded by defensive wall and dominated by a central watch-tower, hence name.

Talmud
Interpretation and elaboration of Mishnah.

Tannaim
Jewish sages of the Mishnaic Period (1st-3rd c.).

Tegart police fort
Network of police forts established during British Mandate, named after Sir Charles Tegart, British specialist on terrorist raids.

Tel
Artificial mound composed of layers of ruins from ancient settlements.

Tumulus (pl. Tumuli)
Mound of earth or stones used to cover a dolmen.

Undressed stone
Unhewn building stone.

Yishuv
Jewish cummunity in Ereẓ Israel during pre-State period.

ABBREVIATIONS

b.	—	ben (son of)
c.	—	century
ca.	—	circa
d.	—	dunam
E	—	east, eastern
Kh.	—	Khirbet (ruin)
N	—	north, northern
pop.	—	population
S	—	south, southern
W	—	west, western

CHRONOLOGICAL TABLE

PREHISTORIC PERIODS

Paleolithic (Early Stone Age) ca. 500,000-15,000 BCE
Lower — 500,000-120,000
Middle — 120,000-35,000
Upper — 35,000-15,000

Mesolithic or Epipaleolithic (Middle Stone Age) 15,000-8,000 BCE

Neolithic (New Stone Age) 8,000-3,150 BCE
Pre-pottery — 8,000-5,500
Pottery — 5,500-4,000
Chalcolithic — 4,000-3,150

HISTORICAL PERIODS IN EREẒ ISRAEL

Early Bronze Age 3150-2200 BCE

I A-C	3150-2850	
II	2850-2650	
III	2650-2350	
IV	2350-2200	

Middle Bronze Age 2200-1550 BCE

I	2200-2000	
IIA	2000-1750	
	ca.1800-1570	Patriarchal Period
IIB	1750-1550	Wanderings of Jacob
	ca. 1720	Hyksos conquer Egypt
	ca. 1570	Hyksos driven from Egypt

Late Bronze Age 1550-1200 BCE

I	1550-1400	
	1468	Hyksos defeated near Megiddo
IIA	1400-1300	
IIB	1300-1200	
	ca. 1250	Moses leads Exodus from Egypt
	ca. 1220	Joshua enters Canaan: Philistines conquer coast

Iron Age 1200-586 BCE

IA	1200-1150	The Judges
IB	1150-1000	
	ca. 1025-1004	Kingdom of Saul
IIA	1000-900	
	1004-965	Kingdom of David
	965-928	Kingdom of Solomon (Building of First Temple)
	928	Israel and Judah separate

IIB	900-800	
	871-851	Ahab King of Israel
IIC	800-586	
	722	Israel destroyed by Assyrians
	722-628	Assyrian rule
	586	Jerusalem and First Temple destroyed by Babylonians

Babylonian and Persian Period 586-332 BCE

586-538	Babylonian Captivity
539	Cyrus of Persia conquers Babylon
538	Cyrus' Edict and Return to Zion
516	Building of Second Temple
332	Alexander the Great conquers Palestine

Hellenistic Period 332-167 BCE

	Diadochi rule
200	Seleucids take Palestine from Ptolemies of Egypt
167	Maccabean Revolt

Hasmonean Period 167-63 BCE

	Hasmonean Kingdom: Roman intervention
63	Pompey subjects Judea to Rome

Roman Period 63 BCE-324 CE

I	63 BCE-70 CE	
	37-4 BCE	Herod the Great
	27-30 CE	Ministry of Jesus of Nazareth
	66	First Revolt against Rome
	70	Destruction of Second Temple
II	70-180	
	73	Fall of Masada
	132	Bar Kokhba revolt
	135	Fall of Bethther
III	180-324	
		Mishnaic Period
	210	Redaction of the Mishnah

Byzantine Period 324-640

I	324-451	
	325	Christianity named religion of Roman Empire
		Christian rule
	ca. 400	Completion of the Jerusalem Talmud
	330	Capital of empire moved to Constantinople
II	451-640	Persian conquest
	529	Samaritan revolt
	610-632	Muḥammad expounds Islam
	614	Persians sack Jerusalem
	622	Muḥammad moves to Medina: beginning of Moslem calendar
	629	Byzantines recover Jerusalem
	634-644	Caliph Omar Ibn el Khattab
	636	Arabs defeat Byzantines at Yarmuk River

Early Arab Period 640-1099

660-749	Umayyad caliphate
749-1258	Abbasid caliphate
996-1021	Fatimid Caliph Hakim the Mad
1071	Seljuk Turks take Jerusalem
1095	Pope Urban II calls First Crusade
1099	Crusaders take Jerusalem

Crusader Period 1099-1291

1171-1193	Saladin
1187	Saladin defeats Crusaders at Horns of Hattin
1189-1192	Third Crusade
1250	Mamluks replace Ayyubids in Egypt
1260	Mamluks defeat Mongols
1291	Mamluks capture last Crusader stronghold

Mamluk Period 1291-1516

ca. 1400	Tamerlane attacks Middle East
1453	Ottomans take Constantinople; end of Byzantine Empire
1516	Ottomans take Palestine

Ottoman (Turkish) Period 1516-1918

1537-1541	Suleiman I the Magnificent rebuilds walls of Jerusalem
1799	Napoleon Bonaparte repulsed at 'Akko
1831	Palestine taken by Muḥammad Ali
1882 ff.	First Aliyah
1897	First Zionist Congress
1904 ff.	Second Aliyah
1917	British capture Jerusalem; Balfour Declaration

British (Mandate) Period 1918-1948

1920	British Mandate over Palestine
1921	Arabs riot
1929	Arabs riot
1936-1939	Arabs riots and strike
1939-1945	Second World War. Six million Jews killed by Nazis
1947	U.N. General Assembly decides on partition of Palestine

State of Israel 1948 ff.

1948	State of Israel proclaimed; War of Independence
1956	Suez Campaign
1967	Six-Day War
1969	War of Attrition at Suez Canal
1973	Yom Kippur War
1979	Peace agreement signed between Israel and Egypt
1982	Completion of Israel's withdrawal from Sinai as part of peace with Egypt
1982	Operation "Peace for Galilee"

HISTORICAL SURVEY

INTRODUCTION

Five kilometres north of the old walled city of Jerusalem, just off the ancient highway to Nablus, is a hill. Looking east from this hill, on a clear day one can glimpse the waters of the Dead Sea in the Rift Valley far below, and across the valley the brown hills that once were Gilead and Moab and today are Jordan.

Travelling west from Jerusalem on the main road to Jaffa and Tel Aviv, one winds around hill after hill, steep and rounded and sparsely covered with new forest, until suddenly one is halfway down the last line of foothills and looking across a broad, flat plain toward a horizon obscured by the dust of the Libyan desert blowing over the sea.

The Crusader castle of Belvoir stood on a 500 metre promontory south of Lake Kinneret, facing the hills of Jordan. Its defenders watched as, from the deep slash of the Yarmuk River Valley that divides the Golan from Gilead, Saladin led his troops to destroy the Crusader kingdom. Standing in the ruins of Belvoir's main gate, one looks down today on the broad, fertile farmland of the northern Jordan Valley, with Lake Kinneret to the left and beyond it in the distance the snow-covered peak of Mount Hermon.

From Masada, Herod's nearly impregnable rock fortress above the Dead Sea where the last of the Jewish rebels fought the Romans in 73 CE, one looks out over sheer towering cliffs to the salt-encrusted flats below, and south to the sea's shallows that in dry years served as a bridge for camel caravans bringing goods from the north and east. The cold winter wind from the Negev is a harsh version of the breezes that once cooled Herod's summer palace.

The uneven topography of Israel provides many high points commanding wide and interesting views. The landscape is impressive in itself, extremely varied in form, in vegetation and in climate. But in addition, one can perceive in its varied features some of the factors behind the events that invest each place with historical significance.

The land of which Israel is a part rises from a Coastal Plain in the west to a central spine of mountains running from Lebanon to the Sinai Desert, and then drops suddenly to the deep depression of the Rift Valley, a geological feature running through part of the continents of Africa and Asia. Across the valley, in Jordan, the land rises to another line of hills, beyond which the vast Syrian Desert stretches into the distance. The Coastal Plain, the western hills, the Rift Valley, and the eastern hills together form a corridor less than one hundred and fifty kilometres wide between the sea and the desert. This narrow strip of country was until recently the only land passage between Egypt, Africa and Arabia to the south and the empires of Asia to the north and east. For centuries it has been the contested frontier of great states, the battleground of tribal kings and huge empires. Many of its sites have been occupied for millennia. Many others, once jealously guarded, are now abandoned.

ISRAEL AND HER NEIGHBOURS

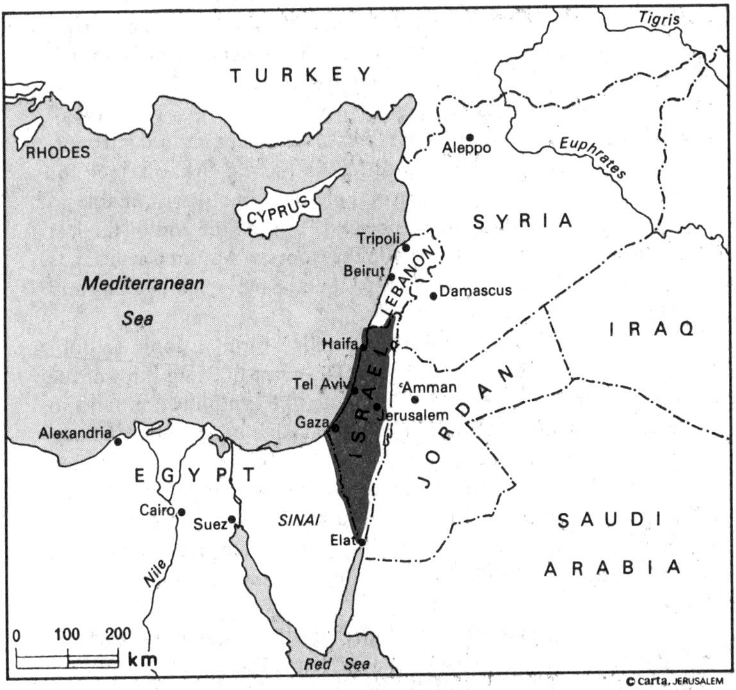

© carta, JERUSALEM

While its position has been the major factor in this area's turbulent political history, the availability of water has always determined the use to which the land itself has been put. Agriculture and husbandry in some form, from vineyards to olive trees to goat herds on the steppes, have long been the occupation of most of the inhabitants, and water decides the possibilities. Rainfall decreases generally from north to south and from west to east. Springs exist in a number of places. Though few of Israel's many rivers flow all year round, people have supplemented their natural supplies by bringing in water through aqueducts, canals and pipes. Where there is fresh water there is growth; and it is the variation in the use of the land as much as in its physical forms that gives such different characters to each part of the country.

THE LAND

The Coastal Plain

The coastline of Israel begins at the Ladder of Tyre, where the mountains of Upper Galilee reach the sea in chalk cliffs. From this point a narrow, crescent-shaped plain, the Zevulun Valley, extends to Haifa, where another mountain spur, the Mount Carmel Range, meets the sea. South of Mount Carmel the littoral gradually widens into the flat, rich Plain of Sharon, with its farmlands, orchards and fishponds. South of Tel Aviv the land rises into the low, rolling hills of ancient Philistia. Beyond these lies another region, the desert wilderness of the Negev. A narrow band of sand dunes runs down the coast, beginning north of Tel Aviv and widening slowly, until it suddenly sweeps eastward into the Negev.

The coastline north of Mount Carmel is broken by the curve of Haifa Bay. Its northern point forms an excellent natural harbour, on which stands the old city of ‘Akko (Acre); ‘Akko served for centuries as the leading port of Palestine, but it was unable to handle the large ships that appeared towards the end of the last century. Haifa, across the bay on the slopes of Mount Carmel, has become Israel's most important port and a major commercial and industrial centre.

South of Mount Carmel the shoreline forms a long, smooth curve. It has no natural harbours. The coast-hugging ships of the ancient world had to follow this route to Egypt, however, and so ports were created wherever any natural advantage offered. Caesarea was an ancient anchorage from which Herod the Great created a splendid port city, for six hundred years the capital of Palestine and later a Crusader port. To the south Ashqelon, now an archaeological park, and Gaza offered ships fresh water from wells. The modern port of Ashdod is a man-made deepwater harbour and industrial centre in the south.

The oldest port on this coast, perhaps the oldest in the world, is Jaffa, near which grew Israel's largest city, Tel Aviv. While Jaffa's old harbour has been restored as a picturesque tourist spot, the new city to the north has become a modern urban centre. With over a million people in its metropolitan area, Tel Aviv is the economic and cultural centre of Israel. Ben-Gurion airport is nearby; no part of the Coastal Plain, in which most of Israel's industry and population are concentrated, is more that 150 kilometres away. The suburbs of Tel Aviv include seaside resorts, museums, Tel Aviv University, and the orthodox town Bene Beraq. Polished diamonds are one of Israel's leading exports, and the diamond exchange at Ramat Gan is one of the biggest in the world.

GEOGRAPHICAL REGIONS

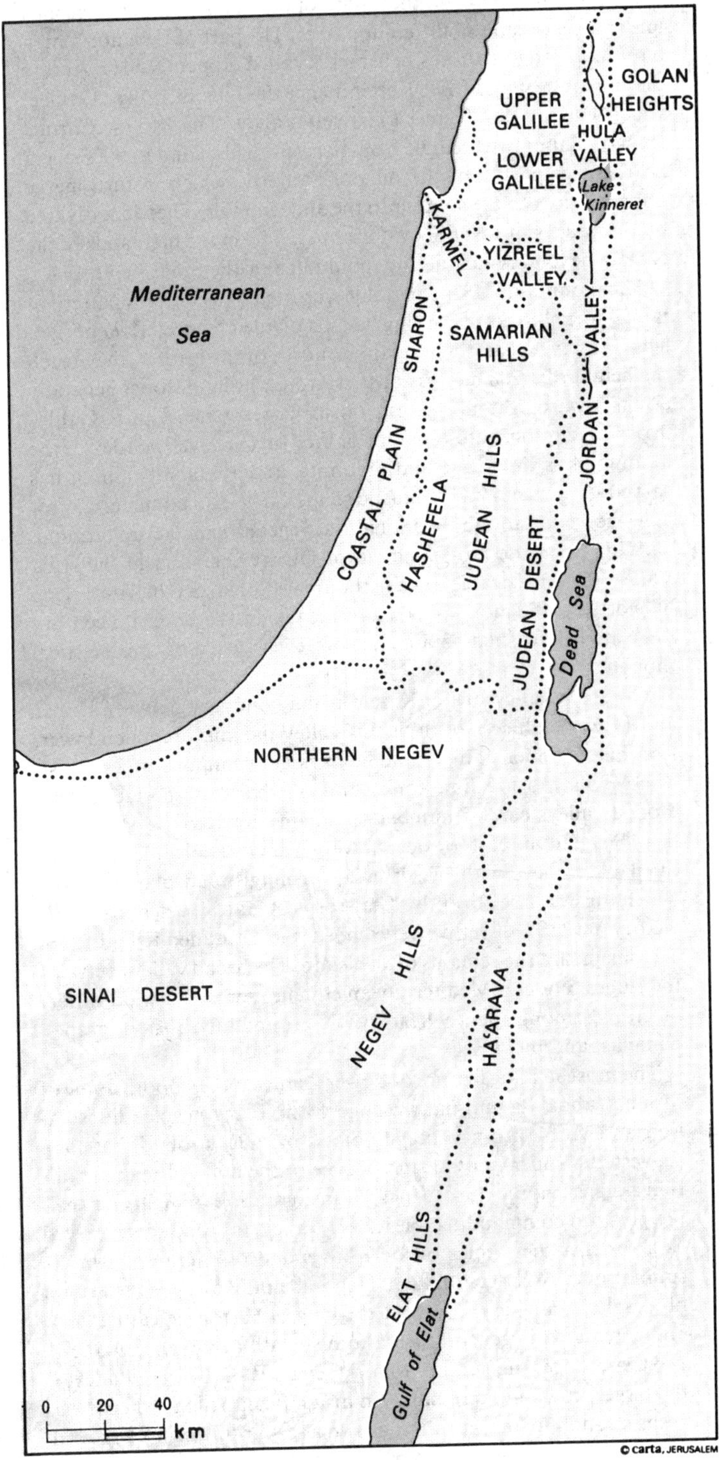
GOLAN
HEIGHTS
UPPER
GALILEE
HULA
VALLEY
LOWER
GALILEE
Lake
Kinneret
KARMEL
YIZRE'EL
VALLEY
Mediterranean
Sea
SHARON
SAMARIAN
HILLS
JORDAN
VALLEY
COASTAL
PLAIN
HASHEFELA
JUDEAN
HILLS
JUDEAN
DESERT
JUDEAN
DESERT
Dead
Sea
NORTHERN
NEGEV
SINAI
DESERT
NEGEV
HILLS
HA'ARAVA
ELAT
HILLS
Gulf
of
Elat
0
20
40
km
© carta, JERUSALEM

The mountains that run the length of the country fall into groups under a succession of different names. The part of Lebanon's high mountain range that lies in Israel is called Upper Galilee. Across the narrow valley of Bet Kerem begin the hills of Lower Galilee, which end at the Jezreel (Yizre'el) Valley. The Mount Carmel Range, running at an angle from the central highland to the sea, is a northern extension of the hills of Samaria, which in turn merge imperceptibly to the south into the Judean Hills. These are divided by the valleys of Be'er Sheva' and 'Arad from the highlands of the Negev, beyond which lie the mountains of the Sinai Peninsula.

The mountains of Upper Galilee, created by a complex pattern of faults, form blocks of varying heights divided by deep river gorges. Though lower than the mountains north of the border, they reach the height of 1,208 metres at Mt. Meron. The land slopes generally down towards the northwest; on its eastern side, Upper Galilee drops precipitously to the floor of the Ḥula valley. The rock of the mountains is limestone and dolomite, and abundant rainfall has carved its surfaces into fantastic shapes. The eroded material provides good soil for abundant natural vegetation and crop farming.

Aside from the modern town of Qiryat Shemona in the Ḥula Valley, the only sizable town in the area is Safed, perched on a steep hillside near the mountains' eastern edge. In the sixteenth century CE, Safed flourished as a centre of Jewish learning and mystical thought.

The steep valley of Bet Kerem is the boundary between Upper and Lower Galilee. South of this valley the hills are much lower, less than 600 metres high, and lie in ridges running east and west. These hills too are limestone,. and on the western side heavily eroded valleys carry a number of streams down to the Mediterranean Sea. On the eastern side, however, ancient volcanic eruptions filled old valleys with basalt lava, forming broad plateaus from which the hills rise abruptly. The Horns of Hattin, where Saladin's victory in 1187 CE effectively ended the Crusader Kingdom of Jerusalem, are the remains of a volcano. The broad valleys between the ridges, under a Mediterranean climate, support a wide variety of crops, among them wheat, beets, groundnuts, cotton, grapes, bananas, and melons.

The most striking feature of Lower Galilee is the smooth dome of Mount Tabor. Its unusually regular form, rising in splendid isolation and visible from vantage points for miles around, has long suggested a super-natural significance to the mind of man. Tradition assigns it as the site of Jesus's transfiguration. A highly defensible position commanding the Jezreel Valley, for centuries it served as a fort for the armies of local kings and of empires. From its summit in the 12th century BCE Deborah and Barak led the armies of Israel against the chariots of the king of Ḥazor, defeatıng them and driving their general Sisera to his death at the tent of Jael.

Nazareth, on the summit of a ridge above the Jezreel Valley, is the largest town in these hills. An insignificant village when it was Jesus's childhood home, it has grown as a spiritual centre for Arab

Christians. A Jewish town too, Naẓrat 'Ilit, has grown up alongside it. The town is connected by a major road with Haifa on the coast and with Tiberias on the western shore of Lake Kinneret.

Across the Rift Valley from Galilee and southern Lebanon is a mountain area that has been administered by Israel since 1967. This is the Golan Heights, a high basalt, plateau of volcanic origin. At its northern end rises Mount Hermon, a snow-capped peak 2,814 metres high; in good winters there is skiing on its slopes. The Golan's southern boundary is the canyon of the Yarmuk River, which flows into the Jordan south of Lake Kinneret. Wild pasture-land in the northern part of the region and rich, flat meadows in the south thrive under abundant rain. Steep river valleys running across the plateau, empty into Lake Kinneret. The Golan's western slopes, though not as steep as those it faces across the valley, nonetheless form an impressive embankment.

Though people have lived on the Golan Heights since prehistoric times, much of the area's history is unknown. In the far north are the site of the Israelite city Dan, now within a nature reserve, and Banyas, at one time Caesarea Philippi, the capital of Herod the Great's son Philip. Later it was guarded by the Crusader castle of Nimrud. Archaeological evidence shows that there were many prosperous Jewish communities on the Golan following the defeat of the Second Jewish Revolt against the Romans in 135 CE, when Jews were forbidden to live near Jerusalem. Today there are more than twenty-five settlements in the area, cultivating chiefly wheat and apples and engaged in some light industry.

The mountain spine between the coast and the Rift Valley is broken by the Jezreel Valley. This broad, fertile plain lies between the ridges of Lower Galilee, the Mount Carmel Range, and the blunt northern end of the Samarian Hills.

Though today the Jezreel Valley has the richest and most intensively cultivated land in the mountain regions, until recently inadequate drainage left much of the land clogged with malarial swamps. It was, however, by far the easiest east-west crossing of the mountain spine, and a number of important trade routes followed its gentle course. One ran from 'Akko and Haifa along the northern side of the valley, crossed it near the modern town of 'Afula, and continued down to Bet She'an, where the valley of the Ḥarod River meets the Jordan Valley. Bet She'an, with the agricultural advantages of a warm, well-watered, fertile plain and the trade advantages of its location on a major caravan route, has been occupied for over 5,000 years. From its Roman period, when it became a free city and a textile centre of the empire, a well-preserved theatre remains.

A second trade route ran from 'Akko along the foot of the Mount Carmel Range to Jenin, where it met the mountain road going south to Jerusalem and Be'er Sheva'. The 'Akko road continued southeast across the Samarian Hills to Wadi el Fari'a, a wide river valley, which it followed to the Jordan. The most important trade route in the area, the Way of the Sea, the *via maris*, led from Damascus southwest across the Jezreel Valley, through the Mount Carmel Range by the narrow 'Iron River Valley to the coast, and on to Egypt. Above the intersection of these two routes, where the 'Iron River Valley enters the Jezreel Plain, stood Megiddo. Because of its strategic position, Megiddo was the site of many battles; the name Armageddon, the final battle of the book of Revelation, derives from Megiddo.

South of the Jezreel Valley rises the central mountain massif. Its northern section, from which the spur of the Mount Carmel Range continues northwestward, is the Samarian Hills. Rising near the coast on the west and falling in dry, eroded slopes to the east, the mountains of this range are gentle and rounded, their winding valleys widening in places into small fertile plains planted with vegetables, fruit trees and tobacco. In the red, rocky soil of the hillside above, whose exposed strata blend with the terracing by generations of farmers, stand long rows of olive trees.

The only good pass across the Samarian Hills lies between the high peaks of Mount Ebal and Mount Gerizim. Occupying this pass is the area's main town, Nablus (Shechem), a market centre with some light industry. At Nablus, the east-west road that comes up Wadi el Fari'a intersects the road along the mountains from the south. Supported by good farmland to the east and a number of springs, people have lived in the vicinity for perhaps six thousand years. The earliest town was Shechem, somewhat to the east. Abraham stopped here on his journey from Sumer (today Iraq) to Egypt; Jacob owned land in the neighbourhood, on which Joseph was buried; and at Shechem Joshua assembled the tribes of Israel to establish the covenant and the laws. Nearly two hundred years after Shechem was finally destroyed and abandoned, Flavia Neapolis — hence Nablus — was founded at its present site by the Romans. The town today is almost completely Moslem, though most of the tiny remnant of Samaritans resides here near their holy place, Mount Gerizim.

No clear physical boundary marks the transition from the hills of Samaria to those of Judea. The southern mountains have a rougher, more forbidding aspect, perhaps because their dryer slopes support less vegetation. The range's western side, sparsely forested and crossed by steep river valleys, is separated from the Coastal Plain by ranges of foothills. A continuous band of high ground, relatively flat, often wide, and of almost constant elevation, forms the watershed of the Judean Hills. On this high ground stand the region's cities — Ramallah, Jerusalem, Bethlehem, and Hebron — linked by the mountain road that comes south from Jenin and Nablus and goes on to Be'er Sheva'. The parched Judean Wilderness, its rainfall blocked by the high ridge, falls away to the east.

The mountains are composed of limestone and dolomite strata. Numerous caves and flint outcroppings encouraged the development of early man. One huge cave, called Khureitun, high in the wall of an ancient riverbed southeast of Bethlehem, contains the earliest indications of the use of fire in Palestine yet discovered; the cave was first occupied between one and five hundred thousand years ago. Other caves along the same wadi are still occupied by Bedouin today.

VEGETATION

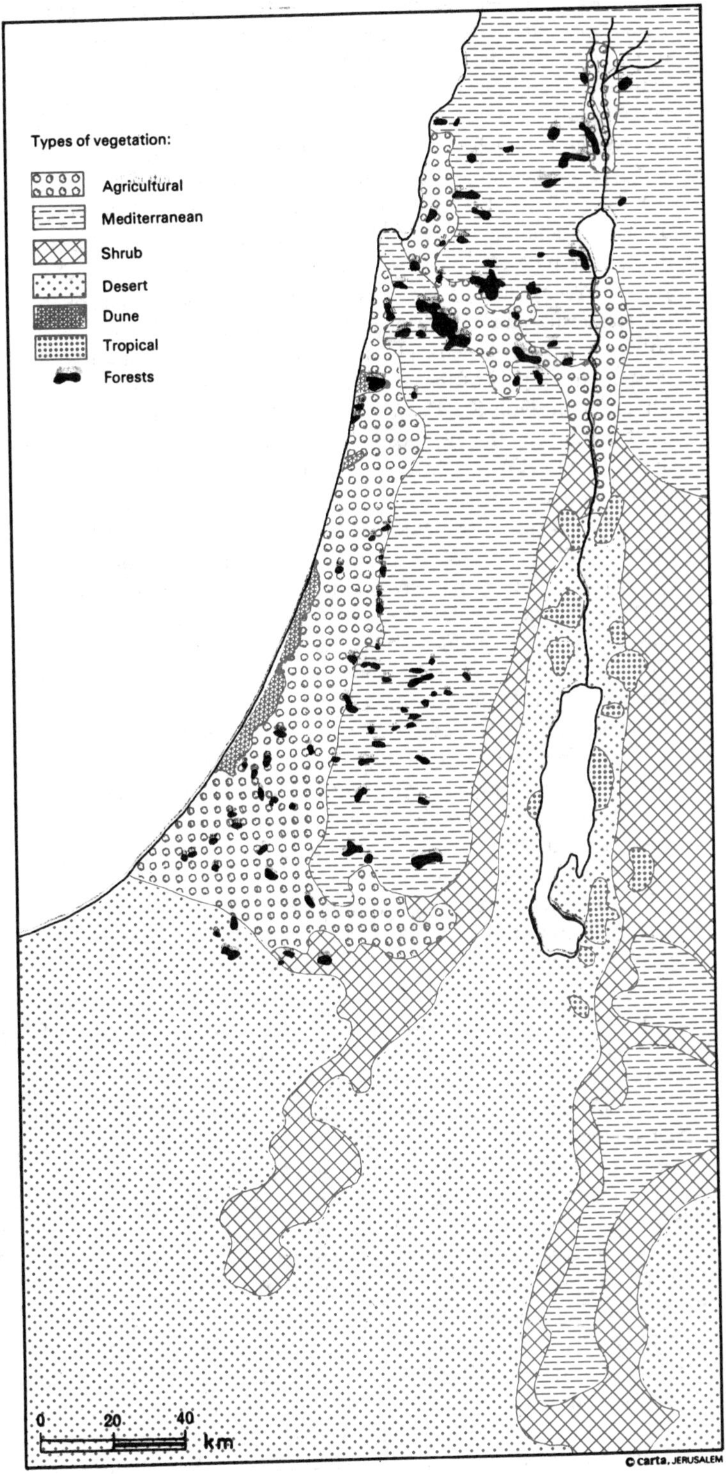

Types of vegetation:
Agricultural
Mediterranean
Shrub
Desert
Dune
Tropical
Forests
0
20
40
km
© carta, JERUSALEM

Vegetables, olives, fruit trees and vineyards grow in the Judean Hills. Much of the land, however, is covered with rather scrubby vegetation, particularly in the east; this provides pasture for herds of sheep and goats. Stone is quarried for building. A number of crafts survive on the tourist trade, among them needlework in the villages, olive-wood and mother-of-pearl in Bethlehem, and in Hebron glass-blowing in a tradition two thousand years old.

There are several major religious sites in the area. In Hebron is the Cave of the Patriarchs (Me'arat HaMakhpela) in which are buried Abraham and Sarah, Isaac and Rebecca, Jacob and Leah; the temple built by Herod the Great above the cave is visited by Jews, Moslems and Christians. Further north is Bethlehem, birth-place of Jesus, and site of Rachel's Tomb. Then there are the many holy places of Jerusalem. The chief of these are the Western Wall, the remaining part of the Second Temple, venerated by Jews; the Church of the Holy Sepulchre, site of Jesus's crucifixion, burial and resurrection; and the two mosques on Temple Mount, the Dome of the Rock and el Aqṣa; the Dome of the Rock marks the spot from where Muḥammad rose on his mystical night visit to heaven.

As the focus of three major religions, Jerusalem acquired additional historical interest as different groups struggled for control over the city. Its people have come from an enormous range of places and backgrounds, producing a complex mixture in both its visitors and its residents. Today Jerusalem has a population of 370,000. It is the nation's capital, seat of the Knesset, Israel's parliament, and of its government.

The Judean Wilderness, to the east and south, is generally too dry to support a settled community. Rainfall in the higher and more northern areas creates pasture for livestock — the extent of the pasture varying with the season. Bedouin with their herds of goats and sheep camp in these areas. Less favoured zones, with neither adequate rain nor springs, are desert.

The descent of these stark hills to the Rift Valley far below sea level is abrupt. Along the Dead Sea it forms an escarpment. The steep, soft limestone slopes, unprotected by vegetation, have been deeply eroded into a wild jumble of heights and valleys. Peaks stand high and alone, with a wide view over the countryside. Many of these naturally became fortresses, like Kypros, which guarded the ancient road from Jericho up to Jerusalem. The most famous of these rock islands is Masada, above the western shore of the Dead Sea. While superbly defensible, Masada in the heart of the wilderness is not a strategic point; its fortress was built solely as a retreat.

The wilderness has long been a refuge for the hunted, who hid in its many caves. The prophet Elijah fled from Queen Jezabel into the wilderness; near the spring of 'En Gedi David hid from the wrath of Saul. The wilderness has also been a refuge for those seeking spiritual purity. A Jewish sect, the Essenes, established a community at Qumeran on the Dead Sea. Their documents, hastily hidden in nearby caves as the Romans approached, are called the Dead Sea Scrolls. Jesus spent forty days in the wilderness, after which he was offered temptations by the devil; tradition assigns a bare mountain-top above Jericho as the location of the encounter. Christians since the fourth century CE have sought spiritual challenge in the Judean Wilderness. The monastery of Mar Saba, founded in the fifth century CE, has functioned continuously to the present day. That of St. George of Koziba, built on the cliff face of Wadi el Qilt, at one time supplied food and religious services to hundreds of hermits living in caves along the wadi.

The Valley of Be'er Sheva', at the southern end of the Judean Hills, is the boundary between the central mountain region and the rugged, arid highlands of the Negev. The land north of the valley has on the whole a Mediterranean climate. The land to the south is desert. With its eastern continuation, the Valley of 'Arad, the Be'er Sheva' Valley forms a passage across the mountains, the first south of the road from Jericho to Jerusalem. It allowed access from Egypt and the south coast to the major highway from Damascus down the Jordanian hills to Arabia. In the middle of the crossing stands Be'er Sheva', from which the mountain road goes north. Once an Israelite frontier town, Be'er Sheva' today is capital of the Negev.

The Negev is a long, narrow triangle of land, its southern point the port city of Elat on the Gulf of Elat. On the East side the land falls sharply to the Rift Valley. On the West it merges into the desert mountains of the Sinai Peninsula. Over half of Israel's land lies in the Negev, but only a small percentage of its population lives here.

The Northern Negev is composed of short ridges of sandstone, low in the north and west and gradually rising to the south. One-third of this area is covered with sand dunes. The loess soil of the remainder is cultivable with adequate water. With careful management of the small amount of water the area receives, this land supported a relatively large settled population in Nabatean and Byzantine times. At other periods the population has been mostly nomadic, a threat to Be'er Sheva' and communities in the Judean Hills. Beyond the Valley of Zin lie the Central Negev Highlands, where long, high ridges of sandstone capped with limestone and dolomite run toward the southwest. An enormous, crater-like depression, Makhtesh Ramon, lies between steep slopes rising nearly 300 metres. Above the southwestern end of the crater, the enclosing ridges culminate in Mount Ramon, at 1,035 metres the highest point in the Negev. The Southern Negev begins with the Paran Plateau, a high tableland whose dry riverbeds carry the waters of flash floods down to the Rift Valley. At the southern tip of the Negev triangle are the spectacular Elat Mountains, continuing westward in the mountains of Sinai. A complex mixture of rock types, each eroding in its own way, has produced a beautiful variety of colours and shapes: sharp, serrated ridges and pinnacles of grey and red granite; small limestone plateaus; and sheer cliffs and dry river gorges in multi-coloured layers of Nubian sandstone.

Besides Be'er Sheva', there are few towns in the Negev. Agricultural settlements, mostly in the north, use imported water to grow mainly cotton and grains. At Dimona there are textile mills. Not far from the site of the ancient town of Arad is the modern development town of the same name. Founded as a petrochemical centre and residential area for people employed in the Dead Sea works, 'Arad, with its clear, dry climate, has become a health resort as well.

The Rift Valley

The valley that runs the entire length of Israel, from the Ḥula Valley to the Gulf of Elat, is part of the Great Rift Valley extending from Turkey to East Africa. The shifting of the earth as Africa and Asia are pushed apart has created this rift; continued movement produces periodic earthquakes in the region.

The Ḥula Valley in the north is a relatively high and wet basin. The sources of the Jordan, which begin with springs and rainfall on the slopes of Mount Hermon, follow steep, irregular courses broken occasionally by waterfalls. In the flat Ḥula Valley, however, the new river's course was so unclear that formerly it divided several times. The floor of the valley was a swamp, with Lake Ḥula at its southern end. Reclamation projects completed in 1958 eliminated both the lake and the surrounding swamps, leaving a nature reserve, fishponds and rich, well-watered farmland.

The lava dam that first created the lake is cut by the steep gorge of the Jordan River, falling 275 metres to Lake Kinneret which is below sea level. Lake Kinneret is also called Lake Genneseret, the Sea of Galilee, and Lake Tiberias. This area was the centre of Jesus's ministry; Capernaum on the lake's northern shore was the home of his first disciples, and Tabgha the site of the miracle of the loaves and fishes. The city of Tiberias, on the western shore, was founded early in the first century CE by Herod Antipas. It later became a centre for Jewish study, and its scholars produced the Palestinian Talmud. Hot springs at Tiberias and elsewhere in the area have supplied hot baths from Roman times to the present.

Lake Kinneret is the largest source of fresh, if hard, water in the country. A series of pipelines, open channels and mountain tunnels called the National Water Carrier, completed in 1964, transports water from this lake to the dry southern regions. The lake also supplies freshwater fish. The warm, wet lands of the southern shores and the Jordan Valley down to Bet She'an produce a variety of subtropical fruits, such as dates, bananas, mangoes and grapes.

The entire stretch of the Rift Valley from Lake Kinneret nearly to the Gulf of Elat lies below sea level. It is the deepest continental depression in the world. This was once the floor of a great inland sea, and consequently the valley floor is composed of easily eroded sediments, often mineral salts. Where there is sufficient fresh water, as around Lake Kinneret, there is considerable vegetation, but further south, where rainfall is scarce, the valley has a remarkably barren look.

The course of the Jordan River from Lake Kinneret to the Dead Sea, 104 km. to the south, meanders through a narrow band lower than the Rift Valley's floor. The Jordan's flood plain is covered with scrub thickets, the "jungle of the Jordan" (Jeremiah 12:5). Between the river's course and the valley floor above it lie heavily eroded salt badlands.

The only city in the lower Jordan Valley is Jericho, the oldest continuously inhabited city in the world. Situated a few kilometres north of the Dead Sea, on the caravan route that crossed the Jordan to go up to Jerusalem, Jericho owes its existence to local springs. Its

NATURE RESERVES

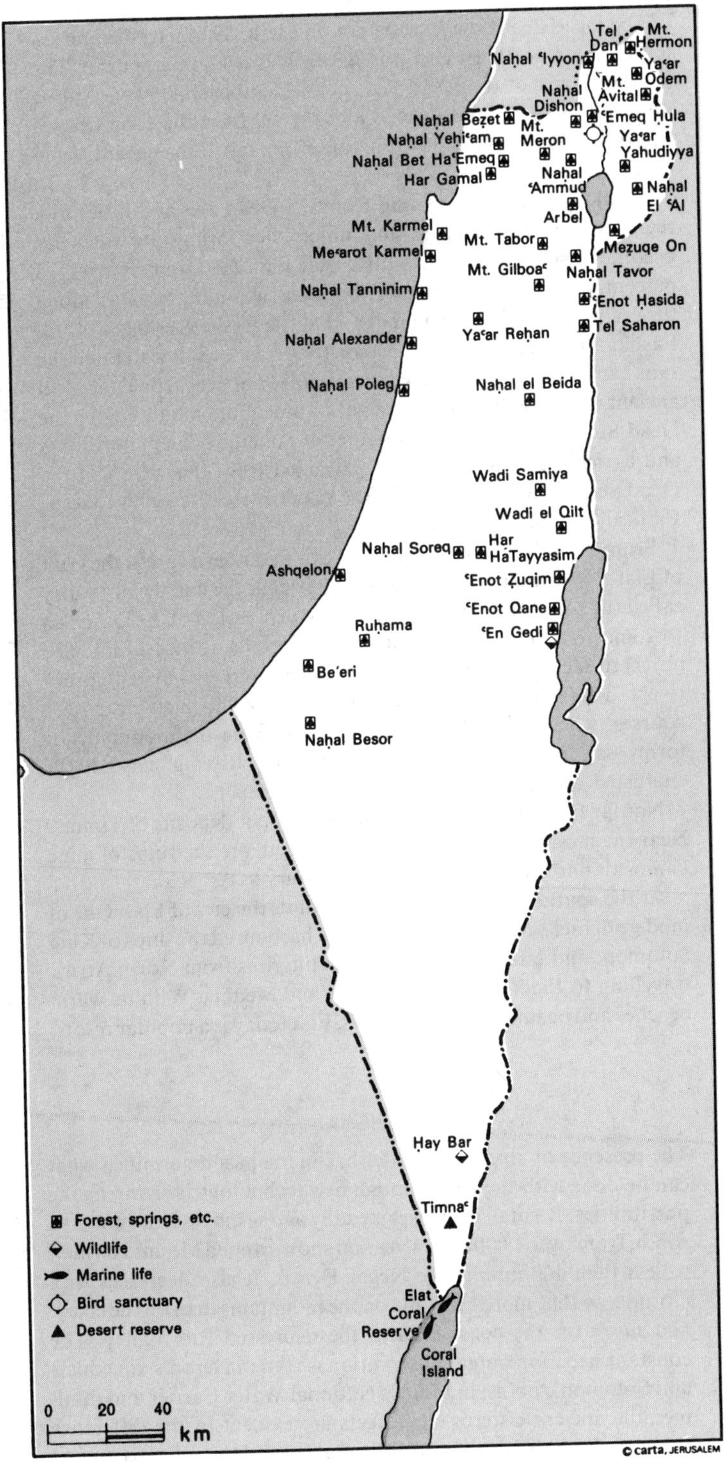

chief produce today are fruits, principally dates, bananas and citrus fruits.

The Dead Sea is the lowest spot on earth, 398 metres below sea level. At its northern end it is about half a kilometre deep. The southern part of the Dead Sea is considerable shallower. At one point a tongue of land reaches into the sea from the east. The sea bed beyond it is now exposed because of a fall in the water level in recent years.

As there is no river exiting from the Dead Sea and it lies in a region rich in mineral salts and mineral hot springs, its water has become extremely dense, with a salt concentration of over 25 percent. There are a number of popular swimming beaches along the sea particularly at 'En Gedi and at the freshwater oasis of 'En Fashka. It is impossible for a person to sink in the salt water, but the salts can be harmful if inhaled or swallowed or gets in one's eyes. In ancient times the Egyptians sought bitumen for embalming on the Dead Sea's shores. today a number of minerals, chiefly fertilizers and agricultural chemicals, are extracted from the waters at the Dead Sea Works, southwest of the sea near the site believed to be Biblical Sodom.

From the salt marsh at the Dead Sea's southern end to the Gulf of Elat, 160 kilometres to the south, stretches the narrow dry valley called the 'Arava. It rises from the deep depression of the Dead Sea to some 183 metres above sea level, then falls again to Elat. The northern section has deeply eroded canyons created by temporary rivers. The southern part, while not flat, has no such clear river courses; when flooded by seasonal rivers from the mountains, it forms salt marshes that quickly dry up, leaving clay sherds encrusted with salt crystals.

Not far from the Gulf of Elat are the copper deposits of Timna'. Near the modern mines, temporarily closed, are the ruins of mine camps dating back to the eleventh century BCE.

At the southern end of the 'Arava stands the city of Elat. One of modern Israel's major ports, Elat once harboured the ships of King Solomon, and later it served Moslem pilgrims from North Africa travelling to the holy cities of Mecca and Medina. With its warm beaches and beautiful fish and corals, Elat today is a popular resort.

Climate

The presence or absence of water has in the past determined what can be done with the land, though new technology is changing the possibilities. Rainfall decreases steadily as one moves from north to south, from over 1,000 mm. a year on snow-capped Mount Ḥermon to less than 100 mm. in the Negev Desert. It also decreases with altitude, so that more rain falls on the mountains than on the coast, and more on the coast than in the depressed Rift Valley. The constant need for water conservation is seen in Herod's aqueducts and Solomon's pools, in today's National Water Carrier and innumerable ancient cisterns. Its effects are evident in the difference between the lush farmlands of the Galilee and the spare pasturage

WINTER CLIMATE

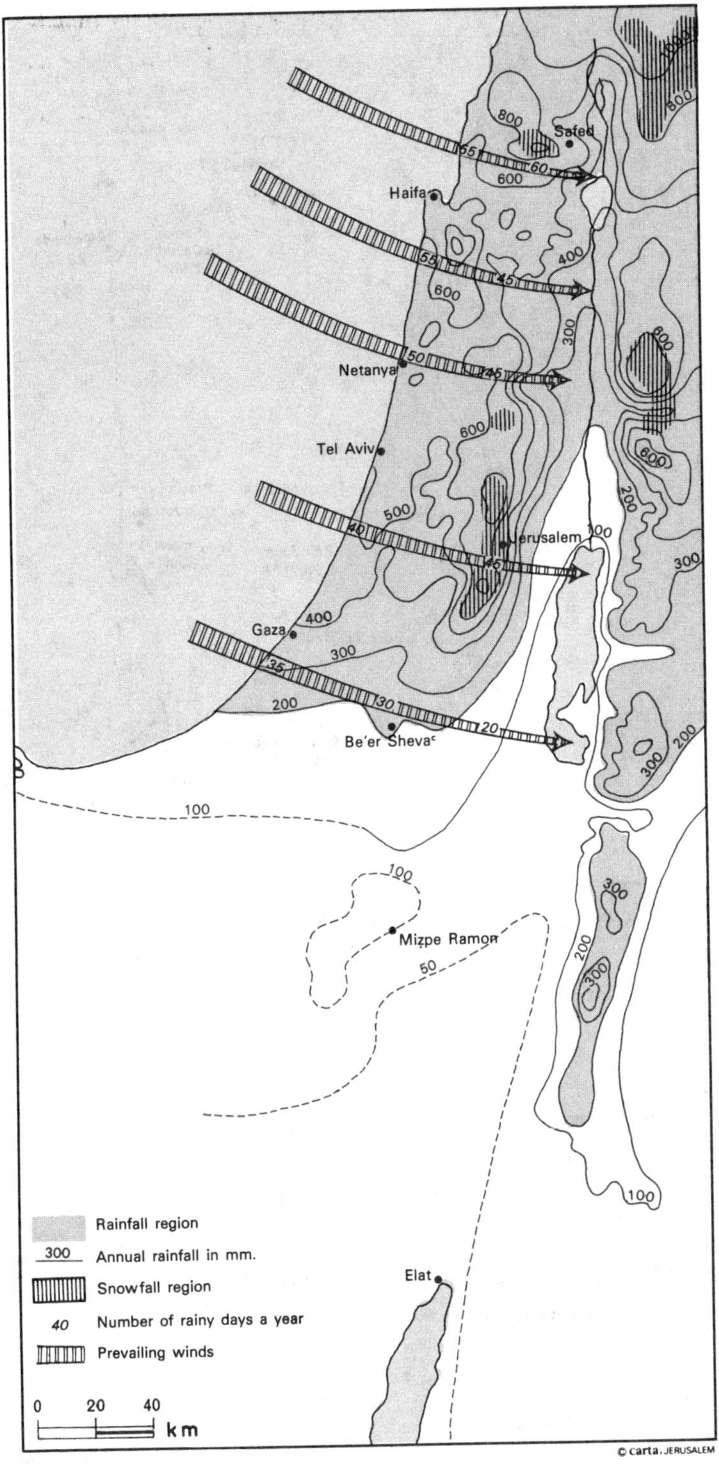
Safed
Haifa
Netanya
Tel Aviv
Jerusalem
Gaza
Be'er Sheva
Mizpe Ramon
Elat
1000
800
600
400
300
500
200
100
50
55
60
45
40
35
30
20
Rainfall region
300 Annual rainfall in mm.
Snowfall region
40 Number of rainy days a year
Prevailing winds
0 20 40
km
© carta, JERUSALEM

SUMMER CLIMATE

Dafna ● 27.1⁰

23.6⁰
Mt. Kena'an

25.0⁰
Nahariyya●

Acre ● 25.7⁰

Haifa
24.3⁰

● Deganya
29.7⁰

Ramat
Dawid ●
26.6⁰

Hefzi
● Bah
29.3⁰

24.7⁰
Tel Aviv ●

Lod 25.4⁰

31.2⁰
Jericho ●

Beit Jimal
26.2⁰ ●

Jerusalem
● 23.6⁰

● Gaza 25.7⁰

Be'er Sheva'
26.2⁰

Sedom ●
33.7⁰

Mizpe Ramon ●
24.0⁰

Summer breezes:

⇢ Morning

⇢ Noon

➡ Afternoon

⇢ Night

⠿ Area with abundant dew

23.6⁰ Mean temperature in July (⁰C.)

Elat ● 30.0⁰

0   20   40
|___|___|___| k m

© Carta, JERUSALEM

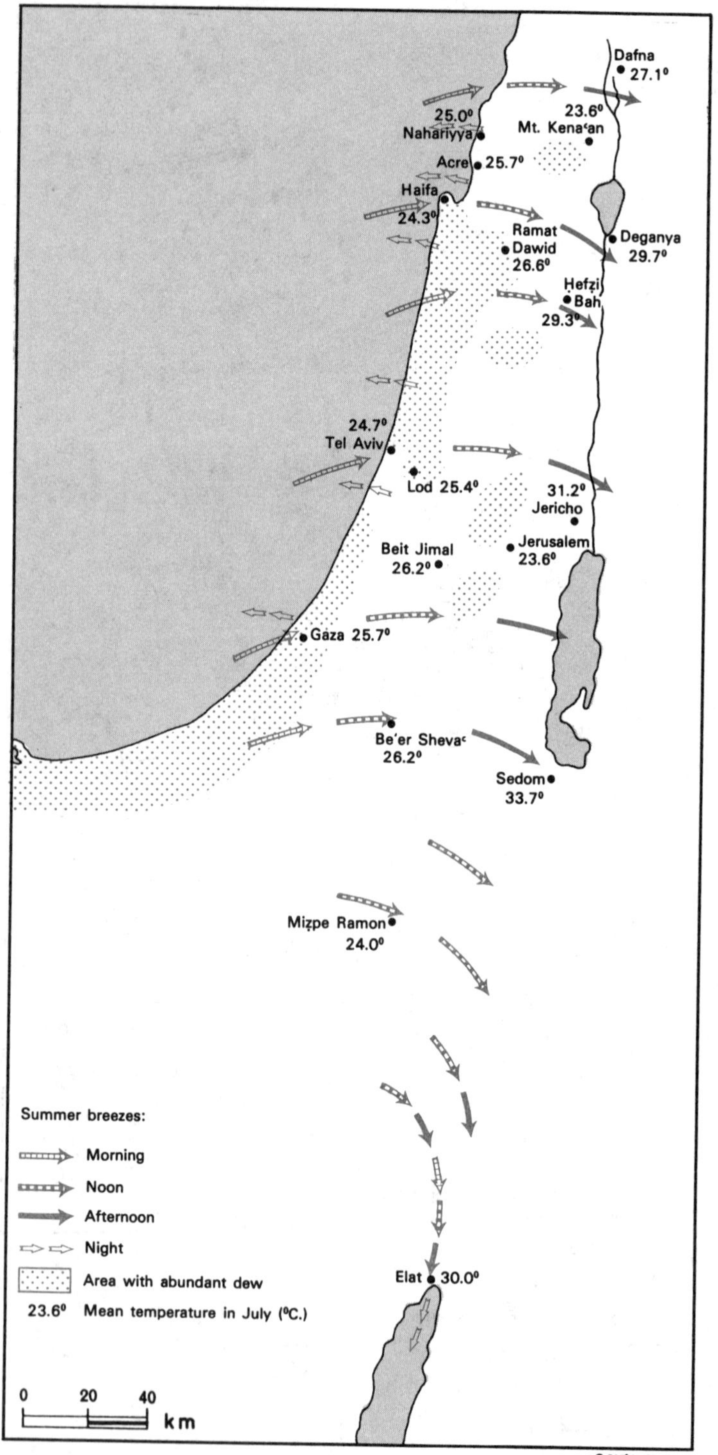

of the Judean Hills, and between the irrigated groves of banana and citrus trees in Jericho and the hardy olives of Bethlehem. Each year the significance of water is demonstrated again, when towards the end of the winter rains the Judean Hills, bare and brown for three quarters of the year, turn green with new growth and bright with spring wildflowers.

Temperature and humidity vary with the topography. The Coastal Plain is hot and humid in the summer and mild in the winter. The hill region of the north and centre have warm summers and cool winters, with the regular snowfalls of Mount Hermon decreasing to an occasional powdering in the centre. In winter, Jerusalem, on the crest of the central ridge, is subject to storms of awesome power. The southern region, the Negev, has a typical desert climate of hot, dry days and cool nights in summer, and mild days and cold nights in winter. The Jordan valley, enclosed between high walls, protected from the winds, and with water down most of its length, is again mild in winter with hot, humid summers. The dry 'Arava has the highest temperatures recorded in Israel.

A climatic affliction of the Middle East is the *ḥamsin*. This is a hot, dry wind from the desert that blows during the dry season. It is usually laden with dust or sand, which can cause anything from a light overcast to an impenetrable fog. "*Ḥamsin*" in Arabic means "fifty". One popular explanation of the name is that this wind blows for a total of fifty days a year.

HISTORY

The Stone Age 600,000-4,000 BCE

Sites*: *Carmel Caves, 'En 'Avdat*

The most ancient human whose remains have been found in Palestine lived in the Jordan Valley around 600,000 BCE. Water was more plentiful then, and people lived by hunting large wild animals in the grasslands. Tools were of flint, and great advances were made in its use during the Stone Age. About 200,000 BCE, it appears, people began using fire. Agriculture began around 14,000 to 12,000, with the farming of grain and domestication of animals. People began to settle in villages, developing a new urban social organization. Jericho, the oldest continuously inhabited site, was settled around 8300. The use of pottery in place of stone vessels appeared about 6700.

* *Note: Many artifacts from all periods have been removed to museums: see especially the Israel Museum and the Rockefeller Museum in Jerusalem.*

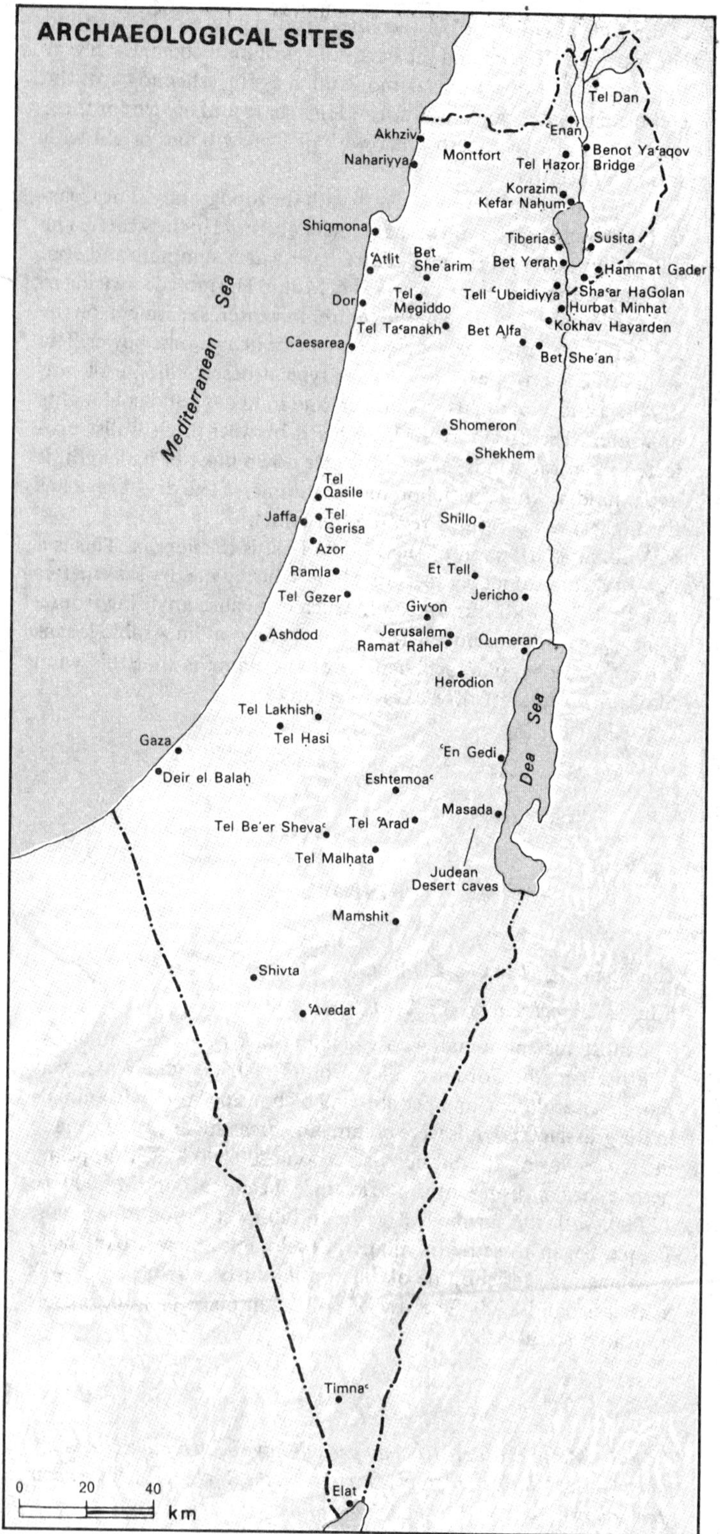

ARCHAEOLOGICAL SITES
Mediterranean Sea
Tel Dan
ʿEnan
Akhziv
Montfort
Benot Yaʿaqov Bridge
Nahariyya
Tel Ḥazor
Korazim
Kefar Naḥum
Shiqmona
Tiberias
Susita
ʿAtlit
Bet She'arim
Bet Yeraḥ
Ḥammat Gader
Tel Megiddo
Tell ʿUbeidiyya
Shaʿar HaGolan
Dor
Ḥurbat Minḥat
Tel Taʿanakh
Bet Alfa
Kokhav Hayarden
Caesarea
Bet She'an
Shomeron
Shekhem
Tel Qasile
Jaffa
Tel Gerisa
Shillo
Azor
Ramla
Et Tell
Tel Gezer
Jericho
Givʿon
Jerusalem
Ashdod
Ramat Raḥel
Qumeran
Herodion
Dead Sea
Tel Lakhish
Tel Ḥasi
Gaza
ʿEn Gedi
Deir el Balaḥ
Eshtemoaʿ
Masada
Tel Be'er Shevaʿ
Tel ʿArad
Tel Malḥata
Judean Desert caves
Mamshit
Shivta
ʿAvedat
Timnaʿ
Elat
0 20 40
km

The Copper and Bronze Ages 4000-1200 BCE

Sites: *'Arad, 'En Gedi, Ḥazor, Megiddo, Shechem, Jerusalem (City of David)*

The new villages began to trade, especially for copper and later bronze, a harder mixture of copper and tin. Trade fostered social and cultural development. Palestine produced numerous small city-states, while in the lusher river basins of the Nile and the Euphrates great empires developed. Recorded history began towards the end of the Early Bronze Age in the 25th and 24th centuries. The Egyptians extended their rule over the Coastal Plain, at this time inhabited by the Canaanites (3150-1220). Semitic nomads began migrating from the east; around 1800 came a group led by Abraham. After crossing the Jordan River from the east, Abraham built his first altar at Shechem and another at Bethel, before travelling on to Egypt. On his return he settled at Hebron, where he and his family are buried. Mount Moriah, on which Abraham prepared to sacrifice his son Isaac, is identified as the hilltop in Jerusalem which is called the Temple Mount. Nomadic herdsmen, the Hebrews roamed the mountain areas, under the loose protection of small local kings, until famine forced them down into the richer lands of Egypt.

In the eighteenth century BCE, the Hyksos appeared from the north with horse-drawn chariots. They conquered Egypt in 1720 and fortified a number of cities in Canaan. In 1570 the Hyksos were driven from Egypt and in 1468 at a battle near Megiddo the Pharaoh Thutmose III defeated the Canaanites and later conquered the Levant. Over the next two centuries local Canaanite rulers appealed to Egypt for help against nomads, called Habiru, invading from the deserts to the east.

Moses led the Israelites out of Egypt around 1250 BCE. They did not travel along the "Way of the Sea" which was the shortest way because of the Egyptian forts along the way. Instead they wandered through the desert approaching Canaan from the south and east.

Under Joshua they crossed the Jordan River near Jericho. The Israelite conquest of Canaan, ascribed to Joshua, actually took place piecemeal over an extended period. At the same time, the Philistines arrived by sea. By 1200 the Egyptians had been driven out, the Philistines occupied the southern coast, and the Israelites held the hills.

The Iron Age (The Israelite Period) 1200-586 BCE

Sites: *Be'er Sheva', Ḥazor, Lachish, Megiddo, Samaria (Sebastiya), Tel Dan, Jerusalem (City of David)*

Iron was introduced to the area by the Philistines, who, with the Canaanites, controlled the open lands with their chariots. In the period of the Judges (ca. 1200-1150 BCE), the Israelites lived as loosely federated tribes in assigned areas extending "from Dan to Beer Sheba," but the pressure of the coastal peoples united them

THE KINGDOM OF DAVID AND SOLOMON

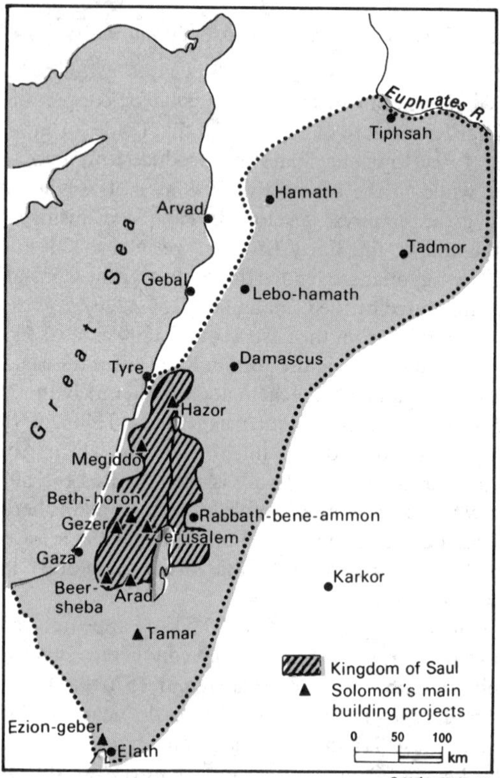

under a monarchy. After Saul, the first king (ca. 1025-1004), and his sons were killed near Beth-shean, David assumed the throne. David conquered Jerusalem and made it his capital; as the home of the Ark of the Covenant Jerusalem became a spiritual centre as well. Under David the kingdom of Israel reached its greatest extent stretching from the Euphrates to Philistia and from Lebo-hamath till Elath. His son Solomon (965-928), who built the First Temple in Jerusalem over the crest of Mount Moriah, consolidated David's political and military successes and built a commercial empire. However, the heavy taxation required to support his projects and his favouritism toward his own tribe of Judah produced increasing dissatisfaction towards the end of his reign.

At Solomon's death the northern tribes seceded, forming the kingdom of Israel under Jeroboam I; Solomon's son Rehoboam retained Jerusalem and the southern lands in the kingdom of Judah. Changes were made in Jewish practice in Israel to remove the focus on Jerusalem and to increase the distinction between Israel and Judah. Thereafter the two kingdoms fought each other and their neighbours. Israel suffered, in addition, internal struggles for the kingship. In 876 BCE King Omri built a new capital, Israel's fourth, at Samaria (Sebastiya). He married his son Ahab (871-851) to the pagan princess Jezebel of Tyre, strengthening his ties with Phoenicia. Jezebel's troubles with the prophet Elijah were but one incident in the efforts of the prophets of Judah and Israel to promote religious conservatism and to condemn social injustice.

In the ninth century BCE the Assyrian empire arose in Mesopotamia. While its influence over Israel and Judah fluctuated, by the 730s both had become vassal states of Assyria. On the death of the Assyrian Tiglath-pileser III Israel revolted. After a three-year siege, the new Assyrian king captured the capital, Samaria, in 722 and deported its inhabitants to the east. In 721 foreigners resettled the city. The kingdom of Israel came to an end; the descendants of its remaining Jews became the Samaritans.

Judah revolted against Sennacherib, and in 701 BCE the Assyrians destroyed a number of its western cities. From Lachish Sennacherib advanced on Jerusalem, but on the advice of the prophet Isaiah the city resisted. The Assyrians withdrew, and Judah remained a vassal state.

Over the next century Assyria declined. As the Babylonian empire rose in the east, Egypt sought to take Assyria's western provinces. In 609 BCE, when the Egyptians marched north, Josiah, the last great Judean king of the House of David, tried to stop them at Megiddo and was defeated and killed. Nebuchadnezzar, king of Babylon, defeated the Egyptians in 605 and took Judah from them. Against the advice of Jeremiah, Judah revolted against Nebuchadnezzar in 598 and again in 590. The second time, Egypt's support

THE DIVIDED MONARCHY

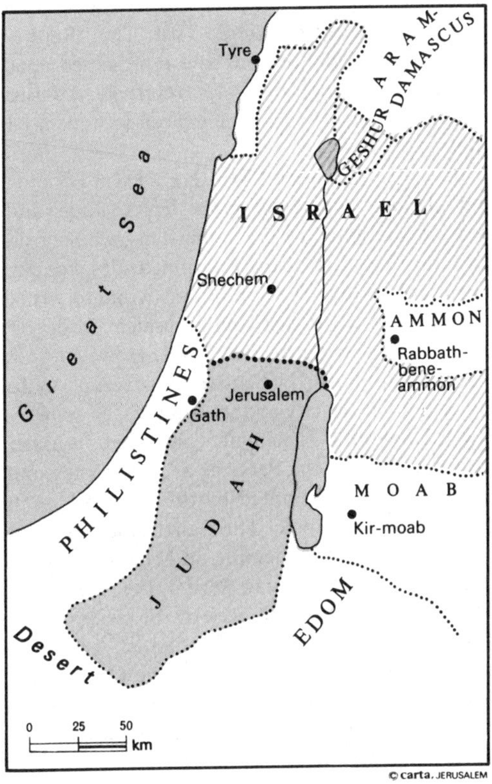

© carta. JERUSALEM

protracted the war, but after a long siege Jerusalem fell to the Babylonians in 586. The city and the Temple were destroyed, and the inhabitants of Judah were carried off into Babylonian Captivity.

The foundations of Israelite culture were laid during the First Temple Period. From the 10th century BCE, Jewish traditions and laws, chronicles of the kings and sayings of the prophets were put into writing to form the basis for the Old Testament. The Bible's universal value derived, among other factors, from the poetic and moral force of the scribes of Psalms and the preaching prophets — Amos, Hosea, Isaiah, Micah, Jeremiah and others. Their struggle to better society gave the prophecy of Israel a unique quality, and their uncompromising fight to proclaim God as a God of justice nurtured the precept of monotheism, never before known in the Ancient East.

The Persian Period 586-332 BCE

Site: *Jerusalem (City of David)*

Cyrus, king of Persia, conquered the Babylonian empire in 539 BCE. In 538 Cyrus' Edict was issued allowing the captive Jews to return to Judea, which like Samaria became a small province in an empire covering the entire Middle East. The "Return to Zion" began when some 40,000 people, who represented about half the number of second generation exiles, returned to Jerusalem. The first wave of returning Jews built a temple in Jerusalem, begun in 520 and completed in 515.

In 458 BCE, the Persian king Artaxerxes I sent Ezra to Jerusalem to impose religious conformity on the Jews of Judea and Samaria. This was deeply resented by the Samaritans, who considered their Judaism purer than that of the returning exiles, contaminated by the sojourn in Babylon. The Samaritans wrote to Artaxerxes that the returning Jews were fortifying Jerusalem to defy Persia; the king sent them to destroy the new walls. However, in 445 Artaxerxes sent his cup-bearer Nehemiah as governor to Judea, with authority to rebuild the city and its defences. In spite of the resistance of local interests, Nehemiah completed Jerusalem's walls. Judah continued under the Persians as a theocracy under Jewish law, with a governor appointed by the Persian king and a high priest of the line of Zadok. The Samaritans, under a separate govenment, built their own temple on Mount Gerizim.

With the close of the Persian Period, the Age of the Prophets came to an end. They were followed by the scribes who spread the word of the Torah among the people of Israel. A central institution which existed for some 300 years was the Great Synagogue (or Great Assembly) composed of leaders and elders who assembled at times of important events. Several synagogues were also established during this period.

The Hellenistic Period 332-167 BCE

Sites: *Bet Guvrin, Lachish, Samaria (Sebastiya), Jerusalem (Bethesda Pools)*

Alexander the Great of Macedon marched through Palestine in 332 BCE with little opposition. The following year he conquered the Persian empire. In 331 the Samaritans rebelled; in response Alexander drove them from their capital Samaria and in their place settled a colony of Greek veterans.

Alexander's death in 323 BCE was followed by devastating wars among his generals. Palestine finally was annexed to Egypt by Ptolemy I. It remained part of the Ptolemaic kingdom for a century, forming the frontier against the descendants of Alexander's general Seleucus, who held Babylon and Syria. Under the Ptolemies the hereditary high priest of Jerusalem continued to govern Judah; but outside of the Judean Hills, and especially in the cities, Greek culture was imposed, led by an influx of Greek colonists.

By 200 BCE the Seleucid Antiochus III (223-187) had gained control over Palestine, holding it against continued Ptolemaic assaults. He was defeated in 188 by the Romans and was required to pay tribute. In need of treasure, his successors began to look at religious caches. Antiochus IV Epiphanes (175-164), while fighting the Ptolemies at the Egyptian border, made efforts to Hellenize Jerusalem, and, after taking the Temple treasures in 169, he sought further control over Judah by banning the external practices of Judaism. The Temple was turned over to Zeus.

The Hasmonean Period 167-63 BCE

Site: *Modi'in*

The response to religious persecution was a revolt in 167 BCE led by Mattathias HaCohen of the Hasmonean house of Modi'in. After four victories over the Greeks, Judah the Maccabee took most of Jerusalem. In 164 he purified the Temple, an act commemorated today in the feast of Hanukkah — the celebration of the inauguration of the Temple. The religious struggle became a political one. The Seleucids, fighting Babylon in the east and the Romans in the west and hampered by internal political struggles, were unable to crush the rebels. The Hasmonean state had been recognized by the Romans in 160. In 142 the last of the five Maccabee brothers, Simeon, received recognition from the Seleucid king for Judea's independence.

Simeon's son John Hyrcanus, after the collapse of the Seleucids in 129 BCE, embarked on conquest. In 128 he took the new Samaritan capital, Shechem, and destroyed the temple on Mount Gerizim. His harshness in imposing Jerusalem's observances on the Samaritans made the rift in Judaism permanent. In the south Hyrcanus's conquests included Idumea (Edom), which was required to convert to Judaism. Prominent Idumeans entered the Hasmonean government.

THE HASMONEANS

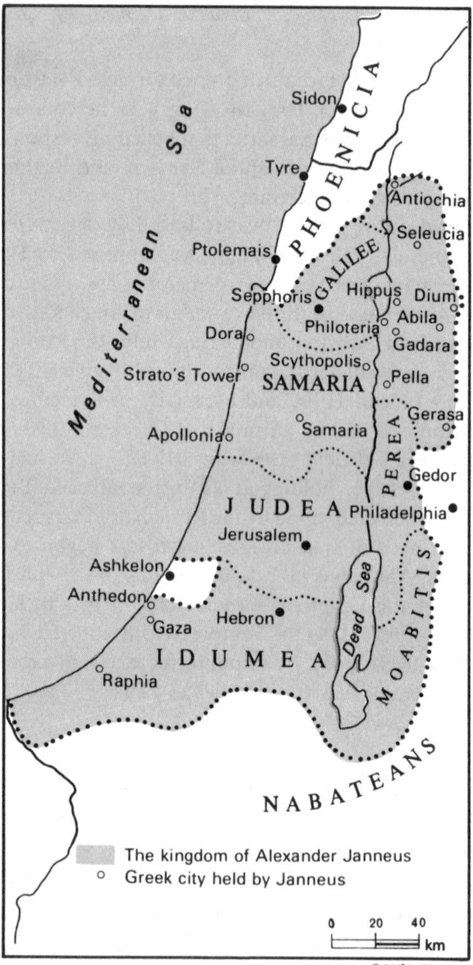

Simeon's successors, particularly Alexander Janneus, son of Hyrcanus, extended the boundaries of Judea almost to those of David's time and made the country a kingdom, which enjoyed some forty years of success. However, at the death of queen Salome Alexandra, widow of Alexander Janneus, in 67 BCE her two sons, Hyrcanus II and Aristobolus II, began a struggle for the throne that was to destroy the Hasmoneans and end the new kingdom.

The Roman Period 63 BCE-324 CE

Sites: *Bet She'an, Caesarea, Capernaum, Hebron, Herodion, Masada, Qumeran, Samaria, Tiberias, Jerusalem (Citadel, Ecce Homo Arch, Temple Mount)*

The kingdom of Judea served the Romans as a buffer state against the Parthians. In conditions of civil war, however, it was useless.

The Roman general Pompey arrived in 63 BCE and settled the conflict in favour of Hyrcanus and his Idumean advisor Antipater. Hyrcanus was made ethnarch of a Judea reduced to its pre-conquest area; Samaria was freed from its control. Thereafter the Romans bestowed the title "king" only on favoured individuals. Antipater and later his son Herod showed astonishing ability in maintaining and even improving Judea's position, through the civil wars that turned the Roman republic into an empire, by their personal friendships with the successive leaders of Rome — Pompey, Julius Caesar, Mark Antony, and Octavian (Augustus Caesar) — and in spite of the hostility of the powerful Cleopatra VII.

Aristobolus II and his sons continued to rebel against Rome. With the aid of the Parthians, Aristobolus's son Antigonus ascended the revived Judean throne in 40 BCE. Herod, who had replaced his assassinated father as advisor to Hyrcanus II, ensconced his family and his fiancée Mariamne, Hyrcanus's granddaughter, first in Herodion and then in Masada, while he went to

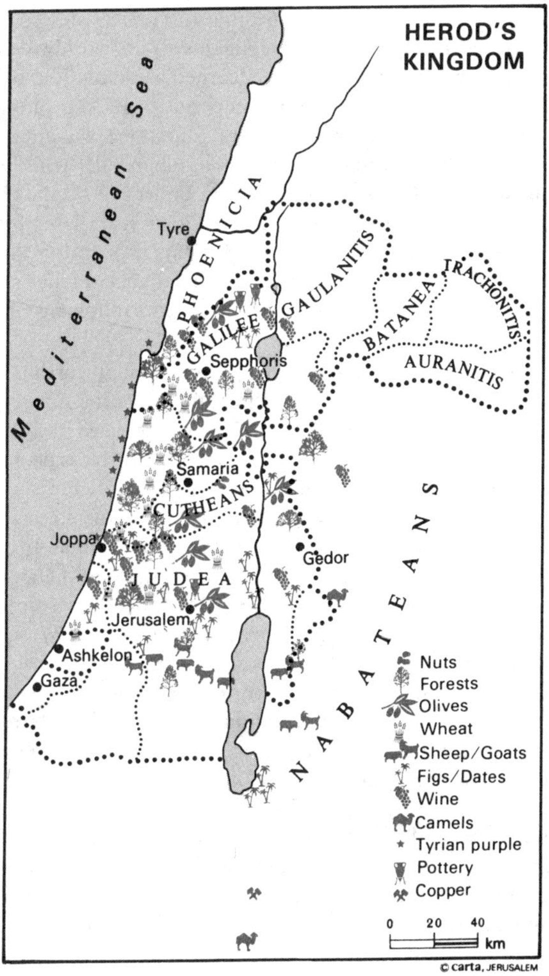

© carta, JERUSALEM

Rome for help. The Roman Senate proclaimed him king of Judea in 39 and sent him back with a small army. By 37 he had conquered the country and Antigonus, the last Hasmonean king, was executed.

Herod the Great ruled as king of Judea from 37 to 4 BCE. In that time he erected architectural monuments all over the country. Among them were the Temple and Citadel of Jerusalem, a palace for himself, and an aqueduct for the holy city, which he made a resplendent capital; the temple over the tombs of the patriarchs in Hebron; works, including an immensely long aqueduct, at Samaria, renamed Sebastiya in honour of Augustus; numerous fortresses and palaces, including Herodion and Masada; and the great port city Caesarea. Not loved by his people, Herod ruled successfully with an iron hand. He was constantly afraid of the palace intrigue, and his fear led him to kill his beloved wife Mariamne (buried at Masada) and four of his sons, though he suffered anguish at his own destruction of his family. He himself died in Jericho and was buried at Herodion.

Soon after Herod's death Judea became a Roman province, with a Roman governor overseeing the rule of Herod's descendants. Internal affairs locally and Jewish religious affairs worldwide were administered by the Sanhedrin, the learned assembly founded by the early Maccabees. There was a brief period of Judean autonomy when Agrippa I, grandson of Herod and Mariamne, was appointed king in 41 CE, he died in 44. The last Herodian ruler died in 92.

Jesus of Nazareth, born in Bethlehem under Herod the Great, began preaching in Galilee in 27 CE. Three years later he was executed outside Jerusalem by the Roman procurator Pontius Pilate (26-36). Jesus's ministry was one of a number of religious and political movements that flourished in the years following Herod's death.

Jewish resistance to Roman dictatorship and idol worship led to increasing tensions and finally to the outbreak of the First Jewish Revolt against Rome in 66. The rebellion was crushed by a Roman army under Vespasian, and later by his son Titus. Jerusalem fell in 70 following a five-month siege. The last pocket of Jewish resistance fell in 73 CE at Masada, where 960 beleaguered Jews had chosen death as free men over surrender to the Roman forces.

Titus destroyed the Temple in Jerusalem. The Herodian foundation stones of the western part of Temple Mount enclosure are its best-known remains, and are venerated today as the Western or formerly the "Wailing" Wall. Professor B. Mazar, the Israeli archaeologist, estimates the number of Jewish inhabitants in the country at the time of the destruction of the Temple to have been close to four million. From Josephus' *The Jewish Wars*, considered the major historical source for the period, it can be inferred that there were at the time approximately three million Jews living in 204 towns and villages throughout Judea and Galilee. Josephus estimated that more than a million died in the siege of Jerusalem alone, while Tacitus, the contemporary Roman historian, placed the number at 600,000. Tens of thousands were sold into slavery and taken to Rome.

JERUSALEM AT THE TIME OF THE SECOND TEMPLE

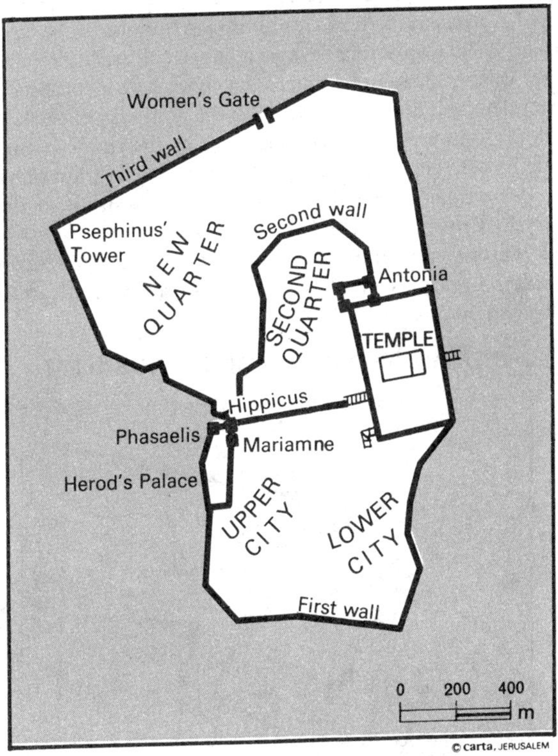

© carta, JERUSALEM

Ever since the destruction of the Temple and the forced exile, the yearning to return to Zion — the Holy Land — has become part and parcel of Jewish life, expressed in its culture, literature, rabbinical writing and prayer, and has become especially prominent in times of persecutions and hardships suffered by Jews throughout the Diaspora.

Despite the depletion of the population, a religious and cultural revival occurred shortly after the end of the Revolt under the influence of Rabban Yohanan Ben Zakkai, believed to have escaped Jerusalem during its siege. Ben Zakkai reestablished the Sanhedrin, the supreme legislative and judicial body, in Yavneh, on the country's southern coast. Tiberias became a centre of religious study and Jewish law.

New laws aimed at Hellenizing Rome's eastern provinces led to the unsuccessful Bar Kokhba revolt (132-135 CE). According to the Roman historian Cassius, more than half a million rebels died, along with those who perished from starvation and disease. Nevertheless, evidence shows that many survived and there was still a sizable Jewish population. Between the years 138 and 161 the condition of the Jews improved greatly. The Mishnah was completed in 210. It is the most comprehensive compilation of Jewish oral law to date, and became the basis for the Talmuds — a compendium for an all-embracing study of Jewish law and life.

After the Bar Kokhba rebellion, the Romans had changed the name of Jerusalem to Aelia Capitolina, in honour of the emperor Hadrian. Aelia Capitolina became a pagan cultural centre and the country was renamed Syria Palaestina. Jews were forbidden to live in Jerusalem and only once a year, on the ninth day of the Hebrew month of Av, were they permitted to enter the city to mourn the destruction of their holy places. The names Aelia Capitolina and Syria Palaestina were enforced until their abolition in the 4th century by Constantine the Great.

For the last two centuries of this period Palestine remained a backwater as various emperors presided over the disintegration of the Roman empire.

ROMAN AND BYZANTINE JERUSALEM

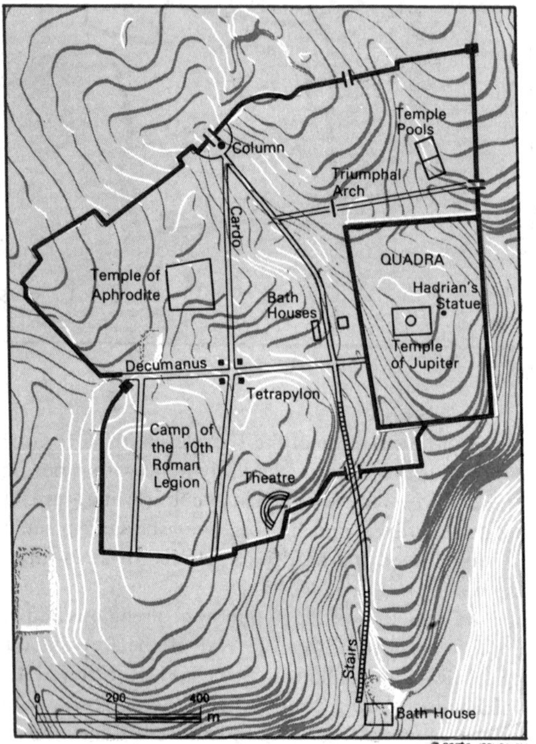

The Byzantine Period 324-640 CE

Sites: *Bet Alfa, Bet She'arim, Bethlehem, Shepherds' Field (Greek Orthodox church), Kursi, Latrun, Mar Saba, Mount Gerizim, Tiberias, Capernaum*

In 330 the emperor Constantine, who had legalized Christianity and made it the official religion of the Roman empire, moved his capital from Rome to Byzantium, renaming it Constantinople. Thus the Roman empire became the Byzantine empire.

The legalization of Christianity had a tremendous impact on Palestine. Constantine's mother Helena visited the Holy Land to identify the sites associated with the life of Jesus, and over these spots churches were built. Christian pilgrims visited their shrines, the monastic movement blossomed, and the devout, seeking enlightenment in isolation, filled the caves of the Judean wilderness. Several Byzantine cities were built; remains of five can be seen today in the Negev.

The condition of Jews throughout this period depended on the inclination of the emperor. Under Julian the Apostate (360-363) there were hopes of rebuilding the Temple, but after his sudden death these hopes vanished.

Growing numbers of Jews lived in agricultural villages in the Galilee, Jezreel Valley and even the Negev. According to various sources, there were at least 43 Jewish villages in the country as well as a Jewish community in Jerusalem. (The Capernaum and Bet Alfa synagogues were built during this period.)

The split in the Christian camp which occurred between 451 and 614 dividing the Orthodox and Monophysite believers resulted in a power struggle which was eventually won by the Orthodox faction. This division led to a weakening of Christian rule in the country which in turn facilitated the revolt in 485 of the Samaritans, who, in ever increasing measure, felt repressed by the Christian presence. The rebellion was quelled with great ferocity by the emperor Justinian (527-565). His reign was the last golden age of Byzantine rule before the onslaught of the Persian forces.

At the beginning of the seventh century the Sassanid empire of Persian with help from the local Jews began to usurp Byzantine territory. In 614 the captured Jerusalem, sacking the city and carrying off its inhabitants and the "True Cross". The Persians rewarded the Jews by handing them the city and subsequently banishing the Christians and their churches. But in 617 the Sassanids recaptured Jerusalem from their former allies. Under the emperor Heraclius, the Byzantines recovered and over a period of several years drove the Persians back, retaking the country in 622. In 629 Heraclius restored the "True Cross" to the Holy Sepulchre. However, the Byzantines held their recovered territory only a few years more.

The Arab Period 640-1099

Sites: *Hisham's Palace (Khirbet el Mafjar), Jerusalem (Dome of the Rock)*

Around the year 610, in Mecca on the western side of the Arabian peninsula, Muḥammad began to set forth the precepts of Islam. Muḥammad regarded himself as the last of God's prophets, of whom Abraham was the first and Jesus another, and Islam as the fulfillment of Judaism and Christianity. Islam's first great success came when the city of Medina requested Muḥammad's help as a peacemaker among feuding tribes, and his migration there in 622 marks the beginning of the Islamic calendar.

THE MOSLEM CONQUEST

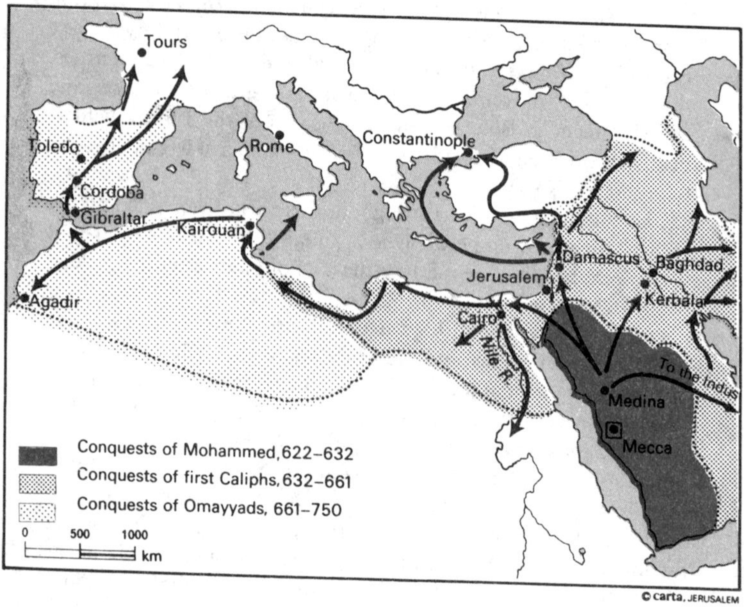

The physical focus of Islam is the Ka'ba, a huge cube of black stone in Mecca purportedly set up as an altar to God by Abraham and his son Ishmael, father of the Arabs. Medina is the second holiest city to Islam, after Mecca. Because of its significance to Judaism and Christianity, Jerusalem was important to Muḥammad. According to the Koran, Muḥammad himself was carried to Jerusalem on a mystical night journey. From the Outer Mosque he rose to heaven, where he prayed with Abraham, Moses and Jesus. The footprint he left in the rock is now enshrined in the Dome of the Rock on the Temple Mount.

The ideology of Islam spread rapidly among the pagans of Arabia. The first serious incursions of the Islamic community into the exhausted Persian and Byzantine empires began in 633, when the Arabs took southern Palestine and parts of Mesopotamia. In 636 they decisively defeated the Byzantines in a battle on the Yarmuk River, which gave them control of Palestine and Syria. Jerusalem surrendered in 638 after a two-year siege; Caesarea held out for seven years until 640, when a Jew showed the Arabs a secret passage into the city. The fall of Ashqelon followed soon after in 641.

Following the conquest, the new rulers rewarded the Jews for their aid by allowing development of Jewish community life. A number of Jews returned from the Arabian peninsula, to which they had fled during the persecutions under Byzantine rule.

After Muḥammad's death in 632, his place as leader of the community was taken by a caliph (successor). The second caliph was the great Omar Ibn el Khattab (634-644), who came to Jerusalem in 638 or 640. Jews, Christians and Zarathustrians were respected by Moslems as fellow People of the Book, who had received God's written revelations. To show his respect, Omar declined to pray in the Holy Sepulchre, lest the church be made into a mosque in his honour by his people.

The murder in 656 of the third caliph, Othman, led to a major split in Islam. The followers of the fourth caliph, 'Ali, became the Shi'ites, a name covering a number of divergent minority sects to the present day. The main line of Islamic thought, followed by the majority of Muslims, would later become the Sunni sect. The Shi'ites were defeated by the governor of Damascus, Mu'awiya, a cousin of Othman, who proclaimed himself the fifth caliph in Jerusalem in 660.

Continued warfare with the Shi'ites in Arabia made Mecca and Medina insecure and at times inaccessible, thus increasing Jerusalem's importance for Islam. The ninth caliph, Abd el Malik (685-705), and his son Walid I built the two great mosques on the Temple Mount. The Dome of the Rock, built above the crown of Mount Moriah, was completed in 691; the external decoration is recent, but the structure and the mosaics inside are the originals. The El'Aqṣa mosque originally built by Walid has been destroyed by earthquakes and rebuilt several times.

A dissident Shi'ite sect, the Fatimids, led by descendants of 'Ali and Muḥammad's daughter Fatima, established itself in North Africa early in the tenth century. In 973 the Fatimids took Egypt from the Abbasids, a dynasty founded by a descendant of Muḥammad's uncle, Abbas, and ruled there until 1171. From 996 to 1021 the Fatimid lands, including Palestine, suffered under Caliph Ḥakim the Mad. After harassing his Sunni subjects for some time, he turned on the Jews and Christians in 1008 and until 1015 persecuted them severely, destroying all their shrines, including in 1009 the Church of the Holy Sepulchre. He then proclaimed himself the incarnation of the deity, attracting a small following, who became the Druze sect, existing today in Lebanon, Carmel, Galilee and the Golan.

Most of the indigenous population had converted to Islam, some by force. Many of the converts were *fellahin* (peasants) who lived in the farming villages; the majority of town dwellers adhered to Christianity. The only town established by the Arabs during this period was Ramla which was founded in 716. Ramla, as its name implies (meaning sand in Arabic), was built on the sand dunes, and became the flourishing capital of the southern region. It lay on the important crossroad between Damascus and Egypt and Jaffa and Jerusalem, and developed into a major commercial centre for the surrounding hinterland.

Jewish and Arab sources, supported by archaeological evidence, tell of several Jewish communities which existed throughout this period namely in Ramla during the 8th century, in the Acre and Haifa region and an extensive community in Caesarea. Tiberias was the Jewish spiritual centre, and Jewish communities existed in various places east of the Jordan. Most were employed in agriculture, trade and crafts.

Various tribes penetrated the region throughout this period; the most distinctive were the Bedouin, who adopted Islam and roamed the desert areas, the Negev, and east of the Jordan. They were often the cause of friction in frontier areas as they raided and looted lands of permanent communities.

Syria and Palestine became a battleground between the Fatimids and the rulers of Baghdad in the eleventh century. War, Bedouin raids and earthquakes (in 1033 and 1067) devastated the country. In the middle of the century the Seljuk Turks, a new vizier dynasty, appeared from Central Asia, capturing Baghdad in 1055 and driving the Fatimids from Jerusalem in 1071. Staunch Sunni Moslems, the Seljuks closed the holy places to Christian pilgrims, creating a frustrated religious fervour in the West that was to contribute, like Ḥakim's destruction, to the origin of the Crusades. Also in 1071, the Seljuks defeated the Byzantine imperial army at Manzikert in Asia Minor, dooming that empire to decline and eventual extinction.

In the last quarter of the eleventh century, the Seljuks' empire was weakened by constant rebellions and by power struggles at all levels of government. The Fatimids in Egypt were suffering civil war, in which political disputes became religious factional struggles. Into this chaotic fragmentation of the Moslem world came the Crusades.

The Crusader Period 1099-1291

Sites: *Abu Ghosh, 'Akko, Belvoir (Kokhav Hayarden), Caesarea, Montfort, Latrun, Nabi Samwil, Nimrod, Jerusalem (Church of the Holy Sepulchre, St. Anne's)*

In spite of the split in 1054 between the Greek and Latin churches, the new Byzantine emperor Alexius Comnenus, finding himself hard pressed by the Turks, asked the Pope for aid, expecting a few bands of mercenaries. In November 1095 Pope Urban II called for help in freeing the holy places for Christendom. The response was overwhelming. Besides a mob of thousands of untrained peasants, eventually massacred by the Turks, four small armies left for the Holy Land. After breaking with Alexius, the Crusaders took Antioch after a long siege.

The advancing armies reached the coastal road leading into Palestine in May, 1099. The Crusaders made their way from Caesarea to Ramla, whose Christian population fled, and then on to Jerusalem. Heroic efforts to defend the city were thwarted by Godfrey de Bouillon, who succeeded in penetrating the Jewish quarter in the north of the city. The Jews, who had gathered to take shelter in the synagogue, were either massacred or expelled. The Holy City fell on July 15, 1099.

Having gained their chief objective, the Crusaders then took the fortified coastal cities, slaughtering Jews along the way; the conquest raged for ten years, till 1110.

The Crusaders set up four separate Latin states: the counties of Edessa and Tripoli, the principality of Antioch, and the kingdom of Jerusalem. They governed their states like European feudal principalities; their administration was among the best the country had known. They built castles and churches, of which St. Anne's in Jerusalem is one of the loveliest churches surviving. In Jerusalem, el'Aqṣa mosque was taken over for a royal residence and later became the headquarters of the Templar Knights, named for Temple Mount. Some of the Crusader kings of Jerusalem were buried in the Church of the Holy Sepulchre, which they had helped rebuild.

The Crusaders, whose numbers were tiny, succeeded only because their opponents were even more divided. A revival of Moslem power began, however, in 1127, with the accession to power of a new emir in Aleppo. He succeeded in taking back Edessa in 1144. Edessa's fall provoked the futile Second Crusade of 1147-1148, led by Louis VII of France and Conrad III of Germany. In 1146 the emir's son, Nur ed Din Zengi, took over his father's domain, expanding it and creating a unified Moslem power.

THE CRUSADER KINGDOMS

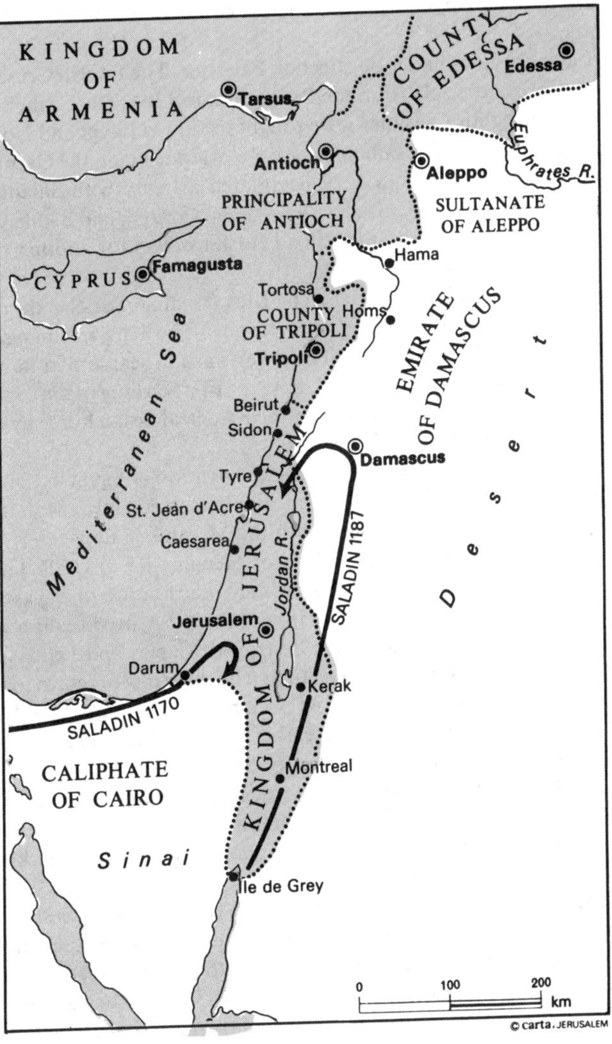

Through the 1160s the king of Jerusalem and Nur ed Din fought for control of Egypt. Nur ed Din's army, commanded by a Kurdish soldier, won in 1169. Two years later the Kurd's nephew, Salah ed Din, or Saladin, took power in Egypt, replacing the Fatimids with his own Ayyubid dynasty.

After early defeats, Saladin developed tactics which proved successful against the armoured knights. In 1187 he lured the Crusaders, distracted by internal dissension, to the Horns of Hattin (Qarne Ḥittim) above Tiberias, where almost the entire Frankish military force was slaughtered. Three months later Saladin took Jerusalem, and when the Moslems ceased fighting for the winter only Tyre remained to the Crusaders.

Europe responded to the fall of Jerusalem with the Third Crusade, led by Richard I the Lionheart of England, Philip II Augustus of France, and Frederick I Babarossa of Germany. Fighting from 1189 to 1192, they failed to take Jerusalem, but they reestablished the Crusader kingdom in the coastal cities for another hundred years.

Later crusades had little effect on Palestine. The Fourth Crusade took Constantinople from the Byzantines in 1204. The Fifth, Seventh and Eighth Crusades were fought mostly in Egypt and North Africa. The Sixth Crusade was hardly a crusade at all; the German emperor Frederick II in 1229 negotiated a treaty with Saladin's successors giving the Crusaders Jerusalem, Nazareth and Bethlehem for ten years. The Crusaders then held Jerusalem for another five years, losing it finally in 1244.

In 1244 Jerusalem was sacked by Khwarasmian Turks in the pay of a contender for the Ayyubid throne. The Khwarasmians, a displaced people moving violently westward in search of a homeland and soon to be annihilated, were the first warning of horrors to come: they had been driven from their Central Asian home by the expanding power of the Mongols.

In the wake of the Seventh Crusade's invasion of Egypt in 1249, a Turkish emir with the support of highly trained slave (Mamluk) troops replaced the Ayyubids with the Mamluk state.

The Mongol Hülagü, grandson of Genghis Khan (1206-1227) and brother of Kublai Khan, brought his hordes to devastate western Asia. Baghdad fell in 1258, and the last Abbasid caliph was executed. In 1260 the Mongols destroyed Aleppo and Damascus with appalling brutality. When Hülagü left his army to return to the east, the Mamluk sultan attacked. At a battle at 'En Jalud (Ma'yan Ḥarod) near Bet She'an in September 1260, the Mamluks defeated the Mongols and drove them out of Syria.

Baybars, who became sultan soon after the victory, gradually captured the remaining Crusader holdings. In 1291, his successor took 'Akko, the last Crusader stronghold, ending the Latin kingdom founded two centuries before.

After the devastation caused by the Crusader conquests had ended, the Jewish communities began to reconstruct their lives. Many refugees were either absorbed into villages, such as Ashqelon, that had to a degree withstood the Crusader onslaughts, or had fled to Egypt. The communities of the agricultural regions of the Galilee suffered minimally from the massacres. The status of Jews, as well as that of Syrian Christians and Moslems, were protected; the well being of the Crusaders depended largely upon the majority of the Moslem population. For a time Jews were forbidden access to Jerusalem but in Acre and Ashqelon major Jewish communities persisted. The remainder of the Jews lived in small, scattered villages throughout the country.

Saladin's conquests wakened the messianic hopes of Jews in Europe and the East to "return" to the Holy Land. The proclamation issued by Saladin inviting Jews to return to Jerusalem engendered a Jewish revival in the 12th and 13th centuries. Newcomers included three hundred rabbis from France and England, arriving in 1211, and a large group of Jews from North Africa.

However, the renewed Jerusalem community was short-lived; the destruction of the city in 1244 virtually extinguished Jewish life here. Despite the efforts of the Spanish born Jewish scholar, Nahmanides (the Ramban), who in 1267 succeeded for a time in resuscitating Jerusalem's synagogue and community; after his death in 1270, these efforts were halted. Renewed Moslem attacks once again brought destruction. Acre's Jewish community gained in importance and existed in relative security until the city's destruction in 1291.

Economically Jews were employed primarily in glass-blowing, pharmacy, shipping and banking. Many pilgrims' hostels and hospitals were set up by various active religious orders during Saladin's rule. The Moslem population were mostly farmers as were some Crusaders who had settled in the rural areas. International trade prospered, especially with Europe and the Far East. The ports too thrived, handling mostly imported mechandise and some few export commodities.

The Mamluk Period 1291-1516

Sites: *En Nabi Musa, Jerusalem (Temple Mount area)*

The Mamluks were not a dynasty; each ruler was bought as a boy, first from the Central Asian Turks and later from the Circassians, and trained as a soldier.

The Mongols under Gazan returned in 1299, taking Damascus in 1300 and briefly setting up an Armenian Christian king in Jerusalem. When Gazan left to meet an attack from the east, the Mamluks regained the lost territory. Late in the fourteenth century Tamerlane appeared out of Central Asia and, like previous Mongol leaders, ravaged the land from India to Europe. He took Aleppo, Damascus and Baghdad but passed by Palestine, dying in Samarkand in 1405.

Palestine, divided among three governors, produced little and had little political importance under the Mamluks. Faded leaders sent to Jerusalem sought sanctity by building houses, schools and hostels, embellished with decorative stonework, against the walls of Temple Mount, while the rest of the country decayed. The coastal cities, together with their flourishing Jewish communities, had been destroyed to prevent further Crusader landings; trade languished.

MAMLUK RULE

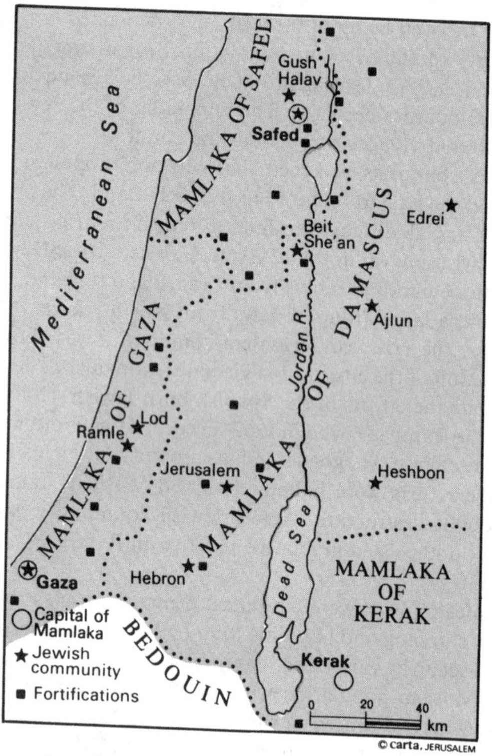

© carta, JERUSALEM

Only Gaza, Ramla and Nablus remained relatively large cities. Local rebellions, Bedouin raids on cities and the coast road, plagues, locusts and two major earthquakes all contributed to the country's decline.

However, at the beginning of the 15th century, Jews began arriving in growing numbers from Italy and central Europe. They were mostly peddlers and petty tradesmen. The Jews received harsh treatment from the Mamluk authorities and in 1440, crippling taxes imposed in Jerusalem compelled many to leave. At the turn of the century, Spanish Jews, faced with persecution or expulsion, began to pour into the country.

The Ottoman Period 1516-1918

Sites: *'Akko, Jerusalem (city walls and gates)*

A small Turkish tribe in Asia Minor began expanding in 1300 under their chief Othman. By 1393 they had an empire in southeastern Europe and Asia Minor. Though temporarily crushed by Tamerlane's passage, the Ottomans recovered. In 1453 Sultan Muḥammad II took Constantinople, ending the Byzantine empire.

The Ottomans fought with artillery and firearms. Sultan Selim I easily defeated the Mamluks in 1516 north of Aleppo and in 1517 outside Cairo; Syria, Palestine and Egypt were added to the Ottoman empire.

Selim's son Suleiman I, the Magnificent, (1520-1566), carried the Ottoman conquest to its greatest extent, reaching the walls of Vienna in the west. Like his father, an able administrator, he rebuilt the walls of Jerusalem. Much of the 16th century walls still stands today.

Palestine was part of the province of Damascus which Suleiman divided into various districts, bringing a sense of order and security to the land. Early in his reign agriculture and industry revived; olive oil and soap were important products. Christians of Jerusalem, Bethlehem and neighbouring villages manufactured religious artifacts from wood and mother-of-pearl, which were sold as souvenirs to pilgrims or exported. Many of the new Jewish immigrants settled in the Galilee. The largest community in the 16th century was in Safed, giving rise to a renaissance of Jewish scholarship, legal codification and mysticism which for generations to come would spread to Jewry throughout the world. Safed also became the economic centre for the hinterland of Galilee.

During the second half of the16th century, an attempt was made by Don Joseph Nasi, duke of the island of Naxos, to resettle Jews in Tiberias and its environs. Though successful at first, the plan to rebuild Tiberias eventually was abandoned due to various political and economic factors. By the end of the century there were 1,000 Jews in Jerusalem and a few Jewish families in Hebron and Nablus.

But unstable conditions caused the position of Jews in most places to deteriorate. However, due to persecutions in the Ukraine in 1648 and the messianic movement of Shabbetai Ẓevi, Jews continued to come to the Holy Land. In 1700, Rabbi Judah Ḥasid led a group of 1,300 Jews from Poland to Jerusalem; most fled to Safed and Tiberias as a result of persecutions.

THE OTTOMAN EMPIRE AT ITS GREATEST EXTENT

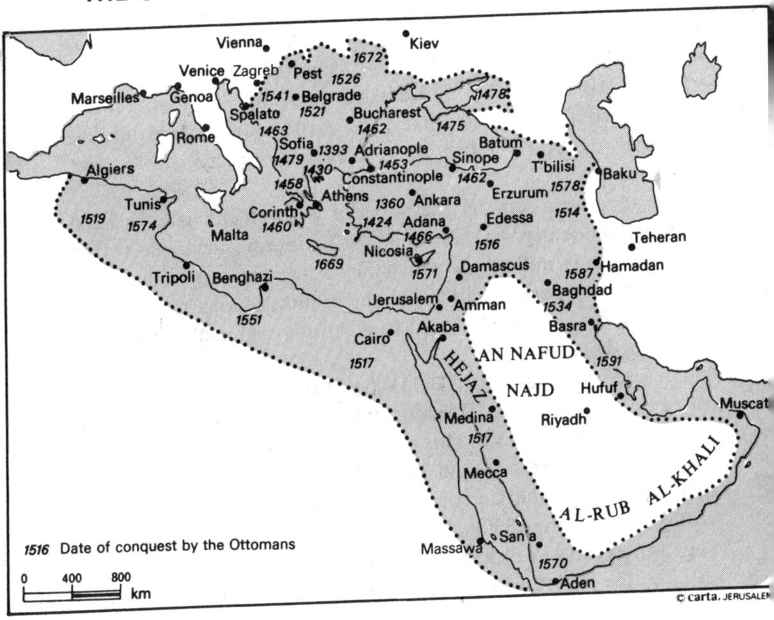

Suleiman's incompetent successors, occupied with controlling Egypt, holding Iraq and later fighting off the expanding Russian empire, allowed Syria and Palestine to decay. The economy collapsed. The major towns, having Ottoman garrisons, generally remained loyal to the empire, but the countryside fell under the control of local tribal chieftains. The tribes attacked towns and traders, and a long-lasting hostility grew up between the rural and urban cultures.

Some chieftains extended their rule over a considerable area. Fakhr ed Din (1590-1635), a Druze, eventually controlled most of Palestine and Lebanon, before he was defeated and executed by the Ottomans. The Bedouin sheikh Dahir el 'Amr (1720-1776) extended his rule over the district of Tiberias, where he helped rebuild the Jewish centre in 1740. From Galilee he expanded into Samaria and Lebanon, until likewise defeated by the Ottomans. Aḥmad Pasha (1776-1804), called el Jazzar (the butcher) due to the harshness of his rule, in turn gained control of all of Palestine and parts of Lebanon and Syria, which he governed from his rebuilt capital at Acre.

It was during el Jazzar's reign that Napoleon Bonaparte, after the destruction of his fleet off Alexandria, began fighting his way back from Egypt to France through Palestine. An unsuccessful three-month siege of Acre in 1799 made him retire to Egypt. The wounded and sick French soldiers left in Haifa were slaughtered by Aḥmad Pasha el Jazzar. Napoleon's brief campaign added to the devastation of the country and destroyed el Jazzar's economic and administrative achievements.

But devout Jews continued to come to the Holy Land. A group of Ḥassidic Jews from Poland and Lithuania, disciples of Israel b. Eliezer Ba'al Shem Tov, arrived during the second half of the 18th century, and were followed by their opponents, the *mitnaggedim*, disciples of Rabbi Elijah, the Gaon of Vilna. By 1800, the Jewish population numbered some 7,000 while the Moslems and Christians numbered 246,000 and 22,000 respectively.

Shortly after 1800 the empire began to disintegrate. Its security remained vulnerable, and great parts of the country were uninhabited due to malaria and dangers of Bedouins attacks in frontier areas.

The governors sent by the imperial government usually acted semi-independently. Subjects had to maintain allegiance to the religious group (millet) into which they were born rather than to the central government. Included in these autonomous millets were Christians and Jews, tolerated to a certain degree although controlled by Moslems.

The rise of Muḥammed 'Ali (1805-1849) in Egypt and incursions into Palestine by his son, Ibrahim Pasha (1832-1840), marked a new era for the Holy Land. This period of Egyptian rule permitted European awareness of and involvement in the Holy Land that literally changed the face of the country.

Beginning in the 1830's, European concern with the holy places began to express itself in research groups and missions despatched to Palestine to stake a claim for any particular sect. Thousands of

Christian pilgrims arrived and churches, monasteries, schools, seminaries and hospitals were established throughout the country. Jerusalem became the focal point of rivalry between various powers and religious orders as it developed into an important pilgrim, administrative and religious centre. The rights of foreign nationals were protected and guaranteed by a growing number of foreign consulates operating under a system of Capitulations (privileges granted to foreign powers by the Turks). Several Jews too enjoyed these same privileges.

The surge of building carried Jerusalem beyond its Ottoman walls in the middle of the century. Sir Moses Montefiore, the Jewish philanthropist, initiated projects beyond the walled city. The introduction of steamships enabled the expansion of international trade; the first road was built for wheeled carriages between Jaffa and Jerusalem. From the 1840s the Jewish population grew, particularly in Jerusalem despite government-imposed obstacles. By 1900, the population of Jerusalem totalled 55,000: 35,000 Jews, 10,000 Moslems and 10,000 Christians.

Towards the end of the century concerted efforts were made to increase Jewish settlement of the land. In 1878 Petaḥ Tiqwa, the first Jewish village, was founded. A major wave of immigration, the First Aliyah, consisting mainly of Jewish pioneers from Russia and Rumania belonging to a group called the Bilu, arrived in 1882 and the following years. There was a steady increase in the number of agricultural villages and the economy flourished. New methods of technology and agriculture were introduced, and home industries, international trade and shipping of citrus and wine expanded. Some of these innovations were prompted by the German Temple Society who immigrated in the 1860's. There was a revival of the Hebrew language, which had not been spoken for centuries, and Jews began to use it both at home and in the schools.

In 1897, the First Zionist Congress met in Basle, Switzerland, under the auspices of Theodor Herzl and advocated the establishment of a Jewish homeland in Palestine. Simultaneously the World Zionist Organization, the Jewish National Fund for purchasing lands in Palestine for Jewish settlement and the Jewish Colonial Bank were set up.

The Second Aliyah (1904-1914) added a new dimension to the Jewish population. Many of the immigrants, coming from Russia, had fervent socialist leanings. They founded the first *kibbutzim* and *moshavim* at the beginning of the century. The first Jewish city, Tel Aviv, was established in 1909; by 1914, the Jewish population had swelled to 85,000, 12,000 of them resided in rural areas and 44 farming villages.

Prior to World War I, the strategic importance of Palestine grew ever more vital for all parties concerned. In the war Turkey sided with Germany, and the population of Palestine found itself isolated. Jews were persecuted, expelled from the Jaffa and some 10,000 expelled to Egypt.

A number of documents were signed by Britain during World War I agreeing to contradictory destinies for the Ottoman Arab lands. In 1915, encouraging Arab nationalist aspirations to provoke a revolt against Turkey, the British promised independence to an ill-defined set of territories. In 1916 the secret Sykes-Picot agreement carved out territories in the Middle East for Great Britain and France. In November 1917 the Balfour Declaration was issued recognizing a Jewish national home in Palestine.

Aided by a revolt in the Arabian Peninsula, the British general Allenby defeated the Turks, entering Jerusalem in December 1917. In the dismemberment of the Ottoman empire that followed the war, the League of Nations gave Great Britain a mandate to govern Palestine.

THE BRITISH MANDATE, 1920

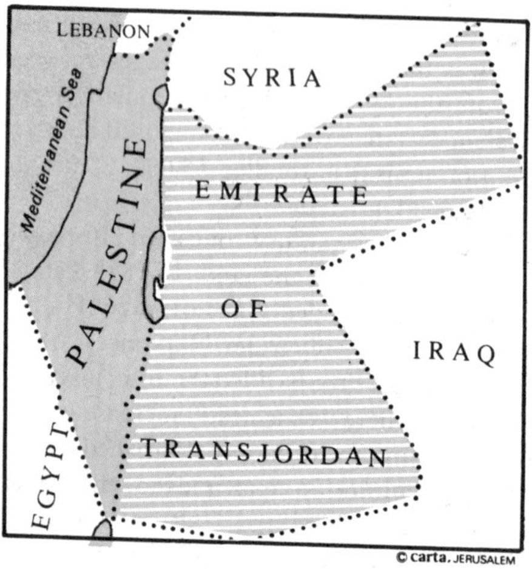

The British (Mandate) Period, 1918-1948

When after the war the French and British took over governing the Middle East and the Balfour Declaration was reaffirmed, many Arabs felt betrayed despite their improved social and economic conditions. Continuing Jewish immigration and settlement produced increasing tensions that resulted in major Arab riots in 1920, 1921 and 1929. The Arab-Jewish strife led to the creation of an underground Jewish self-defence organization, the Haganah. Despite anti-Jewish acts immigration continued and the Third Aliyah (1919-1923) brought 35,000 newcomers, mainly from Russia, Poland and Galicia. With the purchase of the Jezreel Valley the number of Jewish settlements reached one hundred. Many new factories and enterprises were established, including the Electric Corporation founded by Pinḥas Rutenberg, at Naharayim near the mouth of the Yarmuk River, and the Dead Sea Potash Company. Many of the new pioneers were employed in road-building and several more *kibbutzim* and *moshavim* were set up. Together with members of the Second Aliyah they founded the Histadrut (General Federation of Jewish Labour) which created a new Jewish working society in Palestine.

Although an economic recession caused many immigrants to leave the country, the Fourth Aliyah (1924-1928) brought 82,000 newcomers, mostly middle-class shopkeepers and artisans from

THE U.N. PARTITION OF PALESTINE 1947

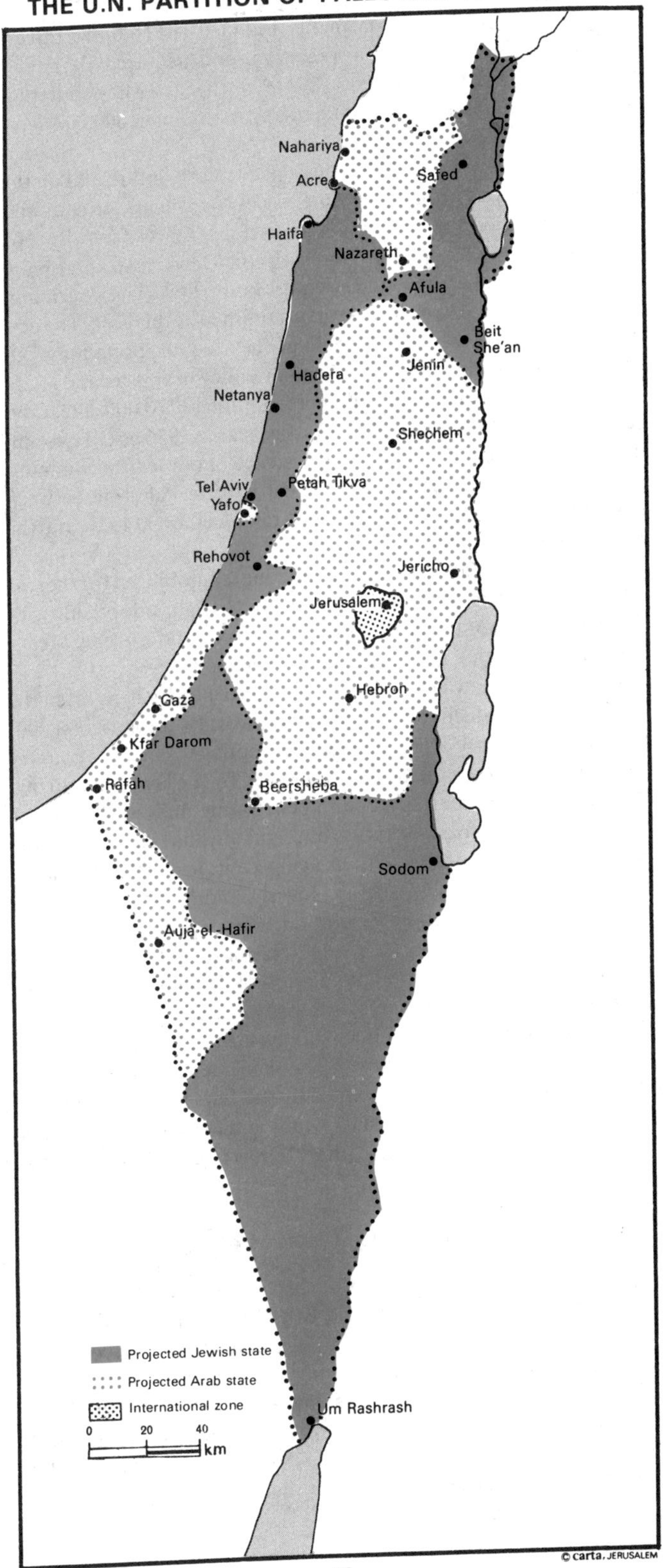

Poland. They set up industrial plants, founded The Hebrew University in Jerusalem and Haifa Technion, and acquired the Ḥefer Valley for Jewish settlement. By 1929 the Jewish population totalled 180,000; there were 140 settlements and over 300,000 acres of land had been purchased.

The Fifth Aliyah (1932-1940) was particularly influential on the local scene. It was prompted by the rise of Nazism in Germany and resulted in a flood of thousands of Jewish refugees from Europe and particularly Germany. Many of the Jews from Germany brought financial capital, and scientific know-how. The Weizmann Institute of Science in Reḥovot was established at this time. The new arrivals totalled 213,000, swelling the Jewish population to 450,000. The acquisition of the Zevulun Valley near Acre and Haifa led to an increase in agricultural land, holdings (370,000 acres) and settlements (256). A renewal of Arab attacks in 1936 lasted two and a half years, and endangered the existence of the Jewish community. The British proposal in 1937 to partition Palestine between Jews and Arabs provoked a serious Arab rebellion in 1938, and the proposal was dropped.

When World War II broke out, the country mobilized for the war effort; 30,000 Palestinian Jews volunteered to fight side by side with British forces and served in North Africa, Asia and Europe. Meanwhile the economic infrastructure burgeoned.

However, mounting tensions came to a head when, after the Holocaust, in which one-third of the world's Jews (6,000,000) perished under the Nazis, survivors attempting to enter the country were turned back by the British. Thwarted by the law, some 30,000 "illegal" immigrants succeeded in penetrating the shores with the help of underground resistance groups, mainly the Haganah. At the same time, Arab terrorist actions against the Jews escalated and a three-cornered struggle — Arab, Jewish, and British — resulted. Unable to find a workable solution, Great Britain decided to hand over the matter to the United Nations. In 1947 there were 615,000 Jews (out of a total population of 2,000,000), 303 Jewish settlements and 470,000 acres of Jewish owned land.

In November 1947 the United Nations General Assembly passed a resolution to divide Palestine into independent Arab and Jewish states. This resolution was accepted by the Jews but rejected by the Arabs. Attacks were launched by Arabs and the Jewish population went on the defensive. The British withdrew from Palestine on May 15, 1948.

The State of Israel, 1948

On May 14, 1948 the independence of the state of Israel was proclaimed in Tel Aviv by David Ben-Gurion, head of the provisional government. Armies from Egypt, Jordan, Iraq, Syria and Lebanon immediately invaded. Israel's War of Independence had begun. With two brief intermissions — in June and July — the fighting lasted till the beginning of 1949. The Jews were able to drive the invaders back, but at the cost of many lives and casualties; the death toll reached 8,000, more than one percent of the total Jewish population.

THE WAR OF INDEPENDENCE AND ARMISTICE LINES

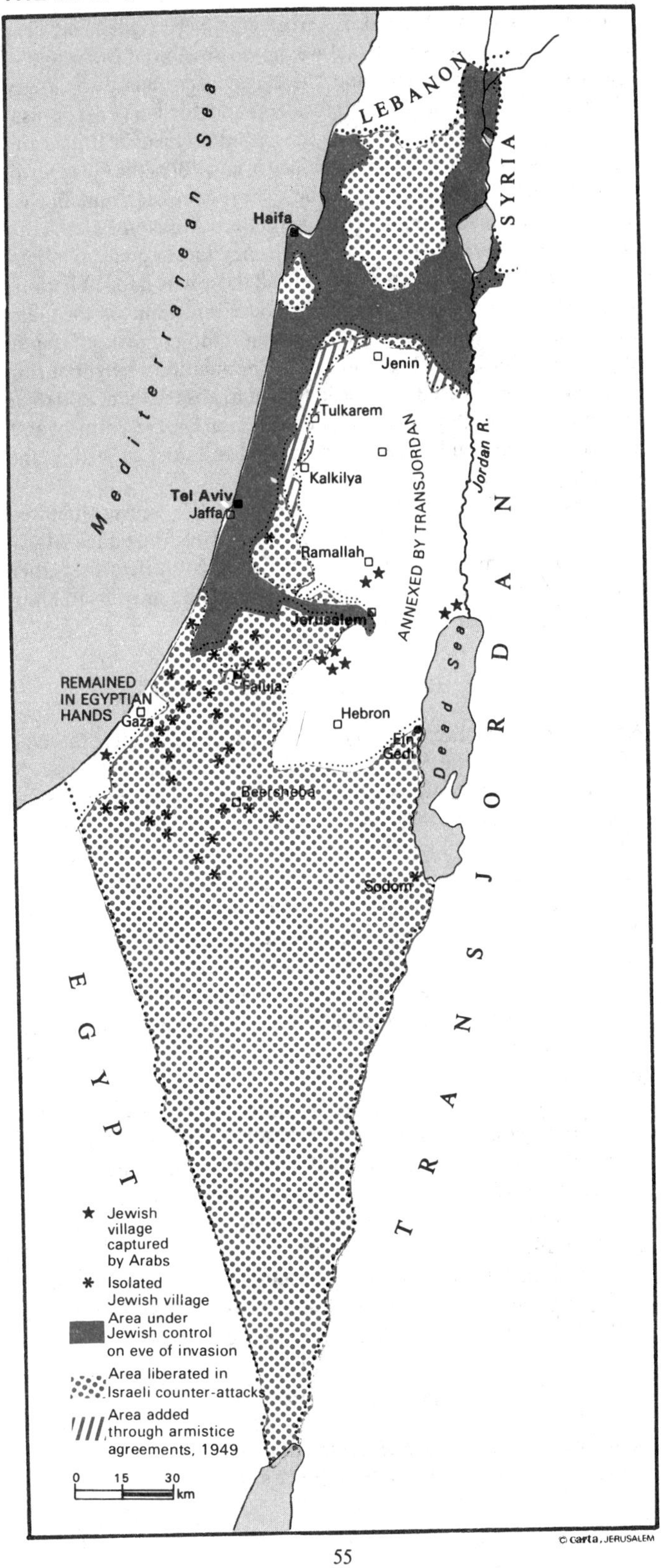

Mediterranean Sea
LEBANON
SYRIA
Haifa
Jenin
Tulkarem
Kalkilya
Tel Aviv
Jaffa
Ramallah
ANNEXED BY TRANSJORDAN
Jordan R.
Jerusalem
Faluja
REMAINED IN EGYPTIAN HANDS
Gaza
Hebron
Ein Gedi
Dead Sea
Beersheba
Sodom
TRANSJORDAN
EGYPT
Jewish village captured by Arabs
Isolated Jewish village
Area under Jewish control on eve of invasion
Area liberated in Israeli counter-attacks
Area added through armistice agreements, 1949
0
15
30
km

By the time the Armistice Agreements were signed, between February and July 1949, Israel was in possession of the whole of Galilee, the Coastal Plain and the Negev. Jerusalem was a city divided between Israel (west Jerusalem) and Jordan (east Jerusalem). Jordan retained control of the mountain areas of Judea and Samaria (West Bank). Egypt remained in control of the Gaza Strip.

In the belief that there would be a short campaign and an easy victory, Arab leaders had persuaded fellow Arabs in Palestine to temporarily leave their homes, which they did in great numbers. There was, however, no way back and all those who had left became refugees. These Arab refugees were housed in camps in the Gaza Strip, the West Bank and the adjoining Arab countries. Despite their proclaimed kinship and sparse populations neighbouring Arab countries refused to resettle them and absorb them into their economies. Their condition and presence soon bred resentment and hatred of Israel and have led to conflict in Israel as well as the Kingdom of Jordan and in Lebanon.

During the first fifteen years of independence, several hundred thousand survivors of war-torn Europe arrived in Israel. Many more came from North Africa and the Arab countries; altogether the newcomers totalled over one and a half million, thereby trebling the Jewish population.

The Sinai Campaign 1956

Despite the Armistice Agreement signed with Israel after the War of Independence, the Arab states continued to consider themselves as being in a state of war with Israel. Incidents along the armistice lines were frequent. "Fidayun" (armed infiltrators on suicide missions) were sent into Israeli territory on murder and sabotage missions to disrupt normal life in the country.

Extending their war against Israel to the economic front, the Arab states organized a trade boycott, while Egypt sought to choke off Israel's maritime link with Africa and Southeast Asia by blockading the Strait of Tiran, at the mouth of the Gulf of Elat.

Things came to a head in October 1956, when the Egyptian ruler, Gamal Abdul Nasser, newly equipped with Soviet weaponry, gathered an army in Sinai to launch an attack.

But Israel struck first and in a matter of days overcame the Egyptian forces, occupied the entire Sinai peninsula and lifted the naval blockade at the Strait of Tiran. Meanwhile, Britain and France (incensed at Nasser for having unilaterally seized the Suez Canal in July of that year) bombarded Egyptian military installations.

Very soon, however, the United States and the Soviet Union, acting together, compelled Israel and its allies to withdraw, and U.N. forces were stationed along the old Egyptian-Israeli border.

The Six-Day War 1967

In May 1967 President Nasser again amassed an army in Sinai, reinstituted the naval blockade of the Tiran Strait and dismissed the

U.N. forces stationed along the Egyptian-Israeli border. He made an alliance with King Hussein of Jordan who, despite urgent messages sent him from Israeli leaders, opened hostilities by occupying U.N. headquarters and shelling Jewish Jerusalem. In the swift campaigns which followed, Israel won, in six days, East Jerusalem, the West Bank, the Golan Heights, the Gaza Strip and the Sinai Peninsula.

The Yom Kippur War 1973

On the Day of Atonement (Yom Kippur), 6 October 1973, the Egyptians crossed the Suez Canal in force; simultaneously Syrians invaded the Golan Heights. After bitter fighting and heavy losses on both sides, the Israel Defence Forces were able to stem the Egyptian advance across the Sinai desert and to drive the Syrians out of the Golan Heights.

On 22 October, the U.N. voted a cease-fire, and the war came to an end. Disengagement of forces agreements were signed between Israel and Egypt, and Israel and Syria, respectively; later an interim agreement was signed between Israel and Egypt. These agreements with Egypt, which grew out of the direct contacts at Kilometre 101 and Dr. Kissinger's "shuttle diplomacy", were destined to blossom, a few years later, into a full peace treaty — the first ever between Israel and an Arab state.

In November 1977, Egypt's President Anwar Sadat made a historic journey to Jerusalem, where he was warmly welcomed, and where he conferred with Israeli Prime Minister Menachem Begin and other leaders and addressed the Knesset.

Negotiations began for a peace treaty between the two nations. On 26 March 1979, the Egypt-Israel Peace Treaty was signed in Washington, D.C. by President Sadat and Prime Minister Begin, with President Jimmy Carter of the United States, who had played an active role in the negotiations, signing as a witness. The treaty provided for the normalization of relations between Egypt and Israel, including the exchange of ambassadors (which took place in February 1980), and Israel's withdrawal by April 1982, from all of the Sinai Peninsula.

"Peace for Galilee" Operation 1982

In order to distance the Palestine Liberation Organization who had set up a mini-military state in southern Lebanon from the civilian settlements of the Galilee, Israel embarked on a campaign against the P.L.O. on June 5th 1982. Fighting raged for more than two and a half months with Beirut besieged for several weeks.

Peace talks were initiated on December 28th 1982 between Israel and Lebanon in the presence of U.S. representatives. Khalde in Lebanon and Qiryat Shemona in Israel were designated as the alternate sites for the talks.

ISRAEL AND THE CAMP DAVID AGREEMENT

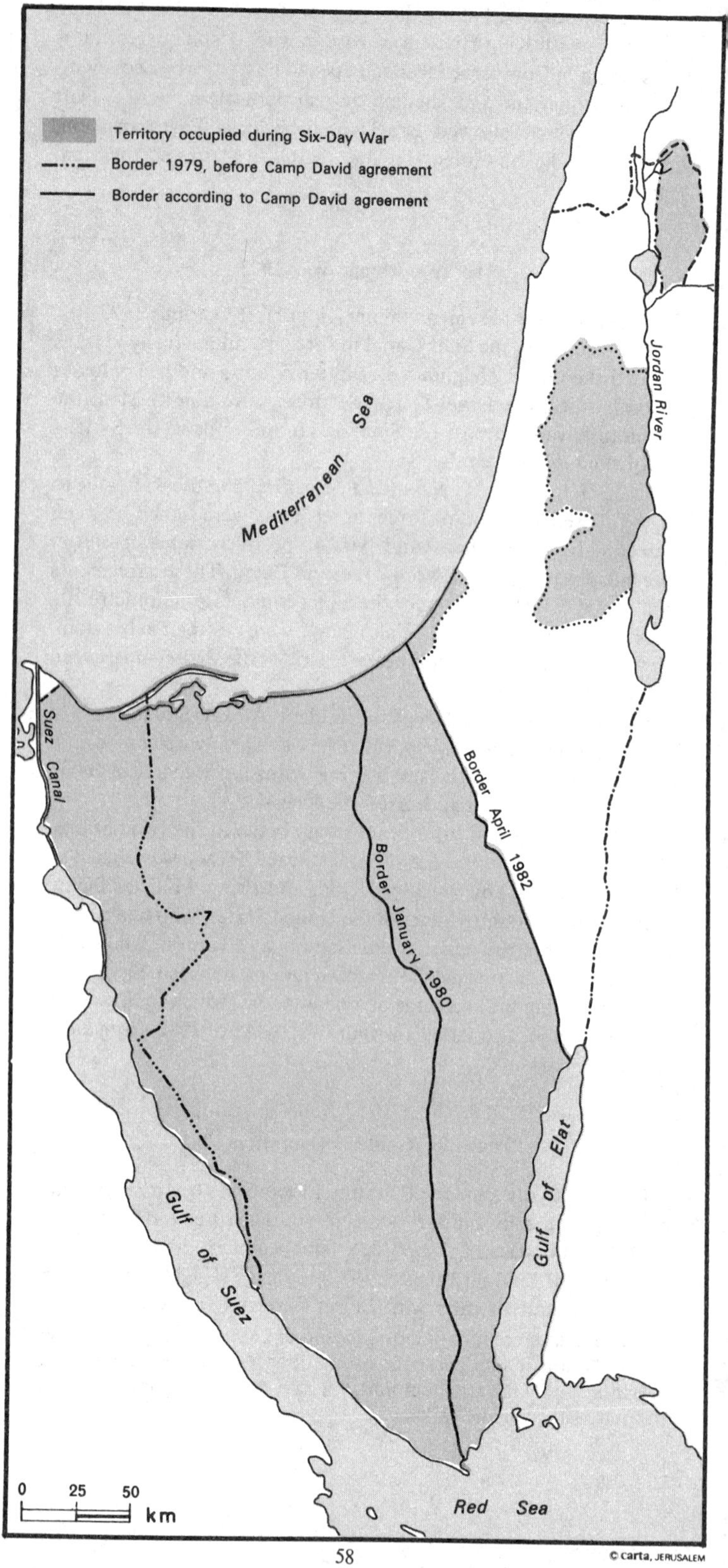

MODERN ISRAEL

The Government

The modern state of Israel is a democratic republic founded on universal suffrage. Its system of government is parliamentary, with a largely ceremonial president, a prime minister and a Cabinet, and a unicameral legislature, the Knesset.

The Knesset's 120 seats are distributed by proportional representation. At each election the various parties offer lists of candidates, and the citizen votes for one party's list. According to the percentage of the vote it wins, each party is allotted a certain number of the Knesset's seats. Members of the Knesset are elected for a four-year term, which may be shortened by the dissolution of the Knesset.

No one party has yet held an absolute majority of the seats in the Knesset, and consequently all governments have been coalitions. From 1948 to 1977 the Labour Party led the government, generally supported by the National Religious Party (NRP) and an assortment of smaller groups and independents. In May 1977, the leadership passed to the Likud party with a coalition of several groups. In 1984, a National Unity Government was formed following elections in which no one bloc of parties received an absolute majority.

It is the responsibility of the president to select a prime minister who can command a majority of the Knesset's votes. The person selected by the president must be a member of the Knesset, and in practice is the head of the party holding the largest number of Knesset seats. The Cabinet is composed of members of the various parties, (not necessarily Knesset members), and is subject to the approval of the Knesset. The Knesset itself is the chief policy-making body of the state and initiates most legislation. If at any time a majority of the Knesset votes lack of confidence in the Cabinet's policies (which to date has never occurred) the government falls, and the president chooses a member of the Knesset to form a new government. Similarly, the Knesset may decide on its own dissolution; the government then becomes a caretaker government until new elections are held.

The judicial system is independent of both the Cabinet and the Knesset. Originally based on British mandatory legislation and remnants of Ottoman laws, it is today derived in the main from Israeli government legislation and a growing influence of original Jewish law. The civil courts are made up of magistrates and district courts and the Supreme Court, which is the highest court of justice and appeal in the land. In matters concerning personal status, jurisdiction is vested in the state courts of the recognized religious communities. Other matters are dealt with in a variety of secular courts. Judges are nominated by select committees and recommended to the president, who then approves their nomination for life, with retirement mandatory at the age of 70.

The People

Israel's population in May 1986 numbered 4,300,000, including 3,530,000 Jews and 770,000 non-Jews. The origin of Israel's people is as diverse as its land; most groups adhere to one of the three major religions — Judaism, Christianity and Islam. Native-born

Israeli Jews total about 55% of the population; those of European and American origin comprise 25%; the remainder are from African and Asian origin.

Jews are often grouped or labelled, according to their origin, Ashkenazi or Sephardi.

The **Ashkenazis** come mainly from eastern and central Europe, although today there is a larger element from the Americas and western Europe. Before 1948, they comprised a majority of the Jewish population of Palestine, but due to the immigration of North African and oriental Asian Jews, the proportion has changed. Among the Ashkenazim, one of the more distinctive communities is the Hassidim, an ultra-orthodox group whose everyday language is mostly Yiddish — a blend of Hebrew and medieval German. A national resurgence of Soviet Jewry following the Six-Day War brought more than 100,000 newcomers to Israel.

The **Sephardis** (meaning Spanish) are descendants of Spanish Jews expelled from Spain and Portugal between 1492 and 1497. They took refuge in various parts of North Africa, Italy, the Balkans and Asia. Many arrived in the country after the Ottoman conquest. The term Sephardi is erroneously applied to all oriental Jews from Asia and Africa, although not all are of Spanish-Jewish origin. Many Sephardis still speak Ladino, a combination of Castillian Spanish and medieval Hebrew.

The largest group of oriental Jews came from North Africa. The **Yemenites** are another large oriental group. They have immigrated to the country from the Arabian Peninsula over the last hundred years; the largest influx arrived in 1949-1950 in operation "Magic Carpet", when almost all of Yemen's Jews (some 50,000) were airlifted to Israel. By 1965 they numbered 150,000.

Iraqi (Babylonian) Jews are a very ancient community, the oldest Jewish community outside Israel. They began settling here in the mid-19th century.

A flood of Iraqi Jews arrived shortly after Israel's independence in operation "Ezra and Nehemiah", when some 120,000 Jews were airlifted to Israel; once again this was almost the sum total of Iraqi Jewry. Other sizable communities are from Iran and India from where two closely knit communities have immigrated: the Bene Israel and Jews from Cochin. The Bukharan quarter in Jerusalem was settled in the nineteenth century by Jews from Soviet Uzbekistan who speak a Persian dialect.

The **Karaite** community was formed in the ninth century CE. They accept the Bible but not its oral law. They are forbidden to marry outside of their sect. So too are the **Samaritans**, the descendants of Israelites of the 8th century BCE Northern Kingdom. They are a tiny group, fewer than 500, living in Nablus and Holon; they maintain their own ritual, customarily sacrificing lambs at Passover on Mount Gerizim.

The **Arabs** in Israel live mostly in mountain villages, though many, especially Christians, live in larger towns. **Bedouin** continue to live their traditional, nomadic lifestyle among the hills, mainly in the south. More recently a substantial number have formed permanent settled communities.

DENSITY OF POPULATION

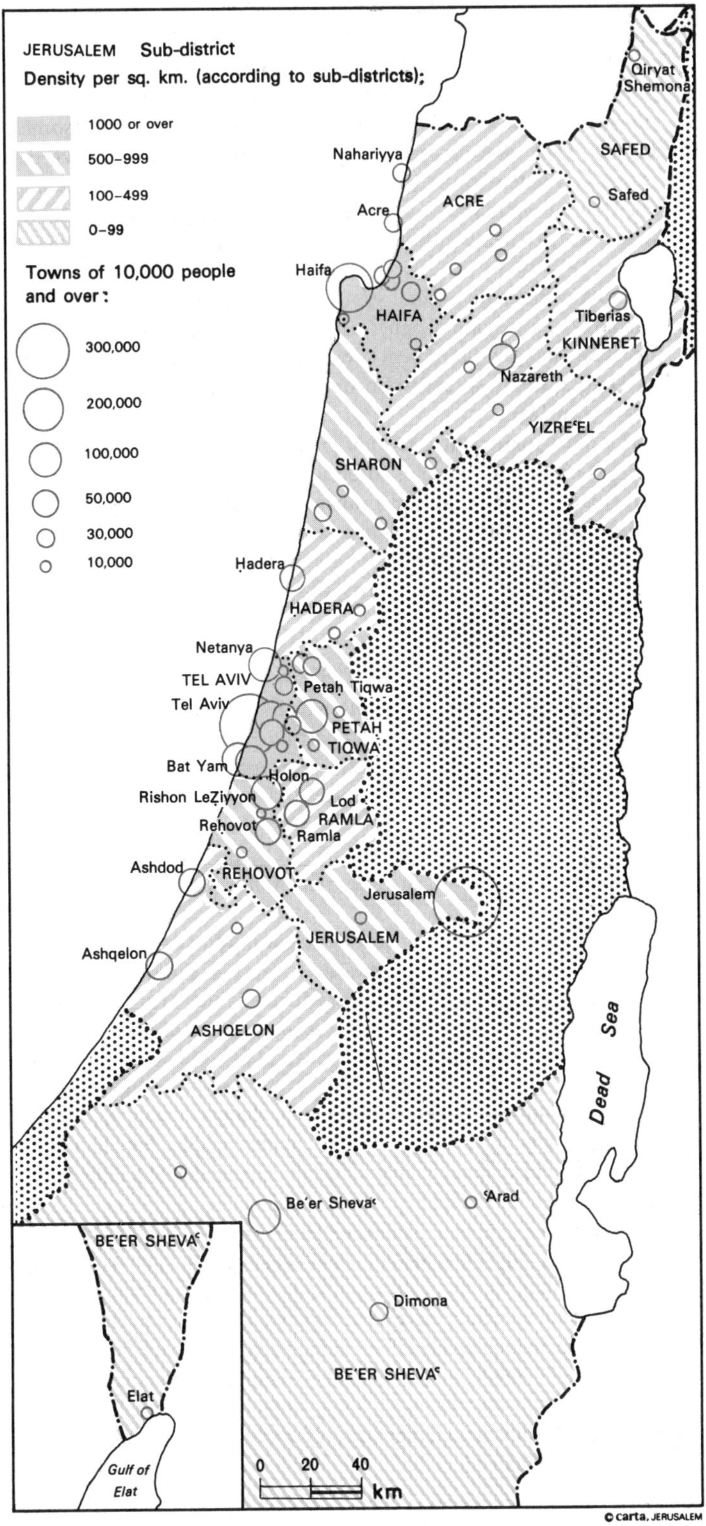
JERUSALEM Sub-district
Density per sq. km. (according to sub-districts):
1000 or over
500–999
100–499
0–99
Towns of 10,000 people and over:
300,000
200,000
100,000
50,000
30,000
10,000
Qiryat Shemona
SAFED
Safed
Nahariyya
Acre
ACRE
Haifa
HAIFA
Tiberias
KINNERET
Nazareth
YIZRE'EL
SHARON
Hadera
HADERA
Netanya
TEL AVIV
Tel Aviv
Petah Tiqwa
PETAH TIQWA
Bat Yam
Holon
Rishon LeZiyyon
Lod
RAMLA
Rehovot
Ramla
Ashdod
REHOVOT
Jerusalem
JERUSALEM
Ashqelon
ASHQELON
Dead Sea
Be'er Sheva'
'Arad
BE'ER SHEVA'
Dimona
BE'ER SHEVA'
Elat
Gulf of Elat
0 20 40
km
© carta, JERUSALEM

The large majority of Arabs are Sunni Moslems. There are a few small communities of Shi'ite Moslems. The Circassian Moslems came from the Caucasus Mountains of Russia and maintain their own language in two villages in Galilee. Of the sects derived from Islam, the largest in Israel are the Druze who live in eighteen villages throughout Galilee and on Mr. Carmel; they number some 50,000. They are descendants of an eleventh century sect in Lebanon; the tenets and practices of their religion are kept secret. The Druze hold the status of a self-governing religious community. Since 1957, Druze youth have been serving in the Israel Defence Forces.

Another distinctive small group are the **Bahais** who follow the teachings of a Persian prophet who was shot in 1850. Although his successor, Baha-u -llah, spent twenty-four years in a Turkish prison in 'Akko, his faith spread to Europe and America. The Bahai world centre is in Haifa.

The most important **Christian** groups are the Greek Catholics, Greek Orthdox, Roman Catholics, Maronites, Protestants and Armenian Orthodox, as well as ancient Middle Eastern sects. Most of the Christians are Arabs. Christian institutions have been plentiful in the Holy Land, proportionate to the size of the community, ever since the 19th century. Christians constitute about 14% of the non-Jewish population.

The Economy

The economy of Israel presents a colourful mosaic of various approaches. Side by side, often in partnership, usually in harmony, are cooperative, capitalist and state-run enterprises — whether in co-operative or private agriculture and services, transport and banking.

The largest enterprises tend to be run by the government or the cooperative sector. Still, the majority of all enterprises are in private hands.

Israel today is practically self-sufficient in food except for grain, fodder and agricultural raw materials, which are imported. Israel on her part exports agricultural produce, mainly citrus fruits and vegetables but also flowers, preserves and processed foods. Foodstuffs constitute about ten percent of total exports. Because of her highly mechanised agriculture, Israel has been in a position to export agricultural expertise. A thriving diamond industry exists which, at its peak, employed about 20,000 people. Polished diamonds are the country's largest single export ($1,213 million in 1984).

Israel manufactures or assembles from imported parts a growing portion of its durable consumer and other goods, such as household appliances. Being poor in natural resources, most raw materials, from oil to wood, have to be imported. Counter to this Israel exports a growing variety of manufactured goods. Immense progress is being made in the fields of computers, electronics and defence-based industries, with some firms being world leaders in their chosen field. Altogether some 26 percent of the work force is engaged in industry.

INDUSTRY AND NATURAL RESOURCES

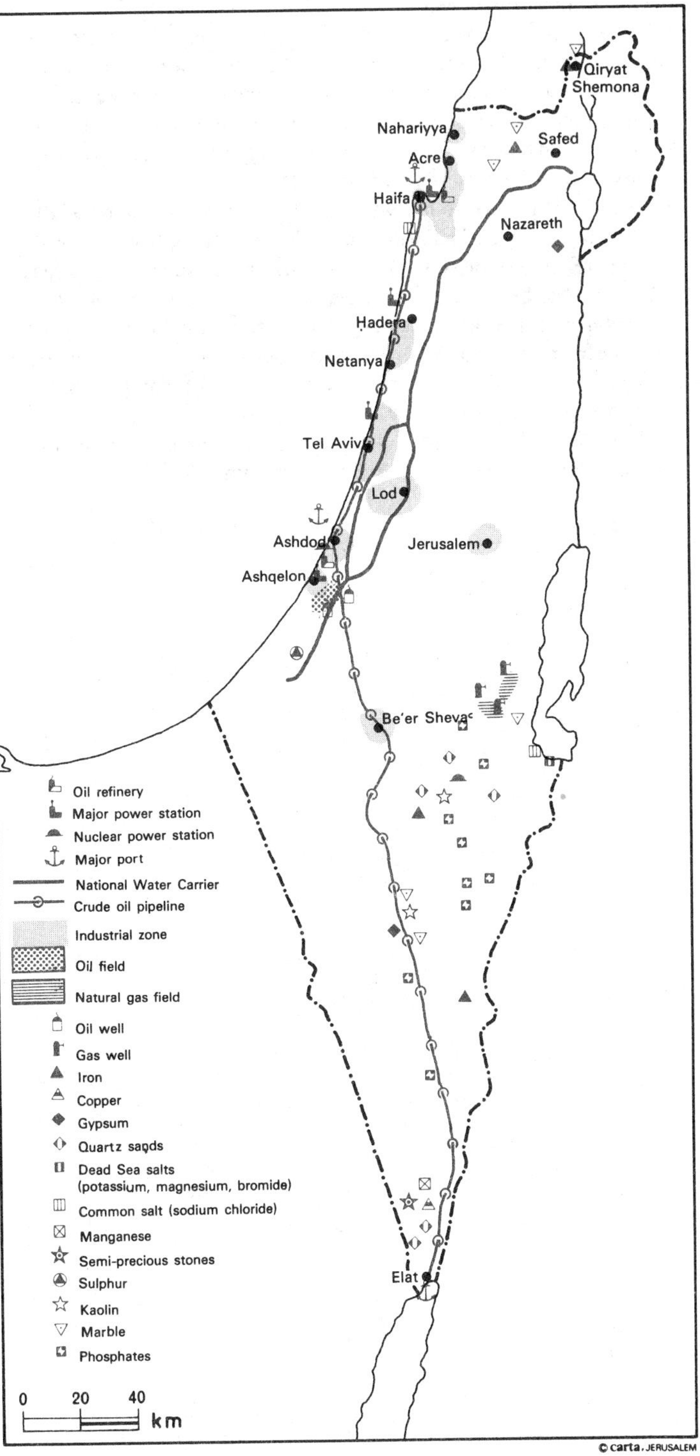
Qiryat Shemona
Nahariyya
Safed
Acre
Haifa
Nazareth
Hadera
Netanya
Tel Aviv
Lod
Ashdod
Jerusalem
Ashqelon
Be'er Sheva
Elat
Oil refinery
Major power station
Nuclear power station
Major port
National Water Carrier
Crude oil pipeline
Industrial zone
Oil field
Natural gas field
Oil well
Gas well
Iron
Copper
Gypsum
Quartz sands
Dead Sea salts (potassium, magnesium, bromide)
Common salt (sodium chloride)
Manganese
Semi-precious stones
Sulphur
Kaolin
Marble
Phosphates
0 20 40 km
© carta, JERUSALEM

Another major source of employment and foreign currency income is tourism, as the country's manifold attractions draw over a million visitors a year.

The banking system is highly specialized. It is divided into commercial banks — which in the main deal with short-term transactions — and specialized institutions — which handle medium and long-range transactions in such fields as agriculture, industry, housing and shipping. These institutions are either state-owned or cooperatives held by the banks and the government.

Israel has learned to live with an inflation rate of two digits. By a workable method of indexing partically everything from interest to wages relative stability is achieved. One major social commitment has always been to avoid unemployment. Through the years, sometimes in the face of great difficulties, almost full employment has been maintained. With the development of various industries, improving education and greater demand, Israel today suffers from a shortage of skilled labour.

Israel's gross national product, per capita income and standard of living place her squarely in the western camp.

GAZETTEER

The LORD said
to Abram,
"Lift up your eyes,
and look
from the place
where you are,
northward
and southward
and eastward
and westward;"

Genesis 13:14

A

o **'Abasan el Kabira** *087:081*

Large Arab village in Gaza Strip 5 km. SE of Khan Yunis. Pop.: 4,000 of Bedouin origin. Columns and masonry fragments from Roman fortress re-used in village buildings.

o **'Abasan eṣ Ṣaghira** *087:082*

Arab village in Gaza Strip 4 km. E of Khan Yunis. Pop.: 1,500 of Bedouin origin.

o **'Abda** *151:097*

Small Arab village (pop.: 150) in Judean Hills 10 km. SW of Hebron. Tel in village (mostly cultivated), has caves and cisterns. Sherds indicate Byzantine and Medieval settlement.

'Abdallah Bridge *202:134*

Demolished bridge over Jordan River 4 km. N of Dead Sea mouth. Built by Jordanians after War of Independence and named after 'Abdallah, first king of Jordan. Destroyed in air strike during Six-Day War.

o **'Abud** *156:158*

Arab village in Samarian Hills 17 km. NW of Ramallah. Pop.: 1,100, Christians and Moslems. Has Greek Orthodox church built on foundations of 5th c. church renovated in 11th c. Ancient masonry re-used in village buildings. In confines of village are other remains of Byzantine churches and monasteries.

o **Abu Dis** *175:130*

Arab village on fringe of Judean Desert 3 km. E of Jerusalem, next to Bethany. Origin of name believed to be Abudison, mentioned in book describing life of the monk, Mar-Saba. Some believe it to be site of the Biblical city of Bahurim (II Sam. 16:5). Pop.: 3,000, belonging to et Ta'amra Bedouin tribe.

∴ **Abu Fula** *211:266*

Abandoned Arab village on S Golan Heights, 3 km. SE of Benot Ya'aqov Bridge. Concentrations of impressive dolmens nearby.

o **Abu Ghosh** *160:135*

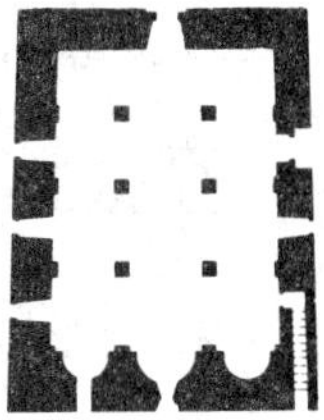

Large Arab village 10 km. W of Jerusalem. Named after Moslem family, Abu Ghosh, who settled in area in 16th c. and imposed toll on travellers to Jerusalem. Descendants of family still live here. Pop.: 3,000, mostly Moslem, few Christians. Dig on nearby hill uncovered remains of Neolithic buildings, Bronze Age and Iron Age sherds, Second Temple Period cisterns, wine press, graves and remnants of Byzantine mosaic. Overlooking village on W side is tel with modern church; the site of Biblical Kiriath-jearim, one of four Gibeonite cities that signed treaty with Israelites, and where Ark of Covenant was brought after its recapture from Philistines (I Sam. 7:1; II Sam. 6:3-4). Arabs call site Deir el 'Azar, apparently after Eleazar, son of Abinadab, to whose home Ark was brought. New church built in 1924 by French monks on foundations of

Byzantine church of which a mosaic floor, capitals and Roman inscriptions remain. In village is a French Benedictine monastery, built 1899, on foundations of 12th c. structure — one of best examples of Crusader architecture in Israel — where, according to tradition, Richard the Lion-Heart prayed before ascending to Jerusalem. Built over Roman pool used by travellers en route to holy city. Village also contains remains of Hospitallers' monastery and Abbasid khan (mid-9th c.) rebuilt in Mamluk Period (1187-1517 CE). Outside village is British Mandatory police fort that served as Palmaḥ base during War of Independence. Near fort is memorial to General David Marcus (Mickey Stone), a West Point graduate killed in vicinity. Jewish housing development, Qiryat Telshe-Stone, located 1 km. W of village.

Abu Juwei'id *148:066*

Bedouin encampment 15 km. NW of Dimona. Pop.: 2,000.

Abu Qash *169:151*

Arab village 5 km. N of Ramallah. Conjectured site of Bet Meqoshesh where one of priestly Israelite families resided (Tosefta Yev. 1:10). Pop.: 500.

Abu Qureinat *146:060*

Bedouin encampment 9 km. NW of Dimona. Pop.: 3,000.

Abu er Riqaqi *153:219*

Remains of Middle Bronze Age settlement near Naḥal Barqan, 4 km. NE of Karkur. Prehistoric site, Dhahrat el 'Anza, on nearby hill.

Abu Rubei'a (Abu Rabi'a) *155:071*

Bedouin encampment 15 km. W of 'Arad. Pop.: 3,250.

Abu Ruqayyiq (Rugeig) *141:071*

Bedouin encampment 10 km. E of Be'er Sheva'. Pop.: 5,000.

Abu Shukheidim *165:152*

Arab village in Samarian Hills 7 km. NW of Ramallah. Pop.: 500.

Abu Sinan *166:262*

Arab village in W Galilee 9 km. SE of Nahariyya. Pop.: 4,700 (50% Druze, 40% Christian, 10% Moslem). Druze and Arab folklore museum. Two churches.

'Abwein *169:160*

Arab village 14 km. N of Ramallah. Pop.: 1,000.

Acre ('Akko) *(Judg. 1:31) 157:258*

Ancient port beside modern city with population of 37,000; 9,000 of whom are Arab (mostly Moslem, some Christian). A cluster of Ottoman mosques and khans, surrounded by ramparts, and the harbour area constitute the most picturesque cityscape in Israel after Jerusalem. Recorded as 'Akko or 'Akka in ancient Egyptian documents. On account of its strategic and commercial significance (on byway between Egypt and Syria), it has been an object of conquest throughout history. Originally a fortified Canaanite city; remains uncovered at Tel 'Akko, E of present-day Acre. During Israelite conquest included in tribal area of Asher. Israelites never captured it, however. In 701 BCE conquered by Sennacherib, King of Assyria, and again in 333 BCE by Alexander the Great, when it became a Hellenistic settlement called Ptolemais. City centre then moved to seashore. The Hasmoneans failed to conquer this hostile

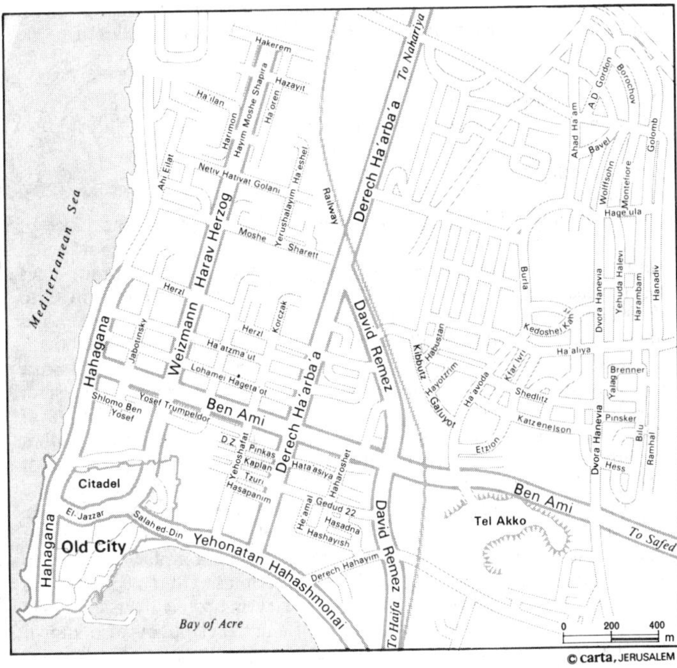

Hellenistic city. During Roman Period it was major settlement in Galilee — Colonia Ptolemais — and served as a naval base. At this time Jews settled here, though many were killed in Jewish Revolt against Rome (66 CE). During Roman and Byzantine Periods, city had large Jewish community and many great scholars either resided or spent time here. In Byzantine Period large Samaritan community developed and city was called Samaritiki. In 614 it was conquered by the Persians who ruled it for two decades. After Arab conquest its original name was restored. In 1104 conquered by Crusaders who fortified it and turned it into naval base. After loss of Jerusalem it served as last Crusader capital and, contrary to their usual custom, they allowed Jews to reside here. The Rambam visited in 1165, Alharizi in 1212 and the Ramban in 1266. In 1291 conquered and destroyed by Egyptian Sultan el Malik el Ashraf. City was rebuilt only in middle of 14th c. and then Jews returned to settle. Due to Bedouin wars the city was impoverished and declined until 18th c. when the Bedouin Dahir el 'Amr made the city his capital, fortified it and built hostels and mosques. He invited Jews to take up residence. They came from Safed and abroad. During Ottoman Period, Acre was seat of government for Syria and Palestine. **1775-1804** Reign of Pasha Ahmad el Jazzar who built mosque bearing his name; rebuilt city walls, which remain to this day and built the aqueduct from the springs of Kabri. In 1799, with aid of British fleet, he repelled Napoleon's attack. Ibrahim Pasha, son of Muḥammad 'Ali, ruler of Egypt, conquered city in 1831 and ruled it until his expulsion by a combined European fleet in 1840. Captured in 1918 by the British, it became the administrative centre for the N sector of the country. During Riots of 1936-1939 the remaining Jews fled and in War of Independence Acre's Arab inhabitants harassed neighbouring Jewish settlements in W Galilee. In May 1948 captured by the Haganah and most Arab inhabitants left. After establishment of State it became an immigrant city which eventually spread beyond the old city walls. The merchant marine officers' school, the Kefar Philadelphia Youth Aliyah Educational Institute, and artists' centre are in this area. Acre is resting place of Baha'u'llah at Bahji mansion, considered holiest spot in Bahai world. Gardens here are loveliest in the country. **Sites in Acre: Crypt of St. John**, 12th c. underground hall W of Great Mosque. Believed to be either reception hall of Crusader Order of Knights of St. John, or burial site of notable Crusaders. **City walls** Remains of walls renovated during reign of Pasha Aḥmad el Jazzar; still preserved today. Remains of 19th c. cannons visible on S wall. **Fortress** Built in W part of city, near seashore, during reign of Aḥmad el Jazzar at end of 18th c.; served as his headquarters and administrative centre. During British Mandate Period served as central prison and place of execution where Jewish underground Haganah, the Irgun Ẓevai Leumi and Leḥi fighters were imprisoned and executed. In 1947 Irgun forces broke into the prison and freed many inmates. (Dramatized in Otto Preminger film "Exodus".) Today part of building is a museum and memorial for underground heroism, and part a mental hospital. A number of 19th c. cannons are located on roof. **Great Mosque** Turkish-style mosque at the entrance to old city, built at behest of Aḥmad el Jazzar; completed 1781. The mosque — best example of Ottoman religious architecture in Holy Land — contains a box with a few hairs which, according to Moslem tradition, are from the beard of the prophet Muḥammad. In the courtyard is a garden, sun-dial and fountain. **Bazaar** Traditional oriental market near Great Mosque, one section of which has been rebuilt from an old khan and lined with gift shops. **Khan el Faranj** Hostel in old city, E of market-place, on way to port. Name means Hostel of the Franks (a term used for Europeans and Jewish travellers). **Khan el 'Umdan** Hostel, recognizable by its columns, at entrance to port. Built during reign of Aḥmad el Jazzar; also known as Khan el Jazzar. Above entrance to hostel is an early 20th c. tower erected in honour of Sultan Abdul Ḥamid. **Port** Ruins of Crusader port SW of city. Remains of breakwater and lighthouse. Today serves as fishing port. **Tel 'Akko** Tel E of city on road to Safed. Site of Canaanite city. Called Toron during Crusader Period; it was from here that Richard the Lion-Heart set out to conquer heavily fortified port city. Napoleon also tried to conquer Acre from this tel; also known as Napoleon's Hill. During War of Independence used by the Israel Defence Forces to launch attack on city. Known as Tell el Fukhkhar (tel of sherds) in Arabic. Site was rich in sherd finds from many periods; an earth embankment from Middle Bronze Age and a Hebrew seal have been uncovered.

Adam Bridge (Damiya) *(Josh. 3:16) 200:167*

One of largest bridges on Jordan River near Jiftlik junction, where roads from Shekhem, 'Amman, Jericho and Bet She'an cross. Named after nearby tel, Damiya. Apparently site of city called Adam, mentioned in narrative of Israelite crossing of Jordan. During Mandate, was one of bridges destroyed by Haganah in "night of the bridges" operation (June 1946). Bombed and destroyed in Six-Day War and later replaced by bailey bridge. One of two crossing points — Allenby Bridge is second — between Israel and Jordan as part of "open bridge policy".

★ Adamit *170:276*

Kibbutz in W Galilee, between Ḥanita and Elon. Origin of name: Idmith, Arab ruin on site. Founded 1958 by HaShomer HaẒa'ir youth movement members who later abandoned the site. Now run by groups of kibbutz youth who spend one year here. Area: 1,350 d. Archaeological finds: Byzantine mosaic floor, Bronze Age and Iron Age sherds.

● 'Adanim *141:172*

Moshav in Sharon 4 km. S of Kefar Sava. Founded 1950 and first called Yarqona HaReḥava. Area: 1,850 d. Pop.: 180.

● **Adderet** 149:118

Moshav in Judean Foothills 9.5 km. S of Bet Shemesh. Settled in 1961. Resettled in 1963 by Rumanian immigrants after original settlers abandoned site. Pop.: 330.

● **Addirim** 175:217

Moshav in Ta'anakh region, 6 km. S of 'Afula. Name from Song of Deborah (Judg. 5:13) "Then down marched the remnant of the *noble*." Founded 1956 by Moroccan immigrants as part of operation "from ship to settlement". Pop.: 400.

'Ad Halom Bridge *119:132*

Bridge on Naḥal Lakhish SE of Ashdod. Arabic name: Jisr Isdud (Ashdod Bridge). Alongside is railway bridge destroyed by Haganah in "night of the bridges" operation (June 1946). Rebuilt but again destroyed before Egyptian invasion in 1948, whose northern thrust was halted at this bridge, hence its name. (*'Ad halom* = up to this point.) Rebuilt 1949.

'Adi *(Josh. 19:25) 166:243*

Look-out post in Lower Galilee. Named after nearby Tell el Ḥali: (*'adi* being a synonym for *hali*, meaning adornment). Site included in Asher tribal allotment: "Its territory included Helkath, Hali, Beten, Achshaph," (Josh. 19:25). Established 1979.

Adorayim → Dura

'Adullam Region *(Josh. 15:35)*

Settlement region between Bet Shemesh and Bet Guvrin. Named after ancient city of Adullam, mentioned often in Bible, and whose ruins have been identified at Ḥurvot 'Adullam. The region was planned to fill gap in settlement along Israel-Jordan border opposite Hebron Hills. In 1957 land development and settlement began.

Afeq (near Rosh Ha'Ayin) → **Tel Afeq**

★ **Afeq** (in Zevulun Valley) *(Josh. 19:30) 162:249*

Kibbutz 3 km. E of Qiryat Bialik. Name Biblical — Aphek, city in territory of tribe of Asher. First settlers organized in 1935 and settled S of Acre at Mishmar HaYam in 1939. Later joined by immigrants from Poland and Germany. Before 1948, it served as base for Palmaḥ fighters. In 1948 moved to present site. Area: 9,200 d. Pop.: 450. **Tel Afeq (Kurdani)** Ancient settlement near sources of Na'aman, W of kibbutz. Sherds indicate occupation in Late Bronze Age and Early Iron Age. Believed to be site of Biblical Aphek. In Crusader Period there were water-mills at Kh. Kurdani near the tel. **Afeq swamps** Nature reserve of 300 d. E of tel.

★ **Afiq** *(I Kings 20:26) 215:242*

Kibbutz in S Golan Heights 6 km. E of 'En Gev off el Ḥamma-Quneitra road. Named after abandoned Arab village Fiq. Name similar to Aphek or Aphik which was Jewish city in Golan during Byzantine Period. Founded by *nahal* settlers from Naḥal Golan outpost; became civilian settlement in 1972 and in 1973 moved to present site. Area: 4,500 d. **Archaeological remains** Ancient synagogue and Bronze Age and Ottoman Period remnants. **Afeq (Fiq)** Within former Syrian army camp is abandoned town of Fiq, with remains of ancient settlement. Perhaps Biblical site of Aphek where Benhadad, King of Aram, fought the Israelites. Houses of abandoned town studded with ancient remains (capitals, bases of columns and carved stones). At the end of 19th c. a column was found with engraved 7-branched *menorah* and Aramaic inscription "I, Judah the cantor". Sherds indicate occupation from

Middle Bronze Age onwards, particularly during Roman and Byzantine Periods.

★ **Afiqim** *204:232*

Kibbutz in Jordan Valley off Ẓemaḥ-Bet She'an road. Name means riverbeds — Jordan and Yarmouk Rivers are nearby. Founded 1932 by HaShomer HaẒa'ir group organized in 1924. Original site was in Upper Galilee; in 1932 it moved to present location. On eve of War of Independence, served as Palmaḥ base and after establishment of State as *naḥal* base. Area: 6,000 d. Pop.: 1,400 — one of largest *kibbutzim.*

■ **'Afula** *177:224*

City in Yizre'el Valley at important junction between Coastal Plain and Samarian Hills. Origin of name from Arabic el 'Afule. According to one opinion, site of Biblical city of Ophel (II Kings 5:24). In WWI a Turkish and German army camp was located here; it was captured by British in 1918. Jewish city founded 1925 by American Zion Commonwealth with the intention to make it an urban centre for Jewish settlements in Yizre'el Valley. In fact it began to develop thus only after founding of State. Area: 29,000 d. Pop.: 20,000. **Ancient tel** within city. Excavations uncovered remains from various periods of occupation including utensils and other objects from end of Chalcolithic Period. (These finds served to classify a special culture called Yizre'el Culture.) Remains of buildings from Early Bronze Age; remains of settlements from Iron Age and from Roman to Arab Periods.

Agam Eshkol → Ma'agar Bet Netofa

Agam HaQishon → Ma'agar Kefar Barukh

● **'Agur** *141:122*

Moshav on border of Judean Hills and Foothills. Founded 1950 on lands of abandoned village of 'Ajjur, hence its name (*'agur* = crane). Area: 2,000 d. Pop.: 370, mostly from Kurdistan. **Ḥurbat Ḥaruvit (Kh. el 'Innab)** Ruins of Byzantine settlement including remains of late 4th c. church with coloured mosaic floor.

● **Aḥi'ezer** *138:154*

Moshav in Judean Foothills 3 km. NW of Lod. Named after Ahiezer, son of Ammishaddai, chieftain of Dan tribe (Num. 1:12). Founded 1950 by Yemenite immigrants. Area: 2,500 d. Pop.: 900. Near *moshav* is Giv'at Dani, memorial site for Dani Mas, commander of "The 35" soldiers who were killed en route to Gush 'Eẓyon during War of Independence.

● **Aḥihud** *166:257*

Moshav in W Galilee 9 km. E of Acre. Name Biblical: (Num. 34:27) "And of the tribe of the sons of Asher a leader, *Ahihud* the son of Shelomi." Founded in 1950 after water was discovered in the area allowing not only Aḥihud but another settlement near kibbutz Yas'ur to be viable. Area: 1,800 d. Pop.: 550, Yemenite immigrants. Nearby are remains of Arab village of Birwa.

● **Aḥisamakh** *141:149*

Moshav in Judean Foothills 4 km. E of Ramla. Named after the Danite Ahisamach, father of Aholiab (Ex. 35:24). Founded in 1950 by Tripolitanian immigrants. Area: 2,000 d. Pop.: 700.

● **Aḥituv** *149:199*

Moshav in N Sharon 8 km. SW of Ḥadera. Named after Ahitub, father of Ahimelech (I Sam. 14:3). Area: 3,000 d. Pop.: 600, Iraqi immigrants.

Aḥmadiyya (**'Amudiyya**) *216:267*

Abandoned Arab village in Golan Heights 2 km. N of Qaẓrin. Also called 'Amudiyya. Nearby ruins of ancient Jewish settlement from Roman and Byzantine Periods. Westwards is 'En Shemer (spring). Arab village partly built on old ruins and in some houses ancient remains were used as building materials.

Aḥuzzam *128:107*

Moshav in Lakhish region 7 km. S of Qiryat Gat. Name Biblical: member of tribe of Judah (I Chron. 4:6). Founded 1950 by immigrants from Morocco. Previously called Ma'ggalim. Area: 7,000 d. Pop.: 570. **Tel Qeshet** — 2 km. S of *moshav*.

Aḥuzzat Naftali *194:244*

Educational institute in Lower Galilee, 6 km. W of Tiberias. In Biblical times area included in territory allotted to Naphtali tribe, hence the name. Established 1949 as *moshav shittufi*, originally called Ereẓ Naftali; it later became an educational institute. Nearby is **Qarne Ḥittim** where Moslems defeated Crusaders in 1187.

Aḥuzzat Shoshanna *198:222*

Cattle-raising farm near Kokhav HaYarden (Belvoir fortress). Established in 1959 by Meir Har-Ẓion in memory of his sister, Shoshanna, murdered by Jordanian Bedouin in 1954 while hiking in Judean Desert.

'Ai → **(Et) Tell** (near Ramallah)

'Ajja *168:196*

Arab village in Samarian Hills 15 km. SW of Jenin. Pop.: 1,300. Located on ruins of ancient settlement. On site are wine presses, cisterns and Byzantine rock-cut tombs.

'Ajjul *167:158*

Arab village (pop.: 520) in Samarian Hills, 13 km. N of Ramallah. Site contains rock-cut tombs and remains of buildings. Sherds indicate occupation from Iron Age to Ottoman Period.

'Akbara *197:260*

Small Arab village (pop.: 350) in Upper Galilee 2 km. S of Safed. **'Akhbera** Ancient Jewish town. One of places fortified by Joseph b. Mattathias in preparation for Jewish Revolt against Rome. Residence of Rabbi Eleazar son of Simeon b. Yoḥai (who was buried in Meron). Sources claim that in 11th c. Jewish community still present here. Jewish 15th c. traveller, Moses Bassola, found ruins of synagogue. According to tradition the sages Yannai, Nehorai and Dostai were buried here. Nearby is **'Akbara boulder.** Large boulder cliff with many caves and crevices. Mentioned in *The Jewish Wars* by Josephus Flavius (Joseph b. Mattathias). Designated as nature reserve. Area: 440 d. Eagles nest in manifold crevices.

Akhziv *159:272*

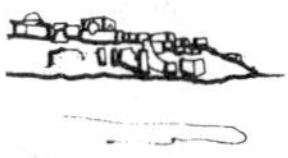

Remains of ancient settlement and port 3 km. N of Nahariyya. Occupied from Bronze Age to Roman-Byzantine Period. In Byzantine Period was a fortified town on Acre-Antioch highway with a Jewish community. Fortress built in Crusader Period. Nearby, two large cemeteries with rock-cut tombs were excavated. Most of tombs from Iron Age and some 6th c. BCE and Roman Period. Tombs contained many ritual objects: masks, incense burners, figurines, chalices and many sherds of Phoenician type. Museum and hostel run by only permanent resident, Eli Avivi. Nearby is **French Village**, one of the Club Mediterrané holiday camps, and diving club named after Oded Amir, from kibbutz Gesher HaZiv, who fell in the Yom Kippur War. Memorial to "the Fourteen"

— youth hostel and memorial on coast 5 km. N of Nahariyya, commemorating 14 Palmaḥ men killed while blowing up bridge over Keziv River on "night of the bridges" (June 17, 1946).

Akhziv Island *157:272*

One and a half km. off coast of Akhziv.

∴ **'Aleiqa** *216:273*

Abandoned village on Golan Heights 3 km. W of Kafr Naffakh. In W part of village is a double storey house; the first storey is of ancient origin.

Alexandrion → Sartaba

'Ali el Muntar *100:100*

Hill 90 m. above sea level, in SE Gaza, 5 km. from shore. Commands E approaches to city. Tomb of Sheikh 'Ali el Muntar at summit. Site of battles between British and Turks in WWI. Egyptian position after War of Independence. Captured by Israeli paratroopers in Six-Day War.

Allenby Bridge *201:142*

One of largest bridges on Jordan River 10 km. E of Jericho. Bridge existed here in ancient times (depicted as boat bridge in Madaba map). Retreating Turks burnt the wooden bridge in WWI. British replaced it with pontoon bridge and later with permanent one which was named after General Allenby, commander of British forces. Jordanians changed name to Ḥussein Bridge (named after King 'Abdullah's father). Destroyed by Haganah in "night of the bridges" operation (June 1946). Bombed and destroyed in Six-Day War and later replaced by bailey bridge. One of two crossing points (Adam Bridge is second) between Israel and Jordan.

● **Allone Abba** *166:237*

Moshav shittufi in Lower Galilee. Named in memory of Abba Berdiczew, Haganah parachutist who died in Europe on mission during WWII; and *allonim* (oaks) due to the many oak trees in region. Founded in 1948 on lands of Waldheim, a German Templer village. Area: 5,000 d. Pop.: 270. **Umm el 'Amad** Remains of ancient settlement within *moshav*. Pillars of Templer church, hence Arabic name (*'amad* means pillars). **Allone Abba Forest** Nature reserve with remains of former forest. Tabor oak common. Area: 960 d.

■ **Allone Yiẓhaq** *150:213*

Youth village and junior and senior high school in N Sharon. Named after Yiẓhaq Gruenbaum, Polish Zionist leader and Israel's first minister of interior. Area: 170 d. Pop.: 350 pupils and 50 adults.

Allon HaGalil *171:241*

Observation site in Lower Galilee 3 km. SW of Ma'agar Bet Netofa. Established 1980.

★ **Allonim** *163:236*

Kibbutz in W Lower Galilee N of Haifa-'Afula road. Named after oak forests in region. In pre-State years served as Palmaḥ staff headquarters, housed its Arab section, and was a Haganah training centre. Kibbutz split in 1953 as a result of major 1951 rift in HaKibbutz HaMe'uḥad movement. Area: 8,000 d. Pop.: 600. **Tell Qusqus** Remains of ancient settlement.

"Allon" Road (Derekh Sefar HaShomeron)

Samarian Hills-Judean Desert border road, fully paved. Also called Derekh Ereẓ HaMirdafim (the pursued) because of many terrorist chases in area during War of Attrition (1969-70). Called "Allon" Road because it presides over the strategic security buffer of Israeli settlements along Jordan River which constitutes the main feature of the late Yigal Allon's solution for the West Bank. **Settlements along route:** Mekhora, Kokhav HaShaḥar, Naḥal Rimmonim. **Sites:** 'Ein Samiya, Kh. el Marjama, Kubat en Nejima (observation point).

Allon Shevut *163:118*

Regional council for Gush 'Ezyon (Bloc) settlements. Origin of name: *allon* — single oak tree in centre of Gush 'Ezyon which could be seen across pre-1967 border and symbolized the bloc after it was captured in War of Independence. *Shevut* — the hope to return and resettle the region. Founded in 1970 by Cooperative Society for Development and Settlement. Settlers, mainly religious, number a thousand, mostly native-born. College for Ereẓ Israel studies. Area: 1,200 d.

'Alma *197:272*

Moshav in Upper Galilee 9 km. N of Safed. Named after ancient Jewish town whose name was retained in abandoned Arab village of 'Alma. Founded 1949 by Tripolitanian immigrants, joined in 1953 by a community of proselytes from San Nicandro, Italy. Later, immigrants from Cochin joined the *moshav*. Area: 8,000 d. Pop.: 780. **'Alma** Abandoned village built over Roman and Byzantine town whose Jewish community was mentioned in *Itinerary* of Benjamin of Tudela — a 12th c. traveller, in 13th c. Hebrew document, and in 15th c. travelogue of Jewish traveller. The community appears to have existed until 17th c. According to a Medieval tradition the sages Simeon b. Gamaliel, Eleazar b. Arakh, Eliezer b. Hyrcanus, Eleazar b. Azariah, Judah b. Tema and others were buried here. Finds within the village include remains of 3rd c. synagogue, fragment of lintel with inscription "peace be on this place and on all the places of Israel His people," a large Jewish cemetery, and an inscribed lintel stone which has been re-used in a village house.

Almagor *206:257*

Moshav in Upper Galilee near Jordan River outlet to Lake Kinneret. Founded in 1961 as *naḥal* outpost which became civilian settlement in 1965. Pop.: 200. A memorial exists to commemorate soldiers and JNF workers who were killed in area. Nearby is Giv'at Qela' (Tell Mutilla) where Syrians tried to gain a foothold and were routed after heavy battle (May 1-4, 1951). **Ancient and prehistoric remains** Four km. W of *moshav*, ancient city of Korazim with remains of Byzantine synagogue. SE of *moshav* by Jordan River an attempt was made at Jewish settlement in 1905. Area also has Megalithic structures and dolmens with tumuli.

Almog *196:133*

Kibbutz N of Dead Sea 8 km. SE of Jericho. Named after Yehuda Almog, chairman of regional council of Tamar. Established 1977 as *naḥal* outpost and became a civilian settlement in 1978.

'Alumim *103:095*

Kibbutz in NW Negev. Founded in 1966 by graduates of Bene 'Aqiva youth movement near ruins of kibbutz Be'erot Yiẓḥaq; destroyed during War of Independence. Area: 7,100 d. Pop.: 260.

Alumma *125:118*

Rural centre for religious *moshavim*: Rewaḥa, Zavdi'el and Qomemiyyut, 5 km. NW of Qiryat Gat.

Alummot *201:234*

Collective settlement (*qevuẓa*) in Lower Galilee 3 km. W of Deganya "A". First group of settlers organized in 1937 at Zikhron Ya'aqov;

settled in Poriyya in 1940 and moved to Bitanya 'Illit (Alummot) in 1947. Site abandoned in 1968 because of social crisis within group. In 1969 new immigrant group from Argentina resettled here. Area: 9,300 d. Pop.: 200.

• **Amaẓya** *142:104*

Moshav shittufi in S Lakhish region, 15 km. SE of Qiryat Gat. Named after Amaziah, King of Judah, killed in Lakhish (II Kings 14:19). Started as *naḥal* outpost in 1955 near abandoned Arab village of ed Dawayma close to cease-fire line. Pop.: 125.

Ambar *084:088*

Settlement bloc under construction in Gaza Strip, 5 km. S of Khan Yunis.

★ **'Amir** *208:287*

Kibbutz in N Ḥula Valley 5 km. SE of Qiryat Shemona. Name means sheaf of corn. Founded in 1939 — the last of "stockade and tower" settlements — by 'Aliyah Bet group of HaShomer HaẒa'ir movement in Lithuania and Poland. At first they resided in Ḥadera and in the early years suffered from malaria. During War of Independence 'Amir was under siege. Area: 3,800 d. Pop.: 530. Near kibbutz is bridge over Jordan River, called Gesher Yosef after 2 kibbutz members who died in War of Independence.

• **Amirim** *192:260*

Moshav in Upper Galilee 5 km. SW of Safed. Name means treetops. When founded in 1950 by Yemenite immigrants it was called Parod 'Illit. In 1956 split into 2 *moshavim*, Amirim and Shefer. In 1958 settled by vegetarians and naturalists intending to establish a national vegetarian-naturalist centre. Pop.: 250. Site has British Mandatory police fort as well as an ancient fort.

★ **'Ammi'ad** *201:258*

Kibbutz in Upper Galilee 4 km. S of Rosh Pinna. Founded in 1946 by native-born group of Palmaḥ trainees, and called HaḤoshlim. Served as Palmaḥ base during War of Independence. Area: 3,600 d. Pop.: 350. **Antiquities** Near kibbutz — ruin of Medieval wayfarers' hostel whose Arabic name is Jubb Yusuf (Joseph's cistern). According to Arab tradition this was cistern into which Joseph, son of Jacob, was thrown by his brothers. Opposite kibbutz, across road, are a number of dolmens alongside which Early Bronze Age flint implements were found.

• **'Amminadav** *163:128*

Moshav SW of Jerusalem 7 km. from city centre. Origin of name: Amminadab, father of Nahshon, chieftain of Judah tribe (Num. 1:7). Founded in 1950 by Yemenite immigrants near abandoned village of Walaja. Pop.: 300.

• **'Ammi'oz** *094:073*

Moshav in NW Negev 4 km. SW of Magen junction. First settlers abandoned it and 2 further attempts at settlement failed. Finally settled by Moroccan immigrants in framework of movement "from city to settlement". Area: 3,300 d. Pop.: 300.

• **'Ammiqam** *152:219*

Moshav in Menashe Hills 5 km. E of Zikhron Ya'aqov. Founded in 1950 by immigrants from China (Harbin and Manchuria) who were joined by N African immigrants, on lands of abandoned village es Sindiyana. Area: 3,000 d. Pop.: 180. About 1 km. N of *moshav* on site of abandoned village Ṣabbrin are remains of 4th c. Samaritan synagogue built by Baba Rabba, a Samaritan leader. Near *moshav* is beginning of an aqueduct leading to Caesarea.

∴ **'Ammuqa** *199:268*

Abandoned village in Upper Galilee, above bed of Naḥal Dalton, 5 km. NE of Safed. Site of ancient settlement of same name, mentioned in accounts of Medieval travellers. Local tradition claims that the sage Jonathan b. Uzziel was buried here. Caves, decorated tomb and other tombs.

o **'Ammuriyya** *170:163*

Small Arab village (pop.: 150) in Samarian Hills.

● **'Amqa** *165:265*

Moshav in W Galilee 6 km. SE of Nahariyya. Named after Jewish village of 'Amqoi from Roman and Byzantine Periods, a name which was also retained in abandoned village of 'Amqa. Founded in 1949 by Yemenite immigrants. Area: 2,500 d. Pop.: 650. **Antiquities** Rock-cut caves and chambers, remains of buildings and sherds from Byzantine and Arab Periods. On hills opposite village are remains of quarries and houses.

'Amram's Pillars * *143:895*

Natural stone columns, resembling palace columns, in Naḥal 'Amram 10 km. N of Elat. Formed by water and wind erosion on blocks of Nubian sandstone. In area are pits and tunnels indicating copper mining. Remains of buildings from Roman and Byzantine Periods found in stream bed.

o **'Anab eṣ Ṣaghira** *(Anab: Josh. 11:21) 146:091*

Arab village (pop.: 400) in Judean Hills, 2 km. W of edh Dhahiriyya. Site of Anab, the city of the Anakim who were destroyed by Joshua (Josh. 11:21) and gave their property to tribe of Judah as part of their allotment (Josh. 15:50). Has tel that extends over an area of 15 d. Finds include: caves, wine presses, heaps of stones, columns and church remnants. Sherds indicate occupation from Iron Age until Middle Ages.

o **'Anabta** *161:191*

Arab town in Samarian Hills 9 km. E of Tulkarm. Pop.: 3,500. Ancient cisterns and pool, rock-cut tombs and sacred Moslem tomb.

o **'Anata (Anathoth)** *(Josh. 21:18) 174:135*

Arab village in Judean Hills 4 km. NE of Jerusalem. Pop.: 1,300. S of village is a hill called Ras el Ḥaruba in Arabic. **Anathoth** Believed to be site of ancient Anathoth which was Levite city in Benjamin tribal allotment (Josh. 21:18), and birthplace of Prophet Jeremiah (Jer. 1:1) and of two of King David's stalwart men. Remains of tombs from Iron Age and Second Temple Period.

● **Ani'am** *219:262*

Industrial *moshav* in Golan Heights 6 km. SE of Qaẓrin. Founded in 1973 by Russian immigrants. Originally located near *moshav* Ramot and called 'Aliyah 70; in 1978 moved to present site.

o **'Anin** *165:211*

Arab village (pop.: 1,000) in W Samarian Hills, 2 km. E of Umm el Faḥm.

Antipatris → **Tel Afeq** (near Rosh Ha'Ayin)

o **'Anza** *171:196*

Arab village (pop.: 850) in Samarian Hills, 15 km. N of Shekhem.

o **'Aqqaba** *183:195*

Arab village in Samarian Hills 4 km. NW of Tubas. Pop.: 1,200.

○ 'Aqraba *182:170*

Large Arab village in Samarian Hills 12 km. SE of Shekhem. Pop.: 2,500. Jewish city during Second Temple Period until Bar Kokhba revolt. Jewish inhabitants expelled by Emperor Hadrian. Samaritan village called Qiryat 'Aqraba during Arab Period. Finds in village: remains of ancient buildings, rock-cut tombs, Greek inscriptions.

Aqua Bella → 'En Ḥemed

○ 'Ara *157:212*

Arab village in Naḥal 'Iron (Wadi 'Ara). Site of ancient city Aruna (Aran), located at tel above village. Pop.: 2,300. **Tell Wadi 'Ara ('Iron)** On slope above village is large tel dominating W approach of Naḥal 'Iron. Believed to be site of Aruna mentioned in memoirs of Thutmose III and in lists of Shishak, King of Egypt. Sherds found on tel and its slopes are from Bronze and Iron Ages and Hellenistic Period. Quarry from Late Bronze Age found on SW slope. Many remains from Roman and Byzantine Periods found in village.

'Arab el 'Aramsha *169:276*

Bedouin settlement in Upper Galilee, near Lebanese border, 2 km. W of kibbutz Adamit. Pop.: 400. Previously a tent settlement; in last decade inhabitants transferred to permanent dwellings.

○ 'Arabbuna *184:213*

Arab village (pop.: 300) on slopes of Mt. Gilboa', 10 km. NE of Jenin.

'Arab es Samniyya *164:241*

Bedouin tribe located in Lower Galilee 5 km. NE of Qiryat Tiv'on. Pop.: 250.

'Arab es Sawa'id (Kammana) *181:257*

Bedouin tribe located in Lower Galilee in Shezor Hills, 2 km. SE of Karmi'el. Pop.: 2,700.

'Arab es Sawa'id (Shuweiki Ḥamriyya) *164:243*

Bedouin tribe located in Lower Galilee 4 km. SW of Shefar'am. Pop.: 600.

'Arab esh Shibli → Kafr Shibli

■ 'Arad *(Josh. 12:14) 170:074*

Urban settlement in NE Negev, 37 km. E of Be'er Sheva' on road to Dead Sea. Named after ancient city located in this area (see Tel 'Arad). In 1921 a group of Jewish Legion veterans tried to settle here but were forced to leave for lack of water. Development of 'Arad region, between Be'er Sheva' Valley and Hebron Hills, began in 1961 with 'Arad as its centre. Pop.: 10,000, mainly native-born (60%) and others from English speaking countries, USSR and South America. 'Arad was built according to a comprehensive town plan. It is considered among Israel's most successful development towns. The dry heat and high elevation make it an ideal health resort. See p.79

○ (El) 'Araqa *169:208*

Arab village (pop.: 600) in Samarian Hills, 9 km. W of Jenin.

'Ar'ara *159:211*

Rural Arab town (with local council) in Naḥal 'Iron, 7 km. NE of 'Iron junction. Pop.: 5,400. Ancient burial caves found near 'Ar'ara, and several finds from Roman and Byzantine Periods.

'ARAD

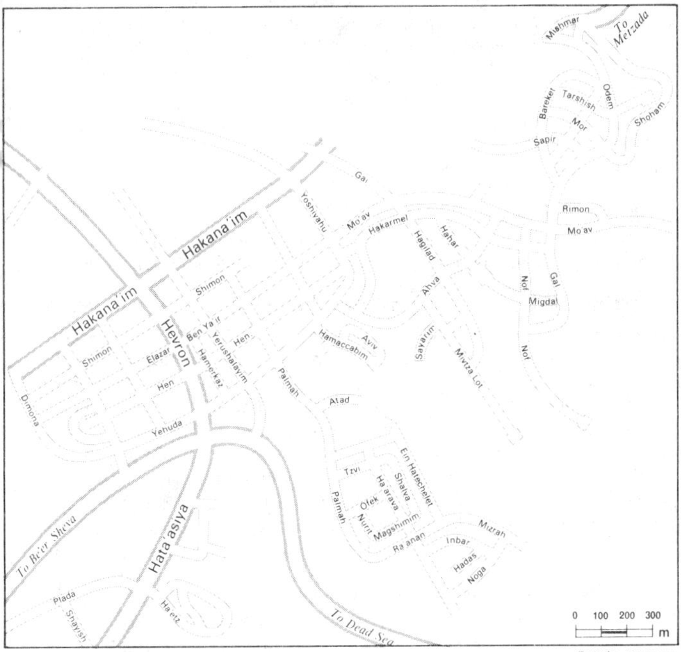

'Arav → **'Arraba** (in Galilee)

'Arava → **Ha'Arava**

Arbel *(Hos. 10:14)* *196:246*

Forbidding promontory 4.5 km. NW of Tiberias providing magnificent look-out on Lake Kinneret. Associated with Biblical Beth-arbel, mentioned in Book of Hosea. Ridge riddled with caves fortified by forces of Judah Maccabee in 2nd c. BCE. Rebels captured, however, by Seleucid general Bacchides who seized slope, or "steps" as it was then called. Caves later occupied by Jewish Zealots fighting Herod in 39 BCE. King's soldiers lowered in cages by ropes extending from brow of hill. They used torches to block cave entrances and burn Zealots. In Jewish revolt of 66 CE against Rome, rebels again hid out in Arbel caves only to be killed by enemy forces. Thriving Jewish community here in Roman and Byzantine Periods. **Moshav** founded in 1949 by de-mobilized Israeli soldiers' organization. Pop.: 200. **Ruins** NW of *moshav* ruins and remains of synagogue from Roman Period (Kh. Irbid). Nearby, remains of ancient fortress, one of 17 erected by the Zealots of Galilee during Revolt against Rome. In Arab Period the fortress was called Qal'at Ibn Ma'an and was used by Dahir el 'Amr, the Arab governor. The ruins and caves are part of a nature reserve which extends over 1,500 d.

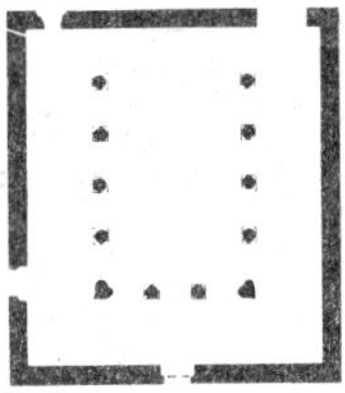

Ard Qibliyya *204:269*

Archaeological site in Upper Galilee near kibbutz Ayyelet HaShaḥar. Rock-cut wine presses of various sizes including pressing ground and vats. Sherds from Bronze Age, Roman, Byzantine and Arab Periods.

Argaman *199:175*

Moshav shittufi in Jordan Valley 8 km. N of Damiya Bridge. Origin of name: acronym for *A*rik *R*egev and *Ga*d *Man*elah, two commanders in

Israel Defence Forces killed in area while conducting chase after terrorist infiltrators. In 1968 *nahal* outpost established; became civilian settlement in 1971. Crisis in 1973 caused most members to leave. After Yom Kippur War renewed development and in 1974 it became a regular *moshav*. Area: 4,500 d.

Ariel *167:168*

Civilian outpost (future town) in Samarian Hills, 15 km. SW of Shekhem. Established 1977.

Ariq Bridge *208:256*

Bridge on Jordan River near outlet of Lake Kinneret, built in 1976 and named after Ariq Shamir, paratrooper officer who fell in area.

'Arraba (in Galilee) *182:250*

Arab town in Lower Galilee; site of Jewish town, 'Arav, from Second Temple Period. Pop.: 8,000, mostly Moslem. **'Arav** One of larger cities in Galilee during Second Temple Period. Simeon the Hasmonean transferred inhabitants from 'Arav to Judah. The sages Rabbi Johanan b. Zakkai and Rabbi Hanina b. Dosa resided and taught here. After destruction of Second Temple one of priestly families of Temple wards, Petahiya, resided here. Jewish tradition from Middle Ages holds that grave of Hanina b. Dosa is in 'Arav. Finds in town: cave with tombs from 2nd and 3rd c. (Roman Period), remains of ancient buildings, columns and cisterns, sherds from Roman, Byzantine and Arab Periods.

○ **'Arraba** (in Samarian Hills) *169:201*

Large Arab village in Samarian Hills 12 km. SW of Jenin. Pop.: 4,300. According to one opinion — site of Arubboth — capital of 3rd administrative district in Solomon's kingdom (I Kings 4:10). Mentioned in sources as existing during Early Arab and Crusader Periods.

○ **'Arrana** *180:211*

Arab village (pop.: 650) at foot of Mt. Gilboa', 5 km. NE of Jenin.

○ **Artas** *167:121*

Moslem Arab village 4 km. S of Bethlehem. Origin of name: distortion of *hortus*, Latin for garden. Herod built aqueduct from nearby Eitam spring to supply water to Jerusalem. Remains of aqueduct can be seen along road. In 1848, Yohanan Meshullam, a Jewish apostate, together with a group of Americans attempted unsuccessfully to settle here. Wall of village mosque has Mamluk inscription from 1306. In village is the convent of *Hortus Conclusus* (closed garden), built in 1901 and staffed by nuns from S America.

● **'Arugot** *128:126*

Moshav in Judean Foothills, Lakhish region. Founded in 1949 by immigrants from Poland and Rumania. Area: 5,000 d. Pop.: 350. **Tell et Turmus** Tel of ancient settlement within boundaries of *moshav*; occupied during Chalcolithic Period and Early Bronze Age.

○ **'Arura** *166:160*

Arab village in Samarian Hills (pop.: 900), 15 km. N of Ramallah.

'Arvat Sedom **(Sedom Plain)**

Part of the 'Arava S of Dead Sea. Saline soil and sparse vegetation. Evaporation pans of the Dead Sea Potash Works cover most of area.

'Arvot Yeriho **(Jericho Plains)** *(Josh. 5:10)*

Part of 'Arava N of Dead Sea; with city of Jericho at its centre, it forms an oasis, receiving water from Wadi Qilt and Nahal Nu'eima. Here Joshua and the Israelites started their campaign for conquest of Canaan (Josh. 5:10 ff.). Pioneers who founded Petah Tiqwa in 1878 first tried to settle here but were prevented by Turkish authorities. In 1940 kibbutz Bet Ha'Arava was established but abandoned during War of Independence.

Arza *164:133*

Sanatorium in Moẓa 'Illit 5 km. W of Jerusalem, belonging to Sick Fund of Histadrut. Named after cedar tree — *erez* — that Herzl planted in Moẓa during his visit to Palestine in 1898. (Actually he planted a cypress, the trunk of which still exists.) Arbour of trees planted by Israel's presidents and a bust of David Ben-Gurion. Near sanatorium is part of old road to Jerusalem called Seven Sisters because of seven hairpin bends. Area is wooded and has nature reserve. Above Arza is Mt. Castel, scene of heavy fighting in War of Independence.

Asaf HaRofe *135:152*

Government hospital by Ẓerifin off Tel Aviv-Ramla road. Named after a Jewish doctor (possibly Asaf b. Berachiah) who wrote a book on medicine in Hebrew in the 6th c. which included a "physician's oath" taken by students of medicine. Founded in 1949, it was first a military hospital. Now services districts of Lod, Ramla, Rishon LeẒiyyon and Reḥovot.

'Asakir *171:119*

Small Bedouin village on border of Judean Hills and Judean Desert, 5 km. SE of Bethlehem.

'Asaliyya *213:263*

Abandoned Syrian village on Golan Heights 3 km. SW of Qaẓrin. Remains of ancient synagogue, including a lintel engraved with two 7-branched candelabra. N of village is oak grove.

'Aseret *126:137*

Rural settlement and regional centre on central Coastal Plain, 2 km. E of Bene Darom junction. Named after 10 founders of Gedera (*'aseret* = ten). Founded in 1954. Pop.: 700. Tomb within settlement, en Nabi Shit, which according to Arab tradition is that of Seth, son of Adam.

Ashalim *120:041*

Moshav shittufi in Negev Hills 10 km. S of Revivim. Founded in 1977. Named after *naḥal* outpost founded in 1956, 4 km. SW of *moshav*. Abandoned a year later. First called Paqua' (gourd). Later name changed to Ashalim (tamarisks) because of their abundance in area. Pop.: 110.

Ashdod *(Josh. 15:47) 116:135*

New port city in S outlet of Naḥal Lakhish. Ancient harbour was situated at Ashdod Yam, S of new city; built near site of Biblical Ashdod, one of the five cities of the Philistines. After War of Independence, a number of *ma'barot* (immigrant transit camps) and agricultural settlements were established in area. Only in 1957 was it decided to build a city and port for S part of country. The new port was inaugurated in 1966 and from then on the city developed rapidly. Municipal area today is 34,000 d. Pop.: 60,000. **Tel Ashdod** *117:129* Ancient tel, 7 km. S of modern Ashdod within abandoned Arab village of Isdud. Site of ancient Ashdod — important Canaanite city along *via maris* taken by Philistines. It was to Ashdod that the Philistines brought the Ark of the Covenant after capturing it at the battle of Aphek. Wars between Judah and Ashdod continued through the time of the Judges and Kings and First and Second Temple Periods. Conquered by Hasmoneans it became an independent city with its own port (Ashdod-on-the-sea). Subsequently it succumbed to various

ASHDOD

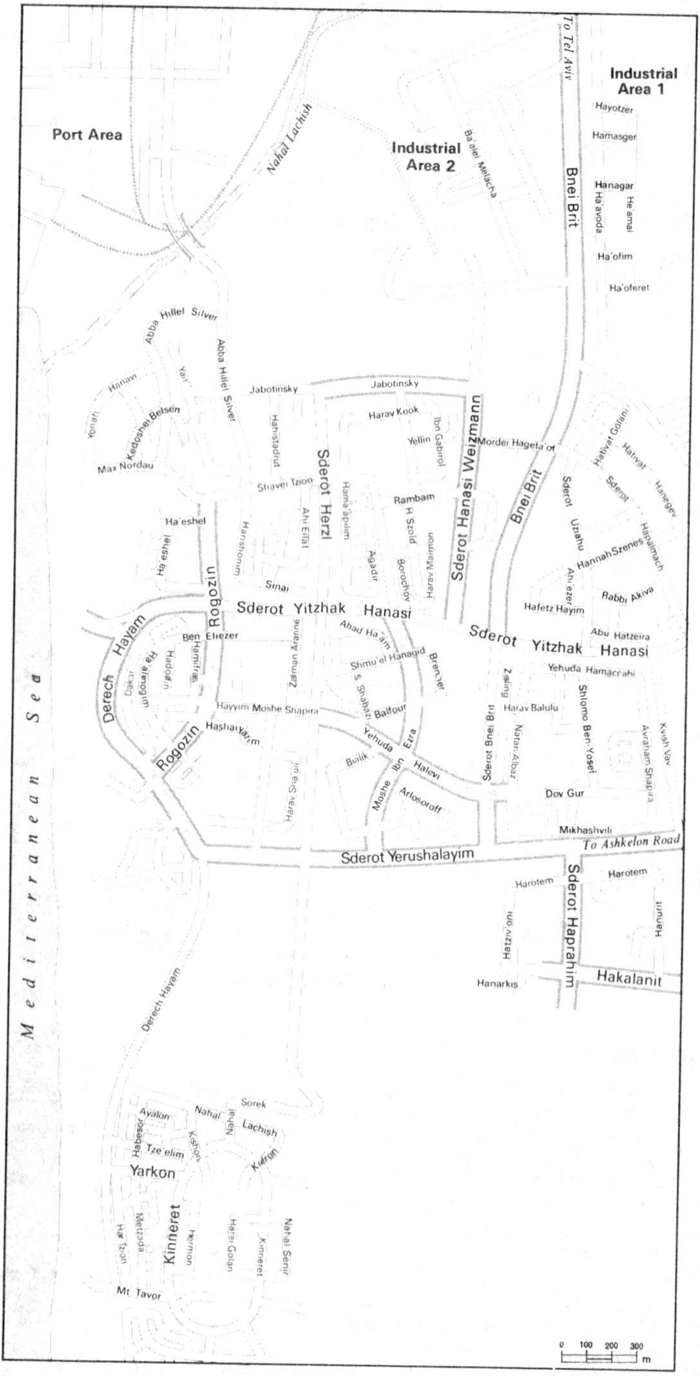

c carta, JERUSALEM

conquerors and was one of the sites of battle between Crusaders and Moslems. The Arab village of Isdud was built on its ruins. During War of Independence, Egyptian army reached Ashdod and heavy fighting ensued until Egyptians were almost encircled. With difficulty they managed to extricate themselves. **Ashdod Yam** (Ashdod-on-the-sea), Minat el Qal'a, 4.5 km. S of Ashdod. Port of ancient Ashdod. Along coast, 600 m. breakwater built of large stones. On shore, remains of Arab fortress built on remains of city from Roman and Byzantine Periods. S of ancient city is high sand mound, semi-circular in shape. This may have been site of bay which served the ancient port. Arab fortress measures 45x60 m. with circular corner towers. Additional towers in W and E walls and at land and sea gates. During Late Bronze Age and Iron Age the hill S of Arab fortress was inhabited but due to shifting sands it is difficult to estimate the size of the town. **Mizpe Yona** Within city of Ashdod on sand mound. Sherds and other remains from Late Iron Age, post-Babylonian Exile, Roman and Byzantine Periods. Ruins of Moslem shrine, Nebi Yunis, and ancient Moslem cemetery.

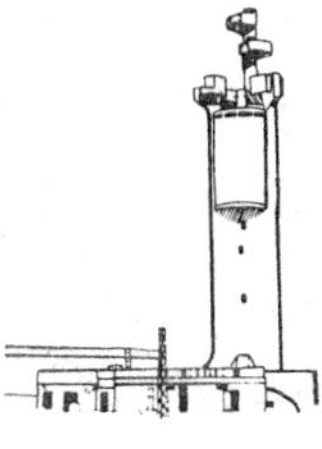

Ashdot Ya'aqov — *204:299; 205:230*

Two adjoining *kibbutzim* in Jordan Valley 5 km. S of Lake Kinneret. Origin of name: *ashdot* (waterfalls) of nearby Yarmouk River; *Ya'aqov* after James (Ya'aqov) de Rothschild, son of Baron Edmond. Originally founded as one kibbutz by members of Latvian HeHaluz movement who settled in 1924 where kibbutz Gesher now stands. In 1935 moved to present site on lands purchased from Dalhamiyya village. Prior to War of Independence, served as Palmah base. After split in movement in 1952, kibbutz divided into two. During War of Attrition after 1967, settlers suffered from terrorist raids; since Yom Kippur War the area has enjoyed quiet. **Ihud** *204:229* Area: 4,200 d. Pop.: 600. **Me'uhad** *205:230* Area: 4,300 d. Pop.: 550.

Asherat — *164:264*

Industrial village under construction in Galilee, 6 km. SE of Nahariyya. During ancient times this area was included within Asher tribal allotment, hence name.

Ashmura — *210:273*

Abandoned settlement in Upper Galilee, on site which was called Dardara in Arabic. Name Biblical "...and meditate on thee in the *watches* of the night..." (Ps. 63:6). Settled in 1946; completely destroyed in War of Independence and members moved to Kefar Sava area. In 1953 it was resettled and in 1956 became a *nahal* outpost. Since the early 60's it is no longer inhabited.

Ashqelon — *(Josh. 13:3) 110:119*

City in S on Mediterranean coast, near site of major Philistine city. Herod the Great was born here. Jews and Christians enjoyed prosperity through Byzantine times, Jews leaving only after Crusaders driven out by Moslems. Old city wall extant by shore. Ancient tel dominated by Roman and Byzantine remains. Modern Ashqelon established after War of Independence. Original intention was to build agricultural settlement called Migdal 'Aza. Afterwards, new immigrant settlers housed in buildings of abandoned town, Majdal. In 1950, new entity of Migdal Ashqelon adopted by South African Zionist Federation who financed establishment of new neighbourhood called Afridar. Town developed and granted city status in 1955 encompassing 45,000 d. Pop.: 50,000. **Ancient Ashqelon** *107:117* S of new city, large tel

ASHQELON

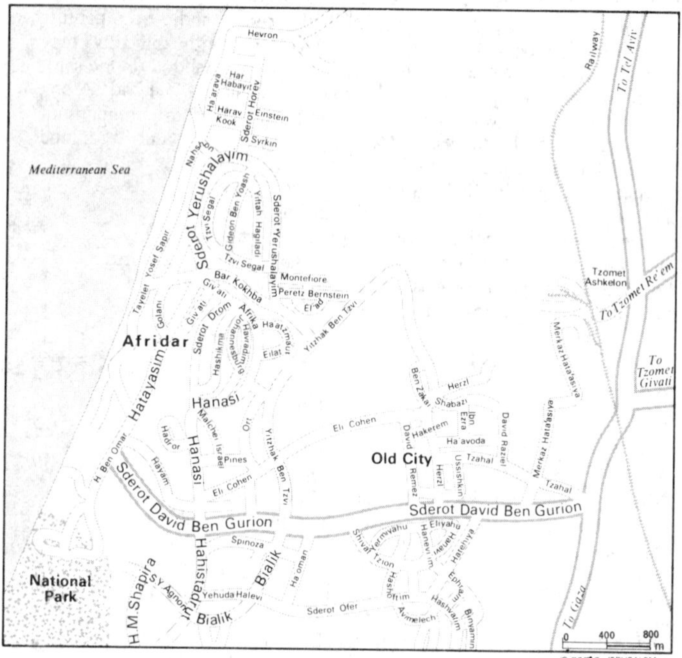

© carta JERUSALEM

on seashore surrounded by park. Important ancient city. Ashqelon's revolt against Ramesses II was quelled (1280 BCE) and its defeat is depicted on walls of Karnak temple. Joshua failed to conquer city but it was conquered after his death and later retaken by the Philistines who made it one of their 5 city-states and seat of one of their princes. By end of First Temple Period it was a large kingdom extending to Jaffa and Bet Dagan. At beginning of Hellenistic Period it was inhabited by Greeks and made a centre of Greek culture. Hasmoneans failed to conquer it although many Jews lived here. Herod was fond of the city and built many beautiful buildings here. During Arab Period it was an important commercial centre with a large Jewish community. Crusaders conquered it in 1153 and strongly fortified it; Crusader remains can still be seen. In 1270 it was captured and completely destroyed by Mamluk Sultan Baybars. Arab town of Majdal was built on these ruins. Majdal served as important base for invading Egyptian army during War of Independence. Archaeological finds indicate occupation levels from Middle Bronze Age onwards and many objects from various periods: marble columns and statues from Roman and Byzantine Periods; many tombs, some decorated with wall paintings; large marble and lead sarcophagi; remains of large Roman council house (*bouleuterion*); a synagogue with Hebrew and Greek inscriptions; Byzantine and Crusader churches; city wall with Byzantine (and possibly Roman) foundations which served until the destruction in Crusader Period.

o **'Aṣira el Qibliyya** *170:176*

Arab village in Samarian Hills, 7 km. SW of Shekhem.

o **'Aṣira esh Shamaliyya** *175:184*

Arab village 3 km. N of Shekhem. Pop.: 3,200. Within village remains of Iron Age settlement reoccupied in Byzantine Period, Middle Ages and

Ottoman Period. Believed to be site of Hazeroth, mentioned in Samaria Ostraca.

'Askar *178:180*

Arab village and refugee camp E of Shekhem. Pop.: 1,800. Site of Jacob's Well (**Be'er Ya'aqov**), a pool and rock-cut canal with well nearby. Not only associated with Hebrew patriarch, but also with Jesus who met the woman of Samaria here. Over the well is Crusader church built on ruins of Byzantine one. N of well is Joseph's Tomb, where Jacob's son is believed buried. White-domed structure over tomb restored by Moslems in 19th c. NW of village at foot of Mt. Eyal is large cemetery with tombs from Iron Age, Hellenistic, Roman and Byzantine Periods. Magnificent 6th c. tomb (apparently Samaritan) discovered and restored. **'En Sukar** Site of ancient 'En Sukar or Sukar, mentioned in Hasmonean battle accounts, and of Samaritan settlement called Yiskar or 'Askar, which persisted until Crusader times.

'Atarot *170:141*

Site of Jerusalem airport. Formerly *moshav*, 11 km. N of Jerusalem off road to Ramallah. First attempt at settlement in 1914 but abandoned during WWI. Resettled in 1922, it became a *moshav* in 1925. During War of Independence 'Atarot and Newe Ya'aqov were surrounded by Arab forces and inhabitants were evacuated. 'Atarot members later settled on lands of German colony Wilhelma and called their *moshav* Bene 'Atarot. After Six-Day War, a small airfield built by British on the site was enlarged and became the Jerusalem airport. 'Atarot Industrial Area lies S of airport.

Atar Sapir (Eshed Kinnarot) *200:252*

Main pumping station of National Water Carrier 9 km. N of Tiberias. Named after Pinḥas Sapir, past minister of finance of Israel. Huge pumps dug into a tel raise water pumped from the Kinneret to a height of 200 m. i.e. sea level. From this height it is either pumped or allowed to gravitate to S.

'Atlit *144:233*

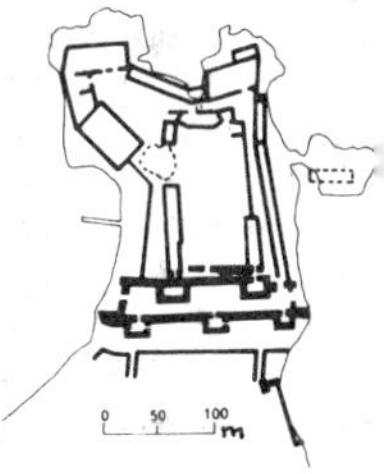

Settlement on Karmel coast, 14 km. S of Haifa, next to Crusader city and ancient tel. Name derived from Arab ruins to the N. First started as farming village in 1903. Area: 10,400 d. Pop.: 3,000. To W are large evaporation pans belonging to company which manufactures table salt from sea water. To E are remains of British army camps which were used as detention camps for "illegal" immigrants during last years of British Mandate. **Ruins of 'Atlit** To N on coast of 'Atlit Bay *144:234*. Origin of ancient name unknown. Archaeological finds indicate occupation from Late Bronze Age until Hellenistic Period. Excavations of tel uncovered Phoenician cemetery containing many sherds. Site resettled during Crusader Period. In 1218 the Templar Knights completed building a castle called Castrum Peregrinorum or Château des Pèlerins (the pilgrims' fortress) to protect pilgrims en route from Acre to Jerusalem. Crusader city evacuated in 1291 after Acre fell to Sultan Baybars and was destroyed by Moslems. Site has remains of Crusader fortress, port, walled city with streets, churches, stables, a bath and other structures. **Experimental station** *146:235* Near 'Atlit, Aaron Aaronsohn's agricultural experimental station was founded in 1911. It also served as centre of operations for Nili during WWI and was abandoned in 1916 when Nili activities were uncovered by Turks. The building has been renovated and now serves as a youth centre — Bet Aaronsohn.

o **(El) 'Attara** (in Jenin district) ⛫ *165:192*

Small Arab village (pop.: 300) in Samarian Hills, 12 km. E of Tulkarm.

o **'Attara** (in Ramallah district) ⛫ *169:156*

Arab village in Samarian Hills 11 km. N of Ramallah. Pop.: 900. Built on ruins of ancient settlement. One theory identifies village as site of Biblical Ataroth-addar which was included in Benjamin's tribal allotment. Ancient stones re-used in modern village. A number of springs with water conduits located N of village. Sherds indicate occupation in Iron Age, Byzantine Period and Middle Ages.

o **'Attil** ⛫ *157:197*

Arab village in W Samarian Hills 7 km. NE of Tulkarm. Pop.: 3,800. Within village are scattered column fragments, well, cisterns and rock-cut tombs indicating ancient settlement.

'Auja el Ḥafir → Nizzana

● **'Avdon** *(Josh. 21:30) 167:273*

Moshav in W Galilee 9 km. NE of Nahariyya. Origin of name: Levite city from tribal allotment of Asher whose name is retained in nearby Kh. 'Abda. Founded in 1952 by Tunisian immigrants. First called Kefar 'Avdon. Area: 700 d. Pop.: 330.

⛫ **'Avedat** *128:023*

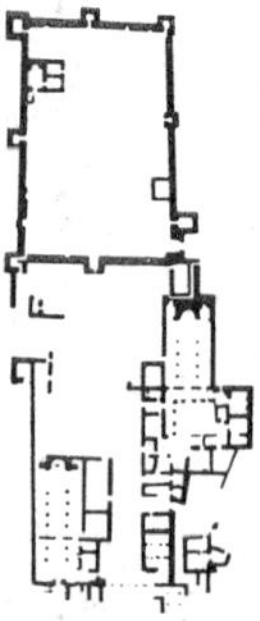

'Avedat was the greatest Nabatean city in the Negev. The ruins lie 9 km. S of Sede Boker on a limestone hill standing sentinel over a sea of desert. Founded in 2nd c. CE and built where the ancient roads from Petra-to-Gaza and Jerusalem-to-Eilat meet. Named after Nabatean king revered as a god who is buried here. Bloody history due to strategic location. First conquered by Romans. Reached zenith in Byzantine era. Conquests by Persians in 614 and Moslems in 634 left it partially a ruin. Decline continued until 10th c. when site was abandoned. Rediscovered in 19th c. archaeological excavations and partial reconstruction in 1958. Easy 10-minute climb from entrance to plateau's summit. Sides of hill dotted with ancient burial caves. Walk from caves to S entrance of fortress is through Roman residential quarter. Two 6th c. churches located within Byzantine fortress. Remnants of Byzantine monastery outside ramparts. Behind fortress are sparse ruins of kiln and workshop, where Nabateans manufactured their famous eggshell pottery. From fortress terrace is view of experimental farm, established by Hebrew University in 1960, which employs 2,000 year-old irrigation techniques to raise wheat, barley, almonds, apricots and pistachios. Between here and Sede Boker is 'Avedat Spring ('En 'Avedat), a steep waterfall where ibex drink in morning and evening.

⛫ **Avel Bet Ma'akha** *(II Sam. 20:19) 205:296*

Ancient tel in Upper Galilee 2 km. S of Metulla. Biblical city. (Joab, King David's commander-in-chief, besieged Abel-beth-maachah when Sheba son of Bichri took refuge here.) Citadel on the N corner of tel, with stone wall on slope below. At summit, sherds found from Early and Middle Bronze Ages and to the S, sherds from Iron Age.

● **Avi'el** ⛫ *150:215*

Ḥerut *moshav* in Samaria, NE of Binyamina. Originally called Yad HaAreba''esre (Memorial to the Fourteen). Avi'el was underground name of Israel Epstein, Irgun agent, imprisoned in Italy for bombing British Embassy in Rome and killed while attempting escape. Founded in 1949. Pop.: 250. Area: 3,000 d. NW of *moshav* are remains of water tunnels hewn out of mountain. Believed to be part of water supply system to Caesarea.

● **Avi'ezer** *152:121*

Moshav 9.5 km. SE of Bet Shemesh. Named after Avi'ezer Sigmund Gestetner, English Zionist. Founded 1958. Pop.: 250, mainly immigrants from Persia and Cochin, India. **Ḥurbat Bet Bad** (ruins of olive oil press) *152:121*. Ruins of church from 6th and 7th c.

● **Avigedor** *125:124*

Moshav in S, 11 km. N of Qiryat Gat. Named after English Zionist, Sir Osmond D'Avigdor-Goldsmid and his son Henry. Founded in 1950 by WWII veterans of British army Jewish Transport Unit. Area: 3,400 d. Pop.: 350.

● **Aviḥayil** *137:195*

Moshav in Sharon 4 km. N of Netanya. Founded in 1932 by WWI veterans of Jewish Legion. Area: 4,000 d. Pop.: 600. Jewish Legion museum and cultural centre — Bet HaGedudim.

● **Avital** *179:218*

Moshav in Yizre'el Valley near Mt.Gilboa'. First settlement in Ta'anakh region; founded in 1953. Pop.: 400, immigrants from Persia.

● **Avivim** *194:277*

Moshav in Upper Galilee, near Lebanese border. Founded in 1958. Abandoned by original founders; resettled in 1962 by immigrants from N Africa. Settlers suffered from Arab terrorist attacks and on May 22, 1970, twelve children were murdered on their way to school by terrorists.

● **Avne Etan** *221:248*

Moshav on S Golan Heights. Founded 1974 by religious scout group. Name is acronym of initials of members of *naḥal* group who died in Israel's wars. Area: 3,500 d.

◆ **Avuqa** *200:209*

Farm S of Bet She'an; founded by group organized in 1941 and disbanded 15 years later.

○ **'Awarta** *177:174*

Arab village in Samarian Hills 6 km. S of Shekhem. Pop.: 1,700. In past, Samaritan village, mentioned in Samaritan Book of Joshua and in poetry of Samaritan priest Abisha b. Phinehas. Cluster of ancient tombs on low hill in village which, according to Samaritan tradition, contains graves of priests Eleazar, Ithamar, Phinehas and his son Abisha. Jewish sources refer to site as Giv'at Pinḥas. Samaritan tradition also claims the 70 elders chosen by Moses are buried here (Num. 11:24 ff.).

■ **'Ayanot** *128:147*

Educational institute in central Coastal Plain off Rishon LeẒiyyon-Ashdod road. Belongs to Pioneer Women. Founded in 1930; 400 pupils and staff. Area: 2,200 d. Has courses in agriculture for boys and nursing for girls. Opposite 'Ayanot are ancient sycamore trees by a fountain built by Turkish governor of an area called Abu Nabut (father of terebinth).

'Ayanot (in Yizre'el Valley) → **Ramat Dawid**

Ayyalon Valley → **'Emeq Ayyalon**

★ **Ayyelet HaShaḥar** *204:269*

Resort and kibbutz in Upper Galilee 8 km. N of Rosh Pinna, with museum consisting mostly of finds from nearby Tel Ḥazor. Name means morning star as does the name of the Arab village Nijmat eṣ Ṣubḥ. Site purchased by ICA in 1892, abandoned and then given to Rosh Pinna farmers for cultivation. In 1917, leased to collective settlement Ḥoreshim. In 1918 land given over to settlers who later made it a kibbutz. During War of Independence it was an important defensive position against Syrian army and served as a Palmaḥ base. In Six-Day War it was badly damaged by Syrian shelling. Area: 9,300 d. Pop.: 1,000. **Antiquities** in museum: Neolithic, Iron Age and Byzantine remains of buildings and sherds. Dig uncovered remains of Assyrian palace, water drainage and supply network.

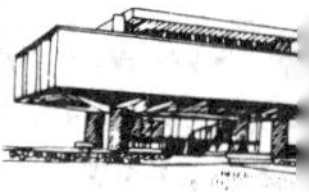

● **'Azarya** *141:144*

Moshav in Judean Foothills 5 km. SE of Ramla. Founded 1949 by immigrants from Zakho (city in Kurdistan) who moved here from Jerusalem. Name is acronym from Hebrew for "Zakho immigrants saw the deliverance of the Lord." Area: 2,900 d. Pop.: 470.

Azor *131:159*

Urban settlement near Tel Aviv on Tel Aviv-Jerusalem road. Location of Yazur, abandoned Arab village; ancient site bears evidence of almost continuous occupation from prehistoric times. Name mentioned in *Annals of Sennacherib* as one of cities conquered in 701 BCE. Remains of synagogue indicate Jewish residence during Byzantine Period. In Crusader Period, Richard the Lion-Heart built a small fort which was later given to Templars. Arab name, Yazur, first mentioned in 13th c. CE sources. Afterwards mentioned in writings of pilgrims and visitors to Holy Land. Non-Moslem travellers were made to pay toll. During 1936-1939 Riots Arab gangs based in Yazur harassed transportation and killed Jewish travellers. During War of Independence, Arabs blocked road and in a battle to open it, 7 Haganah men were killed. Memorial erected to them alongside road. After Arabs abandoned site, Jewish immigrants settled here and the village expanded. Pop.: 6,000. **Antiquities** Prehistoric site, Chalcolithic burial tomb with clay ossuaries, remains from Bronze and Iron Ages and Roman Period, beautiful architectural remains including carved candelabrum and inscription from Byzantine synagogue, ancient sycamore alongside Byzantine water storage pools, remains of Crusader fort, one tower of which later served as mosque, domed building from Arab Period — one of Moslem holy places named after Imam 'Ali.

● **'Azri'el** *147:185*

Moshav in Sharon 7 km. E of Tel Mond junction. Named after Rabbi 'Azri'el Hildesheimer, German rabbi, scholar, leader of Orthodox Jewry and supporter of Ḥoveve Ẓiyyon movement. Founded in 1951 by Yemenite immigrants. Area: 2,000 d. Pop.: 530.

● **'Azriqam** *121:129*

Moshav in central Coastal Plain 7 km. SE of Ashdod. Named after Azrikam, a descendant of Zerubbabel (I Chron. 3:23). Founded in 1950. Area: 3,000 d. Pop.: 660.

'Azza → Gaza

'Azzata → Netivot

'Azzun ⛰ *155:175*

Arab village in Samarian Hills at Shekhem-Qalqilya and Tulkarm-Ramallah junction. Pop.: 2,200. Built on ruins of ancient settlement which existed from Iron Age to Ottoman Period. During WWI site of German-Turkish army base.

'Azzun 'Atma ⛰ *151:170*

Arab village in W Samarian Hills 7 km. NE of Rosh Ha'Ayin. Pop.: 300. Built on ruins of ancient settlement whose stones have been re-used in modern village. Sherds indicate occupation from Iron Age until Ottoman Period.

B

Ba'al Ḥaẓor * *(II Sam. 13:23)* *176:153*

Mountain on N border of Samarian Hills 10 km. NE of Ramallah. Height: 1,016 m. above sea level. Called Tell 'Asur in Arabic. On its summit is a group of ancient trees — preserved because it is considered holy by local inhabitants; remains of ancient houses and church. Mentioned in Bible as place where Absalom's servants killed Amnon (II Sam. 13:23 ff.). This is probably the Mt. Ḥaẓor associated with last battle of Judah Maccabee (I Macc. 9:15).

Bab el Hawa (Tell el Gharam) *222:283*

Large ruin on N Golan Heights. Name means gate of the winds. Called thus owing to prevailing strong W winds. Also called Tell el Gharam after tel to S. Remains of buildings and scattered hewn stones indicate settlement during Roman and Byzantine epoch. In Manṣura, neighbouring village to SE, 2 Greek inscriptions were found; probably brought from Bab el Hawa. To S is water reservoir where flint tools from Paleolithic and Mesolithic Periods were found. Site has small nature reserve with pool supporting rare water plants and striped salamanders.

Bab el Wad → Sha'ar HaGay

★ **Baḥan** *152:195*

Kibbutz in NW Samarian Hills 4 km. N of Tulkarm. Name means watch-tower. Founded as *naḥal* outpost in 1953 on site of War of Independence military "outpost 83". Area: 3,600 d. Pop.: 370. Mosaic floor with Greek inscription found here. In area of ancient cities of Socoh and Yaham, mentioned in City Lists of Thutmose III (15th c. BCE) and centre of King Solomon's third province.

(El) Bahja *158:260*

Garden N of Acre, with grave of Mirza Ḥusayn 'Ali, known as Baha'u'llah, 2nd leader of Bahai faith. Exiled by Turkish government from Baghdad, he reached Acre in 1863 where he died in 1892. Next to his tomb is a museum. Loveliest gardens in Israel. Considered holiest spot in Bahai world.

Baiyada *173:122*

Bedouin village on border of Judean Desert, 3 km. E of Bethlehem. Pop.: 250.

o **(El) Baiyada** *166:218*

Arab village 3.5 km. SW of Megiddo junction. Name means white and refers to local white soil. Pop.: 200.

o **Bal'a** *160:193*

Arab village in Samarian Hills 7 km. NE of Tulkarm. Served as base for Arab gangs during Disturbances of 1936-1939. Pop.: 2,400.

o **(El) Balata** *177:179*

Arab village and refugee camp at SE entrance to Shekhem. Named after nearby Tell Balata. **Joseph's tomb** (en Nabi Yusuf) where, according to tradition, Joseph's bones were buried after being brought from Egypt

(Josh. 24:32). Revered as such since 4th c. and confirmed by discovery of Egyptian relics nearby from 1500 BCE. Restored by Moslems in 1868. Inscriptions in Hebrew and Samaritan. Pillars at each end of grave are traditionally believed to be tombs of Joseph's sons, Ephraim and Manasseh, from whom Samaritans claim descent. **'Ein Balata** Near village mosque is a tunnel-opening through which water from Balata spring was directed to ancient Shekhem at foot of Mt. Gerizim. **Church of Jacob's Well** W of village is Greek Orthodox church built over opening of ancient well which, according to tradition, was dug by Jacob (Gen. 33:19).

Balfour Forest *174:230*

JNF-planted forest 3 km. SW of Nazareth. Named after Lord Balfour, author of Balfour Declaration. Original trees planted 1928.

Balfouriyya *178:226*

Moshav in Yizre'el Valley 2 km. N of 'Afula. Named after Lord Balfour, author of Balfour Declaration. Founded 1922. Area: 8,000 d. Pop.: 230. **Ancient tel** NE of *moshav* is site of one of string of ancient towns which ran along Naḥal 'Adashim. Finds include sherds from Late Bronze Age, Early Iron Age and Hellenistic through Arab Periods. **Nature reserve** At S foot of tel are many springs and remains of ancient buildings, including thick walls built of two rows of large unhewn stones.

Bani Na'im *165:102*

Arab village 6 km. E of Hebron. According to Arab tradition, named after 2 brothers to whom Prophet Muḥammad promised district of Hebron. Site of settlement called Kafr Berekha, or Kafr Berukha, mentioned in Christian church writings. (Named after Valley of Berachah — II Chron. 20:26.) Pop.: 4,500. Local mosque has tomb purported to be that of Lot and called by Arabs — en Nabi Lut.

Bani Suheila *085:083*

Arab village in Gaza Strip 2 km. E of Khan Yunis. Name means: sons of the star Suheil (Canopus). Called Bani Suheil by Christian pilgrim in 1839. Pop.: 8,000.

Banyas *215:294*

A source of Jordan River running through lush woodlands and ending in broad lagoon overlooked by Mt. Ḥermon snows, and flanked by rock-hewn caves and an ancient temple dedicated to goat-footed Pan. Now part of nature reserve 12 km. NE of Qiryat Shemona. Called Paneas in Hellenistic age in honour of the Greek god; Banyas, being Arab mispronunciation of Paneas. It was here that in the Roman Period Philip the Tetrarch, son of Herod, established the city of Caesarea Philippi — mentioned in New Testament and Talmud. Games held here in 70 CE to celebrate Titus' victory over Jews. Many Jewish captives killed here. Had large Jewish community and called Dan in Middle Ages. Called Belinas by Crusaders. Arab village captured by Israel Defence Forces in Six-Day War was called Banyas. **Naḥal Ḥermon** Source of Naḥal Banyas, one of 3 major sources of Jordan River. Evident are rock-cut grottos where Greeks placed statues of their gods. **Sheikh el Khadr** Above springs is purported tomb of Sheikh el Khadr, Arab name for Prophet Elijah. **Banyas waterfall** Further along Banyas stream. Entire area has been designated a nature reserve.

Baptist Village ▲ *142:173*

Rural settlement with educational institute and hostel for Baptists. Located off Petaḥ Tiqwa-Kefar Sava road, near Yarqon River. Founded 1956.

○ **Baqa** **(Baqa Bani Ṣa'ib)** *161:179*

Arab village (pop.: 600) in Samarian Hills, 15 km. W of Shekhem.

Baqa el Gharbiyya *154:202*

Arab village in N Sharon 12 km. SE of Hadera. Origin of word *baqa* not known; *el gharbiyya* means western. Founded some 200 years ago by inhabitants of nearby village, 'Illar. Pop.: 10,000. Seat of Shari'a Moslem religious court. Within village is tel with cisterns, rock-cut tombs, fragments of mosaics and remains of buildings.

○ **Baqa esh Sharqiyya** *157:202*

Sister Arab village to E of Baqa el Gharbiyya in N Sharon. Until Six-Day War it was in Jordanian territory. Pop.: 1,500. Remains including cisterns, column fragments and capitals.

★ **Bar'am** *190:273*

Remains of 2nd c. CE synagogue that is one of the best-preserved in Israel, though not mentioned in ancient sources. Nearby, 5 km. NE of Hiram junction close to Lebanese border is a kibbutz of same name. A second ancient synagogue here was destroyed in 19th c. Two Hebrew inscriptions relating to synagogue building found: "Eleazar b. Yudan built it," "Peace be on this place and on the places where His people, Israel, dwell. Yose HaLevi built this lintel, blessed be his deeds, amen." Written about by Medieval travellers, among them Rabbi Samuel b. Simeon in 13th c. and Rabbi Moses Basula in 16th c. Surviving structure measures 15.2 by 20 metres. Facade preserved almost whole up to upper corniche. Indications that there was once a second storey. Giant ashlars, similar to ones used on Temple Mount in Jerusalem, were utilized here. Unlike other synagogues of period, it has porch along length of S wall supported by eight pillars. Other ancient buildings on site. Abandoned Maronite village of Bir'am constructed on remains of Roman-Byzantine Period Jewish settlement. Kibbutz founded in 1949 by Palmaḥ veterans, 2 km. NE of Maronite town and ancient site, whose Arab Christian inhabitants were evacuated during War of Independence. Pop.: several hundred. Area: 1,750 d. **Allone Bar'am Forest** Nature reserve which covers 1,000 d.

● **Baraq** *175:216*

Moshav in Ta'anakh region in Yizre'el Valley. Named after Barak, son of Abinoam, who fought against Sisera in this area. Founded in 1956 by Moroccan immigrants. Pop.: 300. Area: 1,700 d.

○ **Bardala** *195:199*

Arab village 12 km. S of Bet She'an. Near village is Kh. Bardala, probably site of Bardala, well-known during Roman and Byzantine Periods for the many *Tannaim* and *Amoraim* who resided here. Remains of buildings and caves from Roman Period and Middle Ages.

● **Bareqet** *145:158*

Moshav in Lod Foothills 5 km. NE of Ben-Gurion Airport. Name means precious stone in breastplate. Founded 1952. Pop.: 1,100. Area: 2,500 d. E of *moshav*, near Kh. el Bira, are ancient caves.

● **Bar Giyyora** *157:126*

Moshav in Judean Hills named after Simeon bar Giyyora, one of leaders of great Revolt against Rome (66-70 CE). Pop.: 280. Area: 700 d.

★ **Barqay** *153:209*

Kibbutz in N Sharon, at approach to 'Iron Valley. Name means: morning star. Founded in 1947 by graduates of HaShomer HaZa'ir youth movement in Rumania. Pop.: 500. Area: 2,750 d. Within kibbutz are prehistoric remains.

Barta'a 159:209

Arab village in W Samarian Hills 7 km. W of kibbutz Barqay. Named after Sheikh Barta'a whose tomb is on hill above village. Until Six-Day War, village was divided in two: N part in Israel and S part in Jordan. Pop.: 1,000.

Bar Yoḥai 192:266

Regional centre in Upper Galilee named after Shim'on bar Yoḥai.

Basmat Tab'un 165:238

Permanent Bedouin settlement 4 km. N of Qiryat Tiv'on. Founded in 1962 as first attempt by Israel to settle migrant Bedouin.

Batn el Yamani 144:152

Family tomb from Roman Period 7 km. E of Lod. Ten niches in walls, frescoes and plaster reliefs. Two graves dug in floor of tomb.

Bat Shelomo 151:222

Farming village (*moshava*) in Ramat Menashe 5 km. NE of Zikhron Ya'aqov. Named after Betty, daughter of Solomon (Shelomo) de Rothschild, mother of Baron Edmond. Founded 1889 by ICA. Pop.: 240.

Battir 163:126

Arab village in Jerusalem Hills 7 km. SW of Jerusalem. Built on ruins of ancient town, Bethther. Pop.: 1,500. Still in existence within village is spring and pool from which a complex system of canals conducts water to neighbouring fields. Not mentioned in Bible but in Septuagint. Was important centre after Second Temple destruction. Bar Kokhba fortified it and made it headquarters of revolt against Romans (132-135 CE). It was here that he fell. Ancient tel is located high above village and called by Arabs, Kh. el Yahud. Most of remains are buried but remnants of wall, towers and rock-hewn agricultural structures are visible. Sherds indicate occupation in Iron Age and in Roman and Byzantine Periods.

Bat Yam 126:159

City on coast, S of Jaffa. Land was purchased in 1923 to build urban suburb of Bayit WeGan. First houses built in 1926. Temporarily abandoned during 1929 Arab Riots. Inhabitants returned in 1932. Name changed to Bat Yam in 1936. Suffered badly during 1936-1939 Disturbances and at beginning of War of Independence it was cut off from other Jewish settlements. In 1950 it started growing rapidly as a result of mass immigration. Area of jurisdiction: 7,000 d. Pop.: 130,000. Mainstays of economy are manufacturing, merchandising and services. City has art museum, Ryback House (collection of paintings and sculpture), Sholem Asch House, large bathing beach with promenade and memorial to fallen soldiers.

Baẓra 138:179

Moshav in Sharon 4 km. N of Ra'ananna junction. Named after Iraqi city of Basra where founders of *moshav* served in British army during WWII. Founded 1946. Pop.: 400. Area: 2,500 d.

Bazzariya 165:190

Arab village in Samarian Hills 5 km. N of Sabastiya. Pop.: 500. Village has Moslem holy tomb — en Nabi Na'aman.

Bedolaḥ 079:081

Moshav in Gaza Strip 3 km. N of Rafah. Established 1980.

Be'er Ḥafir (Bir Ḥafir) 110:014

Well in Naḥal Nizzana channel. Restored by British. Nearby are remains of Iron Age fortress.

★ **Be'eri** 101:092

Kibbutz in W Negev 8 km. S of Gaza. Named after Be'eri (Berl Katznelson). Founded in 1946 as part of operation to settle 11 sites in one night. Heavily attacked during War of Independence and settlers had to live for many months in underground bunkers. Area: 18,000 d. Pop.: 650. Large cultural centre and bibliography library of Kibbutz HaMe'uḥad movement and Tel Aviv University. Near kibbutz are abandoned sulphur mines. Nature reserve, (5,000 d.), N of kibbutz, surrounding crater-shaped valley. **ANZC memorial** In Be'eri forest, 3 km. E of kibbutz, is memorial to WWI and WWII expeditionary corps from Australia and New Zealand. (Hence ANZC — Australia-New Zealand Corps.) Look-out point.

Be'er Mash'abbim (Bir 'Asluj) 126:047

Ancient well in Negev, alongside Be'er Sheva'-Nizzana road. Called Bir 'Asluj in Arabic. Used to be central settlement for 'Azazmeh Bedouin tribe. Near well are remains of railroad and station built by Turks and Germans in WWI. Later served British army as base for attack on Be'er Sheva'. During Mandate, British built police fort, later used by invading Egyptian army in War of Independence. Fort blown up by Israeli army at end of first truce. However, it was liberated during Ḥorev operation in which invaders were evicted from entire area. Site has memorial to soldiers who died here.

Be'er Menuḥa 162:968

Well in 'Arava 30 km. N of Qetura junction, at foot of Giv'at Menuḥa. Name from Arabic Bir el Muleiḥa (the good well) — a sweet water well supplying needs of local Bedouin. Served as departure point for adventurous youth who secretly tried to reach the Red Rock (Petra) 30 km. E across border in Jordan. Site has 2 memorials for those who died in the attempt. W of well is a small tel.

◆ **Be'er Ora** 147:902

Gadna farm in S Negev 20 km. N of Elat. Name means well of light — contrary to former Arabic name Bir Hindis (well of great darkness). Established 1950. Has Gadna training camp run by permanent Israel Defence Forces staff.

Be'erotayim (in Negev) → **'Ezuz**

● **Be'erotayim** (in Sharon) 148:191

Moshav in Sharon named after Arabic Bir Burin. Founded 1949. Area: 3,500 d. Pop.: 250. Pool and ancient wells.

★ **Be'erot Yizḥaq** 141:160

Religious kibbutz 5 km. N of Ben-Gurion Airport. Named after Rabbi Isaac Nissenbaum, leader of religious Zionist movement in Poland who died in Holocaust. During War of Independence, kibbutz was razed by Egyptian shelling and suffered many casualties. In 1949 settlers moved to lands of former German Templer village, Wilhelma, founded in 1903; its German settlers were evicted during WWII. State acquired possession of land in 1948. Moved to present site in 1952. Area: 3,000 d. Pop.: 400.

■ **Be'er Sheva'** *(Gen. 21:32)* 130:072

Israel's 4th largest city lies between the Negev prairies and the cultivated fields to the N. It is considered the nation's most successful development town, an accomplishment largely due to the presence of Ben-Gurion University of the Negev — Israel's most recently built university. Known as the City of the Patriarchs, Beer-sheba was where Abimelech, King of Gerar, made covenants with both Isaac and Abraham (Gen.

21:32; 26:33). Here, too, Jacob made sacrifices. Within city is site known as **Abraham's Well.** The Thursday morning Bedouin market recalls the age when semi-nomads ruled the region. **City of Patriarchs** First mentioned in description of Patriarchs' wanderings. However, exact location in that period has not yet been found. Remains of ancient settlements from Chalcolithic Period have been located in the area: Hurbat Matar *128:071*, Bir es Safadi *128:070*, Kh. el Bitar *129:071*, Bir Ibrahim *130:071* and others. Excavations have uncovered underground dwellings, indications of agriculture and metal-working that belonged to a special culture from 4th millennium BCE. After Israelite conquest, was allotted to tribe of Judah (Josh. 15:28) and then to tribe of Simeon (Josh. 19:2). During period of Judges, was district capital and seat of court (I Sam. 8:2). Its importance can be learned from expression "from Dan to Beer-sheba" (Judg. 20:1 et al). **Tel Sheva'** Possible location of ancient Beer-sheba (Arabic name: Tell es Saba') situated E of present-day Be'er Sheva' *134:071*. Excavation at tel uncovered a well-planned and fortified city dating from the period of Judges and reaching its zenith during time of David and Solomon. Other excavations near present-day Bedouin market uncovered ancient wells from Roman Period, and beneath them tools from Iron Age until end of First Temple Period. **Second Temple Period** It seems that from Second Temple Period onwards city was located at present site. During Roman Period, it was in centre of *Limes Palaestina* (series of Roman fortresses built between Rafah and Dead Sea). During Byzantine Period served as bishopric and a number of churches were built. Town abandoned in Arab Period and rebuilt by Turks in 1880. In 1901 became district and administrative centre for Negev. Captured by British in WWI (1917) after heavy fighting. (There is a British war cemetery in the city.) Until Arab Disturbances of 1936-1939, a few Jewish families lived in Be'er Sheva'. During War of Independence served as headquarters for invading Egyptian army. Captured and liberated by Israel Defence Forces in Yoav operation on 21 October, 1948. Until War of Independence it was a small Bedouin town, but developed rapidly afterwards. Area of municipal jurisdiction: 54,000 d. Pop.: 110,000. Serves as industrial, commercial and administrative centre for entire Negev. City has University of the Negev, Negev Medical Centre, Negev Institute for Arid Zone Research, theatre, museum, arts centre and sports stadium. NE of city on "Hill 369" is a memorial complex for Negev Brigade (Palmaḥ) that liberated Be'er Sheva' in War of Independence.

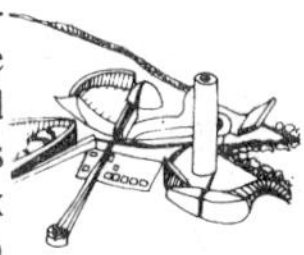

Be'er Sheva' HaGelilit (Ḥurbat Be'er Sheva') *189:259*

Ruins of ancient settlement in Upper Galilee 8 km. SW of Safed. Apparently site of ancient Beer-sheba (in Galilee) that was located at one of important Galilee junctions. Known to be one of cities fortified in Revolt against Rome at end of Second Temple Period. Many sherds from Iron Age and Byzantine Period have been found. Remains of fortress (date as yet unknown).

Be'er Toviyya *124:127*

Moshav on Coastal Plain W of Qiryat Mal'akhi. Name from Arabic — Bir et Tabiyya. Founded in 1887 on lands purchased by Baron de Rothschild and called Qastina after neighbouring Arab village. Abandoned due to Arab harassment and scarcity of water; resettled in 1896 and called Be'er Toviyya. In 1929 Riots attacked by Arabs and again abandoned. Present *moshav* established in 1930. Area: 15,000 d. Pop.: 700. During War of Independence served as Israel Defence Forces' base from which Egyptians were driven out of Negev. Memorial to fallen soldiers.

Be'er Ya'aqov → Askar

BE'ER SHEVA'

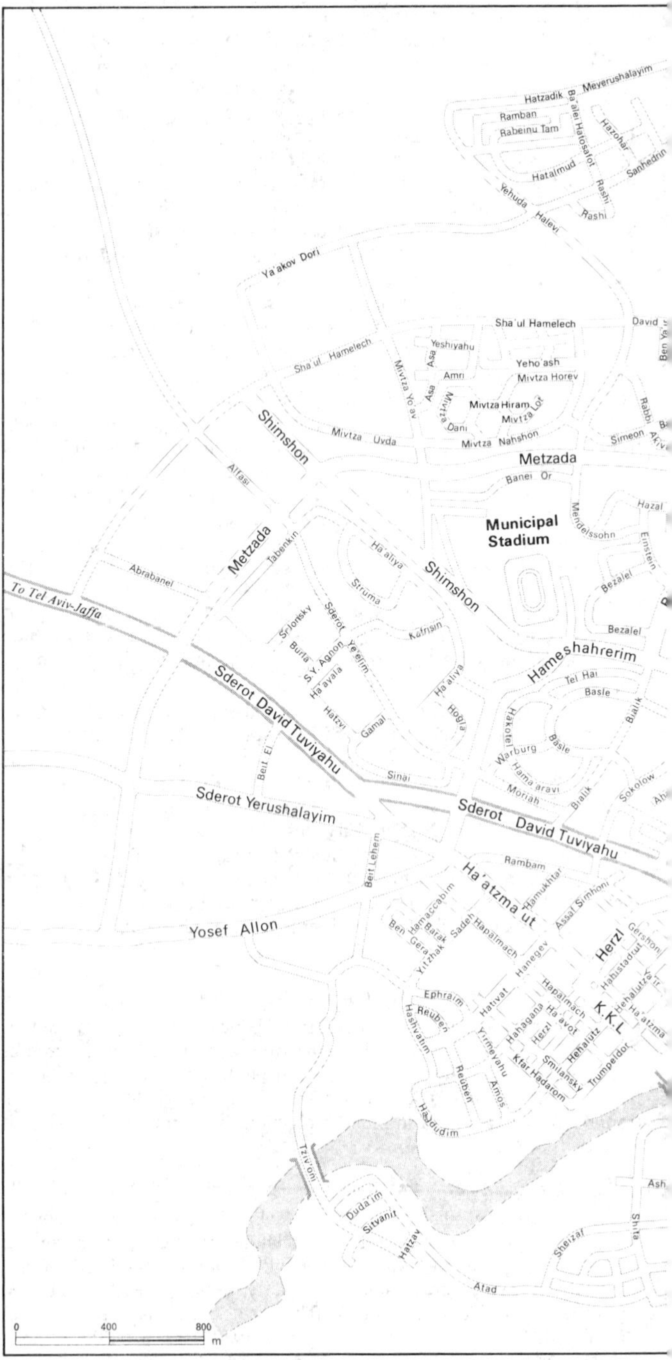
Hatzadik
Meyerushalayim
Ramban
Rabeinu Tam
Ba'alei Hatosafot
Hazohar
Hatalmud
Sanhedrin
Yehuda Halevi
Rashi
Ya'akov Dori
Sha'ul Hamelech
David
Yeshiyahu
Yeho'ash
Asa
Amri
Mivtza Horev
Mivtza Yo'av
Mivtza Hiram
Mivtza Lot
Dani
Rabbi Akiva
Shimshon
Mivtza Uvda
Mivtza Nahshon
Simeon
Metzada
Banei Or
Alfasi
Hazal
Mendelssohn
Municipal Stadium
Einstein
Tabenkin
Ha'aliya
Abrabanel
Struma
Bezalel
To Tel Aviv-Jaffa
Sderot
Kafrisin
Hameshahrerim
Ye'elim
S.Y. Agnon
Burla
Ha'ayala
Tel Hai
Basle
Bialik
Hatzvi
Gamal
Hogla
Hakotel
Sderot David Tuviyahu
Warburg
Beit El
Hama'aravi
Moriah
Sokolow
Sinai
Sderot Yerushalayim
Beit Lehem
Rambam
Ha'atzma'ut
Hamukhtar
Assaf Simhoni
Yosef Allon
Hamaccabim
Ben Gera
Barak
Yitzhak Sadeh
Hapalmach
Herzl
Gershon
Histadrut
Hanegev
Hativat
Ephraim
Hehalutz
Ha'atzma
Reuben
Hashvatim
Hahagana
Ha'avot
K.K.L.
Yirmeyahu
Smilansky
Trumpeldor
Kfar Hadarom
Amos
Hadudim
Tzivoni
Duda'im
Sitvanit
Hatzav
Ash
Shita
Sheizaf
Atad
0
400
800
m

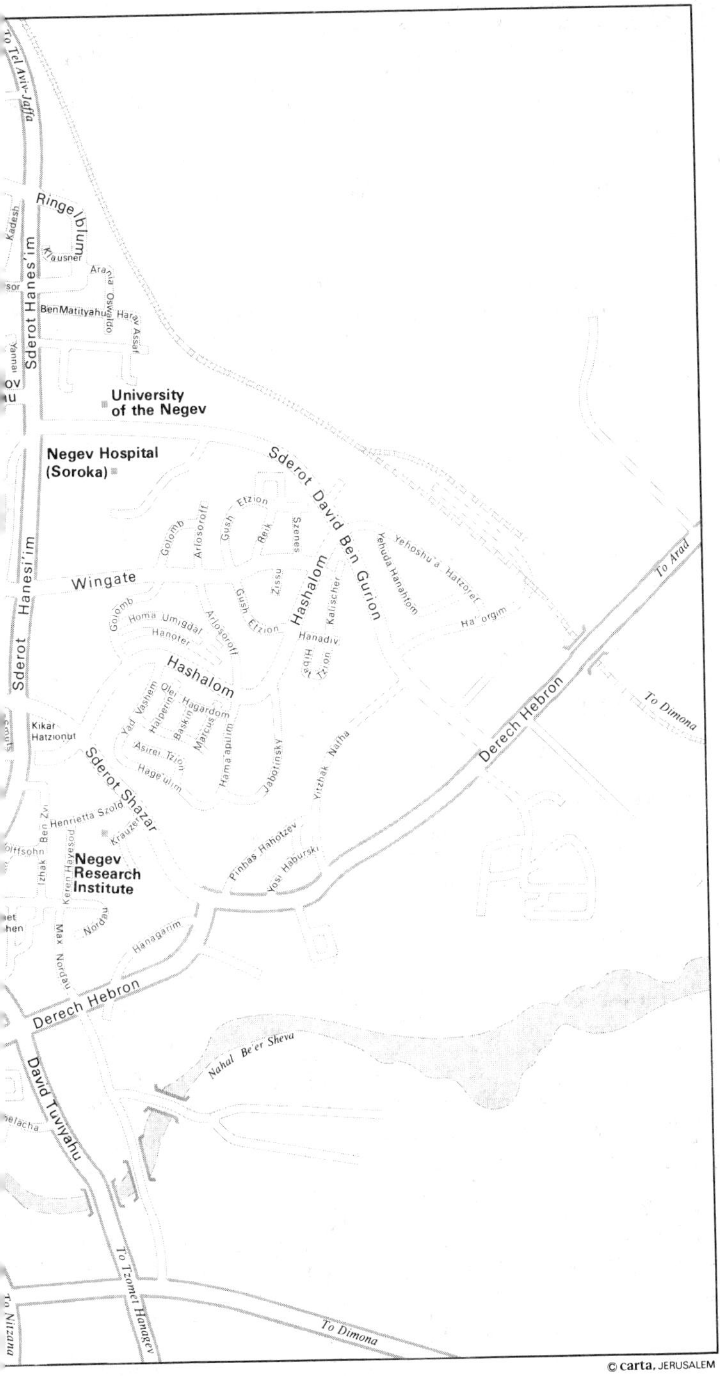
To Tel Aviv-Jaffa
Ringelblum
Kadesh
Klausner
Arania
Oswaldo
Sderot Hanes'im
BenMatityahu
Harav Assaf
Yannai
University of the Negev
Negev Hospital (Soroka)
Sderot David Ben Gurion
Gush Etzion
Golomb
Arlosoroff
Reik
Szenes
Yehoshu'a Hatzorer
Yehuda Hanahtom
Wingate
Zissu
Hashalom
Kalischer
Ha'orgim
To Arad
Homa Umigdal
Hanoter
Hanadiv
Hiba
Tzion
Sderot Hanesi'im
Hashalom
Yad Vashem
Olei Hagardom
Halperin
Baskin
Marcus
Kikar Hatzionut
Asirei Tzion
Hage'ulim
Hama'apilim
Jabotinsky
Yitzhak Nafha
Derech Hebron
To Dimona
Sderot Shazar
Henrietta Szold
Ben Zvi
Krauze
Izhak
Keren Hayesod
Negev Research Institute
Pinhas Hahotzev
Yosi Haburski
Nordau
Max Nordau
Hanagarim
Derech Hebron
Nahal Be'er Sheva
David Tuviyahu
To Tzomet Hanagev
To Nitzana
To Dimona

Be'er Ya'aqov (near Ramla) *134:149*

Settlement W of Zerifin. Named after Rabbi Ya'aqov Yizhaqi, spiritual leader of founders of the farming village in 1907. They came from the Caucasus. At outset of War of Independence settlers were harassed by Arab gangs of Hasan Salame. Today town includes settlements of Talme Menashe, Johanna Jabotinsky youth village and Hoter. Area: 10,000 d. Pop.: 4,200.

Be'er Yeroham *141:045*

Mound near well by Yeroham junction in Negev. Sherds indicate Iron Age occupation.

o **Beita** *177:172; 177:171*

Arab village in Samarian Hills 8 km. S of Shekhem. Village divided in two: Beita el Fauqa (upper) and Beita et Tahta (lower). Pop.: 2,300.

o **Beit Amin** *152:171*

Arab village in W Samarian Hills, 8 km. SE of Qalqilya.

o **Beit 'Amra** *155:095*

Arab village in Hebron Hills 10 km. SW of Hebron. Pop.: 300. Site has ruins and remains of 2 churches.

o **Beit Aula** *152:111*

Arab village in W Hebron Hills 10 km. NW of Hebron. Built on site of ancient settlement; according to one theory site of Biblical Beth-el. Pop.: 1,700.

o **Beit 'Awwa** *145:102*

Arab village in S Judean Hills 15 km. W of Hebron. Pop.: 1,500. Built on ruins of ancient settlement that existed, according to sherds, from end of Babylonian Exile to Byzantine era. Baptismal font in shape of cross found among remains of ancient buildings.

o **Beit Dajan** *185:177*

Arab village in E Samarian Hills 10 km. E of Shekhem. Pop.: 1,200. In the past it was a Samaritan settlement where Baba Rabba built a synagogue in 4th c. CE. Remains of ancient buildings, caves and cisterns.

o **Beit Duqqu** *162:140*

Arab village NW of Jerusalem. Pop.: 500.

o **Beit Fajjar** *164:114*

Arab village in Hebron Hills 5 km. SE of Kefar 'Ezyon. Pop.: 5,000.

o **Beit Furik** *181:175*

Arab village in Samarian Hills 10 km. SE of Shekhem. Formerly Samaritan village called Farkha. Pop.: 2,500

Beit Ghur → **Bet Horon**

o **Beit Hanina** *169:137*

Arab village in Jerusalem Hills 3 km. N of Jerusalem. Pop.: 1,200. Believed to be site of Ananiah, mentioned in Neh. 11:32.

Beit Hanun *105:105*

Arab town in N Gaza Strip. Pop.: 5,000. Site of great battle between Moslems and Crusaders — Battle of Beit Hanun — in 13th c. Moslems won the battle and commemorated victory by building mosque on site (en Nasr — victory — mosque). During War of Independence Israelis captured the Beit Hanun wedge, but returned it to Egyptians after Armistice Agreements.

o **Beit Iba** *169:182*
Arab village in Samarian Hills 5 km. W of Shekhem. Pop.: 1,000.

o **Beit Ijza** *164:139*
Arab village 10 km. NW of Jerusalem. Pop.: 120.

o **Beit Iksa** *167:136*
Arab village in Jerusalem Hills 4 km. NW of Jerusalem. Pop.: 650. Captured in War of Independence and later evacuated.

o **Beitillu** *161:153*
Arab village in S Samarian Hills 12 km. NW of Ramallah. Pop.: 900.

o **Beitin** *172:148*
Arab village in Samarian Hills 4 km. NE of Ramallah. Pop.: 1,000. Popular theory identifies site as ancient city of Beth-el, whose name was retained in distorted form of Beitin. Near village is army camp which served as Jordanian army headquarters in West Bank until Six-Day War. (See Bet El.) **Burj Beitin** *173:147* Ruins of ancient settlement within boundaries of Beitin village Sherds found on site indicate settlement in Roman, Byzantine and Crusader Periods. Remains of partly preserved Crusader basalt-stone fort, monastery and church.

o **Beit I'nan** *161:140*
Arab village in Jerusalem Hills 5 km. N of Qiryat 'Anavim. Believed to be site of Elon-beth-hanan (I Kings 4:9). Pop.: 1,300.

□ **Beit Jala** *167:125*
Arab town S of Jerusalem adjacent to Bethlehem. Believed to be site of ancient city of Giloh, birthplace of Ahithophel the Gilonite (II Sam. 15:12). Pop.: 6,500, mostly Christians and some Moslems. Town has churches, monasteries and many Christian schools. Its antique stores are frequented by Jerusalem residents. **Er Ras** Near town on summit of mountain (923 m. above sea level) is er Ras or Ras Beit Jala and the Judean Hills held school on premises of abandoned Jordanian army camp.

Beit Jann *186:263*
Druze village in Upper Galilee, on slope of Mt. Meron, 10 km. NE of Karmi'el. Origin of name is possibly from *gan* = garden, reminiscent of parks in area; or perhaps a distortion of Beth-dagon, a city within Asher tribal allotment (Josh. 19:27). Present settlement founded in 18th c. Pop.: 4,700.

Beit Jimal *147:125*
Italian Salesian agricultural school in Judean Hills 3 km. S of Bet Shemesh. Arab name means house of beauty. According to Christian tradition the site is named after Rabban Gamli'el HaZaken (the elder), president of Sanhedrin early in 1st c. CE. Mentioned in New Testament as teacher of St. Paul. Present church built in 1881 on remains of 5th c. church. Destroyed during Persian conquest in 614. In church is a burial cave with supposed tombs of Rabban Gamli'el and St. Stephen. Also uncovered were remains of 5th c. building, mosaic and Greek inscriptions. **Deir 'Asfura** Remains of circular monastery. **En Nabi Bulos** Tomb of St. Paul.

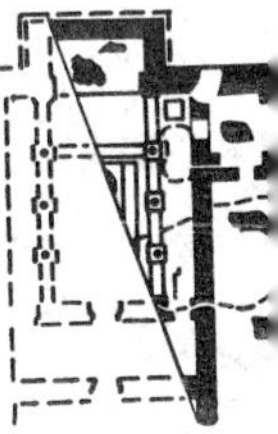

o **Beit Kahil** *156:108*
Arab village in Hebron Hills 4 km. NW of Hebron. Pop.: 1,000.

o **Beit Lahiya** *102:106*
Arab village in N Gaza Strip. Pop.: 3,700. Site has Mamluk Period shrine of Sheikh Salim Abu Muslam.

○ **Beit Lid**

163:185

Arab village in Samarian Hills 18 km. W of Shekhem. Pop.: 2,000.

Beit Lid junction (Sharon junction) *141:192*

Former name of Sharon junction of Kefar Sava-Ḥadera and Netanya-Tulkarm roads. Named after Arab village that existed here. Near junction is Tegart police fort which is now a prison.

○ **Beit Liqya**

156:141

Arab village on border of Judean Hills and Ayyalon Valley, 13 km. SW of Ramallah. Name Beit Lija, of unknown origin, mentioned in 12th c. Crusader document. Pop.: 2,000. Near village is holy Moslem tomb of esh Sheikh Laqani.

○ **Beit Mirsim**

141:096

Arab village on border of Hebron Hills and Judean Foothills. Pop.: 200. Nearby is **Tell Beit Mirsim.**

Beit Naballa → Bet Neḥemya, Kefar Truman

Beit Natif → Ḥurbat Bet Natif

○ **Beit Qad**

183:208

Arab village S of Mt. Gilboa' 5 km. E of Jenin. Believed to be Biblical city of Beth-eked of the Shepherds (II Kings 10:12). Pop.: 250. Its mosque is constructed of re-used building materials from Roman Period. Near village is experimental agricultural station. Close by is sister village, Mashru' Beit Qad with 220 inhabitants.

○ **Beit Rima**

159:160

Arab village in W Samarian Hills, 18 km. NW of Ramallah. Borders on N with neighbouring village of Deir Ghassana. Ruins of settlement occupied in following periods: Iron Age, Roman, Byzantine, Middle Ages and Ottoman. Apparently site of ancient town Bet Rima mentioned in Mishnah (Menaḥot 8:6) where superior wine was produced. Pop.: 1,500.

○ **Beit er Rush**

143:096; 143:095

Arab village in S Judean Hills, 17 km. SW of Hebron. Village has two parts: upper (Beit er Rush el Fauqa) and lower (Beit er Rush et Taḥta). Pop.: 400.

○ **Beit Ṣafafa**

169:128

Arab village in S Jerusalem, within latter's municipal jurisdiction. Pop.: 1,800. During War of Independence served as base for attacks on Jewish Jerusalem. Between War of Independence and Six-Day War, S half of village was in Jordan and N half in Israel. A 5th c. family tomb was discovered here containing a prayer niche with mosaic floor, lead coffin decorated with crosses and Greek inscriptions.

Beit Saḥur

170:123

Arab town in Judean Hills E of Bethlehem. Pop.: 6,000 (majority Christian, rest Moslem). Town has two important sites: Field of Boaz, where, according to tradition, Boaz met Ruth, as recounted in Book of Esther; Shepherds' Field, where, according to Christian tradition, shepherds received tidings of birth of Jesus. Here Christmas carols are sung by pilgrims every Christmas eve. Byzantine church called Shepherds' Field built in 5th c. over ancient grotto with 2nd c. mosaic floor. Originally a chapel stood here but only the mosaic floor survived. In 6th c. a magnificent basilica was built to replace chapel. It was destroyed in 7th c.; rebuilt and again destroyed and abandoned in 10th c.

○ **Beit Sira** *154:144*

Arab village in N Ayyalon Valley. Possibly site of Uzzen-sheerah, one of three cities built by Sheerah, daughter of Ephraim, son of Jacob. The other two are Lower Beth-horon and Upper Beth-horon (I Chron. 7:24). Pop.: 700.

○ **Beit Surik** *164:136*

Arab village in Jerusalem Hills 6 km. NW of Jerusalem. Near village is source of Naḥal Soreq — perhaps the origin of the town's name. Pop.: 700. Byzantine mosaic floor located here.

○ **Beit Ummar** *160:114*

Arab village in Hebron Hills 3 km. S of Kefar 'Eẓyon. Pop.: 3,000. During War of Independence village served as one of the bases for attack on 'Eẓyon Bloc. Within village is tomb of en Nabi Matra which, according to Arab tradition, is tomb of Amittai, father of Prophet Jonah. A Roman rock-cut tomb was uncovered under courtyard of mosque, apparently part of cemetery.

○ **Beit Umrin** *171:188*

Arab village in Samarian Hills 3 km. NE of Sabastiya. Pop.: 1,200. Remains of settlement from Roman Period have been found in village.

Beitunya *166:143*

Arab town in N Judean Hills 4 km. SW of Ramallah. Possibly site of Biblical Beth-aven. Pop.: 2,300. Remains of buildings, pools and Medieval mosaic fragments.

○ **Beit Wazan** *170:182*

Arab village in Samarian Hills 4 km. from Shekhem. Pop.: 350, all Moslem. According to Samaritan tradition, 7 Samaritan families who converted to Islam lived here, hence its name (*wazan* means seven).

Belvoir → Kokhav HaYarden

● **Ben 'Ammi** *161:267*

Moshav in W Galilee 2 km. E of Nahariyya. Named after Haganah commander, Ben 'Ammi Pechter, who, with 46 of his men, was killed while attempting to relieve siege of Yeḥi'am in War of Independence. Founded 1949. Pop.: 300. Area: 3,000 d. **Tell en Nahr** Ancient tel in *moshav*. Finds: Mesolithic and Neolithic flint tools, sherds from Early and Middle Bronze Ages and Iron Age.

● **Benaya** *126:139*

Moshav on Coastal Plain 2 km. S of Yavne. Founded 1949. Area: 2,600 d. Pop.: 250.

Ben Dor → Nesher

● **Bene 'Atarot** *141:159*

Moshav in Sharon 5 km. N of Ben-Gurion Airport. Founded 1948 on lands of former German colony, Wilhelma. Area: 4,000 d. Pop.: 350. Memorial to former *moshav* 'Atarot and its members who died in War of Independence. **Wilhelma-Hamidya** German colony named after Kaiser Wilhelm II and Turkish Sultan Abdul Ḥamid II. Founded 1903. During WWII served as internment camp for German citizens later deported to Australia.

Bene 'Ayish *127:133*

Settlement 2 km. S of Gedera. Name is acronym for *A*kiva *J*oseph *Sch*lesinger (1837-1922), spokesman of extreme religious elements who advocated rural settlement in Ereẓ Israel. Founded 1958 to accommodate immigrant residents of Naḥal Soreq transit camp. Pop.: 1,100.

Bene Beraq *(Josh. 19:45) 134:166*

City in country's centre between Ramat Gan in W and Petaḥ Tiqwa in E. Same name as ancient city, Bene-berak, apparently located to S of present city. Mentioned in Bible in territory of Dan and in Assyrian inscriptions as one of cities conquered by Sennacherib. Important centre in Roman and Byzantine Periods and site of *yeshiva* established by Rabbi 'Aqiva. Also mentioned in sources from Crusader Period. Modern city founded in 1924 by group of Ḥasidim from Warsaw (Ḥevrat Bayit WeNaḥala), on lands purchased from Arabs. Has always had an orthodox religious character. Area: 7,200 d. Pop.: 83,000. Some archaeological remains have been found, mainly sarcophagi.

Bene Berit → Moledet

Bene Darom *121:136*

Moshav shittufi on Coastal Plain 4 km. E of Ashdod. Originally kibbutz, in 1961 became *moshav shittufi*. Area: 3,100 d. Pop.: 250. **Kh. Sukreir** Small tel in *moshav* with remains of aqueduct, khan and Medieval ruin. Sherds indicate habitation during Byzantine and Arab Periods.

Bene Deror *140:185*

Moshav in Sharon 1 km. E of Even Yehuda. Founded 1946 by soldiers discharged from British army, hence its name (*deror*: freedom). Area: 2,800 d. Pop.: 200.

Bene Re'em *130:130*

Moshav 5 km. S of Gedera. Name is acronym for Ḥasidic *R*abbi of Gur, *A*braham *M*ordekhay. Pop.: 400.

Bene Yehuda *215:245*

District centre on Golan Heights 5 km. NE of 'En Gev. Named after earlier settlement, Bene Yehuda, abandoned in 1920. (See Bir esh Shuqum.) Settled 1972.

Bene Ẓiyyon *138:181*

Moshav on Coastal Plain 4 km. N of Ra'ananna. Named after Bene Ẓiyyon Order from USA. Area: 1,500 d. Pop.: 400.

Benot Ya'aqov Bridge *209:268*

Bridge over Jordan River in Upper Galilee 15 km. N of Lake Kinneret. Legend claims that Jacob's daughters crossed the Jordan at this point when entering the land of Israel. One of most important crossing points throughout history, and major branch of *via maris* that connected Egypt with Fertile Crescent through Israel and Syria. Near present structure are remains of Roman bridge and Crusader fortress, captured and destroyed by Saladin in August 1179. Napoleon's army reached here in 1799 and in 1918 it was scene of battle between Turks and British troops. Bridge demolished by Haganah in "night of the bridges" (June 1946). In War of Independence Syrians captured it and nearby settlement of Mishmar HaYarden which was later returned to Israel. After Six-Day War, a bailey bridge was constructed. **Ancient remains** Paleolithic remains: fossilized bones of prehistoric animals, cracked skull of man and flint tools. Also sherds from Middle Bronze Age, Byzantine and Arab Periods.

● **Ben Shemen** *(moshav)* 142:151

Moshav 4 km. E of Lod. Name from Biblical verse "My beloved had a vineyard on a *very fertile* hill" (Isa. 5:1). Established 1922. Settlers suffered badly in 1929 Riots and in same year a defensive wall was built around *moshav* which still exists. During War of Independence *moshav* surrounded and inhabitants evacuated. Siege lifted with capture of Lod but only in 1952 was *moshav* re-established near Ben Shemen Youth Village. Pop.: 250. Area: 2,500 d. E of *moshav* is Herzl Forest (Ben Shemen Forest).

■ **Ben Shemen** (Youth Village) 143:151

Educational institute and youth village 4 km. E of Lod. In 1906 agricultural school, Qiryat Sefer, established by Israel Belkind for children orphaned in Russian pogroms. The school closed after a year. In 1909 served as work camp for planters of Herzl Forest. In 1927 youth village was established which still exists. The educational institute includes elementary, rural junior and senior high schools with boarding facilities, some 800 students and 200 teachers and staff.

● **Ben Zakkay** 124:140

Moshav on Coastal Plain near Yavne. Named after Rabbi Johanan b. Zakkai, founder and head of *yeshiva* Kerem deYavne after destruction of Second Temple. Area: 3,800 d. Pop.: 620.

● **Beqa'ot** 192:183

Moshav in el Buqei'a Valley in Samarian Hills. Founded 1972. Area: 1,800 d. Nearby are ruins of ancient settlements (Kh. eṣ Ṣufeira, Kh. Umm el Qatan) and rock-cut tombs from Byzantine Period (Kh. Muqeisima).

● **Beqoa'** 143:137

Moshav on border of Judean Hills 2 km. NE of Naḥshon junction. Nearby is "Burma Road", constructed to relieve besieged Jerusalem during War of Independence. Founded 1951 on lands of abandoned village, Deir Muḥeisin. Pop.: 450. **Mizpe Beqoa'** N of *moshav* *141:138* an observation point overlooks Ayyalon Valley, Latrun area and Jerusalem Hills. Near look-out is holy Moslem site called Musa et Tali'; remains of building and olive tree.

Berekhat 'Amal (Sakhne) 192:212

Natural pool in Bet She'an Valley at foot of Mt. Gilboa'. Called Sakhne (hot in Arabic) because it is fed by warm water spring. In centre of pool is waterfall flowing from pool to Naḥal 'Amal ('Asi in Arabic) which then empties into Jordan River. Alongside is camping and recreation site called Gan HaShelosha in memory of 3 local settlers: Ḥayyim Sturman, Aaron Etkin and David Mossinsohn who were killed here by a land mine in 1938.

Berekhat HaMeshushim 212:261

Pool in Naḥal Meshushim (Wadi el Hawa) in Golan Heights, 6 km. NE of Jordan outlet. Size 20x30 m. enclosed by hundreds of hexagonal and pentagonal basalt columns, hence its name (*meshushe* = hexagon). Above pool is waterfall. All part of Ya'ar Yahudiyya (forest) nature reserve.

Berekhat Ya'ar 140:202

Pool in Coastal Plain 5 km. S of Ḥadera junction. Arabic name is Birkat 'Ata and in Hebrew named after Ḥadera forest (*ya'ar*) to the N.

Berekhot Shelomo (Solomon's Pools) — *165:122*

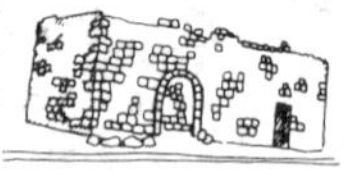

Complex of 3 large pools partially carved out of the living rock, 4 km. S of Bethlehem, which store spring water and catch rain-water. Known as Solomon's Pools since Medieval times but actually built in Second Temple Period — perhaps by Herod to improve Jerusalem's water supply. The water was conducted by aqueducts and pipes by means of gravitation to Jerusalem and to the Herodion fortress further S. Total capacity was 180,000 cub. m. Names of Roman army commanders were found on several stone pipes. In 1617 Turks built a fortress to protect water sources. The fortress, Qal'at el Burak, which also served as a khan, can be seen today near the upper pool. During British Mandate a metal pipe was laid to conduct water from pools to Jerusalem. Today this water is used only by inhabitants of immediate vicinity.

● **Berekhya** — *114:119*

Moshav 3 km. E of Ashqelon. Named after personal name in Bible — Berechiah (I Chron. 3:20). Pop.: 800. Area: 2,400 d.

★ **Beror Ḥayil** — *116:107*

Kibbutz in Negev 6 km. NE of Sederot. Named after ancient site of Beror Ḥayil where Rabbi Johanan b. Zakkai lived after his stay in Yavne. The Talmud relates that when Roman Emperor Hadrian forbade circumcision rite, the Jews of Beror Ḥayil would perform it secretly and announce the celebration by lighting a candle. Kibbutz founded 1948. Pop.: 650, mostly from Brazil. Area: 16,000 d. Kibbutz has cultural centre named after Brazilian statesman, Oswaldo Aranha, who presided over UN General Assembly in 1947 that voted for partition of Palestine. Two tombs uncovered in kibbutz, one decorated with drawings of animals and Greek inscriptions, apparently from Byzantine Period.

● **Berosh** — *115:086*

Moshav in Negev 6 km. N of Ofaqim. Name from "I will set in the desert the *cypress*, the plane and the pine together;" (Isa. 41:19). Neighbouring settlements are called Tidhar (plane) and Te'ashur (pine). Pop.: 350.

◆ **Berurim** — *129:130*

Seed nursery 7 km. S of Gedera. Name from Hebrew root word meaning to sort seeds. Nearby is memorial to policemen and workers of Electric Corporation who were killed on the site during Disturbances of 1936-1939.

★ **Bet Alfa** (kibbutz) — *190:213*

Kibbutz in Yizre'el Valley at foot of Mt. Gilboa'. Name from Arab village Beit Ilfa that probably derived from more ancient Hebrew name of Bet Ulpana, Bet Ulfa and Bet Halifa. First kibbutz of HaShomer HaẒa'ir movement. Organized 1921. Settled 1922 and withstood Arab attacks in Riots of 1929 and 1936-1939 and served as departure base for "stockade and tower" settlements established in area. Before War of Independence served as Haganah base which was attacked and shelled by Arabs at start of war. Pop.: 850. Area: 10,300 d. Kibbutz has educational institute (founded 1943), cultural centre in memory of fallen in War of Independence and assembly hall in memory of all who fell in Israel's wars.

Bet Alfa Synagogue → **Ḥefẓi Bah**

Betar (Bethther) → **Battir**

Bet 'Arif — *144:155*

Moshav 4 km. E of Ben-Gurion Airport. Same name as town in Roman Period and mentioned in Onomasticon of Eusebius from 4th c. CE.

Founded in 1949 on lands of abandoned village, Deir Tarif. Area: 1,600 d. Pop.: 560. Tombs and remains of Byzantine settlement.

Bet Berl *143:178*

Ideological and educational centre of Israel Labour Party and educational institute 3 km. N of Kefar Sava. Named after Berl Katznelson, one of great leaders of Israel Labour movement. Founded 1947 on 1,500 d. and maintained by permanent staff. Includes: institute for education and research, institute for youth leaders, district high school, state seminary for school and nursery teachers and dormitories.

Bet Dagan *134:156*

Town S of Tel Aviv off Ramla road. Name from Arab village of Beit Dajan, abandoned during War of Independence. One theory claims it is on site of ancient city Beth-dagon, named after Philistine god Dagon who was half man and half fish. Another theory claims source of name to be that of god of corn (*dagan* = corn). Blocking Tel Aviv-Jerusalem road at start of War of Independence, this Arab village was captured by Haganah in 1948. After war became Jewish immigrant settlement, inhabited mainly by Bulgarian emigres. Pop.: 3,000. **Bet HaKeren HaKayemet** Near Shiva' junction are remains of Bet HaKeren HaKayemet, a Haganah post during War of Independence guarding road to Jerusalem. Blown up by Arabs but not abandoned by defenders until liberated. Memorial to fallen.

Bet El *(Gen. 35:14-15)* *172:148*

Tel in area of village of Beitin 4 km. NE of Ramallah. Accepted site of ancient Beth-el, major holy city mentioned many times in Bible: Abraham built an altar here; site of Jacob's dream; after Joshua's conquests it was included in tribal allotment of Benjamin; housed sanctuary and was seat of Judges; after division of kingdom, Beth-el was incorporated into Kingdom of Israel, but from time to time passed hands. Importance of sanctuary in Beth-el was enhanced during reign of King Jeroboam I (928-907 BCE) who also introduced worship of golden calf. Sanctuary was destroyed during reign of Josiah (640-609 BCE). After destruction of First Temple the site was abandoned; resettled by returnees from Babylonian Exile and continuously occupied during Second Temple Period. At beginning of Hasmonean revolt city was fortified by Syrian general Bacchides. During Revolt against Rome, Vespasian captured city and garrisoned troops here. Fell into decline after destruction of Second Temple. **Excavations** Archaeological evidence indicates that city was occupied from Middle Bronze Age until Byzantine Period. Finds include: remains of sanctuary, palace and fortress; foundations of ancient wall, sherds, seals, hewn building stones (one of which had a star of David chiselled on it).

Bet El (temporary name) *171:149*

Civilian outpost on border of Judean and Samarian Hills, 4 km. NE of Ramallah near village of Beitin. Named after historical site. Established 1977.

Bet El'azari *131:139*

Moshav 3 km. S of Bilu junction. Named after the agronomist Yizhaq Elazari-Volcani (Wilkansky), one of the planners of the country's agriculture. Founded 1948. Area: 4,700 d. Pop.: 500.

Bet Eshel *132:071*

Abandoned settlement in Negev 2 km. S of Be'er Sheva'. Name from Biblical story of tamarisk (*eshel*) planted by Abraham in Beer-sheba (Gen. 21:33). One of the 3 first observation points established in Negev in 1943; (the others are Gevulot and Revivim). During War of Independence was encircled by Egyptians and heavily shelled. Defenders held on but the settlement was destroyed. When Be'er Sheva' was captured by Israel Defence Forces, settlers moved to Yizre'el Valley and founded new *moshav*, HaYogev.

• Bet 'Ezra — *117:127*

Moshav 10 km. S of Ashdod. Named after Ezra the Scribe. Area: 1,200 d. Pop.: 650. **Hill 69** Outpost S of *moshav* dating from War of Independence where battles were fought to stop advancing Egyptian army. Nearby, 'Ad Halom Bridge where Egyptian advance was halted. Tel Ashdod is 2 km. N of *moshav*.

• Bet Gamli'el — *127:140*

Moshav 2 km. SE of Yavne. Named after Rabban Gamli'el II, president of Sanhedrin at Yavne. Area: 3,400 d. Pop.: 300.

Bet Gan — *197:235*

Agricultural settlement within Yavne'el in Lower Galilee. Founded 1903 and called Bet Gan after Arabic name of nearby ruin, Beit Jann (ruin of the demons).

★ Bet Guvrin (Beit Jibrin) — *140:113*

Ruins of ancient city and limestone caves near kibbutz 14 km. E of Qiryat Gat. Kibbutz named after Jewish city that existed during Second Temple Period. Founded 1949 by Palmaḥ veterans on fields of abandoned village of Beit Jibrin. Pop.: 200. Area: 20,000 d. **Meẓudat HaḤamisha** Off the road, Tegart police fort built by British, now named after the five (*ḥamisha*) soldiers who were killed when it was captured (23.10.48). **Ancient Bet Guvrin** E of kibbutz, across road, are ruins of abandoned village, Beit Jibrin, site of important ancient city Betogabris, located on junction of roads from Judean Foothills to Hebron and Jerusalem. During Roman Period was given status of "city of freemen" and named Eleutheropolis. A large Jewish community existed during Roman and Byzantine Periods and famous *Tannaim* and *Amoraim* resided here. Seat of bishop during Byzantine Period. Crusaders fortified city and built many churches. Remains from many periods: 2 mosaic floors, one Roman and other Byzantine (transferred to Jerusalem), remains of churches including Church of St. Gabriel and of St. Anne (name corrupted in Arabic to Ṣandaḥanna); fragments of walls and ancient buildings and Aramaic inscription; mosque and rock-cut tombs. The 63 limestone bell-shaped caves are in nearby Tel Maresha. Hollowed out by the Phoenicians, the largest measures 22x17.4 m. The niches, pillars and carved ornamentations evince a mixture of Greek and Egyptian styles. There are many Greek inscriptions from the 2nd c. BCE. Markings can also be discerned from Christian hermits who inhabited these cavities in Byzantine times. Written sources mention 2 aqueducts that brought water to Bet Guvrin: one from Adorayim district, a distance of 25 km., and the other from Tel Goded district (Tell el Judeida). S of Bet Guvrin is Tel Maresha.

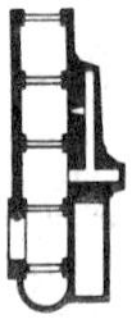

Bet Ha'Arava — *200:134*

Ruins of kibbutz at N end of Dead Sea, near 'Abdallah Bridge. Founded 1939 in area of very high soil salinity that could not be cultivated. After many years of hard work the soil was desalinated by flushing and a farming unit was established. During War of Independence the kibbutz was evacuated and the Arabs subsequently destroyed it.

★ Bet Ha'Arava (Almog "C") — *197:135*

Kibbutz under construction in Jordan Valley 7 km. SE of Jericho. Named after settlement abandoned during War of Independence.

Bet HaBeq — *208:255*

House enclosed by eucalyptus grove near mouth of Jordan River. In past, home of Abdul Rahman Pasha el Yusuf, owner of lands of Buteiḥa

Valley and his son Fuad who succeeded him. Syrians built military positions in vicinity and harassed Israeli fishermen in Kinneret and neighbouring Israeli settlements. In December 1955 Israel Defence Forces destroyed positions in retaliatory raid.

★ **Bet Ha'Emeq** *(Josh. 19:27)* *164:264*

Kibbutz 6 km. SE of Nahariyya. Named after ancient city located in vicinity and included in Asher tribal allotment. Area: 3,300 d. Pop.: 400. Archaeological and zoological museum. **Tell Mimas** nearby is apparently site of ancient city Beth-emek. **Naḥal Bet Ha'Emeq** In nearby stream bed are remains of water-works from Crusader Period, including tunnel with ditches and 2 hewn parallel canals 4 km. in length.

● **Bet HaGaddi** *112:093*

Moshav in W Negev near Netivot junction. Named after ancient city that appears on Madaba map of 6th c. CE. Founded 1949 by Tunisian immigrants from island of Djerba and first called BeNetiv HaMoledet. Area: 7,500 d. Pop.: 700. Ruins of Bet HaGaddi 1 km. to E.

● **Bet HaLevi** *144:195*

Moshav 3 km. NE of Sharon junction (Beit Lid). Named after Yehuda HaLevi, renowned Medieval Jewish poet. Area: 2,000 d. Pop.: 300.

Bet HaMekhes → Custom's House

● **Bet Ḥanan** *129:149*

Moshav 2 km. W of Nes Ziyyona. Named after Elon-beth-hanan, one of Solomon's twelve officers (I Kings 4:9). Founded 1930 by Bulgarian pioneers. Area: 3,000 d. Pop.: 350. Mosaic floor with Greek inscription uncovered within *moshav*. Small nature reserve (35 d.) W of *moshav* with local purple iris.

● **Bet Ḥananya** *143:215*

Moshav near coastal road 2 km. N of Or 'Aqiva. Area: 4,200 d. Pop.: 250. Near *moshav* is section of Roman aqueduct, with Roman Legion inscription, that carried water to Caesarea.

Bethany → (El) 'Eizariyya

★ **Bet HaShitta** *(Judg. 7:22)* *191:217*

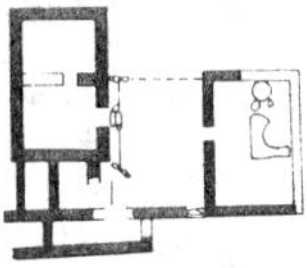

Kibbutz in Yizre'el Valley 8 km. NW of Bet She'an. Name mentioned in book of Judges and retained in name of abandoned village, Shatta. Founded 1935. Pop.: more than 1,000. Area: 15,000 d. W of kibbutz is Shatta prison. Remains found within kibbutz of 6th c. Byzantine church with mosaic floor (removed to Jerusalem). Nearby is a wine press. One km. W of kibbutz is **Kh. Shatta.** Tel containing column fragments, remains of ancient cemetery and Roman road. Sherds indicate occupation during Roman and Arab Periods.

Bet Ḥashmonay *142:144*

Regional centre for settlements affiliated to Gezer regional council, 5 km. SE of Ramla. Named after Simeon the Hasmonean who captured nearby Gezer (142 BCE). Founded 1972.

● **Bet Ḥerut** *137:198*

Moshav shittufi 8 km. from Netanya. Named after agricultural organization Ḥerut of USA. Founded 1933 by American immigrants and initially called Ḥerut America "B". Area: 2,700 d. Pop.: 280.

● **Bet Hillel** *207:291*

Moshav in Upper Galilee 3 km. E of Qiryat Shemona. Named after Dr. Hillel Joffe, pioneer doctor in Erez Israel during Second Aliyah. Founded 1940. Area: 3,500 d. Pop.: 180.

BETHLEHEM

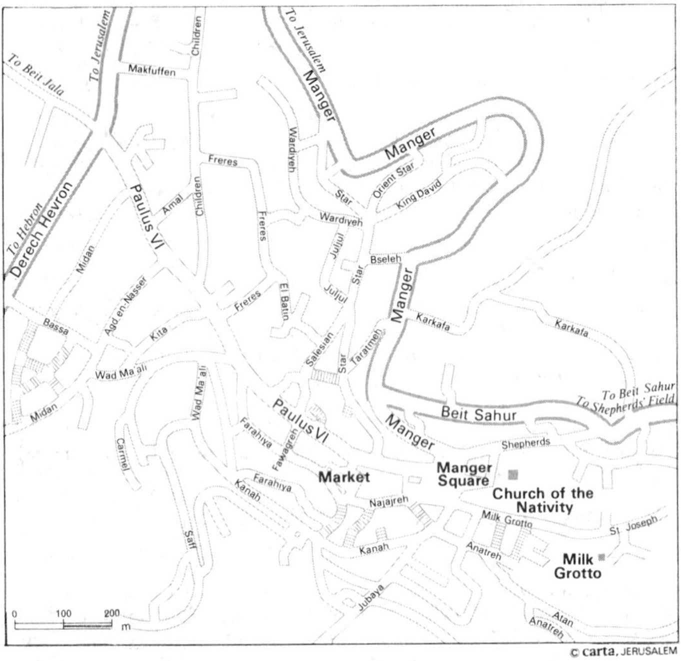

● **Bet Ḥilqiyya** *132:133*

Moshav 4 km. SE of Gedera. Named after Hilkiah, the prophet Jeremiah's father (Jer. 1:1). Area: 3,200 d. Pop.: 220. *Moshav* has magnificent synagogue and Torah institute, Yad Binyamin, named after the late Benjamin Minz, a former minister of posts.

□ **Bethlehem (Bet Leḥem)** *(Gen. 35:19) 169:123*

Christian Arab city in Judean Hills 7 km. S of Jerusalem, where Jesus was born and thus holy to Christians the world over; Roman Catholic, Greek Orthodox, Syrian Catholic and Armenian churches in the vicinity of Manger Square. The Church of the Nativity dates from 4th c. when Queen Helena marked it as site of Jesus' birth. Mother-of-pearl items sold in local shops. Pop.: 15,000. **History** Mentioned in Bible by several names: Ephrath, Bethlehem-ephrath, Bethlehem in Judah. Burial place of matriarch Rachel (Gen. 35:19). Levite youth in story of Micah's idol came from Bethlehem (Judg. 17:7 ff.). Scene of story of Ruth. Birthplace of David, son of Jesse, and place where he was anointed king. During Second Temple Period it was captured by Edomites who were later expelled by John Hyrcanus, the Hasmonean. According to Christian tradition, it was the birthplace of Jesus. During Byzantine Period, Jews were forbidden to live in Bethlehem. Appears on 6th c. Madaba map. Captured in 1100 by Crusaders; destroyed in wars between Crusaders and Moslems and then rebuilt. In 1170, the Jewish traveller, Benjamin of Tudela, visited the city. In 1244, destroyed by Turks and then rebuilt. At end of 15th c. it was badly damaged in fighting between Christians of Bethlehem and Moslems from Hebron. City developed as pilgrimage centre for Christians, during British Mandate and later Jordanian rule. Since Six-Day War it has been under Israeli jurisdiction. In vicinity are remains of 2 aqueducts which carried water from Solomon's Pools to Jerusalem. **Sites: Church of Nativity** City has many Christian holy places, churches, monasteries, religious institutes, etc. The Church of Nativity was built upon the cave where Jesus is believed to have been born. Church first built in days of Constantine in 330, destroyed in 6th c. and rebuilt in days of Justinian. Place where Crusader Baldwin was crowned king in 1100. Built in form of fortress and divided into sections: central part held by Greek Orthodox, S section by Armenians and N section divided between Catholics and Protestants. Today's Basilica dates from 6th c. with extensive repairs from Crusader Period. Adjoining church of St. Catherine to W is site of midnight mass for the Latins every Christmas eve. Fragments of 12th c. murals visible on Basilica walls. Fifty-three lamps hang from Nativity Grotto. Disappearance of silver star from Grotto was pretext for outbreak of Crimean War. **Rachel's Tomb** At N entrance to city is tomb purported to be that of matriarch Rachel. According to Medieval Jewish travellers, consisted of 11 stones laid by Jacob's 11 sons topped by larger stone laid by Jacob himself. Walls date from 18th c. Visited traditionally by Jewish women wanting to conceive a child. Restored in 19th c. by Sir Moses Montefiore. Near Bethlehem is **David's Well** believed to be the well mentioned in II Sam. 33:16.

Bet Ḥogla → Deir Ḥajla

Bet Ḥoron *(I Sam. 13:18) 160:143*

Mountain pass and settlement on ancient road from foothills to mountain ridges. (Today Latrun-Ramallah road runs through pass.) At beginning of ascent is Arab village of Beit Ghur et Taḥta *158:144* or Lower Bet Ḥoron; at top of ascent is Arab village of Beit Ghur el Fauqa *161:143* or Upper Bet Ḥoron. Besides obvious resemblance between names Beit Ghur and Bet Ḥoron, the lower village has a holy Moslem tomb called en Nabi Ghur. Because of its strategic importance, Bet Ḥoron ascent was site of battles throughout the ages. After Joshua defeated the Amorite kings at Gibeon he pursued them through Beth-horon ascent (Josh. 10:10-11). Site is mentioned in Shishak City Lists (925 BCE). One of 3 Philistine forces ascended via Beth-horon to attack Saul (I Sam. 13:18). II Chron. (8:5) relates how King Solomon built "...Upper Beth-horon and Lower Beth-horon, fortified cities with walls, gates and bars." Here Judah Maccabee defeated army of Seleucid general Seron. Site mentioned in Talmud and other sources. During WWI, Bet Ḥoron ascent was one of routes used by British on their way to capture Jerusalem. After War of Independence, Jordanian army strongly fortified area but their defences were pierced by Israel Defence Forces in Six-Day War.

Bet Ḥoron (temporary name) *162:142*

Civilian outpost in W Judean Hills, 8 km. SW of Ramallah. Named after Biblical Beth-horon. Established 1977.

• Bet Leḥem HaGelilit *(Josh. 19:15) 168:237*

Moshav in Lower Galilee 7 km. NE of Qiryat Tiv'on. Named after ancient city belonging to Zebulun tribal allotment. In Byzantine Period was known for its ceramic industry. Founded 1948, on lands of abandoned German colony of same name. Area: 4,000 d. Pop.: 260. Site has Jewish cave tombs. **German Colony** Founded in 1906 by German Christian Templers.

• Bet Meir *153:134*

Moshav in Judean Hills 3 km. SE of Sha'ar HaGay. Named after Rabbi Meir Bar-Ilan (Berlin) a Mizraḥi leader. Founded 1950 on lands of abandoned village — Beit Maḥsir. Pop.: 320. Ramot Shapira field school located in *moshav*. **Archaeological remains** Arab village, now abandoned, was built on ruins of ancient settlement. Site has been occupied almost continuously since Hasmonean Period. Remains of ancient Crusader or Arab building with olive oil press. **HaMasreq** Near *moshav* at summit of hill, that served as military post during War of Independence, is grove of pine trees which looks like a giant comb (*masreq*) from a distance. Today a nature reserve and picnic site with a look-out over Jerusalem Foothills. At foot of *moshav* is **Jeep path**, a section of "Burma Road" to Jerusalem. (See "Burma Road".) Near road is a large Byzantine wine press.

● **Bet Neḥemya** *145:153*

Moshav 4 km. E of Ben-Gurion Airport. Named after Biblical Nehemiah who left Persia for Ereẓ Israel, rebuilt Jerusalem and was a major force in the Return to Zion, as related in book of Nehemiah. Founded 1950. Until Sinai Campaign (1956) it was vulnerable to terrorist infiltration from across the border. Area: 2,000 d. Pop.: 300.

● **Bet Neqofa (Beit Naqquba)** *162:134*

Moshav in Jerusalem Hills near kibbutz Qiryat 'Anavim. Name mentioned in Talmud where a priestly family of same name originated. Ancient name seems to have been preserved in that of abandoned village, Beit Naqquba, on whose land the *moshav* was established. Pop.: 260.

★ **Bet Nir** *138:117*

Kibbutz in Lakhish region 5 km. N of Bet Guvrin. Named after Hebrew rendering of name of Dr. Max Bodenheimer, German Zionist leader. Area: 42,000 d. (including natural pasture). Pop.: 250.

★ **Bet Oren** *151:237*

Kibbutz on Mt. Karmel 10 km. S of Haifa. Abundant pine forests, hence name (*oren* = pine). Founded 1939. During struggle against British Mandate, served as Haganah training base, from where operation was launched to free immigrants from 'Atlit internment camp (1945). Area: 3,000 d. Pop.: 300. Kibbutz has memorial Hekhal HaKarmel for parachutists from Palestine who died in WWII on European missions behind Nazi lines.

● **Bet 'Oved** *128:147*

Moshav in Coastal Plain 5 km. S of Rishon LeẒiyyon. Founded 1933. Area: 1,000 d. Pop.: 250.

★ **Bet Qama** *127:095*

Kibbutz in N Negev 20 km. N of Be'er Sheva'. Name based on quotation from Isa. 17:5, "And it shall be as when the reaper gathers *standing grain*." Founded 1949 by group in Hungary. Area: 15,500 d. Pop.: 300. Near Qama junction, memorial to soldiers of Palmaḥ's Yiftaḥ Brigade who fell in Negev during War of Independence.

Bet Qaẓir → Tel Qaẓir

★ **Bet Qeshet** *188:236*

Kibbutz 5 km. N of Mt. Tabor. Name based on verse in II Sam. 1:18, "...teach the children of Judah the use of the *bow*." Founded 1944 by demobilized Palmaḥ soldiers on PICA lands. Area: 15,000 d. Pop.: 340. Monument to 7 kibbutz members who fell in battle at foot of Mt. Tabor as well as to members who died in War of Independence. **Ḥanot Taggarim** Two km. E of kibbutz are remains of Turkish caravanserai. N of kibbutz is tel, perhaps site of Biblical city Aznoth-tabor.

■ **Bet Rabban** *124:136*

Religious educational institute 6 km. W of Gedera. Named after sages of Yavne called *rabbanim*. Includes state religious seminary and comprehensive girls' high school. Pop.: 600.

★ Bet Rimmon *181:243*

Kibbutz in Galilee on ridge of Har Tir'an 4 km. NW of Golani junction. Established 1977 as *nahal* outpost and received civilian status in 1979.

Bet She'an *(Josh. 17:11) 197:211*

City in Bet She'an Valley on site of ancient city Beth-shean, one of the oldest inhabited sites in the Holy Land. The Roman theatre is the best preserved in Israel. After War of Independence became a development town populated by new immigrants, mostly from oriental countries. Area: 7,000 d. Pop.: 14,000. **History of Bet She'an** Ancient city was an important commercial and military centre throughout almost every historical period in the country. It is situated in heart of a fertile region, on border of Yizre'el and Jordan Valleys, controls one of the fords of Jordan River and is located on an important artery of the *via maris*. Its name seems to be derived from a god called Shean or Shan worshipped by local inhabitants. Finds from digs indicate occupation already from Chalcolithic Period. Name first mentioned in 19th c. BCE Egyptian execration texts. Also mentioned in 15th c. BCE City Lists of Thutmose III and in lists of conquests of other pharaohs. Mentioned in 'Amarna letters of 14th c. BCE. During Israelite conquest, Beth-shean was allotted to tribe of Manasseh but Canaanites continued to occupy it. During reign of King Saul Philistines occupied city. Conquered during reign of King David. During Second Temple Period it was a Hellenistic city called Scythopolis. The sons of John Hyrcanus, the Hasmonean, conquered the city and expelled gentiles, but it once again became a gentile city with Roman conquest. During Roman Period was granted "free city" status and included in federation of 10 Greek cities (Decapolis). During Byzantine Period was capital of Galilee and Golan and had a considerable Jewish population. During Middle Ages city had important Jewish community. Estori HaParḥi, the famous 14th c. Jewish topographer, resided here. City was later impoverished as result of many wars. During British Mandate was Arab town and district capital; a small Jewish community lived here until 1936. During Disturbances of 1936-1939 served as a base for attacks on Jewish settlements in area. Captured by Haganah at beginning of War of Independence and, after Arab residents fled, it became a Jewish city. **Tel Bet She'an and environs** The ancient city was mainly located at Tel Bet She'an (Arabic: Tell el Ḥuṣn) N of present-day city. However, many remains from various periods have been found in and around other parts of city. Archaeological digs uncovered 18 levels of occupation, from Chalcolithic to Arab Periods. Among important finds: remains of Egyptian temples and palaces from Late Bronze Age. Digs to S of tel uncovered large Roman theatre — original seating capacity of 8,000, remains of magnificent buildings from Roman and later periods, Roman villa, House of Leontius and alongside it, remains of 4th-5th c. basilica-type synagogue in use for 200 years. E of tel are remains of 6th c. church with mosaic floor and Greek inscriptions. Additional synagogue, Samaritan, with mosaic floor depicting Ark of Law was discovered N of the city. **Other sites** Khan el Aḥmar (the Red Inn), remains of caravanserai from 1308 in N of city; building served as centre of Turkish administration; its entrance is skirted with columns and capitals; Jisr el Khan — a Turkish bridge near Khan el Aḥmar, over road leading to 'Afula; Roman bridge (actually built during Turkish Period) over road leading N out of Bet She'an; the severed bridge (Jisr el Maktu'a) has Byzantine foundations.

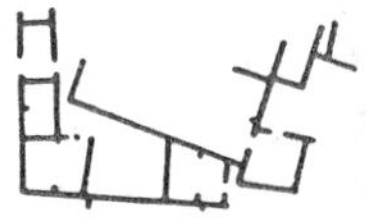

BET SHE'AN

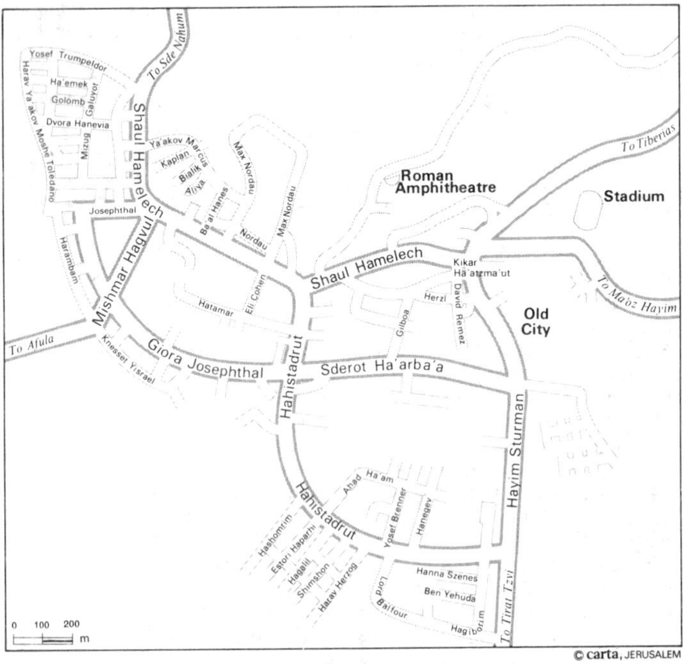

Bet She'arim (antiquities) *162:234*

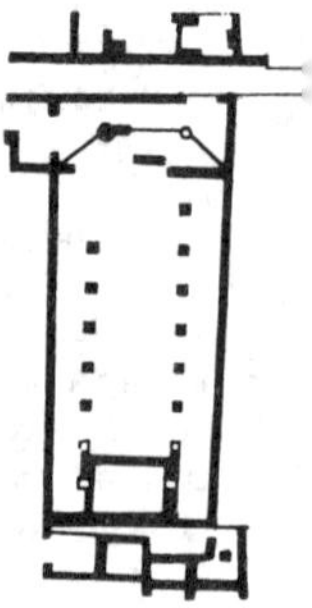

Remains of ancient Jewish city on border of Yizre'el Valley and Lower Galilee, near Qiryat Tiv'on. Site has catacombs filled with sarcophagi. Most extensive Jewish remains outside of Jerusalem. Known during Second Temple Period but became famous during Roman and Byzantine Periods, after Bar Kokhba revolt, when centre of Jewish settlement moved from Judea to Galilee. The Sanhedrin was located here for a while and Rabbi Judah HaNasi and other sages resided here. Due to ill health Rabbi Judah was obliged to move to Zippori in his last years. However, he was buried in Bet She'arim. From that time city became a central burial site for local and diaspora Jews. It was totally destroyed by Gallus during suppression of Jewish revolt in 352 CE. Excavations have thus far uncovered 26 networks of tombs, of which a few were family vaults but the majority were for the general public and could be purchased as burial sites. Largest catacomb contained 400 tombs. In one of the catacombs a magnificent courtyard was discovered — perhaps the tomb of Rabbi Judah HaNasi. The wall of the tomb was inscribed with names "Rabbi Simeon and Rabbi Gamliel", the names of Judah HaNasi's 2 sons. Also excavated were remains of many houses, workshops, living quarters and a large 3rd c. synagogue converted into a Byzantine church. Ancient city spread over 40 d. of soft chalk hills which facilitated tunnelling. Rich in bas relief carvings of animals. Leda and the Swan, Achilles and bearded personages reminiscent of Greek gods depicted. Decorations illustrate evolution of Hellenistic influence among Jews. Many depictions of Jewish motifs in naive artistic style. Jews came from Antioch, Beirut, Mesopotamia and southern Arabia to be buried here.

Bet She'arim *(moshav)* *167:233*

Moshav in Lower Galilee 2 km. W of Nahalal. Named after ancient city of Beth-shearim located in vicinity. Founded 1936 by Yugoslav immigrants. Pop.: 330. Area: 4,500 d.

Bet Shemesh (Josh. 15:10) *148:128*

Town on border of Judean Hills and Foothills, 5 km. S of Shimshon junction. Same name as ancient Beth-shemesh located in vicinity. Founded 1950 on site known during War of Independence as Mishlat HaMeshutaf (military outpost held alternately by Israel Defence Forces and Jordanian army). First settlers were Rumanian and Iraqi immigrants. Area today: 10,000 d. Pop.: 14,000. **Sites in vicinity:** Cave of the Twins, Netifim (stalactite) Cave, Naḥam wood and Tel Bet Shemesh excavations. **Tel Bet Shemesh** W of new town *147:128* beyond Bet Guvrin is ancient tel, site of Biblical Beth-shemesh which controlled important ancient road from Judean Foothills to Jerusalem. Beginnings in Early Bronze Age, only enclosed by city wall in Middle Bronze Age. In Late Bronze Age it was a prosperous city having commercial relations with neighbouring countries. During Israelite conquest of Joshua was allotted to Dan tribe but apparently not at first conquered. In I Sam. 6 it is related how Philistines returned Ark of the Law to Beth-shemesh after its capture in battle of Aphek. King Saul conquered and burned the city. Resettled during reign of King David and prospered again. Jehoash, King of Israel, defeated Amaziah, King of Judah, at Beth-shemesh (II Kings 14:11). City destroyed in days of destruction of First Temple (586 BCE). Apparently resettled later and in 5th c. a large Byzantine monastery was built. Excavations of tel have uncovered remains of Canaanite city conquered by Joshua. Temple remnants could be those of "House of the Sun", from which town gets its name. Other ruins include walls, buildings, cultic vessels, weapons, ceramic utensils, seals, inscriptions, olive oil presses, wine presses, large granary and other finds. A Byzantine monastery was also excavated. Ancient tombs found near tel with abundant offerings for dead. **Er Rujum** Within city is rectangular tomb of stones, apparently from Arab Period. **Kh. 'Ein Shams** Small tel N of Bet Shemesh. At its N side is curved wall built of large rough stones. Flint tools from Early Bronze Age found nearby.

Bet Shiqma *113:116*

Moshav 5 km. SE of Ashqelon. Named after the many sycamore (*shiqma*) trees in vicinity. Area: 2,400 d. Pop.: 600. **Ruins** In *moshav* are ruins of ancient settlement from Iron Age and Byzantine Period.

Bet 'Uzi'el *141:142*

Moshav in Judean Foothills 7 km. from Ramla, 1 km. S of Tel Gezer. Named after Ben-Zion Meir Ḥai Ouziel, late Sephardi Chief Rabbi (Rishon LeẒiyyon) of Ereẓ Israel. Area: 2,600 d. Pop.: 360.

Bet Yannay *137:198*

Moshav in Sharon by seashore 6 km. N of Netanya. Named after Hasmonean king, Alexander Yannai, who annexed the Sharon to Hasmonean kingdom. Founded 1933. Area: 1,300 d. Pop.: 300.

Bet Yehoshua' *137:185*

Moshav 7 km. S of Netanya. Named after Yehoshua' Thon, Polish Zionist leader. Founded 1938. Area: 2,000 d. Pop.: 300.

Bet Yeraḥ *203:235*

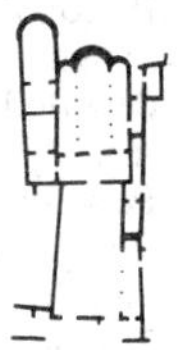

Large tel on S shore of Lake Kinneret near outlet of Jordan River. Site of ancient Beth-yerah or Bet Ariaḥ. Excavations have uncovered 16 levels of occupation from Early Bronze Age. Destroyed in Middle Bronze Age and rebuilt during Second Temple Period. In Hellenistic Period was called Philoteria after Ptolemy II's sister, Philadelphus. During Roman Period declared "city of freemen" and called Ariaḥ. The special privilege of Bet Yeraḥ and its adjacent sister city Zinabri (Sennabris) are also mentioned in the Talmud. Most of inhabitants in this period were Jews. Arabs called site

Karak. **Oholo** Near tel is Oholo, a seminar and regional school for Jordan Valley settlements.

• **Bet Yizhaq-Sha'ar Hefer** *139:192*

Cooperative village 3 km. E of Netanya. Named after German Zionist Yizhak Feuerring. Pop.: 1,500. **Gan Hefer** *Moshav* founded 1935. **Bet Yizhaq** *Moshav* founded 1939. **Sha'ar Hefer** *Moshav* founded 1940. **Nira** *Moshav shittufi* founded 1942. Within settlement, *139:192*, are ruins of large town from Roman and Byzantine Periods. Also cemetery, fragments of buildings, wells and other finds.

• **Bet Yosef** *202:218*

Moshav in Bet She'an Valley. Named after one of Israel's labour leaders, Yosef Aharonovitch. Founded 1937 as "stockade and tower" settlement. In War of Independence it was on front battle line. Area: 3,000 d.

• **Bet Zayit** *165:132*

Moshav 5 km. from Jerusalem. Named after the many olive (*zayit*) trees in vicinity; also perhaps name of ancient settlement N of Jerusalem. Area: 1,100 d. Pop.: 500. Footprints of dinosaur were discovered in *moshav*. Museum contains reconstruction in wood of dinosaur. Nearby in channel of Nahal Soreq is a dam to store winter flood waters. **'En Beroshim** Nearby is spring, with tunnel and irrigation pools. Alongside are ruins of a Byzantine building. **'Ein Tut** E of *moshav*, ruin with cistern and trough.

Bet Zeid **(Giv'ot Zeid)** *161:234*

Former settlement site on border of Yizre'el Valley and Lower Galilee, S of Qiryat Tiv'on, adjacent to ruins of Bet She'arim. Named after HaShomer watchman Alexander Zeid who lived and was murdered here by Arab gangs. On one of hills is memorial statue of a mounted watchman. Today there is a closed educational institution, Kefar Tiqwa, on site.

★ **Bet Zera'** *204:232*

Kibbutz in Jordan Valley 3 km. S of Degania "A". Founded 1927 by early pioneers from Germany. Area: 6,400 d. Pop.: 700. Museum of local archaeological finds.

■ **Bet Zevi** *147:236*

Educational institute 5 km. S of Tirat HaKarmel. Named after Zevi Sitrin, American Po'el Mizrahi leader. Includes agricultural school, vocational school and *yeshiva*. Staff and students: 350.

Bet Zur *(Josh. 15:58)* *159:110*

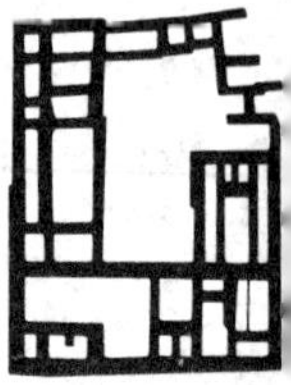

Tel (Kh. et Tubeiqa) in Judean Hills 6 km. N of Hebron. Site of ancient city of Beth-zur that controlled Hebron-Jerusalem road and was consequently a battlefield in various periods. During Israelite conquest allotted to tribe of Judah (Josh. 15:58). Was one of cities fortified by King Rehoboam (II Chron. 11:7). In 165 BCE Judah Maccabee defeated Syrian general Lysias at Beth-zur, but was later defeated by Lysias (162 BCE) in battle of Beth-zechariah, just N of Bet Zur. City recaptured by Simeon the Hasmonean in 150 BCE who strengthened its fortifications. Bet Zur is mentioned during the Persian Period as important city whose inhabitants participated in rebuilding Jerusalem. Excavations at Kh. et Tubeiqa uncovered Iron Age remains. At Kh. Burj es Sur remains of Crusader defence tower built on ruins of Byzantine fortress. Other finds indicate occupation from post-Babylonian Exile until Ottoman Period.

Bezet *162:275*

Moshav 8 km. N of Nahariyya. Site of Jewish city mentioned in 2nd and 3rd c. writings. Pop.: 260. Area: 2,200 d. **Ancient Bezet** Large tel S of village. Finds include flint tools and remains from Chalcolithic Period, Early and Middle Bronze Age sherds and tombs, and wine presses of Roman and Byzantine Periods. Some of ancient building stones re-used in houses of el Bassa village, whose inhabitants fled during War of Independence.

Biddu *164:138*

Arab village NW of Jerusalem. Situated adjacent to ancient route from Coastal Plain to Jerusalem. Pop.: 1,400. Giv'at HaRadar (see entry) is situated between Biddu and Ma'ale HaḤamisha.

Biddya *157:168*

Arab village in W Samarian Hills 12 km. E of Rosh Ha'Ayin. Pop.: 2,300. Remains of ancient settlement: ruined tower, pools and rock-cut tombs.

Bikura *196:206*

Rural centre in S Bet She'an Valley. Excels in early ripening (*bikur*) fruits.

Bil'in *156:148*

Arab village 13 km. W of Ramallah. Pop.: 550.

(El) Bi'na *175:259*

Arab village in W Galilee, N of Acre-Safed road. Pop.: 2,700, majority Moslems, rest Christian. Village has mosque, Greek Catholic and Orthodox churches. **Bet 'Anat** Within village is large, elongated tel where Hellenistic and Roman sherds were found. Believed to be site of Beth-anath, Canaanite city mentioned in Egyptian documents and conquered by Israelites. An estate called Bet 'Anat is also mentioned in Hellenistic documents.

Binyamina *145:214*

Settlement (local council) 7 km. S of Zikhron Ya'aqov. Named after Baron Binyamin (Edmond) de Rothschild. Founded as a *moshava* (farming village) in 1922 on lands of Burj village purchased by the Baron. Over years additional quarters founded: Naḥalat Jabotinsky (1946), Newe 'Oved (1947); and after 1948: Amidar, Warburg, Shikun 'Ovedim and Shikun 'Oleh. Area: 15,000 d. Pop.: 3,000. Near Shekhunat HaPo'alim a section of ancient aqueduct that carried water to Caesarea was uncovered.

Biq'at Be'er Sheva' (Valley)

Large depression in central Negev. Boundaries: Judean Foothills in N, Negev Plateau in S, Judean Hills in E and Coastal Plain in W. Crossed by a number of streams, mostly seasonal, the major one being Naḥal Be'er Sheva'. The soil is parched and area is sparsely settled. In centre is city of Be'er Sheva'.

Biq'at Bet Kerem (Valley)

Valley in Galilee with Acre-Safed road running its length from W to E. Named after ancient city of Beth-hakerem on whose site today is Arab village, Majd el Kurum. Other Arab villages in valley: el Bi'na, Deir el Asad, Naḥf, er Rama, Sajur, and 2 Jewish settlements: town of Karmi'el and *moshav* Shezor.

Biq'at Bet Netofa (Valley)

Valley in Galilee 12 km. N of Nazareth. Size: 4x17 km. General direction: NE-SW. Named after ancient settlement whose name is preserved in Kh. Beit Natuf (Ḥurbat Netofa — *186:248*). Has abundance of water and fertile soil. Important link in National Water Carrier: in E end of valley near 'Eilabun village is rock-cut tunnel whose W end forms a reservoir from where water is directed southwards.

Biq'at Bet Ẓayda (Valley) (Biq'at Buteiḥa) * Λ

Valley on NE shore of Lake Kinneret. Area: 25,000 d. Intersected by many streams descending from Golan and flooding area in winter, hence Arab name — el Buteiḥa (flat flooded land). Hebrew name from ancient town of Beth-saida. Rich alluvial soil. At beginning of 20th c. most of valley was still owned by a Kurdish family who leased land to tenant farmers. In 1905 Crimean Jews attempted settlement in valley but were forced to abandon site because of harsh conditions. After WWI it was included in area of French Mandate over Syria with exception of a strip 10 m. from water line, that remained in area of British Mandate over Palestine. After 1948 the Syrians established military posts in valley preventing Israeli fishing in NE Lake Kinneret. In 1955 Israelis attacked and destroyed some of these posts. In Six-Day War entire area captured and Syrian inhabitants fled. Area is slated for agricultural, tourist and recreational development. Part of valley, particularly the stream beds, has been declared a nature reserve. **Park HaYarden** National park stretching 20 km. E of Jordan River between Benot Ya'aqov Bridge in N and Jordan River estuary in S. At present only S part is open to public. Reconstructed water-powered flour mills. At Tel Mishpa' potsherds found from Early Bronze Age, Middle Bronze Age, Iron Age, Byzantine and Ottoman Periods. **Kh. ed Dikka** Ruins of ancient Jewish village with remains of 3rd c. synagogue.

Biq'at Buteiḥa → Biq'at Bet Ẓayda

Biq'at Ginnesar (Valley)

Valley on NW shore of Lake Kinneret. Size: 3x3 km. Important route through which *via maris* passed on way to Benot Ya'aqov Bridge. Three streams flow through valley into Kinneret: Naḥal 'Ammud, Naḥal Arbel and Naḥal Ẓalmon. Soil is fertile and valley was continuously occupied during most historical periods. Part inhabited in prehistoric era. (Skull of prehistoric [Palestine] man found in cave of Naḥal 'Ammud.) Remains of Second Temple Jewish settlement have been found on edges of valley. Josephus describes and extols valley and the sages were overwhelming in their praise of it. They claimed Ginnesar means *gane sar* (gardens of the minister). After destruction of Temple it became swamp and haunt of Bedouin. In 19th c. most of the lands were purchased by German religious orders who tried to settle here but were forced to abandon their homes because of malaria. In 1910 colony of Migdal was established here by Russian Zionists, and in 1937 kibbutz Ginnosar founded alongside it.

Biq'at HaYareaḥ (Valley) * *135:894*

Plateau surrounded by sharp granite rocks 15 km. NW of Elat. This desert, with its reddish coloured earth, seemed to resemble a moonscape to Israeli soldiers in War of Independence; hence its name — moon valley.

Biq'at Hureqanya (Valley) (El Buqei'a)

Valley in Judean Desert 6-8 km. from N shore of Dead Sea. Size: 3x11 km. Drained by Naḥal Qidron and Naḥal Sekhakha into Dead Sea. Indications of ancient agriculture (irrigation channels and terracing) and remains of Iron Age settlements.

Biq'at 'Iron (Valley)

Narrow valley joining Sharon with Yizre'el Valley along bed of Naḥal 'Iron which drains to S into Naḥal Ḥadera. Strategic route since ancient times. It was through this valley that Thutmose III passed on his way to conquer Megiddo, 15th c. BCE In WWI General Allenby broke through here into Yizre'el Valley. During War of Independence area seized and controlled by Iraqi forces and after war included within Israel. Valley has a string of prosperous Arab villages.

Biq'at Man (Valley) *

Valley in Mt. Ḥermon near ascent from Majdal Shams to Ketef Ḥermon. About 1,500 m. above sea level. Formed by dissolution of rocks (doline in geological terminology). **Berekhat Man** Round pool (100 m. in diameter) which collects flood waters of Naḥal 'Ar'ar. Pool filled most of the year round and frozen over in winter.

Biq'at Megiddo (Valley)

Name for port of Yizre'el Valley near Megiddo. Site of many famous battles throughout history. Christians believe it to be site destined for battle between Gog and Magog which would herald the end of days. (See Megiddo.)

Biq'at Qanna'im (Valley)

Small valley in Judean Desert 10 km. W of Masada. Name commemorates Zealot fighters in Revolt against Rome, who continued to fight in Judean Desert after uprising had been quelled in rest of country.

Biq'at Rimmon (Valley) (Biq'at Tur'an)

Valley in Galilee NE of Nazareth. General direction: W-E, with Nazareth-Tiberias road intersecting it. Named after ancient city, Rimmon, which was included in Zebulun tribal allotment (Josh. 19:13).

Biq'at Sanur (Valley) (Marj Sanur)

Small fertile cretaceous valley in Samarian Hills, between Shekhem and Jenin. Lacks drainage, thus filling up with water during winter.

Biq'at Sayyarim (Valley) * *136:917*

On border of Negev and Sinai 30 km. N of Elat. Size: 3x6 km.; general direction: S-N. One of the two routes used in the capture of Elat during War of Independence ('Uvda operation) passes through this valley. Named in honour of scouts (*sayyarim*) who led the Israel Defence Forces. NW of valley is Miẓpe Sayyarim (observation point — *132:932*).

Biq'at 'Uvda (Valley) *143:926*

Valley in Negev 40 km. N of Elat. Size: 5x10 km.; general direction: SW-NE. Named after 'Uvda operation to capture Elat during War of Independence. Adjacent to valley on W, a temporary airfield was built, Sede Avraham, to assist Israeli army in drive to Elat.

Biq'at Yavne'el (Valley)

Valley in Lower Galilee. Size: 3x6 km. General direction: NW-SE. Borders: N — Nazareth-Tiberias road, S — Jordan Valley, E — Yavne'el Hills, W — Ramat Poriyya. Traversed lengthwise by Naḥal Yavne'el that drains into Jordan River near kibbutz Deganya. Has a number of agricultural settlements: Yavne'el, HaZor'im, Mishmar HaShelosha and others.

Biq'at Ẓin (Valley)

Valley in Negev 10 km. S of HaMakhtesh HaGadol, SE of Sede Boqer. General direction: W-E along Naḥal Ẓin. The Sultan's Way, an ancient route, passes from N Negev Hills to 'Arava through valley.

o (El) Bira (in Hebron Hills) *143:093*

Arab village 20 km. SW of Hebron. Pop.: 3,500.

(El) Bira (near Ramallah) *170:146*

Neighbouring town of Ramallah 15 km. N of Jerusalem. Conjectured site of ancient Beeroth (Josh. 9:17), and the place where Joseph and Mary lost the child Jesus on way back to Galilee. (They later found him in the Temple in Jerusalem listening to the teachers.) Pop.: 10,000, mainly Moslem with small number of Christians. Mentioned in early Christian legends. In 12th c. French Crusaders settled here. Remains of Crusader church.

Biranit *182:274*

Regional centre in Upper Galilee 8 km. NW of Sasa junction. Name means small fortress. Founded as *nahal* outpost in 1964. Has institute for training Gadna youth leaders and fencing centre.

Bir 'Asluj → Be'er Mash'abbim

Biriyya *197:265*

Moshav in Galilee 1 km. N of Safed. Named after town of Biriyya mentioned in Talmud and later known as residence of Rabbi Joseph Caro, author of the Shulḥan Arukh. Founded 1945 by Bene 'Aqiva group on lands purchased by Baron de Rothschild in 1893. Became famous during struggle between the Jews of Palestine and the British Mandate authorities in last years before founding of the state. On 5 March, 1946 British forces entered settlement and arrested all settlers, claiming they had fired on nearby Arab Legion camp. On 14 March 3,000 people from all settlements in Galilee staged a march up to Biriyya and on a nearby hill established camp called Biriyya "B". This was demolished by the British and on following night a new camp, Biriyya "C" was set up. Finally, the British allowed 20 settlers to remain in camp. Besieged during War of Independence; in 1949, an immigrant *moshav* was established here. Area: 1,500 d. Pop.: 400. Site has remains of ancient synagogue and tomb attributed to Benaiah, son of Jehoiada, one of King David's commanders.

Birkat Ram *221:293*

Natural pool on N Golan Heights, near Mas'ada village. Elliptic in shape, measures 600x900 m., 8 m. deep and has capacity of 3 million cub. m. Water sources both from underground flow and from rains. Serves as irrigation reservoir for settlements in area. Also has fish. Known in ancient times as Lake of Panias or Phiale (bowl). Legend claims an underground connection between lake and sources of Banyas. Investigations turned up a link between lake and 'Ein Fit.

Birkat el Waqa' *146:157*

Ancient pool 5 km. E of Ben-Gurion Airport, S of *moshav* Bareqet. Hewn out of rock wall; one side has constructed wall. Still stores water today. (See Me'arot Bareqet.)

Bir el Maksur *171:242*

Bedouin village 10 km. W of Nazareth. Its 2,500 inhabitants, members of the 'Arab el Ḥajeirat tribe who settled here in permanent buildings in 1960's. Within village: ruins of cistern (Kh. Bir el Maksur) with ruined walls, foundations, door posts, column fragments and rock-cut tombs.

Bir el Muleiḥa → Be'er Menuḥa

Bir Nabala *168:139*

Arab village 8 km. N of Jerusalem. Pop.: 1,000. Within village, foundations of ancient buildings, wine presses and remains of Arab buildings from Middle Ages.

Birqin 174:206

Arab village in N Samarian Hills 3 km. W of Jenin. Pop.: 2,200. Village built on ruins of Byzantine and Medieval settlement. Ancient stones, including capital have been re-used in village buildings. About 1 km. NW of village is Kh. Birqin containing ancient settlement remains.

Bir eṣ Ṣafadi → Be'er Sheva'

Bir esh Shuqum 212:245

Abandoned village at foot of Golan 3 km. NE of 'En Gev. Built on ruins of Byzantine settlement; also occupied in Ottoman Period. **Bene Yehuda** Ancient stones re-used in village houses. At end of last century an attempt was made at settlement on this site by Jews of Safed. It gradually became impoverished. In 1913 only one family was left and after their son was murdered the family abandoned site in 1920. Syrian Arabs took control of their lands until its recapture in Six-Day War.

Bir es Sikka 153:196

Arab village 5 km. N of Tulkarm. Pop.: 600. Village has Moslem holy tomb — Jamal ed Din.

Bir Zabala 151:053

Two ancient pools in Negev 1 km. NW of Dimona. Built of dressed stone with many layers of plaster. Sherds from site indicate use in Hellenistic, Roman and Byzantine Periods.

Bir ez Zeibaq 139:149

Ancient well near Ramla prison. Name means well of mercury. Over well is Mamluk structure and nearby is group of ancient sycamore trees.

Bir Zeit 169:153

Arab town in Samarian Hills 6 km. N of Ramallah. Origin of name: apparently, olive oil well. (The area abounds with olive trees.) Perhaps site of ancient Beth-zaith mentioned in descriptions of Maccabean wars. Birzaith was name of one of descendants of Asher (I Chron. 7:31). Pop.: 2,500, mainly Christian and some Moslems. Town has a college. **Khan and ruin** On hill within town are ruins from Mamluk and Ottoman Periods with khan in centre. Three long halls, with arched ceilings, encompassed a courtyard on 3 sides. Sherds found on hill-slope indicate site was also occupied in Iron Age and Hellenistic and Roman Periods.

Bitan Aharon 138:197

Moshav 5 km. N of Netanya. Named after Aharon Freiman, Canadian Zionist leader. Founded 1936. Area: 800 d. Pop.: 100. **Nature reserve** Next to *moshav* a reserve of 50 d. encompasses 2 coarse sandy hills with indigenous plant life. Remains of Roman and Byzantine cemetery.

Bitanya 203:234

Abandoned farm and experimental station, previously in Jordan Valley, near Deganya "A". Founded 1913.

Bitanya 'Illit 201:235

Monument in Lower Galilee near Poriyya-Alummot junction. In 1920, in a camp on this site, HaShomer HaẒa'ir movement founded HaKibbutz HaArẓi. A monument to the event, a large concrete tent, was unveiled in 1964, the 50th anniversary of HaShomer HaẒa'ir.

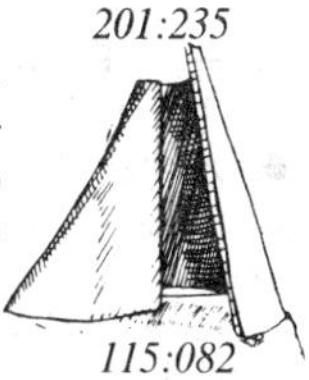

Bitḥa 115:082

Moshav in Negev 2 km. N of Ofaqim. Name from Biblical passage "in quietness and in *trust* shall be your strength" (Isa. 30:15). Area: 4,000 d. Pop.: 800.

• Biẓẓaron *124:133*

Moshav 6 km. E of Ashdod. Founded 1935 by group of Prisoners of Zion from USSR and hence name: "Return to your *stronghold*, O prisoners of hope;" (Zech. 9:12). Pop.: 480. Area: 4,600 d.

o Budrus *149:152*

Arab village 10 km. E of Lod. Some believe this to be site of city Petrus mentioned in Talmud. Pop.: 500. **Kh. Budrus** Near village are remains of Byzantine walls and agricultural installations. Between village and ruin is large sheikh's tomb.

o Bu‘eina *184:246*

Arab village in Lower Galilee 5 km. NW of Golani junction. Believed to be site of ancient city Beth-anath, mentioned in Ugarit tablets. Pop.: 1,300.

o Buq‘ata *223:289*

Druze village on N Golan Heights 4 km. S of Birkat Ram. Pop.: 2,000. Built on ruins of Byzantine settlement.

(El) Buqei‘a (Peqi‘in) *181:264*

Settlement in Upper Galilee 7 km. SE of Ma‘alot-Tarshiḥa, which has traditionally had Jewish presence since 70 CE Temple destruction. This is the one place in Israel from which Jews have never gone into exile. Mentioned in Talmud under several names: Tekoa‘, Peqa‘, Baqa‘ and in the Zohar as Peqi‘in — the origin of Arabic name Buqei‘a or el Buqei‘a. Pop.: 2,600, 67% Druze, 29% Christian, 4% Moslem and one Jewish family (Zeynati). Moslem settlement began about 900 years ago, the Christians came with Crusades, and Druze about 200 years ago. The village has a Druze *khilwa* (place of seclusion), Greek Catholic and Greek Orthodox churches and a synagogue. The synagogue was only built in 1873 but one of walls has stones used from a more ancient synagogue; local tradition has it as stones from the Temple. One stone is decorated with a *menorah*, *shofar*, *etrog* and *lulav*. Since no ancient remains have been found within the village itself, one can assume that ancient Peqi‘in was located nearby. Near village spring is cave whose opening is covered by a very old carob tree. Tradition has it that Rabbi Simeon b. Yoḥai and his son Eleazar hid in this cave from their Roman pursuers and it was here that he wrote the Zohar. Near village are a number of ancient tombs including those attributed to Joshua b. Hananiah and Rabbi Yose of Peqi‘in. **Ḥurbat ‘Evad (Kh. Ras ‘Abad)** *180:265* Ruin of ancient settlement within new Peqi‘in. Site has many remains from Hellenistic, Roman and Byzantine Periods: remains of buildings, door posts and lintels, stone mounds, rock-cut tombs and cisterns. One theory identifies site as that of ancient Peqi‘in.

(El) Buqei‘a (in Samarian Hills)

Valley in Samarian Hills SE of Tubas. After Six-Day War two new settlements were established: Beqa‘ot and Ro‘i.

(El) Buqei‘a (in Judean Desert) → **Biq‘at Hureqanya**

• Buregeta *146:192*

Moshav 9 km. E of Netanya. Same name as city of Burgeta, mentioned in Talmud and retained in name of abandoned village, el Burj. Area: 2,600 d. Pop.: 400. *Moshav* has district school for settlements in ‘Emeq Ḥefer regional council, cultural centre and district packing station for agricultural produce. Near *moshav* are remains of Roman building and Crusader fort (the Red Tower). Nearby, a Roman milestone was found. **Tel Buregeta** In *moshav* are remains of settlements from Iron Age, post-Babylonian Exile and Roman and Byzantine Periods. Apparently site of the Burgeta mentioned in Talmud.

(El) Bureij *093:094*

Refugee camp in Gaza Strip 10 km. SW of Gaza. In 1967 inhabitants numbered 13,000 refugees, mostly from villages in S of country. Name means small fortress.

Burham *166:155*

Arab village 10 km. NW of Ramallah. Pop.: 200. One theory claims this is ancient site of Barhum, birthplace of Azmareth the Barhumite, one of King David's commanders.

Burin *173:176*

Arab village 4 km. S of Shekhem. Pop.: 1,400. Near village is tel with remains of ancient buildings.

(El) Burj *141:094*

Arab village on border of Judean Desert 20 km. SW of Hebron. Site has ruins scattered over large area. Some of ancient ruins and caves still serve as dwelling places. In centre of village, remains of Crusader fortress identified as Castellum Ficuum (Fortress of Figs). Sherds indicate occupation from Byzantine Period to Middle Ages.

Burj Bardawil *173:154*

Remains of Crusader road fort 10 km. NE of Ramallah. Possibly built by Crusader King Baldwin who was called Bardawil by Arabs. Remains of fort and other contemporary fortifications. Sherds indicate Iron Age occupation.

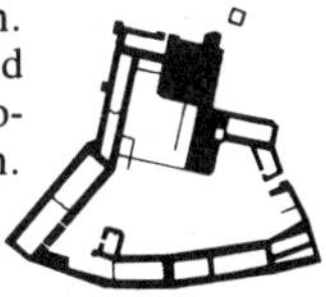

Burj Beitin → Beitin

Burj Dayqat el 'Amirin *121:035*

Ruin of ancient hill fortress in Negev 10 km. NW of Sede Boqer. Remains of round structures from Bronze or Iron Age.

Burj el Fari'a *183:188*

Ruins of ancient settlement in Samarian Hills 4 km. SW of Tubas. Remains of Crusader tower. Occupied from Iron Age until Middle Ages.

Burj el Maliḥ *193:193*

Remains of Mamluk fort 10 km. E of Tubas. Intended to guard entrance to Wadi el Maliḥ. Outer wall of hewn stones has been preserved. **Ḥammam el Maliḥ** Two km. E of Burj el Maliḥ is small oasis with hot springs enclosed by simple bathhouses with living quarters alongside.

"Burma Road" (Derekh Burma)

Track in Judean Hills constructed during War of Independence (May 1948) in order to bring supplies and reinforcements to besieged Jerusalem. Name was borrowed from original "Burma Road" — a hidden road cut through the jungles of Burma by Allied forces in WWII. The road was secretly built in the no-man's-land between the Israeli and Jordanian armies that surrounded Jerusalem. The track passed through the captured villages of Beit Jiz and Beit Susin (today between Naḥshon and Beqoa'), detoured Latrun in the S and crossed Sha'ar HaGay-Hartuv road (near Mesillat Ẓiyyon), ran S of Beit Maḥsir (Bet Meir of today) and joined Sha'ar HaGay-Jerusalem road near Kafr Saris (Shoresh of today). The last section was steep and narrow and was nicknamed "Derekh HaJeepim" because only jeeps could manoeuvre on it.

Burqa *168:189*

Arab village 3 km. N of Sabastiya. Pop.: 650.

○ **Burqa** 174:144

Arab village 5 km. E of Ramallah. Pop.: 2,500.

○ **Buruqin** 159:164

Arab village 20 km. NW of Ramallah. Pop.: 1,200.

● **Bustan HaGalil** 158:261

Moshav 2 km. N of Acre. Founded 1948 on the site where in 1941 the French Vichy army in Syria and Lebanon signed their surrender to the British army. Area: 1,600 d. Pop.: 350. N of *moshav* is educational institute Berit Aḥim (formerly Philadelphia Village).

Buteiḥa → Biq'at Bet Ẓayda

∴ **Butmiyya** 233:262

Abandoned village on central Golan Heights, situated on tel. Remains found nearby of ancient buildings and an inscription which includes symbol of the cross. Site occupied in Roman and Byzantine Periods.

○ **(El) Buyuki** 082:076

Arab village in Gaza Strip 2 km. SE of Rafah. Pop.: 1,400.

C

Caesarea *(Acts 8:40)* 140:212

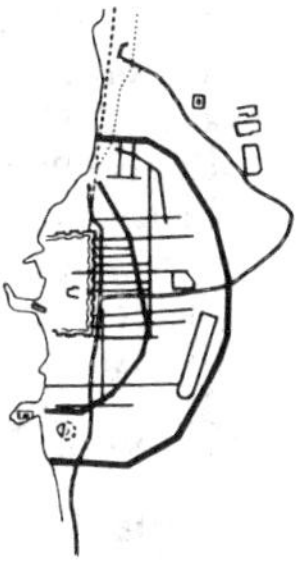

This quintessential, ancient Mediterranean port is now an archaeological site and resort centre 10 km. N of Hadera. Though the city was small during the Crusader Period, it is from this era that most of the ruins date. Site of ancient Sidonite city, Straton's Tower. Conquered in 90 BCE by Alexander Yannai and annexed to his kingdom. In 63 BCE Pompey excluded the city from Judea and gave it autonomy. The Emperor Augustus gave city as a present to Herod who proceeded to build a large and magnificent fortified city called Caesarea in honour of Emperor Augustus. To distinguish it from Caesarea Philippi (Banyas) the city was sometimes called Caesarea Maritima (Caesarea-near-the-sea) or Augusta. Jewish sources called it Qesari, Qesarin or Qesariyon. During Roman Period it was the largest city in the country, seat of the Roman Procurator of Judea and headquarters of the Roman occupation army. It had a mixed population, Jews and gentiles (chiefly Greeks and Syrians) and often there were disputes between them. One of the clashes between the 2 communities that took place in the synagogue in 66 CE, sparked the Jewish Revolt against Rome. According to Josephus, 20,000 Jews were killed in an hour. During the war, the gentiles slaughtered many Jewish inhabitants and the survivors fled to Narbata. After the revolt and the destruction of the Second Temple, Caesarea became a Roman colony and capital of Province of Judea. Jewish settlement was renewed in 2nd c. and, during Roman and Byzantine Period, many *Tannaim* and *Amoraim* lived here. According to legend, during days of the Bar Kokhba revolt (132 CE), the Ten Martyrs (among them Rabbi 'Aqiva) were arrested, tortured and slain here. Caesarea also had a large Samaritan community at that time. During Byzantine Period it was important Christian centre. In fact Christianity became an established force here as early as the 2nd c. and Caesarea was site of a famous Christian school. From school's library came early translation of Bible called Hexapla. Eusebius, author of the Onomasticon, was Archbishop of Caesarea in the 4th c. Emperor Justinian made it the capital of *Palaestina Prima* and oppressed the Jewish and Samaritan inhabitants. At this time the city reached its zenith and was the most important urban centre in the Holy Land. In 640 it was captured by the Arabs, who, according to Arab historians, were led via a secret passage into the fortress by a Jew named Joseph. The city continued to prosper during the Arab Period. In 1107 it was conquered by the Crusaders. Benjamin of Tudela visited the city in 1170 and found 10 Jewish families and about 200 Samaritan families in residence. In 1187 it was conquered and destroyed by Saladin. The Crusaders retook the city at beginning of 13th c. and refortified it. In 1265 it was taken by the Mamluk Sultan Baybars, and in 1291 after the fall of Acre (the last Crusader stronghold) the city was completely destroyed by Sultan el Ashraf in order to prevent possibility of another Crusader invasion by sea. Since then city remained in ruins. In 1878 Moslem refugees from Bosnia were settled here and established a fishing and farming village. Some left and part of their land was purchased by PICA. It was on these lands that kibbutz Sedot Yam was established in 1940. During War of Independence the last of the

Moslems left. **Restored sites** After War of Independence, excavations in Caesarea began and in 1961 restoration work started. Prominent features of this work are buildings attributed to the Sidonite city, Straton's Tower; amphitheatre, theatre, stadium (hippodrome), remains of port and wall from Roman Period; remains of large building (perhaps a market) with 2 statues from Byzantine Period; remains of synagogue with large courtyard paved with marble and mosaic from 5th and 6th c.; majority of extant remains are from Crusader Period: city walls with towers and gates, glacis and moat, ruins of port and sea fort; remains of 2 Roman aqueducts from time of Herod, the lower one carrying water from Naḥal Tanninim *142:217*, a distance of 5 km., and the higher one from springs in area of ʿAmmiqam *152:219* and Kefar Shumi *145:215*. The total length of the upper aqueduct is 17 km. and includes a tunnel and open canal. **Resort and tourist site** Concurrent with restoration of ancient Caesarea, the remaining area was developed under Baron de Rothschild's initiative and has become a holiday, recreation and tourist centre. Restaurants, shops, galleries and bathing beach in old city. E of ruins are hotel, villa residential quarter and golt course. The Roman theatre — mentioned by Josephus — has been renovated and is host to the Israel Music Festival each summer.

Canada Park → Emmaus, Latrun

Cape Costigan → HaLashon

Cape Molineux → HaLashon

Capernaum → Kefar Naḥum

Castellion → Hureqanya

Castellum Merle → Dor

Cremisan → Deir Kirmizan

Custom's House (Bet HaMekhes) *209:268*

In past was border checkpost between Ereẓ Israel and Syria, on E side of Benot Yaʿaqov Bridge. NE of Lower Custom's House, at top of winding road, is Upper Custom's House *210:269*, used as headquarters for Syrian positions in area until Six-Day War. In Yom Kippur War, Syrian salient reached this point.

D

∴ Dabbura — *212:272*

Abandoned village in Golan Heights 5 km. NE of Benot Ya'aqov Bridge. Built on ruins of Jewish town from days of Mishnah and Talmud (Roman and Byzantine era). Dressed and decorated stones with Hebrew and Aramaic inscriptions were re-used in village houses. Nearby is nature reserve with Naḥal Gilbon, a perennial stream with two waterfalls — Gilboa and Devora.

∴ Dabiya — *218:268*

Abandoned village in central Golan. Built on ruins of ancient settlement from Roman-Byzantine Period whose remains were found on site (columns, capitals, bases and lintels). One lintel fragment was decorated with 2 seven-branched candelabra, apparently from local synagogue.

Daburiyya (Dabburiya) — *185:234*

Arab village at foot of Mt. Tabor. According to tradition, named after the prophetess Deborah. Pop.: 4,000. **Kh. Dabura** NE of village, apparently site of Biblical Daberath, a city in Issachar tribal allotment. During Byzantine Period there was Jewish village called Dabira on site and during Crusader Period a settlement called Buria. Site has remains of Crusader fortress, church foundations and mosaic floor. Sherds indicate occupation in Early Bronze Age and from post-Babylonian Exile through Middle Ages.

★ Dafna — *209:292*

Kibbutz in Galilee 7 km. NE of Qiryat Shemona. The city of Dafna or Dafni was located in this area (mentioned in writings of Flavius). Founded in 1939 in framework of "stockade and tower" settlements. Served as Palmaḥ base. Area: 5,000 d. Pop.: 750.

Daheisha — *167:122*

Refugee settlement 2.5 km. SW of Bethlehem. Pop.: 4,200. Across road is building called Nabi Danyal, after name of a battle in War of Independence.

o Daḥi — *182:225*

Arab village on summit of Giv'at HaMore, 5 km. NE of 'Afula. Named after 7th c. Arab personage — en Nabi Daḥi, whose tomb is near village. Pop.: 250, of Bedouin origin.

o (Ed) Dahiriyya — *147:090*

Arab village 18 km. from Hebron. Named after 13th c. Sultan Baybars ed Dahr. Pop.: 5,000. Site has remains of Iron Age fortress. Near village is British police fort which later served as Jordanian Legion post. Today, site of Naḥal Zohar.

★ Daliyya — *157:222*

Kibbutz in Ramat Menashe 12 km. NE of Zikhron Ya'aqov. Name means: long trailing branch. Founded 1939 in framework of "stockade and tower" settlements. On eve of War of Independence served as Palmaḥ base. Area: 10,000 d. Pop.: 650. Kibbutz has cultural centre, Bet Miriam, that includes concert hall, library and reading rooms; open air theatre that hosted first Israeli folk dance festival in 1944.

Daliyyat el Karmil *154:233*

Traditional Druze settlement in Karmel mountains off Elyaqim-Haifa road where old men wear traditional dress of black robe with white turban. Colourful bazaar in village. Founded some 250 years ago on remains of ancient settlement by Druze family from Syria. Growth of town associated with Druze chieftain Fakr ed Din who rebelled against Turks and established his rule in Galilee in late 16th c. Area: 30,000 d. Pop.: 7,400 (90% Druze and rest Moslem and Christian). Site has remains of ancient buildings, cisterns, wine presses and building materials; a structure in memory of Abu Ibrahim; the house where Sir Lawrence Oliphant resided between 1882–1887. (His secretary at that time was N. H. Imber, the author of HaTiqwa, the Israeli national anthem.)

● **Dalton** *196:269*

Moshav 5 km. N of Safed. Named after ancient settlement Dalton. Nearby abandoned village of Dallata also preserves part of ancient name. Area: 2,000 d. Pop.: 700. Remains of building foundations, caves, cisterns, tombs (attributed to Talmudic sages: Rabbi Yose HaGelili, Rabbi Eleazar b. Arakh, Rabbi Eleazar b. Azariah and others), and remains of synagogue from beginning of Middle Ages. Also 2 prehistoric dolmens. **Dalton Lake** Two km. W of *moshav*. Seasonal lake.

Damiya Bridge → Adam Bridge

(Ed) Damun *152:237*

Prison on Mt. Karmel. Built on site of Byzantine and Crusader settlement (Kh. ed Damun). In prison courtyard a mosaic floor was found, as well as column fragments, cisterns and rock-cut tombs discovered nearby.

★ **Dan** *(Gen. 14:14)* *211:294*

Kibbutz 10 km. NE of Qiryat Shemona. Named after ancient city of Dan identified with nearby Tel Dan. Founded 1939 in framework of "stockade and tower" settlements. In years prior to 1948 served as transit station for "illegal" immigrants from Syria and Lebanon. During War of Independence Syrians tried to capture it but were repelled. Border incidents with Syrians continued for many years and in Six-Day War it was again subject to attack. Pop.: several hundreds. Area: 4,500 d. Kibbutz has a cultural centre and national history museum, Bet Ussishkin. N of kibbutz is archaeological site and nature reserve (see Tel Dan).

★ **Daverat** *(Josh. 21:28)* *182:228*

Kibbutz in Yizre'el Valley 6 km. NE of 'Afula. Named after Biblical Daberath a city in Issachar tribal allotment, identified with Kh. Dabura near Daburiyya. Founded 1946. Area: 10,000 d. Pop.: 350.

∴ **(Ed) Dawayima** *141:104*

Abandoned village 16 km. SE of Qiryat Gat. Site has Chalcolithic remains, cisterns, Roman and Byzantine building walls and subterranean rock-cut caves (like those in Bet Guvrin).

Dead Sea (Yam HaMelaḥ)

Salt sea in S Jordan Valley, the lowest point on earth (398 m. below sea level). Known from ancient days and called by various names: Yam HaQadmoni, Sea of Sedom, Salt Sea, Arabah Sea and others. Bounded in E by hills of Moab, in W by Judean Desert, in N by Jericho Plain and in S by Sedom Plain. Length: about 80 km.; maximum width: 17 km.; area: about 1,000 sq. km.; maximum depth: about 400 m. Major water sources: Jordan River, Naḥal Zarqa,

Nahal Arnon and many other seasonal streams. In SE is peninsula called the Tongue (see HaLashon) with 2 bays at its tip: Cape Costigan at N and Cape Molineux at S. Its salty waters do not enable any life in the sea but it is rich in minerals. Along its coastline are a number of sulphur springs, some of them hot. Its W shore is within Israel while the E shore is within Jordan. Along W coast from N to S on the shore are: Qalya, remains of Palestine Potash Company, ruins of Qumran, ‘Enot Zuqim (‘Ein el Fashkha) resort, swimming and nature reserve, ‘Enot Qane reserve, ‘En Gedi reserve, hot springs, Ḥamme Yesha‘, Ḥamme Zohar, ruins of Masada, ‘En Boqeq, Newe Zohar and the Dead Sea works at Sedom. Because of over-taxing of Jordan waters and slackening rainfall, the S basin is gradually drying up. This has necessitated an artificial canal which brings water from the N basin to the evaporation pools at Sedom.

★ **Deganya “A”** *204:235*

Oldest kibbutz in Israel. Pioneer agricultural commune at S end of Lake Kinneret 10 km. S of Tiberias. Name originates from *dagan*: corn or grain. Called Mother of the Pioneer Communes — *qevuẓot*. Situated on lands of Umm Juna, possibly site of ancient town of Gun. Originally, in 1909, a farm was set up here. In 1911 settled by group of pioneers called Hadera. In early years settlers suffered from the harsh climate, isolation and attacks by local Bedouin. Over the years it has become a significant landmark in labour and settlement history. During Disturbances of 1936-1939 it served as a base for *peluggot sade* (field companies) and as Palmaḥ base on eve of War of Independence. During the war its defenders and those of its neighbour, Deganya “B”, repelled Syrian attackers who reached gates of kibbutz. Pop.: 530. Within kibbutz is Bet Gordon — a natural science museum named after A.D. Gordon who lived and worked here; small planetarium, educational institute; Gan HaMeginnim (Defenders' Park) in memory of Deganya members who fell in War of Independence; a Syrian tank which was stopped at gates of Deganya has been left as a memorial. In local cemetery a number of famous people are buried, among them: A.D. Gordon, Joseph Bussel, Otto Warburg, Arthur Ruppin and others.

★ **Deganya “B”** *204:234*

Pioneer agricultural commune (*qevuẓa*) in Jordan Valley adjacent to Deganya “A”, 10 km. S of Tiberias. Founded in 1920 by ‘Avoda pioneer group from Second ‘Aliyah. During Disturbances of 1936-1939 served as base for “stockade and tower” settlements established in area. During War of Independence its members, together with those of Deganya “A”, repelled Syrian invaders. Area: 2,600 d. Pop.: 700.

o **Deir Abu Da‘if** *184:206*

Arab village on slope of Mt. Gilboa‘ 6 km. E of Jenin. Name means monastery of the weak father. Pop.: 1,500.

o **Deir Abu Mash‘al** *156:156*

Arab village 17 km. NW of Ramallah. Pop.: 900.

o **Deir ‘Ammar** *159:152*

Arab village 12 km. NW of Ramallah. Pop.: 1,400. Remnants of ancient settlement. Adjacent to village is tomb of Moslem holy person, Nabi Gheit.

Deir el Asad *175:260*

Arab settlement in W Galilee. Name means monastery of the lion. Local tradition claims that the village was founded about 400 years ago. Pop.: 4,000. **Antiquities** Rock-cut caves and tombs from Roman and Byzantine Periods, and remains of 12th c. Crusader church.

o Deir el 'Asal *144:097*

Small Arab village in Judean Hills 17 km. SW of Hebron. Name means monastery of honey. Village has 2 parts: Fauqa (upper) with 370 residents and Taḥta (lower) with 200 residents. Upper village is built on ruin near deep well (Bir Deir el 'Asal) and tunnel. Sherds found on site from Middle Bronze Age I and II and Roman Period.

Deir 'Aṣfura → Beit Jimal

Deir 'Aziz *217:252*

Abandoned village in Golan 12 km. NE of 'En Gev. Built on ruins of border village of Roman and Byzantine Periods. From ancient settlement one large structure has remained, built of dressed stones and alongside it a building roofed with panels of basalt (now underground). Underneath these are remains of a synagogue. Near village, on bank of Naḥal Kanaf, is a well covered with dressed stone structure. Near well are additional remains: column fragments, capitals and carved stones.

Deir Baghal *159:122*

Remains of fortress in Judean Hills with square casemate wall, 30x30 m., internal courtyard, tower on NW corner and opening in E wall. Sherds indicate it was built in Iron Age and reoccupied in Roman Period.

□ Deir el Balaḥ *088:092*

Arab town in Gaza Strip 15 km. from Gaza with important antiquities. Named after fruit of palm trees (*balaḥ* in Arabic) abundant in area. Pop.: 11,000. **Antiquities** Excavations uncovered ancient tombs from 13th c. BCE with anthropoid coffins containing work tools and jewellery. In 1978 a hoard of Bronze Age Philistine pottery was found here. A Crusader city, Darom or Darum, was located in area. Site has remains of 12th c. church. Within the town is a WWI British military cemetery.

o Deir Ballut *152:163*

Arab village 13 km. E of Petaḥ Tiqwa. Mentioned in writings of 13th c. Moslem geographer. Pop.: 1,100.

Deir Daqla *152:162*

Remains of large ancient farm 13 km. SE of Petaḥ Tiqwa. Occupied in Iron Age and again in Middle Ages. Remains of buildings, rock-cut cisterns, mosaic fragments and tombs.

o Deir Dibwan *175:146*

Arab village 6 km. E of Ramallah. Pop.: 3,000. N of village is Kh. et Tall believed to be site of Biblical Ai (Josh. 7:2).

o Deir Ghassana *159:161*

Arab village 20 km. NW of Ramallah. Pop.: 900. Birthplace of writer Omar Ṣalaḥ Albarghuti who described Ereẓ Israel and Bedouin judicial customs. Remains of Iron Age settlement, apparently site of Biblical Zeredah (I Kings 11:26) and in Mishnah (Sot. 9:9). Site was also occupied in Byzantine Period, Middle Ages and Ottoman times.

o Deir Ghazzala *183:211*

Arab village on border of Samaria and Yizre'el Valley 5 km. NE of Jenin. Name means monastery of the gazelle. Pop.: 500.

o Deir el Ghuṣun *157:195*

Arab village 7 km. NE of Tulkarm. Pop.: 3,700.

Deir Ḥajla *198:136*

Greek Orthodox convent on N shore of Dead Sea 5 km. SE of Jericho, named after St. Gerasimus a monk who settled here in 5th c. The

Biblical city of Beth-hoglah (Josh. 15:6), depicted in Madaba map, is believed to be located nearby. Near convent is a spring, 'Ein Ḥajla.

Deir Ḥanna *184:252*

Arab village in Lower Galilee 10 km. NW of Golani junction. Pop.: 4,000, mostly Moslem and some Christians. Apparently site of Kefar Yoḥanna or Kefar Ḥannun from Roman and Byzantine Periods. Remnants of fort built by Bedouin ruler Dahir el 'Amr in 18th c.

Deir el Ḥatab *180:180*

Arab village 4 km. E of Shekhem. Name means monastery of trees. Pop.: 550.

Deir Ibzi' *161:146*

Arab village 8 km. W of Ramallah. Pop.: 500.

Deir Istiya *163:170*

Arab village 16 km. SW of Shekhem. Pop.: 1,500. Has holy tomb called en Nabi Istiya.

Deir Jarir *178:152*

Arab village in Samarian Hills adjacent to Mt. Ba'al Ḥaẓor. Pop.: 1,300. Site of ancient settlement containing building stones, wine presses, olive oil presses, Crusader fortress and church remnants.

Deir Kirmizan (Cremisan) *166:126*

Salesian theological seminary and noviciate on slope of Mt. Jala (Beit Jala), SW of Jerusalem, with a farm and winery. Their wines have a fine reputation.

Deir Mar Jiryis → St. George's Monastery

Deir Mar Saba → Mar Saba

Deir Me'adal *223:260*

Abandoned village in Golan 10 km. SE of Qaẓrin. Established in Ottoman Period on ruins of settlement from Byzantine Period, remains of which have been re-used in village buildings. Area contains many dolmens.

Deir el Mir *154:163*

Ruins of Iron Age settlement (over 25 d.) 9 km. SE of Rosh Ha'Ayin. Also occupied in Persian Period and reoccupied in Byzantine Period and Middle Ages. Impressive layout of village can be seen on ground. The large building with the arched hall is from a later period.

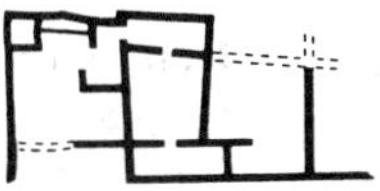

Deir Muḥeisin → Beqoa'

Deir el Muḥraqa → Qeren Karmel

Deir Nidam *160:156*

Arab village 15 km. NW of Ramallah. Pop.: 220.

Deir Qaddis *154:150*

Arab village 20 km. W of Ramallah. Name means holy monastery. Pop.: 500. Near village is British Mandate Tegart police fort.

Deir Qal'a *154:163*

Remains of monastery or Byzantine farm 15 km. SE of Petaḥ Tiqwa. Parts of walls of 2-storey building have been preserved, 4 plastered pools, tombs and building fragments.

Deir el Qaruntul ♠ *191:143*
(Monastery of the Temptation or of the 40 Days)

Greek Orthodox monastery 4 km. NW of Jericho built onto side of sheer cliff, overlooking the Jericho oasis; one of the most fabulous locations in the Holy Land. Name derives from the Arabic word *quarantena* meaning forty. According to Christian tradition it was here that Jesus fasted for 40 days and was tempted by Satan. The original monks who moved here early in 4th c. lived in the natural caves in the cliff. Later a monastery was built but it was destroyed by the Persians. The present building was constructed by the Russian Orthodox church between 1875 and 1905. Inside is a stone on which Jesus is believed to have sat during the Temptation. Also Byzantine art treasures.

Deir Rafat ♠ *145:135*

Latin Patriarchate monastery 5 km. NW of Bet Shemesh. On walls and ceiling of church the *Ave Maria* prayer is written in 350 languages. Nearby is a remedial school, Giv'at Shemesh.

o **Deir Raziḥ** *153:097*

Arab village in S Judean Hills. Pop.: 120.

Deir Sami'an *155:163*

Remains of Byzantine farm 10 km. SE of Rosh Ha'Ayin. Building remains, plastered pools and water canal.

o **Deir Ṣamit** *147:103*

Arab village in W Judean Hills 12 km. W of Hebron, with thatched-roof houses. Pop.: 700.

o **Deir Sharaf** *168:184*

Arab village 8 km. NW of Shekhem. Name means monastery of honour. Pop.: 1,000. Site has tombstone from 3rd or 4th c. with Greek inscription.

∴ **Deir esh Sheikh** *156:128*

Abandoned village in Judean Hills. Tomb of local Moslem holy person, Sheikh Badr.

o **Deir es Sudan** *164:160*

Arab village 15 km. NW of Ramallah. Name means monastery of the blacks, however, origin of name not known. Pop.: 550.

Deir Tantura ♠ *168:126*

Hospice off Jerusalem-Bethlehem road 2 km. N of Bethlehem. Established in 1876 by Knights of Malta. In 1971 an ecumenical university was inaugurated on hospice lands.

∴ **Deir Yasin** *166:132*

Abandoned village W of Jerusalem, now incorporated in Giv'at Shaul "B", suburb of Jerusalem. Captured by Irgun and Leḥi forces in War of Independence. During fighting, many Arab villagers were killed and battle is known to Arabs as the Deir Yasin massacre. Remains of buildings and rock-cut tombs from Roman Period and Middle Ages. Leading to village from Moẓa is an ancient Roman road.

● **Deqel** *087:067*

Moshav in Besor region 7 km. SE of Kerem Shalom. Established 1980.

Derekh Avraham

Track in central Negev that descends from Sede Boqer to HaMakhtesh HaGadol (the big crater). Built by a paratrooper unit in 1964 and named after Avraham Krinitzi, mayor of Ramat Gan.

Derekh Burma → **"Burma Road"**

Derekh Ereẓ Pelishtim *(Ex. 13:17)*
(Way of the Land of the Philistines)
Ancient route which passed through length of Philistine territory (S Coastal Plain) and became part of the *via maris* which joined Egypt with kingdoms of Fertile Crescent passing through Ereẓ Israel. Mentioned in the Bible in account of journeys of Children of Israel. "God did not lead them by way of the land of the Philistines" (Ex. 13:17).

Derekh Ha'Arava (Way of the Arabah) *(Deut. 2:8)*
Ancient route along length of 'Arava from S of Dead Sea to Gulf of Elat. Mentioned in Bible in account of journeys of Children of Israel. During War of Independence was one of routes taken to capture Elat. Present 'Arava road follows same course.

Derekh HaAtarim (Way of the Atharim) *(Num. 21:1)*
Ancient route between Negev and Sinai passing through Be'er Sheva', Makhtesh Ramon and central Sinai. When Israelites left Egypt they took this route to enter Canaan but were repelled by king of 'Arad. It is possible that this was route used by spies sent out by Moses.

Derekh HaBesamim (Perfume Route)
Ancient route used by Nabateans for perfume trade from Arabian Peninsula. Road passed through Petra, crossed 'Arava and Negev (Naḥal Neqarot-'En Saharonim-Ma'ale Maḥmal-'Avedat-Ḥaluẓa) until coast of Gaza. Along its course hostels were built; some of their remains can be seen today.

Derekh HaHar (Way of the Mountain)
Ancient internal route between N Sinai and Yizre'el Valley through Qadesh Barnea', Be'er Sheva', Hebron, Jerusalem and Shekhem.

Derekh HaḤogegim (Darb el Ḥaj) (Pilgrims' Route)
Name given by Moslems to routes used by pilgrims (*ḥogegim*) to Mecca. One of them is 2nd c. Roman road used by pilgrims from Damascus to Elat and from Elat to Mecca. At beginning of 20th c. the Hejaz railroad was built along this route. Another route crossed Sinai and was used by pilgrims from Egypt and N Africa: it passed from Suez through Ras en Naqb to Elat, from Elat to 'Aqqaba and from 'Aqqaba, usually by ship, to Mecca.

Derekh HaJeepim → **"Burma Road"**

Derekh HaNasi
Section of road E of Lod at tip of Herzl Forest near Ben Shemen to tombs of Maccabees in Modi'im. Named after 2nd president of Israel — Yiẓḥaq Ben-Ẓevi.

Derekh HaNeft (T.A.P.-Line Road)
Track in Golan, parallel to Aramco oil pipeline. Fierce battles were fought along this track in Six-Day War and Yom Kippur War.

Derekh HaSultan (Darb es Sultana) (Sultan's Way)
Trade route from Coastal Plain to Hills of Edom. Course: Gaza-Ḥaluẓa-area of Sede Boqer-Naḥal Ẓin-'En Yahav-Ma'on (Ma'an).

Derekh HaYam *(via maris)*
An important ancient route which connected Egypt to Aram Naharaim and, in part, passed through Ereẓ Israel. Its course from S to N was: Egyptian Plain, W coast of Sinai, area of El 'Arish, Gaza, Ashdod. Here it split into 2 branches, one E through Lod and the other W through Jaffa. In N Samaria, near Pardes Ḥanna, the two joined and route

continued N on E side of Coastal Plain, passed through Biq'at 'Iron and reached Yizre'el Valley. Once again it split into 2 branches, one passed through Bet She'an Valley, Bet Yeraḥ, the Golan and on to Damascus; the second through Lower Galilee, Upper Galilee, Benot Ya'aqov Bridge and on to Damascus. From Damascus it again split into 2 branches, one E to Aram Naharaim and the other N to Heth.

Derekh Shur (Way of Shur) *(Gen. 16:7)*

Ancient route from Egypt to Be'er Sheva' that passed through Shur Desert (Sinai Desert). Mentioned in Bible story of Hagar.

Derekh Yair

Track in Negev and Sinai on course — Nizzana-Har Saggi-Ma'ale Elat. Named after late Yair Peled, an Israeli army officer and scout, under whose command the track was forged.

★ **Devira** *(Josh. 15:49) 133:091*

Kibbutz 17 km. N of Be'er Sheva'. Named after Biblical city, Debir, which is identified with nearby Tell Beit Mirsim. Identified today with Kh. Rabud in Hebron Hills. Area: 20,000 d. Pop.: 330. Area has many tels and ancient sites.

● **Devora** *175:217*

Moshav in Yizre'el Valley 8 km. SW of 'Afula. Founded 1956 by Moroccan immigrants from city of Marrakesh. Named after prophetess Deborah who was active in this area (Judg. 4:4). Area: 2,500 d. Pop.: 300.

○ **Dhannaba** *154:191*

Arab village E of Tulkarm. Pop.: 1,400. Remains of Roman settlement.

■ **Dimona** *(Josh. 15:22) 152:052*

Negev development town 35 km. E of Be'er Sheva'. Named after Biblical city of Judah tribal allotment. Biblical name Dimonah also preserved in nearby Kh. Umm Dumne. Founded 1955 as residence for workers in Sedom Dead Sea potash works and phosphate works at Oron. Israel's Nuclear Laboratories also located here. City developed rapidly because of full employment and geographical location – on route to Elat. Municipal boundaries encompass 30,000 d. Pop.: 30,000, 60% from N Africa. Has community of Black Hebrews from America.

● **Dishon** *198:276*

Moshav 13 km. N of Safed. Name means antelope and in Hebrew retains sound of nearby abandoned village of Deishum. Pop.: several hundreds. Because of proximity to border, has suffered from terrorist attacks.

● **Dor** *(Josh. 12:23) 143:224*

Moshav on shore of Mediterranean, S of the Karmel. Area where the Tjeker league of the Sea Peoples settled. Plentiful remains from many periods. Named after ancient royal city of the Canaanites. Founded 1949 on lands of abandoned village, Tantura, by Greek immigrants. Initially a fishing village. Area: 1,500 d. Pop.: 160. Memorial to soldiers who died in capture of Tantura. **Ancient Dor (Dora)** N of *moshav* are remains of important ancient port city Dor or Dora. Archaeological finds indicate Early Bronze Age, Iron Age, and Hellenistic to Arab Period occupation. Joshua defeated king of Dor but failed to occupy city. Conquered by King David and was residence of one of King Solomon's governors. Became capital of Assyrian coastal province and a Greek city during Hellenistic Period. Conquered by Alexander Yannai. Jewish population declined after destruction of Second Temple. Destroyed in 4th c. CE but resettled in 7th c. Had a Crusader fortress called Castellum Merle. After its destruction was called Kh. el Burj in Arabic. During Ottoman Period Arab village of Tantura located here. Remains include ancient port, burial caves, Hellenistic temple, Roman theatre, large and splendid Byzantine basilica-type church paved with mosaics, Crusader fortress, city wall and mosque.

Dor Island *143:224*

Group of 4 islands off coast of Dor which form one island during ebb tide. Names are: Dor, Shaḥafit (after sea terns who nest here), Taphath (after daughter of King Solomon, wife of Governor of Dor, I Kings 4:11) and Ḥofami (for plovers who nest here).

★ **Dorot** *116:101*

Kibbutz 5 km. SE of Sederot. Name is an acronym for *D*ov, *R*ivqa and *T*irza — in memory of Dov Hos, labour leader and one of founders of Aḥdut Ha'Avoda, and his wife and daughter who were killed in a road accident. Founded 1941. Served as Haganah and Palmaḥ base before War of Independence and for Negev Brigade during war. Area: 20,000 d. Pop.: 500. Nearby is Tell Huj with remains from Roman-Byzantine Period.

◆ **Doshen** *201:217*

Farm 7 km. NE of Bet She'an. Name means fertile soil.

Dotan (temporary name) *169:193*

Civilian outpost in Samarian Hills 7 km. N of Sabastiya. Established 1977 near British Mandate Tegart police fort.

● **Dovev** *188:273*

Moshav adjacent to Lebanese border. Name is acronym of *D*avid *B*loch *B*lumenfeld, a former labour leader. Founded 1963 by Moroccan immigrants.

o **(Ed) Duma** *184:162*

Arab village on E slope of Samarian Hills 17 km. SW of Adam Bridge. Pop.: 550. Perhaps site of Biblical city of Arumah (Judg. 9:41).

o **Duma (Kh. Dumat ed Deir)** *(Josh. 15:52) 148:093*

Arab village 17 km. SW of Hebron and Be'er Sheva' road. Pop.: 650. Perhaps site of ancient Dumah, one of 9 cities in Hebron district.

o **Dura (Adorayim)** *(II Chron. 11:9) 152:101*

Arab village 8 km. SW of Hebron. Pop.: 5,000. **Adorayim** Mentioned in Bible as one of cities of Judea fortified by Rehoboam. John Hyrcanus captured city and forced its inhabitants to convert to Judaism. Today's village has remains of ancient buildings and nearby are cave tombs. Sherds indicate occupation in Iron Age II B, Hasmonean Period, Roman and Byzantine Periods and Middle Ages. Local tradition has it that Noah was buried here.

∴ **(Ed) Dura** (on Golan Heights) *212:266*

Abandoned village 4 km. SE of Benot Ya'aqov Bridge, on site of ancient settlement. Sherds indicate Bronze Age occupation. Remains of city wall and buildings from Hasmonean, Roman-Byzantine and Ottoman Periods.

o **Dura el Qari'** *172:151*

Arab village 8 km. N of Ramallah. Pop.: 600. Ancient settlement remains.

E

Eder *177:271*

Look-out point in Galilee 3 km. NE of Ma'alot-Tarshiḥa. Named after type of tree grown in area. Established 1979.

o **'Eilabun** *187:249*

Arab village 13 km. NW of Tiberias. Established more than 100 years ago by residents of Deir Ḥanna village. Pop.: 2,000, mostly Christian (95%). Has 2 churches. Nearby is 'Eilabun tunnel of National Water Carrier. Water is pumped through this tunnel from Ma'agar Ẓalmon to Ma'agar Bet Netofa. **'Eilabo** Roman-Byzantine town. Residence of one priestly Temple clan. Mentioned in poetry of Eleazar Kallir (7th c. CE). During Middle Ages pilgrims visited local tomb of Tanna Mattiah b. Ḥeresh. Burial caves and other ancient remains not as yet investigated.

o **'Eilat 'Ali** *171:120*

Arab village 5 km. S of Bethlehem.

o **'Einabus** *173:172*

Arab village, pop.: 550, 8 km. S of Shekhem.

o **'Ein 'Arik** *163:146*

Arab village, pop.: 650, with flowing spring, 6 km. W of Ramallah. Remnants of Paleolithic settlement discovered within village.

o **'Ein el Asad** *187:260*

Druze village in Upper Galilee 9 km. E of Karmi'el. Established about 80 years ago by residents of Beit Jann village. Pop.: 440.

o **'Ein el Beida** *180:185*

Arab village in Samarian Hills 8 km. SW of Tubas. Local springs within nature reserve constitute one of water sources of Naḥal Tirẓa.

'Ein ed Dirwa *159:111*

Spring in Judean Hills 6 km. N of Hebron, near ruins of Bet Ẓur. Name means spring of the peak. (Spring originates 960 m. above sea level.) According to Christian tradition believed to be St. Philip's fountain. Ruins of Roman way-station, burial caves and Byzantine church.

'Ein ed Duk **('Ein ed Duyuk)** *190:144*

Flowing spring 3 km. NW of Jericho with pools and aqueduct nearby.

'Ein Fara *179:138*

Large spring in bed of Wadi Fara 8 km. NE of Jerusalem. Over spring is defunct pumping station used to supply water to Old City of Jerusalem. Nearby are 2 monasteries (Greek and Latin), partially built out of the living rock. The Greek one, St. Chariton's, is still inhabited by one monk and the monastery is 1,650 years old, the oldest monastery in the Holy Land. Kh. 'Ein Fara, 1.5 km. from spring, is a small tel and perhaps site of Biblical Parah (Josh. 18:23). Excavations revealed remains of city wall, watch-tower, moat, dam and other buildings — one of stone and another of bricks. Finds indicate occupation from Early Bronze Age until Byzantine Period.

‘Ein el Fari‘a *183:188*

Large spring in Samarian Hills 4 km. SW of Tubas. Major water source for Naḥal Tirẓa (Wadi el Fari‘a) that drains into Jordan River. Near spring is ancient tel, Kh. el Fari‘a. Conjectured site of ancient city of Tirzah. Nearby are remains of 12th c. Crusader fortress, Burj el Fari‘a.

‘Ein Fashkha → ‘Enot Ẓuqim

‘Ein el Fawwar *183:138*

Spring in Jerusalem Hills at ascent of Wadi Qilt 3 km. NW of Ma‘ale Adummim. Name means bubbling spring — its flow is not uniform. During British and Jordanian rule its waters were piped to Jerusalem. Next to spring is ancient pool and canal. Nearby, remains of a 5th or 6th c. church with mosaic floor have been uncovered.

∴ **‘Ein Fit** *216:292*

Abandoned village in Golan Heights 2 km. SE of Banyas. In centre of village is spring covered by constructed dome. Ancient building stones have been re-used in village houses.

‘Ein Ghadyan → Yotvata

‘Ein el Ghuweir → ‘Enot Qane

‘Ein Ḥajla *198:137*

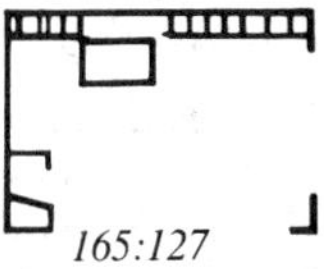

Spring 6 km. NE of Jericho. Alongside it are remains of large Roman structure which was used till Arab Period. The building is rectangular, around a central courtyard with rows of rooms leading off it.

‘Ein el Ḥaniyya *165:127*

Spring in Judean Hills 2 km. NE of Battir village. Alongside are remains of 6th c. Byzantine church. Christian tradition identifies this spring with the St. Philip's fountain mentioned in New Testament.

‘Ein Ḥusb → Ḥaẓeva (oasis)

o **‘Ein Ibrahim** *164:215*

Arab village (pop.: 250) in Biq‘at ‘Iron 3 km. NW of Umm el Faḥm. Named after Patriarch Abraham who is also revered by Arabs and who, according to local tradition, passed by here.

‘Ein el Khandaq *163:129*

Spring in Judean Hills, near *moshav* Even Sappir. Name means tunnel spring. Used in ancient days for step irrigation. Has remains of tunnels hewn out of rock, which led water to small pools and from there to irrigated lands.

‘Ein el Khirba *192:275*

Ruins of ancient settlement near Lebanese border, adjacent to Yir'on. Site has column fragments and lintel with inscription.

‘Ein Mahil *183:236*

Arab village 5 km. NE of Nazareth. Name means quiet waters. On site of settlement called ‘Ein Mahir in Crusader Period. Perhaps site of town called Mahir and mentioned in Talmud. Pop.: 4,400.

‘Ein Miri‘ *191:272*

Spring in Galilee 4 km. NE of Ḥiram junction, adjacent to tel with remains from Chalcolithic Period and Middle Bronze Age. Also scattered flint artifacts from Paleolithic Period.

‘Ein en Nu‘aima *190:144*

Flowing spring 4 km. NW of Jericho, adjacent to Ein ed Duk. Alongside it is an aqueduct.

‘Ein el Qilt *185:138*

Gushing spring in Judean Desert 3 km. NE of Ma‘ale Adummim. Some sections of the aqueduct carrying its waters to Jericho can be traced to ancient times.

○ **‘Ein Qinya** *164:148*

Arab village (pop.: 100) 6 km. NW of Ramallah.

‘Ein el Qudeirat → Qadesh Barnea‘

○ **‘Ein Qunya** *218:293*

Druze village on Golan Heights 3 km. NW of Mas‘ada junction. Pop.: 600. Has tomb believed to be that of sister of en Nabi Shu‘ayb, Jethro, father-in-law of Moses. Within village is tel which was inhabited in Early Bronze Age and Roman-Byzantine Period. S of village is new bridge across stream built to replace the one destroyed by retreating Syrian army during Six-Day War. Called Bridge of Friendship to commemorate Israeli-Druze friendship.

○ **‘Ein Rafa** *161:133*

Arab village in Judean Hills, 2 km. SW of Ḥemed interchange. Pop.: 600.

○ **‘Ein es Sahla** *161:210*

Arab village in Samarian Hills 4 km. SW of Umm el Faḥm. Pop.: 600.

‘Ein Samiya *182:155*

Large spring on border of Judean Desert 15 km. NE of Ramallah. Its waters flow into small fertile valley. Archaeological survey indicates ancient settlement on this site. On hill N of spring is Kh. el Marjana — remains of Late Bronze Age settlement with 30 tombs with pottery and weapons. Most important find was a silver goblet decorated with scenes from Mesopotamian mythology. Also remains of Late Bronze and Iron Age settlements, including tomb and structure believed to be a ritual platform. Believed to be site of Baal-shalishah, mentioned in description of one of Elisha's miracles (II Kings 4:42). Remains of Roman and Byzantine settlement uncovered other side of spring (Kh. Samiya), including dam walls, aqueducts, a church and cemetery.

∴ **‘Ein Simsim** *216:270*

Abandoned village 8 km. E of Benot Ya‘aqov Bridge. Built on ruins of Roman settlement. Ancient building stones, some of them carved, have been re-used in village houses. Among stones is a large carved lintel depicting a mythological scene of a man standing between a lion and lioness suckling her cub.

○ **‘Ein Sinya** *171:153*

Arab village (pop.: 350) 6 km. N of Ramallah. Perhaps site of ancient city Jeshanah (II Chron. 13:19). In 1908 the Shertok family (parents of Moshe Sharett, Israel's first foreign minister and second prime minister) settled in village. In one of tomb caves in village is an inscription with Hebrew name.

‘Ein Sitt Maryam → Jerusalem — Pool of Siloam

‘Ein Wazani *207:297*

Large spring in ravine of Naḥal Senir (Ḥaṣbani) adjacent to Lebanese border.

○ **‘Ein Yabrud** *173:151*

Arab village 7 km. NE of Ramallah. Pop. 1,500.

‘Ein ez Zeitun → ‘En Zetim

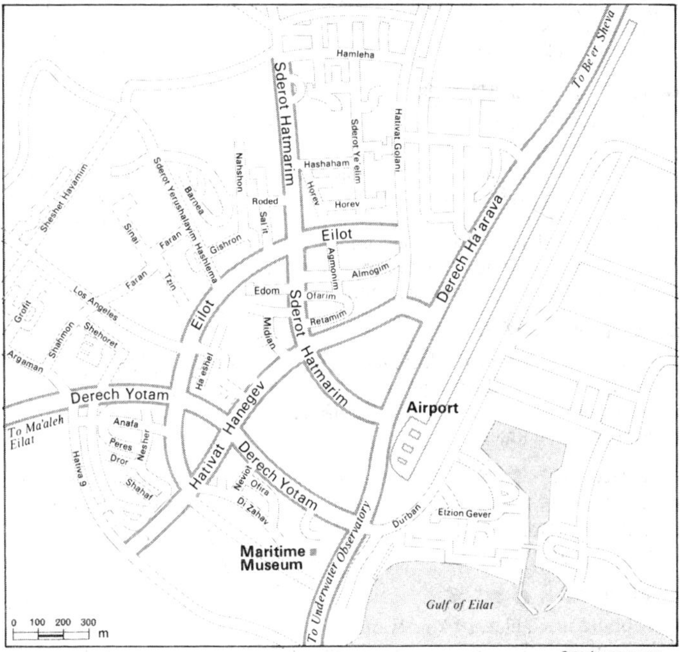

o (El) 'Eizariyya *174:130*

Arab village at E approach to Jerusalem. Pop.: 3,600, Christian and Moslem. Purported to be site of Bethany where Jesus resurrected Lazarus, brother of Mary and Martha, as related in New Testament. The grotto on the site of Lazarus' tomb was enshrined in 4th c. Has 27 steps leading down to tomb. In 16th c. Moslems built a mosque over grotto; in 17th c. Christians were allowed to pray inside. Nearby tower is last remnant of fortified monastery built in 12th c. by Crusader Queen Melisande. Orthodox school and Anglican refugee centre are also located here. Today, the Franciscan Church of St. Lazarus, built 1952, stands by the grotto.

■ Elat *(II Kings 14:22)* *145:885*

Port on Gulf of Elat. Ancient settlement mentioned several times in Bible as Eloth or Elath. Important during kingdoms of Judah and Israel. Solomon built large navy at Ezion-geber, apparently near here. Because of strategic position on major trade and travel route, many vied to control Ezion-geber. Captured and held by Edomites for short while and then taken by Azariah, king of Judah and son of Amaziah, who rebuilt Elath in place of the destroyed Ezion-geber. During Roman Period it was called Aila and a military garrison was stationed here. Conquered by Byzantines, Arabs, Crusaders, Mamluks, Ottomans and finally by British who built a police station here called Umm Rashrash. On March 10, 1949, it was captured in operation "'Uvda" by Negev and Golani Brigades. Modern town of Elat was founded in 1951, but did not develop until 1956 when Egyptian blockade of Red Sea was lifted. After Sinai Campaign it developed rapidly. Present pop.: 17,500. **Archaeological sites** 'Ezyon Gever, near Jordanian border; Coral Island with Crusader fortress. Elat Coral Reserve — underwater aquarium 8 km. S of town. Resort centre with international airport.

● El'azar ✿ *163:118*

Moshav shittufi in N sector of 'Ezyon Bloc 8 km. SW of Bethlehem. Founded 1975. Named for Eleazar the Hasmonean who died in battle with Greeks in area.

● Eli 'Al *219:245*

Moshav on Golan Heights 10 km. NE of 'En Gev. Named in memory of Israel's most famous spy, Eli Cohen, who was hanged in Syria. Founded in 1968 as *moshav shittufi* on abandoned Syrian village of El 'Al. Adopted its present name in 1973. Area: 4,500 d. Pop.: several tens. **El 'Al** Just SE of Eli 'Al is abandoned Syrian village built on ruins of ancient settlement from Hasmonean, Roman and Byzantine Periods. Dwellings in village built partly from sections of ancient pillars and capitals, some bearing inscriptions.

● Elifelet *202:261*

Moshav 3 km. S of Rosh Pinna. Name refers to return of Jews to their land of refuge. Also name of one of King David's sons (I Chron. 3:8). Pop.: 400, mainly of N African origin. Nearby at Kh. Duvshan is a prehistoric dolmen.

● Elishama' *143:173*

Moshav 2 km. S of Kefar Sava. Name Biblical — a man from tribe of Ephraim (Num. 1:10). Area: 1,600 d. Pop.: 650. Byzantine pottery remains found here.

★ Elon ✿ *171:274*

Kibbutz in Galilee 10 km. E of Rosh HaNiqra junction. Name means oak; many oaks and terebinths in surrounding area. Organized in 1935 by Polish groups; settled in 1938 as a "stockade and tower" kibbutz. Cut off for 6 months in War of Independence. Children evacuated to Haifa in "Ben Ami" operation. After war, area of kibbutz increased and is today 3,200 d. Pop.: several hundred.

Elone Mamre *(Gen. 13:18) 161:107*

Ruins 2 km. N of Hebron. Believed to be site of Biblical Elone Mamre, the *oaks* of Mamre, site of Abraham's dwelling place. Remains of enclosure, 50x65 m., built by Hadrian. Two courses of large stones, some measuring 6 m. in length, are all that remain today. Site of Botnah (mentioned in Talmud and Midrash) where trade fairs were held. Captives of Bar Kokhba War were sold here into slavery. Emperor Constantine built church on site, remains of which can still be seen.

Elon More *(Gen. 12:6) 182:180*

Jewish settlement in Samarian Hills, 5 km. E of Shekhem, on hill Jebel el Kabir. Name Biblical (Gen. 12:6). Abraham's first stop in Canaan. Founded in 1980 by a group of settlers from Gush Emunim. In 1975 the settlers were allowed to reside temporarily in Qadum army camp, 10 km. E of Shekhem. In 1979 they moved to their designated permanent residence near the Arab village of Rujeib, 4 km. SE of Shekhem. As a result of a court injunction accompanied by a political and public storm, the settlers were forced to move to their present site.

★ Elot ✿ *(I Kings 9:26) 146:887*

Kibbutz 5 km. N of Elat. Name Biblical, "...Ezion-geber which is near Eloth on the shore of the Red Sea..." Area: 1,000 d. Pop.: several hundred.

Elqana *153:168*

Civilian outpost in W Samarian Hills 8 km. E of Rosh Ha'Ayin. Named after Elkana, father of Samuel (I Sam. 1:1). Founded in 1977. Has library named after Amihai Paglin, who planned Acre prison-break and was made famous in Otto Preminger's film, Exodus.

● **Elqosh** (*Nah. 1:1*) *180:271*

Moshav in Galilee 8 km. W of Sasa junction. Name Biblical — birthplace of Prophet Nahum, assumed to be reflected in name of Arab village Deir el Qasi. Flowing spring, 'Ein Elqosh, near *moshav*. **Antiquities** Small cave tomb, Hebrew inscription on wall of abandoned house. Finds indicate occupation in Roman, Byzantine and Arab Periods.

Elro'i *160:235*

Neighbourhood within Qiryat Tiv'on. Originally a *moshav* founded in 1935 by Kurdistan immigrants. Named after David Elro'i, leader of 12th c. messianic movement in Kurdistan.

★ **Elrom** *223:287*

Kibbutz at foot of Mt. Hermonit 8 km. NW of Quneitra. *Rom* means height, and Elrom is the highest settlement in country (1,050 m. above sea level). Area: 5,000 d. Most members are native-born and some are immigrants from N America.

Elyakhin *143:203*

Rural settlement 3 km. S of Ḥadera. Pop.: 1,800.

● **Elyaqim** *156:226*

Moshav in Ramot Menashe 5 km. SW of Yokne'am. Named after Eliakim, master of Hezekiah's household (Isa. 36:3). Area: 2,200 d. Pop.: 600.

● **Elyashiv** *141:198*

Moshav 7 km. S of Ḥadera. Founded in 1933. Pop.: 450, Yemenite immigrants.

'Emeq 'Akko → 'Emeq Zevulun

'Emeq Ayyalon (Valley) (*Josh. 10:12*)

Valley in Judean Foothills between central Coastal Plain and Judean Hills. Runs NE to SW as far as Latrun junction. Course of 2 important routes from Coastal Plain to mountain ridge: through Sha'ar HaGay and through Ma'ale Bet Ḥoron. Because of geographic position and strategic importance, it has always been a military and political objective and therefore often a battlefield. Mentioned in one of Tell el 'Amarna letters as route for caravans to Egypt. Here Joshua smote the Amorite kings (Josh. 10:12) and Saul and Jonathan pursued the Philistines (I Sam. 14:31). Fierce battles raged here in days of Hasmoneans and Romans, during Arab conquest (7th c. CE) and Crusader Period. During War of Independence, Arab Legion succeeded in blocking passage through the valley and Israeli attempts to break through failed. Valley was taken in Six-Day War. Since then, a number of new settlements have been established here, a new highway has been paved which has shortened the distance between Jerusalem and Ben-Gurion Airport. At its S end is the recently laid out Canada Park.

'Emeq Bet She'an (Valley) (*Josh. 17:11*)

The central and widest part of Jordan Valley. Boundaries: N — Naḥal Tavor, E — Jordan River, S — Wadi Maliḥ, W — Mt. Gilboa'. Named after ancient city of Beth-shean located in centre of valley. Because of its width, it forms a convenient course for the Jordan River and has always been an important junction. Has good soil and many water sources and was therefore densely settled from Chalcolithic Period until Middle Ages. During Ottoman Period settlement dwindled and valley was covered with swamps. During British Mandate Jews attempted to revive settlement but British authorities obstructed them. Jews finally began settling area in 1936-1939, but the new settlement suffered from Arab attacks during War of Independence. After Six-Day War the entire area was wrested from Jordanian control.

'Emeq Dotan (Valley) **(Sahl 'Arraba)** *(Gen. 37:17)*

Narrow valley in N Samarian Hills, SW of Jenin. General direction: NE-SW; the Shekhem-Jenin road passes through SE side of valley. Name derived from ancient city located here (see Tel Dotan). During Six-Day War a tank battle took place here between Israeli and Jordanian armies.

'Emeq HaEla (Valley) *(I Sam. 17:2)*

Small valley on border of Judean Hills 8 km. S of Bet Shemesh. Important route from foothills to hills. Origin of name is ancient, probably after indigenous terebinth trees (*ela* = terebinth). Three streams: Sansan, 'Ezyona and HaEla descend from Hebron Hills, drain into valley and join with Naḥal Lakhish in Coastal Plain. In ancient days it was a battlefield between Israel and Philistines, where David slew Goliath (I Sam. 17). In centre of valley is kibbutz Netiv HaLamed He and nearby a Ministry of Communications satellite receiving station. Valley is populous with post-War of Independence settlements: Ḥevel HaHar in N and E, Ḥevel 'Adullam in S and Ḥevel Lakhish in E.

'Emeq HaMikhmetat (Valley) **(Sahl Makhna)** *(Josh. 16:6)*

Fertile valley S of Shekhem at foot of Mt. Gerizim. Name mentioned in Bible as boundary of Ephraimites.

'Emeq HaYarden **(Biq'at HaYarden) (Jordan Valley)**

Narrow and long valley along Jordan River; part of Syrian-E African rift. Divides the Jordan area in two: Cisjordan and Transjordan. It runs from slopes of Mt. Ḥermon to N of Dead Sea for 168 km. and its rate of descent from N to S is 725 m. Its major sections from N to S: Upper Jordan Valley (or Ḥula Valley), Lake Kinneret Basin, Middle Jordan Valley (includes Bet She'an Valley) and Lower Jordan Valley ending at the Jericho Plains. The name Jordan Valley is sometimes used for middle and lower sections and sometimes only for the middle section. Archaeological surveys indicate that the area was occupied as early as Neolithic Period and, according to historical records, was a battle zone in almost every age. When Jewish settlement was revived in Ereẓ Israel, most of the Jordan Valley was desolate swampland. The first Jewish settlement — Yesud HaMa'ala — in Ḥula Valley was established in 1883. The first settlements in Middle Jordan Valley were established at beginning of 20th c. (Menaḥemya — 1902, Kinneret Farm — 1908, Kinneret Moshava — 1909, and Deganya "A" — 1909). Later, Jewish settlement continued to develop chiefly in Ḥula Valley, Lake Kinneret Basin and Middle Jordan Valley. In War of Independence Arab armies from Syria, Iraq and Jordan invaded Jordan Valley. Armistice agreements left Lower Jordan Valley within Kingdom of Jordan, but it was recaptured by Israel in Six-Day War. After the war Jewish settlements were established here, most of them *naḥal* outposts. The valley is commonly called the Biq'a (the valley).

'Emeq Ḥefer (Valley) **(Wadi el Ḥawarith)** *(I Kings 4:10)*

Valley (also known as Ḥefer Plain) in Central Sharon through which last section of Naḥal Alexander passes (Wadi el Ḥawarith). Hebrew name based on assumption that this was Hepher district during King Solomon's reign. In 1930 swamp drainage and land reclamation begun. In 1933 the first settlement — Kefar Vitkin — was established.

‘Emeq Ḥula (Valley)

Valley at E end of Upper Galilee. Boundaries N and W — mountains of Upper Galilee, E — Golan Heights, S — mountains of Galilee and Golan Heights. Length from N to S — 20 km., average width — 7 km. The Jordan sources enter the valley in the N and emerge in S as single river. Known in Talmud as Hulata and in Midrashim as Hulat Antokhia. The lake in centre has been known by many names: Agam Ḥula, Yam Ḥula, Yam Samkhi and Me Merom. During Israelite conquest, the N part was in Dan's tribal allotment and the S part in Naphtali's. According to sources, also settled during Roman and Byzantine Periods. These settlements were destroyed and valley became a desert as a result of wars between Crusaders and Moslems. Jewish settlers in modern period found area full of swamps and malaria, and sparsely populated with Bedouin. In 1883 the farming village of Yesud HaMa‘ala was established S of lake but intensified settlement in the area began after JNF purchased concession for S section of valley. In 1951 a drainage project got under way, encompassing an area of 37,000 d. After the 7-year project was completed, large tracts of fertile land became available for cultivation. **Nature reserve** Part of lake and swamp (3,100 d.) has been preserved as a reserve of typical local flora and fauna. Until Six-Day War settlements in valley suffered from Syrian shelling.

‘Emeq Maharal

Small valley S of Mt. Karmel. Named thus because of Kerem Maharal situated at its W end.

‘Emeq Yizre‘el (Valley) *(Josh. 19:18)*

Large fertile valley that extends the width of the country between the hilly regions of the Galilee and Samaria. Named after ancient city of Jezreel. It is crossed by vital arteries including ancient international routes (through Naḥal ‘Iron and Naḥal Yoqne‘am). It was, therefore, during all periods, a battleground against invading armies from N, S, E and W. When the Israelites entered the country, the valley was inhabited by Canaanites whom Joshua failed to dislodge. Only after their defeat at the hands of Deborah and Barak, son of Abinoam, did valley come under Israelite control providing territorial continuity between the Israelite tribes in N and in central regions. Valley was scene of battle between Israelites and Philistines in which Saul and his sons were killed. It became one of 12 districts under King Solomon and he built cities and fortifications here. After division of the kingdom, it was included in Kingdom of Israel. In 733 BCE, it was conquered by Tiglath-pileser III and turned into an Assyrian province. For a long period the valley remained desolate until settlement was renewed during Hellenistic Period. Captured from the Greeks by John Hyrcanus, the Hasmonean, and annexed to his kingdom. At beginning of Roman Period it was detached from Kingdom of Judah, but was later returned. An important Jewish centre after destruction of Second Temple and during Roman and Byzantine Period. Laid waste during Arab conquest in 7th c. Once again the valley served as a battlefield for Crusaders and Moslems, and then for Mamluks and Seljuks. During Ottoman Period became property of Sultan (lands of Jiftliq). In 1799 Napoleon's armies fought here against the Turks. Renewal of Jewish settlement in the country at end of 19th c. found valley completely desolate, partly covered with deadly swamps. Turks thwarted attempted settlement in 1890. Only at beginning of 20th c. did Yehoshua Hankin succeed in purchasing a small tract of land upon which Merḥavya (1911) and Tel ‘Adashim (1913) were established. During WWI it was again a battlefield, this time between the Turks and Germans against the British. After the war Hankin was able to purchase larger tracts of land upon which in 1921, ‘En Ḥarod in the E and Nahalal in the W were established. From that year onward the valley flourished.

'Emeq Zevulun (Valley)

Valley in N of country along Haifa Bay. Length 14 km. and maximum width 9 km. Boundaries: N — Naḥal Na'aman, E — Hills of Lower Galilee, S — Mt. Karmel and W — Mediterranean Sea. To N of valley is ancient port city of Acre; to S is Haifa, largest port in country and an industrial centre. Name from Jacob's blessing: "Zebulun shall dwell at the shore of the sea" (Gen. 49:13). Also known as 'Emeq 'Akko, Shefelat Haifa-'Akko and Mifraẓ Haifa. A battlefield during Arab conquest (7th c.) and Crusader Period (12th and 13th c). In 1920 Jewish settlement here was renewed. Today valley accommodates suburban communities and industrial complexes.

∴ Emmaus ('Imwas) *(Luke 24:13)* *149:138*

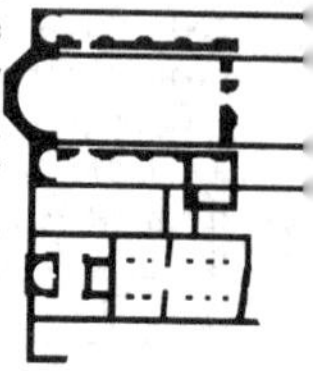

Ruins of settlement and archaeological site within Canada Park 2 km. N of Latrun junction. Some believe it to be the New Testament Emmaus, where Cleopas and Simon saw the risen Jesus, as told in Luke's Gospel. Strategic site from ancient times. Encampment of Seleucid army soundly routed by Judah Maccabee in 166 BCE. Important road fortress during Roman conquest and Fifth Macedonian Legion camped here during the great Revolt against Rome. Site of health resort with hot springs during Roman Period. Called Nicopolis (city of victory) on Madaba map indicating its importance in Byzantine Period. Major camp of invading Arab armies of 639 CE. Site of 12th c. Crusader fortress called Le Toron des Chevaliers (knights'- fortress), hence the name Latrun. Captured by Israel Defence Forces during Six-Day War. Remains of almost completely preserved Roman villa and bathhouse; incriptions of Fifth Roman Legion; Byzantine and Crusader churches. Nearby is the French Trappist Monastery. Monks belong to ascetic order founded at Soligny-la-Trappe, France. In 1927 they built Italianate building which graces hillside. Here they make wine from grapes of surrounding vineyards. The monks maintain vow of silence.

● Emunim *119:128*

Moshav 7 km. SE of Ashdod. Name taken from Biblical passage "the Lord preserves the *faithful*" (Ps. 31:23).

'Enan (Mallaḥa) *203:277*

Large spring in Upper Galilee 3 km. S of Koaḥ junction. Remains of prehistoric settlement nearby. Excavations uncovered 3 levels from Mesolithic Period containing circular dwellings, the most ancient discovered to date in this area. All levels contained graves with skeletons, basalt and stone artifacts, bone implements, beads and other objects.

'En 'Aqev *132:025*

Oasis in ravine of Naḥal Ẓin 5 km. NE of 'Avedat. Has dense growth of tamarisks, a large and deep pool, and 12 m. high waterfall.

'En 'Aqrabbim → 'En Ẓin

★ 'Enat *145:165*

Kibbutz in Sharon 3 km. E of Petaḥ Tiqwa. Origin of name: its proximity to sources of Yarqon River (*'enot* = sources). Area: 5,100 d. Pop.: 520.

'En 'Avedat *127:026*

Spring in Negev Hills 5 km. SW of Sede Boqer. Its waters flow into Naḥal Ẓin and form beautiful steep waterfalls and pools along its way. In the early morning and evening a herd of ibex drink here and can be seen climbing up sheer face of cliff.

'En 'Avrona *149:894*

Salt water spring in 'Arava 15 km. NE of Elat. Nearby are remains of farm from beginning of Arab Period. Consists mainly of 2 perpendicular rows of rooms, brick-built on stone foundation, with large courtyard between them containing kitchen and large granary. Excavations uncovered pottery, remains of food and bits of cloth. Near farm is a chain of wells connected by an underground canal.

'En Awwazim *203:284*

Nature reserve in Ḥula Valley, 2 km. W of Ne'ot Mordekhay. Area: 80 d. *Pistacia atlantica* trees grown here.

● **'En Ayyala** *144:226*

Moshav on Karmel coast 6 km. N of Zikhron Ya'aqov. Name taken from abandoned village of 'Ein Ghazal. (*Ghazal* in Arabic means gazelle and *ayyala* in Hebrew means roe-deer.) Area: 2,600 d. Pop.: 240.

'En Beroshim → Bet Zayit

'En Boqeq *184:067*

Health and holiday resort on W coast of Dead Sea 13 km. S of Masada. Hotels, health spas, camping sites, observation point and swimming beach. Nearby is ancient site (see Meẓad Boqeq).

★ **'En Dor** *(Josh. 17:11) 189:229*

Kibbutz in Galilee 4 km. SE of Mt. Tabor. Name from Biblical city En-dor, a name which was possibly retained in that of abandoned village, Indur. Area: 10,500 d. Pop.: 640. Within kibbutz, on stony hill, are remains of rock-cut tombs and many sherds from Roman and Byzantine Periods. **Ḥurbat Zafzafot** (Kh. Ṣafṣafa). SW of kibbutz *187:227* adjacent to spring now called 'En Dor are remains of settlement that according to sherds was occupied in Early Bronze Age, Iron Age, Roman and Arab Periods. Perhaps site of Biblical En-dor, referred to in story of King Saul and the witch (I Sam. 28:7 ff.).

★ **'En Gedi** *(Josh. 15:62) 186:095*

Oasis on Dead Sea shore 17 km. N of Masada. En-gedi, fountain of the kid, is where the Shulamite watered her flocks and King Solomon sought her among the cascades of water, banana groves, rosebeds and vineyards. Among the most beautiful oases in the Middle East, 'En Gedi is mentioned in Song of Songs (1:14): "My beloved is unto me as a cluster of camphire in the vineyards of En-gedi." Near the 200 m. high waterfall is a stalactite cave, where David had his famed meeting with King Saul (I Sam. 24:1-17). Adjacent kibbutz named after ancient settlement whose remains were excavated at nearby Tel Goren (Tell el Jurn). Founded as *nahal* outpost in 1953, on 400 d., it was developed for cultivation by washing saline soil with fresh water. Pop.: several hundred. N of kibbutz *187:097* is youth hostel and field school with local museum, swimming beach and picnic site. To W is 'En Gedi nature reserve incorporating springs of Naḥal David and Naḥal 'Arugot, observation point and antiquities. **Ancient En-gedi** Findings in excavations at Tell el Jurn (site of ancient En-gedi) indicate area was already settled in Chalcolithic Period. Bible identifies site with Hazazon-tamar (II Chron. 20:2). First mentioned in story of Abraham's victory over Chedorlaomer and other kings (Gen. 14:7), it later fell within Judah's tribal allotment. David hid from Saul in "strongholds of En-gedi" (I Sam. 23:29) and battle between men of Judah, Ammon and Moab was fought nearby (II Chron. 20:1-31). En-gedi was apparently destroyed during Nebuchadnezzar's siege of Jerusalem, but renewed following Babylonian Exile. Eusebius mentions a Jewish community in En-gedi in 4th c. CE which existed until

Byzantine Period. **Antiquities** Tel Goren *187:096* excavations uncovered 5 occupation levels dating intermittently from First Temple Period until Byzantine Period. NE of tel remains of 6th c. synagogue mosaic floor with Hebrew inscription: "Peace on Israel" were discovered, as well as remains of a large Chalcolithic enclosure. Iron Age remains of tower were found close to observation point, where remnants of Israelite and Roman fortress are still extant. Above Naḥal 'Arugot, at 2 different locations are remains of long buildings with many rooms. These were possibly dwellings for Essene sect. On slope of hill N of 'En Gedi field school, buildings of undressed stone containing ovens, pottery and food traces were found. Sherds indicate occupation from Roman until Arab Periods.

★ **'En Gev** *210:243*

Kibbutz on E shore of Lake Kinneret 10 km. NE of Zemaḥ junction. Restaurant on shore offers famous St. Peter's fish. Boats make regular crossings to Tiberias and back. Name from nearby site known in Arabic as en Nuqeib (the tunnel or passage). Founded in 1937 as "stockade and tower" settlement. Lacking a suitable land approach, the first settlers came by boat from Tiberias. During War of Independence and until Six-Day War, kibbutz often attacked by Syrians. Area: 4,800 d. Pop.: 430. Large concert hall in which the annual 'En Gev Music Festival takes place during Passover. Statue of mother and child by Chana Orloff. **Antiquities** Discoveries at tel within kibbutz of sherds and other remains from Iron Age, post-Babylonian Exile, Hellenistic, Byzantine and Arab Periods. Olive oil press also uncovered.

'En Ha'Emeq *158:226*

Rural settlement 4 km. SW of Yoqne'am junction. Area: 1,600 d. Pop.: 320.

★ **'En HaḤoresh** *145:199*

Kibbutz 6 km. S of Ḥadera. Founded 1931 by members of HaShomer HaẒa'ir in Poland. Served as Palmaḥ base before 1948. Area: 13,300 d. Pop.: 740.

'En HaMe'ara *106:980*

Spring in high Negev Hills 35 km. SE of Mizpe Ramon. Flows in underground cave, hence its name (*me'ara* = cave).

★ **'En HaMifraẓ** *159:256*

Kibbutz in Haifa Bay 3 km. SE of Acre. Founded in 1938 as "stockade and tower" settlement by HaShomer HaZa'ir group from Galicia. Served as Palmaḥ base before War of Independence and during war as a base for capture of Acre. Area: 8,000 d. Pop.: 750.

★ **'En HaNaẓiv** *195:208*

Kibbutz 3 km. S of Bet She'an. Named after Rabbi Naphtali Zevi Judah Berlin, head of Volozhin Yeshiva and supporter of Ḥoveve Ziyyon. Founded in 1946 by religious youth group from Germany as part of Youth Aliyah movement. Area: 8,200 d. Pop.: 500.

★ **'En Ḥarod** *186:219; 187:218*

Two adjacent *kibbutzim* with same name in Yizre'el Valley. Founded as one kibbutz in 1921 by pioneers of Joseph Trumpeldor's Labour Legion. First located at foot of Gilboa' near Ḥarod spring, hence its name. In 1927, settlers moved to Qumi ridge *187:218*, where Kibbutz Me'uḥad 'En Ḥarod is now located. After 1953 ideological

split, a second kibbutz *186:219* was established N of first kibbutz. **'En Harod (Me'uhad)** Area: 11,000 d. Pop.: 850. **'En Harod (Ihud)** Area: 11,000 d. Pop.: 760. **Cultural institutions** shared by both *kibbutzim*: Hayyim Atar Mishkan LaOmmanut (museum for Jewish art and artifacts), Bet Sturman Museum and Study Centre housing collections and documents on history and natural history of region and Aharon Zisling Cultural Centre. In Ihud kibbutz is Shelomo Lavi Cultural Centre. **Antiquities** Six Roman milestones were found in Me'uhad kibbutz; one of them dates from reign of Septimius Severus (195-211 CE) and marked 10th mile between Bet She'an and Legio (near Megiddo).

★ 'En HaShelosha ❀‼●🖬ˮ⅄   *093:084*

Kibbutz opposite Gaza Strip 6 km. NW of Ma'on junction. Named after 3 members of founding group who died in War of Independence (*shelosha* = three). Area: 15,000 d. Pop.: 380.

★ 'En HaShofet ❀‼●🖬ˮ⅄🚍   *159:222*

Kibbutz 7 km. S of Yoqne'am junction. Named after Louis Brandeis, Justice of US Supreme Court and American Zionist leader. Founded 1937 as "stockade and tower" settlement by HaShomer HaZa'ir groups from USA and Poland. Area: 13,800 d. Pop.: 680.

'En Hawwa   *142:015*

Spring in Negev Hills, 15 km. SE of 'Avedat, in bed of Nahal Hawwa. Flows to foot of 15 m.-high waterfall, and into small concrete tunnel.

'En Hay → Kefar Mallal

● 'En Hazeva ●⅃   *174:023*

Farm in 'Arava, 31 km. S of Sedom SE of Hurbat Hazeva ('Ein Hasb), hence its name. Area: 2,000 d. Pop.: 40.

✶ 'En Hemed (Aqua Bella)   *161:133*

Nature reserve in Judean Hills 7 km. W of Jerusalem. A landscaped meadow divided by a brook breaking into series of rock-cut pools. Spring called Iqbala in Arabic, a distortion of Latin name, *aqua bella* (pleasant water); Hebrew name is a translation. At meadow's end lie ruins of a Crusader fortified farm. Arab name is Deir el Banat (monastery for women), but there is no proof that it was a convent. The site has been restored; 40 m.-long walls enclose courtyard and hall, with a campsite alongside.

'En Hod ⌂   *148:234*

Artists' village in S Mt. Karmel, 4 km. SE of 'Atlit interchange. Named after previous Arab village on site, 'Ein Hawd. Set up as a *moshav* of Algerian immigrants in 1949. Since 1954 it is an artists' village. Pop.: 180. Many art galleries and workshops for ceramics, mosaics and lithography. Open air theatre as well. Venue for seminars on arts and handicrafts.

● 'En 'Iron ‼●ᵗ🖬ˮ⅄   *151:210*

Moshav on border of Samarian Hills-Ramat Menashe 2 km. W of 'Iron junction. Origin of name: Nahal 'Iron. Founded 1934. Area: 2,600 d. Pop.: 240.

★ 'En Karmel ❀‼●⅃🖬ˮ⅄   *146:231*

Kibbutz on Karmel coast 4 km. S of 'Atlit interchange. Established in 1947 by members of kibbutz 'En HaYam located till then on temporary site. Area: 3,500 d. Pop.: 430.

'En Kerem → Jerusalem

'En Moda' **('Ein el Maddu')** ⛰ *193:210*

Group of springs at foot of Mt. Gilboa' 4 km. SW of Bet She'an. Near springs are remains of Roman farm and aqueduct.

'En Nashut ⛰ *215:268*

Spring on Golan Heights on E bank of Naḥal Meshushim, 2 km. N of Qazrin. Nearby are remains of Second Temple Jewish settlement, small 5th c. synagogue and oil press. Apparently abandoned after Arab conquest.

'En Netafim **('Ein el Qatr)** *137:889*

Spring in Elat Hills in bed of Naḥal Netafim, 7 km. NW of Elat. Spring seeps out slowly, hence name (*netafim* = drops).

'En Nimfit *160:254*

Nature reserve in Galilee S of kibbutz Kefar Masaryk. Area: 60 d. Has natural pool containing rare water plants.

'En Notera *210:276*

Nature reserve on slopes of Golan Heights 4 km. NE of Yesud HaMa'ala. Area: 300 d. Has spring creating several shallow pools with manifold water plants. Near spring is ancient flour mill.

'Enot Ḥasida → Ḥamadya

'Enot Qane **('Ein el Ghuweir)** ⛰ *189:115*

Spring enclosed by thick foliage on W shore of Dead Sea 4 km. NE of Miẓpe Shalem. Included in 'Enot Qane nature reserve. Nearby are remains of Iron Age fortress.

'Enot Samar **('Ein et Turaba)** ⛰ *188:112*

Spring enclosed by thick foliage on shore of Dead Sea 3 km. NE of Miẓpe Shalem. Alongside it are ruins of Iron Age fortress called Qaṣr et Turaba. Excavations revealed remains of building of undressed stones with 8 rooms around a courtyard, containing column bases, cooking stove and much pottery. Near fortress are remains of other buildings. Some believe this to be the City of Salt (Josh. 15:62). The spring and fort are part of 'Enot Qane reserve.

'Enot Timsaḥ *142:216*

Natural pool in Naḥal Tanninim nature reserve near Ma'agan Mikha'el. Spring water pool is remnant of Kabara swamps, drained between 1925 and 1934.

'Enot Ẓuqim **('Ein el Fashkha)** ⛰ Λ *193:124*

Group of springs on NW shore of Dead Sea and favourite bathing resort for Jerusalemites who enjoy the mineral-rich mud packs here. Believed to be site of En-eglaim, mentioned in vision of Ezekiel (Ezek. 47:10). Remains similar to those of small Second Temple villages dotted on W shore of Dead Sea found near springs. Contemporary sherds and coins found on site. Included in area of 'Enot Ẓuqim reserve. **PEF Rock** Half km. S of springs, near road, is a rock on which Dead Sea's oscillating height was recorded between 1910 and 1913. The measurements were taken by Palestine Exploration Fund (PEF).

'En Petel *200:233*

Group of springs 4 km. SW of Deganya "A". Alongside springs are 3 ancient devices for raising water to higher level of aqueduct. One of them flows from a small cave and alongside it are remains of an ancient pool, around which Byzantine sherds were found.

'En Rogel *(Josh. 15:7)* *173:130*

Spring in Naḥal Qidron, SE of Jerusalem, near Shiloaḥ Pool. One of

Jerusalem's water sources in ancient days; mentioned in Bible several times. Arabs call it Bir Aiyub (Job's well).

'En Saharonim *143:001*

Oasis in Makhtesh Ramon next to Mount Saharonim. Formed as a result of high ground-water reservoir in bed of Naḥal Ramon. Plant-growth: palm trees, reeds and rushes. Nearby are remains of Nabatean outpost (40x40 m.) located alongside ancient "perfume route" from Arabian Peninsula past Petra and 'Avedat to Gaza coast.

'En Sarid *144:186*

Rural settlement in Sharon 6 km. SE of Sharon junction. Area: 850 d. Pop.: 410.

'En Sarig → Ora

'En Senunit ('Ein el 'Alaq) *155:219*

Prehistoric site in Ramat Menashe, 8 km. E of Zikhron Ya'aqov. Many flint tools found on site mostly from Neolithic Period and some from Chalcolithic Period. Also many Early Bronze Age sherds.

'En Shemer *150:207*

Kibbutz on border of Samarian Hills and Sharon 3 km. SW of 'Iron junction. Named after Shemer, who was owner of land upon which city of Samaria was built (I Kings 16:24). Founded in 1927 by 'En Gannim group of HaShomer HaẒa'ir from Poland. From 1942 served as Palmaḥ base. Area: 4,600 d. Pop.: 670.

'En Shemesh ('Ein el Ḥod) *(Josh. 15:7) 176:131*

Spring in Judean Hills 3 km. E of Jerusalem, N of el 'Eizariyya village on way to Jericho. Apparently site of city En-shemesh on tribal borders of Benjamin and Judah. In Christian tradition this is the Fountain of the Apostles, mentioned in New Testament. Alongside spring an abandoned building served in past as a caravanserai for travellers from Jerusalem to Jericho and Transjordan.

'En Sheva' → (Et) Tabkha

'En Shoqeq *192:211*

Ancient site SE of Mt. Gilboa' 6 km. W of Bet She'an. Has remains of Byzantine building and man-made pool.

'En Sukar → 'Askar

'En Tamar *184:043*

Moshav in N 'Arava 5 km. E of 'Arava junction. Named after nearby spring *183:044*.

'En Te'o *204:282*

Nature reserve in Ḥula Valley 2 km. N of Koaḥ junction. Area: 30 d. Spring, water plants and *pistacia atlantica* trees.

'En Tut → Bet Zayit

'En Wered *144:185*

Moshav in Sharon 2 km. NE of Tel Mond. Founded 1930. Area: 5,000 d. Pop.: 530. Within *moshav* sherds and other remains were discovered indicating ancient occupation of site.

'En Ya'aqov *171:268*

Moshav in Galilee 4 km. W of Ma'alot. Name taken from Biblical passage (Deut. 33:28) "So Israel dwelt in safety, the *fountain of Jacob* alone." Area: 550 d. Pop.: 280.

● 'En Yahav *172:007*

Moshav in 'Arava 13 km. S of Ḥaẓeva. Name similar to that of Arabic name of nearby spring, 'Ein el Weiba. Important road junction in ancient times, site of Nabatean settlement and British guard post during Mandate. Captured during operation "'Uvda" (1949). First settlement attempt was in 1950 by members of Shaḥal (pioneer service for Israel); became Gadna camp in 1953; 1954-1959 — agricultural observation station; 1959 — *naḥal* outpost of *moshav* youth and permanent *moshav* in 1962. Moved to present site in 1967. Area: 3,000 d. Pop.: several hundred. Near *moshav* is Sapir Regional Centre, named after Pinḥas Sapir, for 'Arava settlements. Near spring are remains of Nabatean irrigation system.

'En Yorqe'am **('Ein Yarqa)** *153:039*

Large water depression in Negev Hills, 5 km. E of HaMakhtesh HaGadol. Has water all year round. Rock-hewn steps lead to bottom of depression. Ruins of Roman-Byzantine fortress nearby.

'En Zetim *195:266*

Abandoned settlement 3 km. NE of Safed. Founded as farming village in 1891 by Russian immigrants near now-abandoned Arab village of 'Ein ez Zeitun. Has rather a long list of being settled and then abandoned. Resettled 1925 — abandoned and destroyed in 1929 Arab Riots; resettled 1932 — abandoned 1937 during Disturbances of 1936-1939; kibbutz established 1946 — abandoned at outbreak of War of Independence; *moshav* established 1955 — but it too was abandoned and replaced by a Gadna farm that was also abandoned. Next to abandoned village at top of hill is metal statue in shape of the letter "ש" commemorating the armoured division that fought in Golan during Six-Day War. **'Ein ez Zeitun** Nearby, abandoned Arab village built on ruins of Medieval village which, according to sources, had Jewish community from 11th to 18th c.

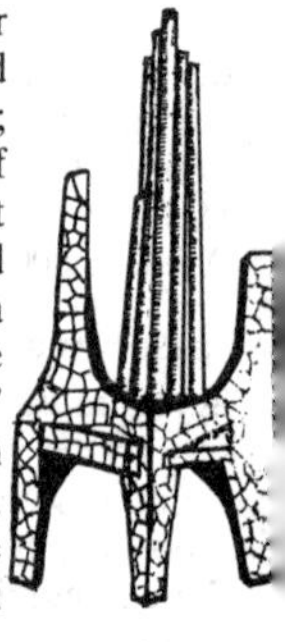

'En Ẓin *165:033*

Large oasis in Negev Hills in bed of Naḥal Ẓin, 3 km. SE of Ma'ale 'Aqrabbim. Has spring flowing over small waterfalls into pools; also large grove of palm trees. One km. SW is another oasis — **'En 'Aqrabbim.**

'En Ziq **('Ein esh Shahabiyya)** *135:023*

Oasis in ravine of Naḥal Ẓin 8 km. E of 'Avedat. Grove of poplar trees.

★ 'En Ziwan *224:278*

Kibbutz on Golan Heights 5 km. SW of Quneitra. Name originates from adjacent Circassian village, 'Ein Ziwan, meaning a type of wheat. Founded 1968 within abandoned Syrian army camp. Area: 5,000 d. Pop.: several hundred.

★ 'En Ẓurim *123:123*

Kibbutz 5 km. SW of Qiryat Mal'akhi. Named after kibbutz 'En Ẓurim in 'Eẓyon Bloc captured in War of Independence and whose members were taken as prisoners of war. Founded 1949 on lands of abandoned village Sawafir el Gharbiya by members of 'En Ẓurim freed from captivity. Area: 8,000 d. Pop.: 500.

■ Ephrata *(Gen. 35:16)* *166:119*

City under construction in Judean Hills 6 km. SW of Bethlehem. Bethlehem also called Ephrata in Bible (Gen. 35:16, Micah 5:2, Ruth 4:11).

Erez *109:107*

Farming collective (*qevuẓa*) 11 km. S of Ashqelon. Founded 1947 by group of Working and Student Youth from Petaḥ Tiqwa. Area: 8,300 d. Pop.: 300. Byzantine mosaic uncovered here.

Ereẓ Peleshet → HaShefela

Eshbol *118:096*

Moshav 7 km. NE of Netivot. *Eshbol* means ear of corn or cluster of flowers. In 1954 Eshbol company established farm on site. Area: 4,500 d. Pop.: 420.

Eshed Kinnarot → Atar Sapir

Eshel → Nir Avraham

Eshel Avraham → Hebron

Eshel HaNasi *121:081*

Agricultural high school in Negev 15 km. NW of Be'er Sheva'. Named in memory of Israel's first president, Dr. Chaim Weizmann. Founded 1952. Area: 5,000 d.

Eshkolot *117:124*

Farm 9 km. NE of Ashqelon owned by Neti'ot HaDarom company. Founded 1951. Mainly grows grapes, hence its name (*eshkolot* = bunches).

Eshta'ol *(Josh. 15:33) 151:132*

Moshav in Jerusalem corridor 4 km. NE of Bet Shemesh. Biblical Eshtaol located in this area. Pop.: 420. Nearby, district tree nursery. Ancient rock-cut tombs in area.

Eshtemoa' → Sammu'

Etan *126:109*

Moshav in Lakhish region 5 km. S of Qiryat Gat. Name Biblical "...Enduring (*etan*) is your dwelling place..." (Num. 24:21). Area: 4,000 d. Pop.: 460. Tels in the district: Tel Ḥasi, Tel Sheqef, Tel Qeshet.

Etanim *159:131*

Psychiatric hospital 8 km. W of Jerusalem. Name Biblical: "...enduring (*etanim*) foundations of the earth..." (Micah 6:2). Previously Arab agricultural school called Deir 'Amr. In War of Independence, captured by Har'el Brigade. In 1950 established as hospital for lung diseases. Now a psychiatric hospital with child and adult wards. Television relay station also situated here. **Antiquities** Remains of stone wall and many water cisterns, one with white mosaic floor; Byzantine sherds. Air Force memorial nearby, Pilots' Hill.

Even Menaḥem *177:275*

Moshav in Galilee 6 km. NW of Ma'alot. Named after Arthur (Menaḥem) Hantke, one of directors of Keren HaYesod. Pop.: 200.

Even Sappir *162:130*

Moshav in Jerusalem corridor 3 km. SW of 'En Kerem. Named after Jacob Halevi Sappir, author of *Even Sappir* and harbinger of Jewish immigration from Yemen in 1882. Founded 1950. Pop.: 500.

Even Shemu'el *127:109*

Rural centre 4 km. S of Qiryat Gat. Named after Samuel Bronfman of Canada, one of great contributors to development of Israel. Founded 1957. Pop.: 360. Services settlements belonging to Shafir local council:

Etan No'am, 'Uza and Shalwa. Elementary and junior high school, library, health centre, senior citizens club and offices of local council.

Even Yehuda *139:186*

Rural settlement 8 km. SE of Netanya. Named after Eliezer Ben-Yehuda, reviver of Hebrew language in modern times. Founded 1932 by children of veteran settlers. Pop.: 5,000. Local council includes villages of Be'er Gannim, Hadassim and Tel Zur. Memorial centre, 'En Ya'aqov, for members who fell in Israel's wars.

★ Even Yiẓḥaq (Gal'ed) *157:218*

Kibbutz in Ramat Menashe 4 km. S of kibbutz Daliyya. Founded 1945 by HaBonim group from Germany formed in 1938 on lands of Ḥubeiza village. Named after Yiẓḥaq Hochberg, South African Zionist leader. Former name was Gal'ed. Pop.: 300. Area: 14,500 d. Remains in surrounding area indicate occupation from Bronze Age to Arab Period.

★ 'Evron *(Josh. 19:28) 159:266*

Kibbutz SE of Nahariyya. Same name as Biblical Ebron located in the area. Established 1945 by immigrants from Poland, Germany and Transylvania. Before 1948 it served as Palmaḥ base and absorption centre for "illegal" immigrants. Area: 3,600 d. Pop.: 580. **Ancient remains** Local archaeological collection. Within kibbutz remains of Byzantine settlement with foundations of 5th c. church and mosaic floor. Nearby, traces of Paleolithic settlement were found.

★ Eyal *148:180*

Kibbutz 10 km. NE of Kefar Sava. Name means strength. First group, organized 1946 at Kefar Sava, settled at Ashmura in Galilee, E of Lake Ḥula. Moved in 1949 to present site. Area: 5,500 d. Pop.: 160.

'Ezer *119:128*

Inter-rural centre 3 km. SE of Ashdod. Established 1960. Pop.: 90.

'Eẓyon Gever → Elat

'Ezuz *099:021*

In past, kibbutz outpost on border of Negev and Sinai 2 km. S of Qeẓi'ot. Abandoned after Six-Day War.

F

o Fahma *167:198*

Arab village 15 km. SW of Jenin. Pop.: 660. Built on ruins of ancient Jewish settlement. Remains of 3rd or 4th c. synagogue have been found in village. Also remains of Crusader church; village mosque built on its ruins.

o Falama *152:181*

Arab village (pop.: 160) in Samarian Hills 6 km. NE of Qalqilya.

o (El) Fandaqumiya *169:192*

Arab village in Samarian Hills 4 km. N of Sabastiya. Pop.: 1,000. Site of ancient settlement mentioned in mosaic floor inscription found in Reḥov excavations. Called Pentakomia in Byzantine Period (five villages). Finds in village: ancient remains, caves, tombs and collection of 6th c. coins.

o Faqqu'a *187:210*

Arab village 10 km. NE of Jenin. Jebel Faqqu'a is Arabic name for Mt. Gilboa'. Pop.: 1,150. Built on site of ancient settlement. Finds include building remains, rock-cut tombs and cisterns from Roman Period.

o Far'ata *165:177*

Arab village (pop.: 150) 10 km. SW of Shekhem. Believed to be site of Biblical Pirathon, birthplace of Judge Abdon (Judg. 12:13) and of Benaiah, one of David's "mighty men" (II Sam. 23:30). Also mentioned in Macc. I, 9. Village has remains of ancient buildings and cisterns. Sherds indicate occupation in Iron Age, and from Roman to Ottoman Periods.

o Fari'a el Jiftliq *197:172*

Village and refugee settlement in Jordan Valley, 4 km. NW of Adam (Damiya) Bridge.

∴ Farj *228:262*

Abandoned village in Golan Heights 2 km. W of Mt. Peres (Tell Faras). Built on ruins of Byzantine settlement. Some houses are preserved. Stones decorated with crosses, rock-cut cisterns and walls and steps from basalt block.

o Farkha *164:164*

Arab village in Samarian Hills 10 km. W of Ma'ale Levona (el Lubban Sharqiyya). Pop.: 500. Village has holy tomb. According to local tradition it is resting place of Seth, son of Adam.

Farradiyya → Amirim, Parod

o Far'un *152:188*

Arab village 3 km. S of Tulkarm. Pop.: 1,200.

Farush Rummana *180:243*

Bedouin settlement in Lower Galilee, in Biq'at Bet Netofa. Pop.: 400.

o **(El) Faṣayil** *192:159*

Arab village in Jordan Valley 18 km. N of Jericho. Name originates from ancient city of Phasaelis, remains of which are at nearby Kh. Faṣayil. Pop.: 450.

Fassuta *179:272*

Arab settlement in Galilee 4 km. NW of Ma'alot-Tarshiha. Founded 150 years ago on site of older town. At first inhabited by both Moslems and Christians. Today, the 1,800 inhabitants are all Christians. **Mifshata** At NE corner of village are ancient remains. Apparently Mifshata was residence of priestly clan of Harim, mentioned in an elegy by Ele'azar HaKallir. In courtyard of present church are remains of a synagogue. Sherds indicate occupation in Early Bronze Age, Iron Age, and from Roman Period through the Middle Ages.

o **(El) Fawwar** *156:098*

Arab village and refugee camp 5 km. SW of Hebron. Pop.: 2,500. Local springs provide water supply for Hebron and its surroundings.

Fiq → **Afiq**

o **Firasin** *160:203*

Arab village in Samarian Hills 8 km. SE of 'Iron junction. Believed to be site of Kefar Parshai — mentioned in Talmud. Fragments found of olive oil press, church and ancient buildings. Sherds indicate occupation in Iron Age and Persian, Roman, Byzantine and Ottoman Periods.

o **(El) Funduq** *163:177*

Arab village (140 people) 13 km. SW of Shekhem. Name means inn. Mentioned as Pandokeion in Byzantine sources. Samaritans lived here at beginning of Middle Ages. In village ancient stone fragments have been re-used in modern houses; sherds from Iron Age, Byzantine and Arab Periods.

(El) Fureidis *146:222*

Rural Arab settlement 2 km. N of Zikhron Ya'aqov. Name means fruit orchard or is perhaps a distortion of *Hordos* (Herod). Present village was established about 100 years ago by Bedouin of el 'Awarna tribe on ruins of ancient settlement. Pop.: 4,400. Remains indicate existence of Jewish settlement in Byzantine Period and Middle Ages.

G

★ **Ga'ash** ✿ ⁝ ● ▬ ⚘ ⚲ *(Josh. 24:30)* *134:182*

Kibbutz 10 km. S of Netanya. Named after Biblical mountain of Gaash. Area: 2,700 d. Pop.: 600. **Ga'ash pool** Small nature reserve (6 d.) near entrance to kibbutz containing small pool with rare amphibians (triton).

Gada Ma'aravit → Judea and Samaria

● **Gadish** ⁝ *173:218*

Moshav 6 km. SW of 'Afula. Name means stack of grain. Pop.: 500. Area: 3,000 d.

★ **Gadot** ✿ ⁝ ● ▬ ⚘ *208:269*

Kibbutz in Hula Valley 1 km. N of Benot Ya'aqov Bridge. Situated on W bank of Jordan, hence its name (*gada* = bank). Up to and during Six-Day War was subjected to Syrian bombardments. Pop.: 400. Area: 6,300 d. Indications of ancient settlement from Roman and Byzantine Periods found in kibbutz. Nearby: Mezad 'Ateret, Benot Ya'aqov Bridge and remains of the old farming village of Mishmar HaYarden.

Galilee (Upper and Lower) **(HaGalil)** *(Josh. 20:7)*

Hilly region in N associated with life of Jesus, Crusader battles and Jewish settlement following Second Temple destruction. Boundaries: N — Litani River in Lebanon, E — Jordan Rift, S — Yizre'el Valley, W — N Coastal Plain (also known as Galilee Coast). Divided into 2 regions, Upper and Lower Galilee with Biq'at Bet Kerem separating them. **Upper Galilee** The highest region in W Erez Israel. Abounds with valleys, gorges, basins, water sources and rich vegetation. Settled from most ancient times. During Israelite conquest was allotted to tribes of Asher and Naphtali, later also to Dan. Insignificant during periods of Judges and Kingdoms of Judah and Israel, when centre was in Judea and Samaria. Partially destroyed during wars between Egypt and the N kingdoms. Sizeable Jewish settlement during Hasmonean Period, and vital community during Revolt against Rome and after Bar Kokhba rebellion. Even after destruction of the Second Temple, the region supported a dense Jewish population, which only decreased as a result of persecutions during Byzantine Period. After Arab conquest (7th c.) the situation of Jewish population worsened and later, Crusaders expelled Jews from Upper Galilee (except for Peqi'in). In 16th c. Safed became Kabbalah centre and attracted Jews to settle in Upper Galilee. However, during first half of 19th c. it again declined. Renewed Jewish settlement began at end of 19th c. with establishment of village of Rosh Pinna (1882) followed by a few others. After WWI Jewish settlement burgeoned throughout country and expanded rapidly after War of Independence during which entire Galilee was liberated and included within Israel. **Lower Galilee** This hilly region also abounds with water sources and fertile soil. During Israelite conquest occupied by Asher, Naphtali, Issachar and Zebulun tribes. After destruction of Kingdom of Judah became spiritual centre of entire people. Its population was active in Revolt against Rome in 1st c. CE. Jewish presence severely eroded during Crusader Period (11th c.) and all but disappeared. It was only renewed at end of 19th c. with Baron de Rothschild's villages. During War of Independence Lower Galilee was liberated by Israel Defence Forces and included in Israel. Today it is populated with many Arab villages, some Moslem and some Christian, and relatively fewer Jewish settlements.

★ **Gal'on** *135:115*

Kibbutz in Lakhish region 7 km. NE of Qiryat Gat. Founded 1946. During War of Independence attacked by Arabs from Beit Jibrin and Egyptian army. Later served as base for attack and capture of Beit Jibrin. Area: 14,000 d. Pop.: 500.

Gamla *219:256*

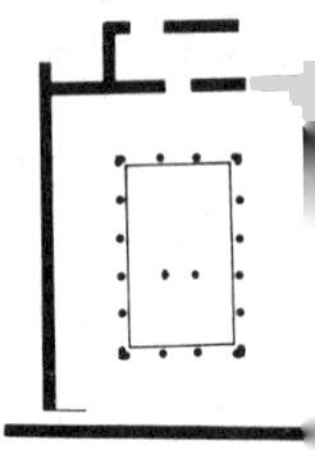

Ruins of ancient settlement on Golan Heights on hill above Naḥal Daliyyot 8 km. NE of *moshav* Ramot. Known as Masada of the north because here thousands of Jews leapt to their death rather than face Roman capture. The hill looks like the hump of a camel, hence its name (*gamal* = camel). Captured by Alexander Yannai in 90 BCE, Gamla was significant during Revolt against Rome in 68 CE. Josephus Flavius related how Romans killed 4,000 Jewish fighters, and 5,000 others died by jumping into an abyss. Excavations have revealed remains of synagogue — one of oldest in country, 2 dykes, city wall, watch-towers, sherds from Early Bronze Age, Hasmonean and Roman Periods, catapult stones and coins from days of Alexander Yannai.

● **Gan HaDarom** *121:134*

Moshav 5 km. E of Ashdod. Founded 1953 by Iraqi immigrants. Pop.: 300.

◆ **Gan HaSharon** *141:177*

Private farm in Sharon, N of Kefar Sava. Founded 1936

Gan HaShelosha → Berekhat 'Amal

● **Gan Ḥayyim** *141:178*

Moshav in Sharon, N of Kefar Sava. Named after Chaim Weizmann, first president of Israel. Founded 1935. Pop.: 240. Area: 3,400 d.

Gan Ḥefer → Bet Yizḥaq — Sha'ar Ḥefer

Gan Meged → Hod HaSharon

◆ **Gan Menashe** *140:178*

Private farm in Sharon, 2 km. N of Kefar Sava. Named after Baron de Menasce of Egypt, founder and first owner of farm, 1932.

● **Ganne'am** *140:173*

Moshav in Sharon, S of Hod HaSharon. Founded 1933. Pop.: 270. Area: 350 d.

Ganne Hadar → Ramot Meir

● **Ganne Tal** *083:086*

Moshav in Gaza Strip 2 km. N of Khan Yunis. Established 1979.

Ganne Tiqwa *138:163*

Urban settlement in Sharon, 2 km. S of Petaḥ Tiqwa. Founded 1953 and initially called Shikun HaYovel. Area: 1,500 d. Pop.: 5,500.

● **Ganne Yehuda** *138:161*

Moshav in Sharon, 4 km. S of Petaḥ Tiqwa. Founded 1950 by Yakhin company and initially called Gannot Yakhin. Pop.: 700.

● **Ganne Yoḥanan** *134:140*

Moshav on central Coastal Plain 4 km. SE of Rehovot. Named after

Johann Kremenetzky, first head of JNF. Founded 1950. Area: 2,100 d. Pop.: 300.

• **Gannot** *133:158*

Moshav on central Coastal Plain. Name from Biblical passage "plant *gardens* and eat their produce" (Jer. 29:5). Founded 1950 by war veterans' organization. Area: 500 d. Pop.: 300.

Gannot Hadar *141:192*

Village 3 km. E of Netanya. Area abundant in citrus groves, hence the name (gardens of citrus). Founded 1954 by Yakhin company. Pop.: 75.

• **Gan Or** *080:082*

Moshav under construction in Gaza Strip 4 km. SW of Khan Yunis.

Gan Raḥel *203:235*

Palm tree grove on shore of Lake Kinneret within *qevuẓat* Kinneret. Named after poetess Raḥel, who loved to walk in area.

★ **Gan Shelomo** *131:142*

Kibbutz on central Coastal Plain 1.5 km. S of Reḥovot. Named after Shelomo Schiller, writer and educator. Founded 1927 by group formed in Galicia in 1923, and who emigrated to Ereẓ Israel in 1925. First called Qevuẓat Schiller. Served as Palmaḥ base and had clandestine workshop for manufacture of arms. Area: 6,900 d. Pop.: 330.

★ **Gan Shemu'el** *145:206*

Kibbutz on border of Samaria and Ramat Menashe 3 km. E of Ḥadera. Named after Rabbi Shemu'el Mohilewer, a leader of Ḥoveve Ẓiyyon. In 1896 a citron orchard was planted here. First pioneers arrived 1913 but left at outbreak of WWI. Present kibbutz founded 1921 by Polish and Bessarabian immigrants. Later joined by HaShomer HaẒa'ir group from Czechoslovakia and S America. Area: 6,000 d. Pop.: 930. Ulpan for foreign students and Bet Uri — a cultural centre in memory of Uri Ilan, a kibbutz youth who died in Syrian captivity.

Gan Shomeron *150:208*

Village in W Samaria. Founded 1934 by German immigrants. Pop.: 350. Area: 2,700 d.

• **Gan Soreq** *127:150*

Moshav on central Coastal Plain 4 km. SW of Rishon LeẒiyyon. Named after Naḥal Soreq, S of *moshav*. Founded 1950. Area: 700 d. Pop.: 140.

Gan Yavne *123:133*

Town (with local council) on S Coastal Plain 5 km. SE of Ashdod. Named after Biblical Jabneh located in area. Founded 1932 by Aḥva society from USA who sold land to settlers. During War of Independence was on front-line. Pop.: 3,000. Area: 9,500 d. **Barqa** *121:131* Ruins and plastered cistern — remains of settlement from Roman and Byzantine Periods.

• **Gan Yoshiyya** *149:195*

Moshav on border of Samaria and Sharon 5 km. NW of Tulkarm. Named after Josiah Wedgwood, British statesman and Zionist. Founded 1949 by organization of war veterans Naḥal Reuven. At first called by that name. Pop.: 230. Area: 2,500 d.

★ **Gat** *(Josh. 13:3) 130:115*

Kibbutz in S Judean Foothills 2 km. N of Qiryat Gat. Named after ancient city of Gath, one of 5 Philistine cities located in area, but whose exact site has not yet been identified. Founded 1942 by members of kibbutz Manof who left their original site near Kefar Sava and settled here. (Kibbutz Manof founded 1933.) During War of Independence the kibbutz was surrounded by Egyptian army, and only combatants remained to defend it. The rest, mainly women and children, were evacuated in operation "Tinok". Pop.: 520. Area: 10,000 d. Memorial to soldiers of Giv'ati Brigade who fell here; memorial to partisan fighter, Lili Neuman; and archaeological museum with local finds.

★ Ga'ton *170:268*

Kibbutz 10 km. E of Nahariyya. Named after village of Ga'ton mentioned in Talmud along with other villages settled on N border by returnees from Babylon. Apparently name retained in that of nearby Kh. Ja'tun. Founded 1948 by HaShomer HaZa'ir group who arrived in country as "illegal" immigrants and then served in Palmaḥ. Area: 2,300 d. Pop.: 400. **Kh. Ja'tun** Natural flattened hill 2 km. W of kibbutz *168:268*. Finds include remains of Hellenistic camp and aqueduct, and khan and rock-cut cellars from Arab Period. At foot of hill are sources of Naḥal Ga'ton, which bisects Nahariyya on its way to the sea.

Gat Rimmon *(Josh. 19:45) 139:164*

Suburb in form of *moshav* SW of Petaḥ Tiqwa. Named after Biblical Gath-rimmon, in Dan tribal allotment. Founded 1926. Pop.: 160.

☐ Gaza ('Azza) *(Josh. 15:47) 099:101*

Arab city on S Coastal Plain in heart of Gaza Strip. The Hebrew *'azza* is from ancient Semitic word meaning might. Tel of ancient city is located near shore, but within boundaries of modern Gaza. Pop.: 120,000, some refugees from War of Independence. City has small port and some industry. Gaza is the city most associated with Samson, who, blinded by his captors, pushed out the centre pillars of the Temple of Dagon here, killing himself along with more Philistines than he had killed during his entire life. **History** In ancient times it was an important city at SW entrance to Canaan, an important station on *via maris* from Egypt to the N kingdoms and a port city on Mediterranean coast. Mentioned in Egyptian and Assyrian records as Azat or Ḥazat; mentioned in Bible many times. In period of Israelite conquest it was the greatest of the 5 Philistine cities. Included in Judah tribal allotment but for most of the time remained a pagan and hostile city. At time of Judges and First Temple Period it was a Philistine city; in Second Temple Period — a Hellenistic city. Taken by Alexander Yannai in 96 BCE. During Roman Period it prospered. Held shortly by Herod and then placed under jurisdiction of Roman Proconsul of Syria. During Revolt against Rome, Gaza was partially destroyed by rebels. In Byzantine Period it was an important and flourishing city with a growing Jewish community, and focal point for Jewish communities in S during 3 pilgrim festivals when Jewish presence in Jerusalem was forbidden. Taken by Arabs in 7th c., but Jews continued to reside here during entire Arab Period. During Crusader Period it became a fortified port city. Captured by Saladin in 1170. The existence of Jewish and Samaritan communities in middle of 15th c. was related by Obadiah of Bertinoro and Meshullam of Volterra. In 1665 it became a centre of the Shabbatean movement through Nathan of Gaza, assistant of Shabbetai Ẓevi. Captured by Napoleon in 1799. Jewish community continued to exist here until 1811; in 1880 a few Jewish families returned to reside here. In WWI taken by British after hard fighting. In 1929 Riots the last Jews left Gaza. In 1948 it served as base for invading Egyptian army. After War of Independence it was a base for terrorist activities against Israel. Taken by Israel Defence Forces in Sinai Campaign (1956) and again in Six-Day War. Since then it has been under Israeli jurisdiction. **Ancient remains** At Tel Gaza *100:100* part of ancient city has been uncovered. Remains of city wall and building from various periods. Within Great Mosque is a column with inscriptions in Hebrew and Greek. The inscription which appears

underneath the relief of a seven-branched candelabrum, ram's horn, *lulav* and *etrog*, is "Ḥananiah son of Jacob". Adjacent to the Great Mosque is a gold jewellery bazaar. On shore S of port, a mosaic synagogue floor was discovered showing an Orpheus-like King David in Byzantine robes, playing the harp. Inscriptions show the building was erected in 508-509. Tombs with Hebrew and Greek inscriptions, Samaritan inscriptions and a Samaritan bath-house were found within city. Another tomb is purported to be that of Samson and called Abu el 'Azzam (father of might).

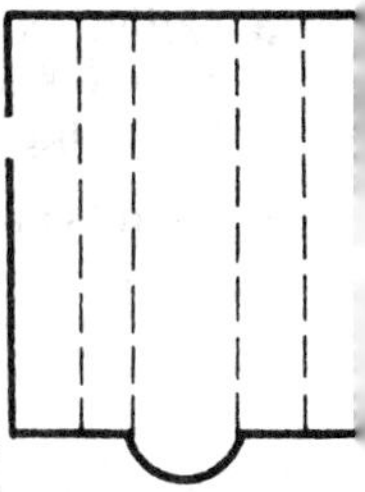

Gaza Road **(Derekh 'Azza) (Darb el 'Azza)**

Ancient trade route between Gulf of Elat and Gaza following Negev-Sinai border.

Gaza Strip

Coastal strip in S of country between S Coastal Plain and N Sinai. Length: 40 km., width: 6-14 km. Population Arab, many refugees. Has 3 cities: Gaza, Khan Yunis, Rafah; rural and urban refugee camps and many villages. Part of Palestine during British Mandate, in War of Independence it was captured by Egyptians. After war served as base for terrorist attacks against Israel and was, therefore, target for retaliatory attacks by Israel Defence Forces. Taken by Israel in Sinai Campaign (1956), but returned to Egypt. Retaken in Six-Day War; after the war a number of *naḥal* outposts were established, some of which became permanent civilian settlements.

★ **Gazit** *192:227*

Kibbutz 5 km. S of Kefar Tavor. Founded 1947 by Rumanian and Polish immigrants. Pop.: 520. Area: 21,800 d. (15,000 d. is natural pasture land).

● **Ge'a** *112:115*

Moshav 5 km. SE of Ashqelon. Founded 1949 by new immigrants on abandoned village of Jiyya. Perhaps site of Biblical Gath(?) (I Sam. 17:52). Pop.: 240. Area: 5,000 d. **Kh. el Jiyya** Near *moshav 111:115*, remains of settlement from Byzantine Period. In 13th c. served as first station on highway from Gaza to Damascus.

● **Ge'alya** *128:144*

Moshav on central Coastal Plain 3 km. W of Reḥovot. Founded 1948 by Bulgarian immigrants. Pop.: 420. Area: 2,000 d. **Tel Shalaf** Within *moshav* is a tel of ancient settlement identified with Eltekeh, a city in Dan tribal allotment (Josh. 19:44). Sherds indicate occupation in Middle Bronze Age and post-Babylonian Exile.

Gedera *(Josh. 15:36) 129:136*

Urban settlement in S Judean Foothills 8 km. SW of Reḥovot. Origin of name is Biblical, Gederah, a city in Judah's tribal allotment, whose name was perhaps retained in that of Qatra, the abandoned village. One of first farming villages, founded 1884 by a group of 10 Bilu pioneers. During early years, settlers had tough struggle with both the elements and Turkish authorities. British and Turks fought in vicinity during WWI. Eventually became regional centre for settlements of S Judean Foothills. Pop.: 6,500. Area: 13,000 d. Original Bilu hut and cave, Harzfeld Home — a hospital for incurable diseases, and Uri'el — a village for the blind. **Ancient Gederah (Qatra)** Tel within Gedera with remnants from Early and Middle Bronze Age, and Iron Age until Byzantine Period. Apparently site of Biblical Gederah, also mentioned in Hasmonean wars and in Byzantine Period.

● **Gefen** 138:127

Moshav in Judean Foothills 12 km. E of Qiryat Mal'akhi. Founded 1955 by Moroccan immigrants. Area: 2,800 d. Pop.: 400.

★ **Gelil Yam** 134:174

Kibbutz 1 km. SW of Herzliyya. Name taken from ancient Samaritan literature where a place Gelilon the Sea is mentioned. Name preserved in nearby abandoned village, Jalil. Founded 1943 by Russian pioneers. Area: 3,250 d. Pop.: 300.

Geranot HaGalil *172:273*

Regional centre in W Galilee 7.5 km. SE of Ḥanita, near *moshav* Goren.

★ **Gerofit** *156:928*

Kibbutz in 'Arava 45 km. N of Elat. Name means a cutting (of olive or sycamore tree for replanting). Founded as *naḥal* outpost in 1963. Became permanent civilian settlement in 1966. Area: 1,250 d. Pop.: several hundred. In 1949 a clash between Jordanian army and Golani Brigade, on their way to take Elat, ("'Uvda" operation) took place N of kibbutz.

★ **Gesher** *202:225*

Kibbutz in Jordan Valley near mouth of Yarmouk River. Named after nearby bridge (*gesher*), Naharayim. Founded 1939 by native-born settlers and German immigrants. During War of Independence was in front-line fighting against Iraqi invaders and was destroyed. Rebuilt after war on adjoining hill. Seriously troubled by terrorist attacks during War of Attrition that followed Six-Day War.

Gesher ..... → for all Gesher ..... (Bridge) see proper name of Bridge

★ **Gesher HaZiv** *161:272*

Kibbutz on coast of Galilee 5 km. N of Nahariyya. Named after nearby bridge and "night of the bridges" operation. Founded 1949 by evacuees from Bet Ha'Arava and HaBonim pioneers from USA. Area: 3,500 d. Pop.: 500. **Naḥal Keziv Bridge** N of kibbutz, near ruins of Akhziv. It was demolished by Haganah in "night of the bridges" operation (June 1946), with loss of 14 men.

★ **Geshur** *(Josh. 13:13) 217:247*

Kibbutz in S Golan. Named after Biblical site. Founded 1968 as *naḥal* outpost. After Yom Kippur War and subsequent Separation of Forces Agreement, settlement was removed from original location on lands of abandoned village, Tannuriyya; in 1975 it occupied temporary site near Fiq (Afiq) junction until taking up its permanent site adjacent to Eli 'Al. Area: 2,000 d.

● **Ge'ulle Teman** *141:200*

Settlement in N Sharon. Partly *moshav* and partly an urban housing complex. Core group of *moshav* was made up of Yemenite immigrants organized at Kefar Ya'betz in 1947; settled here after War of Independence. Pop. of *moshav*: 200; of housing complex: 150.

● **Ge'ullim** *144:189*

Moshav in N Sharon. Founded 1936 by German immigrants and called Bene Ge'ullim. In 1945 original settlers replaced by Yemenite immigrants, members of Talmon organization, and name changed to Talmon Ge'ullim, and later to Ge'ullim. During War of Independence was near front-line and Iraqi troops held it for a few hours before being repulsed. Pop.: 550. Area: 2,400 d.

★ **Geva'** *185:219*

Kibbutz in Yizre'el Valley 10 km. SE of 'Afula. Settlement built on hill, hence its name (*geva'* = hill). Founded 1921 by pioneers from Russia and Poland of Second and Third 'Aliyah. First called Qevuzat Geva'. Area: 9,400 d. Pop.: 650. Kibbutz runs a popular choir called the Gevatron. Has recreation centre named after kibbutz member Yosef Ben-Gurion, and memorial to those who fell in Israel's wars.

● **Geva' Karmel** *146:229*

Moshav on Karmel coast 3 km. S of 'Atlit. Named after ancient Geba (mentioned by historians of 1st and 4th c. CE) whose name was retained in that of now-abandoned village of Jaba'. Founded 1949. Pop.: 400. Area: 2,300 d. Within abandoned village ancient remains and mosaic fragments were uncovered. A Middle Bronze Age rock-cut tomb was discovered nearby.

★ **Gevar'am** *113:111*

Kibbutz on S Coastal Plain 5 km. E of Mordekhay junction. Founded 1942 by members of group called Maḥar, immigrants from Germany and Czechoslovakia. Served as Palmaḥ base and was in front-line of battles with Egyptian army in War of Independence. Pop.: 300. Area: 6,800 d. S of kibbutz is Rekhes Gevar'am reserve, with largest deposits of coarse sand in country.

★ **Gevat** *170:231*

Kibbutz in Yizre'el Valley 3 km. E of Migdal Ha'Emeq. Name from ancient Gabata (Aramaic for hill) which has perhaps been retained in name of Arab village Jubata. Founded 1926 by pioneers from Pinsk, Poland. Area: 9,500 d. Pop.: 760. **Ancient remains** within kibbutz of building with mosaic floor from Roman Period. Near building is rock-cut wine press.

★ **Gevim** *112:101*

Kibbutz on S Coastal Plain 1.5 km. S of Sederot. Name means hollows in rock where rain-water collects. (One of the water pipelines to Negev passes near kibbutz.) Founded 1947. First called Sede 'Aqiva. During War of Independence, headquarters of Negev Brigade was located in kibbutz. Pop.: 350. Area: 12,000 d.

★ **Gevulot** *099:068*

Kibbutz in N Negev. First of three observation outposts established in Negev in 1943 to explore settlement conditions. (The other 2 were Revivim and Bet Eshel.) Founded by HaShomer HaZa'ir groups and called Mizpe Gevulot because of its proximity to the border. In 1947 it moved to present site and was called Gevulot. During War of Independence served as base for Palmaḥ 8th battalion. Pop.: 170. Area: 12,500 d.

Gev Yam → Qiryat Yam

★ **Gezer** *(Josh. 10:33)* *142:143*

Kibbutz in Judean Foothills, 7.5 km. SE of Ramla near remains of a strategic city of same name dating from Canaanite and Israelite eras. Here, the famous 10th c. BCE "Gezer calendar", the earliest example of Hebrew writing, was discovered. Founded 1945. During War of Independence it was taken by Jordanian Legion, but after a few hours it was retaken. In this battle 28 defenders were killed and others taken as prisoners of war. In 1964 kibbutz disbanded and since then it has been run by relief groups. Pop.: 100. Area: 5,000 d. **Tel Gezer** Ancient Gezer is identified with tel 2 km. S of kibbutz. Sherds indicate occupation as early as Chalcolithic Period (4000 BCE). Strategically important as it is located on main thoroughfare from Judean Foothills into Judean Hills. One of cities taken by Joshua. Mentioned in Tell el 'Amarna letters from 14th c. BCE and on "Israel Stele" of Pharaoh Merneptah which describes his conquests in the country. King Solomon received city from Egyptian Pharaoh as part of dowry for latter's daughter. Simeon the Hasmonean captured it (140 BCE), built a palace, fortified it and appointed his son John Hyrcanus as city commander. Had a Jewish community during Roman and Byzantine Periods. Large battles fought here in 1177 and 1191 between Crusaders and Moslems. Later served as headquarters for Saladin. **Finds** Archaeological excavations have uncovered sherds and remains from all periods of Gezer. Includes the Gezer agricultural calendar from 10th c. BCE, city wall and water tunnel from Late Bronze Age, remains of Hasmonean fort, and famous 10 monoliths of Canaanite Gezer High Place. Some are more than 3 m. high. A holy Moslem tomb — Sheikh Maḥmud el Jazari — is located on tel.

Ghadir en Naḥas → (El) Majami'

○ Ghajar (El Ghazar) *208:297*

Arab village in Galilee 4 km. SE of Metulla, near Lebanese border. In past was Lebanese village that was transferred to Syria. After Six-Day War residents, who belong to 'Alawite sect, requested to remain within Israel. Pop.: 4,000. Village has many architectural remains (columns, capitals and dressed stones) from Byzantine Period. These were probably brought here from another site.

(El) Ghayada *214:236*

Ancient site on Golan Heights 3 km. SE of Mevo Ḥamma. Middle Bronze and Iron Age wine presses, caves and shaft tombs. Perhaps cemetery of nearby ancient settlement, now called Kh. el 'Ayun.

● Gibbeton *(Josh. 19:44) 131:144*

Moshav W of Reḥovot. Named after Biblical city, Gibbethon, in Dan tribal allotment. Founded 1933. Pop.: 170. Today within municipal boundaries of Reḥovot.

● Gid'ona *184:217*

Moshav in Yizre'el Valley at foot of Mt. Gilboa' near Ḥarod spring. Named after Biblical Judge, Gideon Jerubbaal, who camped in area before battle with the Midianites (Judg. 7:1 ff.). Founded 1949. Pop.: 140. *Moshav* has Gilboa' field school, youth hostel and tombs of Yehoshua Hankin, "redeemer" of lands in Yizre'el Valley, and his wife, Olga. Nearby is **'En Ḥarod** (Ḥarod spring) — national park with spring, swimming pool and campsite.

● Gilat *117:082*

Moshav in Negev 3 km. NE of Ofaqim. Name from Biblical passage "it shall blossom abundantly, and rejoice with *joy* and singing" (Isa. 35:2). Founded 1949. Area: 2,500 d. Pop.: 650. **Experimental station** Near *moshav 118:083* is agricultural research station for Negev. Founded 1953 by Volcani Institute and called Yivula. Major areas of research: irrigated wheat, industrial crops, persimmon and citrus groves, raising calves and sheep.

Gilboa' Hills *(I Sam. 31:1)*

Block of hills running SE to NW (offshoot of Samarian Hills) between Yizre'el and Bet She'an Valleys. Length: 18 km.; width: 9 km. Its highest peak (Mt. Malkishua') is 536 m. above sea level. Has minimal rainfall (400-500 mm. annually) and sparse vegetation. Mentioned in

Bible many times: included in tribal allotments of Issachar and Manasseh; the battles of Deborah and Gideon were fought in this region. King Saul and his sons died on these mountains and in their memory one of its peaks has been named Mt. Sha'ul. Modern Jewish settlement seems to have overlooked area. During Arab Disturbances, it served as base for attacks on Jewish settlements in valley below. During War of Independence the slopes up to the ridge line were captured by Israel Defence Forces and in Six-Day War the rest of the range was taken. Today it has 3 Jewish settlements: Ma'ale Gilboa', Naḥal Malkishua' and Nurit. Large tracts on hills have been covered with forests planted by JNF and parts have been designated as nature reserves.

Gilgal *(Josh. 4:19) 192:156*

Kibbutz in Jordan Valley 16 km. N of Jericho. Named after Biblical Gilgal, identified with Tell Ghalghala (or Tell Jaljul), 2 km. SE of Jericho. Founded as *naḥal* outpost in 1970 by religious youth and called Naḥal Gilgal. Became permanent civilian settlement in 1973. Area: 1,400 d.

Gillo → Beit Jala

Gilon *172:256*

Community settlement in Lower Galilee 7 km. SW of Karmi'el. Named after adjacent mount. Established 1980.

Gimzo *(II Chron. 28:18) 144:148*

Moshav 6 km. SE of Lod. Site of Biblical Gimzo whose name has been retained in that of abandoned village, Jimzu. Founded 1950. Pop.: 130. **Ancient Gimzo** Within abandoned village of Jimzu *145:148* is tel of ancient settlement with rock-cut tombs. Believed to be site of Biblical and Second Temple Gimzo, birthplace of Naḥum of Gimzo mentioned in Mishnah. Site contains sherds from Ḥasmonean, Roman and Byzantine Periods.

Ginnaton *142:152*

Moshav 1 km. NE of Lod. Founded 1949. Pop.: 300.

Ginnegar *174:230*

Pioneer agricultural commune in Yizre'el Valley 2 km. SE of Migdal Ha'Emeq. Named after settlement mentioned in Talmud as residence of Rabbi Joḥanan b. Nuri and apparently retained in Arabic site name, Jinjar. Established 1922 by group of Second 'Aliyah pioneers, organized in 1920, who settled in Deganya "C" (adjacent to Deganya "B"). However, due to shortage of land, they moved to Yizre'el Valley. On eve of War of Independence it served as a Palmaḥ base. Area: 7,000 d. Pop.: 500. Ancient wine presses and water cisterns were discovered here. Nearby is Balfour Forest.

Ginnosar *199:250*

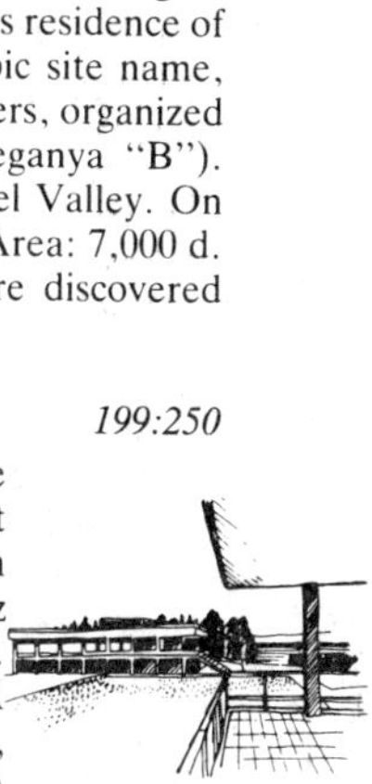

Kibbutz in Ginnesar Valley on NW shore of Lake Kinneret. (In Roman and Byzantine Periods the Kinneret was called Yam Ginnesar.) Burial site of late Israeli foreign minister, Yigal Allon, head of Palmaḥ and one of kibbutz founders. Named after ancient Jewish settlement in area. Founded 1937 by No'ar 'Oved youth movement on PICA lands. After split in HaKibbutz HaMe'uḥad movement, Ginnosar absorbed members who left kibbutz 'En Gev. On eve of War of Independence it served as Palmaḥ and Haganah base. Pop.: 650. Area: 5,260 d. **Ancient finds** Excavations on site uncovered Bronze Age remains: tombs, pottery, tools, weapons, seals and jewellery.

GIV'ATAYIM — RAMAT GAN — BENE BERAQ

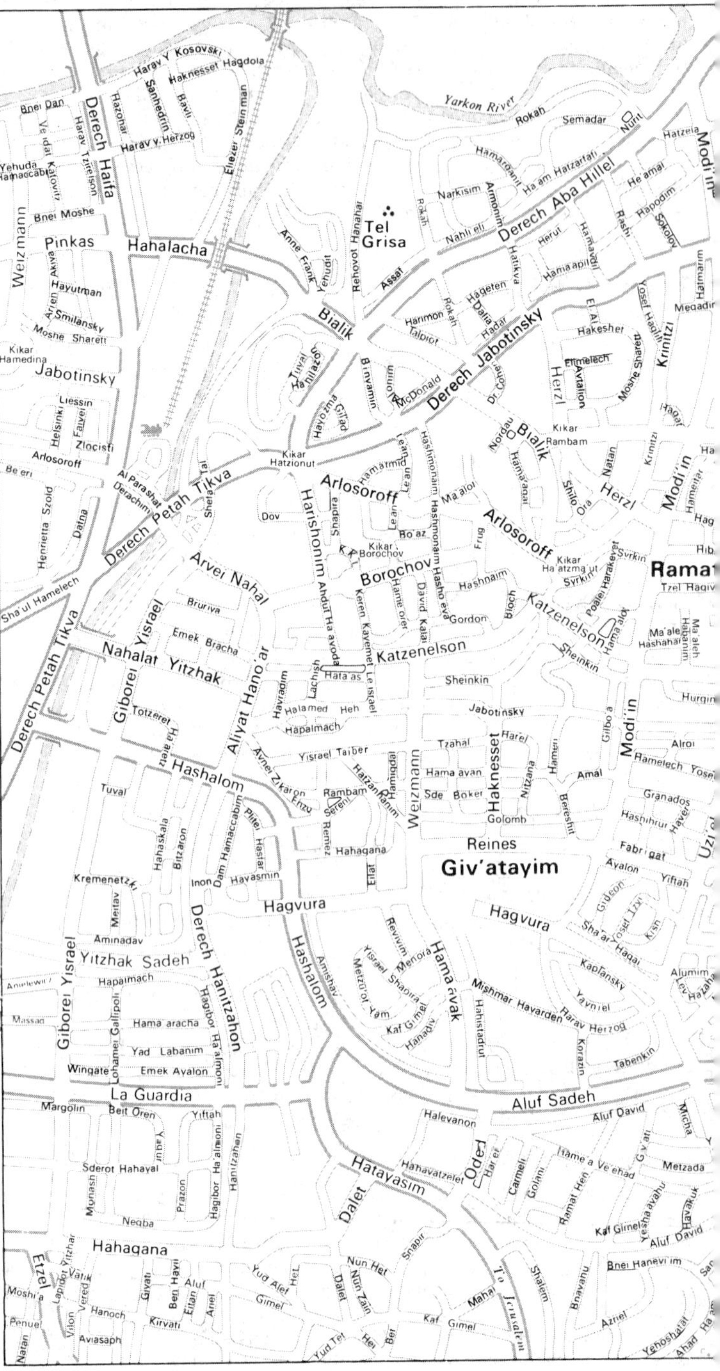

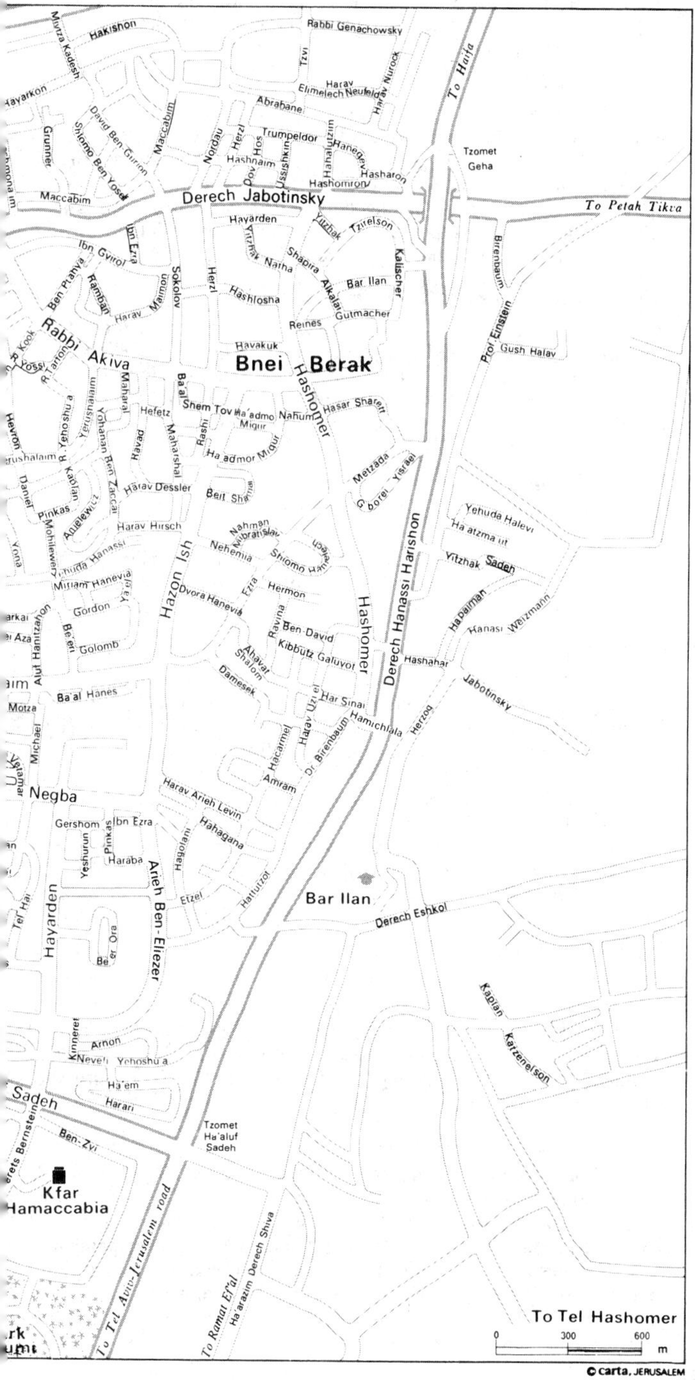
Bnei Berak
Derech Jabotinsky
To Petah Tikva
To Haifa
Tzomet Geha
Rabbi Genachowsky
Hakishon
Mivtza Kadesh
Hayarkon
Harav Elimelech Neufeld
Harav Nurock
Abrabane
Tzvi
Trumpeldor
Hanegev
Hasharon
Hashomron
Hashnaim
Herzl
Nordau
Dov Hos
Ussishkin
Hahalutzim
Maccabim
David Ben Gurion
Shlomo Ben Yosef
Grunner
Hayarden
Tzirelson
Ibn Gvirol
Ibn Ezra
Ben Prahya
Ramban
Harav Maimon
Sokolov
Hashlosha
Shapira
Alkalai
Bar Ilan
Kalischer
Gutmacher
Reines
Birenbaum
Prof. Einstein
Gush Halav
Rabbi Akiva
Havakuk
Hashomer
Maharal
Hefetz
Shem Tov
Ha'admo Nahum
Hasar Sharett
Rashi
Maharshal
Ha'admor Migur
Yohanan Ben Zaccai
Havad
Harav Dessler
Beit Shearim
Metzada
G'borei Yisrael
Hevron
Derech Hanassi Harishon
Yehuda Halevi
Ha'atzma'ut
Yitzhak Sadeh
Harav Hirsch
Hazon Ish
Nehemia
Shlomo Hamelech
Yehuda Hanassi
Miriam Hanevia
Gordon
Dvora Hanevia
Ezra
Hermon
Habanim
Hanasi Weizmann
Ben David
Kibbutz Galuyot
Golomb
Hashahar
Jabotinsky
Ba'al Hanes
Damesek
Har Sinai
Hamichlala
Herzog
Harav Uziel
Dr. Birenbaum
Hacarmel
Amram
Negba
Harav Arieh Levin
Hahagana
Gershom
Ibn Ezra
Pinkas
Haraba
Yeshurun
Hagolani
Arieh Ben-Eliezer
Hattutzot
Bar Ilan
Derech Eshkol
Etzel
Hayarden
Tel Hai
Be'er Ora
Kaplan
Katzenelson
Kinneret
Arnon
Neveh Yehoshu'a
Ha'em
Harari
Sadeh
Tzomet Ha'aluf Sadeh
Ben-Zvi
Kfar Hamaccabia
To Tel Aviv-Jerusalem road
To Ramat Ef'al
Ha'arazim
Derech Shiva
To Tel Hashomer
0
300
600
m
© carta, JERUSALEM

Gittit 187:167

Moshav on border of Samaria and Jordan Valley. Founded as *naḥal* outpost by kibbutz youth in 1972. Became permanent civilian settlement in 1975. Area: 1,500 d.

Giv'ah "69" 117:126

Hill in S Coastal Plain 1 km. E of Ashdod-Ashqelon road. Named thus owing to height of hill (*giv'ah*) above sea level. Called Thlat el Pantis in Arabic (3 towers) for 3 water towers built on hill during British Mandate. Important military vantage point during War of Independence and therefore site of fierce battles between Egyptian force and Giv'ati Brigade. Taken by Egyptians during battle in which 20 defenders were killed. Later Israel Defence Forces retook hill. On site is memorial.

Giv'at 'Ada 150:214

Farming village 8 km. SE of Zikhron Ya'aqov. Named after wife of Baron Edmond de Rothschild, Ada (Adelaïde). Founded 1903 by ICA on lands purchased from Maraḥ village. The first settlers lived in an old khan. Because of its isolation, they suffered from Arab attacks in 1920 and during Disturbances of 1936–1939. Developed only after 1948. Pop.: 1,500. Area: 7,000 d.

Giv'at Admot (Kh. Idma) 200:226

Small tell on hill dominating surrounding area, on border of Jordan Valley and Lower Galilee, 2 km. NW of kibbutz Gesher. Flint implement from Chalcolithic Period and sherds from Chalcolithic and Early Bronze Age were found at foot of tel, and on slopes ancient building stones of basalt and limestone were found.

Giv'atayim 133:164

City between Tel Aviv and Ramat Gan. Located between 2 hills hence its name (*giv'atayim* = two hills). Founded 1942 when several adjacent quarters joined together to form a municipal unit. In 1959 it received city status. The uniting quarters were: Borochov, founded 1922; Sheinkin, founded 1925; Qiryat Yosef, founded 1934; Arlosoroff, founded 1936; Giv'at HaKerem, founded 1936; and Giv'at Rambam, founded 1953. Area: 3,500 d. Pop.: 50,000. Archaeological museum, Haganah archives. **Antiquities** Ancient site in former Rambam quarter *132:164*. Excavations uncovered remains of sarcophagi and cave-tombs from Chalcolithic Period. Indications of agricultural settlement from Hellenistic Period, foundations of fortress from days of Alexander Yannai.

Giv'at Ayyala (Ghuweir Abu Shusha) 198:251

Tel 2 km. NW of kibbutz Ginnosar alongside bed of Naḥal Ẓalmon. Sherds indicate occupation in Early and Middle Bronze Ages and Roman and Byzantine Periods. Remains of flour mill, built on ancient foundations, from Arab Period. At foot of tel, Middle Bronze Age tombs were discovered.

Giv'at 'Azaz (Tell el 'Azaziyat) 212:292

Hill on border of Golan Heights and Ḥula Valley. At 290 m. above sea level it dominates E part of Ḥula Valley. Hebrew name derives from Arabic Tell el 'Azaziyat, which is named after Bedouin tribe of that name who reside in area. Battle fought here in War of Independence. After conquering hill, Israel Defence Forces returned it to Syrians for it to remain in demilitarized zone according to Armistice Agreement. After war, Syrians reoccupied area and established a military position here, from where they frequently fired on settlements of Ḥula Valley. Retaken in Six-Day War by Golani Brigade.

Giv'at Bazaq (Tell el Bazuq) 221:257

Basalt hill in Golan Heights 10 km. SE of Qaẓrin. SW of hill is large dolmen field.

Giv'at Brenner *131:141*

Kibbutz on central Coastal Plain 2 km. W of Bilu junction. Named after the writer, Joseph Ḥayyim Brenner, who was murdered by Arabs in Jaffa during Riots of 1921. Founded 1928 by pioneers from Lithuania and Poland. After split in Kibbutz HaMe'uḥad movement some of members left for kibbutz Neẓer Sereni. Pop.: 1,500 (largest kibbutz); its members originate from over 20 countries. Area: 7,800 d.

Giv'at Dani → Yagel

Giv'at Golani → Tel Dover

Giv'at Ḥablanim (Ras Ḥablein) *130:066*

Ancient tel in Negev 4 km. S of Be'er Sheva'. Hebrew name similar in sound to that of Arabic one: Ras Ḥablein. Sherds indicate occupation in following periods: Iron Age, post-Babylonian Exile, Hellenistic, Roman and Byzantine. One hundred m. W of tel is small Byzantine ruin.

Giv'at Ḥadasha *166:140*

Community settlement N of Jerusalem 5 km. SW of Jerusalem airport. Established 1980. Site of Hadashah (name preserved in Kh. 'Adasa), where Judah the Maccabee defeated Nikanor's army in 161 BCE. Nikanor was killed in this battle (I Macc. 7:40).

Giv'at HaEm *211:290*

Hill in N Ḥula Valley 196 m. above sea level. Named after Henrietta Szold "Mother (*em*) of Youth 'Aliyah". Arabic name: Tell Abu Ḥanzira. Battles fought here during War of Independence. Front-line Israeli post on Syrian border until Six-Day War. From here Israel Defence Forces broke through to Golan Heights in Six-Day War.

Giv'at HaMeshuryan (Tell Waqiyya) *166:269*

Tel 7 km. E of Nahariyya, off road to Ma'alot. Arabic name: Tell Waqiyya. Nearby an armoured (*meshuryan*) car with guardsmen was ambushed while on its way to the aid of Yeḥi'am, which was being attacked by the Arab Liberation Army (20 Jan. 1948). On tel are remains of settlement from Iron Age and Byzantine Period.

Giv'at HaMore * *(Judg. 7:1) 181:225*

Mountain in Yizre'el Valley E of 'Afula, 515 m. above sea level. Name mentioned in Biblical description of Gideon's battle against Midianites. Arabic name: Jebel ed Daḥi, after Moslem holy man of 7th c. whose tomb is on summit of mountain. Also called Little Ḥermon by Medieval Christian pilgrims who ascribed to the following passage: "Tabor and Hermon joyously praise thy name" (Psalms 89:12). At foot of mountain is agricultural school first called Kefar Yeladim and now called Giv'at HaMore.

Giv'at HaQerav *162:121*

Hill in Judean Hills 6 km. NW of Gush 'Eẓyon. It was here that the 35 Israeli fighters sent to aid 'Eẓyon Bloc during War of Independence made their last stand (16 Jan. 1948). Site has memorial to them.

Giv'at HaRadar * *162:137*

Dominating hill in Jerusalem Hills 2 km. N of kibbutz Ma'ale HaḤamisha. During WWII a radar installation was located here, hence the name. In War of Independence a Jordanian Legion military post on hill thwarted the Palmaḥ Har'el Brigade's attempts to take the position. During Six-Day War it was taken by Har'el armoured Brigade on its way to capture the Jerusalem-Ramallah mountain ridge. Large memorial to Har'el Brigade.

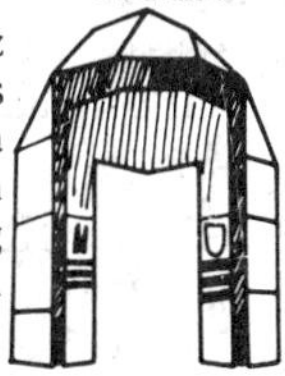

★ **Giv'at HaShelosha** *142:167*

Kibbutz 2 km. E of Petaḥ Tiqwa. Named after 3 (*shelosha*) Jewish labourers from Petaḥ Tiqwa who were executed by Turks in WWI on charges of espionage. Founded 1925 and located in Petaḥ Tiqwa. After split in Kibbutz HaMe'uḥad movement, some members moved to present site while others established kibbutz 'Enat. Pop.: 500. Area: 4,000 d.

Giv'at Ḥatul (Kh. Khatula) *151:135*

Hill on border of Judean Hills and Foothills 1 km. SW of Sha'ar HaGay. Contains remains of fortified settlement from Roman and Byzantine Periods, rock-cut wine presses and remains of *maqam* (Moslem holy place) from Arab Period. When Sha'ar HaGay road was widened after Six-Day War, earth was dumped on hill giving it shape of artificial mound.

■ **Giv'at Ḥaviva** *152:207*

Educational seminar and library of HaShomer HaẒa'ir and Mapam movements on border of Sharon and Samaria 2 km. S of 'Iron junction. Named after Ḥaviva Reik, a member of adjacent kibbutz Ma'anit, who parachuted on a mission to Slovakia during WWII. She was captured and killed by Germans. Founded 1949.

★ **Giv'at Ḥayyim** *143:199; 143:200*

Two neighbouring *kibbutzim* 5 km. S of Ḥadera and belonging to different kibbutz movements. Named after Ḥaim Arlosoroff, head of Jewish Agency's political department, murdered in Tel Aviv in 1933. Founded as one kibbutz in 1932 and first called Kibbutz "C" (Wadi Ḥawarith). Settled mainly by members of European pioneer groups. Made headlines in 1945 during struggle against British. The kibbutz was surrounded and searched by British troops looking for stores of Haganah weapons. In ensuing clash 7 of the defenders were killed and others wounded. In 1950 the kibbutz split. The Me'uḥad members remained on and the Ihud members left and founded a new kibbutz nearby. **Me'uḥad** *143:200* Pop.: 900. Area: 4,300 d. Memorial to fallen in battle against British. Cultural centre named after Moshe Sharett. **Ihud** *143:199* Founded 1952 by former members of Giv'at Ḥayyim and Kefar Szold. Pop.: 850. Area: 4,300 d. "Theresienstadt House" commemorates concentration camp; large community centre, ulpan and sports centre.

● **Giv'at Ḥen** *138:175*

Moshav in Sharon, S of Ra'ananna. Named after famous poet, H. N. Bialik. Founded 1933 by immigrants from Russia, Poland and Lithuania. Pop.: 260. Area: 1,300 d.

● **Giv'ati** *119:126*

Moshav in Coastal Plain 4 km. W of *moshav* Be'er Toviyya. Named after Giv'ati Brigade who fought in area during War of Independence to halt Egyptian invasion. Founded 1950 by Israel Defence Forces' veterans and Egyptian immigrants on lands of abandoned village, Beit Daras. First called Bet Daras, later Mesillat 'Oz, and then Gan Giv'ati. Pop.: 420. Area: 2,200 d.

● **Giv'at Koaḥ** *143:159*

Moshav 5 km. NE of Ben-Gurion Airport. Named in honour of 28 soldiers who died here during War of Independence. Founded 1950. Pop.: 400. Area: 1,450 d.

■ **Giv'at Mikha'el** *130:149*

Jewish Agency training institute near Nes Ẓiyyona. Named after Michael Helpern, labour Zionist, pioneer and one of founders of Nes Ẓiyyona.

Giv'at Napoleon (near Acre) → **Acre, Tel 'Akko**

Giv'at Napoleon (near the Yarqon) → **Tel Gerisa**

Giv'at Nili *154:217*

Moshav 10 km. E of Zikhron Ya'aqov. Named after Nili (Hebrew acronym for "the Glory of Israel will not lie" — I Sam. 15:29), a Jewish espionage organization during WWI serving the British against the Turks. *Moshav* founded 1953. Pop.: 220. Area: 3,000 d.

Giv'at Noaḥ (Ju'ara) *160:223*

Hill in Ramat Menashe near kibbutz 'En HaShofet. Named after member of kibbutz who died in a plane crash. Ju'ara is Arabic name of site. At summit of hill is old building in which founders of kibbutz 'En HaShofet lived for first years. Later served as Haganah and Palmaḥ training base. After War of Independence was a Golani and Gadna training base. **Ḥurbat Zahura (Kh. Ju'ara)** Remains of buildings, tombs and sherds from Roman and Byzantine Periods and Middle Ages.

Giv'at Olga *139:205*

Suburb of Ḥadera on shore, 2 km. W of Ḥadera. Named after Olga, wife of Yehoshua Hankin, known as "redeemer of the lands". During British Mandate, a coast guard station was located on hill-top to prevent "illegal" immigration. Demolished by Haganah at beginning of 1945. Suburb founded 1950. Pop.: 15,000. Remains of large buildings, coloured floor mosaic from Roman Period, and ancient Moslem cemetery.

Giv'at Orḥa (El Jukhadar) *230:259*

Tel on E Golan Heights near abandoned Bedouin village, el Jukhadar, apparently a distortion of Jukhandar — respected title for governor of Safed in 14th c. Rises to height of 697 m. above sea level. Excavations have uncovered remains of buildings from Roman, Byzantine and Mamluk Periods. Also found was a tombstone with Greek inscription: "Consoleme Antonia, year 27". At foot of tel are springs whose waters the Syrians collected in a pool and channelled S. Near village are remains of a khan.

Giv'at 'Oz *169:218*

Kibbutz on border of Yizre'el Valley 2 km. S of Megiddo junction. Founded 1949. Until Six-Day War it was a frontier settlement. Pop.: 450. Area: 7,200 d.

Giv'at Rabi (Jebel el 'Ein) *175:237*

Hill in Lower Galilee 5 km. NW of Nazareth. Named after Rabbi Judah HaNasi. Arabic name is Jebel el 'Ein, after spring at foot of hill ('Ein Rabi). On E slope of hill is broad tel in which sherds indicating Bronze and Iron Age occupation were found.

Giv'at Refed *148:047*

Hill in Negev 6 km. SW of Dimona. Site has ruins of large rural settlement from Late Iron Age. At foot of hill are foundation remains of many buildings. Nearby, *150:046*, there was an Israelite fortress.

Giv'at Seled (Abu Ṣundeiḥ) *143:119*

Hill on border of Judean Hills and Foothills adjacent to Li On. On E side of hill is site dating from Early Bronze Age and perhaps to Chalcolithic Period. On summit of hill are two large carob trees surrounded by small hollows. Sherds and other evidence, including sickle blades, indicate the presence of a flint-tool workshop. Nearby is **Giv'at Shama,** *143:118*, where more recent water cisterns and a large underground hall were found.

Giv'at Shapira *138:196*

Moshav 4 km. N of Netanya. Named after Prof. Ẓevi Hermann Schapira, originator of idea of Jewish National Fund and Hebrew University. Founded 1958. Pop.: 110. Area: 900 d.

Giv'at Shashan *143:117*

Ancient hill site on border of Judean Hills and Foothills, off Bet Shemesh-Bet Guvrin road. Foundations of late Second Temple Period structure, which probably served as watch-tower to secure nearby Roman road (on route of present road). The square tower (12x12 m.), built of dressed stones with chiselled borders, was enclosed by a wall. To E and W are 2 caves and to N, off road, is a collection of Roman milestones (see Giv'at Yesha'yahu).

Giv'at Sha'ul (Tell el Ful) *172:136*

Hill 4 km. N of Jerusalem off road to Ramallah; 840 m. above sea level. Arabic name: Tell el Ful. Believed to be site of Biblical Gibeah (also known in Bible as Gibeah of Benjamin, Geba of Benjamin and Gibeah of Saul). Until Six-Day War it was in Jordanian administered territory. On summit of hill is shell of King Ḥussein's incomplete summer palace. Excavations uncovered remains of Israelite fortress and many sherds.

Giv'at Sha'ul → Jerusalem (neighbourhoods)

Giv'at Shemesh → Deir Rafat

Giv'at Shemu'el *136:165*

Urban complex in central Coastal Plain near Bene Beraq. Named after religious Zionist leader, Samuel Pineles. Suburb set up in 1942 by E European immigrants. Later joined with other suburbs: Qiryat Yisra'el, Giv'at Yehuda and Pardes Rosenblum. Since 1948 it has a local council. Area: 3,600 d. Pop.: 7,500.

Giv'at Washington → Bet Rabban

Giv'at Yardinnon (Sheikh Muḥammad) *212:284*

Small ruin in Ḥula Valley 1 km. S of kibbutz Shamir. Site has building and cistern remains. Finds indicate settlements in Roman, Byzantine and Arab Periods.

Giv'at Yasaf (Tell es Sumeiriyya) *159:262*

Ancient tel on Galilee coast adjacent to kibbutz Loḥame HaGeta'ot. Sherds indicate occupation in Early Bronze Age and from Iron Age to Byzantine Period. Also remains of skull and bones of prehistoric man from Mesolithic Period.

Giv'at Ye'arim *158:133*

Moshav in Judean Hills off Ẓuba-Shimshon junction. Founded 1950 on lands of abandoned village, Jaba' — perhaps site of Biblical Gibeah (hill) mentioned in account of wanderings of Ark of the Covenant. Pop.: 550.

Giv'at Yehonatan *184:216*

Hill in Mt. Gilboa' chain 1 km. E of Gid'ona; 131 m. above sea level. Named after Jonathan, son of King Saul, who, together with his father and brother, died in battle on Mt. Gilboa' (I Sam. 31:1-2). Memorial on hill to 7 residents of Yizre'el Valley who died in battles on Gilboa' during War of Independence.

Giv'at Yesha'yahu *144:120*

Moshav 10 km. S of Bet Shemesh on road to Bet Guvrin. Named after Yesha'yahu Press, historian and topographer of Ereẓ Israel. Founded 1958. Pop.: 180. Original name of site: Umm el 'Adas. Site contains column fragments and

ancient decorations. Off road is collection of Roman milestones from nearby Roman road (on route of present road). One stone has inscription from days of Emperors Septimius Severus and Caracalla (3rd c.).

Giv'at Yo'av *214:245*

Moshav on Golan Heights 5 km. NE of 'En Gev. Named after Lt. Col. Yo'av Shaham who fell in Israeli raid on Sammu' village in 1966. Founded 1968 and was temporarily located in abandoned village of Fiq. In 1972 moved to abandoned village of Sequfiyya. Pop.: several hundred. Area: 4,500 d.

Giv'at Zafit *168:050*

Remains of square fort tower in Negev Hills, 15 km. E of Dimona. Walls built of straight courses of dressed stone. Finds date tower to Roman Period (2nd c.).

Giv'olim *111:089*

Moshav in Negev 4 km. S of Netivot. Founded 1952. Pop.: 200. Area: 3,000 d.

Giv'on *166:139*

Civilian outpost in Judean Hills 8 km. SW of Ramallah. Established 1978.

Giv'on → (El) Jib

Giv'ot Etun (Rujm el 'Atawina) *107:092*

Ancient site in Negev 3 km. W of Netivot. Many mounds of broken pottery. Similar heaps found in bed of adjacent Nahal Bohu, mostly from Byzantine Period. Apparently there was a pottery industry here which supplied utensils to neighbouring Byzantine settlements. In bed of stream *108:092*, remains of Chalcolithic underground settlement were discovered.

Giv'ot Zayd → Bet Zeid

Golan Heights

Plateau in N. Boundaries: N — Mt. Hermon, S — Yarmouk Valley, E — Nahal Ruqqad and W — Hula Valley and Lake Kinneret. During Israelite conquest partially included in allotment of Manasseh, and in Hasmonean Period conquered by Alexander Yannai. Golan settlements participated in Revolt against Rome. Even after destruction of Second Temple, Jewish settlements continued to exist on Golan. In Byzantine times close to one million Jews may have lived in as many as 100 settlements here. After its conquest by Arabs, it was attached to Damascus district. Populated mainly by Bedouin during Turkish Period. At end of 19th c. several Circassian villages were established, while a number of attempts at Jewish settlement failed owing to harsh climate and enmity of population and government. After WWI included in French Mandate of Syria. During War of Independence, Syrians tried from Golan Heights to invade Hula and Jordan Valleys. After the war, they continued to harass front-line Jewish settlements. In 50's and 60's Israel Defence Forces carried out reprisal attacks against Syrian military positions on Golan Heights. Taken by Israel in Six-Day War; most of inhabitants fled. After war, Jewish settlement, based on farming and industry, was renewed. During Yom Kippur War, Syrians broke through Golan Heights but were repulsed by Israel Defence Forces after fierce battles. Under Separation of Forces Agreement (May 1974) a section of Golan Heights was returned to Syria and a UN buffer zone was established between Syrian and Israeli forces.

★ **Gonen** *210:281*

Kibbutz in E Ḥula Valley on border of Golan Heights. Founded as *naḥal* outpost in 1951 on lands of abandoned village Gorba by Scouts from Tel Aviv and Jerusalem. A year later it became a permanent civilian settlement. Until Six-Day War, it was a border settlement and suffered from Syrian harassment. Area: 4,000 d. plus 17,000 d. of pasture land on Golan Heights. Pop.: several hundreds.

● **Goren** *172:273*

Moshav in Galilee 13 km. SE of Rosh HaNiqra. (*Goren* = threshing-floor.) Founded 1950. Pop.: 360. Nearby is Ḥurbat Galil *173:273* — ruins from Roman Period. Remains of a church were found here.

Gush ‘Eẓyon *161:118*

Jewish settlement bloc founded in 1967, on ruins of previous settlements destroyed in 1948 war. A group of Jewish settlements isolated in heart of Arab territory 20 km. S of Jerusalem, W of Bethlehem-Hebron road. Before War of Independence, it included: Kefar ‘Eẓyon (founded 1943), Massu'ot Yizḥaq (founded 1945), ‘En Ẓurim (founded 1946), and kibbutz Revadim (founded 1947). At outbreak of War of Independence, the bloc was besieged and after several attempts to break out, the settlers were finally cut off. After a long siege and fierce battles, the settlements fell and were destroyed (14 May 1948 — one day before the declaration of the state); 240 defenders were killed and 260 taken prisoner. After the war, the returning prisoners established new settlements, with similar names, in other parts of the country. Gush ‘Eẓyon was liberated in Six-Day War and Jewish settlement was renewed here. (See Kefar ‘Eẓyon, Rosh Ẓurim, Allon Shevut, El‘azar, Migdal ‘Oz.)

Gush Ḥalav → Jish

H

Ha'Arava *(Deut. 1:1)*

Long and narrow valley extending from S Dead Sea until Gulf of Elat, separating Hills of Edom on E from Negev Hills on W. Part of great rift in earth's surface stretching from Syria to E Africa. The name is ancient (mentioned in Bible in account of wanderings of Israelites) and means dry and desolate area — synonym for desert. Water is sparse. The region contains some copper and other minerals. However, the 'Arava's importance is primarily as a transit area. In ancient days traversed by important routes from centre of country and Negev Hills to Gulf of Elat and E to Transjordan. In days of Judges area was controlled by Edomites until conquered by King David. King Solomon established a port in Elat and mined copper in the 'Arava. When kingdom split, Edomites re-established control over the 'Arava until they were expelled by Nabateans. At beginning of 2nd c., Romans conquered it and built forts and guard posts to protect strategic routes. After Arab conquest, the 'Arava lost its significance, a situation which persists almost to this very day. Included in Israel by virtue of "'Uvda" operation (1949) in War of Independence. Since then, its importance has increased. Port city of Elat established 1951. Afterwards Timna copper mines were opened and settlements established along major 'Arava routes. The completion of Kvish Ha'Arava, the 'Arava road, allowed for major developments in region.

HaBesor → Ḥevel Eshkol

HaBiq'a →'Emeq HaYarden

o **Ḥabla** *148:174*

Arab village on border of Samaria and Sharon 3 km. S of Qalqilya. Pop.: 1,200.

● **HaBonim** *143:226*

Moshav shittufi on Karmel coast 6 km. S of 'Atlit. Named after HaBonim youth organization, whose members were among founders of *moshav*. Established 1949. Area: 2,700 d. Pop.: 170. Within *moshav* is abandoned Arab village, called Kafr Lam, and an 8th c. Arab fortress later converted by Crusaders. Rock-cut tombs and quarries from Roman Period nearby.

o **(El) Ḥadab** *155:098*

Arab village in Judean Hills 8 km. SW of Hebron. Pop.: 350. N of village is **tel** of ancient settlement with remains of city wall, fragments of Mesolithic flint implements and columbarium at summit. Sherds indicate occupation during Early Bronze and Iron Ages, and Hellenistic and Byzantine Periods. **Qaṣra** In village are two Second Temple Period rock-cut burial caves, one decorated and another with two square columns on facade. Ancient water cistern nearby.

Hadar → Hod HaSharon

● **Hadar 'Am** *140:195*

Moshav 4 km. NE of Netanya. Name refers to citrus (*hadar*) groves in area. Founded 1933. Pop.: 230.

Hadar Ramatayim → Hod HaSharon

Hadassim *139:187*

Youth village in Sharon 6 km. SE of Netanya. Named after Hadassah Women's Zionist Organization of America. Founded 1947 by Hadassah and WIZO of Canada. Has elementary school, junior high and high school. Staff and students total 700.

Ḥadera *142:204*

City in N Sharon. Name from Arabic el Khudeira (*khadra* = green). Founded as farming village in 1890 by pioneers from Vilna, Kovno and Riga. First settlers suffered from malaria. Many died. In 1895 swamps were drained, with support from Baron de Rothschild, and supplanted by groves of eucalyptus trees, today known as Ḥadera Forest. During WWI served as base for British army in its N offensive. During Riots of 1929 was subject to attacks by Arab gangs. Gained in importance over the years. City quarters: Naḥli'el (1912) founded by Yemenite immigrants; Newe Ḥayyim (1936) named after Chaim Arlosoroff; Giv'at Olga (1950) named after wife of Yehoshua' Hankin and Ḥefẓi Bah (founded in 1914). Area of Ḥadera: 30,000 d. Pop.: 37,000. Ḥadera Forest is SW of city. **Ancient remains** Finds within city: house-shaped pottery ossuaries from Chalcolithic Period (first of its kind discovered at that time in country), series of Second Temple tombs, mausoleum from Roman Period and various remains from Byzantine Period.

Ḥafeẓ Ḥayyim *131:132*

Kibbutz in Coastal Plain 4 km. S of Gedera. Named after Rabbi Israel Meir HaKohen, known as Ḥafeẓ Ḥayyim. Founded 1944 (first settlement founded by Po'ale Agudat Yisra'el) by 'Ezra youth movement group from Germany. Area: 6,000 d. Pop.: 400. Attractive synagogue.

HaGada HaMa'aravit → Judea and Samaria

HaGalil Ha'Elyon → Galilee

HaGalil HaTaḥton → Galilee

HaGilboa' → Mt. Gilboa'

HaGolan → Golan Heights

Ḥagor *145:171*

Moshav in Sharon 5 km. SE of Kefar Sava. Name from Biblical passage: "*Gird* your sword upon your thigh, O mighty one, in your glory and majesty!" (Ps. 45:3). Founded 1949 by veterans of 9th Palmaḥ Battalion. Pop.: 360. Area: 3,000 d.

HaGosherim *208:291*

Kibbutz in Galilee 5 km. E of Qiryat Shemona. Founded 1948. Area: 5,000 d. Pop.: 530. Naḥal Dan passes through *moshav*. Nearby is Ḥureshat Tal — a nature reserve and national park. Finds here include: flint tools and other prehistoric remains, cemeteries from Middle Bronze Age and Hellenistic Period and remains from Roman, Byzantine and Arab Periods. Other ancient sites nearby: **Tell Zuq** *205:291* with remains mainly from Hellenistic and Mamluk Period; **Tell Khizaz** *208:292* with remains from Middle Bronze Age, Hellenistic and Arab Periods.

HaḤoterim *146:239*

Kibbutz on Karmel coast 10 km. S of Haifa. Settled 1948, but in 1952 moved to permanent site on lands of abandoned village of Tira. Area:

3,600 d. Pop.: 450. Cultural centre named after parachutist, Zevi Ben Ya'aqov, who died in WWII while on secret mission in German-occupied Europe.

Haifa

Israel's third largest city, its main port, and large industrial and commercial centre. Situated along shore of Haifa Bay; built partly on Coastal Plain at foot of Karmel, and partly on N and W offshoots of Karmel. Area: 52,000 d. Pop.: 230,000, of whom 14,000 are Arab. Composed of many quarters, major ones being: Hadar HaKarmel in city centre, founded 1912; Newe Sha'anan in E part of city, founded 1922; Aḥuza on Mt. Karmel, founded 1922; Bat Galim at S entrance to city, founded 1923; and Qiryat Eliyahu in S. Haifa is divided geographically and economically into 4 major sections: lower city near port — hub of port activity; Bay area — industry and workshops; Hadar HaKarmel — commercial and business centre and Har HaKarmel — area of present expansion. Two major institutes of higher learning: Technion (founded 1925) and Haifa University (founded 1963). Moshe Stekeles Museum of Prehistory and Oceanography Institute. Many parks; largest are Gan HaEm and Gan HaParsi (see below). Major museums: National Maritime Museum, Naval and Illegal Immigration Museum and Japanese Art Pavilion. Holy sites: Elijah's Cave (see Me'arat Eliyahu), Bahai Temple (see below) and Carmelite Monastery of Stella Maris — star of the sea — marking spot where the prophet Elisha is purported to have sat and meditated. The grotto is lavishly decorated. **History** During Second Temple Period two Jewish communities inhabited area of present-day city: Shiqmona, identified with Tell es Samak (fisherman's tel) at S entrance to city, and the other on the E side of Haifa. The 2 communities continued to exist during Roman Period and even later; Shiqmona appears to have been destroyed in 7th c. In Middle Ages Jewish community of Haifa grew. In 1100 city was taken by Crusaders who slaughtered Arab and Jewish population. During Crusader Period Haifa was a small town. In 1291 it was taken and destroyed by Mamluks. Over the years it was rebuilt. In 1517 taken by Turks but remained a poor town. In 1750 taken by Bedouin Sheikh Dahir el 'Amr, who at first destroyed the town and then rebuilt and fortified it. Dahir el 'Amr's rule came to an end in 1775 and Haifa remained under Turkish authority until WWI (with exception of 1799, when it was captured by Napoleon, and between 1831 and 1840 when it was taken by Ibrahim Pasha of Egypt). At beginning of 19th c. Sephardi Jews from N Africa settled in Haifa and established a small quarter which Arabs called Harat el Yahud (Jewish quarter). In 1868 German Templers established a modern quarter called HaMoshava HaGermanit (German Colony). In 1870 Ashkenazi Jews settled in city. The population influx and construction of Hejaz railway (Haifa-Damascus) accelerated development; eventually Haifa replaced Acre as economic and business centre. In 1918 it was taken by British and after modern port was built it became most important city in N of country. On eve of War of Independence population of Haifa was 156,000, of whom 80,000 were Jews and rest Moslem and Christian Arabs. When war broke out the Arabs initiated acts of terror. As British forces began leaving city, the Haganah took over evacuated areas. After fierce battles the Arabs surrendered and most left (only 3,000 remained). **Rushmiya fort** Nearby, *149:243*, adjacent to Elizabeth Square, are ruins of Byzantine road fort. A Crusader fort was built on its foundations and in 18th c. Dahir el 'Amr rebuilt Crusader remains. Remains of a hall and a tower. Nearby are remains of Roman olive oil press. Opposite is Tell Abu Huwwam (today site of refineries) where finds include: a Late Bronze Age cemetery and remains from Iron Age and post-Babylonian Exile. At Kh. Qastra finds include: remains of buildings, cisterns, olive oil press and sherds, mostly from Byzantine Period. **Shiqmona** At Tell es Samak *146:247* remains of

HAIFA

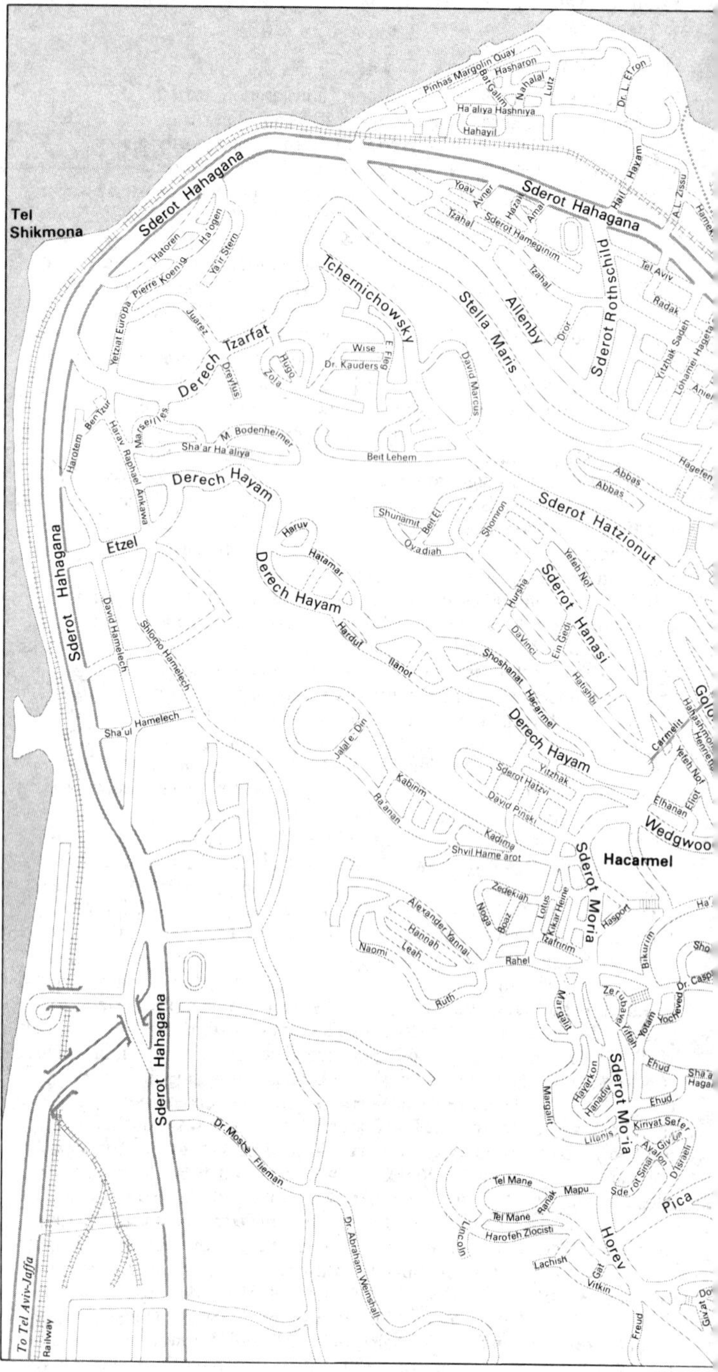

Tel Shikmona
Pinhas Margolin Quay
Hasharon
Bat Galim
Nahalal
Lutz
Dr. L. Efron
Ha'aliya Hashniya
Hahayil
Sderot Hahagana
Hatoren
Ha'ogen
Ya'ir Stern
Pierre Koenig
Yetziat Europa
Juarez
Derech Tzarfat
Dreyfus
Hugo
Zola
Tchernichowsky
Wise
E. Fleg
Dr. Kauders
Stella Maris
Allenby
Dror
Sderot Rothschild
Yoav
Avner
Hazak
Amal
Tzahal
Sderot Hameginim
Hai
Hayam
A.L. Zissu
Tel Aviv
Radak
Yitzhak Sadeh
David Marcus
Ben Tzur
Harotem
Harav
Raphael
Ankawa
Marseilles
M. Bodenheimer
Sha'ar Ha'aliya
Beit Lehem
Derech Hayam
Abbas
Hageten
Sderot Hatzionut
Shunamit
Beit El
Shomron
Ovadiah
Haruv
Hatamar
Etzel
David Hamelech
Shlomo Hamelech
Sha'ul Hamelech
Yefeh Nof
Sderot Hanasi
Hursha
DaVinci
Ein Gedi
Hatishbi
Hardufi
Ilanot
Shoshanat Hacarmel
Jalal e-Din
Kabirim
Ra'anan
Sderot Hatzvi
Yitzhak
David Pinski
Kadima
Shvil Hame'arot
Carmelit
Elhanan
Eliot
Wedgwood
Hacarmel
Sderot Moria
Zedekiah
Alexander Yannai
Noga
Boaz
Lotus
Kikar Heine
Hasport
Hannah
Leah
Naomi
Tzafririm
Rahel
Ruth
Bikurim
Margalit
Zerubavel
Yiftah
Yotam
Yocheved
Ehud
Hayarkon
Hanadiv
Kiriyat Sefer
Lilianis
Aya
Sderot Sinai
D'Israeli
Pica
Tel Mane
Mapu
Ranak
Harofeh Zlocisti
Lincoln
Horev
Lachish
Gat
Vitkin
Freud
Dr. Moshe Flieman
Dr. Abraham Weinshall
To Tel Aviv-Jaffa
Railway

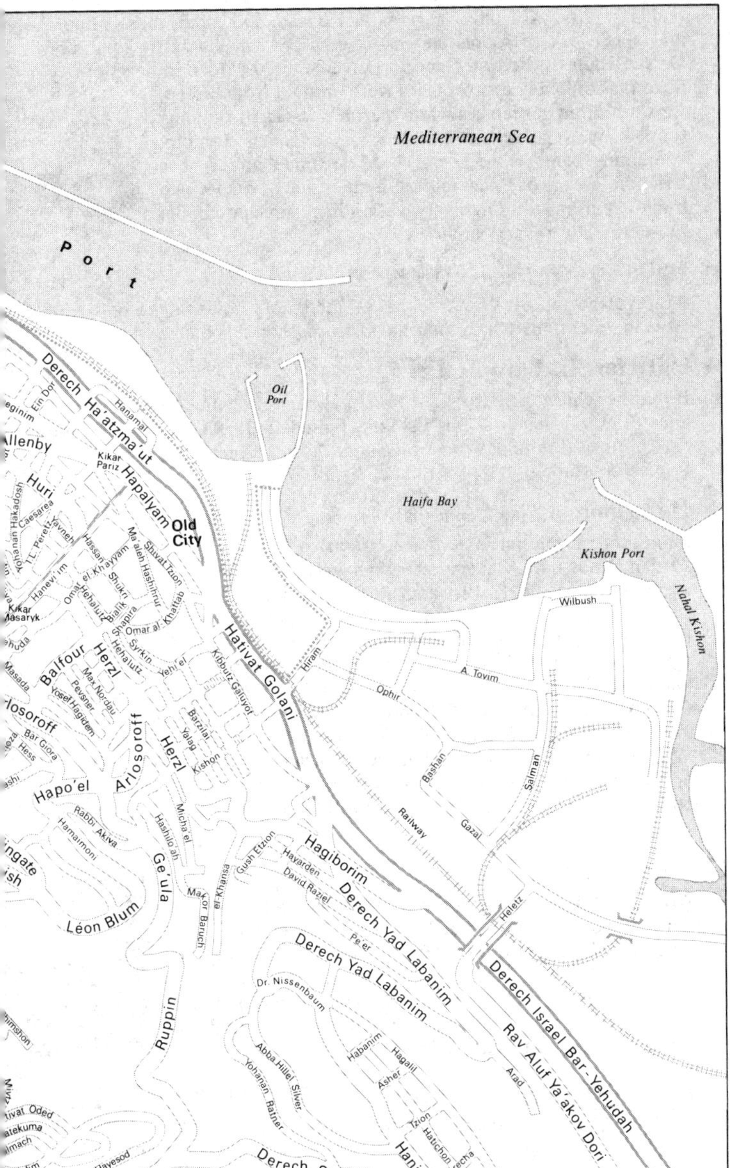
Mediterranean Sea
Port
Oil Port
Haifa Bay
Kishon Port
Nahal Kishon
Derech Ha'atzma'ut
Hapalyam
Old City
Hativat Golani
Hiram
Wilbush
A. Tovim
Ophir
Bashan
Salman
Railway
Gazal
Heletz
Hagiborim
Derech Yad Labanim
Derech Israel Bar-Yehudah
Rav Aluf Ya'akov Dori
Arad
To Nazareth
Derech Simha Golan
Hanita
Trumpeldor
Harav Maimon
Wilbuschewitz
Pinsker
Gilbo'a
Aleikhem
Borochov
Hankin
Pica
Keren Hayesod
Ruppin
Ge'ula
Léon Blum
Hapo'el
Arlosoroff
Herzl
Balfour
Allenby
Huri
Kikar Pariz
Kikar Masaryk
Hanamal
Ein Dor
Caesarea
Yavneh
T.L. Peretz
Yohanan Hakadosh
Hanevi'im
Hassan Shukri
Ma'aleh Hashihrur
Shivat Tzion
Omar al-Khayyam
Omar al-Khattab
Hehalutz
Bialik
Shapira
Syrkin
Yehi'el
Kibbutz Galuyot
Barzilai
Yalag
Kishon
Max Nordau
Pevsner
Yosef Hagalili
Masada
Bar Giora
Hess
Rabbi Akiva
Hamaimoni
Hashilo'ah
Micha'el
Ma'kor Baruch
el Khansa
Gush Etzion
Havarden
David Raziel
Pe'er
Dr. Nissenbaum
Habanim
Hagalil
Asher
Abba Hillel Silver
Yohanan Ratner
Tzion
Hatichon
Habrecha
Feuerberg
Katzenelson
Mendele Mokher Sfarim
0
400
800
m
© carta, JERUSALEM

ancient Shiqmona were uncovered, revealing continuous settlement from Iron Age until the Persian Period. Among finds were columned buildings, Iron Age olive oil press and Byzantine church, mosaic floors, and a network of rooms and pools used for some industrial purpose. **HaGan HaParsi (Persian Garden)** Large cultured garden in heart of city. Seedlings of lovely cypress trees were brought from Shiraz, Persia. Within garden is a white marble neo-classic building topped by a golden dome that is the Bahai Temple, containing tombs of Mirza Ali Muḥammad and Abbas Effendi, leaders of Bahai faith. On other side of road which bisects garden is Greek-style building housing Bahai museum, library and archives.

○ **Ḥajja** **(Qaryat Ḥajja)** *162:179*

Arab village 13 km. W of Shekhem. One theory holds this to be site of Hoglah, mentioned in Samarian Ostraca. Pop.: 900.

■ **HaKefar HaYaroq** *134:171*

Boarding school in Sharon S of Ramat HaSharon. Named in memory of late Prime Minister Levi Eshkol. Founded 1950. Studies include agriculture, technology and mechanical agriculture. Area: 2,700 d. Pop.: 600 students, 100 permanent staff.

HaLashon **(Lissan Peninsula)** *(Josh. 18:19)* *195:075*

Peninsula resembling a tongue (*lashon*) on E shore of Dead Sea in Jordan. Known in Arabic as el Lissan — (the tongue). Hebrew name as mentioned in Josh. 18:19: "and the boundary ends at the northern bay (*lashon* in Hebrew text) of the Salt Sea." Size: 10x14 km. Area: 74 sq. km. The N tip of the Lashon is called Cape Costigan after Irishman, Christopher Costigan, who in 1835 explored Jordan River and Dead Sea and died while doing so. He is buried on Mt. Zion. The S tip is called Cape Molineux after the British naval officer, Thomas Molineux, who explored the Dead Sea in 1847. The strait between the Lashon and the W shore of the Dead Sea is called Lynch Straits after Captain Lynch who headed an American expedition to explore the Jordan and Dead Sea in 1848. The Lashon is not inhabited but there are some small villages on its E fringes.

□ **Ḥalḥul** *(Josh. 15:58)* *160:109*

Arab city 5 km. N of Hebron on the road to Bethlehem. Pop.: 6,200. **Ancient Halhul** The present settlement is built on ruins of ancient city of Halhul, which was allotted to tribe of Judah. Inhabited also during Middle Ages. According to Jewish tradition Prophets Nathan and Gad were buried here, and according to Islamic tradition Prophet Jonah was buried here.

Ḥallamish (temporary name) *162:157*

Civilian outpost in Samarian Hills 15 km. NW of Ramallah. Nearby is village of Nabi Ṣaliḥ. Name means hard rock. Founded 1977.

Ḥaluẓa → **Ḥurvot Ḥaluẓa**

★ **Ḥamadya** *199:213*

Kibbutz 3 km. NE of Bet She'an. Name derives from that of abandoned village of Ḥamidiyya (in honour of Turkish Sultan 'Abdul Ḥamid). Founded in 1939 as "stockade and tower" settlement. During War of Attrition (1967–1970) kibbutz suffered badly from bombardments and other terrorist activities. Area: 24,000 d. Pop.: several hundreds. **'Enot Ḥasida** One km. E of kibbutz is a holiday site near a spring ('Ein Abu Farida). **Dabayib et Tuwwal** S of kibbutz are ancient remains scattered across surface of 50 d. Finds include: flint tools, sherds, remains of aqueduct, buildings and fragments of mosaic floor indicating occupation from Neolithic and Chalcolithic Periods, and later from Iron Age until Middle Ages.

HaMakhtesh HaGadol **(Wadi Ḥathira)** * *146:038*

Large crater running NE to SW in Negev Hills between Dimona and Yeroḥam. Length: 15 km.; width: 7 km.; depth: 400 m. Naḥal Ḥatira drains into it, hence Arabic name Wadi Ḥathira. The crater has deposits of quartz sand used in glass industry. To E is phosphate works at Oron.

HaMakhtesh HaQatan **(Wadi el Ḥadira)** * *168:042*

Small crater running NE to SW in Negev Hills 20 km. SE of Dimona. Length: 8 km.; width: 6 km.; depth: 450 m. Naḥal Ḥazira drains into it and hence Arab name Wadi el Ḥadira. Above crater is an observatiom point that can be reached from Ma'ale 'Aqrabbim.

★ **HaMa'pil** *148:198*

Kibbutz 12 km. NE of Netanya. Founded 1945. Area: 3,500 d. Pop.: 500.

HaMasreq → Bet Me'ir

HaMeshar **(Qa'at el Qireiq)** *146:982*

Flat basin in Negev between Makhtesh Ramon in N and Paran in S. Area: 40 sq. km., mostly alluvial soil and areas of *hamada* (desert areas covered with gravel). A section of road from Mizpe Ramon to Elat crosses the basin, as straight and level as a ruler.

(El) Ḥamma → Ḥammat Gader

Ḥammam el Maliḥ → Burj el Maliḥ

Ḥammat *(Josh. 19:35) 201:241*

Remains of excavated ancient city 2.5 km. SE of Tiberias. Identified with city of Hammath or Hammath-Tiberias that was included in Naphtali tribal allotment. Home of priestly clan of Ma'zia and Talmudic sages. Excavations of 1920 and 1963 uncovered remains of two synagogues from 1st and 4th c. The latter has remains of mosaic floor depicting zodiac, names of the months in Hebrew, seven-branched *menorah*, Holy Ark, palms and citrus. In fact this is one of the most beautiful mosaic floors in the Middle East. The 17 hot springs here have been famous since Trajan's day, when a coin was minted in honour of the springs.

Ḥammat Gader **(El Ḥamma)** * Λ *212:232*

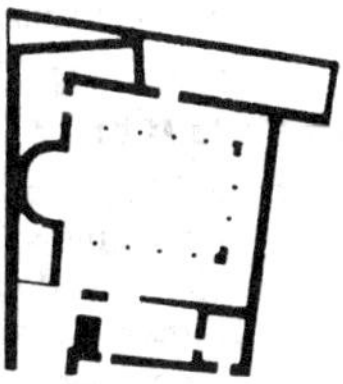

Hot spring in bed of Yarmouk River on S Golan Heights, 10 km. SE of Zemaḥ. Name from ancient city of Gadara. (Jordanian village of Umm Qeis, on other side of Yarmouk, is built on ruins of Gadara.) Even in ancient times springs were known for their medicinal properties. Rabbi Yehuda HaNasi was reputed to have used them. Near baths, remains of a bath complex, a Roman theatre and a 6th c. synagogue with a mosaic floor were uncovered. Area of springs was included within boundaries of Israel after War of Independence, but Jordanians took control of site and later gave it to Syrians. After Six-Day War, it was renovated with intention of converting it to a health spa and resort, but because of border incidents it was not opened to public. In 1977 it was again renovated and opened to public. It has baths and services and pleasant gardens.

Ḥamme Zohar Λ ⫪ *185:064*

Health and holiday resort on W shore of Dead Sea 20 km. S of Masada. Medicinal hot springs, hotels and other services for bathers.

Ḥamra *191:178*

Moshav in Samarian Hills off Adam Bridge–Shekhem road. Named after nearby tel called ʻAraq el Ḥamra in Arabic. Founded 1971. Area: 3,500 d.

Ḥanita *166:277*

Kibbutz in Galilee 7 km. E of Rosh HaNiqra, near Lebanese border. Named after ancient town of Hanita mentioned in Tosephta (7:4,9); kibbutz is built on its ruins. Original name has also been preserved in nearby site of Kh. Ḥanuta. Founded 1938, as a "stockade and tower" settlement, 2 km. from present location. During its first year, 10 of its members were killed in Arab attacks. At beginning of War of Independence it was cut off from surrounding Jewish settlements. Only after capture of Galilee did kibbutz expand and absorb new members. Area: 3,000 d. Pop.: several hundreds. **Ancient Hanita** Finds within kibbutz include flint tools and sherds from Chalcolithic Period, tombs from all Bronze Age Periods, cave tomb from Roman Period, remains of church with mosaic floor and remains of large buildings from late Byzantine Period. **Hanita observation point** E of Ḥanita on Jebel el Mared *167:277.* Nature reserve of 1,200 d.

Ḥanni'el *145:193*

Moshav 8 km. E of Netanya. Named after Biblical Hanniel (Num. 34:23), son of Ephod, a leader of Manasseh tribe who settled in this area. Founded 1950. Pop.: 300. **Tell en Nashaf** Small tel within *moshav* with Iron Age sherds.

Ḥanot Qira *159:227*

Ruins of Mamluk khan on border of Yizreʻel Valley and Menashe Hills 3 km. SW of Yoqneʻam. Apparently dates from 14th c. Square in shape. The arches in the N wall have been preserved.

Ḥanot Taggarim *188:236*

Caravanserai and fortress ruins in Lower Galilee off Kefar Tavor-Golani junction road. In ancient times the *via maris* passed alongside these buildings. Arabic name: Khan et Tujur, meaning caravanserai of the merchants. Also called Suq el Khan (*suq* = market); apparently a market was held here, either within khan or nearby.

Ha'Ogen *143:196*

Kibbutz in ʻEmeq Ḥefer NE of Netanya. Founded by a group of Czechoslovakian immigrants formed in 1939 and who first settled near Kefar Sava. Settled on permanent site in 1947. Area: 3,000 d. Pop.: 660. **Ancient remains** Near kibbutz are remains of large Byzantine town with fragments of columns, glass and sherds.

HaOn *208:237*

Kibbutz on E shore of Lake Kinneret 3 km. S of ʻEn Gev. Name means strength. Founded initially as *naḥal* outpost in 1949 by Polish and Hungarian immigrants. Pop.: several hundred. Area: 3,300 d. Memorial to 2 Turkish pilots who crashed here in 1914. Nearby is beach and camping; remains of Byzantine church containing 6th c. mosaic floor.

HaQirya, Jerusalem → Jerusalem

HaQirya, Tel Aviv → Tel Aviv

Harabat es Suʻeidani *134:048*

Settlement ruin from Byzantine Period in Negev 5 km. S of Negev junction. Alongside is a large pool with opening in rock and rock-cut steps of same period. Next to pool are rock-cut troughs.

Har Ardon *145:005*
Mount on E edge of Makhtesh Ramon, between Biq'at Maḥmal and Biq'at Ardon. Height: 713 m. above sea level. Look-out point over Makhtesh and surroundings.

● **Hararit** *184:250*
Moshav under construction in Lower Galilee 3 km. E of 'Arraba.

Ḥarashim *181:262*
Look-out point in Galilee 3 km. S of Peqi'in. Remains of Iron Age metal workshop found nearby. Hence its name (*ḥarash* = craftsman). Established 1979.

Har 'Aẓmon *175:247*
Mountain in Lower Galilee NW of Biq'at Bet Netofa. Height: 548 m.

Har Ben Ya'ir *180:081*
Mountain in Judean Desert 4 km. NW of Masada. Named after Ele'azar Ben Yair, commander of Masada during the great Revolt against Rome. At its summit is look-out point over entire area.

Har Dov *217:302*
Mountain range W of Ḥermon. Highest peak is 1,529 m. above sea level. Extends over Lebanese border and nicknamed Fataḥland because of the number of PLO (Fataḥ) terrorists who have their bases in this area. Arabic name is Jebel Ros (mount of heads). Mt. Dov is named after Dov Rudberg who fell in battle with terrorists in 1970.

★ **Har'el** *145:135*
Kibbutz in Jerusalem corridor, off Ramla-Jerusalem road. Named after Palmaḥ Har'el Brigade, which fought in area during War of Independence. Founded 1948 by Palmaḥ veterans on site of abandoned village, Beit Jiz. Area: 12,000 d. Pop.: 150. Near kibbutz is Miẓpe Har'el. Probably site of ancient Giza (whose name has been retained in that of Beit Jiz), one of dwelling places of David's mighty men (I Chron. 11:34).

Hare Yehuda → Judean Hills

Har Gamal *170:258*
Mount in Galilee 3 km. W of Majd el Kurum. Included in nature reserve of Mediterranean-type wood (300 d.).

Har Gillo *166:125*
Settlement S of Jerusalem near Arab town of Beit Jala, on Mt. Gillo, called Ras Beit Jala in Arabic. Height: 923 m. above sea level. Before WWI, building of a Russian church was started, but was discontinued when Russian Revolution broke out. In WWII a British army broadcasting station was established here. Up to Six-Day War it was a Jordanian army camp. Now it is the Hare Yehuda and Jerusalem field school; also used as national centre of Nature Preservation Society and army academy. Within settlement are remains of a Roman mausoleum and collection of agricultural installations from different periods.

Har HaAri *184:262*
Mountain in Galilee off Acre-Safed road N of Rama village. Height: 1,047 m. above sea level. Named after the Ari of Safed (Isaac b. Solomon Ashkenazi Luria; 1534–1572; Kabbalist). Arabic name: Jebel Haidar.

Har HaBetarim **(Mash-had et Teir)** *216:299*

Mountain and holy place on Si'on shoulder of Mt. Hermon. Height: 1,296 m. Arabic name means witness of the bird, mentioned in Covenant of Abraham: "but the *birds* divided he not" (Gen. 15:10). On southern slope, according to ancient Jewish and Moslem traditions, there is a holy site called in Arabic Maqam Ibrahim el Ḥalil (shrine of beloved Abraham). Domed structure next to a water reservoir and ancient oak trees. In past practicing Jews would visit site; after Six-Day War this pilgrim custom was renewed.

Har HaOsher **(Mt. of Beatitudes)** *202:254*

Mountain NW of Lake Kinneret near Kefar Naḥum (Capernaum). Height: 125 m. above lake and 70 m. below Mediterranean sea level. Here, according to Christian tradition, Jesus gave his Sermon on the Mount. The opening words of the sermon were "Blessed are", hence the name of the mountain. Also called Har Naḥum. In the 4th c. a monastery and church were built at foot of mountain, but they were destroyed by Moslems in the 7th c. The modern octagonal church on summit was built in 1937. A hostel and Italian convent are also located here.

Har HaQefiẓa → Nazareth Ridge

Har Ḥarif *107:989*

Mountain in Negev 30 km. SW of Miẓpe Ramon. Arabic name: Jebel Ḥaruf. On summit are remains of round structures and many Middle Bronze Age finds.

Har HaRuaḥ *159:136*

Summit in Judean Hills 2 km. W of Ma'ale HaḤamisha. Height: 771 m. above sea level. Name derives from its location in path of strong westerly wind (*ruaḥ* = wind). Mostly forested by Red Army Forest, planted in commemoration of Soviet army's victory over Nazis in WWII.

Har HaTayyasim *158:131*

Mountain W of Jerusalem off 'En Kerem-Ẓuba-Kesalon road, S of Etanim. Height: 795 m. above sea level. During War of Independence an Israeli air force plane crashed nearby killing 2 pilots and 4 crewmen. On mountaintop is a memorial to them and all fallen pilots. Once a year a memorial service is held here. The mountain is part of a nature reserve called Har HaTayyasim Reserve. **Kh. Akrad** S of memorial are remains of an ancient building from 6th c. BCE, possibly a watch-tower or central farm building. Remains of walls and stairs.

Har HaZikkaron → Jerusalem

Har Ḥazon *188:256*

Mountain in Galilee off Acre-Safed road, 10 km. E of Karmi'el. Height: 584 m. above sea level. At its summit are remains of fortress built by Joseph b. Mattathias during Revolt against Rome. Finds indicate occupation during Roman and Byzantine Periods. In 1969 a *moshav* called Ḥazon was established here.

o **Ḥaris** *163:169*

Arab village 15 km. SW of Shekhem. Pop.: 700. Perhaps site of Arus mentioned in Jewish Revolt against Rome. Remains of houses, towers, rock-cut cisterns, tombs and sherds from Iron Age, Persian, Roman and Byzantine Periods.

Har Kammon *183:257*

Mountain in Galilee off Acre–Safed road, 5 km. E of Karmi'el. Height: 598 m. above sea level.

Har Karkom (Jebel 'Adeid) *125:964*

Mountain in Negev 40 km. S of Mizpe Ramon. Height: 847 m. above sea level. Some of its cliffs have rock drawings from 4th and 3rd c. BCE.

Ḥarmala, Ḥaramil *171:118*

Bedouin village (pop.: 250) on border of Judean Desert 7 km. SE of Bethlehem. Name means a type of desert plant.

Har Mattat *183:272*

Look-out point in Galilee 3 km. NW of kibbutz Sasa. Same name as nearby mount. Established 1979.

Har Miḥya *123:025*

Mountain in Negev 8 km. SW of Sede Boqer. Height: 610 m. above sea level. Traces of ancient farming at foot of mountain and on slope 3 groups of rock drawings and Nabatean inscriptions. On summits of surrounding hills are remains of round structures and courtyards. Sherds indicate occupation in Early and Middle Bronze Ages, and Roman and Byzantine Periods.

Har Nezer *202:286*

Mount in Galilee 2 km. S of kibbutz Menara. Height: 760 m. above sea level. Look-out point over Ḥula Valley and S Lebanon. Part of mountain falls within small nature reserve (90 d.) with many orchids.

Har Peres (Tell Faras) *231:263*

Extinct volcano on Golan Heights in Rafid area near Syrian border. Height: 929 m. above sea level and mouth of crater is 200 m. in diameter, with a depth of 35 m. Hellenistic tombs were found here — among the very few found on Golan Heights. The small number of sherds found indicate occupation in Middle and Late Bronze Ages, Iron Age, Roman, Byzantine and Ottoman Periods.

Har Qarantal → Deir el Quruntul

Har Qedumim → Nazareth Ridge

Har Ramon *114:990*

Highest mountain in Negev Hills. Height: 1,035 m. above sea level. On its summit are tumuli from Middle Bronze Age.

Har Rotem *157:048*

Mountain in Negev 7 km. SE of Dimona. Arabic name: Jebel Zuleiqa. On E slope are remains of ancient buildings from various periods: round ones from Early Bronze Age; square ones from Middle Bronze Age; square watch-tower from Iron Age, rock-cut tomb from Roman and Byzantine Periods.

Har Sha'ul → Mt. Gilboa'

Har Shifon (Tell Abu el Khanzir) *222:275*

Extinct volcano on Golan Heights 4 km. NE of Kafr Nafakh. Height: 977 m. above sea level. Arabic name means father of the pigs and is called thus because of wild boars in area. Hebrew name from rye (*shifon*) which was grown here. At foot of tel is a memorial to 74 men of tank brigade who fought and died on Golan Heights during Yom Kippur War.

Har Shomeron → Samarian Hills

Hartuv *150:130*

Railway station between Shimshon junction and Bet Shemesh. In 1895 a farming village was founded here by immigrants on lands purchased from Anglican mission of Jerusalem. The mission tried unsuccessfully to establish a settlement in 1883. The name Hartuv is taken from the name of nearby Arab village, 'Artuf. The village was destroyed in Riots of 1929, rebuilt but evacuated during War of Independence; again destroyed by Arabs but shortly thereafter taken by Israel Defence Forces. The *moshav* Naḥam and regional school Even Ha'Azar were built on its ruins. Part of lands were used for industrial zone of Bet Shemesh.

Ḥaruẓim ● *138:182*

Rural settlement in Sharon 5 km. N of Ra'ananna. Name taken from Biblical verse (Prov. 10:4) "the hand of the *diligent* makes rich." Originally an immigrant transit camp established in 1951 and called Ḥof HaSharon. Pop.: 600. Area: 200 d.

Har Warda *223:290*

Extinct volcano on N Golan Heights 1 km. N of Buq'ata. Height: 1,226 m. above sea level (highest on Golan Heights).

Har Ya'ala ✱ *154:128*

Summit in Judean Hills 4 km. E of Bet Shemesh. Height: 631 m. above sea level. Arabic name: Deir el Hawwa (home of winds). Observation point overlooking Judean Foothills.

Har Yedidya ⛰ *142:889*

Mountain in S Negev 6 km. NW of Elat. Remains of building apparently used as workshops for manufacture of millstones. This theory is based on unfinished millstones found scattered over area.

Har Yehuda → Judean Hills

⛰ **Har Yoresh** *143:116*

Ruins of settlement in 'Adullam region 4 km. NE of Bet Guvrin. Apparently dates from Byzantine Period. Site has columbarium in form of cross, and other ruins.

Har Yosifon (Tell Yusuf) *225:273*

Extinct volcano on Golan Heights 5 km. E of Kafr Nafakh. Height: 981 m. above sea level. Hebrew name same as designation in Middle Ages for writings of Josephus b. Mattathias.

Har Ẓin (Hor HaHar) *156:027*

Mountain in Negev, in Biq'at Ẓin 10 km. SW of Ma'ale 'Aqrabbim Height: 278 m. above sea level. Good view of entire area seen from summit. According to one theory it is site of Mount Hor, burial site of High Priest Aaron during Israelite wanderings in desert. (Other theories claim the location of Hor HaHar to be at Jebel Harun, in Transjordan, or Jebel el Muweilaḥ, W of Qadesh Barnea'.) **Potato field** Wide field of circular limestones, with diameter of 20 to 50 cm., in shape of potatoes, SE of mount. Some of the stones bear animal shapes. According to one theory, these stones were formed as a result of a build-up of minerals from animal skeletons.

HaShefela → Judean Foothills

o **(El) Hashimiyya** *171:207*

Arab village 7 km. W of Jenin. Pop.: 450, mainly farmers.

★ **HaSolelim** *172:239*

Kibbutz 8 km. NW of Nazareth. Founded 1949. Area: 6,000 d. Pop.: 220. **HaSolelim Forest** Nature reserve with remains of large ancient forest. Area: 1,500 d. Indigenous Tabor oak.

∴ **Ḥaspin** *224:250*

Regional centre for Golan Heights religious settlements: Ramat Magshimim, Nov and Avne Etan. Founded 1973. Origin of name: abandoned village of Khisfin which retained name of Second Temple Jewish settlement, Hisfiya.

HaTannur → Mappal Naḥal 'Iyyon

● **Ḥavaẓẓelet HaSharon** *137:196*

Moshav 3 km. N of Netanya on seashore. Named after a common flower of region, Sharon lily. Founded 1935 by Polish immigrants. Area: 1,000 d. Pop.: 350.

◆ **Ḥawwat 'Eden** *196:208*

Government farm 4 km. S of Bet She'an. Name based on legend that Bet She'an Valley was entrance to Garden of Eden.

■ **Ḥawwat HaShomer** *188:240*

Religious educational institute in Galilee. Founded 1956. Pop.: 260, staff and students. Within grounds is Sejera, where HaShomer organization was founded.

Ḥawwat Kinneret → Kinneret *(moshava)*

◆ **Ḥawwat Mattityahu** *190:273*

Agricultural experimental station in Galilee near kibbutz Bar'am. Founded 1972. Named after Mattityahu Kahanovich, director of hill region in Settlement Department of Jewish Agency.

◆ **Ḥawwat Mordekhay** *127:147*

Agricultural experimental station on central Coastal Plain near Nes Ẓiyyona. Affiliated to National University Institute. Founded 1935 and named after agronomist, Mordekhay Wilkansky.

◇ **Ḥawwat Musa el 'Alami** *197:140*

Farm and agricultural school 4 km. E of Jericho. Founded 1952 by Musa el 'Alami for refugee children in Jericho area.

◆ **Ḥawwat Noy** *142:196*

Government farm in Sharon near kibbutz Ma'barot.

◆ **Ḥawwat Shalem** *132:161*

Seed-improvement farm near Kefar Shalem in Tel Aviv area. Founded 1949.

◆ **Ḥawwat Shemu'el** *202:220*

Experimental farm in Jordan Valley 10 km. N of Bet She'an. Named after Sam Hamburg, Jewish farmer from California, pioneer of cotton growing in Israel. Founded 1952.

◆ **Ḥawwat Shikmim (Mar'it)** *115:105*

Ranch for sheep-breeding in Negev 3 km. SE of Sederot. Established 1954 by Jews from Australia who attempted to foster a new breed of sheep. The ranch was sold in 1960 and named Mar'it. In 1976 Ari'el Sharon purchased farm and gave it its present name, after plentiful sycamore trees in area.

Ḥay Bar → Yotvata

● **HaYogev** *169:224*

Moshav in Yizre'el Valley 6 km. W of 'Afula. Founded 1949 by members of Bet Eshel whose settlement in N Negev was destroyed during War of Independence. Area: 6,500 d. Pop.: 360.

● **Ḥazav** *128:132*

Moshav on central Coastal Plain 4 km. S of Gedera. *Ḥazav* is name of flower (squill). Founded 1949 by Libyan immigrants. Area: 3,200 d. Pop.: 780.

★ **Ḥazerim** *(Deut. 2:23)* *122:072*

Kibbutz 6 km. W of Be'er Sheva'. Named after Biblical site where the Avvim are said to have lived. Founded 1946, one of 11 settlements set up at the time in Negev, by Scouts and Youth 'Aliyah (from Teheran). During War of Independence it was cut off from rest of country for a short while. Area: 12,750 d. Pop.: 550. **Hurbat Sufa and Be'er Sufa** Within kibbutz are two adjacent ancient sites: Ḥurbat Sufa (Kh. eṣ Ṣufi) remains from the Israelite Period and Be'er Sufa (Bir eṣ Ṣufi) remains from Roman and Byzantine settlement. Between the two sites are remnants of a Byzantine bathhouse.

● **Ḥazeva** *(moshav)* *176:019*

Moshav in 'Arava 35 km. S of Sedom. Named after ruins of Ḥazeva, 6 km. NW of *moshav*. Founded as *naḥal* outpost in 1962. Became permanent civilian settlement in 1970. Pop.: several hundred. W of *moshav* off main road, is field school.

Ḥazeva (oasis and ruins) *173:024*

Ancient ruins near oasis in Naḥal 'Arava, 30 km. S of Sedom off road to Elat. Name Ḥazeva in its Greek form is mentioned in 6th c. Greek writings found in Be'er Sheva'. Site of way-station at time of Nabateans, Romans, Byzantines and British. Has water source — 'En Ḥazeva ('Ein Ḥusb). Near spring is large jubjube tree, considered to be oldest tree in country. Nearby are remains of Roman-Byzantine fort and building from Iron Age and Hasmonean Period. Some believe it to be site of Tamar, built by King Solomon.

● **Ḥazon** *187:256*

Moshav in Galilee 3 km. SW of Ḥananya junction. Named after Mt. Ḥazon on whose slopes *moshav* lies. Founded 1949. Area: 3,000 d. Pop.: 360.

◆ **Ḥazon Yeḥezqel** *124:119*

Training farm for Agudat Yisra'el on S Coastal Plain. Named after Rabbi Yeḥezqel Abramsky of London.

Ḥazor → Tel Ḥazor

★ **Ḥazor Ashdod** *124:131*

Kibbutz 8 km. SE of Ashdod. Origin of name: ancient city of Hazor included in Judah tribal allotment (Josh. 15:23 and 24). Founded in 1937 by groups from HaShomer HaZa'ir, Tel Yosef and 'En Ḥarod. During War of Independence it was on front-line opposite Egyptian army. Area: 8,000 d. Pop.: 650. In 1956 a mosaic floor from a 5th and 6th c. Byzantine church was uncovered here.

★ **HaZorea'** *161:227*

Kibbutz in Yizre'el Valley, S of Yoqne'am. Founded 1936 by members of German youth movement. Under attack by Arab bands during Disturbances of 1936–1939, and prior to 1948 served as Palmaḥ base. Area: 6,500 d. Pop.: 850. Art and antiquities museum, Bet Wilfred Israel, which houses

Wilfred Israel Far Eastern art collection. **Antiquities** in area: houses, caves, tombs and rock-cut tombs. Flint implements and sherds indicate occupation from Chalcolithic Period until Middle Bronze Age and again from Hellenistic and Roman Periods.

● **HaZore'im** *197:239*

Moshav in Galilee 6 km. SE of Tiberias. Founded 1939 on PICA lands. Area: 6,000 d. Pop.: 350.

Ḥazor HaGelilit *201:264*

Town in Galilee 2 km. N of Rosh Pinna. Origin of name: Biblical city of Hazor whose remains have been excavated at nearby Tel Ḥazor. Founded 1953. Pop.: 6,500, mainly immigrants from N African countries. An ancient tomb exists in the town, believed to be that of Ḥoni HaMa'agel and his grandchildren.

□ **Hebron** **(Hevron)** *(Num. 13:22)* *160:104*

City in Judean Hills 36 km. S of Jerusalem; one of the oldest continuously inhabited cities in the world. Almost as rich as Jerusalem in Biblical associations. Height: 950 m. above sea level. Also mentioned in Bible as Kiriath-arba and Mamre. Abode of Patriarchs Abraham, Isaac and Jacob, who were buried in Me'arat (cave) HaMakhpela. Canaanite city before Israelite conquest and dwelling place of descendants of Anak, as described in Biblical story of spies (Num. 13:22). In tribal allotment of Judah. Capital of David's kingdom — he reigned here for seven years until he took Jerusalem. After destruction of First Temple the Edomites dominated city until Judah Maccabee expelled them (162 BCE). During Revolt against Rome, Romans captured city from Simon Bar Giora and set it on fire. During Roman Period it was a small town called Avramyus, but in Byzantine Period it began to develop anew. In 7th c. it was conquered by Arabs who called it el Khalil (the friend), name of Patriarch Abraham in Koran. Arabs allowed Jews to return and settle here. In 1100 Crusaders captured city and expelled Jews. After Mamluk conquest at beginning of 13th c., Jews were again allowed to return to Hebron but a Jewish community did not grow until middle of 16th c. after Ottoman conquest. During British Mandate there was a fairly large Jewish community in Hebron that was destroyed during 1929 Riots, when many Hebron Jews were slaughtered. From 1930 an attempt was made to renew Jewish settlement, but this was frustrated by the 1936 Disturbances. During Six-Day War, the Israel Defence Forces took Hebron without any resistance. In 1968 work began on the Jewish quarter of Qiryat Arba' in NE part of city. Hebron today is a large Arab city with a population of 39,000. **Me'arat HaMakhpela** Site of ancient Hebron on Tell Rumayda where Iron Age remains were uncovered. At its centre was Me'arat HaMakhpela bought by Abraham from Ephron the Hittite (Gen. 23:7 ff.). According to tradition the patriarchs and matriarchs: Abraham, Sarah, Isaac, Rebekah, Jacob and Leah, are buried here. Legend has it that Adam and Eve are also buried here. The structure above the cave, known as the Haram el Khalil, shrine of the friend, was built in days of Herod and expanded during Crusader Period. During Mamluk Period it was divided into several mosques, embellished with slabs of marble, coloured plaster and inscriptions. From 13th c. Jews were forbidden to enter the cave; they were only allowed up to 7th step leading to the cave. After Six-Day War cave was opened to Jews. However, it continued to remain a source of feuding between Jews and Moslems. **Elon Mamre** At entrance to Hebron, to N, are ruins of ancient settlement believed to be site of ancient Mamre, where Abraham sat while the 3 angels came to visit him (Gen. 18:11 ff.). Remains of building similar to that over Me'arat HaMakhpela and a well called Abraham's Well. **Eshel Avraham** In W of city *158:105* is an ancient oak tree, called Eshel Avraham. A popular legend associates this tree with Abraham. The tree and land around it

HEBRON — QIRYAT ARBA'

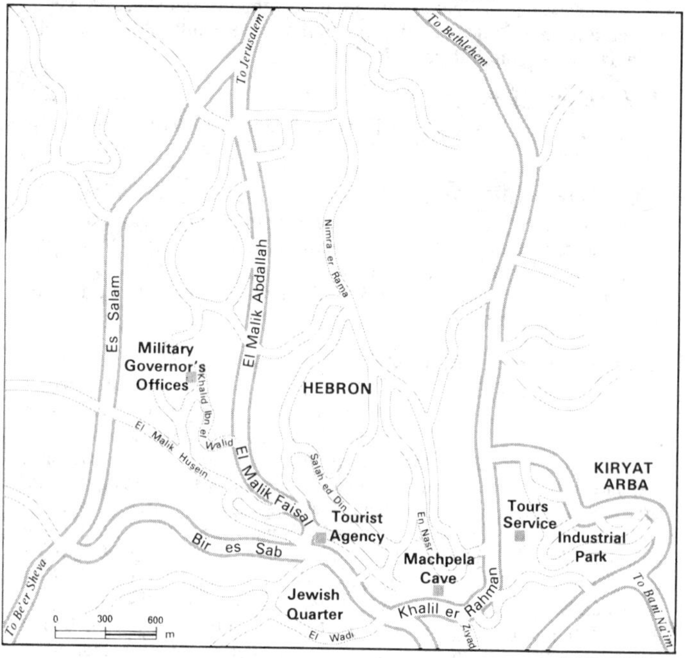

© carta, JERUSALEM

belong to the Russian church which built a church and hospice for pilgrims here. **Jewish quarter** Ruins of Jewish quarter destroyed in 1929 Riots. Jewish and Karaite cemeteries nearby. **Qiryat Arba'** Jewish quarter in NE part of Hebron. Founded 1970 by group called Hebron settlers, organized in 1968, who first settled in a local hotel and military government building in Hebron. Qiryat Arba''s population is 1,500.

Ḥefẓi Bah (Ḥadera) — *140:207*

Plantation within Ḥadera off old road to Haifa. Founded in 1908 by Agudat Neta'im. Origin of name: "but you shall be called *My delight in her*" (*ḥefẓi bah*), (Isa. 62:4). The plantation was a training site in 1921 for founders of kibbutz Ḥefẓi Bah in Yizre'el Valley (see below).

★ Ḥefẓi Bah (Yizre'el Valley) — *190:214*

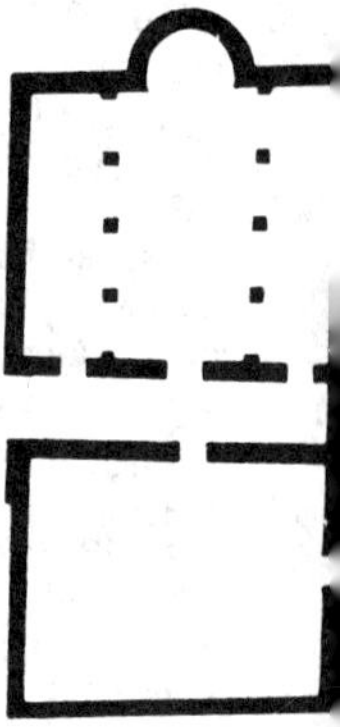

Kibbutz in Yizre'el Valley at foot of Mt. Gilboa'; site of the 6th c. CE Bet Alfa synagogue. Name from a Biblical phrase (Isa. 62:4); same as name of plantation (Ḥefzi Bah in Ḥadera) where founders of kibbutz received their training. Founded in 1922 by members of Blau-Weiss movement from Germany and Czechoslovakia. Pop.: 600. Area: 8,700 d. Kibbutz has a Japanese garden planted by members of Japanese Makuya sect who maintain a special relationship of friendship with kibbutz. **Ancient synagogue** Within kibbutz a coloured mosaic synagogue floor was unearthed in 1928. The synagogue from 6th c. CE was a basilica-type structure with entrance from N and ark of law in S. The mosaic covered the entire floor space. In centre of nave is zodiac wheel arranged around the sun-god Helios. In 4 corners are figures depicting the seasons. The aisle is covered with geometric patterns. On N side of zodiac is a drawing depicting attempted sacrifice of Isaac. On S side are drawings of 2 seven-branched candelabra, *lulavim* (palm branches), *etrogim* (citrons), censers and 2 lions. The nave mosaic is bordered by drawings of animals and flowers.

∴ **Ḥeitil** *223:245*

Abandoned village on Golan Heights 3 km. E of *moshav* Eli 'Al. Was built on ruins of ancient settlement from Roman and Byzantine Periods. Also occupied during Arab Period and Middle Ages. Ancient stones were re-used in village buildings.

• **Ḥeleẓ** *117:109*

Moshav in Lakhish region 8 km. S of Giv'ati junction. Named after one of King David's mighty men (II Sam. 23:26). Founded 1950. During War of Independence, fierce battles raged here in attempt to break through to Negev. Pop.: 630. Area: 5,000 d. Near *moshav* is memorial to soldiers of Giv'ati Brigade who fell in Negev battles (inscription on memorial reads: "You who go to the Negev, remember us"); also a memorial to soldiers of 52nd Battalion from War of Independence. Adjacent to *moshav* *116:110* is first oil field discovered in Israel (22 September 1955). Nearby are drilling sites from Mandatory Period.

• **Ḥemed** *135:158*

Moshav on central Coastal Plain near Or Yehuda. Name from Hebrew acronym for veteran religious soldiers. Founded 1950. Pop.: 480. Area: 1,400 d.

Ḥeres *164:167*

Civilian holding-point in Samarian Hills 18 km. SW of Shekhem. Established 1978 by Gush Emunim supporters. Designated as principal Jewish city in Samarian Hills.

• **Ḥerev Le'et** *142:200*

Moshav in Sharon 4 km. S of Ḥadera. Origin of name: "they shall beat their *swords into plowshares*" (Isa. 2:4). Founded 1947 by veterans of British and Czechoslovakian armies. Pop.: 220. Area: 1,750 d.

Ḥermon → **Mt. Ḥermon**

Herodium *(Rom. 16:11)* *173:119*

Mountain in Judean Desert 6 km. SE of Bethlehem, off Bethlehem-Za'tara-Hebron road. Height: 758 m. above sea level. Named after King Herod who built a fortress on summit and a settlement at its foot. According to Joseph b. Mattathias, Herod was also buried here. After great Revolt against Rome was quelled in 70 CE, the fort served as a refuge for fighters who fled from Jerusalem, until it too fell — like Masada 3 years later. During the Bar Kokhba war, the fortress was used by rebels. Also occupied during Byzantine Period. Excavations uncovered remains of fortress: a double circular curtain wall with 4 towers jutting out of wall and a gateway from the NE. Inside the walls were storerooms and water reservoirs. Remains of a hall with pillars and a bathhouse were found within fortress. Aqueducts brought water from Artas region. During the Revolt, water cisterns were hewn in rocks and tunnels cut into bowels of mountain. During this period, one of the rooms was converted into a synagogue, similar in style to the one found at Masada. A mosaic floor from the Byzantine church built here still exists today. Lower Herodium, at foot of mountain to N, includes remains of palaces, storerooms, hippodrome and pool.

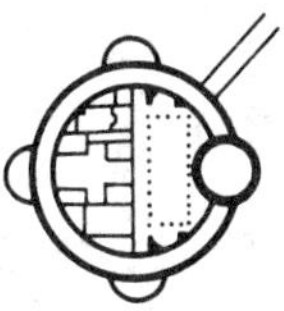

• **Ḥerut** *142:183*

Moshav in Sharon 5 km. N of Kefar Sava. Founded 1930. Pop.: 440. Area: 3,800 d.

HERZLIYYA

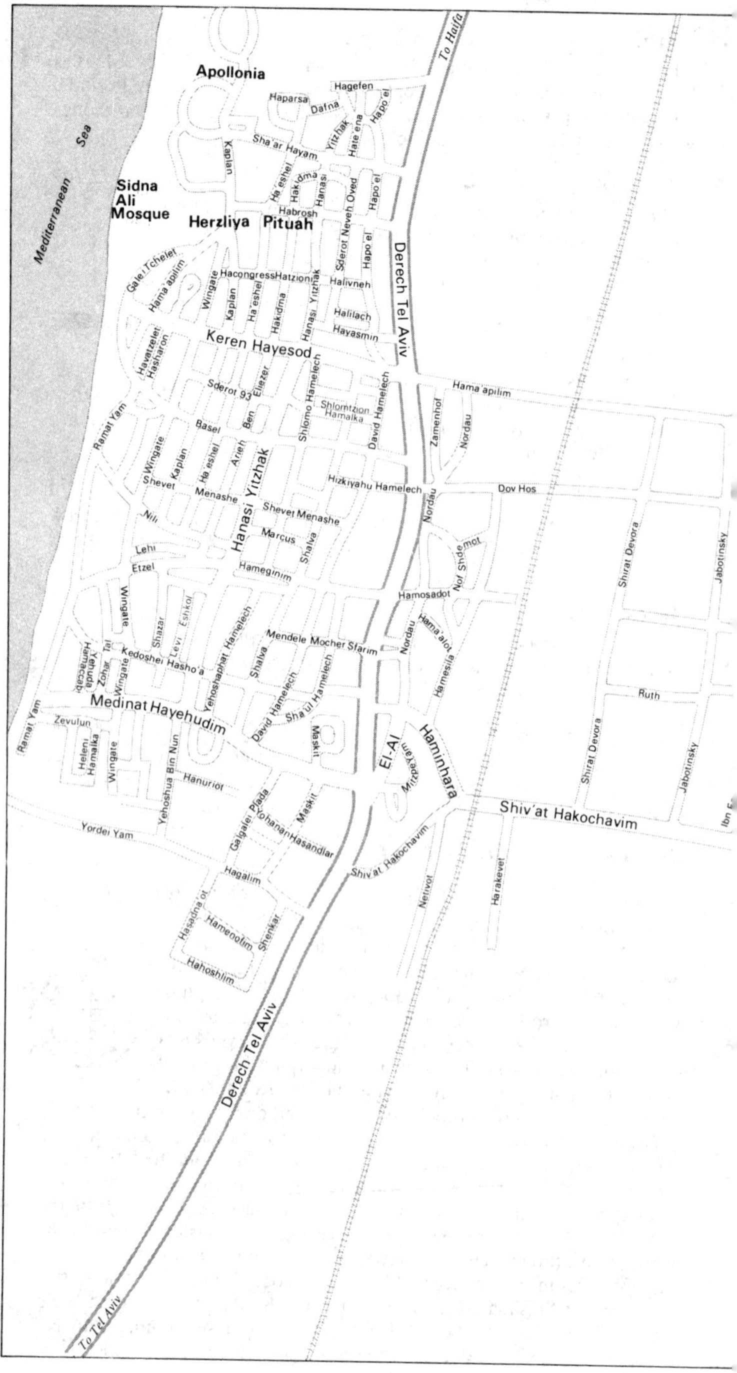
To Haifa
Apollonia
Hagefen
Haparsa
Dafna
Hapo'el
Yitzhak
Hate'ena
Mediterranean Sea
Sha'ar Hayam
Kaplan
Sidna Ali Mosque
Ha'eshel
Hakidma
Hanasi
Neveh Oved
Habrosh
Herzliya Pituah
Derech Tel Aviv
Galei Tchelet
Hama'apilim
Wingate
Hacongress
Hatzioni
Sderot
Halivneh
Halilach
Hayasmin
Havatzelet Hasharon
Keren Hayesod
Eliezer
Sderot 93
Shlomo Hamelech
Shlomtzion Hamalka
David Hamelech
Basel
Ben
Ramat Yam
Arieh
Zamenhof
Nordau
Hanasi Yitzhak
Hizkiyahu Hamelech
Dov Hos
Shevet Menashe
Nili
Marcus
Shalva
Lehi
Nof Shdemot
Etzel
Hameginim
Shirat Devora
Jabotinsky
Hamosadot
Shazar
Levi Eshkol
Hama'alot
Mendele Mocher Sfarim
Yehuda Hamaccabi
Tal
Zohar
Kedoshei Hasho'a
Yehoshaphat Hamelech
Hamesila
Ruth
Medinat Hayehudim
David Hamelech
Sha'ul Hamelech
Maskit
Zevulun
Heleni Hamalka
Bin Nun
El-Al
Haminhara
Mitzpe Yam
Hanuriot
Yehoshua
Galgalei Plada
Yohanan Hasandlar
Shiv'at Hakochavim
Ibn
Yordei Yam
Hagalim
Netivot
Harakevet
Hasadna'ot
Hameoofim
Shenkar
Hahoshlim
To Tel Aviv

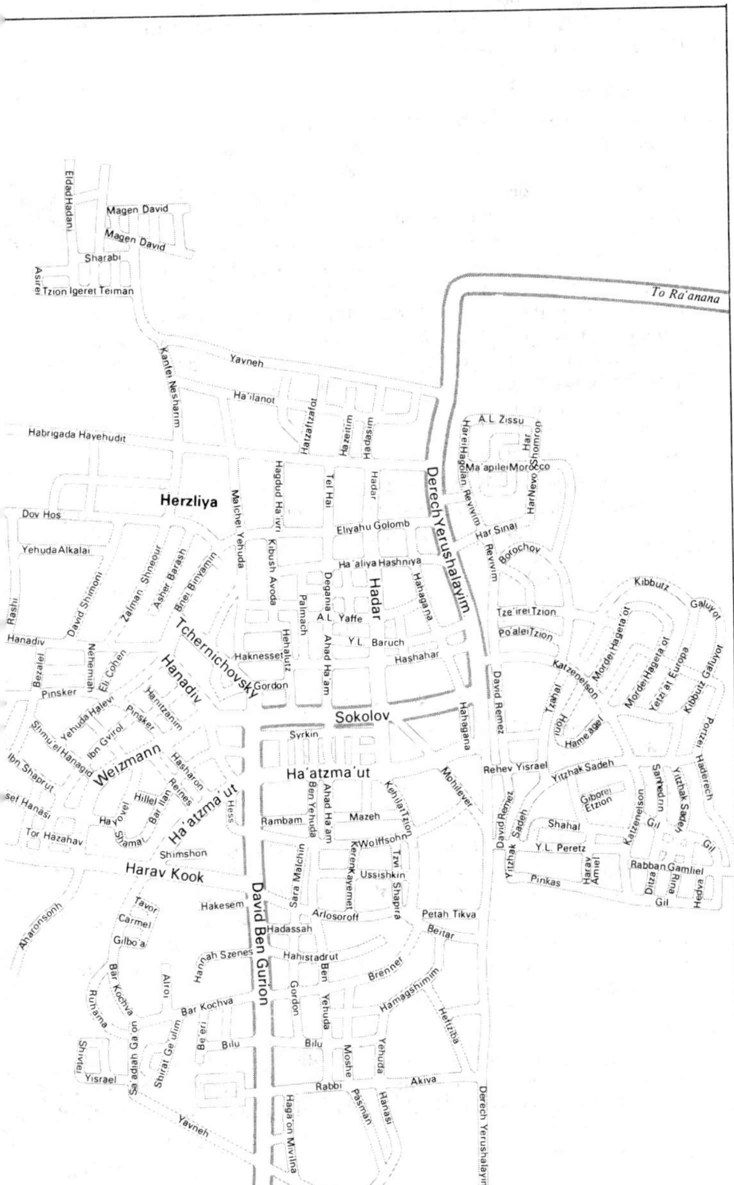

© carta, JERUSALEM

Herzl Forest **(Ya'ar Herzl)** *144:151*

Large forest in Judean Foothills SE of Ben Shemen. Named after Theodor Herzl, father of political Zionism. Planting started in 1908. Recreation area within forest.

Herẓliyya *135:174*

City on Sharon coast between Tel Aviv and Netanya. Named after Theodor (Binyamin Ze'ev) Herzl, father of political Zionism. Founded 1924 by American Zion Commonwealth Corporation. Initially an agricultural settlement. After War of Independence it developed with giant strides. Over the years it was united with neighbouring quarters: Nof Yam, Shaviv, Newe 'Amal, Newe 'Oved and Gelilot. Municipal area is 24,000 d. with a population of 70,000. Youth village named after David Raziel, Irgun commander who was killed while on a mission in Iraq. Within city is a cave tomb, rock-cut tombs and a rock-cut tunnel 165 m. long that drained swamp waters which collected between coarse sand ridges and the sea. Probably constructed during Byzantine Period.

Ḥevel Eshkol **(HaBesor)**

Settlement region in W Negev. Boundaries: N — Netivot area; E — Sa'ad-HaNasi junction road; S — Ḥurvot Ḥaluẓa and W — Gaza Strip. Region is bisected by Naḥal Besor. The W section is more fertile than the E section and the whole region has a number of agricultural settlements as well as the more recent Negev settlements. First called Ḥevel HaBesor but in 1969 its name was changed to Ḥevel Eshkol, in memory of Levi Eshkol, Israel's third prime minister.

Ḥevel Tefen

Region in W Upper Galilee, N of Acre-Safed road. Extends SW to NE, between Aḥihud and Ma'alot-Tarshiḥa. Name based on Arabic name for nearby ancient ruin — Kh. Tufaniyya.

Ḥevel Yattir

Region in NE Negev. Boundaries: N — Hebron Hills; E — 'Ira Hills; S — Be'er Sheva'-'Arad road; W — Be'er Sheva'-Hebron road. Area: 200,000 d. The region is rocky with little water. Partly forested. **Ḥurbat Yattir** (Kh. 'Attir) *152:084* — site of ancient city of Jattir, birthplace of 2 of David's mighty men (II Sam. 23:38). Mentioned in Onomasticon of Eusebius and appears on Madaba map. Apparently destroyed in 7th c. Remains of buildings, wells, burial caves and wine press. To E is a forest observation post.

Ḥever *175:217*

Rural centre for settlements: Addirim, Baraq and Devora in Ḥevel Ta'anakh, in Yizre'el Valley. All these names are derived from a story of battle of Prophetess Deborah. (Heber, the Kenite, was husband of Jael.)

Ḥeẓron *160:086*

Civilian holding-point in Judean Hills 5 km. SE of Eshtemoa' (Sammu'). Founded 1977.

Ḥibbat Ẓiyyon *142:200*

Moshav in Sharon. Named after Ḥibbat Ẓiyyon, a movement founded in Russia in 1882, whose aim was Jewish national revival and immigration to Ereẓ Israel. *Moshav* founded 1933 by pioneers from Russia. Area: 2,200 d. Pop.: 320.

Ḥifar *214:277*

Abandoned village on Golan Heights 12 km. NE of Benot Ya'aqov Bridge. Built on ruins of ancient settlement and ancient dressed building stones have been re-used in village houses. Stone decorations include crosses, an eagle and fragmentary Greek inscriptions. Also preserved here are remains of ancient arched buildings and a cellar built of stone slabs.

Hilla *175:271*

Observation site in Upper Galilee 2 km. N of Ma'alot-Tarshiḥa. Name synonymous with that of adjacent mount Ziw. Established 1980.

Ḥilluf *164:239*

Name of Bedouin tribe and its place of residence in Lower Galilee, 3 km. N of Qiryat Tiv'on. Pop.: 900.

Ḥinnanit *165:210*

Community settlement in N Samaria 4 km. S of Umm el Faḥm. Named after plant which flourishes in area. Established 1980.

Hisham's Palace → Kh. el Mafjar

Ḥizma *175:138*

Arab village in Judean Hills 5 km. NE of Jerusalem. Pop.: 1,000. Possibly site of Biblical Bethazmaveth — in Benjamin tribal allotment (Neh. 7:28; 12:29); also called Azmaveth (Ezra 2:24). In 19th c. wheat was grown in village for Jews of Jerusalem to be used in baking *mazza shemura* ("guarded flour" used in making unleavened Passover bread; closely supervised from time wheat is harvested). At foot of village are ancient tombstones called by Arabs Qabur Bani Israil (tombs of Israelites).

Hodayot *191:243*

Religious agricultural school 9 km. W of Tiberias, adjacent to kibbutz Lavi. Founded 1950. Its first students were children of Indian immigrants, hence name (*hodu* = India). Courses of study: mechanics, automobile electronics and sewing. There are 150 pupils. School caters to new immigrants and development areas.

Hod HaSharon *140:173*

Town with local council off Petaḥ Tiqwa-Kefar Sava road. Conglomeration of several neighbourhoods. Ramatayim and Hadar amalgamated in 1951, and called Hadar-Ramatayim; in 1963 they were joined by Ramat Hadar, in 1964 by Magdi'el and then took on the name of Hod HaSharon. Later joined by Gane Ẓevi, Newe Ne'eman and Gan Meged. Area: 22,000 d. Pop.: 17,000.

Hodiyya *115:120*

Moshav on Coastal Plain 5 km. E of Ashqelon. Founded 1949 on lands of abandoned village, Julis, by immigrants from India (*hodu* = India) hence the name. Today there are 500 settlers from Persia, Yemen and Kurdistan.

Ḥofit *137:199*

Village in Sharon 6 km. N of Netanya. Located on shore, hence its name (*ḥof* = coast). Founded 1955. Pop.: 700.

Ḥogla *143:199*

Moshav in Sharon 10 km. NE of Netanya. Named after Hoglah (Josh. 17:3), one of daughters of Zelophehad who demanded and received an allotment within tribe of Manasseh who settled in this area. Founded 1933 by Hadera labourers from Russia, Poland and Bulgaria. Area: 2,000 d. Pop.: 220.

ḤOLON – BAT YAM – AZOR

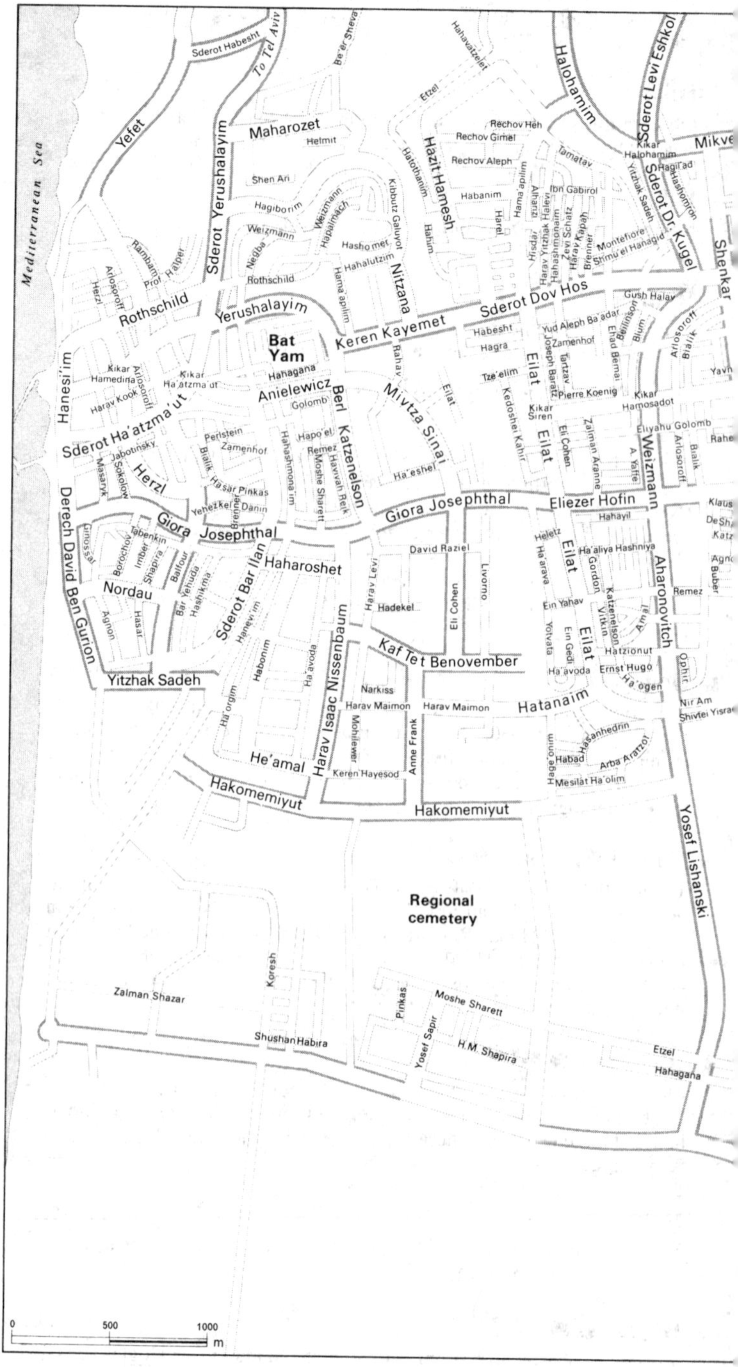

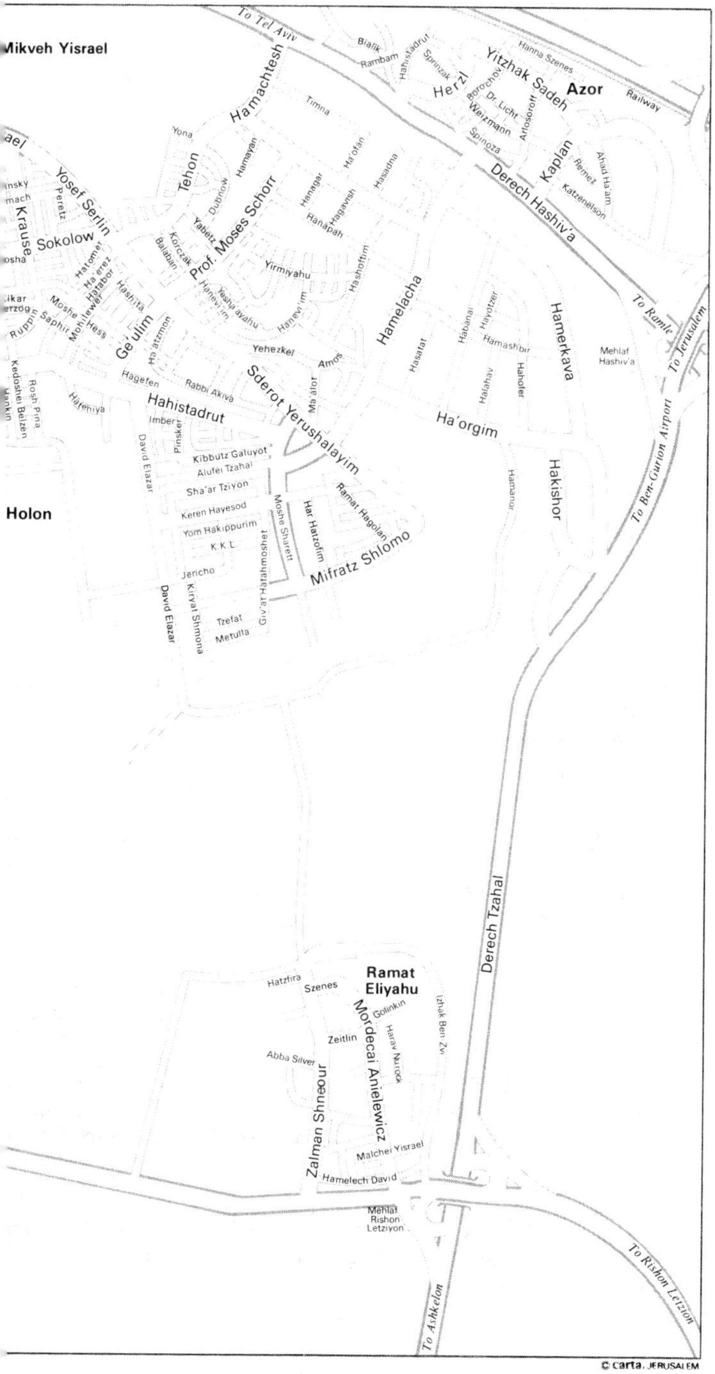
Mikveh Yisrael
To Tel Aviv
Bialik
Rambam
Hahistadrut
Sprinzak
Herzl
Borochov
Dr. Licht
Weizmann
Spinoza
Arlosoroff
Yitzhak Sadeh
Hanna Szenes
Azor
Railway
Kaplan
Remez
Ahad Ha'am
Katzenelson
Derech Hashiv'a
Hamachtesh
Timna
Yona
Tehon
Hamayan
Dubnow
Ha'ofan
Hasadna
Hanagar
Hagavish
Hanapah
Yosef Serlin
Peretz
Krause
Sokolow
Hatomer
Ha'erez
Hatabor
Hashita
Moshe Hess
Mohilewer
Saphir
Ge'ulim
Yabetz
Korczak
Balaban
Prof. Moses Schorr
Yirmiyahu
Hashoftim
Yesha'ayahu
Hanevi'im
Ha'atzmaut
Yehezkel
Amos
Hamelacha
Hasatat
Habanai
Hayotzer
Hamashbir
Hahofer
Halahav
Hamerkava
Mehlaf Hashiv'a
To Ramle
To Jerusalem
Hagefen
Rabbi Akiva
Harehiya
Hahistadrut
Imber
Pinsker
David Elazar
Sderot Yerushalayim
Ma'alot
Ha'orgim
Hamanor
Hakishor
To Ben-Gurion Airport
Kibbutz Galuyot
Alufei Tzahal
Sha'ar Tziyon
Keren Hayesod
Yom Hakippurim
K.K.L.
Jericho
Moshe Sharett
Har Hatzofim
Ramat Hagolan
Mifratz Shlomo
Giv'at Hatahmoshet
Kiryat Shmona
Tzefat
Metulla
Rosh Pina
Kedoshei Belzen
Holon
Derech Tzahal
Ramat
Eliyahu
Hatzfira
Szenes
Golinkin
Mordecai Anielewicz
Harav Nurock
Izhak Ben-Zvi
Zeitlin
Abba Silver
Zalman Shneour
Malchei Yisrael
Hamelech David
Mehlaf
Rishon
Letziyon
To Ashkelon
To Rishon Letzion

■ **Ḥolon** *(Josh. 15:51)* *130:158*

City on central Coastal Plain S of Tel Aviv. Name derives from sands (*ḥol* = sand) upon which city was built. (Same name as Biblical city in tribal allotment of Judah.) Founded as a suburb in 1933. In 1941 united with a number of other quarters: Qiryat 'Avoda, Agrobank and Moledet. At beginning of War of Independence it was cut off from Tel Aviv by Arab forces who established themselves on hill of Tell er Rish, until Israel Defence Forces took hill. Acquired municipal status in 1950. Area: 20,000 d. Pop.: 122,000. **Tel Gibborim** (Tell er Rish) — park with 3 memorials in memory of those who fell in battle for tel, Israel's wars, and victims of "illegal" immigrant ship, Struma. **Tel Ḥolon** Within city *128:156* is tel of ancient settlement with remains of many buildings. Sherds and flint implements indicate occupation in Chalcolithic Period, Bronze Age, Iron Age and Hasmonean, Roman and Byzantine Periods.

★ **Ḥoreshim** *147:171*

Kibbutz in Sharon 7 km. SE of Kefar Sava. Name derives from Biblical Valley of Charashim (I Chron. 4:14). Founded 1955. Pop.: 180. Area: 3,000 d.

Hor HaHar → Har Ẓin

● **Ḥosen** *178:267*

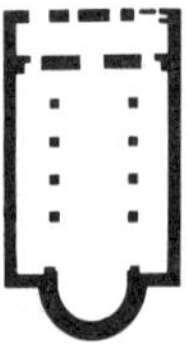

Moshav in Galilee 2 km. SE of Ma'alot. Founded 1949 by former Irgun members on lands of abandoned village Suḥmata. First called Naḥalat Shelomo in memory of Shelomo Ben Yosef, member of Betar who was hanged by British in 1938. Pop.: 230. **Ancient remains** Byzantine church with mosaic floor from 5th c., tomb caves, rock-cut cisterns and pool.

Hosha'ya *178:240*

Observation site in Lower Galilee 1 km. NE of Ẓippori. Named after Rabbi Hoshaiah Rabbah, one of sages of Ẓippori during 2nd c. Established 1980.

○ **Ḥubeila** *160:118*

Arab village (pop.: 400) in Gush 'Eẓyon. Established on ruins of kibbutz Massu'ot Yiẓḥaq, destroyed in War of Independence. Remains of 4th c. Byzantine church.

○ **Ḥujeila** *174:124*

Arab village on border of Judean Desert 4 km. E of Bethlehem. Name means small partridge. Pop.: 150.

★ **Ḥulata** *207:273*

Kibbutz in Hula Valley. Origin of name: sea of Ḥulata, i.e. the now-drained Ḥula lake. Founded 1936 by a Youth 'Aliyah group from Germany together with a local HaNo'ar Ha'Oved group. Settlers suffered from malaria carried by mosquitoes which bred in Ḥula swamps. On eve of War of Independence served as base for Palmaḥ platoon. Kibbutz was in front-line of Syrian invasion during War of Independence. Until Six-Day War it suffered from continuing Syrian attacks across border. Area: 6,000 d. Pop.: 500. Kibbutz has natural museum named after Zionist leader, Ya'aqov Thon.

★ **Ḥulda** *138:137*

Collective settlement in Judean Foothills 4 km. NW of Naḥshon junction. Name same as that of adjacent Arab village abandoned during War of Independence. Started 1907 as a farm for labourers planting Herzl Forest. Attacked and destroyed in 1929 Riots, but resettled in

1931 by Gordonia group. Moved to present site in 1937, about 1.5 km. W of farm. During Disturbances of 1936–1939 it was attacked several times by Arab gangs. In 1943 British army and police conducted a massive search here for Haganah arms. During War of Independence it served as departure base for convoys to besieged Jerusalem. Also served as Israel Defence Forces base for attack on Latrun. Area: 7,000 d. Pop.: 350. Bet Herzl — the Iḥud HaKevuẓot We HaKibbutzim archives; Gordonia-Maccabi HaẒa'ir museum in name of Pinḥas Lavon and a statue commemorating Ephraim Chizhik, Haganah commander killed here in 1929. To the E is Ḥulda forest. At nearby ancient site *137:138*, finds include remains of Byzantine synagogue with mosaic floor containing drawings of *menorah*, *shofar*, censer, *lulav*, *etrog* and short inscription.

Ḥuleyot → Sede Neḥemya

Ḥuqoq *(Josh. 19:34) 197:254*

Kibbutz in Galilee 12 km. NW of Tiberias. Named after Biblical city Hukok in Asher tribal allotment. Its name was preserved in that of abandoned Arab village, Yaquq. Also mentioned in travel books of Middle Ages when it was believed to be burial place of Prophet Habakkuk. Founded 1945 by Palmaḥ group, graduates of Miqwe Yisra'el agricultural school and HaNo'ar Ha'Oved group. Area: 4,700 d. Pop.: 320. The open canal of the National Water Carrier starts here.

Ḥurbat Admut (Tell Idma) *201:226*

Large ancient site 2 km. NW of kibbutz Gesher in Jordan Valley. Finds include basalt architectural fragments, remains of aqueduct running N to S, tombs, caves and wine presses. Sherds from Early Iron Age, Roman, Byzantine and Arab Periods.

Ḥurbat 'Afrat (Kh. et Taiyyiba) *169:243*

Remains of rural settlement in Galilee 3 km. SE of Shefar'am. Remains of foundations, column fragments, rock-cut tombs and cisterns from Roman Period.

Ḥurbat 'Agalgal *152:142*

Large settlement remains in Ayyalon Valley 3.5 km. E of Sha'alvim. Occupied in Middle Bronze Age, Persian and Hellenistic Periods.

Ḥurbat Aḥlai (Kh. er Rasm)' *143:115*

Ruins of ancient settlement on border of Judean Hills and Foothills 3 km. NE of Bet Guvrin. Remains of fortress (towers and traces of walls) apparently from Roman Period. Sherds indicate occupation in Hellenistic, Roman and Byzantine Periods.

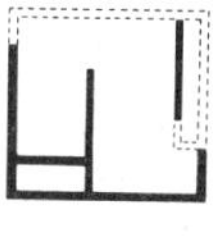

Ḥurbat 'Akin (Kh. 'Ein el Ḥayya) *199:225*

Large ruin of ancient settlement near small spring in Jordan Valley 2.5 km. W of kibbutz Gesher. Remains of buildings with some walls intact to a considerable height. Most of sherds are from post-Babylonian Exile, some from Early and Middle Bronze Age and Hellenistic Period.

Ḥurbat 'Al (Kh. Deir 'Ala) *149:159*

Remains of Roman-Byzantine settlement 10 km. NE of Ben-Gurion Airport. Remains of cisterns, pool, rock-cut tombs and Roman road.

Ḥurbat 'Ammudim (Kh. Umm el 'Umdan) *143:108*
(Judean Foothills)

Concentration of stone pillars near ancient way in Judean Foothills, 6 km. SE of Bet Guvrin. Opposite pillars is a sealed cave, rock-hollows and cuttings. A survey in area uncovered sherds from Early Bronze Age, Byzantine and early Arab Periods.

Ḥurbat ʻAmmudim **(Kh. Umm el ʻAmad)** *188:246*
(Lower Galilee)

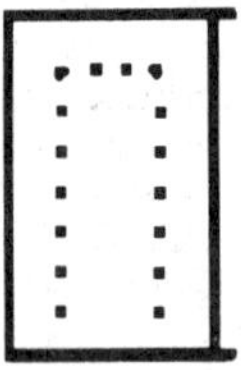

Remains of ancient settlement in Lower Galilee 4.5 km. N of Golani junction. One theory identifies site as that of ʻUzi'el, residence of priestly clans of Abijah and Iddo. Site has remains of late 3rd c. synagogue with mosaic floor and a double column on broad base. An Aramaic inscription was also found. NE of ruin is Tel Za'ir where Iron Age, Roman and Byzantine sherds were found.

Ḥurbat ʻAnav **(Kh. ʻAnnab el Kabira)** *143:089*

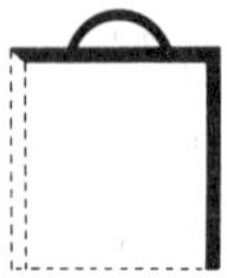

Ruins of large settlement in Judean Hills 5 km. SW of edh Dhahiriyya village. It was a Jewish village in Byzantine Period. Remains of many buildings, various installations, church remnants, caves, cave-tombs, cisterns, and a mosque built on ancient foundations. Nearby is Kh. ʻAnnab eṣ Ṣaghira, identified with Biblical Anab, the city of the Anakim that was included in Judah tribal allotment (Josh. 11:21).

Ḥurbat ʻAnim *(Josh. 15:50)* *156:084*

Ruins of ancient settlement in NE Negev 5 km. S of Sammuʻ. Mentioned in Bible and in Onomasticon of Eusebius as large Jewish settlement. Remains of a building on summit of hill — perhaps a fortress — among other structural remains. Sherds indicate occupation in Iron Age and from Hellenistic Period through Middle Ages.

Ḥurbat Anusha *149:161*

Ruin in Samaria 6 km. SE of Rosh HaʻAyin. Remains of buildings grouped around a courtyard. Site occupied from Roman-Byzantine Period until Middle Ages.

Ḥurbat ʻAqrav *179:274*

Ruins of ancient settlement in Galilee 7 km. NE of Maʻalot. Many buildings, a pool and sherds from Iron Age, Byzantine and early Arab Periods remain.

Ḥurbat Aristobulya **(Kh. Istabul)** *163:097*

Large ruin 7 km. SE of Hebron. Apparently site of Aristobalius, mentioned in late Christian literature. Remains of buildings, cave-tombs and various installations indicating occupation in Iron Age, Roman, Byzantine and Arab Periods.

Ḥurbat ʻArpad **(Kh. ʻIrbada)** *189:236*

Ruin in Galilee 5 km. NE of Mt. Tavor. One theory identifies site as that of Heleph — a city on border of Naphtali tribe (Josh. 19:33). On S side of site are building foundations. Sherds indicate settlement in Iron Age and post-Babylonian Exile.

Ḥurbat Baʻalan *136:122*

Ruin in Judean Foothills 11 km. SE of Qiryat Mal'akhi. On summit of hill are fragments of olive oil presses, Roman tomb caves, underground passages and Arab building. Finds also include Roman and Byzantine sherds.

Ḥurbat Badid *185:272*

Settlement ruins in Galilee 3.5 km. NW of kibbutz Sasa. Remains of many buildings and rock-cut steps at a nearby spring. Sherds indicate occupation from Roman Period and thereafter.

Ḥurbat Baqar *125:085*

Settlement ruins 12 km. NW of Be'er Shevaʻ. Building foundations, wells, cisterns, pools and workshop remains. Finds indicate occupation from Roman to Crusader Periods.

Ḥurbat Barir **(Rujm el Barara)** *164:069*

Roman-Byzantine ruin in NE Negev 8 km. SW of 'Arad. Remains of unknown structure on a hill dominating area.

Ḥurbat Be'er Sheva' → Be'er Sheva' HaGelilit

Ḥurbat Berakhot **(Kh. Bureikut)** *163:116*

Ruins of ancient settlement in Judean Hills 4 km. E of Kefar 'Ezyon next to kibbutz Migdal 'Oz. Includes remains of large Byzantine church and Mamluk settlement and agricultural installations.

Ḥurbat Bet Ma'on *152:144*

Ruins of abandoned village, Bir Ma'in, on N fringes of Ayyalon Valley 8 km. NE of Latrun junction. Built on ruins of settlement occupied from Roman until Ottoman Periods.

Ḥurbat Bet Ma'on → Tiberias

Ḥurbat Bet Natif *149:122*

Tel of ancient settlement within abandoned village of Beit Natif on border of HaEla Valley. Site of Second Temple district city Letefa, destroyed during Revolt against Rome. Remains of buildings, coloured mosaic stones and cisterns indicating occupation from Hasmonean Period until Roman-Byzantine Period.

Ḥurbat Bet Pelet → Ḥurbat Mizbaḥ

Ḥurbat Bet Qiq **(Kh. Beit Kika)** *168:135*

Ruin NW of Jerusalem 1 km. S of suburb of Ramot. Remains of buildings, architectural fragments and mosaic stones. At its centre are ruins of a tower. Occupied in Roman, Byzantine and Ottoman Periods.

Ḥurbat Bet Rosh **(Kh. Beit Ras)** *162:221*

Remains of ancient settlement 7 km. NW of Megiddo junction, near 'En HaShofet. Sherds on site from Iron Age and post-Babylonian Exile, Roman, Byzantine and early Arab Periods.

Ḥurbat Bet Shana *148:143*

Ruin in Judean Foothills N of Ayyalon Valley. Remains of buildings and vestibules of Byzantine vaulted tombs.

Ḥurbat Birzayit **(Kh. Barza)** *179:260*

Ruin of settlement in Galilee 4 km. E of Ma'alot. Perhaps named after Biblical Birzaith mentioned in genealogy of Asher (I Chron. 7:31). Building remains and sherds from Roman and Byzantine Periods; however, indications of Iron Age settlement as well.

Ḥurbat Bodeda **(Ha'Ir HaAvuda)** *140:890*

Late Byzantine quarry site in Elat Hills 7 km. NW of Elat. Many piles of stone debris and some building fragments. Excavations uncovered a building with 4 rooms, similar in structure to a chapel with drawings and Greek inscriptions. In one of houses, ostraca were found with Greek writing.

Ḥurbat Bor **(Kh. Zuweirita)** *148:050*

Settlement ruin in Negev 4 km. SW of Dimona. On hill are remains of square structure from Roman and Byzantine Periods. At foot of hill are stone mounds and other remains of Iron Age settlement.

Ḥurbat Bota (Kh. Umm Buteiḥ) *120:099*
Roman-Byzantine ruin 10 km. NW of Qama junction. The ruin, covering a large area, contains building remains and a well with ancient foundations.

Ḥurbat Burggin (Kh. Umm Burj) *147:115*
Roman-Byzantine ruin in Judean Foothills 8 km. NE of Bet Guvrin. Remains of buildings, mosaic floor, cisterns and columbarium.

Ḥurbat Dardar (Kh. el Mudaḥdara) *151:182*
Ancient settlement ruins in E Sharon near Tulkarm-Qalqilya road. Remains of Crusader fortress and smaller buildings. Sherds indicate occupation in Roman, Byzantine, Crusader and Mamluk Periods.

Ḥurbat Deragot (Kh. ed Darajat) *157:079*
Remains of ancient settlement in Hebron Hills, N of Be'er Sheva'-'Arad road. Sherds indicate occupation in following periods: Chalcolithic, Iron Age, post-Babylonian Exile, Hasmonean, Roman and Byzantine. In Roman Period was used as a stronghold to guard Hebron-Kurnub-Elat junction.

Ḥurbat Devela (Kh. Dubil) *154:232*
Roman-Byzantine ruin on Mt. Karmel, adjacent to Daliyyat el Karmil. On site of a more ancient settlement, perhaps Jewish. Contains column fragments, mounds of stones and many cave-tombs, some decorated.

Ḥurbat Dimdumit (Kh. Dimdim) → **Kefar Menaḥem**

Ḥurbat Din (Kh. 'Ala'a ed Din) *158:233*
Ancient settlement remains on E Karmel, off track leading from Qeren Karmel (Deir el Muḥraqa) to 'Isfiya. Site has dressed stones and foundation remains. Few sherds found on site indicate occupation in Byzantine and Arab Periods, and perhaps also in Crusader Period.

Ḥurbat Dubba (Kh. ed Duweiba) *158:231*
Ruin from Roman and Byzantine Periods near Qeren Karmel (Deir el Muḥraqa) on Mt. Karmel. Remains of rows of stones, and on one of the boulders one can see an incomplete rock-cut sarcophagus.

Ḥurbat 'Egla (Kh. 'Ajalan) *123:108*
Ancient settlement remains in Judean Foothills 5 km. SW of Qiryat Gat. Tomb of sheikh. Sherds indicate occupation in Iron Age, Byzantine and Arab Periods.

Ḥurbat Elef (Kh. Ma'aluf) *186:224*
Settlement ruins on E lowlands of Giv'at HaMore 8.5 km. E of 'Afula. Evidence of settlement from Roman, Byzantine and Arab Periods. In area are cave-tombs and rock-cut cisterns from these periods.

Ḥurbat Esel (Kh. es Sahla) *183:262*
Remains of ancient settlement in Upper Galilee 13.5 km. W of Safed. Alongside is a spring, 'Ein Esel. Sherds indicate occupation in Early Iron Age.

Ḥurbat Eshkar *177:266*
Ruin on summit of Mt. Eshkar in Galilee 2 km. S of Ma'alot. This and nearby Ḥurbat Balu'a were apparently twin settlements occupied alternately in different periods. Sherds indicate occupation in post-Babylonian Exile, Hasmonean and Roman-Byzantine Periods.

Ḥurbat Galemat (Kh. Jalama) *162:249*
Remains of ancient settlement in Zevulun Valley 4 km. E of Qiryat Bialik. Occupied from Roman until Arab Periods.

Ḥurbat Galil (Kh. Jalil) *173:273*

Ruin of large ancient settlement in Galilee 5 km. NW of Ma'alot. Believed to be site of Meẓuda mentioned in Talmud. Foundations of large buildings, cave-tombs and cisterns. Sherds indicate occupation in Hasmonean, Roman, Byzantine and Arab Periods.

Ḥurbat Geduda (Kh. Judeida) *189:213*

Ruin of large fortified settlement on Mt. Gilboa' 2.5 km. W of Bet Alfa. Situated on route of Roman road. Building foundations and heaps of stones from Roman and Byzantine Periods.

Ḥurbat Gemama (Kh. Jammama) *120:101*

Ruins of Roman-Byzantine settlement in Judean Foothills W of kibbutz Ruḥama. Excavations uncovered a coloured mosaic floor and water supply system to nearby farm.

Ḥurbat Gemila *179:271*

Settlement ruins from Roman and Byzantine Periods in Galilee 4.5 km. NE of Ma'alot. Near ruins *180:271* are pool and ancient steps.

Ḥurbat Gerarit (Kh. Umm Jarar) *096:091*

Settlement ruins in NW Negev 10 km. SW of Sa'ad junction. Remains of large structure, mosaic floor, building rubble, cisterns built of unhewn stone and sherds from Roman and Byzantine Periods.

Ḥurbat Gevul *198:219*

Settlement ruin on border of Jordan Valley and Lower Galilee plateau, alongside N bank of Naḥal Yissaskhar. Remains of many structures. Sherds indicate occupation in Middle Bronze Age, Persian and from Byzantine until early Arab Periods.

Ḥurbat Gidora (Kh. Jidru) *159:247*

Settlement ruin in Zevulun Valley 1 km. NW of Qiryat Ata. Perhaps site of city Gedora or Gidora, mentioned in Talmud and Midrashim. Located along ancient *via maris*. Remains indicate occupation from Roman Period until Arab conquest.

Ḥurbat Gov (Kh. el Jauq) *178:272*

Settlement ruin in Galilee 4.5 km. NE of Ma'alot. Remains of Crusader tower and buildings, cisterns, olive oil press and other finds from Byzantine Period. Stone-cut sarcophagi containing skulls and bones were also found.

Ḥurbat Gov Yosef (Khan Jubb Yusuf) *200:258*

Ruins of Medieval Arab khan N of Lake Kinneret off Tiberias-Safed road. Alongside ruin is a domed cistern. Arab tradition claims this to be well into which Joseph was cast by his brothers, hence name of site (*gov* = pit). Near ruin is a dolmen field.

Ḥurbat Ḥadasha (Kh. 'Adasa) *170:139*

Roman-Byzantine ruin in Judean Hills 6 km. N of Jerusalem. Possible site of Hadashah where Judah Maccabee defeated army of Nicanor, killed in this battle (I Macc. 7:40). Remains of tower, large pool, cisterns, water canals, rock-cut tomb and segment of mosaic floor.

Ḥurbat Ḥaluqim *131:032*

Fortress ruins from days of Judean kings, in Negev Hills 3 km. N of Sede Boqer. The fortress, elliptical in shape, contains 8 rooms enclosed around a central courtyard. Excavations revealed stone bowls and pottery in the rooms. Near fortress are remains of a settlement in which a typical house has been excavated.

Ḥurbat Ḥamama (Kh. el Ḥumeima) *187:268*

Ancient settlement ruins in Upper Galilee on N slope of Mt. Meron. Alongside are 2 destroyed Arab houses. Sherds indicate occupation in Iron Age and post-Babylonian Exile.

Ḥurbat Ḥanot (Kh. el Khan) *154:124*

Ruin of caravanserai in Judean Hills off Bar Giyyora-HaEla junction road. Built during Ottoman Period off ancient way from Bethlehem to Coastal Plain. Near ruin is rock-cut reservoir.

Ḥurbat HaRo'a *136:035*

Remains of Iron Age fort in Negev Hills 7 km. NE of Sede Boqer. It is oval in shape with a wall surrounding a courtyard. Nearby are several small structures.

Ḥurbat Ḥasif (Kh. el Khasif) *112:074*

Remains of Roman fort in NW Negev 6 km. S of Ofaqim. Part of chain of Roman border defence forts (*limes*). Remains of contemporary settlement around fort.

Ḥurbat Ḥaẓaẓa *134:034*

Roman-Byzantine way-station in Negev Hills 5 km. NE of Sede Boqer. Station building had 2 wings, each with separate entrance and central courtyard around which were halls and rooms. Some of rooms had stone-slab floors. In one room there was a plastered cistern and in one entrance room a rock-cut basin. Finds from excavation in 1971 include: pottery, decorated clay candles and millstones. E of way-station are 5 rock-cut cisterns, and the banks of Naḥal HaRo'a were terraced for agriculture.

Ḥurbat Hoga (Kh. Huj) *114:102*

Tel of ancient settlement in Negev 3 km. SE of Sederot. Moslem cemetery from period of Arab conquest. Beginnings of occupation date to Iron Age and continue, with interruptions, until Byzantine Period.

Ḥurbat Karemet (El Karm) *185:216*

Ancient settlement ruins in Yizre'el Valley on N slopes of Mt. Gilboa' (Giv'at Yehonatan). Sherds and other remains indicate occupation in Stone Age, Bronze Age, Iron Age, Byzantine and Arab Periods.

Ḥurbat Karkor *131:081*

Settlement remains 7 km. N of Be'er Sheva'. Remains include aqueduct and buildings from Roman Period; cisterns, rock-cut tombs and sheikh's tomb.

Ḥurbat Karkor 'Illit *126:081*

Ancient settlement ruins in N Negev 5 km. E of HaNasi junction. Remains of buildings and cisterns from Roman-Byzantine Period. Sherds and other finds indicate occupation from Iron Age until Hellenistic Period. At summit of hill is Arab cemetery.

Ḥurbat Kasif (Kh. Keseifa) *155:073*

Ruins of large Roman-Byzantine settlement in Negev 15 km. W of 'Arad. Remains of churches, mosaic floor, buildings, etc.

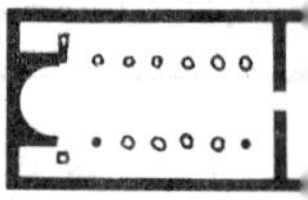

Ḥurbat Kefar 'Annot (Kh. Kafr 'Ana) *138:133*

Remains of Byzantine farm in Judean Foothills 5 km. SW of Naḥshon junction. Scattered on surface of site over large area are Iron Age sherds and other remains.

Ḥurbat Kefar 'Azziz (Kh. el Uzeiz) *158:093*

Settlement ruins in Judean Hills 10 km. S of Hebron. Site of Jewish settlement Kefar Aziz mentioned in Talmud. Remains of buildings, streets, wine presses and sherds from Byzantine Period. Nearby is ancient cave-tomb in front of which are rock-cut steps.

Ḥurbat Kefar 'Otnai *168:220*

Settlement ruins on W fringe of Yizre'el Valley SW of Megiddo. Believed to be site of Kefar Otnai, a Samaritan village in Roman-Byzantine days. After Bar Kokhba revolt the 6th Roman Legion was stationed here, and the site was later called Legio. Arab name of site was el Lejun. Building remains, mosaic floor, wine press, tomb and sherds from Roman and Byzantine Periods.

Ḥurbat Kefar Rut (Kh. Kafr Rut) *154:145*

Large settlement ruins in Samarian Hills 15 km. W of Ramallah. Appears as Capheruta in Madaba map. Remains of buildings, caves and cisterns, indicating occupation from Roman until Ottoman Periods. Nearby is Kh. Ḥuriyya, probably part of the ancient site.

Ḥurbat Kenes (Kh. el Kana'is) *178:258*

Ancient tel in Lower Galilee W of Karmi'el. On tel are remains of 4th and 6th c. church, and building remains that indicate occupation even after Arab conquest. Flint tools from Chalcolithic Period were found on S side of tel.

Ḥurbat Kishor (Kh. Umm Kashram) *136:097*

Ruin from Roman-Byzantine Period on summit of hill in Judean Foothills 8 km. E of Qama junction. Remains of 2 square structures built of large rough stones at distance of 100 m. from each other. Large dressed stone with *menorah* incised on it also found. Apparently lintel of synagogue or *bet midrash* (house for Torah study) from 3rd or 4th c.

Ḥurbat Kones (Kh. el Kanisa) *146:241*

Ruin of ancient settlement on Karmel shore 7 km. S of Haifa. Remains of Crusader church, shaft tombs, cave-tombs, quarries and other remains indicating occupation from Byzantine till Crusader Periods. Sherds found from 6th and 5th c. BCE and flint tools from Paleolithic Period.

Ḥurbat Kukhim (Kh. el 'Ijliyya) *178:278*

Settlement ruins in Upper Galilee 10 km. N of Ma'alot. Occupied during Second Temple, Roman and Byzantine Periods. Remains include beautifully preserved houses, agricultural installations (chiefly wine presses and mills), tombs and a mausoleum with 2 coffins (apparently from 2nd and 3rd c.).

Ḥurbat Kush (Kh. Ḥusha) *202:233*

Ruin of ancient settlement S of Lake Kinneret. Remains of large buildings and aqueduct from Roman and Byzantine Periods, as well as earlier Iron Age remains.

Ḥurbat Labnin (Kh. Tell el Beida) *145:116*

Tel in Judean Foothills 6 km. NE of Bet Guvrin. Building remains, including a decorated lintel. Sherds and other finds indicate occupation in Iron Age, post-Babylonian Exile, Hasmonean and Roman till Arab Periods.

Ḥurbat Leved (Kh. Umm el Labad) *148:161*

Ruin in Samarian Hills 5 km. SE of Rosh Ha'Ayin. Walls still extant up to height of 8 rows of stones; remains of large buildings with mosaic floor, olive oil press and plastered rock-cut cisterns. Sherds indicate occupation in Byzantine and early Arab Periods.

Ḥurbat Luvim (Kh. Lubya) *150:238*

Large ruin on Mt. Karmel 8 km. S of Haifa, near Bet Oren. Building remains. Sherds indicate occupation from Hasmonean Period until Arab conquest.

Ḥurbat Ma'aravim (Kh. Barrata) *123:088*

Roman-Byzantine ruin in Negev 3 km. SW of Shuval. Apparently a sister city to nearby Tel Shera'. Remains of round tower, building stones, cisterns, wells, rock-cut caves and tombs. Sherds and other remains indicate occupation from Iron Age until Mamluk Period, at which time it was destroyed.

Ḥurbat Manoaḥ *116:078*

Tel in Negev 4 km. SE of Ofaqim. Ḥurbat Manoaḥ is one link in a chain of hills, and most of its finds date from Byzantine Period. At summit are remains of buildings, constructed with soft limestone — apparently from Hellenistic Period. Iron Age sherds were found on the slopes indicating an archaeological level below the Hellenistic one. In bed of Naḥal Manoaḥ are some wells called Be'erot Manoaḥ.

Ḥurbat Ma'on BaNegev (Kh. el Ma'in) *093:082*

Settlement ruins in NW Negev 1 km. SE of kibbutz Nirim. Beautiful mosaic floor of 6th and 7th c. synagogue (since removed to Department of Antiquities in Jerusalem). Nearby are traces of ancient track, and W of it, off Nirim-Magen road, tombs from same period.

Ḥurbat Ma'on BiYehuda *(Josh. 15:55) 162:090*

Tel on border of Judean Desert 13 km. S of Hebron. Site of Biblical city Maon. David hid from Saul in Maon desert. Even after destruction of Second Temple a Jewish community continued to exist here. Finds include: to W — remains from Roman and Byzantine Periods, to E — remains from Iron Age, to N — cave-tombs some of which served as dwellings; and at its summit — remains of Roman outpost used to guard Hebron-Kurnub road. Flint tools were also found, indicating prehistoric occupation.

Ḥurbat Matar → Be'er Sheva'

Ḥurbat Meẓudat Hunin (Qal'at Hunin) *201:291*

Remains of Crusader castle, Castellum Novum (new castle), in Galilee 3 km. W of Qiryat Shemona, within abandoned village of Hunin. Built in 1106 by Hugh of St. Omer on ancient tel believed to be site of Biblical Janoah. The 1837 earthquake in Galilee destroyed remains of castle which was surrounded by a rock-cut moat. An Arab geographer has described Hunin as a "fort which stands on a single rock." Overlooking main route to Damascus, it was created to protect vulnerable N flank of Crusader kingdom. Following Battle of Ḥittin in 1187, it was one of three castles in Galilee to remain in Crusader hands.

Ḥurbat Midras (Kh. Durusiyya) *144:118*

Settlement ruins in Judean Foothills 4 km. SW of HaEla junction. Site of small town in Hellenistic Period, and important city in Roman and Byzantine Periods. Building remnants, columbarium, underground hall, cisterns and remains of ancient road. Nearby is cemetery, including a tomb in shape of a graded pyramid.

Ḥurbat Migdalit *135:091*

Settlement ruins in Negev 8 km. SE of Bet Qama junction. Remains from Late Bronze and Iron Ages, and ruins of synagogue (apparently from Byzantine Period).

Ḥurbat Minḥat (Kh. el Manḥata) *201:223*

Settlement remains in Jordan Valley 2 km. SW of kibbutz Gesher, alongside ascent to Kokhav HaYarden. Flint tools and sherds indicate occupation in late Neolithic Period, and Chalcolithic Period.

Ḥurbat Minnim (Kh. Minya) *200:252*

Remains of ancient palace on shore of Lake Kinneret between Ginnosar and et Tabkha. Built by 8th c. Umayyad Caliph el Walid, but not completed. Probably destroyed by earthquake. Architectural and decorative detail indicates Greek Christians may have been employed as artisans. Like all provincial Umayyad fortresses, austere exterior masked magnificent interior. Some walls and towers rise to 10 m. One of best examples in Israel of early Moslem architecture. Finds from site include mosaic floor and remains of bathhouse from 8th c.; also remnants of fortified palace from Roman and Byzantine Periods. Nearby are remains of ruined caravanserai, **Ḥanot Minnim** (Arabic: Khan Minya or Kh. el Khan). Lake Kinneret is known as Baḥr el Minya by the Arabs, after name of this site. The khan is mentioned in the writings of 17th c. Karaite, Samuel b. David. Ruins of khan were covered over when Eshed Kinnarot pumping station was built here.

Ḥurbat Mizbaḥ *144:065*

Settlement ruins on hill 15 km. SE of Be'er Sheva' off road to Dimona. Perhaps site of Beth-pelet, Biblical city in Judah tribal allotment on border of Edom (Josh. 15:27). Also mentioned as existing during post-Babylonian Exile days (Neh. 11:26). At foot of hill are caves and Iron Age building remains. Sherds indicate occupation in Roman and Byzantine Periods as well.

Ḥurbat Molada (Kh. el Watan) *(Josh. 19:2)* *142:074*

Large ruin 10 km. E of Be'er Sheva' on hill adjacent to Naḥal Yattir. One theory identifies site as that of Biblical city Moladah, in tribal allotment of Simeon (Josh. 19:2); it was one of cities resettled after Babylonian Exile (Neh. 11:26). Scattered sherds, found on S slope of hill, are from following periods: Chalcolithic, Middle Bronze Age, and Iron Age through Arab conquest.

Ḥurbat Ner *190:203*

Ruin of Byzantine settlement within abandoned village of Umm Sirḥan 10 km. SW of Bet She'an, at foot of Mt. Gilboa'. Building remains, column sections, capital fragments, a few cisterns and a rock-cut cave.

Ḥurbat Neriyya *186:268*

Ancient ruin in Galilee on NW offshoot of Mt. Meron. Remains of building foundations and perhaps remains of defensive walls. Sherds indicate occupation in Iron Age and post-Babylonian Exile. Included in Mt. Meron reserve; half km. from ruin is Neriyya field school.

Ḥurbat Nevoraya (Kh. en Nabratein) *198:267*

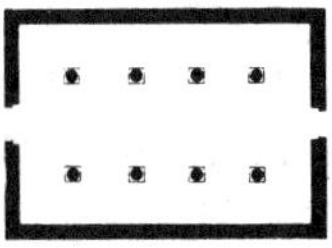

Settlement ruin in Galilee 4 km. NE of Safed. Site of Kefar Nevorya from Roman-Byzantine Period that also existed in Middle Ages. Remains of 4th-6th c. synagogue. A stone with incised *menorah* and inscribed lintel stone were found amid ruins.

Ḥurbat 'Ovesh (Kh. 'Abbasiyya) *164:274*

Settlement ruin in Upper Galilee SE of Ḥanita junction. Remains from Chalcolithic Period and Early Bronze Age, burial caves from Early and Middle Bronze Ages, wall remnants from Roman and Byzantine Periods and wine presses and cisterns.

Ḥurbat Paqqu'it (Kh. Fuqeiqi'a) *187:212*

Ruin of settlement on Mt. Gilboa' 3 km. NW of Ma'ale HaGilboa'. Built in crater. Building remains, rock-cut and plastered cisterns, Moslem holy place esh Sheikh Barqan. Sherds indicate occupation after Babylonian Exile, and during Byzantine and Arab Periods.

Ḥurbat Pattish **(Kh. Futeis)** *114:081*

Ruins of Byzantine settlement Photis in Negev 1 km. NE of Ofaqim. Appears on Madaba map of 6th c. Apparently site of Patash mentioned in lists of cities conquered by Shishak, King of Egypt. Remains of plastered buildings, water cisterns, and fortress (Arabic — Qal'at el Futeis; see Mezudat Pattish). Nearby, *115:018*, a large Chalcolithic site was discovered.

Ḥurbat Pelaḥ **(Kh. el Fallaḥ)** *143:113*

Remains of 3rd c. Roman villa in Judean Foothills 3 km. NE of Bet Guvrin. Building foundations, stone-cutting and coloured mosaics.

Ḥurbat Qamal **(Kh. Qummal)** *194:229*

Ruin of ancient settlement on Galilee hill 8 km. SE of Mt. Tavor. On summit are building remains; to E — remains of defensive wall and to N and S — remains of towers. Finds also include wine presses and rock-cut tombs. Sherds indicate occupation after Babylonian Exile, Byzantine Period and Middle Ages.

Ḥurbat Qashta **(Kh. Qasta)** *188:237*

Roman army camp remains in Galilee off Kefar Tavor-Golani junction road. Remains of defensive walls, tent bases, cisterns and sherds from Roman and Arab Periods.

Ḥurbat Qav **(Kh. el Qabu)** *176:257*

Settlement ruins in Galilee 1.5 km. SW of Karmi'el. Remains of building with hall surrounded by rooms and rock-cut and masonry cisterns. Seems to have been occupied in Byzantine and Arab Periods.

Ḥurbat Qedem **(Kh. el 'Ein)** *150:240*

Prehistoric site on Mt. Karmel 2 km. E of Tirat HaKarmel. Nearby is a broad flat area with Neolithic remains.

Ḥurbat Qedesh **(Qedesh Naftali)** *(Judg. 4:6)* *202:237*

Settlement ruins in Galilee 6 km. SE of Tiberias. Site of Biblical city Kedesh whose name has been retained in that of the Arabic — Kh. el Kidish. Called Kedesh in Naphtali because of its location within tribal allotment of Naphtali and to distinguish it from Kedesh in Upper Galilee. Birthplace of Barak, son of Abinoam, and city from whence he set out with 10,000 men to battle against Jabin, King of Hazor.

Ḥurbat Qove *161:126*

Ruins of a settlement called Qove in Judean Hills 2 km. NE of Mevo Betar. Name retained in that of abandoned village of el Qabu. Situated on ancient route from Judean Foothills to Jerusalem and mentioned in Talmud (Sanhedrin 95:71). Remains of ancient buildings (including a Byzantine church), and a spring ('En Qove) with conduit surrounded by fruit gardens.

Ḥurbat Radum *166:066*

Fort remains apparently from Iron Age in Negev 9 km. SW of 'Arad.

Ḥurbat Raḥba **(Kh. Irdeiha)** *152:051*

Remains of small fortress in Negev 1 km. S of Dimona. Excavations revealed oval-shaped fortress from time of Kings of Judah and on top of it a structure built in Roman Period, which existed until Byzantine Period. Israelite fortress was apparently one of a string of fortresses along the ancient Way of the Atharim. E of ruin is a cistern. In adjacent tributaries of Naḥal Mamshit one can see traces of ancient farming.

Ḥurbat Raqiq **(Kh. Abu ir Riqayyiq, Abu Irqaiq)** *121:078*

Settlement ruins 10 km. NW of Be'er Sheva'. Remains of thick defensive wall and buildings; cisterns and sherds from Chalcolithic,

Hellenistic, Roman and Byzantine Periods. Also found on site were small flint tools (microlithic) and complete bowls from Chalcolithic Period.

Ḥurbat Rimmon **(Kh. Umm er Ramamin)** *137:086*

Settlement ruin in N Negev 2.5 km. SW of kibbutz Lahav. Abandoned village built on ruins of ancient settlement mentioned in Onomasticon of Eusebius. Remains of architectural fragments, synagogue, ancient building stones which have been re-used in modern village, cisterns, wells and caves. Sherds indicate occupation in Roman and Byzantine Periods. W of the ruin is an ancient cemetery.

Ḥurbat Ritma **(Abu Ruteimat)** *128:034*

Ruins of large Israelite fortress in Negev Hills 4 km. NW of Sede Boqer. Remains of building walls up to height of 1.5 m.; some sherds from post-Babylonian Exile and abundance of sherds from Roman and Byzantine Periods. Nearby are two cisterns.

Ḥurbat Rom **(Kh. el Jarmaq)** *188:266*

Settlement ruin in Galilee 8 km. NW of Safed on SW slope of Mt. Meron (Arabic: Jebel Jarmaq). Remains of houses, foundations, floors, cisterns and stone-cutting. In first half of 19th c. there was a Jewish village on site founded by Jews who fled Safed after Arab and Druze rebels attacked city. Israel Bak, one of founders, transferred his printing press from Safed to this village. In 1839 Moses Montefiore visited. Abandoned after Safed earthquake.

Ḥurbat Ruma **(Kh. er Ruma)** *177:244*

Settlement ruins in Galilee at SW fringes of Biq'at Bet Netofa. Many building remains. NW of ruin is an extensive network of water installations. A row of steps leads to one of them through decorative entrance incised in the rock.

Ḥurbat Sa'ar *221:294*

Ruin on Golan Heights 1 km. NW of Birkat Ram. Remains of buildings and many sherds from Hasmonean, Roman-Byzantine and Ottoman Periods. Many sherds, typical Golan finds.

Ḥurbat Saddan **(Kh. esh Sheikh Sandaḥawi)** *153:211*

Small ruin in S Ramat Menashe 1 km. N of 'Iron junction. Sheikh's tomb next to wine press and mosaic floor. Excavations have uncovered dressed stones and Byzantine and Arab sherds.

Ḥurbat Sartaba *185:265*

Settlement ruins in Galilee within boundaries of Mt. Meron reserve. Few sherds from Iron Age and many others indicating occupation from Hellenistic until Arab Periods.

Ḥurbat Se'adim **(Kh. Su'eida, Qaryat Sa'ida)** *162:128*

Ancient remains in nature reserve in Judean Hills 6 km. W of Jerusalem, near Kennedy Memorial. Remains of Byzantine buildings and Crusader fortress amongst ancient oak and carob trees.

Ḥurbat Seraḥ 'Illit **(Kh. Ṣuruḥ el Fauqa)** *177:275*

Settlement ruins in Galilee N of *moshav* Even Menaḥem. Remains of buildings, including a large one where columns, mosaic floor and Greek inscriptions were found. Also cisterns and rock-cut tombs. Sherds indicate occupation in Roman, Byzantine and Arab Periods.

Ḥurbat Shammot *191:216*

Settlement remains in Yizre'el Valley 1 km. S of Bet HaShitta. Remains of basalt stone walls. An inscribed stone slab from time of Antiochus III (223-187 BCE) was found and removed to Department of Antiquities in

Jerusalem. Sherds indicate occupation from Iron Age until Hellenistic Period. Some sherds from Arab Period were also found.

Ḥurbat Shamrit → Sede Terumot

Ḥurbat Sharaq (Kh. esh Sharqiyya) *157:235*

Tel on Mt. Karmel SE of 'Isfiya village. Remains of steps, walls and foundations. Sherds indicate occupation in Hellenistic, Byzantine and early Arab Periods.

Ḥurbat Sharav *140:016*

Ruins of ancient Arab village in Negev Hills 13 km. SE of 'Avedat. Established in 7th c. (one of the oldest Arab villages in the country). Remains of circular brick structures; nearby are remains of a small mosque.

Ḥurbat She'eri (En Nabi Thari) *143:163*

Ruin on central Coastal Plain 5 km. SE of Petaḥ Tiqwa. Remains of 14th c. Arab holy place, Byzantine church with fragment of coloured mosaic floor, and fortress walls.

Ḥurbat Shefannim (Kh. Shufnin) *186:263*

Settlement ruin in Galilee within Mt. Meron reserve. Situated on summit of high, steep mountain with stone steps on upper reaches. Sherds indicate occupation in Middle Bronze and Iron Ages.

Ḥurbat Sheizaf *202:258*

Remains in Galilee off Tiberias-Rosh Pinna road. Building remnants from Roman and Byzantine Periods, and remains of ancient highway. Neolithic flint tools also found on site.

Ḥurbat Shema' *191:264*

Settlement ruins in Galilee 6 km. W of Safed. One theory identifies site as that of Tekoa (in Galilee), mentioned in Talmud. Excavations have uncovered remains of buildings including a 4th c. synagogue, and coins from Hasmonean, Roman and Byzantine Periods. Also remnants of olive oil press and large tomb that many attribute to Shammai, his daughter-in-law, or various other *Tannaim* (scholars and teachers in 1st and 2nd c. CE — Mishnaic Period).

Ḥurbat Shemarya (Kh. Abu Samara) *119:087*

Large ruin in Negev 6 km. NE of Ofaqim. Tomb of en Nabi Samara, caves, cisterns, marble columns and Bedouin cemetery. Byzantine coins found within Arab tomb. Roman and Byzantine sherds.

Ḥurbat Shenuna (Kh. Shanna) *179:276*

Settlement ruins in Galilee 9 km. NE of Ma'alot. Remains of defensive walls, houses, columns, cisterns and rock-cut tombs.

Ḥurbat Shoqef (Kh. Umm esh Shuqaf) *152:233*

Prehistoric site on Mt. Karmel 2 km. W of Daliyyat el Karmil, at foot of Mt. Shoqef. Two groups of hollows.

Ḥurbat Shovav (Kh. Deir Shubeib) *148:133*

Settlement remains in Judean Foothills 3 km. NW of Shimshon junction. Building ruins from Iron Age, tombs, cisterns and columbarium from Roman Period. Sherds indicate occupation in Early Bronze Age, Iron Age and Hellenistic Period. Settlement was renewed on adjacent site in Roman and Byzantine Periods.

Ḥurbat Siv *152:194*

Settlement ruin in Samarian Hills 3 km. N of Tulkarm. Believed to be site of Yeshev mentioned in Samarian Ostraca. Building fragments, olive oil press and sherds indicate occupation in Roman-Byzantine Period, Middle Ages and Ottoman Period.

Ḥurbat Soreqa (Kh. es Sawarika) *120:107*

Settlement ruin in Judean Foothills 9 km. SW of Qiryat Gat. Building remains of undressed stones and sherds from Iron Age and post-Babylonian Exile days.

Ḥurbat Sumaq (Kh. Summaqa) *154:230*

Ruin of settlement in heart of Mt. Karmel, 2 km. S of Daliyyat el Karmil. Remains of ancient synagogue, foundations and walls of large buildings, many fluted columns and cave-tombs. At mouth of one cave is an incised seven-branched *menorah*. About 600 m. S of ruin is a group of cave-tombs. At mouth of one cave is a relief of an ox and a lion with a chalice between them. Remains date from reign of Herod and Byzantine Period.

Ḥurbat Suseya *159:090*

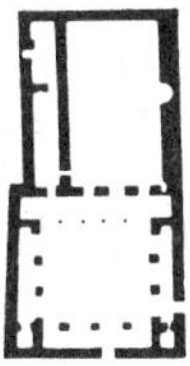

Ruins of large Byzantine settlement in S Judean Hills 3 km. NE of Eshtemoa‘ (Sammu‘). Cisterns and caves scattered over a large area. In centre of ruin are remains of one of the most splendid synagogues yet discovered in the country. Apparently built in 4th c., it was in use until 8th or beginning of 9th c. It constitutes one of the first proofs of a flourishing Jewish community this far south in country after Arab conquest. After its destruction, a small mosque was built in its courtyard. The synagogue was excavated and restored. Finds include: many marble fragments, some incised with designs and inscriptions, a mosaic floor with 3 sections depicting a hunt, Daniel in the lions' den, part of a zodiac surrounded by a wreath with patterns of birds and plants, Ark of the Law, *menorot*, animals and geometric patterns. The Hebrew inscription is one of the few dating from the early Byzantine Period.

Ḥurbat Tefen (Kh. Tufaniyya, Qal‘at et Tufaniyya) *174:262*

Large fortress ruins in Galilee 7 km. S of Ma‘alot. Defensive walls — remaining intact to height of several metres, gates, pools and other installations. Fortress is believed to have been built during Herod's reign. In 4th c. a Roman fortress called Tufaniyya stood here.

Ḥurbat Tittora (El Burj) *152:145*

Ruins of Arab village in Judean Foothills 5 km. N of Mevo Ḥoron. Built on remains of ancient settlement that existed from Early Bronze Age until Middle Ages. Site has 2 ancient colour pestles (large stones used to pulverize colour dyes), column bases and fragments of coloured mosaics.

Ḥurbat ‘Uza (Kh. Ghazza) *165:068*

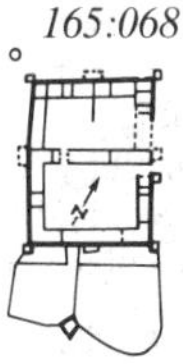

Ruins of Israelite fortress from 9th or 8th c. BCE in Negev 7 km. SW of ‘Arad, off ancient Way to Edom. Rectangular in shape, 53x41 m., surrounded by casemate wall with towers at its corners and at centre of its sides. Part of walls have been preserved, some up to a height of 1 to 2 m.; the rest has been covered by collapsed stones.

Ḥurbat ‘Uẓa (Kh. el ‘Ayyadiyya) *164:257*

Flat tel in Galilee 7 km. E of Acre. Inhabited during Roman and Byzantine Periods.

Ḥurbat Weradim (Kh. Wadi el Ḥamam, Kh. el Wureidat) *196:248*

Remains of ancient structure 6 km. NW of Tiberias, on N promontory of Mt. Arbel. Perhaps remains of synagogue from Roman and Byzantine Periods.

Ḥurbat Yarḥa‘ **(Kh. Subei‘)** *145:118*

Settlement ruins on hill in Judean Hills near *moshav* Ẓafririm. Remains of buildings, large two-tiered columbarium with square and triangular niches and Roman tomb built of dressed stones with decorated lintel. Nearby are traces of an ancient highway. To the N sherds were found from Chalcolithic Period and Early Bronze Age; and on summit sherds from Middle and Late Bronze Age and Iron Age were found. Reoccupied in Roman Period.

Ḥurbat Yattir **(Kh. ‘Attir)** *(Josh. 15:48) 151:084*

Settlement ruin in S Judean Hills 12 km. NE of Shoqet junction. Site of Biblical Jattir, a priestly city in Judah tribal allotment (Josh. 15:48; 21:14). Birthplace of Ira and Gareb, two of David's mighty men (II Sam. 23:38). Mentioned in Onomasticon of Eusebius and appears on Madaba map. Site has remains of buildings, cisterns, caves, tombs, wine press and building rubble. E of ruins is a forest watch-tower and Jewish National Fund forest.

Ḥurbat Yavne Yam **(Minat Rubin)** *121:148*

Tel and ruins of ancient port of Jabneh on central Coastal Plain, near mouth of Naḥal Soreq (Wadi Rubin), 2 km. S of kibbutz Palmaḥim. Sherds and other remains indicate port was in use, and site was occupied in Middle Bronze Age and from Iron Age till Arab Period.

Ḥurbat Yavnit **(Kh. Ibnit)** *198:266*

Settlement ruin in Galilee 1 km. N of Safed. Site of settlement Jamnia or Jamnith from days of Second Temple. Fortified by Joseph b. Mattathias in anticipation of Revolt against Rome. One of the places where beacons were lit to announce the new moon and festivals. Site has tombs of the Babylonian *Amoraim* (Talmudic scholars) Abbaye and Rava, and the tomb of Rabbi Judah HaNasi's grandson.

Ḥurbat Yiftaḥ El **(Kh. el Khalladiyya)** *173:241*

Prehistoric site 8 km. NW of Nazareth. Flint tools from Paleolithic and Chalcolithic Periods, and remains of pavings and sherds from Roman and Byzantine Periods.

Ḥurbat Zaggag **(Kh. Qazaz)** *177:257*

Ruin from Byzantine Period in Galilee 2 km. SW of Karmi'el. Situated on dominant hill. On W is rock-cut and plastered cistern. In fields, towards nearby Ḥurbat Qav are rock-cuttings, remains of olive oil press, cisterns and many pieces of glass.

Ḥurbat Ẓalmon **(Kh. es Sallama)** *185:254*

Settlement remains in Galilee 5 km. SW of Ḥananya junction. Site of Zalmon, a city during time of Second Temple that was fortified by Joseph b. Mattathias in preparation for Revolt against Rome. It was also the city where the priestly clan of Ginnethon resided after destruction of Second Temple. Remains of buildings, rock-cuttings, an aqueduct and tombs.

Ḥurbat Zawit **(Kh. ez Zawiya)** *176:271*

Ancient ruin on hill summit in Galilee 2 km. N of Ma‘alot. Thresholds from houses, rock-cut wine presses and cisterns. Sherds indicate occupation in Byzantine and Arab Periods. Nearby, along Naḥal Keziv, some flint tools were found.

Ḥurbat Zed **(Kh. Ibn Zayd)** *144:118*

Ancient domed tomb built of dressed stone located in a once-walled cemetery. Sherds from late Roman Period. Nearby are remains of large structure from Byzantine and Arab Periods.

Ḥurbat Zikhri (Kh. Dhakar) *138:121*
Mound of stones in ʻAdullam region 13 km. NE of Qiryat Gat. Part of network of mounds in Judean Foothills.

Ḥurbat Ẓiyya (Kh. Bayud) *161:079*
Roman fortress remains in Negev 11 km. NW of ʻArad. One of Roman border fortresses (*limes*).

Ḥurbat Ẓonam (Kh. eṣ Ṣuwwana) *175:274*
Ruins of settlement from Roman and Arab Periods in Galilee 6 km. N of Maʻalot. Remains of buildings, column fragments, rock-cut cisterns and tombs.

Ḥurbat Ẓura (Kh. eṣ Ṣura) *142:117*
Settlement ruins in Judean Foothills 4 km. NE of Bet Guvrin. Remains of defensive walls, buildings, architectural fragments, cisterns and caves, mostly from early Arab Period; some pre-date this time. Under ruins, near road, are group of Roman milestones.

Hureqanya *184:125*
Remains of ancient fortress and a monastery in Judean Desert between Bethlehem and Dead Sea, W of Biqʻat Hureqanya. Probably built by order of John Hyrcanus, hence name of site. Arabic name is el Mird, from the Aramaic word *marda* for fortress. Monastery built at end of 5th c. by the monk, Saba, and called Castellion (fortress). Excavations have uncovered remains of buildings, Herodian water system and Aramaic and Greek papyrus documents.

Ḥureshat HaArbaʻim *153:239*
Ancient oak wood on Mt. Karmel off Haifa-ʻIsfiya road. Named after the Arabic Shajarat el Arbaʻin (40 revered heroes in Moslem tradition). The wood is part of a nature reserve. Haganah observation point is located here.

Ḥureshat HaShivʻa *198:262*
Wood in Galilee 1 km. S of Safed. Named in memory of 7 soldiers, killed in an attempt to relieve besieged Safed during War of Independence. There is a memorial in the wood.

Ḥureshat Khazuri *217:295*
Ancient wood on Golan Heights 5 km. NW of Birkat Ram. Site of tomb of Druze holy man, Sheikh Uthman Khazuri.

Ḥureshat Tal *209:291*
Ancient oak wood in Galilee 5 km. E of Qiryat Shemona, on banks of Naḥal Dan. Arabic name is Shajarat el ʻAshara (wood of the ten), based on Arab legend that 10 of Muḥammad's companions rested here and from the staffs that they stuck in the ground on which to tie their horses, large oak trees miraculously grew. The site was designated as a nature reserve and a swimming pool was built, lawns planted and day campsite equipped.

Ḥureshat Yaʻala *201:232*
Remains of ancient wood in Lower Galilee 4 km. SW of Deganya "A". Arabic name is Shajarat el Kalb (wood of the dog). Wood has 10 ancient jujube trees and remains of ancient tropical plants.

Ḥurfeish *182:269*
Druze village in Galilee 5 km. W of kibbutz Sasa. Name means brier (a type of indigenous thorn bush). Pop.: 2,400; 90% Druze, rest Moslem and Christian. Village contains a Druze *khilwa* (cemetery), Greek Catholic church and memorial to Druze soldiers who fell in Israel's

wars. Within the village are scattered building foundations, ancient tombs, columns and remains of Roman till Arab Period settlement. Near village, on summit of hill, *182:268*, is a Druze *maqam* (holy place) of en Nabi Sabalan (the prophet Zevulun).

Ḥurvot 'Aro'er **(Kh. 'Ar'ara** in Negev) *(I Sam. 30:28)* *148:062*
Tel in Negev 12 km. NW of Dimona. Believed to be site of Biblical Aroer, a city of Judah tribal allotment. Sherds indicate occupation in Iron Age, Roman and Byzantine Periods. Excavations uncovered Iron Age finds: remains of buildings, city wall, fortress built with dressed stones, pottery and seals; remains of defensive walls from Roman Period. A large Arab cemetery is located on tel. S of tel is **Be'erot 'Aro'er** — 2 large wells.

Ḥurvot Ḥaluẓa *117:056*
Ancient city ruins of Haluza 20 km. SW of Be'er Sheva'. One of important Nabatean cities, located on trade route between Gaza and Petra. During Byzantine Period it was spiritual centre and army base. City was surrounded by vineyards and in 5th c. was famous for its wines. Haluza began its decline before Arab conquest; desert sands gradually covered it over. During Arab Period it was completely abandoned. Today's remains are from Byzantine Period. (Most of its dressed building stones were taken for buildings in Gaza and Be'er Sheva'.) Excavations uncovered Aramaic and Nabatean inscriptions and an early 1st c. theatre. A cemetery with elaborate family graves was uncovered 1 km. from ruins. Kibbutz Mash'abbim, founded 1947, was located nearby. In 1949 the kibbutz moved to its present site and was called Mash'abbe Sade.

Ḥurvot Mamshit → Mamshit

Ḥurvot Qumeran → Qumeran

Ḥurvot Reḥovot (in Negev) *(Gen. 26:22)* *108:048*
Large settlement ruins in Negev E of Ḥurvot Ḥaluẓa, 15 km. W of Revivim. Name mentioned in Bible as site where Isaac dug a well. Name has been retained in the Arabic — er Ruḥeiba. Nabateans established a way-station at this ancient crossroad; it became a city during Roman Period and reached pinnacle of its development during Byzantine Period (10,000 inhabitants). Remains of many buildings whose walls reach considerable heights, remains of 3 churches, tombstones with Greek inscriptions and fragments of columns and capitals. S of ruins is an ancient well with man-made upper section.

Ḥurvot Sokho **(Kh. Shuweika)** *147:121*
Tel on border of Judean Hills and Foothills, 2 km. SE of HaEla junction. Believed to be site of "Socoh, which belongs to Judah" (I Sam. 17:1-2), mentioned in story of battle between David and Goliath. Biblical name has been retained in that of adjacent Kh. Shuweika. Remains of buildings, defensive wall and glacis.

o **Ḥusan** *162:124*
Arab village in Judean Hills 7 km. W of Bethlehem. Pop.: 1,200. Believed to be site of Biblical Hushah, birthplace of 2 of King David's mighty men (II Sam. 21:18; 23:27). Near village are ruins of police fort which served as terrorist base on eve of Sinai Campaign and was destroyed by Israel Defence Forces in retaliatory operation (25 September 1956). Within village are remains from Iron Age and from post-Babylonian Exile until Middle Ages.

∴ **Ḥutiyya** *215:248*
Abandoned village on tel on Golan Heights 7 km. NE of 'En Gev. Ancient building stones have been re-used in modern village. Sherds

indicate occupation in Early and Middle Bronze Age, Iron Age and Byzantine Period. Flint tools from Chalcolithic and Upper Paleolithic Periods also found in area.

o **Ḥuwara** *174:173*

Arab village in Samarian Hills 8 km. S of Shekhem. Perhaps site of Horon, residence of Sanballat I, the Horonite, who tried to prevent Nehemiah from rebuilding walls of Jerusalem (445 BCE). Pop.: 2,000.

(El) Huzayyil *126:091*

Bedouin settlement in Be'er Sheva' region off Be'er Sheva'-Qiryat Gat road. Headquarters of tribe. Pop.: 600. Dam nearby for catching flood and rain-waters.

I

Ibbim *115:105*

Regional council centre in W Negev 4 km. NE of Sederot. Was once a farm. Name derived from verse "I went down to the nut orchard to look at the *blossoms* of the valley" (Song 6:11). Founded 1953.

I'billin *168:247*

Arab village in Galilee near Zevulun Valley, 8 km. E of Qiryat Ata. Name may be distortion of Evlayim, ancient Jewish city in area, mentioned in Talmud. Pop.: 4,800 — 60% Christians, 40% Moslems. Family of Dahir el 'Amr, ruler of Galilee in 18th c., is buried in local mosque. **Evlayim** Ruins near the village *168:247* was Jewish city during Roman-Byzantine Period. Nearby was Roman road from Acre to Upper Galilee and Jordan Valley. Site contains rock-cut tombs, synagogue lintel with Hebrew-Aramaic inscription, and stone decorated with five-branched *menorah*. Remains of Crusader fortress.

Ibthan *154:196*

Arab village in Samaria 6.5 km. NE of Tulkarm. Perhaps name is associated with the ancient city of Apadan, mentioned in description of campaign of Thutmose III, king of Egypt in 15th c. BCE. Pop.: 500. Remains of ancient settlement.

Ibtin *160:241*

Arab village, containing large farm, located on W border of Lower Galilee, 5 km. S of Qiryat Ata. Origin of name: Beten — ancient Hebrew settlement bordering on territory of tribe of Asher (Josh. 19:25). Pop.: 700.

'Idan *178:024*

Moshav in 'Arava, 5 km. NE of 'En Ḥaẓeva. Founded 1976.

Idhna *147:107*

Arab village 10 km. NW of Hebron. Believed to be site of Dannah, a city in territory of Judah between Socoh and Debir (Josh. 15:49). Another theory holds it to be site of Ashnah (Josh. 15:43). In N part of village is a hill with ancient tel on summit and spring at its foot.

Idmith *169:276*

Bedouin village of 'Aramsha tribe in Galilee near kibbutz Adamit on Lebanese border.

Ijnisinya *170:186*

Arab village 7 km. NW of Shekhem. Pop.: 250.

Iksal (Kislot Tavor) *180:232*

Arab village in Galilee 2 km. SE of Nazareth. Name is possibly a distortion of ancient Hebrew name of Chisloth-tabor or Chesulloth (Josh. 19:12, 18). Founded 250 years ago by inhabitants of neighbouring village, Nein. Pop.: 3,300 — all Moslem.

Iktaba *155:192*

Small Arab village 2 km. E of Tulkarm.

Ilaniyya **(Sejera, Esh Shajara)** 188:240

Moshav in Galilee 2.5 km. S of Golani junction. Name from Arabic Sejera meaning tree (*ilan* in Hebrew). Originally a farm established on land bought by ICA (Jewish Colonization Association) in 1899. During Second 'Aliyah served as centre for Galilee labourers and transit camp for immigrants (among them David Ben-Gurion). In 1907, HaḤoresh, the first Jewish agricultural workers' organization, was founded; they were the first to employ Jewish guards. (This was some time before HaShomer was set up.) During War of Independence it was front-line post in fighting against heavy troop concentration of Arab Liberation Army. An Israeli counter-attack in July 1948 freed the entire area. Pop.: 200. **Antiquities** Prehistoric mill with flint implements from Paleolithic Period. Large ruin, probably remains of Byzantine church.

Ilanot 140:188

Government tree nursery 6 km. SE of Netanya.

'Illar 160:197

Arab village in Samarian Hills 10 km. NE of Tulkarm. Pop.: 2,400. Perhaps site of Aner, a Levite city in allotment of half tribe of Manasseh. Ancient cave-tombs found near village. Above entrance to one of caves a Hebrew inscription was discovered: "tomb of Menashe son of Yani."

'Illut 174:236

Arab town in Galilee 4 km. NW of Nazareth. Perhaps site of 'Aitalo, a Jewish town during Roman-Byzantine Period and residence of priestly clan of Seorim (I Chron. 24:8). Pop.: 2,500. Ancient settlement remains and rock-cut tombs.

Imam 'Ali 155:135

Moslem holy tomb 3.5 km. SE of Sha'ar HaGay. Imam 'Ali, a holy man, is subject of famous Arab legend. One day he met a young girl who was crying. She had spilled a pot of cream which she was carrying and was afraid to return home. Imam 'Ali collected the cream-soaked soil, squeezed it and refilled the pot. At that moment a divine voice called out from the soil, "Just as you have squeezed me so I will reject your body when you die." When the Imam died, wherever he was buried the soil rejected the body. Consequently there are a number of places in the country which are designated as his tomb. However, Sha'ar HaGay is most commonly accepted as his place of burial.

Immatin 165:177

Arab village 16 km. W of Shekhem, apparently the site of Elmattan mentioned in Samarian Ostraca. On W slope of village hill Iron Age and Byzantine remains were found.

Intiṣar 181:266

Small Druze village in Galilee by Peqi'in. Arab name means victory. Inhabitants were originally from village of Peqi'in.

Iqrit 176:275

Abandoned village with tel of ancient settlement in Galilee, 6.5 km. N of Ma'alot. Greek Catholic Arab inhabitants were evacuated during War of Independence and to this day are campaigning to return. Site of Yoqerat from Roman-Byzantine Period (where Yosse from Yoqerat was born). Greek Catholic church built apparently on Crusader foundations. Sherds indicate occupation in Early and Middle Bronze Age, Iron Age and Byzantine Period. Some springs W of tel.

'Iraq Burin 172:178

Arab village (pop.: 250) 9 km. SW of Shekhem. Within village is tel with ancient building fragments.

★ **'Ir Ovot** *(Num. 21:10) 173:024*

Kibbutz in 'Arava 30 km. SW of Sedom near ruins of Ḥazeva. Named after Oboth, where the Israelites camped in wilderness (Num. 21:10-11; 33:44). Founded 1966. Area: 80 d.

o **Irtaḥ** *151:189*

Arab village in Samaria 2 km. S of Tulkarm. Pop.: 900. Name means rest. Legend has it that Patriarch Jacob camped here while on his travels. Shrine — Maqam en Nabi Ya'qub. **Kh. Irtaḥ** Ruins in village of settlement from Byzantine Period, Middle Ages and Ottoman Period: column fragments, capitals, stone door posts and rock-cuttings.

'Isfiya, 'Isifya *156:236*

Druze village on Mt. Karmel 8 km. SE of Haifa. Founded about 1600 by Druze family from Lebanon. About 200 years ago a few Christian families from Bethlehem and Ramallah settled in village. Pop.: 7,500 — 77% Druze, 22% Christian and rest Moslem. Druze prayer house, Greek Catholic church and military cemetery for Druze soldiers who fell in service. **Ḥusifa** Village located on ruins of ancient settlement, perhaps site of Husseifa, mentioned in an ancient lamentation. Remains of a 6th c. synagogue with an attractive mosaic floor depicting seven-branched *menorah*, vine tendril, *etrogim*, *lulav*, *shofar*, zodiac, Hebrew inscription "Shalom 'al Yisrael" and fragments of other inscriptions. Also located in village are ancient caves and olive oil presses.

o **Iskaka** *171:167*

Arab village 13 km. SW of Shekhem. Pop.: 300, all Moslem.

'Iyye Kidon *140:117*

Settlement ruins in Judean Foothills 4 km. N of Bet Guvrin, above abandoned village of Kidna. Sherds indicate occupation in Iron Age and Roman and Byzantine Periods.

'Iyye Qeratya *124:116*

Tel in Judean Foothills 5 km. NW of Qiryat Gat, adjacent to abandoned village of Qeratya. Remains of an Iron Age settlement that also existed from Persian Period until Middle Ages. Remains of Byzantine church.

o **'Izmut** *179:181*

Arab village 4 km. E of Shekhem. Pop.: 800. Tomb of Sheikh Ḥamud and remains of ancient olive oil press. Sherds indicate settlement in Byzantine and Arab Periods.

J

o **Jaba‘** (Judean Hills) *175:140*

Arab village 8 km. N of Jerusalem. Thought to be site of ancient Geba; or Geba in Benjamin, mentioned several times in Bible. Pop.: 3,000.

o **Jaba‘** (Samarian Hills) *171:192*

Arab village 13 km. NW of Shekhem. Pop.: 3,000. Served as headquarters for Arab nationalist Fawzi al-Kaukji during Disturbances of 1936-1939, and during War of Independence. After Six-Day War a cave was discovered near village that contained the bones of Barukh Mizrahi, a converted Moslem and member of the Irgun, who, while on a mission to Jenin, was caught and executed. Ruins of ancient settlement that was continuously inhabited from Middle Bronze Age until Ottoman Period.

□ **Jabaliya** *101:104*

Arab town and refugee camp in N Gaza Strip. Founders came from hill region, hence name (*jebel* means mountain). Pop.: 11,000. Refugee camp, located 2 km. NE of town, has pop. of 35,000.

■ **Jaffa (Joppa; Yafo)** *(II Chron. 2:15)*

City on Mediterranean shore S of Tel Aviv, considered the world's oldest port and the place from where the prophet Jonah set sail for Tarshish. According to Greek myth, Andromeda was held captive by Poseidon on the rocks off Jaffa. Jaffa is also associated with the deeds of St. Peter. Here the woman disciple Tabitha was resurrected by Peter. Today the city is within the municipal boundaries of Tel Aviv. Legend claims Jaffa was built by Japheth, son of Noah, hence its name. Mentioned in Bible, Egyptian and Assyrian documents. Not captured by Joshua during his conquest. During reign of King Solomon served as port for united kingdom of Judah and Israel. After return from Babylonian Exile it was under Phoenician control, like the other coastal cities. During Hellenistic Period was at first an autonomous city and later subject to district of Samaria. During Hasmonean Period it was populated mainly by gentiles and their relationship with the local Jewish community was strained. One day the gentiles forced some 200 Jews out to sea and then drowned them. For this act, Judah Maccabee razed the port and slaughtered many inhabitants. Simeon the Hasmonean annexed it to his kingdom and during reign of King Yannai the city prospered, particularly as a vital port. During Revolt against Rome, Jewish sailors from Jaffa tried to prevent the Romans from sending supplies by sea. However, after Roman victory, Jaffa became a Roman city and was called Flavia Ioppa. Jews continued to live here after destruction of Second Temple, and in Roman and Byzantine Periods it was the home of many sages and scholars. Jaffa rose in importance during Crusader Period. In 1268 it was taken by Mamluk Sultan Baybars who destroyed its fortifications and killed its inhabitants. It was rebuilt only in 17th c., serving mainly as an entry port for Christian and Jewish pilgrims. Captured and destroyed in 1799 by Napoleon after he besieged it. In 19th c. pilgrim traffic to Holy Land swelled and Jaffa recuperated. By beginning of 20th c. its population was mainly Arab, but it became a gateway for Jewish immigration and base for building Tel Aviv. As Tel Aviv grew and expanded, tension increased between Arab inhabitants of Jaffa and Jewish inhabitants of Tel Aviv. The Riots of 1920 were its first manifestation; it was later followed by Disturbances of 1936-1939. The port was closed to Jews, and this resulted in the creation of Tel Aviv port. The partition plan proposed that Jaffa remain a free zone between Jewish and Arab areas. But with the outbreak of War of Independence Jaffa was a base for Arab forces attacking Tel Aviv and Jewish settlements to the S. In the course of the war Jaffa was taken by Irgun and Haganah forces, and most of the inhabitants fled. In 1950 Jaffa was amalgamated with Tel Aviv. When the Ashdod port was opened, the port of Jaffa ceased its commercial operations and became a harbour for fishing and sailing boats. Part of old city has been renovated and turned into an arts, crafts and entertainment centre. **Antiquities of Jaffa** Excavations at Tel Jaffa uncovered Late Bronze Age and post-Babylonian Exile defensive walls. Within the old city a glacis, possibly dating from Iron Age, was uncovered. The many Medieval remains found include a synagogue, Jewish cemetery, churches, monasteries, mosques, Moslem tombs and a Crusader structure. The old port is today characterized by Ottoman architecture.

o **Jalama** (Yizre'el Valley) *179:212*

Arab village in S Yizre'el Valley 5 km. N of Jenin. Pop.: 800.

Jalazun *170:150*

Arab refugee camp 5 km. N of Ramallah. Pop.: 3,200.

o **Jalbun** *189:207*

Arab village in Samarian Hills S of Mt. Gilboa'. Its name is a distortion of that of Biblical Gilboa. Mentioned as Gelbus in Onomasticon of Eusebius and in Estori HaParhi's book. Pop.: 1,000. **Gilboa'** Village built on ruins of ancient town identified as Gilboa. Sherds indicate occupation in Iron Age, Byzantine and Ottoman Periods.

Jaljulya *145:173*

Arab village in Sharon 4 km. E of Kefar Sava. Founded about 200 years ago on ancient ruins — perhaps site of Gilgal in Sharon, mentioned in Bible as one of Canaanite cities captured by Joshua (Josh. 12:23). Pop.: 3,500. **Ancient remains** Within village are ruins of large Arab khan from Middle Ages, mosque and pool from Mamluk Period, tomb attributed to Shams ed Din, one of Saladin's commanders, and other remains from Late Bronze Age, Iron Age, Persian, Arab and Crusader Periods.

o **Jalqamus** *184:203*

Arab village in Samarian Hills 7 km. SE of Jenin. Pop.: 500.

o **Jalud** *180:164*

Arab village in Samarian Hills 8 km. E of Ramallah-Shekhem road. Pop.: 250.

o **Jamma'in** *169:170*

Arab village 13 km. SW of Shekhem. Pop.: 1,800. Birthplace of 'Abd el Ghani en Nabulusi, late 17th c. Arab writer who wrote travel books about Palestine.

o **Jammala** *158:153*

Arab village 13 km. NW of Ramallah. Pop.: 300. Some believe it to be site of Kefar Gamla. A Christian tradition designates this as burial site of 1st c. Rabban Gamaliel HaZaqen.

o **(El) Janiya** ⚔ 161:149

Arab village 10 km. NW of Ramallah. Pop.: 300. Mentioned in Byzantine sources as Ginta. Finds include Greek and Arabic inscriptions from Byzantine and Mamluk Periods.

o **Jarba** ⚔ 174:199

Arab village in Samarian Hills 10 km. SW of Jenin. Pop.: 100. Ancient remains of buildings, tombs and cisterns.

Jarmaq → **Mt. Meron**

⌂ **Jatt** (Gat Karmel) ⚔ ● ⚘ ⚕ 154:200

Arab village in Samarian Hills 9 km. N of Tulkarm. Founded in last century by residents of Baqa el Gharbiyya on ancient remains, apparently of Gat Karmel, mentioned in ancient Egyptian documents. The *via maris*, connecting Egypt to the kingdom of the Fertile Crescent, passed alongside this village in ancient times. Pop.: 4,100. Remains from Late Bronze Age.

o **Jatt** (Upper Galilee) ⚔ 🖐 ✓ ⚕ 172:264

Druze village in Galilee 5 km. SW of Ma'alot. Pop.: 800. **Ancient settlement** Within village to the N, remains of ancient stone wall and many cisterns were found. Sherds indicate almost continuous occupation from Early Bronze Age until Arab Period. A Jewish settlement existed here during Second Temple Period.

Jebel 'Askar → **Mt. 'Eval**

Jebel Haidar → **Har HaAri**

Jebel el Muntar 183:127

Mountain in Judean Hills 12 km. SE of Jerusalem. Height: 524 m. above sea level. Arabic name means mountain of the guard, because it towers above its surroundings and forms an impressive observation point. Some scholars think this is cliff of Mt. 'Azazel, where one of goats (scapegoat) in Temple service on Day of Atonement was cast off the cliff. A monastery and tower were built here in Byzantine Period. During WWI served as headquarters for ANZAC (Australian and New Zealand) forces, in their campaign to conquer Transjordan.

Jebel Ros → **Har Dov**

Jebel esh Sheikh → **Mt. Ḥermon**

Jebel et Tur → **Mt. Gerizim**

▢ **Jenin** ✿ ⚏ ⚵ ⚑ 178:207

Arab city on border of Samarian Hills and Yizre'el Valley. Perhaps site of 'En Gannim mentioned in Tell el 'Amarna letters, or possibly of Biblical Ginath (I Kings 16:21). Served as transit station on road from Samarian Hills to the N. During WWI a Turkish-German army base was located here. During Disturbances of 1936-1939 Arab gangs had bases here. In War of Independence Israeli forces captured area around city but failed to take Jenin itself. Taken by Israel Defence Forces in Six-Day War. Pop.: 15,000, mostly Moslem, some Christians.

▢ **Jericho** ⚔ ✿ ● ⚕ ⚑ ⚑ (Josh. 3:16) 193:140

Arab city in S Jordan Valley at junction of major N-S and E-W arteries. Considered the oldest city in the world and the lowest on earth (250 m. below sea level); the first place conquered by Joshua after crossing the Jordan. Desert climate but abundant water sources give it the character of an oasis. Pop.: 5,500, mostly Moslem. **History of Jericho** Inhabited

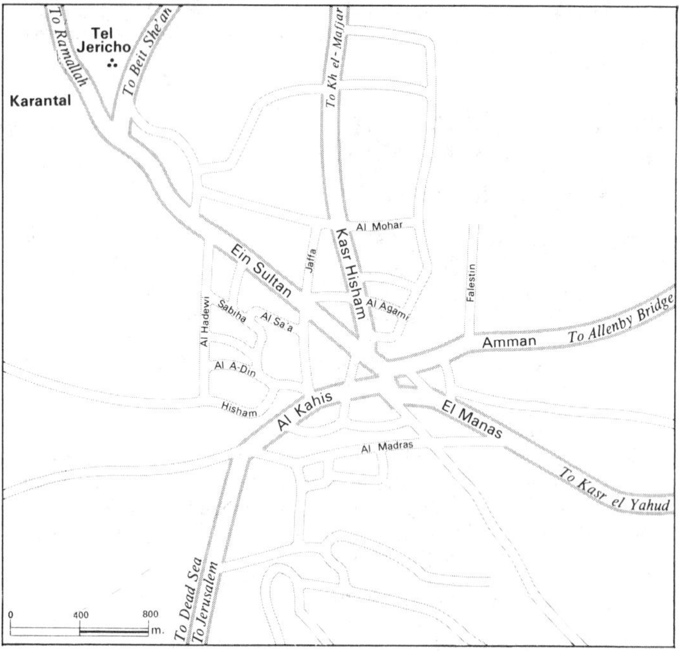

during Mesolithic Period. One theory attributes derivation of name from moon (*yareaḥ*) cult practised here. Another theory attributes name to the pleasant fragrance (*reaḥ*) of its flora. Captured by Joshua and included in Benjamin tribal allotment. Mentioned several times in texts dealing with the Monarchy and Hasmoneans. District centre during Roman conquest. Antony gave city as present to Cleopatra; Augustus Caesar returned it to Herod who built his winter palace and other buildings here. Destroyed during Revolt against Rome but rebuilt by Hadrian. Even after destruction of Second Temple a Jewish community still persisted here. After Arab conquest in 7th c., Jews who were expelled from Arabia were settled in Jericho. It was destroyed in clashes between Moslems and Crusaders, remaining desolate until 19th c. when settlement was renewed. Several Jews tried to settle here but were forced to leave when the 1936 Disturbances broke out. **Tel Jericho** Site of ancient Jericho (Tell es Sultan) NW of present city. Record habitation going back to prehistoric Natufian culture of 11th-9th c. BCE. In 8000 BCE Neolithic Jericho was a city of 2,000 protected by fortifications. In the many excavations on the site, finds include a round tower from pre-pottery Neolithic Period, tombs from Chalcolithic Period, walls from Early and Middle Bronze Ages and ensuing periods. These walls may have in fact been the ones destroyed by Joshua's trumpet blasts, since destroyed sections have been unearthed bearing no traces of battle damage. **Spring of Elisha** At foot of Tel Jericho is a spring (Arabic: 'Ein es Sultan) whose waters Elisha miraculously purified (II Kings 2:22). Herod's winter palaces were discovered W of present city on both banks of Wadi Qilt. **Palaces from Hasmonean Period and Herod's time** on site called Tulul Abu 'Alaiq *191:140.* On S bank remains of one palace were found with garden and pool alongside it. On N bank remains of second palace were found; it contains a magnificent bathhouse. The two palaces were protected by a fortress called Cypros after Herod's mother. Recently, remains were found of a third magnificent palace NE of the first palace. Nearby, at Tell es Samrat, remains of large cemetery and hippodrome were found. **Remains of synagogue** Within Jericho a mosaic floor from 6th c. synagogue was found. Depictions include: Ark of the Law, underneath a seven-branched *menorah*, and at the sides a *lulav* and *shofar*. Below is a Hebrew inscription: "peace upon Israel". **Kh. el Mafjar** Three km. to N *193:143* are remains of Byzantine city and of 8th c. Arab Umayyad palace (see Kh. el Mafjar).

Jerusalem *(Josh. 10:1)*

The capital of the State of Israel and ancient capital of the Kingdom of Israel and later of Judah. A city sacred to the three principal monotheistic religions. From 1000 BCE to 586 BCE, and from 515 BCE to 70 CE, it was the political, commercial and religious centre of the Jewish nation. For over 100 years now, Jews have constituted the majority of the city's population. For Christians, Jerusalem is associated with the life of Jesus. For Moslems, with Muḥammad's nocturnal journey to heaven. Situated in the heart of the Judean Hills, 800 m. above sea level on the crossroads of 2 major arteries: the N-S mountain route, and the road ascending from Coastal Plain and Judean Foothills in W and descending to Jordan Valley and Transjordan in the E. Occupies an area of 107 sq. km. (107,000 d.). Pop.: 379.000 (275,000 Jews and 104,000 non-Jews). Divided into Old City, surrounded by a wall, and the new city, outside the wall. The Old City has 4 quarters: Jewish, Armenian, Moslem and Christian. The new city is composed of many quarters, mostly Jewish. Major employment is in industry, crafts, tourism, commerce, clerical work, teaching, research and religious and secular services. The following institutes and administrative bodies are located in Jerusalem: the Knesset, official residence of President of the State, the government centre (Qirya), government offices, the central offices of the Zionist movement, Jewish, Christian and Moslem holy sites, religious centres and institutes, cultural and educational facilities (the Hebrew University) and archaeological and historical sites. Jerusalem has the highest rate of natural increase in Israel — 20 births per 1,000 — and is thus faced with a number of social and economic challenges: 15.5% of its families have seven or more children; 39% of the population is of school age. To house this growing population and provide it with a livelihood, extensive residential and industrial building has taken place in the city in recent years. Extreme care has been taken in planning this development, in order to retain the unique beauty and special historical atmosphere of Jerusalem.

GROWTH OF THE POPULATION OF JERUSALEM

	1844	*1896*	*1948*	*1967*	*1980*
Jews	7,120	28,112	100,000	195,700	275,000
Moslems	5,000	8,560	40,000	54,960	92,000
Christians	3,390	8,748	25,000	10,800	12,000
TOTAL	15,510	45,420	165,000	261,460	379,000

History of Jerusalem Flint tools found near Jerusalem demonstrate the area was inhabited as early as **Paleolithic Period**. Sherds indicate permanent habitation from Early Bronze Age (approximately 3000 BCE). Some of these sherds were found on the E hill of the ancient city, S of Old City walls of today, above the Giḥon spring. In its most ancient form, the name of Jerusalem appears in the Egyptian Execration Texts, 19th-18th c. BCE as Rushalimum. In **Middle Bronze Age** its name was possibly a combination of 2 Canaanite words: Yru (foundation) and

JERUSALEM

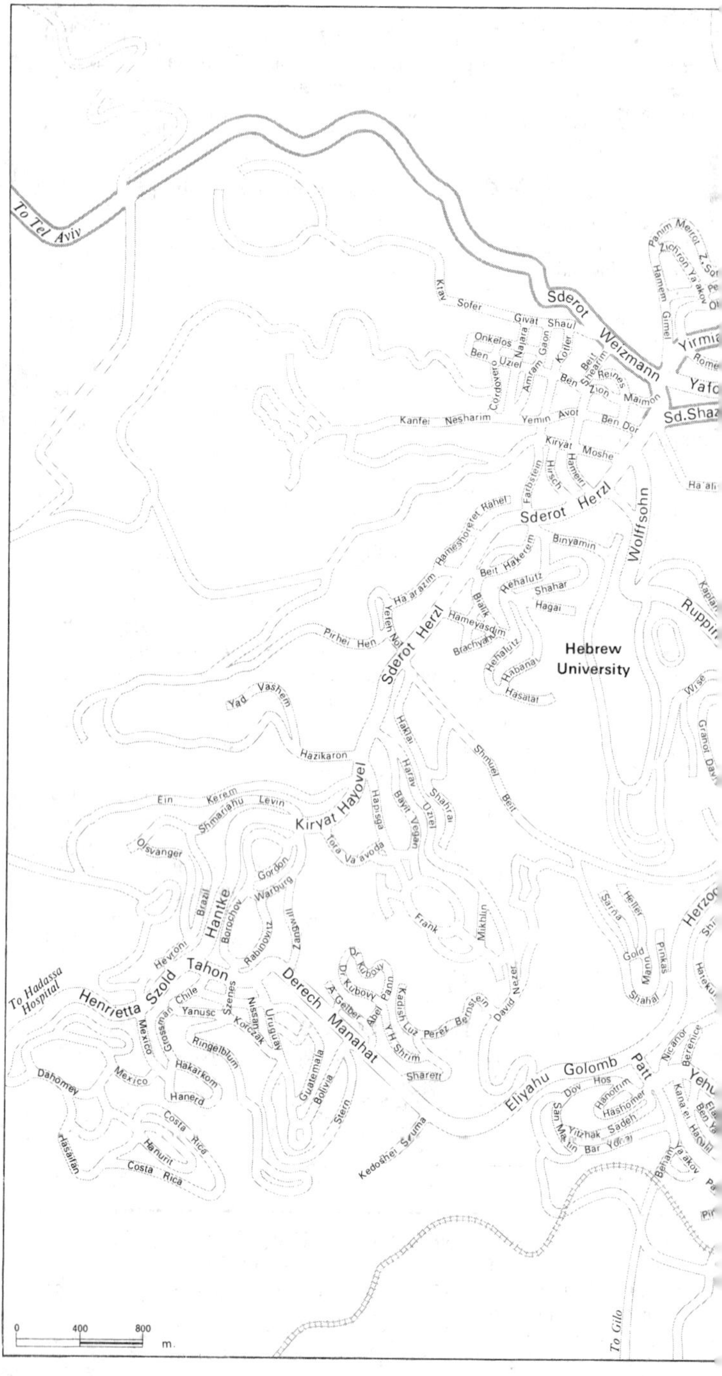
To Tel Aviv
Sderot Weizmann
Krav
Sofer
Givat Shaul
Onkelos
Ben Uziel
Kanfei Nesharim
Yemin Avot
Kiryat Moshe
Sderot Herzl
Binyamin
Wolffsohn
Hebrew University
Yad Vashem
Hazikaron
Pirhei Hen
Shmuel Beit
Kiryat Hayovel
Ein Kerem
Olsvanger
Hantke
Tahon
Henrietta Szold
To Hadassa Hospital
Derech Manahat
Eliyahu Golomb
Dahomey
Mexico
Costa Rica
Hanurit
Hakarkom
Hanerd
Ringelblum
Uruguay
Guatemala
Bolivia
Stern
Kedoshei Struma
Sharett
Herzog
Sd.Shaz
Yafo
Ruppin
Granot
Patt
Yitzhak Sadeh
To Gilo
0
400
800
m.

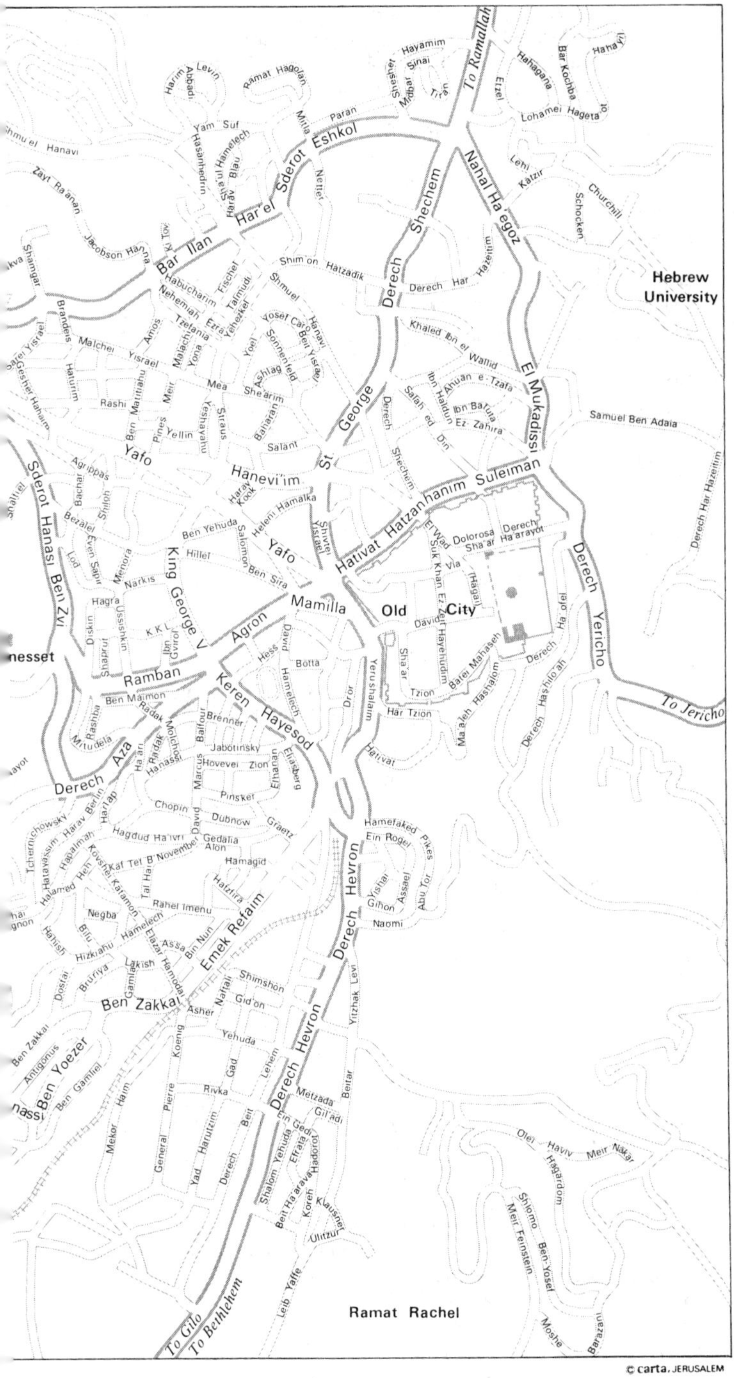

Hayamim
Hahaganah
Bar Kochba
Hanavi
Sinai
Sheshet
Midbar
Tiran
To Ramallah
Etzel
Lohamei Hageta'ot
Harim Abbadi
Levin
Ramat Hagolan
Paran
Mitla
Yam Suf
Shmu'el Hanavi
Hasanhedrin
Hamelech
Sha'ul
Blau
Harav
Sderot Eshkol
Netter
Nahal Ha'egoz
Leh'i
Katzir
Churchill
Schocken
Zayt Ra'anan
Har'el
Jacobson Hanna
Bar Ilan
Kol Tov
Shim'on Hatzadik
Derech Shechem
Derech Har Hazeitim
Hebrew University
Shamgar
Habucharim
Fischel
Talmudi
Shmuel
Nehemiah
Ezra
Yehezkel
Brandeis
Tzefania
Amos
Yosef Caro
Hanavi
Beit Yisrael
Khaled Ibn el Wallid
Sarei Yisrael
Malchei Yisrael
Malachi
Yona
Sonnenfeld
Yoel
Ashlag
Gesher Haha'im
Haturim
Matitiahu
Meir
Mea She'arim
Ibn Haldun
Anuan e-Tzafa
El Mukadissi
Rashi
Ben
Pines
Yellin
Yeshayahu
Straus
Baharan
Salah ed Din
Derech Shechem
Ibn Batuta
Ez-Zahira
Samuel Ben Adaia
Yafo
Salant
St. George
Agrippas
Hanevi'im
Harav Kook
Sderot Hanasi Ben Zvi
Bachar
Shiloh
Heleni Hamalka
Hativat Hatzanhanim
Suleiman
Derech Har Hazeitim
Bezalel
Ben Yehuda
Shivtei Yisrael
El-Wad
Dolorosa
Via
Derech Sha'ar Ha'arayot
Derech Yericho
Even Sapir
Lod
Menora
Hillel
Salomon
Yafo
Ben Sira
Suk Khan Ez Zeit
Hagai
King George V
Narkis
Mamilla
Old City
Hagra
Ussishkin
K.K.L.
Diskin
Ibn Gvirol
Agron
David
Hayehudim
David
Knesset
Shaprut
Hess
Botta
Sha'ar Tzion
Batei Mahaseh
Ha'ofel
Ramban
Hamelech
Yerushalaim
Derech Hashilo'ah
Ben Maimon
Radak
Keren Hayesod
Dror
Tzion
Har Tzion
Ma'aleh Hashalom
To Jericho
Rashba
Brenner
Mitudela
Molcho
Balfour
Jabotinsky
Aza
Radak
Ha'ari
Hanassi
Hovevei Zion
Marcus
Elhanan
Eliasberg
Hativat
Derech
Harlap
Harav Berlin
Pinsker
Chopin
Dubnow
Tchernichowsky
Hapalmah
Hatayassim
Hagdud Ha'ivri
David
Gedalia
Graetz
Hamefaked
Ein Rogel
Pikes
Kaf Tet B'November
Alon
Halamed Heh
Kovshei Katamon
Hamagid
Derech Hevron
Tal Hai
Hatzfira
Yishai
Assael
Abu Tor
Rahel Imenu
Emek Refaim
Gihon
Naomi
Negba
Hamelech
Bilu
Assa
Bin Nun
Hanish
Hizkiahu
Elazar Hamodai
Lakish
Shimshon
Dostai
Bruriya
Gamla
Gid'on
Naftali
Ben Zakkai
Derech Hevron
Asher
Yitzhak Levi
Ben Zakkai
Antigonus
Ben Yoezer
Koenig
Yehuda
Ben Gamliel
Lehem
Gad
Haim
Pierre
Rivka
Beitar
Hanassi
Beit Lehem
Metzada
Gil'adi
Mekor
General
Harutzim
Derech
Yad
Ein Gedi
Efrata
Hadorot
Olei Hagardom
Haviv
Meir Nakar
Shalom Yehuda
Beit Ha'arava
Koreh
Klausner
Shlomo Ben Yosef
Meir Feinstein
Ulitzur
Leib Yaffe
To Gilo
To Bethlehem
Ramat Rachel
Moshe Barazani

Slm (the name of local god); combined — foundation of god Shalem. During days of Abraham it was called Shalem (Gen. 14:18). In Tell el 'Amarna letters from 14th c. BCE the city is called Urusalim similar to the Biblical Yerushalem or Yerushalayim. During period of Israelite conquest (**Late Bronze Age II B**) Joshua was not able to take the city and it remained a wedge separating the central tribes from those of the N and S. Only in 1005 BCE, **Iron Age I B**, did King David capture the city of Jebus (as it was then called after its Jebusite inhabitants) and change its name to the City of David making it capital of his kingdom.
The following are the major dates in the history of Jerusalem from ancient times until today:

Israelite Period (from conquest of city by David until destruction of First Temple):

969 BCE	Solomon builds the Temple.
930 BCE	Division of the kingdom; Jerusalem capital of Judah.
925 or **924** BCE	Shishak, King of Egypt, enforces heavy tribute on city.
701 BCE	Sennacherib, King of Assyria, besieges city.
586 BCE	Nebuchadnezzar, King of Babylon, destroys city and burns Temple; destruction of First Temple.

Babylonian and Persian Periods (586-332 BCE):

538 BCE	Beginning of Return to Zion in reign of Cyrus, King of Persia, under leadership of Zerubbabel, son of Shealtiel.
515 BCE	Consecration of Second Temple.
445 BCE	Rebuilding of Jerusalem and its walls by Nehemiah.

Hellenistic and Hasmonean Periods (332-37 BCE):

332 BCE	According to legend Alexander the Great visited Jerusalem; beginning of Greek political and cultural dominance and Hellenization programme.
169 BCE	Antiochus IV Epiphanes, King of Syria, storms and plunders Jerusalem, profanes Temple and outlaws practice of Judaism.
167-165 BCE	Hasmonean (Maccabean) revolt, conquest of Jerusalem, cleansing of Temple and resumption of Temple service.
63 BCE	Pompey enters Jerusalem at head of Roman army.

Roman Period (**37** BCE-**324** CE):

37 BCE	Herod, King in Jerusalem under Roman protection; physical splendour and beauty of city reaches a peak.
22 BCE	Herod rebuilds Temple.
44 CE	King Agrippa I extends city to the N and begins to construct the Third Wall. (After his death in the same year, Romans take control of the country.)
66 CE	Beginning of Jewish Revolt against Rome.
70 CE	Siege of Jerusalem; Titus conquers city, demolishes it and burns Temple; destruction of Second Temple.
135 CE	After quelling Bar Kokhba revolt, Romans destroy city, expel Jewish inhabitants and build pagan Roman city called Aelia Capitolina.

Byzantine Period (324-640 CE):
Beginning of Christian Byzantine rule; during this period Jews were forbidden to reside in Jerusalem except during short reign of Emperor Julian the Apostate (**361-363** CE).

614-629	Persians take city and hand it over to the Jews.
629	Byzantines return and retake city.

Early Arab Period (638-1090):

638	Omar ibn el Khattab, known as sword of Islam, conquers city. Jerusalem becomes one of the centres of Islam and is called el Quds (the holy). Rule shifts from one Caliphate to the next.

750 End of rule of Umayyad Caliphate and beginning of Abbasid rule.
878 Egyptian rule.
969 Rule of Fatimid Caliphs.
1071 Conquest of city by Seljuks (Turks).
1098 Return to power of Fatimids.

Crusader Period (**1099-1250**):

1099 Crusaders capture city, slaughter Jewish and Moslem inhabitants and establish Kingdom of Jerusalem.
1171 Jewish traveller, Benjamin of Tudela, visits Jerusalem.
1187 Saladin takes Jerusalem; renewal of Jewish community.
1209-1211 300 rabbis from France and England settle in city.
1241 Crusaders return and conquer city, extending their rule for several years.
1244 Khwarizm Turks attack and destroy city.

Mamluk Period (**1250-1516**):

1260 Mongols invade and destroy city.
1267 Jerusalem annexed to Mamluk kingdom.
1267 Ramban (Naḥmanides) settles in Jerusalem and Jewish community revives.
1488 Rabbi Obadiah of Bertinoro arrives in Jerusalem.

Ottoman Period (**1516-1918**):

1516 Conquest of Jerusalem by Turkish Sultan Selius I.
1538 Building of walls of Jerusalem (still standing today) by Sultan Suleiman I the Magnificent.
1622 Rabbi Isaiah Horowitz (HaShela) founds Ashkenazi Jewish community in Jerusalem.
1700 Rabbi Judah Ḥasid and his disciples settle in Jerusalem.
1807 Disciples of Vilna Gaon (Elijah b. Solomon Zalman) settle in Jerusalem.
1827 Moses Montefiore's first visit to Jerusalem.
1831 Ibrahim Pasha of Egypt gains control of Syria and Palestine (including Jerusalem) from Turkish sultan.
1840 Turks regain control from Muḥammad 'Ali.
1860 Mishkenot Sha'ananim, first Jewish community outside Old City walls, founded.
1869 Completion of road from Jaffa to Jerusalem.
1892 Inauguration of railway to Jerusalem.
1898 Theodor Herzl, founder of Zionist movement, and Kaiser Wilhelm II meet in Jerusalem.

British Mandate (**1917-1948**):

1917 Entry to Jerusalem of British army. Expansion of local Jewish community. Jerusalem becomes national and cultural centre of emerging Jewish State.
1947 UN decision to internationalize Jerusalem.

War of Independence, founding of State of Israel and early decades:

With the outbreak of War of Independence, fighting in Jerusalem. Old City cut off from new city. Siege of Jewish Jerusalem.

2 May 1948 Capture of Qatamon quarter.
14 May 1948 British evacuate Jerusalem.
17 May 1948 Evacuation of N quarters of 'Atarot and Newe Ya'aqov.
19 May 1948 Breakthrough to besieged Old City.
28 May 1948 Fall of Jewish quarter in Old City.
1 June 1948 Opening of "Burma Road" and end of siege of Jewish

Jerusalem. Armistice Agreement after the war left Israel with new city and enclave on Mt. Scopus, and Jordanians with Old City, Mt. of Olives and several quarters in NE part of city.

13 December 1949 Jerusalem proclaimed capital of Israel.

Until 1967 City divided.

28 June 1967 Proclamation of unification of Jerusalem following Six-Day War.

List of major quarters of Jerusalem (alphabetical order):

Abu Tor mixed quarter in S, Jewish part called Giv'at Ḥananya.

Aḥuzat Bene Brit near Bayit WeGan, founded 1929 by members of Bene Brit.

Aḥwa in centre, near Mea She'arim, founded 1908 by Aḥwa society.

Arnona in S, between Talpiyyot and Ramat Raḥel, founded 1931.

Bab ez Zahara Arab quarter in E Jerusalem, N of Gate of Flowers (in Arabic — Bab ez Zahara), also known as Herod's Gate.

Baq'a in S, old Arabic name of Ge'ulim; name means valley.

Batte Goldstein see Bet Yisra'el HaḤadasha.

Batte Hornstein in centre, S of Kerem Avraham, named after philanthropist, built 1905.

Batte Minsk in centre, N of Naḥalat Aḥim, built 1894 by immigrant community from Minsk.

Batte Naitin in centre, S of Maḥane Yehuda, named after philanthropist, built 1907.

Batte Ungarin in centre N of Mea She'arim, built in 1898 by immigrants from Warsaw.

Batte Werner see Ohale Moshe.

Bayit WeGan in SW, name symbolic (house and garden), founded 1921.

Beit Ṣafafa Arab village in S of city.

Bet HaKerem in W, named after Biblical city near Jerusalem, founded 1923.

Bet Ya'aqov in centre, W of Maḥane Yehuda, name symbolic — founders of quarter were 70 in number, same number as Jacob's offspring, founded 1877.

Bet Yisra'el in centre, N of Mea She'arim, name symbolic, founded 1887.

Bet Yisra'el HaḤadasha near Bet Yisra'el, also called Bet Goldstein.

'Emeq Refa'im near centre, named after valley in which suburb is located; formerly called German Colony (HaMoshava HaGermanit) founded 1880.

'En Kerem SW, site of village abandoned during War of Independence. Location of Biblical Bethhaccerem (Jer. 6:1; Neh. 3:14), and traditional birthplace of John the Baptist.

Even Yehoshua' in centre, W of Mea She'arim, founded 1893.

Even Yisra'el in centre, SE of Maḥane Yehuda, name symbolic (*even* in numerological terms [gematria] is equal to 53 — the number of founders), founded 1875.

'Eẓ Ḥayyim at W approaches to city, named after 'Eẓ Ḥayyim Yeshiva located here, founded 1928.

'Ezrat Yisra'el	in centre, SE of Maḥane Yehuda, name symbolic, founded 1892.
Ge'ula	in centre, name symbolic, founded 1926.
Ge'ulim	in S, name symbolic, formerly Baq'a.
Giv'at Bet HaKerem	in W, E of Bet HaKerem, built 1963.
Giv'at HaMivtar	in N, S of Ramot Eshkol, named after split hill (*mivtar*) upon which suburb was built in 1970.
Giv'at HaPorẓim	in S, W of Gonen, battle site in War of Independence, Arabic name was Giv'at Shahin.
Giv'at Mordekhay	in S, named after public figure, Mordekhay Abel of USA, founded 1955.
Giv'at Shahin	see Giv'at HaPorẓim.
Giv'at Shapira	(former name: HaGiv'a HaẒarfatit, French Hill), in N, named after late minister Moshe Ḥayyim Shapira, founded 1971.
Giv'at Sha'ul	in W, named after Rabbi Jacob Saul Elyashar, founded 1914.
Giv'at Weradim	in S, origin of name: nearby Naḥal Weradim (Wadi Wered), also called Rassco, founded 1951.
HaGiv'a HaẒarfatit (French Hill)	see Giv'at Shapira.
HaMeqasher	in W, near Qiryat Moshe, housing estate of members of former HaMeqasher, Jerusalem bus cooperative.
Hebrew University	on Giv'at Ram, SW of Qiryat David Ben-Gurion; also on Mt. Scopus.
'Ir Gannim	in SW, near Qiryat HaYovel, name symbolic, founded 1961.
Kefar HaShiloaḥ (Arabic name: Ṣilwan)	Arab village S of Old City on site of City of David.
Kefar Salma	W of Qiryat HaYovel, youth village named after Swedish writer, Selma Lagerlöf, founded 1956.
Kefar Sha'ul	in W, near Giv'at Sha'ul, mental institution.
Kerem	in centre, E of Meqor Barukh, founded 1885 on vineyard.
Kerem Avraham	in centre, founded 1933 on lands purchased from a mission; Arabic name — Karm el Ḥalil (vineyard of Patriarch Abraham).
Knesset Yisra'el	in centre, N of Naḥalat Aḥim, founded 1891.
Ma'alot Dafna	in N, E of Bukharim quarter, founded 1972.
Maḥanayim	in N, NE of Tel Arza, Biblical place name, founded 1926.
Maḥane Yehuda	main outdoor market of new city, in centre, named after Yehuda Navon, founded 1887.
Manaḥat	in S, Hebrew name of abandoned village of Malḥa.
Mazkeret Moshe	in centre, S of Maḥane Yehuda, named after Moses Montefiore, founded 1883.
Mea She'arim	in centre, ultra-orthodox area, origin of name from Biblical passage: "And Isaac sowed in that land, and reaped in the same year a *hundredfold*" (Gen. 26:12), founded 1874.
Meqor Barukh	in centre, founded 1924.
Meqor Ḥayyim	in S, founded 1925.
Merkaz Mishary	once commercial centre of new city, near Mamilla road, founded 1928.
Me Nefto'aḥ	at W approaches to Jerusalem, on site of abandoned village, Lifta; Biblical place name (Josh. 15:9).

Mishkenot	in centre, SE of Maḥane Yehuda, name from Biblical passage: "how fair are your tents, O Jacob, your *encampments*, O Israel!" (Num. 24:5), founded 1875.
Mishkenot Sha'ananim	near centre, within Yemin Moshe quarter, name symbolic, founded 1860 as first Jewish quarter outside Old City walls. Has artists and music centre.
Morasha	in centre, on border prior to Six-Day War, name symbolic, former Arabic name: Musrara.
Moshava Ameriqanit (American Colony)	in E, S of Sheikh Jarrah, group of buildings from 1881, established by Christians from USA.
Moshava Germanit (German Colony)	near centre, founded 1880 by members of German Templer sect, present name: 'Emeq Refa'im.
Moshava Yewanit (Greek Colony)	in S, now part of Gonen quarter.
Muṣrara	see Morasha.
Naḥalat Aḥim	in centre, N of Sha'are Ḥessed, name symbolic, founded 1924.
Naḥalat Shim'on	in N, near Wadi el Joz, origin of name: tomb of Shim'on HaẒadiq, founded 1891.
Naḥalat Shiv'a	in centre, named for seven (*shiv'a*) founders; established 1869.
Naḥalat Ẓadoq	in centre, near Sha'are Ḥessed, named after Rabbi Ẓadoq HaKohen, a former Chief Rabbi of France, founded 1908.
Naḥalat Ẓevi	in centre, N of Mea She'arim, named after Baron Hirsch, founded 1894 (also called Shekhunat HaTemanim).
Naḥalat Ẓiyyon	in centre, S of Maḥane Yehuda, name symbolic, founded 1908.
Nayot	in SW, S of Israel Museum, origin of name from Bible (I Sam. 19:22), founded 1962.
Newe Beẓalel	in centre, N of Sha'are Ḥessed, named after Beẓalel art school, founded 1927.
Newe Granot	in SW, named after Abraham Granot, founded 1963.
Newe Sha'anan	in W, between Israel Museum and Hebrew University, name symbolic, founded 1925.
Newe Ya'aqov	in N, named after Rabbi Isaac Jacob Reines, founded 1924, destroyed during War of Independence, rebuilt 1972.
Ohale Moshe	in centre, W of Mea She'arim, also called Batte Werner, founded 1902.
Ohale Simḥa	in centre, near Mea She'arim, named after Rabbi Simḥa Bunem Sofer, founded 1892.
Ohel Moshe	in centre, SE of Maḥane Yehuda, named after Moses Montefiore, founded 1883.
Ohel Shelomo	in centre, W of Maḥane Yehuda, founded 1891.
Paggi	in N, founded 1946 by *Po*'ale *Ag*udat *I*srael (*Paggi* is acronym).
Qatamon	former name of Gonen.
Qiryat David Ben-Gurion	in W, on Giv'at Ram, houses Knesset and government offices.
Qiryat Emet	within Bayit WeGan, complex of Torah study institutes, founded 1955 by Iḥud Mif'alim Toraniyim (Hebrew name *Emet* is

	acronym of name of founders).
Qiryat Hadassah	in W, Hadassah University Medical Centre, founded 1960.
Qiryat HaYovel	in SW, founded on 50th anniversary (*yovel*) of Jewish National Fund (1954).
Qiryat Itry	in W, N of Romema, origin of name: acronym of *I*nstitute for *T*orah *R*esearch.
Qiryat Mattersdorf	to E of Romema, named after Jewish community of Mattersdorf and its environs in Austria, founded 1963.
Qiryat Menaḥem	in SW, near Qiryat HaYovel, named after Zionist public figure, Menaḥem Bressler, founded 1958.
Qiryat Moshe	in W, named after Moses Montefiore, founded 1923.
Qiryat Shemu'el	near centre, S of Reḥavya, named after Rabbi Samuel Salant, founded 1928.
Qiryat Wolfson	near centre, W of Sha'are Ḥessed, founded 1975.
Qiryat Ẓanz	in N, NW of Tel Arza, named after town in Galicia that was a Ḥasidic centre.
Qomemiyut	near centre, former Arabic name — Talbiyya.
Ramat Denya	in S, named in honour of Denmark, founded 1970.
Ramat Raḥel	kibbutz to S of city, named after nearby tomb of Rachel, founded 1926.
Ramat Sharett	in S, named after Moshe Sharett, founded 1974.
Ramot	in N, on way to Nabi Samwil, *ramot* = heights, founded 1971.
Ramot Eshkol	to N, named after Levi Eshkol, built 1969.
Reḥavya	near centre, name symbolic, founded 1921.
Romema	in W, name derived from height of location (*romema* = elevation), founded 1921; to its N is Romema 'Illit.
Sanhedriya	in N, named after tombs of Sanhedrin — Second Temple tombs found on site, founded 1926; to its N is Sanhedriya Murḥevet.
Sha'are Ḥessed	in centre, name symbolic, founded 1909.
Sha'are Pinna	in centre, near Bet Yisra'el, *pinna* = corner — located on corner between Mea She'arim and Bet Yisra'el, founded 1889.
Sha'are Yerushalayim	in centre, S of Meqor Barukh, name symbolic, founded 1891.
Shamm'a	near centre, S of Yemin Moshe, on slope of valley of Hinnom; origin of name: distortion of Champs de Mars (field of Mars) from Middle Ages, founded 1909.
Sheikh Jarraḥ	Arab quarter in NE part of city, named after Moslem holy person.
Shekhunat HaBukharim	in centre, founded 1873 by immigrants from Bukhara, previous name, Reḥovot HaBukharim and also Reḥovot.
Shekhunat HaPo'alim	in W, within Bet HaKerem, founded 1928, named after its founders who were labourers (*po'alim* = labourers).
Shekhunat HaTemanim	see Naḥalat Ẓevi.
Shikun Rassco	see Giv'at Weradim.
Shoshanat Ẓiyyon	in SW near Bet HaKerem, name symbolic, founded 1930.
Shu'afat	Arab quarter in N, off road to Ramallah.
Silwan	see Kefar HaShiloaḥ.

Sukkat Shalom	in centre, S of Maḥane Yehuda, founded 1888.
Talbiyya	see Qomemiyut.
Talpiyyot	in S, origin of name: Song of Songs 4:4, founded 1922, adjacent and to N is **Zefon Talpiyyot**, founded 1935, to E is new quarter, **Talpiyyot Mizraḥ**, founded 1972.
Tel Arza	in N, name symbolic, founded 1931.
(Et) Tur	Arab quarter in NE of Jerusalem, named after wadi that passes through quarter (name means wadi of the nut).
Yefe Nof	in W, within Bet HaKerem, name symbolic, founded 1929.
Yegia' Kapayim	in centre, S of Ge'ula, name symbolic, founded 1907.
Yemin Moshe	centre, artists' quarter, named after Moses Montefiore, founded 1892.
Zikhron Aḥim	in centre, N of Naḥalat Aḥim, name symbolic, founded 1934.
Zikhron Moshe	in centre, NE of Maḥane Yehuda, named after Moses Montefiore, founded 1906.
Zikhron Toviyya	in centre, S of Maḥane Yehuda, name symbolic, 11th quarter to be established outside Old City walls, founded 1890.
Zikhron Yosef	in centre, W of Maḥane Yehuda, founded 1931.

List of major sites in Jerusalem (alphabetical order):

Absalom's Monument — magnificent tomb monument, partly rock-cut and partly built of stones, in Qidron Valley, opposite SE corner of Old City wall. Popular legend attributes this monument to the tomb built by Absalom, son of King David (II Sam. 18:18). Legend also maintains that at one time at the top of the monument there was a hand (*yad*), hence the name Yad Avshalom. This symbolized the disapproval of Absalom who "raised his hand (*yad*) in rebellion against his father." For many generations, Jews, Christians and Moslems who passed by would throw stones at it in contempt of the rebellious son. In 1925, the almost submerged monument was cleared of stones and cleaned.

Antonia Fortress — remains that have been found are of the N fortress. The Antonia was erected to guard over the Temple Mount. It was apparently built on foundations of an older fortress called the Citadel (*bira*). Herod renamed it Antonia in honour of Mark Antony. Christian tradition designates this as the first Station of the Cross (on the Via Dolorosa), where Jesus was judged before Pontius Pilate and condemned to crucifixion.

(El) Aqṣa Mosque — silver-domed mosque on S end of Temple Mount; called el Aqṣa, meaning extreme end or distant, because it is furthermost from Mecca and Medina, the holy cities of Islam. The site on which the mosque stands is mentioned in the Koran and is considered one of Islam's holiest places. Built on the site where the royal portico was located during the Second Temple Period, the mosque is square and consists mainly of a large colonnaded hall with the floor covered by giant carpets. At its S end is a mosaic floor, a remnant of the first building erected here in the 8th c. by Abd el Malik, or his son el Walid. During the Crusades, the mosque was used as a palace for European kings and was in the hands of Templar Knights.

Armon HaNaziv → see Government House.

Augusta Victoria — hospital, church and tower located between Mt. of

Olives and Mt. Scopus. Named after wife of German Kaiser Wilhelm II who visited Ereẓ Israel in 1898. Inaugurated by German Catholics in 1910 as a pilgrims' hospice. The building was taken over as Government House for British High Commissioner from 1920-1927. During Jordanian rule, it became a military hospital. Today serves as hospital for local Arab population.

Batte Mahase — in past was a courtyard neighbourhood in S part of Jewish quarter of Old City. Established 1858 by Dutch and German community; destroyed during War of Independence but partly restored after Six-Day War.

Bene Hezir Tomb — rock-cut cave in Qidron Valley, E of Temple Mount. Hebrew inscription on architecture lists names of priestly family of Ḥezir, mentioned in I Chron. 24:15. Dates from late 2nd c. BCE. The entrance is flanked by 2 columns, and inside the tomb are 5 burial chambers with rock-cut niches in their walls. Popular tradition claims the tomb to be site of the "separate house" in which King Azariah, son of Amaziah, dwelt after being struck with leprosy (II Kings 15:5).

Biblical Zoo — situated in N part of city, the zoo has a collection of animals mentioned in the Bible.

Binyanei HaOoma — convention centre and international conference centre. Shows, exhibitions and concerts are held here.

Churches and Monasteries (alphabetical order):

Annunciation, Church of the — Greek Catholic cathedral and seat of the Patriarchate in Christian quarter of Old City. Built in 1848. **Archangels (Convent of the Olive Tree)** — Armenian monastery and church in Armenian quarter of Old City. A 5th c. building restored in 1300. A veritable museum of Oriental art. Armenian tradition claims this to be site of house of High Priest Ḥanan (Annas) where Jesus was first imprisoned. **Ascension, Church of** → see Mt. of Olives. **Assumption, Church of** → see Tomb of Virgin Mary. **Basilica of the Agony** → see Mt. of Olives. **Bethphage, Chapel of** → see Mt. of Olives. **Coenaculum** → see Mt. Zion. **Deir el Ades** — (*ades* = lentils). Small Greek Orthodox convent in Old City, near Lions' Gate. Christian tradition claims this to be site of Herod's house where Jesus was brought by Pilate's soldiers. **Dominus Flevit** → see Mt. of Olives. **Dormition, Church of** → see Mt. Zion. **Ecce Homo Church** — ("this is the man") of Sisters of Zion near 2nd Station of the Cross on Via Dolorosa in Old City. **Eleona, Church of** → see Mt. of Olives. **Gorny** — Russian church and convent of the Moscow Patriarchate, where a special icon of the Annunciation is honoured in a procession each spring. Situated in 'En Kerem. Convent buildings are scattered within large walled garden. **Holy Sepulchre, Church of** — the holiest place in Christendom. Complex of over 30 chambers and chapels, in Christian quarter of Old City. A conglomeration of Byzantine, Crusader and 19th c. Greek construction. According to Christian tradition this is the site of Jesus' crucifixion (golgotha), and his burial. The present-day buildings were constructed over more ancient churches. The earliest one was built in 335 CE by order of Emperor Constantine I, but was destroyed by Persians in 614, and rebuilt in 634. Arab conquest and control of the Holy Sepulchre from 640 was one of the reasons for the First Crusade. The Crusaders built a new church in Romanesque style that included under one roof the site of the crucifixion, and of the tomb. After the Crusaders were expelled, the city and the church were once again in Moslem hands and they hold the keys of the church to this day. Destruction by Tartars in 1240 and a fire in 1808 spurred the Greek Orthodox community to do extensive repairs in the last century. The church is shared by 6 communities: Latins, Greek Orthodox, Armenian Orthodox, Syrian (Jacobite), Copts, and Abyssinians. The church

complex includes the tomb of Queen Helena, the gate of Constantine's basilica in the adjacent Russian convent, and the village of Ethiopian monks on the roof. The compound and its environs evinces the diversity of the Christian community in the Holy Land. **Monastery of Alexander Nevsky** — monastery of exiled Russian church in Christian quarter of Old City. Built 1860. **Monastery of the Cross** — Greek Orthodox monastery located in the Valley of the Cross between Reḥavya and the hill of the Israel Museum. According to Christian tradition, the monastery was built on the site of the tree from which the cross for the crucifixion was made. Established in 5th c., it was destroyed by the Persians in the 7th c. and shortly afterwards rebuilt by the Georgian church. In the 17th c. it was sold to the Greek Orthodox church. Because of its distance from the Old City its shape is that of a fortress. The Georgian national poet Shota Rustaveli lived in the monastery for a while at the end of the 12th c.; here he wrote his famous work *The Knight in the Tiger's Skin* and was also buried here. **Monastery of the Flagellation** — Franciscan monastery in Old City, 2nd Station of the Cross. According to Christian tradition, this is the site where the Roman soldiers scourged Jesus. The monastery has a Bible school and antiquities museum. **Notre Dame de France** — monastery and hospice near Ẓahal square, opposite New Gate. Founded 1887 as a hospice for French pilgrims. The building was partially damaged during War of Independence and until Six-Day War served as an Israeli border post. Restoration of the building began after the war. **Pater Noster Church →** see Mt. of Olives. **St. Anne, Church of** — Catholic church in Old City, near Lions' Gate. According to Christian tradition, site of home of Anne and Joachim, parents of Virgin Mary, and place of her birth. **St. Charalampos, Convent of** — Greek Orthodox convent in Old City, near 8th Station of the Cross. **St. Claire, Convent of** — convent of the order of Poor Claires located between Abu Tor and N Talpiyyot. **St. James, Church of** — the Armenian cathedral in Armenian quarter of Old City. Named after 2 Christian saints: James the Greater, apostle and brother of John the Apostle, beheaded by order of Herod Agrippa and whose head is buried in the church, and James the Less, believed to be the brother of Jesus, and first bishop of Jerusalem, who is buried in the church. The walls of the church are lined with decorated 17th c. ceramic tiles. The church has a priceless collection of religious objects and manuscripts. Among the most magnificent cathedral interiors in the Middle East. Colourful ceremony takes place here at 3 pm each Saturday. **St. John the Baptist, Church of** — ('En Kerem) Franciscan church built on remains of 2 ancient churches: one Byzantine from 5th c. and one Crusader. Within church is a grotto believed by Christians to be part of the house of John's parents, Elizabeth and Zachary. **St. John the Baptist, Church of** — (Old City) Greek Orthodox church with 2 parts: upper church from 11th c. and subterranean church from 5th c. **St. Mark, Church of** — ancient Syrian Orthodox church and convent in Old City, E of Armenian quarter. According to Syrian tradition, site of room of Last Supper. **St. Mary Magdalene, Church of →** see Mt. of Olives. **St. Peter in Gallicantu, Church of →** see Mt. Zion. **St. Saviour, Church of →** (Armenian) see Mt. Zion. **St. Saviour, Church of** — Lutheran church in Christian quarter of Old City, built on ruins of Crusader church St Mary Latine. Inaugurated 1898 by German Kaiser Wilhelm II during his visit to Jerusalem. **St. Saviour, Convent of** — headquarters of Franciscans in Middle East, located in Christian quarter of Old City. Also known as residence of Custodian of the Holy Land (Terra Sancta). **St. Simeon, Monastery of** — Greek Orthodox monastery in Gonen. Site of supposed tomb of Simeon, the Jerusalemite, who recognized the young child Jesus as the Messiah (Luke 2:25). Served as an Arab military post during War of Independence until taken by Israel Defence Forces. **St. Theodorus, Church of** — Armenian church in Armenian

quarter of Old City. Built 1266. Has large collection of ancient manuscripts. **Visitation, Church of** — in 'En Kerem. Built 1939 on remains of ancient destroyed Byzantine church which was rebuilt during Crusader Period; again destroyed and partly rebuilt in 17th c. According to Christian tradition, site of summer home of parents of John the Baptist, Elizabeth and Zachary. It was here that the Virgin Mary met Elizabeth and first felt Jesus stirring in her womb.

Court of the Guard — cave near Damascus Gate opposite Zedekiah's Cave. According to tradition the site of the Court of the Guard into which the prophet Jeremiah was thrown (Jer. 38:6 ff.).
David's Tomb → see Mt. Zion.

David's Tower — fortress with walls of Old City, near Jaffa Gate. Its construction is attributed to King David; rebuilt by King Herod, it served as a stronghold in days of Revolt against Rome. It was used as a fortress during Roman and Crusader Periods and guard tower during Ottoman Period. Military post during Jordanian occupation. Remains of walls from Hasmonean Period; Hippicus' Tower from Herod's fortress; many remains from Crusader Period and a mosque from Ottoman Period. Today it is an archaeological site and theatre for performances and public events.

Dome of the Rock — octagonal structure topped by a golden dome in centre of Temple Mount. Erected in 691 by Caliph Abd el Malik and is one of the few surviving creations of Umayyad art. Used as a church in Crusader Period. Built around a large stone hence its Arabic name Qubbat eṣ Ṣaḥra. According to Jewish tradition the stone is the *even shetiyya* (foundation stone), the centre of the world and site of sacrifice of Isaac. Moslem tradition designates this as the spot from which Muḥammad ascended on his night journey. It is sometimes erroneously called Mosque of 'Omar after the Caliph 'Omar during whose reign the Moslems conquered the country. Inside, the wealth of decoration defies the eyes including arabesque designs in stucco and floral patterns. Outside facade is combination of marble, and green and blue ceramic tiles.
Garden Tomb — rock-cut tomb within garden NE of Damascus Gate. Believed by a number of Protestant denominations to be site of crucifixion and burial of Jesus. Near tomb is a large rock in shape of a skull, i.e. the traditional golgotha. Discovered in 1867 and publicized in 1882 by British General Gordon. The custodians of the site are the Garden Tomb Association, an Anglican organization with its centre in England.

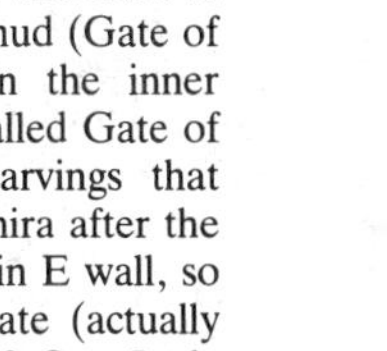

Gates of the Old City The wall of the Old City has 8 gates — 1 on the W, 3 on the N, 2 on the E and 2 on the S. **Jaffa Gate** — in centre of W side of city wall; from here the road to Jaffa began, hence its name. Also called Bab el Khalil (Hebron Gate) by Arabs because the road to Hebron also leads off from here. **New Gate** — (Arabic: Bab el Jadid) near NW corner of city wall. Opened 1887, hence its name. **Damascus Gate** — in centre of N wall, the road to Damascus and also to Shekhem (Nablus) led off from here, therefore is also known by these two names. Arabic name is Bab el 'Amud (Gate of the Column) named for the column that once stood in the inner courtyard. **Herod's Gate** — near NE corner of wall. Also called Gate of the Flowers (Arabic: Bab ez Zahira) for the flower carvings that decorate it. During Middle Ages, Arabs called it Bab es Sahira after the adjacent hill which has a Moslem cemetery. **Lions' Gate** — in E wall, so named because of reliefs of lions on either side of the gate (actually leopards). In Arabic, called Bab Sittna Mariam (Gate of Our Lady Mary) because of proximity to site of birth of Virgin Mary, according to Christian tradition. This is the gate through which Israeli paratroopers entered the Old City, from where they proceeded to the Temple Mount during Six-Day War. **Gate of Mercy** — in E wall, delineates the Temple

Mount. Also called Golden Gate. Blocked up by the Arabs several hundred years ago in order to prevent the Jewish Messiah from entering the city through this gate (as specified in Jewish tradition). **Dung Gate** — in S wall. The name is ancient (Neh. 3:13-14). **Zion Gate** — in S wall, adjacent to SW corner. Arabic name is Bab en Nabi Daoud (Gate of Prophet David). Within area of Mt. Zion, hence its name. It was through this gate that a Palmaḥ unit entered the Old City and linked up with the besieged in Jewish quarter during War of Independence. In the past there were additional gates but these have been blocked up over the years. Some of them have been identified by name and others still remain unidentified.

Gethsemane → see Mt. of Olives.

Giv'at HaMivtar — hill in N of city, between Giv'at HaTaḥmoshet (Ammunition Hill) and HaGiv'a HaẒarfatit (French Hill, now called Giv'at Shapira). A road cleft the hill, hence its name (*mivtar* = cut). Battle site in Six-Day War.

Giv'at HaTahmoshet — hill in N of city, S of Ramot Eshkol. In past a strongly fortified Jordanian position, site of fierce battle in Six-Day War; now a memorial site for those who fell in that war. Memorial, museum and park.

Giv'at Ram — ridge of hills W of Valley of the Cross. Origin of name: acronym of *rikus mefaqdim* (concentration of commanders), name of Gadna training camp in Jerusalem (also housing site for commanders) during War of Independence. The ridge contains the Knesset building, Qiryat David Ben-Gurion (with government buildings and offices) and the Hebrew University campus (in place of original campus on Mt. Scopus which was cut off from Jerusalem after War of Independence).

Golgotha → see Churches and Monasteries — Holy Sepulchre church.

Government House (Armon HaNaẓiv) — palatial building surrounded by garden in SW of city at summit of hill called Ras el Maqabar in Arabic. According to Christian tradition this is the Mt. of Evil Counsel. The building was erected to serve as the official residence of British High Commissioner during Mandate and was therefore called Government House. After War of Independence it remained in demilitarized zone and served as headquarters for UN observers. On first day of Six-Day War it was taken by Jordanian forces but was retaken on same day by Israel Defence Forces. After the war it was returned to UN jurisdiction. Today serves as staff headquarters of UNEF (United Nations Emergency Force) and UNDOF (United Nations Disengagement Observer Force).

Grotto of the Agony → see Mt. of Olives.

Haceldama — site on slope of Valley of Hinnom, between Abu Tor and village of Silwan. Various Christian traditions associate this site with Judas Iscariot, who either committed suicide in this field which he bought with the 30 pieces of silver he received for betraying Jesus, or, that the field was purchased by the priests with the silver returned by Judas, to be used for burying strangers. Name means field of blood. A small Greek Orthodox convent was built here and named after the hermit St. Onuphrius. Nearby are ancient Jewish burial caves.

HaQirya — government centre which includes the Knesset building and the Jerusalem offices of various ministries. Situated on Giv'at Ram. Official name: Qiryat David Ben-Gurion. Also site of Gan HaNasi.

Har HaZikkaron — mountain in W of city, adjacent to Mt. Herzl. Contains the Yad WaShem Holocaust Remembrance complex with the Ohel Yizkor museum, archives and memorial column.

Hebrew University → see Giv'at Ram and Mt. Scopus.

Hekhal HaGevura → see Russian Compound.

Hekhal Shelomo — domed building in centre of city, seat of Chief Rabbinate of Israel. Named after Shelomo Wolfson, father of philanthropist Sir Isaac Wolfson who donated the building. Synagogue,

museum of Jewish religious and secular art objects, and Torah library. A new synagogue is being erected nearby.
Herod's Family Tomb — burial cave N of Yemin Moshe, near King David Hotel. Excavations uncovered a central hall with 4 burial chambers. The chambers are faced with hewn masonry and contained several decorated sarcophagi. The entrance of the tomb was sealed by a rolling stone. It is supposed that this was the family tomb of King Herod and that his wife Mariamne, the Hasmonean, was buried here.
Herzl Museum → see Mt. Herzl.
Ḥulda's Tomb — ancient tomb on Mt. of Olives. According to Jewish tradition, tomb of Huldah the prophetess from days of King Josiah (II Kings 22:14 ff.). According to Christian tradition it is the tomb of 5th c. Pelagia the Penitent, a converted dancing girl from Antioch. According to Moslem tradition, it is the tomb of a 9th c. holy Moslem woman.
Ḥurva → see Ḥurvat Rabbi Judah HeḤasid.
Ḥurvat Rabbi Judah HeḤasid — ruins of magnificent Ashkenazi synagogue in Jewish quarter of Old City. Named after Rabbi Judah HeḤasid who came to Jerusalem together with his disciples in 1700. Inaugurated in 1864. Bombed by Arabs during War of Independence and destroyed after Jewish evacuation of Old City.
Ḥuẓot HaYoẓer — arts and crafts centre at ascent of Hinnom Valley between Yemin Moshe and Jaffa Gate. An arts and crafts fair is held here every summer.
Islamic Art Museum — located at corner of HaPalmaḥ and HaNasi streets. Named after Prof. L.A. Mayer, orientalist and archaeologist. Contains collection of ancient and modern Islamic artifacts and weapons. Also a rich collection of ancient clocks.
Isolated Quarters → see Bene Ḥezir Tomb.
Israel Museum — national museum, in W part of city, opposite Qiryat David Ben-Gurion, E of Hebrew University campus on Giv'at Ram. Opened 1965. Beẓalel National Art Museum (mainly religious artifacts), Bronfman Biblical and Archaeological Museum, Shrine of the Book (where some of the Dead Sea Scrolls and Bar Kokhba letters are exhibited), Billy Rose Sculpture Garden, Youth Wing and changing exhibits and displays.

Jason's Tomb — located in Reḥavya (Alfasi St.), dating from Hasmonean Period. On walls of porch are inscriptions in Greek and Aramaic, the latter mentioning the deceased, Jason. Drawings of ships and incised drawings of a deer and a *menorah*. Other finds in tomb date from period of Alexander Yannai's reign until end of Second Temple Period.
Jehoshaphat's Cave — burial cave in Qidron Valley behind Monument of Absalom. Legend claims this to be tomb of King Jehoshaphat; however, a more accepted theory is that the name derives from its proximity to Valley of Jehoshaphat.
Jehoshaphat Valley — name of small section of Qidron Valley located between Mt. of Olives and Temple Mount. According to Bible (Joel 3:2) it is here that the Lord will judge the nation at the end of days, and it is from here that the redemption will begin.
Johanan Ben Zakkai Synagogue — complex of 4 Sephardi synagogues in Jewish quarter of Old City: Johanan Ben Zakkai, Eliahu HaNavi, Middle Synagogue and Istambuli. According to tradition, this was site of Rabbi Johanan Ben Zakkai's school during Second Temple days. The synagogues were destroyed by Arabs during War of Independence and restored after Six-Day War.
Knesset → see Mishkan HaKnesset.
Lion's Cave → see Mamilla.
Mamilla — old cemetery of city, within Independence Park. Known from Middle Ages and called by Arabs Maman Allah (God's trusted), which was then corrupted to Mamilla. Within cemetery is large rainwater pool — Mamilla Pool. Alongside is Lion's Cave: Christian tradition designates this as burial site of martyrs killed by 7th c. Persian invaders. Jewish tradition holds this to be burial site for bones of Jews

martyred by Greeks. According to legend, a lion came to guard the bones, hence its name.
Mamilla Pool → see Mamilla.
Military Cemetery → see Mt. Herzl.
Mishkan HaKnesset — Knesset (Israel's Parliament) on Giv'at Ram adjacent to Qiryat David Ben-Gurion (government complex). Inaugurated in 1966. A huge Marc Chagall Gobelin tapestry hangs in one of the halls. Opposite entrance to building is a huge, bronze *menorah* by Benno Elkan, depicting in relief significant events in history of Jewish people.

Mishkenot Sha'ananim — two long single-storey buildings and windmill in today's Yemin Moshe quarter. Mishkenot was established in 1860 as first Jewish quarter outside Old City walls, through the initiative and aid of Sir Moses Montefiore and American Jewish philanthropist Judah Touro. Today, the renovated buildings are a guest house for visiting artists and writers. The windmill has been turned into a museum and memorial for Moses Montefiore.
Monasteries → see Churches and Monasteries.
Mosque of 'Omar → see Dome of the Rock.
Mt. Herzl — mountain W of city (830 m. above sea level). Named after Theodor (Binyamin Ze'ev) Herzl, father of political Zionism. At summit is Herzl's grave and nearby are graves of other state leaders. On N part of mountain is military cemetery. Near entrance gate to Mt. Herzl is small museum and reconstruction of Herzl's study. Upper part of mountain has large square where every year, the ceremony to herald Independence Day celebrations takes place. Also used for official state ceremonies.
Mt. of Olives — mountain E of Old City, partly covered with olive trees to this day. Mentioned a number of times in Bible. According to Prophets (Ezek. 11, Zech. 14 and Joel 3) the resurrection will begin in Valley of Jehoshaphat at foot of Mt. of Olives. Thus the mountain was chosen as a location for a cemetery already in ancient times. According to Christian tradition, many events related to life of Jesus took place on Mt. of Olives, hence the many holy sites here. Within village of et Tur is the **Church of the Ascension** — octagonal structure, covered with dome built around a rock from which, according to Christian tradition, Jesus ascended to heaven. On summit of mountain is a Russian church built in 1886 to commemorate the same event. Alongside the church is a large bell tower that can be seen for some distance (erroneously called Tur Malka in Hebrew). **Church of Pater Noster** — according to Christian tradition this is the site where Jesus taught his disciples the Our Father prayer. **The Carmelite Convent** contains the remains of **Church of Eleona** (where Jesus foretold destruction of Jerusalem and his last coming). The church is believed to have been built by Constantine and his mother Helena on slopes of Mt. of Olives. **Chapel of Bethphage** — according to Christian tradition, it was from here that Jesus began his entry into Jerusalem. **Dominus Flevit** — (the Lord wept) a church built in 1955 over remains of 7th c. Byzantine church, on site where Jesus is believed to have wept over the fate of Jerusalem. At foot of Mt. of Olives, on site known as **Gethsemane**, Jesus spent his last hours before his arrest by Roman soldiers. Lovely well-tended garden with 8 very ancient olive trees. **Grotto of the Agony, Basilica of the Agony** — Catholic church and shrine maintained by Franciscan Order. The basilica was built between 1919-24 on remains of Byzantine and Crusader churches (also known as **Church of All Nations** because it was built with contributions from 12 nations corresponding to the 12 cupolas of the church). **Church of the Assumption** — according to Christian tradition this is site of tomb of Virgin Mary. Christian dogma states that Mary did not remain buried here, but was "assumed into heaven." The first church here was built by Crusaders and is now located under-

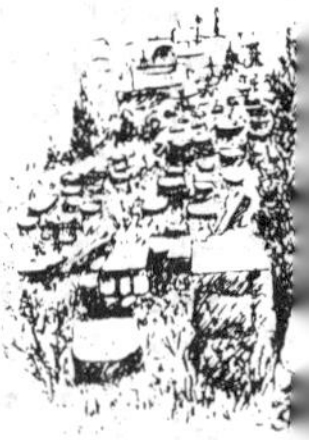

ground. The ashes of Queen Millicent, daughter of Baldwin II and wife of Fulk of Anjou, King of Jerusalem, are buried here. Above the Church of All Nations is the **Church of St. Mary Magdalene** — a Russian church with seven golden onion-shaped domes built in 1888 by Czar Alexander III in memory of his mother.

Mt. Scopus — mountain on NE side of Jerusalem overlooking the city, hence its name (Greek — *scopus*, Arabic — Ras el Mushraf). After WWI the Hebrew University campus was built here (opened 1925) followed later by Hadassah Hospital. After War of Independence it was an enclave of Israeli territory surrounded by Jordanian-held territory. (The new university campus was then built on Giv'at Ram and Hadassah Hospital in 'En Kerem.) After Six-Day War, the ramshackle and pockmarked university buildings were rebuilt and greatly extended and the old Hadassah Hospital was renovated and reopened. Nicanor's Tomb and British Military Cemetery for soldiers killed in WWI are also located here.

Mt. Zion — mountain adjacent to SW corner of Old City. Location of Upper City during Second Temple Period. On mountain is **David's Tomb** which, according to ancient Jewish tradition, is the burial site of King David. Nearby is **Holocaust Chamber** — memorial site for those who died in the Holocaust. Mt. Zion draws many Jewish pilgrims and has synagogues, *yeshivot* and is a tourist site. The holy Christian site on Mt. Zion: **Coenaculum** — room of the Last Supper; the Basilica of Zion was built over the Cenacle, and is believed to have been the first Christian church. **Church of the Dormition** — built 1910 on remains of ancient buildings. According to Christian tradition this is believed to be site where Mary, mother of Jesus, fell into a sleep of death (*dormition* = sleep) before being assumed into heaven. On E slope of Mt. Zion is **Church of St. Peter in Gallicantu** — built 1931 on remains of ancient structures. Tradition designates this as site where St. Peter heard the cock crow (*gallicantu*). **Armenian Church of St. Saviour** — near Zion Gate. This is believed by Christians to be the site of house of Caiaphas, the high priest, where Jesus was imprisoned for a second time. The church was damaged during War of Independence, but restored after Six-Day War. Alongside, a new church is being built. Mt. Zion has cemeteries of many Christian denominations.

Natural History Museum — small museum and pedagogical institute for natural history in German Colony. Collection of stuffed animals and educational instruments.

Nicanor's Tomb — ancient cave-tomb on Mt. Scopus which contained ossuary of Nicanor of Alexandria, who donated money for one of Second Temple gates (Gate of Nicanor); also mentioned in Talmud. Zionist leaders, Menahem M. Ussishkin and J.L. Pinsker, were buried in this cave.

The Old City — refers to Jerusalem within the old walls, as distinct from the new city which began to develop in the 2nd half of the 19th c. The Old City has 8 gates (see **Gates of the Old City**) and is divided into 4 quarters: Jewish, Armenian, Moslem and Christian. **Jewish Quarter** — located in SE part of city, near Western Wall. In past, this was the centre of Jewish life in Jerusalem. During War of Independence it was encircled and besieged, and captured after bitter fighting when the defenders were taken prisoner. The Jewish quarter was almost completely destroyed by the Arabs. After it was taken by Israel Defence Forces in Six-Day War, it was partly reconstructed and partly restored and repopulated. **Armenian Quarter** — located in SW part of Old City. Populated mainly by Armenians, it contains the community's churches, religious and educational institutions, and pilgrim hospices. **Moslem Quarter** — located in NE part of Old City, is the largest of the quarters and is the financial and commercial centre of the Old City. **Christian Quarter** — located in NW, contains the Holy Sepulchre church,

religious institutions of various Christian denominations, many churches and pilgrim hospices.
Old City during reign of Herod — scale model (1:50) of Jerusalem during days of Herod (Second Temple Period) built according to plan of reconstruction by Prof. Michael Avi-Yonah. The open-air model is adjacent to Holyland Hotel, in SW part of new city.
Pontifical Biblical Institute — located near city centre adjacent to King David Hotel. Collection of antiquities from the Middle East, including an Egyptian mummy.
Pool of Siloam (Shiloah) — ancient pool outside Old City walls, within village of Silwan. One of important water sources of ancient Jerusalem. Its water comes from the Giḥon stream, mentioned in the Bible as one of the 4 rivers emanating from Garden of Eden (Gen. 2:13). Solomon was crowned King of Israel near the waters of Gihon (I Kings 1:45). The water was used for drinking and ritual purposes (the Temple libation) and the people attributed medicinal properties to it. Just before siege of Jerusalem by Sennacherib, King Hezekiah had a tunnel bored through solid rock to divert water of the Giḥon Spring into the Pool of Siloam, then outside the city wall (II Kings 20:20). The tunnel, 513 m. long, was constructed by borers working from two ends and meeting in the middle. This meeting and the completion of the work was commemorated on a plaque, discovered in 1880, with an inscription describing the task (Siloam Inscription). The pool is called Pool of Shelah in Book of Nehemiah (3:15). It is also associated with Jesus' miracle of the blind man who washed in the pool and regained his sight (John 9:7). The Greeks called the site Sileus and it was corrupted in Arabic to Silwan. The Giḥon Spring is called Umm ed Daraj (mother of the steps) in Arabic, because of the steps that lead down to it. Christian Arabs call the pool 'Ein Sitt Maryam (Spring of Lady Mary, mother of Jesus).

Qidron Stream — originates in Jerusalem between Mt. Scopus and Old City, with outlet into Dead Sea. On E side, opposite SE corner of Old City are a number of rock-cut tombs (Bene Ḥezir, Zechariah and Pharaoh's Daughter). The upper part of stream was used as a garbage and sewage dump for many generations. Where it traverses the Judean Desert there are many caves, some of which were used in the past as dwelling places for hermits.
Qiryat Hadassah — university medical centre in W Jerusalem, established by Hadassah Women's Organization in 1960. It was built after the Hadassah Hospital on Mt. Scopus was cut off from Jewish Jerusalem. General hospital, medical school, nursing school, school of pharmacy and research centre. Hospital synagogue contains the famous Chagall stained-glass windows depicting the Tribes of Israel.
Rockefeller Museum — antiquities museum in E Jerusalem opposite the NE corner of Old City. Named after American millionaire, J.D. Rockefeller, who financed the building which was opened in 1938. The museum contains a rich collection of archaeological finds from many excavations. During British Mandate the museum and building were administered by the Government Department of Antiquities. Before end of Mandate in 1948 it was entrusted to an international board which included a representative from the Hebrew University. In 1966 the Jordanian government nationalized the museum and its contents. After Six-Day War the building and its contents were entrusted to the Israel Department of Antiquities.
Russian (Moscow Patriarchate's) Compound — a tract of land containing the green-domed Cathedral of the Holy Trinity and other buildings in centre of city, N of Jaffa Rd. The land was acquired by the Russian Orthodox church which erected a church, monastery and hospice here in 1855. During British Mandate the police headquarters and city gaol were located in compound. In 1955 Israel government purchased it and it is now location of Jerusalem police headquarters, law courts, gaol and

Hekhal HaGevura memorial to Jewish fighters executed by the British. Within compound is a large stone column, about 12 m. in length, from Second Temple Period. The column lies horizontally in a trench and quarrying was apparently discontinued at the time due to a fissure in the stone. Children of Jerusalem used to call it the finger of Og, King of Bashan.

Sanhedrin Tombs — group of rock-cut tombs in N Jerusalem, within a park, between Sanhedriya and Sanhedriya Murḥevet. The caves were cut during Second Temple Period. Tradition attributes them to the tombs of the Sanhedrin court of judges.

Solomon's Quarries → see Zedekiah's Cave.

Sultan's Pool — a dried-up pool in valley between SW corner of Old City and Yemin Moshe. Part of the Jerusalem water system in ancient times. In 16th c. it was restored by order of Sultan Suleiman the Magnificent and named in his honour, Birkat es Sultan. Nearby are remains of pipes and aqueducts which transport water here from Solomon's Pools, near Bethlehem.

Tax Museum — small museum in Customs House, located on corner of Agron and HaMelekh David Streets. Recounts history of taxes in the country.

Temple Mount — a walled-in platform site in ancient times of both the First and Second Temple — the religious and national focal point of the Jewish people for many generations. Located in SE corner of Old City. Today occupied by the following structures: Dome of the Rock (sometimes erroneously called Mosque of 'Omar), Mosque of el Aqṣa, Dome of the Chain, Dome of the Prophet and Dome of Elijah. At the NW end of the mount are remains of the Antonia Fortress. On its W flank is the Western Wall, part of retaining wall of Temple Mount. Jewish tradition, as mentioned in the Bible (II Chron. 3:1), designates the site as Mt. Moriah, where Abraham went to sacrifice Isaac. The First Temple was constructed by King Solomon on the threshing floor purchased by King David from Araunah, the Jebusite (II Sam. 24:18 ff.). The First Temple was destroyed by King Nebuchadnezzar of Babylon in 586 BCE. The Second Temple was built by Jews who returned from Babylonian captivity in 515 BCE. During Hellenistic Period, the Temple was used as a place of pagan worship by Antiochus Epiphanes, until it was cleansed by Judah Maccabee in 164 BCE. It was enlarged and embellished by King Herod in 22 BCE. Destroyed by Roman commander Titus in 70 CE. After failure of the Bar Kokhba revolt (131-135 CE) a pagan temple to Jupiter was built here and Jews were forbidden to enter the Temple Mount. For many subsequent generations the area was desolate. After the Arab conquest (638) the Temple Mount (called Haram esh Sharif — the noble sanctuary) became a Moslem religious centre and during reign of Umayyad Caliph Abd el Malik, the Dome of the Rock and el Aqṣa mosques were built. However, these were converted to churches during Crusader Period, and only after the expulsion of the Crusaders did they revert to mosques again. But the area was neglected as a result of wars and power shifts that continued for many generations. Only after the Ottoman conquest (1517) was the mount cleaned and the mosques restored. Shortly after that, Jews and Christians were forbidden entry to the Mount, although for a short period during the Arab conquest this was not the case. The ban continued throughout British Mandate. The Temple Mount was taken by the Israel Defence Forces during the Six-Day War. The problem of free access and right of prayer continues to be a point of religious and political conflict.

Tiferet Israel Synagogue — ruins of Ashkenazi synagogue in Jewish quarter. Founded on initiative of Nisan Bak, and popularly called by his name. The synagogue was inaugurated in 1865 and named after Rabbi Israel Friedmann of Ruzhin. It was destroyed during the War of Independence.

Tomb of Pharaoh's Daughter — rock-cut tomb in form of cube located in rock scarp of Qidron Valley, opposite SE corner of Old City, near Tomb of Zechariah. Its shape is like that of an Egyptian chapel and is called by Arabs Kubr Bint Fara'un (tomb of Pharaoh's daughter). Built during time of First Temple, it is one of the earliest tombs discovered in Jerusalem.

Tomb of Shimon HaẒadiq — ancient burial cave on slope of Qidron Valley, between American Colony and Sheikh Jarraḥ. Traditionally believed to be tomb of Shimon HaẒadiq, 4th c. BCE, one of last members of Great Synagogue; supreme council in period of Second Temple. Up to War of Independence object of pilgrim visits and place for folk festivities.

Tomb of the Virgin Mary → see Mt. of Olives.

Tombs of the Kings — a complex of rock-cut tombs located S of American Colony, on corner of Saladin and Derekh Shekhem Streets. Excavated in 1863 and erroneously attributed to kings of Judah, hence its name. Now ascribed to Helena, Queen of Adiabene (in N Mesopotamia) who converted to Judaism and was brought to Jerusalem for burial with other members of her family in 1st c. CE. A late Jewish tradition holds this to be tomb of Ben Kalba Savu'a, a wealthy 1st c. CE Jerusalemite (father-in-law of Rabbi Aqiva). The tomb has a forecourt with 9 m. wide staircase leading down to main court.

Tombs of the Prophets — rock-cut burial cave on slope of Mt. of Olives, within cemetery and above common grave of those who fell in Old City during War of Independence. Jewish tradition holds it to be burial site of Prophets Haggai and Malachi. Apparently hewn during Byzantine Period.

Valley of Hinnom — to W and S of Old City. Mentioned a number of times in Bible, but origin of name unknown. In ancient days, site of pagan Topheth, where children were sacrificed to Molech. During period of Kings, idolatory altars were erected here. According to Jewish legend this is place for sinners in world to come, in contrast to Garden of Eden for the righteous. Today it is part of the park surrounding the walls of the Old City.

Via Dolorosa — (literally sorrowful road) also called Way of the Cross. A series of narrow lanes in Old City that according to Christian tradition was Jesus' route from Pilate's judgment hall to Golgotha. There are 14 Stations of the Cross, each one commemorating an event along Jesus' route to crucifixion. **First Station** — Jesus is tried and condemned to death in Antonia Fortress (near Lions' Gate of today). **Second Station** — Monastery of the Flagellation, where Jesus was scourged by Roman soldiers. **Third Station** — where Jesus fell for first time under weight of the cross. **Fourth Station** — Our Lady of the Spasm, where Mary fainted on seeing her son. **Fifth Station** — where Simon of Cyrene helped Jesus carry the cross. **Sixth Station** — where St. Veronica wiped Jesus' face. Church and monastery located here. **Seventh Station** — where Jesus fell for second time. Site of Franciscan chapel. **Eighth Station** — where Jesus said: "weep not for me, but weep for yourselves and for your children" (Luke 23:28). Site of Charalampos Convent. **Ninth Station** — where Jesus fell for third time. **Tenth-Fourteenth Stations** — within Church of the Holy Sepulchre (Golgotha).

Walls of Old City — the existing walls were built in middle of 16th c. during reign of Ottoman Sultan Suleiman the Magnificent. Partly built on foundations of older walls. The first and most ancient wall encompassed the City of David that was located on an offshoot hill S of the Temple Mount (outside today's wall). The wall was later extended to include the Temple Mount and Mt. Zion. The 2nd wall included an area on border of N part of the city towards David's Tower (which is Hippicus Tower) in the W, up to Antonia Fortress which was N of Temple Mount. The 3rd wall was built by King Agrippas I in 44 CE and completed in 66 CE by rebels against Rome. It was breached by the Romans in 70 CE. The 3rd wall extended to the N from the present wall and remains have been uncovered along St. George Street in E

Jerusalem, near the American consulate. The present ramparts around the Old City contain stones from previous walls.

Western Wall — part of western retaining wall of Temple Mount from time of Second Temple. After destruction of Temple it became a holy site for Jewish people — a site for prayer and lamentations over the destruction of the Temple, and a symbol of yearnings for salvation. The right to pray at the wall was a source of bitter disputes between Moslems and Jews during the British Mandate. The Armistice Agreement, signed after War of Independence, stipulated that Jews had the right to free access to all their holy places in Jordanian territory including the Western Wall. However, the Jordanians never abided by the agreement. After the Six-Day War the wall became a popular focal point for pilgrimages, prayer and official and public ceremonies. The court in front of the wall was enlarged and additional stone courses were uncovered. Archaeological excavations have been conducted in the adjacent area.

Yad Ben-Zvi — institute in memory of and for continuation of work of Yitzhaq Ben-Zvi, 2nd president of Israel. History of Jewish communities in Israel and Oriental countries is taught and researched.

Yad WaShem → see Har HaZikkaron.

YMCA — Jerusalem branch of Young Men's Christian Association in centre of city. Sport facilities, hostel, concert hall, observation tower and small antiquities museum.

Zalman Shazar Centre — institute of Jewish studies, named after S.Z. Shazar, 3rd president of State of Israel (on Hovevei Zion Street in Qomemiyut).

Zechariah's Tomb — monumental rock-cut tomb on rock scarp of Qidron Valley, between Mt. of Olives and Temple Mount, near the Bene Hezir Tomb. Built during Second Temple Period. Tradition ascribes this tomb to Zechariah, son of Jehoiada, the priest who was stoned by command of King Joash (II Chron. 24:20 ff.).

Zedekiah's Cave — large cave between Damascus and Flower Gates. Length: 200 m. Believed to be the cave through which King Zedekiah fled from Nebuchadnezzer, King of Babylon. He was then captured at the other end of the cave in the plains of Jericho (II Kings 25:4-6). It served as a quarry for building in Jerusalem during various periods. One legend relates that the stones for the Temple were quarried from here and it is therefore known as Solomon's Quarries.

o (El) Jib *167:139*

Arab village N of Jerusalem 2 km. SW of Jerusalem airport. The site of a great Canaanite city where Joshua made the sun stand still. Pop.: 1,200. **Gibeon** Site of ancient Biblical city, on road from Coastal Plain to Jerusalem through Bet Horon. First mentioned in story of Joshua and Hivites (Josh. 9). In Ayyalon Valley, W of Gibeon, Joshua fought battle with 5 Amorite kings and he called sun to stand still (Josh. 10:12). Men of David and Saul fought battle by pool at Gibeon (II Sam. 2:13 ff.). Gibeon was important cult centre before Jerusalem Temple was built. Gibeonites participated in building wall of Jerusalem in days of Nehemiah. Also mentioned by Josephus in *The Jewish Wars*. Excavations at site uncovered remains of buildings, winery, rock-cut pool 25 m. deep with a spiral staircase (mentioned in II Sam. 2:12-17; Jer. 41:12), tombs and pottery from Middle Bronze Age I, Late Bronze Age and a massive city wall from Iron Age I. Also Crusader church.

∴ Jibin *222:244*

Abandoned village on Golan Heights 4 km. SE of *moshav* Eli 'Al. Built on ruins of ancient settlement. Column base with Greek inscription found near mosque. Within village are scattered remains of ancient buildings.

o Jibiya *165:156*

Arab village 12 km. NW of Ramallah. Pop.: 70. Remains of a church and *maqam* (holy place).

Jib Yusif → 'Ammi'ad

∴ Jidiya *220:248*

Abandoned village on Golan Heights 2.5 km. N of *moshav* Eli 'Al. Located above Naḥal El 'Al with 2 springs alongside village. On edge of cliff are remains of large ancient structure (probably a public building). Sherds found from Byzantine and Ottoman Periods. Area included in Naḥal El 'Al nature reserve which also contains Lavan waterfall.

o Jifna *170:152*

Arab village 6 km. N of Ramallah. Apparently site of Ophni, city mentioned in Book of Joshua (18:24) or Gophna, mentioned in battles of Hasmoneans. Pop.: 800, half the inhabitants are Moslems and half Christians. In past, villagers were among the labourers who built Monastery of St. George in Wadi Qilt, and their names are inscribed in documents found in the monastery. Site has three modern churches, remains of two ancient churches, and a Crusader fort. Also burial caves from the Second Temple Period.

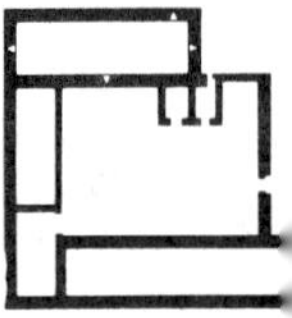

(El) Jiftliq *195:172*

Ottoman building in Jordan Valley near junction of Jericho-Shekhem-Bet She'an roads. Name means sultan's property. During Ottoman Period, housed sultan's property administration. During British Mandate used as police fort to guard nearby approach to Damiya Bridge. Road junction has same name. E of junction is Arab refugee camp, Fari'a el Jiftliq.

o Jiljiliya *171:160*

Arab village 15 km. N of Ramallah. Pop.: 500. One of camps used by Jewish Legion on Samarian front in WWI (1918).

o Jinṣafut *162:176*

Arab village 12 km. W of Shekhem. Pop.: 700.

o Jish *192:270*

Arab village in Upper Galilee off Sasa-Safed road, 4 km. N of Meron junction. Pop.: 1,800, mostly Christians (mainly Maronites). Maronite church, Greek Catholic church and mosque. **Ancient Gush Ḥalav** was located here. During Second Temple Period it was famous for its olive oil, milk and silk. Fortified by Joseph b. Mattathias (Josephus) during Revolt against Rome. One of leaders of revolt, Johanan b. Levi of Giscala (known as John of Giscala), came from this town. A Jewish community existed here during Byzantine Period and Middle Ages. **Ancient sites** Sherds found on site indicate occupation in Iron Age and Persian Period, and from Hasmonean Period until today. Remains include ruins of mausoleum, buildings, city wall, 2 synagogues (one on site of Greek Catholic church of Mar Butrus and the other near village spring) and caves with loculi. A local tradition claims that the tombs of the 1st c. BCE sages, Shemaiah and Abtalyon, are located here.

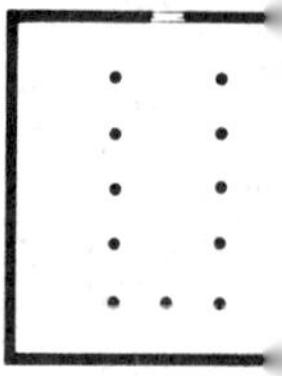

Jisr Ḥusein → Allenby Bridge

Jisr el Majami' → Naharayim Bridge

Jisr esh Sheikh Ḥusein → Ma'oz Bridge

Jisr ez Zarqa *141:215*

Arab village in N Sharon on shore of Mediterranean Sea near mouth of Naḥal Tanninim, which is called Wadi ez Zarqa (blue stream) in Arabic. Founded 1924 by Bedouin of the el 'Awarna tribe who moved here from Kabara Valley after swamps were drained. Pop.: 4,000. **Roman bridge** Near village, at Naḥal Tanninim *142:217*, are remains of bridge and dam from Roman Period. Dam used to control flow from stream to Caesarea; also helped power a flour mill. When swamps were drained the dam broke, and most of the bridge was washed away.

Jit *166:180*

Arab village 9 km. W of Shekhem. Mentioned in Estori HaParḥi's book *Kaftor wa Feraḥ*.

Jordan River *(Gen. 32:10)*

Largest river in Israel, 250 km. long. Its name derives from the Hebrew *Yarden* (the river that descends), since its journey from Mt. Ḥermon foothills to Dead Sea involves a drop of 800 m. to the lowest point on earth. It flows N to S. Its primary sources are: Naḥal Ḥermon (Banyas), Naḥal Dan and Naḥal Senir (Ḥaṣbani). As it flows down to the Kinneret and finally into the Dead Sea it is fed by many lateral tributaries, the largest being the Yarmouk. Crossed by Joshua and repeatedly by Jacob, the Jordan is perhaps the most famous Biblical place name, the river that divides the Promised Land from the desert to the E. It has been sanctified by both Jewish and Christian traditions. In its waters Jesus was baptized by John. As a vital water source and a natural boundary, the river has often been a subject of contention between Israel and her neighbours, Jordan and Syria. In 1922 the Jordan River was designated as the border between Palestine and Transjordan (at first an Emirate and later the Kingdom of Jordan). During War of Independence, the Syrians attempted to gain control over those parts of the river adjacent to her border. After the war, the N reaches of the river were included within boundaries of Israel and the S part, from Tirat Zevi to Dead Sea, came under Jordanian control. After the founding of the State, the new government prepared an overall plan for exploitation of waters of the Jordan and its tributaries — the National Water Carrier. The Arab states rejected the plan as well as an American proposal (known as the Johnston Plan) for distributing the waters between Israel and her neighbours. Syria and Jordan executed their own plan for diverting two of the sources of the Jordan into their own territories. This plan was foiled by the Six-Day War, when Israeli forces took control of the entire river.

Jordan Valley → 'Emeq HaYarden

Ju'ara → Giv'at Noaḥ

Jubata ez Zait → Newe Ativ

Judea and Samaria *(Judea: Ezra 5:8)*
(Samaria: I Kings 16:32)

Area W of Jordan River, known as the West Bank, annexed in 1948 by Hashemite Kingdom of Jordan and under Israel military control since Six-Day War. Includes parts of Jordan Valley, Samarian and Judean Hills. Total area: 5,507 sq. km. Pop.: (excluding residents of E Jerusalem) 700,000, mostly Arabs. During Jordanian rule (1948-1967) used from time to time as base for terrorist activities against Israel. From 1967 until today a number of *naḥal* settlements established, chiefly along Jordan River. Some have since become civilian settlements. Other civilian settlements have also been established in hill area.

Judean Desert *(Josh. 15:61)*

Hilly desert region on Israel's E boundary. Bordered by Judean Hills in W, Dead Sea and Lower Jordan Valley to E, Samarian Hills to N and Negev

Hills to S. It is about 100 km. long and 20 km. wide. Composed of hilly escarpments that descend from W to E, from a height of 1,000 m. above sea level to 400 m. below sea level. In spite of harsh climate and soil conditions the Judean Desert was settled during Chalcolithic Period and for most of Israel's history. During Israelite conquest the Bible mentions 6 cities in the area: Beth-arabah, Middin, Secacah, Nibshan, City of Salt and En-gedi. During the Hasmonean Period and Herod's time a number of fortresses were built in Judean Desert to protect Jerusalem: Herodium, Hureqanya, Alexandrium, Cypros, Dagon, Aristobulias and Masada. The Judean Desert also served as a natural hideaway for rebels, fugitives and hermits who could find shelter in the many wadis and caves. Discoveries were made in a number of caves that attested to communities of the Essene sect living here during the late Second Temple Period (Dead Sea Scrolls), and to the flight of the Jewish fighters to caves during the Bar Kokhba revolt (documents, coins, utensils and human skeletons). During the Byzantine Period the Judean Desert accommodated isolated monasteries (Mar Saba and St. Theodosius) and hermits. With renewed Jewish settlement in recent times a potash works and kibbutz, Bet Ha'Arava, were established at N end of the Dead Sea. They were abandoned during War of Independence and taken by the Transjordanian Arab Legion. In Six-Day War the area was retaken by the Israel Defence Forces, and since then, has undergone development, particularly along the Dead Sea shore.

Judean Foothills (HaShefela) *(Jer. 17:26)*

Hilly region in centre of country between Judean Hills in E and Coastal Plain in W. Bounded by Samarian Hills in N and the Negev in S. Its length is about 100 km. and its width between 20-40 km. Its E rim is designated as the Upper Foothills and the W part as Lower Foothills. During Byzantine Period, the N section was called Shefelat Lod and the S section Shefelat HaDarom or Shefelat Yehuda. Important region economically because of flat areas suitable for farming. Strategically, the area is a thoroughfare from N to S and E to W. Always an objective for domination, and therefore often a battleground. Until mid 13th c. BCE it was controlled by Egypt. During Israelite conquest it was a battleground between Joshua and the Amorite kings, and in 11th c. BCE a battleground between Israelites and Philistines who had previously invaded the Coastal Plain. A flourishing region controlled by Israel during the reigns of David and Solomon and during period of Kings. After the destruction of Jerusalem by Nebuchadnezzar, the villages in the Judean Foothills were also destroyed and were partly resettled after the return from Babylonian captivity. In 4th c. BCE the region was conquered by Alexander the Great, and became Hellenized. The Hasmoneans came from Modi'im in the Judean Foothills and it was here that Judah Maccabee scored his first military victories. Alexander Yannai annexed the Judean Desert to Kingdom of Judea, and the local Jewish communities were strengthened during reign of Herod. Most of these communities perished when the Second Temple was destroyed. The region was a battleground again during the Arab conquest (7th c.) and later during Crusader Period. Modern Jewish settlement was renewed with the arrival of the Bilu pioneers. Important battles were fought here in the War of Independence. After the Six Day War the entire region of the Judean Foothills came under Israel's control.

Judean Hills

The mountainous region that runs from Mt. Ba'al Hazor in the N to Biq'at Be'er Sheva' in the S, and between Judean Foothills in the W and Judean Desert in the E. Historically it was the heart of Kingdom of Judah. Also called Har HaMelekh.

Judeida (Galilee) *164:259*

Arab village in Galilee 8 km. E of Acre. Founded about 400 years ago by settlers of Syrian origin. At beginning of 19th c. the village was leased by Hayyim Selim Farhi, the Jewish adviser to the governor of Acre. Pop.: 3,200, mostly Moslems, some Christians.

(El) Judeida (Samarian Hills) *178:193*

Arab village in Samarian Hills 6 km. W of Tubas, on margin of fertile valley of Marj Sanur. Pop.: 1,500.

Judeira *168:140*

Arab village N of Jerusalem, W of Jerusalem airport. Believed to be site of Biblical Gederah, birthplace of Jozabad, one of King David's mighty men (I Chron. 12:5). Pop.: 700.

(El) Jukhadar → Giv'at Orḥa

Julis *167:261*

Druze village in Galilee, 10 km. E of Acre, seat of spiritual leader of Israel's Druze community. There is evidence that a Jewish community existed here in the 14th c. — the manuscript for a book by Tanḥum b. Yosef of Jerusalem was copied here by Sa'adiah b. Ya'aqov. Pop.: 2,700, mostly Druze, some Moslems.

Juneid *170:181*

Arab village 2.5 km. W of Shekhem. Pop.: 200. Built on ruins of settlement from Ottoman Period. Remains of buildings, cisterns, and broken pottery.

Jurdeiḥ *171:278*

Bedouin village on Lebanese border, N of kibbutz Adamit. Pop.: 400. Belongs to el 'Aramshe tribe.

Jurish *180:167*

Arab village 13 km. SE of Shekhem. According to one theory it is the site of ancient Gerasa, in district of Acrabeta, birthplace of Simeon bar Giora, one of leaders of Jewish Revolt against Rome during Second Temple Period. Pop.: 500.

K

o **Kababir** *148:245*

Arab village on Mt. Karmel included within municipal boundary of Haifa. Centre of a Moslem religious sect, Aḥmadiya, founded in 19th c.

Kabara → 'Enot Timsaḥ

★ **Kabri (El Kabri)** *164:269*

Kibbutz in Galilee 5 km. E of Nahariyya. Same name as nearby abandoned village of Kabiri, which seems to have retained part of the name Kabrita — a N border town in existence following the return from Babylonian Exile. Founded 1949 by members of kibbutz Bet Ha'Arava, who were forced to abandon their kibbutz during War of Independence. Area: 10,000 d. Pop.: 600. At adjacent road junction is a memorial depicting events which befell the Yeḥi'am convey during War of Independence. Nearby are the famous Kabri springs, and within the kibbutz and in surrounding area are many antiquity sites. **Bir el Khazna** Within kibbutz is a small ruin from Roman and Byzantine Periods. Hewn stones and white mosaic stones are scattered around site. Many remains have been found in the area, including rock-cut tomb from Roman Period, mosaic floor from Byzantine Period and an Ottoman aqueduct (built 1814 during the governorship of Suleiman Pasha), which was used to carry water from the Kabri springs to Acre — a distance of 12 km. Nearby are remains of more ancient aqueducts: from Hellenistic and Roman Periods, and from governorship of pasha Aḥmad el Jazzar (1775). S of kibbutz *163:269* is an ancient tel. **Daharat eṭ Tell** The northernmost of 3 tels on N bank of Naḥal Ga'aton. Remains indicate occupation in Chalcolithic Period, Early Bronze Age, Middle Bronze Age and Iron Age. Excavations uncovered courtyard of large house and remains of adjacent rooms. Middle Bronze Age pottery was found and a large collection of 17th c. BCE pottery imported from Cyprus.

o **Kabul (Kavul)** *(Josh. 19:27) 170:252*

Arab village 15 km. SE of Acre. Site of ancient city of Cabul. Pop.: 4,200. **Ancient Cabul** Included in territory of Asher (Josh. 19:27). Mentioned in Egyptian writings of 13th c. BCE. King Solomon gave city to Hiram, King of Tyre. During Second Temple Period it was a large city on outskirts of Jewish settlement facing the gentile communities centred around Acre. An industrial centre and home of many scholars, particularly during Roman and Byzantine Periods. During Middle Ages, pilgrims would come here to prostrate themselves at the local tombs of the sages. Popular tradition claims the poets Judah Halevi, Abraham Ibn Ezra and Solomon Ibn Gabirol are buried here. A 16th c. document states that 15 Jewish families were resident here at the time. Within present-day village are remains of a Byzantine Period synagogue and cemetery with burial caves and rock-cut sarcophagi; 2 tombs from Arab Period — one of a sheikh and one of Banat en Nabi.

■ **Kadoorie Agricultural School** *188:234*

Agricultural boarding school in Galilee, off Kefar Tavor-Golani junction road, at foot of Mt. Tavor. Named after Sir Elly Silas Kadoorie of Hong Kong, from whose legacy the school was funded in 1931. (A similar Arab school was established near Tulkarm from the same legacy and also named after Kadoorie.) The school was attended by children of pioneer settlers in pre-State years. Many of its graduates have played a leading role in administering modern Israel. Area: 400 d. Pop.: 200, including pupils and staff.

o **Kafr 'Abbush** *158:181*

Arab village (pop.: 600) 15 km. W of Shekhem.

o **Kafr 'Aqab** (Judean Hills) *171:142*

Arab village (pop.: 300) 3 km. SE of Ramallah.

∴ **Kafr 'Aqab** (near Lake Kinneret) *210:253*

Abandoned Syrian village on NE shore of Lake Kinneret. One theory identifies it as site of Kefar 'Aqiva, mentioned in Talmud and also inscribed on mosaic floor of synagogue uncovered at Ḥammat Gader.

o **Kafr Bara** *147:171*

Arab village in Sharon 7 km. NE of Petaḥ Tiqwa. Named after Moslem holy person, en Nabi Bara, whose tomb is in village. Pop.: 850. Many remains from Roman Period.

o **Kafr Dan** *174:209*

Arab village in N Samarian Hills 5 km. NW of Jenin. Pop.: 1,500.

o **Kafr ed Dik** *157:163*

Arab village in W Samarian Hills 13 km. E of Rosh Ha'Ayin. Name means village of the rooster. Pop.: 1,600.

o **Kafr 'Ein** *161:161*

Arab village (pop.: 650) 18 km. NW of Ramallah.

Kafr Ḥarib → Kefar Ḥaruv

o **Kafr Jammal** *154:181*

Arab village in W Samarian Hills 10 km. S of Tulkarm. Name means beauty. Pop.: 800.

Kafr Kama *192:236*

Circassian village in Lower Galilee 6 km. SE of Golani junction. Founded 1876 by Moslem Circassians who fled the Caucasus because of Russian persecution. Pop.: 1,600. The villagers had already cast their lot with the State of Israel during the War of Independence, and many of them serve in the Israel Defence Forces, Border Police, and regular police force. **Ancient remains** Excavations in village uncovered remains of a 6th c. church and monastery. The finds include a prayer niche, 2 mosaic floors with drawings of animals, plants and geometric patterns and 3 Greek inscriptions.

Kafr Kanna (Cana) *(John 2:1)* *182:239*

Arab village in Galilee 6 km. NE of Nazareth, where Jesus performed his first miracle. Site of ancient city of Galilean Kanna, mentioned in 20th c. BCE Egyptian Execration Texts, Tell el 'Amarna letters and in Tiglath-pileser III's city lists. One of cities fortified by Joseph b. Mattathias in preparation for Revolt against Rome. In Christian tradition, this is where Jesus performed the miracle of changing water into wine at the wedding feast (John 2:1-11). During Roman and Byzantine Periods it was a Jewish town and residence of one of the priestly clans. During Middle Ages it was a station on the caravan route from Damascus to Egypt. According to travellers' reports there was a large Jewish community in the town up to the 16th c. Today it is a large village with population of 6,700, mostly Moslems (74%), the rest Christians. The Catholic Franciscan church is called Miracle of Jesus and contains a replica of a jar used by Jesus. The church was built at the end of 19th c. on ruins of 6th c. church in which a mosaic floor was found with a 4th c. Aramaic inscription on it reading: "Yose b. Tanḥum." This would indicate that a synagogue once stood here. Near the Latin church is a Greek Orthodox church commemorating the same miracle, which contains two jars, also supposedly used by Jesus.

o Kafr el Labad *160:189*

Arab village in Samarian Hills 8 km. E of Tulkarm. Pop.: 1,200.

o Kafr Laqif *158:176*

Arab village (pop.: 250) in Samarian Hills 13 km. E of Qalqilya.

∴ Kafr el Ma *227:246*

Abandoned Syrian village on S Golan Heights 7 km. E of *moshav* Eli 'Al. Built on ruins of settlement from Roman and Byzantine Periods. Finds include remains of large public building constructed of basalt stones, olive oil press, capitals and other building materials re-used in village houses, and a tombstone with Greek inscriptions. On a nearby tel Early Bronze Age sherds were found. At the foot of the tel a spring flows from a recess in a rock embedded in a stone wall.

o Kafr Malik *179:155*

Arab village 15 km. NE of Ramallah. Pop.: 1,400, mostly Moslems, some Christians. Believed to be site of Beth HaMelekh, mentioned in Josephus Flavius' *Jewish Antiquities*. Holy Moslem tomb of en Nabi Shamail located within village.

Kafr Manda *174:246*

Arab village in Lower Galilee at foot of Mt. 'Aẓmon. Site of Kefar Mandi, a large Jewish settlement in Roman and Byzantine Periods and Middle Ages. An ancient tradition claims this is burial site of Rabbi Akahvyah b. Mahalalel, Rabbi Simeon b. Gamaliel and Issachar of Kefar Mundi. Pop.: 5,200.

o Kafr Miṣr *190:228*

Arab village in Galilee 5 km. S of Kefar Tavor. Named Miṣr (Egypt) because the first inhabitants emigrated from Egypt at beginning of 19th c. Pop.: 850.

∴ Kafr Nafakh *219:274*

Abandoned village on central Golan Heights off Benot Ya'aqov Bridge-Quneitra road. Inhabitants were Moslem Turkomans who abandoned the village during Six-Day War. Architectural fragments from Roman and Byzantine Periods have been re-used in many village houses. A headless statue of a man holding a shield depicting the Medusa's head was found in the village. Kafr Nafakh is an outstanding example of a naturally preserved Roman-Byzantine Jewish town.

o Kafr Na'ma *159:148*

Arab village 10 km. NW of Ramallah. Pop.: 1,300.

o Kafr Qaddum *163:180*

Arab village 15 km. W of Shekhem. Name means village of the brave. Pop.: 1,500.

o Kafr Qallil, Qallin *176:177*

Arab village (pop.: 750) in Samarian Hills at foot of Mt. Gerizim, 3 km. S of Shekhem. Inscriptions found here indicate existence of local Samaritan settlement at least until 13th c.

Kafr Qari' *155:212*

Arab village 6 km. NE of 'Iron junction. Established at beginning of

18th c. on remains of Roman-Byzantine town by an Arab-Turkman Bedouin tribe later joined by Bedouin from Egypt. Pop.: 6,500.

Kafr Qasim *148:169*

Arab village 8 km. NE of Petaḥ Tiqwa. Site of ancient Samaritan settlement mentioned in Mishnah. Established more than 300 years ago by residents of adjacent village, Masḥa. The village made headlines because of Kafr Qasim incident when 49 villagers were killed by a Border Police unit on the eve of the Sinai Campaign. Area: 9,000 d. Pop.: 6,500.

o Kafr Qud *171:206*

Arab village (pop.: 400) in Samarian Hills 8 km. W of Jenin. N of village are tombs of Sheikh Shibil and Sheikh ʻAbdallah.

o Kafr Raʻi *164:197*

Arab village in Samarian Hills, 17 km. SW of Jenin. Perhaps site of Biblical city Beth-eked, where the kinsmen of Ahaziah, King of Judah, were slain by order of Jehu. Pop.: 3,000.

o Kafr Rumman *162:191*

Arab village (pop.: 380) W of Samarian Hills, 9 km. E of Tulkarm. Name means village of pomegranates.

o Kafr Shibli *187:233*

Bedouin settlement in Galilee at foot of Mt. Tabor. Pop.: 1,800.

o Kafr Sumeiʻ *178:264*

Druze village in Galilee 5 km. SE of Maʻalot. Pop.: 1,200, mostly Druze (75%), rest Christians and Moslems. **Ancient remains** Within village are remains of Jewish settlement from days of Second Temple, perhaps Kefar Sama. S of village is an ancient building surrounded by carob trees — considered holy by local residents.

o Kafr Ṣur *156:183*

Arab village (pop.: 600) in Samarian Hills 8 km. SE of Tulkarm.

o Kafr Thulth *154:173*

Arab village in W Samarian Hills 3 km. SW of ʻAzzun. Possibly location of land of Shalishah, mentioned in story of Saul looking for the asses (I Sam. 9:4). Pop.: 1,300.

Kafr Wadi en Nar *191:120*

Ruin of unidentified ancient settlement on N bank of Naḥal en Nar, adjacent to its outlet into the Dead Sea, 4 km. S of ʻEin Fashkha. Remains of small houses, traces of paths between houses and nearby cave dwellings and caves. Sherds indicate occupation in Iron Age, Roman and Byzantine Periods.

Kafr Yasif *166:262*

Large Arab village in Galilee 8 km. E of Acre. Site of ancient Jewish settlement which, according to tradition, was named after Joseph b. Mattathias (Josephus Flavius) commander of Galilee during Jewish Revolt against Rome. Pop.: 4,900 (59% Christians, 38% Moslem, 3% Druze).

o Kafr Zibad *156:181*

Arab village (pop.: 550) in Samarian Hills 10 km. NE of Qalqilya.

● Kallanit *193:253*

Moshav in Galilee 4 km. W of Ḥuqoq. *Kallanit* = anemone. Named thus because of abundant wild anemones in area. Founded 1981.

Kammon *184:257*

Look-out point in Galilee 6 km. SW of Ḥananya junction. Same name as nearby mount (Hebrew name of popular local herb, cumin). Established 1979.

Kannot *126:134*

Agricultural school in central Coastal Plain 1 km. W of Gedera junction. Name means seedlings. Founded 1952 by Council of Women Workers (Mo'eẓet HaPo'alot) and the Pioneer Women's League of the USA. Today affiliated to Na'amat. Pop.: 260.

Kare Deshe ▲ *200:253*

Youth hostel on NW shore of Lake Kinneret, adjacent to et Tabkha. Named after Yoram Katz, killed in battle on the Kinneret before Sinai Campaign. Founded 1955 as a cattle ranch.

Kare Na'aman *161:254*

Cattle raising ranch in Zevulun Valley 6 km. SE of Acre. Name from Naḥal Na'aman on whose banks the ranch is located. Founded 1955.

Karkom *205:261*

Observation point in Upper Galilee 5 km. SE of Rosh Pinna. Named after local wildflower, crocus. Established 1980.

Karkur → Pardes Ḥanna-Karkur

Karme Yosef *141:143*

Settlement under construction in Judean Foothills 6 km. SE of Ramla. Named after Yosef Sappir, one-time head of Liberal Party and government minister.

Karmi'el *178:258*

Town in Galilee. Name originates from ancient Beth-haccherem. Founded 1964 with aim of increasing Jewish population in Galilee. The master plan for Karmi'el calls for a city of 50,000. Today's population is 8,500. Within the town are a number of ruins, including a Byzantine church.

★ **Karmiyya** *106:112*

Kibbutz 7 km. S of Ashqelon, adjacent to kibbutz Yad Mordekhay. Founded 1950 and named after both Adolphe Crémieux, French-Jewish statesman, and the abundant vineyards (*kerem*) in the area at the time when the kibbutz was established. Area: 7,500 d. Pop.: 300. **Ancient remains** Flint tools, Early Bronze Age tomb, Roman tomb, remnants of Crusader tower (in 1244 a battle between Crusaders and Mamluks took place here). **Nature reserve** S of kibbutz is a nature reserve (480 d.) with acacia trees. **Ma'agar Shiqma** SW of kibbutz is an artificial lake of flood waters from Naḥal Shiqma.

Karm es Samra (El 'Ajaz) *187:125*

Archaeological site in Judean Desert 16 km. SE of Jerusalem. Ruins of both an Iron Age and a Roman fortress, and remains of dams for collecting flood waters. Sherds also indicate habitation in Hellenistic Period.

o **Karza** *149:094*

Arab village (pop.: 330) in Judean Hills 15 km. from Hebron. Built on ruins of Byzantine settlement which apparently was also occupied in Middle Ages. Remains of walls and columns.

o **Kaubar** *165:155*

Arab village (pop.: 1,000) 10 km. NW of Ramallah.

○ **Kaukab** ▲ *173:248*

Arab village in Galilee 7 km. N of Ma'agar Bet Netofa, at foot of Har 'Azmon. Perhaps site of Kokhava, a Jewish town in Roman and Byzantine Periods. Pop.: 1,350. Tomb of Sheikh el Ḥija, a 17th c. Moslem holy person.

Kaukab el Hawa → Kokhav HaYarden

○ **Kaziyya er Ratrut** *196:173*

Arab village in Jordan Valley 2 km. N of Jiftliq junction.

Kefar Adummim *182:137*

Civilian outpost on border of Judean Desert 12 km. NE of Jerusalem. Established 1978.

Kefar Aharon *130:146*

A suburb of Nes Ẓiyyona named after Aaron Aaronsohn, agronomist and leader of Nili. Originally set up as a farming village in 1926 by second generation farmers. In 1950 its population was replaced by Bulgarian immigrants, and the village eventually became part of Nes Ẓiyyona.

● **Kefar Aḥim** *127:128*

Moshav on border of Judean Foothills and Coastal Plain 2 km. N of Qiryat Mal'akhi. Named after two brothers (*aḥim*) from Kefar Warburg who were killed in War of Independence. Founded 1949. Area: 3,000 d. Pop.: 240.

Kefar Ata → Qiryat Ata

● **Kefar Aviv** *124:137*

Moshav on central Coastal Plain 1 km. NE of Bene Darom junction. Founded 1951 by Egyptian immigrants on lands of abandoned village Bashshit. Name taken from Biblical passage "for in the month of *Abib* you came out of Egypt" (Ex. 34:18). Area: 2,000 d. Pop.: 320.

■ **Kefar 'Avoda** *144:184*

Educational institute in Sharon 2 km. E of Tel Mond. Founded 1942. Run by Ministry of Social Welfare; 400 students and staff.

● **Kefar Azar** *135:163*

Moshav on central Coastal Plain E of Ramat Gan. Named after the writer Azar (acronym for Alexander Siskind Rabinovitz). Founded 1932. Area: 2,000 d. Pop.: 350.

★ **Kefar 'Azza** *105:099*

Kibbutz in Negev 6 km. E of Gaza. Named after nearby Gaza ('Azza = Gaza). Founded 1951 by Egyptian immigrants.

● **Kefar Barukh** *168:228*

Moshav in Yizre'el Valley 10 km. NW of 'Afula. Named after philanthropist Barukh Kahana. Founded 1926 by Rumanian immigrants. Pop.: 260. Area: 7,000 d. SE of *moshav* is Ma'agar Kefar Barukh — a flood water reservoir. **Tell Thawra** 2 km. to NW *167:229* is a low tel. Sherds indicate habitation in Late Bronze Age, Iron Age, Roman and Byzantine Periods.

■ **Kefar Batya** *136:137*

Youth village and religious school in W Ra'ananna. Founded 1948 by Mizrahi Women's Organization of USA; named after Bessie Goldstein Gotsfeld, one of its founders. Agricultural and vocational school with instruction in agriculture, carpentry, clerical work, mechanics, industrial tool-making and electronics. Pop.: 1,000 students and staff.

Kefar Bialik *158:247*

Cooperative village in Zevulun Valley between Qiryat Bialik and Qiryat Ata. Named after H.N. Bialik who died in 1934, the year the village was founded by immigrants from Germany. Area: 3,000 d. Pop.: 600.

• **Kefar Bilu** *133:143*

Moshav on central Coastal Plain S of Reḥovot. Founded 1932 on 50th anniversary of first Bilu settlers (Bilu — acronym: *Bet Ya'aqov Lekhu Wenelka*: "O house of Jacob, come let us walk..."). Settlers came from Russia, Poland and Rumania. Pop.: 420. Area: 3,000 d. Within *moshav* are ruins of Samaritan settlement.

• **Kefar Bin Nun** *145:141*

Moshav 10 km. SE of Ramla. Named after Joshua, son of Nun (*bin Nun*) who fought one of his most famous battles during the Israelite conquest in Ayyalon Valley E of the *moshav*. Founded 1952. Area: 2,000 d. Pop.: 140.

• **Kefar Blum** *207:286*

Kibbutz in Ḥula Valley 6 km. SE of Qiryat Shemona. Named after Léon Blum, Jewish socialist premier of France before WWII. Founded 1943 by immigrants from England and Baltic countries. Before taking up residence at their permanent site, the settlers lived at neighbouring Na'ama. Area: 4,500 d. Pop.: 600. Natural history museum of flora and fauna of Ḥula Valley.

Kefar Brandeis *143:203*

Suburb of Ḥadera. Formerly a *moshav* founded 1928 and named after Louis Brandeis, Zionist leader and US Supreme Court justice.

• **Kefar Daniyyel** *143:148*

Moshav shittufi 4 km. SE of Lod. Named after Daniel Frisch, former president of ZOA. Founded 1949 by members of Mahal (overseas volunteers during War of Independence) from English speaking countries on lands of abandoned village of Danyal. Area: 2,900 d. Pop.: 180.

⋆ **Kefar Darom** *088:090*

Kibbutz in Gaza Strip 3 km. S of Deir el Balaḥ. Founded as *nahal* outpost in 1970 and became permanent civilian settlement in 1975. Kibbutz located near site of Kefar Darom, founded 1946 and evacuated after long siege in War of Independence. Area: 400 d.

■ **Kefar Eliyyahu** *129:134*

Religious educational institute for girls on central Coastal Plain 1 km. S of Gedera. Named after Rabbi Dr. Eliyyahu Jung, a Po'ale Agudat Israel leader. Founded 1951. Comprehensive high school and teachers' seminary.

⋆ **Kefar 'Eẓyon** *160:117*

Religious kibbutz in 'Eẓyon Bloc 10 km. SW of Bethlehem. Founded 1967 on site of original Kefar 'Eẓyon; founded in 1932 and destroyed during Arab Riots of 1936. It was re-established in 1943 but besieged and destroyed during War of Independence (see Gush 'Eẓyon). Some of the present settlers are children of veterans of original kibbutz. Area: 5,000 d. Pop.: several hundred. Museum of history of Gush 'Eẓyon, field school and youth hostel.

■ **Kefar Gallim** *146:241*

Youth village with educational institute on Karmel coast 6 km. S of Haifa. (*Gallim* = waves.) Founded 1952. Area: 1,500 d. Students are drawn from surrounding area and include Arabs. Pop.: 900 students and staff. The school offers general humanities programme and vocational courses in agriculture and mechanics.

Kefar Gannim *139:164*

Suburb of Petaḥ Tiqwa. Founded in 1926, it was a farming village until 1962.

● Kefar Gid'on *177:227*

Moshav in Yizre'el Valley 4 km. N of 'Afula. Named after Biblical judge, Gideon, who resided in area. Founded 1923 by Transylvanian immigrants. Area: 3,600 d. Pop.: 120.

★ Kefar Gil'adi *203:294*

Kibbutz in Galilee 5 km. S of Metulla. Named after Israel Gil'adi, one of founders of HaShomer movement. Founded 1916 by HaShomer members, who initially engaged in farming and guard duties at nearby Metulla. During WWI all the males were interned by the Turks and the kibbutz was temporarily abandoned. Resettled after the war, it was again abandoned in 1920 after the Tel Ḥay attack in which Josef Trumpeldor (founder of Jewish pioneer movement in Russia) and his companions were killed. Ten months later the settlers returned. In 1926 Tel Ḥay and Kefar Gil'adi merged. During pre-State years the kibbutz was a base for field companies (*peluggot sade*) and Palmaḥ units, and for smuggling "illegal" Jewish immigrants across nearby borders with Syria and Lebanon. Area: 5,400 d. Pop.: several hundred. **Ancient remains** Next to kibbutz are ruins of a mausoleum with 2 burial tombs from 2nd and 3rd c. and tombs from 3rd and 4th c. Sherds and other remains indicate habitation during Hellenistic and Arab Periods. S of kibbutz is monument of Tel Ḥay (see Tel Ḥay).

★ Kefar Glickson *150:212*

Kibbutz on border of Samarian Hills and Sharon 5 km. E of Binyamina. Named after Moshe Gluecksohn (or Glickson), Zionist leader and Hebrew journalist, killed in road accident shortly before kibbutz was founded in 1939. Before 1948, the kibbutz served as a Haganah training base. Area: 4,200 d. Pop.: 320.

Kefar Ḥabad *136:155*

Rural settlement 5 km. W of Ben-Gurion Airport. Founded 1949 by Ḥabad *hasidim* from Russia on lands of abandoned village of Safiriya and called Shafrir. Name was later changed to Kefar Ḥabad. In 1956, Arab infiltrators killed a teacher and 4 children while at prayer in a synagogue. Area: 2,400 d. Pop.: 900 permanent settlers (additional 1,400 external students in various educational institutes). The village has central *yeshiva* and teachers' seminary for girls. Also serves as a centre for Israel's Ḥabad *ḥasidim* and once a year on 19th of the Hebrew month of Kislev, a great gathering and festival is held to commemorate anniversary of release of Ḥabad founder, Rabbi Shneur Zalman of Lyady, from a Russian prison in 1798.

★ Kefar HaḤoresh *176:234*

Kibbutz 2 km. W of Nazareth. Situated in wooded area hence its name (*ḥoresh* = copse). Founded 1933. During War of Independence it was cut off from the rest of Jewish-held territory for a while until relieved in operation "Deqel".

★ Kefar HaMaccabi *161:244*

Kibbutz in Zevulun Valley 2 km. S of Qiryat Ata. Founded 1936 by members of Maccabi HaẒa'ir from various countries, hence its name. During War of Independence an attack by a company of Druze soldiers was successfully repelled. Area: 4,000 d. Pop.: 350.

● **Kefar HaNagid** *126:144*

Moshav on central Coastal Plain 5 km. W of Rehovot. Named after Samuel HaNagid, 11th c. Jewish statesman and poet in Spain. Founded 1949 on lands of abandoned village of Qubeiba. Area: 2,400 d. Pop.: 360.

◆ **Kefar Ḥananya** *189:260*

Experimental station of Ministry of Agricultu e in Galilee, 2 km. NE of Ḥananya junction. Named after ancient village of Kefar Ḥananya whose ruins are located nearby *189:258*, within abandoned village of Kafr ‘Anan. Important Jewish settlement during Roman-Byzantine Period, residence of sages (including Abba Ḥalafta) and famous for its pottery industry. The village, which during the Middle Ages was inhabited by Jewish farmers, existed until the end of the 16th c. Remains of 4th c. synagogue — of the type found at Bar‘am, Kefar Naḥum and Meron. Cave-tombs and remains of buildings from same period have been found in the area.

★ **Kefar HaNasi** *207:264*

Kibbutz N of Lake Kinneret 5 km. E of Rosh Pinna. Named after first president of Israel, Dr. Chaim Weizmann (*nasi* = president). Founded 1948. Until Six-Day War it was a border settlement. Area: 5,300 d. Pop.: 550.

■ **Kefar HaNo‘ar HaDati** *159:238*

Religious educational institute in Galilee 5 km. NW of Qiryat Tiv‘on. Founded 1936. Pop.: 700 students and staff. School offers 2 courses of study: agriculture and technology.

● **Kefar HaRif** *130:128*

Moshav in Judean Foothills 5 km. NE of Qiryat Mal'akhi. Named after Rabbi Isaac b. Jacob Alfasi ("Rif": 1013-1103), talmudic scholar in N Africa and Spain. Founded 1956. Area: 2,250 d. Pop.: 250.

● **Kefar HaRo'e** *141:199*

Moshav in Sharon 5 km. S of Ḥadera. Named after Rabbi Avraham HaKohen Kook (HaRo'e is Hebrew acronym), former chief rabbi of Ereẓ Israel. Founded 1933. Area: 2,300 d. Pop.: 800. Near *moshav* is Bene ‘Aqiva *yeshiva.*

★ **Kefar Ḥaruv** *214:240*

Kibbutz on S Golan Heights 4 km. SE of ‘En Gev. Same name as ancient settlement of Kefar Ḥaruva mentioned in sources from time of Mishnah (Tosefta) and also retained in name of abandoned village Kafr Ḥarb. The Arab village was built on ruins of Kefar Ḥaruva. The kibbutz was founded in 1973. Area: 4,000 d. Within abandoned village are building remains from Roman-Byzantine Period which were re-used in village houses.

● **Kefar Ḥasidim** *159:240*

Moshav in Zevulun Valley 6 km. S of Qiryat Ata. Founded 1924 by Polish *hasidim* from Kozienice and Yablonov. Area: 8,500 d. Pop.: 400. **Kefar Ḥasidim "B"** Rural settlement founded 1950 alongside *moshav.* Pop.: 350.

● **Kefar Ḥayyim** *140:195*

Moshav in Sharon 4 km. N of Sharon junction. Named after Chaim Arlosoroff, Zionist Labour leader murdered in 1933. Founded 1933. Area: 3,800 d. Pop.: 360.

● **Kefar Hess** *144:183*

Moshav situated in Sharon 2 km. to the SE of Tel Mond. Named after Moses Hess (1812-1875) author of *Rome and Jerusalem.*

Founded 1933. During War of Independence it was in front-line of fighting and after the war suffered infiltrator attacks from across nearby Jordanian border. Area: 3,900 d. Pop.: 480. A Roman cemetery has been found within *moshav*, but not as yet investigated.

● **Kefar Ḥittim** *197:245*

Moshav shittufi in Galilee 3 km. NW of Tiberias. Name based on that of Byzantine village Kefar Ḥittayya. First modern settlement here was founded in 1914. The present *moshav* (the first *moshav shittufi* in the country) was established in 1936 within framework of "stockade and tower" settlements. Area: 6,000 d. Pop.: 260.

■ **Kefar Joanna Jabotinsky** *134:150*

Agricultural school on central Coastal Plain 4 km. W of Ramla. Established by Ḥerut movement in 1948 and named after wife of Ze'ev Jabotinsky. Pop.: 600 students and staff.

● **Kefar Kisch** *192:230*

Moshav in Galilee 3 km. SE of Kefar Tavor. Named after brigadier Frederick Kisch, Zionist leader and head of political department of Jewish Agency. He died in WWII while serving with British army in N Africa. Founded 1946 as *moshav shittufi* by group of demobilized British army soldiers. Area: 6,000 d. Pop.: 220.

● **Kefar Mallal** *140:175*

Moshav in Sharon S of Kefar Sava. Mallal is Hebrew acronym for Moses Leib Lilienblum, a Hebrew writer. Founded 1914; abandoned and destroyed during Riots of 1921, but rebuilt in 1922. Area: 1,500 d. Pop.: 320.

Kefar Marmorek *131:143*

Suburb of Reḥovot. Originally a rural settlement founded in 1931. Named after Oscar Marmorek, one of Herzl's assistants. Most residents are of Yemenite origin.

★ **Kefar Masaryk** *159:254*

Kibbutz in Zevulun Valley 5 km. S of Acre. Named after Thomas Masaryk, first president of Czechoslovakia. Founded 1938 in framework of "stockade and tower" settlements by HaShomer HaẒa'ir groups from Czechoslovakia, Lithuania, Poland and Germany. In pre-State years it served as district Haganah base. Area: 8,000 d. Pop.: 600.

● **Kefar Maymon** *106:093*

Moshav in Negev 5 km. W of Netivot. Named after Rabbi Judah Leib Fishman (Maimon), a former minister of Religious Affairs (1949-1951). Founded 1959 by Bene 'Aqiva members — 1st *moshav* of this movement. Area: 5,500 d. Pop.: 350.

★ **Kefar Menaḥem** *134:126*

Kibbutz in Judean Foothills 8 km. E of Qiryat Mal'akhi. Named after Menaḥem Ussishkin. First settled in 1935 but abandoned during Disturbances of 1936 and destroyed by Arabs. Rebuilt as *moshav* in 1937 in framework of "stockade and tower" settlement. Area: 11,000 d. Pop.: 700. Within kibbutz is an archaeological museum. Nearby, prehistoric remains were found. Two km. SE *136:125* is Ḥurbat Dimdumit (Kh. Dimdim) — ruins of ancient settlement. Sherds indicate occupation from Roman Period until Arab conquest. To NE *134:127* is Kh. Abu el Quḥuf where building foundations, cisterns and sherds have been found.

Kefar Mesubbim → Or Yehuda

• Kefar Monash *142:194*

Moshav in Sharon 3 km. N of Sharon junction. Named after Sir John Monash, Jewish general in Australian army in WWI and president of Australian Zionist Federation (1928). Founded 1946 by demobilized British army soldiers on lands of Wadi Kabani in ‘Emeq Hefer. Area: 2,700 d. Pop.: 320. **Kefar Monash Hoard** A hoard of 37 Early Bronze Age copper weapons and tools were found here. The collection, known as Kefar Monash Hoard, is now located in the Israel Museum, Jerusalem.

• Kefar Mordekhay *127:137*

Moshav on central Coastal Plain 3 km. W of Gedera. Named after Mordekhay Eliash, Israel's first official representative in Great Britain. Founded 1950. Area: 1,800 d. Pop.: 230.

Kefar Naḥum (Capernaum) *(Matt. 4:13)* *204:254*

Site of ancient Capernaum on NW shore of Lake Kinneret, 4 km. SW of mouth of Jordan River, where Jesus began his preaching career. Capernaum was located alongside ancient highway from Ereẓ Israel to kingdoms of Fertile Crescent. One Jewish tradition believes the town to have been named after the prophet Nahum. It was well known during Second Temple, Roman and Byzantine Periods. Its residents participated in the Jewish Revolt against Rome. For Christians, it is important as birthplace of Peter, and where Jesus once lived, preached and performed miracles. (It is related in the New Testament that when the town's residents disapproved of Jesus' preaching, he cursed them.) In 4th c. a Jewish apostate, Joseph of Tiberias, built a church here and in time the place became a Christian pilgrimage centre. Kefar Naḥum was apparently destroyed in 6th c. However, it seems to have been resettled. Excavations carried out in 1979 give evidence of its flourishing existence until 10th c. A 16th c. traveller tells of how, when he visited Kefar Naḥum, he found a Jewish settlement whose inhabitants were engaged in fishing and farming. A 3rd c. synagogue was built over an earlier synagogue, possibly the one in which Jesus preached. The typically early Byzantine synagogue was reconstructed in 1921 by Franciscans, who purchased the site in 19th c. and erected a monastery here. The gallery is adorned by stone friezes depicting a *menorah*, vine leaves, bunches of grapes, dates, hexagram, pentagram, *shofar*, Torah ark and tabernacle. A Greek and Aramaic inscription was found on two column fragments. There is also a Greek Orthodox church and monastery on the shores of Lake Kinneret, on the site of a Byzantine Period church dedicated to St. John the Theologian.

• Kefar Netter *138:186*

Moshav in Sharon, off Herzliyya-Netanya road, 1 km. E of Poleg interchange. Named after Charles Netter, founder (1870) of Miqwe Israel agricultural school. Founded 1939 by Miqwe graduates. Area: 2,000 d. Pop.: 300.

• Kefar Pines *150:210*

Moshav on border of Sharon and Ramat Menashe, NE of Pardes Ḥanna. Named after Yeḥiel Michael Pines, writer and leader of Ḥibbat Ẓion movement. Founded 1933. Pop.: 630. Area: 2,400 d.

★ Kefar Rosh HaNiqra *161:276*

Kibbutz on Galilee coast 10 km. N of Nahariyya. Named after adjacent cliff of Rosh HaNiqra (see Rosh HaNiqra). Founded 1949 by demobilized soldiers of Palmaḥ's Yiftaḥ brigade and pioneer youth. Area: 3,000 d. Pop.: several hundred.

★ **Kefar Ruppin** *202:207*

Kibbutz 7 km. S of Bet She'an. Named after Dr. Arthur Ruppin (1876-1943), head of Palestine Office in Jaffa and director of Zionist Executive colonization department. Founded 1938. Before founding of State it served as Palmaḥ base. Area: 14,000 d. Pop.: several hundred. **Tell Masil el Jizl** Within kibbutz is ancient tel. Sherds and other remains indicate occupation in Middle and Late Bronze Age, Iron Age and Roman and Byzantine Periods. Other tels within kibbutz are Tell 'Artal, Tel Karpas and Tel Qataf.

● **Kefar Rut** *154:146*

Moshav in Judean Foothills 5 km. N of Mevo Ḥoron. Name from ancient settlement mentioned in Madaba map and called Capheruta. The name was also retained and somewhat distorted in the now ruined adjacent Kh. Kafr Lut. *Moshav* founded 1977.

■ **Kefar Sava** *141:176*

City in S Sharon 9 km. N of Petaḥ Tiqwa. Same name as nearby ancient settlement. The former Arab village of Kafr Saba (today site of suburbs of Kaplan, Josephthal and Giv'at Eshkol) and Kh. Sabieh, 2 km. NE of Kefar Sava centre and apparently site of ancient settlement, also preserved the original name. Kefar Sava lands were purchased in 1896 by Baron de Rothschild's administration and sold in 1903 to Petaḥ Tiqwa farmers. However, most of them sold their plots mainly to new immigrants. As the Turkish authorities forbade building of houses, the first settlers (in 1905) had to live in mud and straw huts. The first permanent houses were built in 1912. During WWI, residents of Jaffa, Tel Aviv and Petaḥ Tiqwa expelled by the Turks found refuge in Kefar Sava. In 1918 the village was on the front-line between British and Turkish armies, and was completely destroyed during the fighting. After the war it recovered slightly but in 1921 Riots it was again destroyed — this time by Arabs. In 1924 an influx of settlers spurred some development, but again during Disturbances of 1936-1939 it was attacked a number of times by Arab gangs. In War of Independence it was once again on front-line. Accorded municipal status in 1962 and has an area today of 14,800 d. and a population of 35,500. Although it is a sizeable and diversified industrial centre, it still has a rural character. **Ancient Kefar Saba** Mentioned in Talmud (Nid. 61:1). Apparently an important city during Second Temple Period. King Alexander Yannai fortified Kefar Saba valley and built a network of walls and towers from the city to the coast (in order to stall an invasion from the N). A few *Tannaim* resided here. Evidence of a large village here in 10th c. The site of ancient Kefar Saba has been identified with the tel Kh. Sabieh *144:176* — today adjacent to neighbourhood of Ge'ulim. The tel contains foundations, remains of buildings and a paved pool which indicate occupation during Roman, Byzantine and Arab Periods.

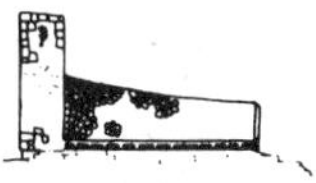

Kefar Shalem *131:162*

Suburb of E Tel Aviv. Established 1949 on site of abandoned Kafr Salama which harboured Arab gangs at outset of War of Independence. Came under Tel Aviv municipality in 1950.

● **Kefar Shammay** *193:262*

Moshav in Galilee 3 km. W of Safed. Named after the sage Shammai (ca. 50 BCE-30 CE) colleague of Hillel. According to tradition Shammai is believed to be buried at nearby Meron. Founded 1949. Pop.: 300.

Kefar Shemaryahu *133:177*

Urban settlement in Sharon N of Herẓliyya. Named after Dr.

Shemaryahu Levin, Zionist leader. At first a farming village, it was founded in 1937 by immigrants from Germany. Area: 2,600 d. Pop.: 1,400. **Antiquities** Caves and rock-cut tombs from 4th c. have been found, but excavation results have not as yet been published.

● **Kefar Shemu'el** *143:144*

Moshav in Judean Foothills 6 km. SE of Ramla. Named after Stephen Samuel Wise (1874-1949), US rabbi and Zionist leader. Founded 1950. Pop.: 240.

Kefar Shumi (Kh. esh Shuma) *145:215*

Ruins of Arab farm house and large ancient settlement, 1 km. N of Binyamina. Believed to be site of Kefar Shemi mentioned in Talmud. Remains of buildings, baths, and water channels from Roman Period. From the two nearby springs, water from Naḥal Tanninim was transported by aqueduct to Caesarea during Roman Period. A 4th c. traveller mentions the place as Mons Sina. In 9th c. there was a Samaritan community here called Bet Masa. Remains of Roman theatre can be seen in the Arab farm house. The house was purchased by ICA in 1913 and was used as residential quarters for original settlers of Binyamina, who called site Giv'at Binyamina, after Baron Edmond (Binyamin) James de Rothschild. In 1930's it was used as an Irgun training camp and operations base.

■ **Kefar Silver** *113:120*

Agricultural high school E of Ashqelon. Named after Rabbi Abba Hillel Silver (1893-1963), US Zionist leader. Founded 1957; today it has 350 students.

● **Kefar Syrkin** *143:164*

Moshav E of Petaḥ Tiqwa. Named after Naḥum Syrkin (1878-1918), Russian Jewish Labour leader. Founded 1936. Pop.: 600. Area: 1,500 d. Nearby, *143:163*, is ancient tomb en Nabi Thari.

★ **Kefar Szold** *211:289*

Kibbutz in Ḥula Valley 8 km. E of Qiryat Shemona. Named after Henrietta Szold (1860-1945), founder of Hadassah and director of Youth Aliyah from 1933. Kibbutz founded in 1942. The first settlement in the N attacked by Syrians during War of Independence. Area: 4,300 d. Pop.: 550.

Kefar Tavor *189:232*

Farming village in Galilee E of Mt. Tabor. Birthplace of the late foreign minister Yigal Allon. Founded 1901 by ICA. Initially called Mesḥa after adjacent Arab village. In early years settlers suffered attacks from their Arab neighbours. This came to an end when the HaShomer (watchman) organization took over the village's security. The organization was officially founded here in 1909 and Kefar Tavor became one of its headquarters. Area: 16,000 d. Pop.: 350.

Kefar Tiqwa → Bet Zeid

● **Kefar Truman** *142:154*

Moshav 3 km. E of Ben-Gurion Airport. Named after Harry Truman, president of USA at the time when the State of Israel was established. Founded 1949 by demobilized Palmaḥ soldiers on lands of abandoned village of Beit Nabala. Area: 1,700 d. Pop.: 330. **Byzantine church** Within *moshav* are remains of church which was repaired in Arab Period. Coloured mosaic floor, stone altar and Greek inscriptions.

● **Kefar Uriyya** *145:133*

Moshav in Judean Foothills 4 km. E of Naḥshon junction. Name from Kafrurieh, a nearby ruin. Began as a workers farm in 1912 to prepare site for a village which was started after WWI. During 1929 Riots the settlers had to abandon their village which was destroyed by Arabs. Resettled in 1944 by Kurdish immigrants — stonecutters by profession. Evacuated during War of Independence and resettled in 1949 by Bulgarian immigrants. Area: 5,700 d. Pop.: 300.

• **Kefar Vitkin** *138:198*

Moshav in Sharon 6 km. N of Netanya. Named after Joseph Vitkin (1876-1912), teacher and member of Labour movement who settled in Palestine in 1897. It was the first settlement in 'Emeq Ḥefer (Wadi Ḥawarith) and the settlers came from Russia and Poland. In the early years they were plagued by malaria and other hardships. Area: 4,500 d. Pop.: 800. There is evidence that the site was inhabited during Byzantine Period, but it has not as yet been excavated.

• **Kefar Warburg** *124:125*

Moshav on S Coastal Plain 2 km. SE of Qiryat Mal'akhi. Named after Felix M. Warburg (1871-1937) US Zionist leader. Founded 1939. Area: 6,400 d. Pop.: 520.

• **Kefar Ya'beẓ** *147:186*

Moshav in Sharon 5 km. E of Tel Mond. Named after historian Ze'ev Jawitz. Founded 1932 initially as a kibbutz. During War of Independence it was in front-line facing Iraqi army. It was evacuated and used as a military base. Resettled 1951. Area: 1,800 d. Pop.: 420.

• **Kefar Yeḥezqel** *184:219*

Moshav in Yizre'el Valley 10 km. SE of 'Afula. Named after Yeḥezqel Sassoon, Jewish philanthropist born in Iraq. Founded 1921 — one of veteran *moshavim*. Area: 9,500 d. Pop.: 450. **Antiquities** Within *moshav*, sherds and other remains were found indicating occupation in Chalcolithic, Early and Middle Bronze, Iron, post-Babylonian Exile and Roman and Byzantine eras.

• **Kefar Yehoshua'** *164:231*

Moshav in Yizre'el Valley 5 km. SE of Qiryat Tiv'on. Named after Yehoshua' Hankin "redeemer" of the Yizre'el Valley. Founded 1927. Area: 9,500 d. Pop.: 700. Regional museum, Bet Ḥankin, has collections of archaeology, fauna and flora; Miẓpe Meir — observatory in memory of a pilot member of *moshav* who died in battle; memorial to fallen in Israel's wars.

Kefar Yeladim → Giv'at HaMore

Kefar Yeroḥam → Yeroḥam

Kefar Yona *143:191*

Rural settlement in Sharon 3 km. E of Sharon junction. Named after Jean (Yona) Fischer, Belgian Zionist leader. It was originally a farming village founded in 1932. During War of Independence was in front battle line facing Iraqi army. Area: 10,000 d. Pop.: 3,300.

• **Kefar Zetim** *193:246*

Moshav in Galilee 7 km. NW of Tiberias. Named after abundant local olive trees (*zetim*). Founded 1950. Site of Kefar Ḥittayya, mentioned in Mishnah. Area: 9,000 d. Pop.: 350. In 1187 the Battle of Ḥittim (Horns of Hattin), between Moslems and Crusaders, was fought in this area. This battle marked the beginning of the end of Crusader rule in the Holy Land. SE of *moshav* is Nabi Shu'eib, tomb of Jethro, revered by the Druze. The tomb is the site of a celebration every spring.

Kefar Ziw → Tel Mond

Kelil *169:266*

Look-out point in Galilee SW of Yeḥi'am, named after nearby Ḥurbat Kalil. Established 1979.

● **Kerem Ben Zimra** *194:271*

Moshav in Galilee 8 km. NW of Safed. Named after Rabbi Yose b. Zimra, 2nd c. scholar. The tombs of Yose and his father Zimra are purported to be near *moshav*. Founded 1949. Area: 1,500 d. Pop.: 270. **Kerem Ben Zimra forest** Nature reserve, area: 70 d.; includes grove of trees grown on basalt ground.

Kerem BeYavne *122:136*

Yeshiva attached to Qevuẓat Yavne 7 km. E of Ashdod. Named after ancient Kerem DeYavne — a spiritual centre after destruction of Second Temple. (Called *kerem* — vineyard — because the scholars used to sit in rows like vines in a vineyard.) Founded 1954. *Yeshiva* has 400 students and staff.

● **Kerem Maharal** *149:228*

Moshav on Mt. Karmel 10 km. N of Zikhron Ya'aqov. Named after the "Maharal" (Judah Loew b. Bezalel, ca. 1525-1609) a chief rabbi of Prague believed to be creator of the *golem* (a dummy which, according to legend, came to life). Founded 1949 on lands of abandoned village. Area: 2,500 d. Pop.: 220. Ancient stones brought from nearby 'Atlit were re-used in houses of abandoned village, Ijzim. Within village is an attractive mosque and a magnificent 17th c. Arab building.

★ **Kerem Shalom** *082:071*

Kibbutz in Negev 7 km. SE of Rafah. Name based on that of nearby village Karm Abu Salem. Initially a religious *naḥal* outpost, established 1956 at Kerem Absalom, a point on border of the Gaza Strip, Egypt and Israel. Named after Absalom Feinberg, Nili member, killed here. Later a *naḥal* outpost of HaShomer HaẒa'ir. Took on civilian status in 1968. Area: 1,750 d.

● **Kesalon** **(Kasla)** *(Josh. 15:10)* *154:131*

Moshav in Judean Hills 7 km. NE of Bet Shemesh. Named after nearby ancient city, Chesalon, located on border between tribal allotments of Judah and Benjamin. Also mentioned in Onomasticon of Eusebius from 4th c. Founded 1952. Area: 2,500 d. Pop.: 240. Tel N of *moshav*. Sherds indicate occupation in Iron Age, Persian Period and Roman until Arab Period. **Scroll of Fire** About 1 km. S of *moshav* is an 8.5 m. tall bronze monument with relief figures depicting history of Jewish People in scroll-form; sculptured by Nathan Rapaport in 1969.

Ketef Ḥermon → Mt. Ḥermon

Ketef Shivta *115:035*

Ruins of Israelite fortress in Negev on N offshoot of Ketef Shivta. The fortress, next to a small settlement, guarded an ancient route which connected many villages in area. Almost square in shape and built of large stones.

(El) Khabiyya *198:271*

Dolmen field in Upper Galilee 8 km. N of Safed.

o **(El) Khadr** *165:123*

Arab village in Judean Hills 4 km. SW of Bethlehem. At turning into village is large stone archway. El Khadr means the green, and is associated with St. George who is parallelled in Moslem tradition with

Prophet Elijah, nicknamed the green. **Ancient remains** W of village are remains of Roman garrison. On nearby hill slopes are burial caves, quarries and wine presses, apparently from Roman Period.

(El) Khalil → Hebron

○ **Khallat el Fula** *194:173*

Arab village in Jordan Valley 3 km. W of Jiftliq junction.

Khan el Aḥmar *182:133*

Ruins of ancient caravanserai from Byzantine Period on Jerusalem-Jericho road, 3 km. SW of Ma'ale Adummim. Name means the red caravanserai because of the red hue of local stones. Built on ruins of 5th c. monastery constructed by the monk Euthymios. A group of skeletons of monks of Byzantine Period were recently discovered here. Near khan (caravanṣerai) are remains of a fortress: Qaṣr el Khan.

Khan el 'Aqaba *210:234*

Ruin of caravanserai on S Golan Heights 2 km. SE of Tel Qaẓir. The abandoned village of Kh. et Tawafiq, where khan was located, was built on ruins of an ancient settlement from which dressed stones were re-used in caravanserai building. One such stone bears the relief of a man and inscriptions in Arabic.

Khan el Ḥatruri *184:136*

Ruin of caravanserai at Ma'ale Adummim on Jerusalem-Jericho road. An Arab milestone was found here dating from time of Caliph 'Abd el Malik (7th c.), builder of Dome of the Rock. The khan was in use until beginning of 20th c. According to Christian tradition, this is site of the Inn of the Good Samaritan (Luke 10:30-37). The parable relates how a Samaritan saved a man who had been beaten by robbers on the road from Jerusalem to Jericho. A Byzantine church was built to commemorate the event. The khan was built by the Mamluks; the Turks used it as a fort.

Khan Jubb Yusuf → Ḥurbat Gov Yosef

Khan el Jukhadar → Giv'at Orḥa

Khan el Lubban → (El) Lubban Sharqiyya

Khan Minya → Ḥurbat Minnim

□ **Khan Yunis** *083:084*

Arab town in Gaza Strip. Name means Yunis caravanserai named after the Emir Yunis who established khan and a mosque here in 1389. A settlement sprang up around the khan and today numbers 30,000, mostly Moslems and some Christians. Remains of khan and mosque still exist. At the entrance to Khan Yunis is a police fort which served as base for Arab infiltrators in the early 50's; destroyed in an Israeli reprisal raid in August 1955.

○ **Kharas** *154:113*

Arab village 12 km. NW of Hebron. Pop.: 1,500. Perhaps site of Hereth mentioned in I Sam. 22:5, "So David departed and went into the forest of Hereth."

○ **Kharasa** *152:098*

Arab village (pop.: 100) in Judean Hills 10 km. SW of Hebron. Name means small wood. Remains of a two-roomed structure built of dressed stones with decorated columns and lintels. Sherds indicate occupation in Byzantine Period and Middle Ages.

o **Kharbata** *156:150*

Arab village 14 km. NW of Ramallah. Name is Aramaic and means ruin. Pop.: 600. Nearby is a tomb of Sheikh Abu Yusuf.

∴ **Khasfin** *226:250*

Abandoned Syrian village on Golan Heights near Ramat Magshimim. Built on ruins of Jewish city Ḥisfiyya or Ḥizpiyya, mentioned in wars of Judah Maccabee. Remains of buildings with arches faced with stone slabs, a mosaic floor, and remnants of a church railing or precinct barrier, lintels and capitals.

Khawaled *165:241*

Bedouin settlement in Galilee 7 km. SE of Qiryat Ata. Pop.: 500.

(El) Khirba *167:184*

Settlement ruins 8 km. NW of Shekhem. Remains of many structures including dressed stone building wall alongside monolithic columns (2.5 m. high). Sherds from Roman–Byzantine Period and Middle Ages.

o **Kh. 'Aba** *181:207*

Arab village in Samarian Hills 3 km. E of Jenin.

o **Kh. Abu Falaḥ** *179:157*

Arab village 15 km. NE of Ramallah. Pop.: 1,200.

Kh. Abu el Ghutsi *166:214*

Ruins of ancient structure 2 km. NE of Umm el Faḥm. Remains of foundations (or building walls) constructed with unhewn stones. Alongside are rock-cut burial caves. At mouth of one cave is an attractively worked stone door. Sherds indicate occupation in Roman, Byzantine and Arab Periods. Excavations uncovered cemetery from Late Bronze Age.

o **Kh. Abu Khumeish** *158:190*

Arab village in Samarian Hills 5 km. E of Tulkarm.

Kh. Abu Leimun *166:137*

Settlement ruins from Byzantine Period, adjacent to tomb of Moslem holy person, 7 km. NW of Jerusalem. Rock-cut cisterns; grove of ancient trees.

Kh. Abu Musaraḥ *177:137*

Ruin 8 km. NE of Jerusalem. Remains of major structure, cistern, caves and stone fences. Sherds indicate occupation in Chalcolithic, Early Bronze Age, Iron Age, Roman, Byzantine and Arab Periods.

o **Kh. Abu Nujeim** *169:118*

Arab village 5 km. S of Bethlehem. Sheikh's tomb in village.

o **Kh. Abu Salman** *149:172*

Arab village in Samarian Hills 6 km. SE of Qalqilya.

Kh. Abu Tuwein *158:119*

Remains of fortress 3 km. NW of Kefar 'Ezyon, perched on plateau of 925 m. hill. Built at end of Israelite Period and restored after Babylonian Exile. The fortress is square with central courtyard and surrounding rooms. On saddle of a hill to the SE are remains of an unfortified settlement that existed until destruction of Kingdom of Judah.

Kh. el 'Adas (Umm el 'Adas) *144:119*

Settlement ruins in Judean Foothills 10 km. SW of Bet Shemesh. Remains from Roman, Byzantine and early Arab Periods. To W are 2

Roman milestones from Jerusalem–Bet Guvrin road. One is inscribed with name of Emperor Septimius Sever (probably from 199 CE) and the other with name of Emperor Caracalla.

Kh. 'Adasa *165:139*

Ruin from Roman and Byzantine Periods 8 km. NE of Jerusalem. Remains of structures, water cisterns and a mosaic floor.

Kh. Aḥmad el 'Auda *151:170*

Settlement ruins on lower slopes of Samarian Hills 6 km. NE of Rosh Ha'Ayin. Beneath some of the stone mounds are structural remains. Sherds from Iron Age and Persian Period found here.

Kh. el 'Ajjuri *128:143*

Settlement ruins on central Coastal Plain near *moshav* Ge'alya. Early Bronze Age tombs. Roman building remains and a well. Nearby are remains of Byzantine church with coloured mosaic floor.

Kh. el 'Alaqa *150:096*

Arab village (pop.: 150) in Judean Hills 14 km. SW of Hebron.

Kh. 'Ali *153:160*

Ruin in Samarian Hills 9 km. SE of Rosh Ha'Ayin. Inhabited from Iron Age and Middle Ages. Remains of walls and olive oil presses. To W are rock-cut shaft tombs; to S — ruins of mausoleum.

Kh. 'Almit *176:136*

Settlement remains in Judean Hills 4 km. NE of Mt. Scopus. Site of Almon or Alemeth, a Levite city in Benjamin tribal allotment (Josh. 21:18; I Chron. 6:60). Remains of walls, caves, rock-cut cisterns and tombs. Sherds indicate occupation in Iron Age, Persian, Roman and Byzantine Periods and Middle Ages. Nearby is tomb of Sheikh 'Abd es Sallam.

Kh. 'Ammar *146:159*

Ruins of a building 6 km. NE of Ben-Gurion Airport. The building is square and constructed of roughly hewn stones. It is as yet undated. Adjacent is a water cistern, small cave and network of rock niches.

Kh. 'Ammuriya *177:159*

Arab village 15 km. NE of Ramallah, adjacent to village of Sinjil. Two stone sarcophagi from Roman Period were discovered in a rock-cut tomb within village. Sherds from Iron Age, Byzantine and Arab Periods.

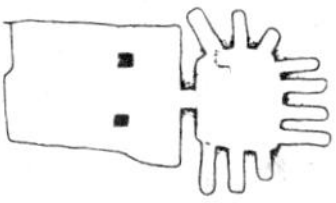

Kh. 'Amra *134:075*

Roman–Byzantine ruin 3.5 km. NE of Be'er Sheva'.

Kh. 'Amuda *113:112*

Small tel on S Coastal Plain 4 km. NE of Mordekhay junction. On slopes of tel descending into adjacent stream are scattered sherds from Early Bronze Age, Byzantine and Arab Periods and Middle Ages.

Kh. 'Annab el Kabira → Ḥurbat 'Anav

Kh. 'Annab eṣ Ṣaghira → Ḥurbat 'Anav

Kh. el Aqra' *182:194*

Arab village in Samarian Hills 4 km. SW of Tubas.

Kh. el 'Aqrabaniyya *186:183*

Arab village in Samarian Hills 8 km. S of Tubas. Pop.: 900.

o **Kh. el 'Arub** *164:114*

Arab village (pop.: 200) in Judean Hills E of refugee camp Mu'askar el 'Arub. Built on ruins of ancient settlement — Qiryat 'Araviyya mentioned in Bar Kokhba letters. Believed to be site of 'Arba DeBet Leḥem Yehuda, where, according to legend, the messiah was born on the day the Temple was destroyed. Within village are several springs ('Ein el 'Arub). In past their waters flowed to Solomon's Pools and Jerusalem by means of an aqueduct. Near refugee camp a ramified tunnel cave was uncovered. Finds inside include coins, pottery, tools and other items from Bar Kokhba Period.

o **Kh. 'Asala** *153:175*

Arab village (pop.: 200) in Samarian Hills 7 km. SE of Qalqilya.

o **Kh. el Ashqar** *152:171*

Arab village (pop.: 100) in Samarian Hills 7 km. SE of Qalqilya. Many caves near village.

o **Kh. 'Atuf** *191:185*

Arab village in Samarian Hills 9 km. SE of Tubas. Built on ruins of ancient settlement. Many relics and sherds from Iron Age and from Roman to Ottoman Period.

o **Kh. el 'Auja et Taḥta** *194:150*

Arab village (pop.: 400) adjacent to refugee camp 10 km. N of Jericho. Site of city Archelais, built by Archelaus, son of King Herod. It was given to Salome, Herod's sister, who in turn bequeathed it to wife of Emperor Augustus. Remains of building from Byzantine and Arab Periods can be found in village and its immediate surroundings. S of village are remains of a monastery and small chapel with mosaic floor and open channel water supply network. Sherds and other remains indicate occupation in Early Bronze Age and Iron Age.

o **Kh. 'Awad** *150:102*

Arab village in Judean Hills 10 km. SW of Hebron.

Kh. el Babariyya *166:186*

Settlement ruin 9 km. NW of Shekhem. Remains of large 3.5 m. structure with walls of dressed stone with drafted margins. Sherds found from Iron Age, Persian, Hellenistic and Roman–Byzantine Periods and Middle Ages.

Kh. Bad 'Isa *154:148*

Byzantine ruins in Judean Foothills 8 km. N of Mevo Ḥoron. Remains of buildings of large dressed stones, some attaining a height of 1.5 m.

Kh. el Balaqiyya *133:181*

Byzantine ruin on central Coastal Plain, 10 km. S of Netanya.

Kh. Bani Dar *164:100*

Tel of ancient settlement in Judean Hills 5 km. SE of Hebron. According to one explanation, it is site of Kain — city within tribal allotment of Judah (Josh. 15:57). The old name is believed to be partially preserved in that of the nearby Moslem shrine en Nabi Yaqin. Remains of buildings, caves and rock niches. At the foot of the tel is a spring and tunnel. Sherds indicate occupation in Iron Age, Hellenistic, Hasmonean, Roman and Byzantine Periods and Middle Ages.

Kh. Barniqiyya *144:172*

Roman Period ruin in Sharon at entrance to *moshav* Ḥagor. Foundation remains, rough stones, mosaic fragments and Roman Period sherds.

Kh. Baṣaliyya *193:177*

Large ruin in E Samarian Hills 2 km. SE of *moshav* Ḥamra. Inhabited during Byzantine Period and Middle Ages. Dwelling remains.

Kh. el Basatin *151:171*

Ruin of large farm from Byzantine Period in Samarian Hills 8 km. E of Qalqilya. Remains of hewn stone wall enclosing a large courtyard with rooms inside. At its centre is a large structure and a complete olive oil press.

Kh. el Batin *164:214*

Small tel in Naḥal 'Iron N of Umm el Faḥm. Strategically placed observation point. On tel are mounds of stones. Iron Age sherds were found at foot of tel.

Kh. Bat el Jabal *163:276*

Remains of Roman–Byzantine settlement in Galilee 3.5 km. SE of Rosh HaNiqra. Remains of large building, apparently a church or monastery, an abundance of mosaic fragments and sherds.

Kh. el Bawati; Kh. el Ḥakmiyya; Umm esh Sharashiḥ *201:215*

Settlement ruins 5 km. NE of Bet She'an. Remains of structure columns, ancient highway and milestones. Sherds from Roman, Byzantine and early Arab Periods.

Kh. Beit ʻAnun *162:107*

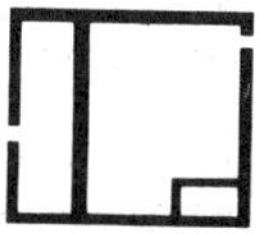

Ruin in Hebron Hills 2 km. SE of Ḥalḥul. Perhaps site of Beth-anoth mentioned in Josh. 15:59 and in Shishak's lists. Remains of church with mosaic floor. Sherds indicate occupation in Iron Age, Hellenistic, Roman, Byzantine and Medieval Periods.

Kh. Beit el Ban *145:105*

Byzantine ruin in Lakhish region 3.5 km. E of Amaẓya. Remains of structures and an olive oil press.

Kh. Beit el Ḥabs *163:165*

Remains of large farm in Samarian Hills 10 km. W of Ma'ale Levona. Established in Roman Period and continued to exist until early Arab Period.

Kh. Beit Ḥasan *188:182*

Arab village in Samarian Hills 10 km. SE of Tubas.

Kh. Beit Maqdum *147:104*

Settlement ruin in Lakhish region 5 km. E of Amaẓya. Site has loculi, cisterns and undressed stones from Second Temple Period. Sherds and other remains indicate occupation in Iron Age, Byzantine Period and Middle Ages.

Kh. Beit Nushif, Beit Naushif *155:142*

Large Roman–Byzantine ruin in Judean Hills 3 km. NE of Mevo Ḥoron. Remains of building walls and ancient stones re-used in modern stone fences and agricultural terraces.

Kh. Beit Ṣama *158:199*

Large settlement ruin (40 d.) in Samarian Hills 10 km. NE of Tulkarm. Many remains of buildings, columns, constructed well, rock-cut cisterns and tombs. Occupied from Middle Bronze Age until Ottoman Period, particularly in Middle Ages.

Kh. Bidra *199:223*

Ruin on border of Lower Galilee and Jordan Valley, 1 km. N of Kokhav HaYarden. Remains of structures, scattered over a large area. Sherds are mostly from Roman and Byzantine Periods, some from Chalcolithic and Iron Age. At foot of ruin is 'En Kokhav.

Kh. Bir el Beidar, Kh. el Beida *165:236*

Tel with remains of fortified settlement in Galilee, 4 km. E of Qiryat Tiv'on. Sherds indicate occupation in Iron Age, post-Babylonian Exile and from Roman Period until Arab conquest.

Kh. Bir ed Dawali *165:143*

Large Roman–Byzantine ruin in Judean Hills 4 km. SW of Ramallah. Remains of structures scattered over large area, including tower, pool and water cisterns.

Kh. el Bitar → Be'er Sheva'

Kh. el Biyar *161:213*

Arab village off Naḥal 'Iron road opposite Umm el Faḥm. Established in 1880 by residents of Umm el Faḥm. Today incorporated within Umm el Faḥm.

Kh. el Biyar *169:137*

Settlement ruins 4.5 km. N of Jerusalem. Water pools and cisterns nearby. The pools are lined with a mix of plaster and sherds and one is partially cut out of the living rock. Sherds and other remains indicate occupation in Iron Age, Byzantine and Arab Periods.

Kh. Bulei'is *135:051*

Roman–Byzantine ruin in Negev 3.5 km. SE of Negev junction. A way-station along an ancient route. Remains scattered over an area of 100 d.; rock-cut cisterns. On surrounding hills are mounds of stones, apparently remains of watch-towers and farming terraces.

Kh. Bura'ish *152:161*

Settlement ruins in Samarian Hills 9 km. SE of Rosh Ha'Ayin. Occupied during Iron Age, Persian, Roman and Byzantine Periods and Middle Ages. Remains of domed structures faced with dressed stones — probably Medieval, re-used building stones and demolished sheikh's tomb which was probably built on foundations of Roman or Byzantine mausoleum. Nearby are rock-cut shaft tombs.

Kh. Burin (near Baqa el Gharbiyya) *153:203*

Tel of ancient settlement in Sharon 10 km. SE of Ḥadera. Possibly site of city of Burit, mentioned in an ancient Egyptian document. Remains include wine presses, cisterns and caves. Sherds indicate occupation in Late Bronze Age, Early Iron Age, Hellenistic, Roman and Byzantine Periods.

Kh. Burin (near Tulkarm) *148:190*

Settlement ruin on low hill in Sharon 4 km. W of Tulkarm. Remains of buildings, wine presses, cisterns and caves. Occupied from Byzantine Period till Middle Ages. A fortress stood here during Crusader Period.

Kh. el Burj (near Beit Iksa) *167:136*

Tel of ancient settlement in Judean Hills NW of Jerusalem, between Beit Ḥanina and Beit Iksa. At centre of tel is a recent building constructed on ancient foundations. Many structural remains and sherds indicating habitation during Iron Age, Persian, Byzantine and early Arab Periods.

Kh. el Burj (near Mazra'at esh Sharqiyya) *174:156*

Settlement ruins 12 km. NE of Ramallah, on summit of hill. Also called Kh. Burj el Lisana — possibly site of Biblical city Jeshanah, in tribal allotment of Ephraim (I Chron. 13:19). Remains of large dressed stone structures, apparently Roman, rock-cut tombs and cisterns. Sherds indicate occupation during Iron Age and from Hellenistic until Arab Periods.

Kh. el Burj (near Sinjil) *173:161*

Settlement ruins 16 km. N of Ramallah. Remains of square tower preserved to height of 6 m., apparently from Byzantine Period, remains of structures, water cisterns and cave-tombs. Sherds indicate occupation during Iron Age and from Roman Period until Middle Ages.

Kh. el Burj (near Tarqumiya) *151:110*

Settlement ruin in Judean Hills 11 km. NW of Hebron. In middle of ruin are remains of square structure, apparently a khan; its walls have been preserved to a considerable height. Many remains of other structures and an olive oil press. Sherds indicate occupation during Byzantine Period and Middle Ages.

Kh. Burj eṣ Ṣur → Bet Ẓur

Kh. Burnat *146:157*

Roman ruin 7 km. NE of Ben-Gurion Airport. Mounds of stones, foundations, caves and pools.

o **Kh. Burqin** *176:208*

Arab village (pop.: 400) in Samarian Hills 2 km. W of Jenin. Nearby are ruins of ancient settlement.

Kh. Buweizi'a *172:121*

Bedouin settlement on border of Judean Hills 5 km. SE of Bethlehem.

Kh. Dajajiyya (Kh. el Ḥashash) *213:248*

Ancient tel near NE shore of Lake Kinneret. In antiquity, settlement served to protect route from shore of Kinneret to Golan Heights. Syrians built a military position here for same purpose. Iron Age sherds found here.

Kh. Dalḥamiyya *203:228*

Ancient settlement ruin in Jordan Valley 1 km. W of Ashdot Ya'aqov, alongside ancient road junction. Excavations uncovered level from Chalcolithic until early Arab Period. Finds include Chalcolithic implements, remains of stone Late Bronze and Iron Age structures and remnants of a Hellenistic street and buildings.

Kh. Dasra *150:155*

Settlement ruins 11 km. NW of Lod. Occupied in Roman and Byzantine Periods and Middle Ages. Remains of ancient walls interspersed with fences and terraces built in later periods.

o **Kh. ed Deir** (E Judean Hills) *170:118*

Arab village 6 km. S of Bethlehem.

o **Kh. ed Deir** (W Judean Hills) *152:118*

Arab village 10 km. W of Kefar 'Eẓyon.

Kh. ed Deir (Samarian Hills) *186:190*

Settlement ruin in Samarian Hills 2 km. SE of Tubas. Inhabited from Middle Bronze Age till Middle Ages, particularly during Iron Age.

Kh. ed Deir (near Yavne) *126:142*

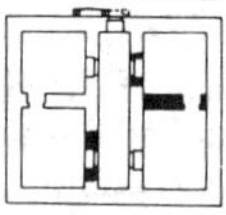

Settlement ruin on central Coastal Plain, N of Yavne. Cave-tombs and building remains made of dressed and undressed stones. Sherds indicate major occupation during Byzantine Period.

Kh. Deiraban *158:188*

Remains of structure from early Arab Period, located on hilltop 7 km. SE of Tulkarm.

Kh. Deir 'Ala *174:110*

Settlement ruin in Judean Desert 16 km. NE of Hebron. Occupied in Roman, Byzantine and Arab Periods. Remains of 3 square structures, 2 stone mounds, channels and water cisterns.

Kh. Deir el 'Arabi *151:157*

Ruin of farm from Byzantine Period 13 km. NE of Lod. Remains of dressed stone structure, 40x80 m., divided into rooms. Inside, a lintel with incised cross and 2 stone basins, 1 round and 1 rectangular, were found. Nearby is a pool, half rock-cut and half built of stones.

Kh. Deir Dusawi *106:101*

Remains of large ancient settlement (approximately 100 d.) in Negev 7 km. E of Gaza. Building remains and sherds from Roman and Byzantine Periods.

Kh. Deir Ḥarrasha *165:150*

Ruins of ancient settlement 6 km. NW of Ramallah. Remains scattered over large area include structures, plastered pool and an olive oil press from Roman, Byzantine and Arab Periods.

Kh. Deir el Qassis *153:166*

Remains of ancient settlement 8 km. E of Rosh Ha'Ayin. Occupied in Iron Age, Byzantine Period and Middle Ages. Building stones re-used in fences and steps, plastered pool, rock-cut tombs and ancient quarries.

Kh. Deir Raṣad *160:158*

Remains of single Byzantine structure on summit of hill 16 km. NW of Ramallah.

Kh. Dhanab el Kalb *154:142*

Large ruin near Ramallah–Latrun road, 15 km. SW of Ramallah. Sherds indicate occupation in Middle Bronze Age, Iron Age, mainly in Persian Period and again in Byzantine Period.

Kh. Dhikkrin *146:163*

Settlement ruin from Roman and Byzantine Periods on a ridge 7 km. SE of Petaḥ Tiqwa. Remains of walls, cisterns, wine presses and rock-cut tombs.

Kh. ed Dikka *218:258*

Ruins of ancient Jewish settlement 4 km. NE of Lake Kinneret. Remains of 3rd c. CE synagogue.

o **Kh. ed Dilba** *154:099*

Arab village (pop.: 80) in Judean Hills, 8 km. SW of Hebron. Within village are ancient building stones, cistern, tomb and caves.

Kh. ed Dureish *154:144*

Settlement remains from Byzantine Period 14 km. W of Ramallah, adjacent to Beit Sira. Ruins of house walls approximately 1 m. high.

Kh. ed Duweir *177:141*

Remains of ancient settlement 9 km. SE of Ramallah. Building remnants from Iron Age, columns, cisterns and drinking troughs from Byzantine Period.

Kh. ed Duweir *152:160*

Iron Age settlement ruins 10 km. SE of Rosh Ha'Ayin alongside Rantis. Remains of structures standing to a height of 1.5 m.

Kh. ed Duyura *152:160*

Byzantine ruin in Judean Foothills 8 km. SE of Rosh Ha'Ayin. Remains of large country house built of dressed stones with capitals. S of ruins are remains of 2 mausoleums.

o **Kh. 'Ein Aiyub** *159:150*

Arab village 11 km. NW of Ramallah.

Kh. 'Ein et Turuq *226:246*

Ancient tel on Golan Heights on summit of cliff above Naḥal Roqed, adjacent to abandoned village of el Ma. Remains of settlement which existed from Hasmonean till Ottoman Periods. Sherds indicate occupation also from Middle Bronze Age until Iron Age.

Kh. Faṣayil *191:159*

Settlement ruins in Jordan Valley N of Arab village el Faṣayil. Site of city Phasaelis (Fazael) built by Herod and named after his older brother. By utilizing spring waters in area, Phasaelis became an oasis famous for its date groves. Herod bequeathed it to his sister Salome, who in turn willed it to Livia, wife of Emperor Augustus. It eventually became a major centre in the area. Remains of many structures. Roman bathhouse, aqueducts and pool. **Water system** NW of ruin is a complex water system, initiated during days of Herod and developed during Arab Period by Umayyad caliphs. **Ruins of Chalcolithic settlement** NW of Kh. Faṣayil, at the source of the stream *191:161*, are remains of large Chalcolithic settlement. Among finds were remains of polygonal house built of large undressed stones. Inside many sherds and flint implements were found.

Kh. Fir'a *151:105*

Settlement ruins in Judean Hills 9 km. W of Hebron. Occupied during Iron Age, Byzantine Period and Middle Ages. Remains of a number of structures, columns and a mosaic floor.

Kh. Fuqeiqis *148:099*

Remains of an ancient structure (perhaps a fortress) 13 km. SW of Hebron. One corner has remained to a height of several stone courses. Cisterns, caves and sherds indicate an Iron Age settlement.

Kh. Fureiḥiyya *153:179*

Ruin of Byzantine mausoleum in W Samarian Hills 6 km. SE of Qalqilya. Square in shape, it was built of dressed stones. Nearby, part of an olive oil press and a rock-cut wine press were found.

Kh. el Ghirur *201:179*

Byzantine ruin in Jordan Valley, 5 km. NE of *moshav* Argaman. Remains of settlement surrounded by stone wall. Remnants of tower built of stones with drafted margins. Alongside is an open courtyard and remains of structures built of both rough and hewn stones.

Kh. Ḥabra *128:139*

Low tel 12 km. NE of Ashdod 1 km. E of *moshav* Benaya. On tel are remains of ancient settlement from Hasmonean Period until Arab Period. To the N is an ancient well — Bir Ḥabra.

o **Kh. el Ḥadab** *149:096*

Arab village (pop.: 150) in Judean Hills 15 km. SW of Hebron. Cisterns, caves and rock-cut tombs attest to an ancient settlement.

Kh. el Ḥadidiyya *196:184*

Solitary Byzantine structure 8 km. SE of Tubas.

o **Kh. Ḥafira** *172:202*

Arab village in Samarian Hills 8 km. SW of Jenin.

Kh. el Ḥafna *166:150*

Settlement ruins from Byzantine Period in Judean Hills 5 km. NW of Ramallah. Remains of structure built of dressed stones and a cistern in middle of ruin.

Kh. el Ḥajj *118:039*

Ruins in Negev 5 km. NE of Ḥurvot Shivta. Sherds from Hellenistic, Roman and Byzantine Periods.

Kh. Ḥammad *155:170*

Remains of Byzantine farm in Samarian Hills 11 km. SE of Qalqilya. Sections of house walls built of dressed stones on slope of small valley.

o **Kh. Ḥarazan** *175:126*

Arab village (pop.: 100) on border of Judean Desert 7 km. NE of Bethlehem. Perhaps site of Harod, birthplace of Shammah and Elika, mighty men of King David (II Sam. 23:25).

o **Kh. el Hijra** *155:099*

Arab village (pop.: 120) in Judean Hills 10 km. SW of Hebron.

Kh. Ḥureisa *162:095*

Large ruin in Judean Hills 10 km. S of Hebron. Occupied in Roman–Byzantine Period and Middle Ages. Remains of many buildings, including church or monastery with mosaic floor, capitals and columns. Close by are caves and cisterns.

Kh. Ibziq *187:197*

Large settlement ruin from Byzantine Period in Samaria 5 km. NE of Tubas. Remains of houses including a typical Byzantine house: a courtyard with cistern and cave, surrounded by rooms. Believed to be site of Biblical Bezek (mentioned in Judg. 1:5 and I Sam. 11:8).

o **Kh. Ikhza'a** *090:080*

Arab village in Gaza Strip 6 km. NE of Khan Yunis. Pop.: 1,600.

Kh. 'Irq *108:086*

Ruins of large Roman–Byzantine settlement in Negev 7 km. NW of Ofaqim. One theory believes this to be site of Orda — a defence station in Roman Period and district centre of Geraritica (area of NW Negev) during Byzantine Period. Site has remains of capitals, pedestal, mosaic stones, pools, wells and bathhouse.

Kh. Jabaris *192:196*

Ruins of large Roman–Byzantine settlement in Samarian Hills 9 km. NE of Tubas. Many remains: structure resembling a basilica in middle of ruins, many walls, 2 plastered pools, one with arches, coloured mosaic floor with inscription (apparently from 6th c. monastery), cisterns, olive oil press, wine press and rock-cut loculi. Further afield are 3 mausoleums, one built in form of stepped pyramid, kerb-stones of ancient road.

o **Kh. Jadur** ⛰ *158:116*

Arab village (pop.: 100) 12 km. N of Hebron. Adjacent to village is tell with remains from Bronze Age through Mamluk Period. Site of Gedor — city in tribal allotment of Judah (Josh. 15:58). Cave-tombs and secret tunnel system from Bar Kokhba days found here.

⛰ **Kh. Jarda** *155:150*

Byzantine ruin in Judean Foothills 10 km. N of Mevo Ḥoron, near village of Deir Qaddis. Remains of structures built of hewn stones with walls still extant to a height of 1.5 m.

o **Kh. el Jarushiyya** *155:195*

Arab village (pop.: 120) in Samarian Hills 4 km. N of Tulkarm.

⛰ **Kh. el Jauf** *155:197*

Tel of large ruin in Samarian Hills 6 km. NE of Tulkarm. In centre is larger structure. Surrounding it and on slopes of tel are remains of building walls, building stones, rock-cut cave-tombs. Sherds indicate occupation in following periods: Middle Bronze Age, Hellenistic and Roman Periods and Middle Ages.

o **Kh. Jubb er Rum** *175:127*

Arab village on border of Judean Desert 7 km. NE of Bethlehem, in ravine of Naḥal Qidron. Pop.: 1,000.

Kh. Juḥdhum *176:123*

Bedouin village (pop.: 100) in Judean Desert 7 km. E of Bethlehem.

⛰ **Kh. Jurish** *161:124*

Settlement ruin in Judean Hills 9 km. W of Bethlehem. Remains of group of structures arranged in a circle and enclosed by a wall. Sherds indicate occupation during Persian Period.

⛰ **Kh. Kabar** *166:123*

Remains of Roman army camp from days of Bar Kokhba revolt, in Judean Hills 3 km. SW of Bethlehem. Remains of square wall encompassing area of 5 d. containing remnants of various buildings. Sherds indicate occupation in Persian, Roman and Byzantine Periods.

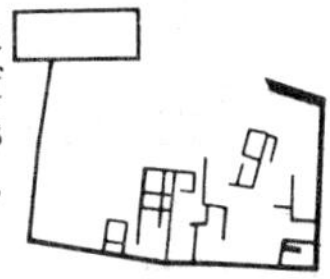

⛰ **Kh. Kafr Jul** (Jawr) *145:093*

Settlement ruin in Judean Hills 4 km. NW of edh Dhahiriyya. Remains of buildings, broken column shafts, rock-cut cisterns and cave-tombs. Occupied in Byzantine Period and Middle Ages.

⛰ **Kh. Kafr Shayan** *165:145*

Settlement ruin on hilltop in Judean Hills, 4 km. W of Ramallah. Remains of large structures, columns, lintels, cisterns, tombs and large building stones. Occupied during Iron Age, Roman and Ottoman Periods.

∴ **Kh. Kafr Ṣum** ⛰ *158:126*

Abandoned village in Judean Hills between Bar Giyyora and Mevo Betar. Remains of Crusader settlement. Moslem shrine and remnants of ancient highway.

⛰ **Kh. Kafrur** *168:178*

Large ruin 9 km. SW of Shekhem. Remains of structures, including a mosque. Sherds indicate occupation in Byzantine, early Arab and Ottoman Periods.

Kh. Kanaf → **Mazra'at Kanaf**

Kh. Kan'an *157:102*

Ruins of Roman settlement off ancient road from Hebron to Bet Guvrin, probably paved in days of Emperor Hadrian. Remains of what appears to have been a road fortress.

o **Kh. Karma** *152:095*

Arab village (pop.: 100) in Judean Hills 12 km. SW of Hebron. Built on ruins of ancient settlement from Byzantine Period and Middle Ages. Remains of buildings, wine presses and caves.

Kh. Karm 'Atrad *188:127*

Settlement ruin in Judean Hills 5 km. NW of 'Ein Fashkha. Remains of Israelite fortress and round building. Sherds indicate occupation in Iron Age, Hellenistic and Roman Periods.

o **Kh. el Karmil (Ḥurbat Karmel)** *163:092*

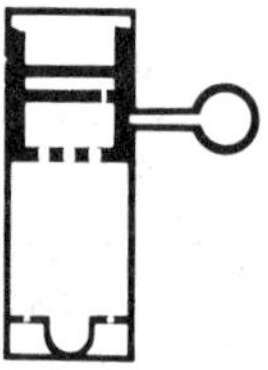

Arab village (pop.: 100) in Judean Hills 10 km. SE of Hebron. **Ḥurbat Karmel** *163:092* Site of Biblical city, Carmel, first mentioned during period of Israelite conquest (Josh. 15:55). Saul came here after his battle with Amalek. Residence of Nabal and birthplace of Hezrai, both mighty men of David. Large town during Roman and Byzantine Periods. Fortified city, protecting route to Negev, in Crusader Period. Sherds indicate occupation in Chalcolithic Period, the Bronze Age, Iron Age, Byzantine and Crusader Periods. A cemetery and storage pool from Roman-Byzantine Period and various tombs (including shaft and pit types) from Roman Period. Also remains of 2 churches and fort from Crusader Period.

o **Kh. el Kawm** *146:104*

Arab village (pop.: 300) in Judean Hills 14 km. W of Hebron. Built on partly excavated ancient tel. Remains of wall and many tombs from Middle Bronze and Iron Ages. A Hebrew inscription was found in one of the tombs. Sherds indicate it was also occupied in Early Bronze Age. Possible site of Saphir — city in tribal allotment of Judah (Micah 1:11).

Kh. Khaybar *176:195*

Tel of ancient settlement in Samarian Hills, 12 km. S of Jenin. Remains of oval wall built of large dressed stones. Site occupied during Middle Bronze Age and from Iron Age until Middle Ages.

Kh. Khiraf *200:176*

Ruins of Byzantine fort in Jordan Valley 1 km. NE of *moshav* Argaman. Large courtyard enclosed by dressed stone wall, with tower near N entrance and rooms along wall.

Kh. Khokha *215:255*

Settlement ruin on Golan Heights, 8 km. E of mouth of Jordan River where it empties into Lake Kinneret. Occupied during Roman-Byzantine Period and then in Ottoman Period. Remains of olive oil press, walls and courtyards of houses, columns and capitals.

Kh. Kufin *160:114*

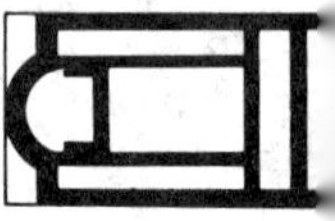

Settlement ruins 10 km. N of Hebron. Remains of large dressed stone structure, apparently from Roman Period. Also underground vaulted structures from Byzantine Period. Sherds indicate occupation in Middle Bronze Age and from Hellenistic until early Arab Periods.

Kh. Kureikur *153:147*

Roman-Byzantine ruin in Judean Foothills 7 km. N of Mevo Ḥoron. Remains of buildings, foundations, rock-cut cisterns and ancient building stones re-used in modern stone fences. Battle site in War of Independence — strong point "318".

Kh. Kuweiziba *164:112*

Settlement ruin 9 km. NE of Hebron. Believed to be site of Biblical city Cozeba that was called Kozva, Koziva or Bet Koziva in Byzantine Period. Apparently birthplace of Bar Kokhba (Bar Kozva). Remains of many Roman-Byzantine structures as well as Medieval remains including hewn stone building still extant to a height of 5 m.

Kh. el Latatin *166:141*

Settlement ruin from Persian and Byzantine Periods in Judean Hills 5 km. SW of Ramallah. Mentioned in Madaba map as To Ennaton (meaning the ninth). Remains of large structure and stone fences, pool and round trough.

Kh. el Lauza *154:103*

Arab village in Judean Hills 5 km. W of Hebron. Built on ruins of Roman and Byzantine settlement. Remains of ancient structures and olive oil press.

Kh. el Mafjar (Hisham's Palace) *193:143*

Extensive remains of winter palace built by Umayyad Caliph Hisham in 8th c., located 1 km. NE of Jericho. Ruined in an earthquake in 747, shortly after its construction; it was never inhabited at all. Architectural design was that of a great courtyard with towers at the corners. The site boasts elaborate stone friezes and mosaic ornamentation. There are intricate plaster moulds of dancers, partridges and floral patterns. Most famous remain is that of a star-shaped window in carved stone. Also remains of decorated slanting structures, mosque, bathhouse, pool and mosaic floor.

Kh. el Maḥma *163:143*

Settlement ruin in Judean Hills 6 km. SW of Ramallah. Remains of large stone structures, lintels, stone columns and other Byzantine remnants.

Kh. Majdal Ba'a (Kh. Majd el Ba') *156:092*

Settlement ruin in Judean Hills 11 km. S of Hebron. Remains of a large structure, apparently a church, whose walls are preserved to a considerable height. Sherds indicate occupation in Byzantine Period and Middle Ages.

Kh. Majduliyya *222:252*

Settlement remains from Byzantine and Ottoman Periods on Golan Heights 5 km. NW of Ramat Magshimim.

Kh. el Majnuna *154:099*

Arab village (pop.: 80) in Judean Hills 8 km. SW of Hebron.

Kh. el Majur *153:099*

Ruin in Judean Hills 9 km. SW of Hebron. Remains of large stone square structure and other building remains. Sherds indicate occupation in Byzantine Period and Middle Ages.

Kh. el Maliḥ *195:192*

Settlement ruins alongside hot springs (Ḥammam el Maliḥ) in Samaria 11 km. E of Tubas. Inhabited during Byzantine Period, Middle Ages and Ottoman Period.

Kh. Maraḥ el Baqar *148:098*

Arab village in Judean Hills 13 km. SW of Hebron.

Kh. Maraḥ el ʻInab *193:179*

Settlement ruin in Samarian Hills 8 km. NW of *moshav* Argaman. Remains of structures, plastered pool and sherds from Iron Age and Byzantine Period.

o **Kh. el Marajim** *152:099*

Arab village (pop.: 100) in Judean Hills 10 km. SW of Hebron. Built on tel from Israelite Period. Identified with Aphekah — city in tribal allotment of Judah (Josh. 15:53). Nearby is a number of springs.

Kh. el Marjama *181:155*

Large tel on border of Samarian and Judean Hills 15 km. NE of Ramallah. At summit are remains of round structure, and alongside, remains of Byzantine church with coloured mosaic floor. Below are remains of flour mill. Sherds indicate occupation in Bronze Age, Hellenistic, Roman, Byzantine and Crusader Periods. Adjacent to tel is a large cemetery with tombs from all these periods. To the E is Kh. Samiya with building remains, columns and foundations from Roman and Byzantine Periods.

Kh. el Minya *170:114*

Permanent Bedouin settlement of er Rashida tribe, near ruin of ancient settlement in Judean Hills, 3 km. S of Teqoaʻ. Remains scattered over wide area: structures, olive oil press, channels, cisterns and tombs, indicating occupation from Roman Period until Middle Ages. Also found were tombs from days of the Patriarchs.

o **Kh. el Miṣbaḥ** *156:143*

Arab village (pop.: 1,000) in Judean Hills S of Ramallah-Latrun junction, near Maʻale Bet Ḥoron.

o **Kh. el Mudawwar** *151:172*

Arab village in Samarian Hills 7 km. SW of Hebron.

Kh. Mufya *198:183*

Ruin of Byzantine settlement in Samarian Hills on fringe of Jordan Valley, 6 km. E of *moshav* Beqaʻot. Remains of houses and a water cistern.

Kh. Mughayyir *218:277*

Ruin of fort on Golan Heights 3 km. N of Kafr Nafakh. Rectangular in shape and built of undressed stones. Oval structures within the fort date from a later period.

Kh. Mugheifir *195:138*

Settlement ruin 2 km. SE of Jericho. Remains of large structure, apparently castle or fortress built around a central courtyard with a pool. Alongside are remains of other buildings. Sherds indicate occupation from Roman until early Arab Period.

Kh. Muneizil *164:099*

Settlement ruin in Judean Hills 6 km. SE of Hebron. Remains of structures and sherds from Roman-Byzantine Period and Middle Ages.

∴ **Kh. Muqeisima** *192:183*

Abandoned village in el Buqeiʻa in Samarian Hills. Built on tel of ancient settlement within area of *moshav* Beqaʻot. Remains of large square structure. Excavations uncovered rooms of a house, corridors and oven rooms. On lower slopes of tel are cisterns and rock-cut shaft tombs. Sherds indicate occupation in Iron Age, Byzantine Period, Middle Ages and Ottoman Period.

o **Kh. el Muraq** *147:104*

Arab village in Judean Hills 13 km. W of Hebron. Built on ruins of ancient settlement. Remains of magnificent columned and frescoed structure from reign of Herod. Nearby are remains of tower built of undressed stones. Sherds and other remains indicate occupation in Hasmonean, Byzantine and Arab Periods.

Kh. el Musheirifa → Mizpe Shivta

Kh. el Mutayyana *155:171*

Ruins of Byzantine farm in Samarian Hills 10 km. NE of Rosh Ha'Ayin. Remains of hewn limestone building with walls still extant to a height of 2.5 m. Alongside is a large courtyard.

o **Kh. el Mutilla** *189:203*

Arab village (pop.: 260) in Samarian Hills 12 km. N of Tubas.

Kh. en Nabi *175:175*

Tel 6 km. S of Shekhem. Also called Kh. Makhna el Fauqa. Known as Makhna in Samaritan writings. Remains indicate occupation in Early Bronze Age, Iron Age, Persian Period and Roman Period till Middle Ages. N of tel is Moslem shrine en Nabi Isma'il.

o **Kh. en Nabi Ilyas** *151:176*

Arab village (pop.: 300) in Samarian Hills, 5 km. E of Qalqilya. Holy Moslem site within village.

o **Kh. en Nabi Ṣaliḥ** *150:107*

Arab village in Judean Hills 10 km. NW of Hebron. Built on ruins of ancient settlement. Tomb of Sheikh en Nabi Ṣaliḥ.

o **Kh. en Najar** (N Samarian Hills) *178:205*

Arab village in N Samarian Hills 2 km. S of Jenin. Built on tel of ancient settlement from Early and Middle Bronze Age. On E side of tel are remains of ancient wall.

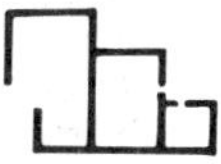

Kh. en Najar (W Samarian Hills) *151:169*

Settlement ruin in Samarian Hills 6 km. NE of Rosh Ha'Ayin. Occupied in Iron Age, Roman and Byzantine Periods. Remains of many structures built of hewn stones still extant to a height of 1.5 m.; door posts, complete olive oil press. W of ruin *150:169* is an ancient cemetery with shaft tombs.

Kh. en Naṣara *158:106*

Settlement ruin on hill 3 km. NW of Hebron. Remains of structures, cisterns and caves. The name hints at its having been a Christian settlement (*naṣṣara* = to convert to Christianity). Sherds indicate habitation in Iron Age, Byzantine Period and Middle Ages.

∴ **Kh. Naṣr ed Din** *199:242*

Abandoned village SW of Tiberias with remains indicating occupation in Early Bronze Age and Hasmonean Period till Middle Ages.

Kh. en Nuqeib *211:243*

Settlement ruin near abandoned village of en Nuqeib NE of 'En Gev. Near village cemetery are remains of prehistoric mill. Middle Bronze Age sherds. E of village, along Naḥal 'En Gev, many flint implements have been found.

Kh. Qarqaf *164:186*

Tel in Samarian Hills near Shekhem-Tulkarm road SW of Ramin village. At summit are remains of fortress from Persian Period. Sherds indicate occupation in Early and Middle Bronze Age, Iron Age and Persian Period.

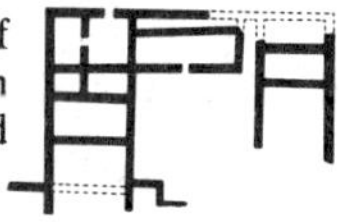

Kh. el Qaryatein → Tel Qeriyyot

Kh. el Qaṣr *167:101*

Remains of Roman-Byzantine fort 8 km. SE of Hebron. Square in shape and built of hewn stones, its remains rise to a height of 3 m. Alongside are cisterns with canals for gathering rain-water. E of fort is an almost complete olive oil press.

Kh. Qaṣr et Taziz *175:145*

Settlement remains from Ottoman Period 5 km. E of Ramallah, near Deir Dibwan village. Ruin of round tower, preserved to height of 4 m., other structures and cisterns.

Kh. el Qatt *160:113*

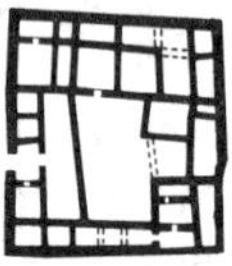

Ruin in Judean Hills 3 km. N of Ḥalḥul. Remains of square fortress (30x30 m.) built of undressed stones and containing rows of rooms enclosing a central courtyard. Sherds indicate occupation in Iron Age, Persian and Byzantine Periods.

o **Kh. Qeis** *166:163*

Arab village (pop.: 120) in Samarian Hills 6 km. E of Ma'ale Levona.

o **Kh. Qila** *150:113*

Arab village in Judean Hills 15 km. NW of Hebron. Pop.: 300. Adjacent to village is Tell Qila, site of ancient city of Keilah, mentioned in Tell el 'Amarna letters as important city kingdom. Included in Judah tribal allotment (Josh. 15:44). David saved city from Philistines but ran away for fear that its citizens would place him in the hands of Saul. After Babylonian Exile, it was district capital and its residents participated in building walls of Jerusalem. During Roman-Byzantine Period was famous for its figs and grain. Christian tradition claims the prophet Habakkuk was buried here. Tell Qila has remains of wall and tombs. Sherds indicate occupation from Middle Bronze Age to Iron Age and from Persian Period until Middle Ages.

Kh. Quma *170:183*

Settlement ruin 4 km. NW of Shekhem. Believed to be site of Azzo, mentioned in Samarian Ostraca. Sherds indicate occupation from Middle Bronze Age through Persian Period.

Kh. el Quṣeir *160:202*

Settlement ruin in Samarian Hills 12 km. NE of Tulkarm. Mounds of stone, remains of structures and olive oil press. Remains indicate occupation in Byzantine Period, Middle Ages and Ottoman Period.

o **Kh. el Quṣur** *151:101*

Arab village (pop.: 200) in Judean Hills 10 km. SW of Hebron.

Kh. Ra'bana *218:291*

Ruin of large settlement on Golan Heights 4 km. SW of Birkat Ram. Remains of structures whose walls have been preserved to a height of many courses, water reservoirs and remnants of ancient highway. Sherds indicate habitation in Byzantine and Ottoman Periods.

Kh. Rabud → Rabud

Kh. er Radana *169:146*

Settlement ruin on low hill N of Ramallah. Excavations uncovered remains of Iron Age village superimposed by large Byzantine watch-tower. Among noteworthy finds are bronze axe and fragment of an iron plough.

Kh. er Rafid *176:161*

Tel in Samarian Hills on fringe of 'Emeq Shillo. Remains of tower, rock-cut tombs, cisterns and street. Sherds indicate occupation in Early Bronze Age, Middle Bronze Age, Iron Age, Persian, Byzantine and early Arab Periods. Flint tools from Chalcolithic Period were also found here.

Kh. er Ras (N of Ramallah) *168:154*

Ruin of Byzantine-Arab fortress 8 km. N of Ramallah, near village of Bir Zeit. On summit of hill are 2 courses of walls of a structure (40x60 m.). Sherds and other remains indicate earlier habitation during Early Bronze Age and Iron Age.

Kh. er Ras (W of Ramallah) *163:143*

Ruin from early Arab Period 5 km. SW of Ramallah, W of Beituniya village. Remains of structures, some vaulted, pit graves, fences. Also sheikh's tomb and ancient building stones re-used in buildings of later period.

o **Kh. Ras 'Attiyya** *149:173*

Arab village (pop.: 120) in Samarian Hills 5 km. SE of Qalqilya.

Kh. Ras Kur *160:188*

Settlement ruin in Samarian Hills 7 km. SE of Tulkarm. Site inhabited during Middle Bronze Age, Iron Age, Byzantine Period and Middle Ages.

Kh. Ras et Tawil *163:108*

Tel 5 km. NE of Hebron, 1 km. SW of Ḥalḥul. Sherds indicate occupation during Iron Age, Hasmonean Period, and Roman-Byzantine Period. Cave-tombs, cisterns and caves, some still occupied today, scattered round about tel.

o **Kh. Ras et Tira** *151:174*

Arab village in Samarian Hills 6 km. SE of Qalqilya. Built on ruin of settlement from Roman and Byzantine Periods and Middle Ages. Many building remains, a complete olive oil press and ancient building stones re-used in Arab village.

Kh. er Rujm *163:247*

Settlement ruin in Zevulun Valley 1 km. NE of Qiryat Ata. Remains of structures and sherds from Iron Age, Persian, Byzantine and Arab Periods.

o **Kh. Ruq'a** *160:096*

Arab village (pop.: 600) on border of Judean Hills 8 km. S of Hebron.

Kh. Sa'ad *151:123*

Settlement ruin from early Arab Period in Judean Hills 6 km. SE of Bet Shemesh. Remains of 2 buildings; one still has a gate and lintel.

Kh. Sab'ein *181:204*

Settlement ruin in Samarian Hills 4 km. SE of Jenin. Remains of ancient structures and building stones re-used in fences and terraces of a later period.

o **Kh. Ṣafa** *159:117*

Arab village (pop.: 250) in Judean Hills 2 km. W of Kefar 'Eẓyon.

Kh. Ṣafra *166:076*

Byzantine ruin in Negev 4 km. NW of 'Arad, near Naḥal Ẓe'elim. Remains of structures and cisterns.

Kh. Ṣaḥiba *171:111*

Ruin of Roman fortress in Judean Desert 5 km. S of Teqoa' on descent to 'En Gedi. Remains of square structure whose walls have been preserved to height of 2 m. Observation point over Judean Desert.

Kh. Sakariya (N) *166:149*

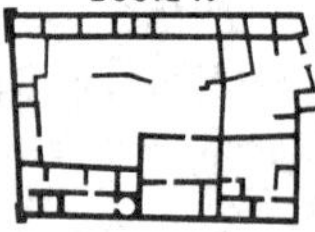

Remains of Roman fortress in Judean Hills 5 km. NW of Ramallah. Size: 40x58 m. In parts, several courses of its walls have been preserved. Sherds indicate earlier occupation in Iron Age.

Kh. Sakariya (S) *165:149*

Roman-Byzantine ruin in Judean Hills 5 km. NW of Ramallah. Remains of crowded structures, streets, round towers and rock-cut cistern.

Kh. es Sakut *201:196*

Large ruin in Jordan Valley 3 km. E of Meḥola. Foundations, sections of wall 3 m. thick and cemetery. Sherds indicate occupation in Iron Age, Byzantine Period and Middle Ages.

Kh. Ṣaliḥ *202:179*

Remains of structures built of undressed stones from Late Bronze Age and Iron Age in Jordan Valley, 3.5 km. NE of *moshav* Argaman.

Kh. Samara *163:204*

Settlement ruin in Samarian Hills 15 km. SW of Jenin. Remains of Byzantine structures built of hewn stones. Sherds indicate earlier occupation in Persian and Hellenistic Periods.

Kh. es Samra *196:146*

Ruin of large fortress 5 km. NE of Jericho. Remains of casemate wall, and at a short distance from fortress — remains of 2 small farms. Finds also include pottery jar-handles impressed with *lamelekh* (of the king) seal, estimated to date from 7th c. BCE (Iron Age).

Kh. Sarmita *173:188*

Settlement ruin from Middle Ages and Ottoman Period in Samarian Hills 7 km. N of Shekhem. Remains of structures built of hewn stones.

Kh. es Sarri, Kh. Ṣirra *149:097*

Arab village in Judean Hills 12 km. SW of Hebron.

Kh. Ṣarṣara *152:163*

Settlement remains in Judean Foothills 8 km. SE of Rosh Ha'Ayin. Remains of structures and sherds from Middle Bronze Age and Iron Age.

Kh. Saylun → Shillo

Kh. esh Shamsaniyat *135:113*

Settlement remains in Judean Foothills 6 km. E of Qiryat Gat. Sherds from Chalcolithic Period, Early Bronze Age and Iron Age were found here.

Kh. Shamsin *157:203*

Ruin in Samarian Hills 9 km. SE of Pardes Ḥanna. Occupied from Iron Age until Byzantine Period. Remains of structures apparently date from Persian Period.

Kh. esh Shaqq *197:194*

Ruin of Byzantine settlement on Muntar esh Shaqq mountain on border of Samarian Hills and Jordan Valley 2 km. SW of Meḥola. Foundations of many hewn and undressed stone structures. E of ruin is observation point over Bet She'an Valley.

Kh. esh Sheikh Aḥmad *150:172*

Arab village in Samarian Hills 6 km. SE of Qalqilya.

Kh. esh Sheikh Maḥmud *140:113*

Moslem holy shrine on site of Byzantine ruin within confines of kibbutz Bet Guvrin. Many remains of structures, including lintels with signs of the cross. Mosque building contains many ancient stones.

Kh. esh Sheikh Sa'd *174:127*

Arab village 6 km. NE of Bethlehem, E of Ṣur Bahir village. Pop.: 460. Sheikh's tomb.

Kh. esh Sheikh Safiriyan *181:200*

Settlement ruin in Samarian Hills 10 km. NW of Tubas. Many remains of structures, scattered around a sheikh's tomb. Sherds indicate occupation from Middle Bronze Age until Middle Ages. Nearby rock-cut tombs with sarcophagi fragments were discovered.

Kh. Shilta → Shillat, Tel Shelat

Kh. esh Shubeika *166:268*

Roman-Byzantine ruin in Galilee 6 km. E of Nahariyya, off road to Ma'alot–Tarshiḥa. Remains of houses, lintels, rock-cut tombs and wine presses.

Kh. esh Shuqqaq *155:225*

Settlement ruin in Ramat Menashe 1 km. S of *moshav* Elyaqim. Late Bronze Age sherds found here.

Kh. Shureim *169:187*

Settlement remains in Samarian Hills 8 km. NW of Shekhem, 1 km. NE of Sabastiya. Occupied in Middle Bronze Age, Iron Age and Byzantine Period. Remains of Byzantine structure.

Kh. Siluqya *217:265*

Abandoned village on Golan Heights adjacent to Qaẓrin. In E part of village is tel of ancient settlement, apparently Seleucia. The city was named after Antiochus IV Seleucus called Epiphanes (175-164 BCE); his predecessor was Seleucus IV Philopater (187-175 BCE). It was captured by the Hasmonean King Alexander Yannai and was one of 3 cities fortified by Joseph b. Mattathias in the Golan, in preparation for Jewish Revolt against Rome. On the tel are remains of Roman wall. Sherds also from Early Bronze Age.

Kh. es Simya *153:092*

Arab village (pop.: 300) in Judean Hills 13 km. SW of Hebron on way to Eshtemoa' (Sammu'). According to one theory, it is site of Biblical city Eshan (Josh. 15:52). Within confines of village are remains of ancient structures and rock-cut cave-tombs from Second Temple Period. One tomb has a row of columns. Sherds indicate occupation in Roman Period and Middle Ages.

Kh. Ṣir *155:178*

Arab village (pop.: 300) in Samarian Hills 2 km. N of 'Azzun village.

Kh. Sirisya *151:168*

Settlement ruin in Samarian Hills 6 km. NE of Rosh Ha'Ayin. Ancient building stones re-used in structures, fences and terraces of later period. Sherds indicate occupation in Roman and Byzantine Periods and Middle Ages.

Kh. eṣ Ṣufeira *193:184*

Settlement ruin in Samarian Hills 11 km. SE of Tubas. Remains of lone structure, apparently Byzantine, in use in Middle Ages. Iron Age sherds were also found.

Kh. Ṣufin *148:177*

Ancient site on hill in Samarian Hills 1 km. E of Qalqilya. Mounds of stones, rock-cut cisterns and fragments of mosaic floor from Roman Period. During Jordanian occupation (1948-1967), it served as a military outpost and artillery position.

Kh. Suq el Khan → Ḥanot Taggarim

Kh. Surgheith *178:152*

Ruin 10 km. NE of Ramallah near Ba'al Ḥaẓor. Remnants of an olive oil press and other remains, mostly from Middle Ages.

Kh. es Suweida *149:218*

Remains of Israelite fortress in Ramat Menashe 3 km. SE of Zikhron Ya'aqov. Size: 70x70 m.; built of large chiselled stones. Several courses of the stone walls still remain. Sherds indicate occupation from Iron Age and up to Byzantine Period.

o **Kh. et Tabaqa** *151:100*

Arab village (pop.: 150) in Judean Hills 9 km. SW of Hebron, 1 km. S of Dura village.

Kh. et Tall (near Ḥaris) *163:169*

Tel 18 km. SW of Shekhem, next to Ḥaris village. According to one theory, site of Timnath-heres or Timnath-serah in tribal allotment of Joshua, son of Nun (Josh. 19:50), and his burial site (Judg. 2:9). Existed from Middle Bronze Age until Middle Ages. Ancient building stones have been re-used in walls of terraces. Site also has tomb of sheikh. At top of hill is a fort from Hellenistic Period, identified with the Timnath fort that Bacchides built.

Kh. et Tall (near Sinjil) *174:158*

Tel in Samarian Hills 4 km. S of Ma'ale Levona (el Lubban Sharqiyya), near Sinjil village. Believed to be site of Geba, mentioned in Bible as on N border of Judah during reign of Josiah (II Kings 23:8) and at beginning of Second Temple Period (Zech. 14:10). Site has caves, olive oil press, rock-cuttings, remains of building walls (apparently of a church from Byzantine Period). Sherds indicate occupation from Early Bronze Age until Middle Ages.

Kh. Tannin *182:202*

Settlement ruins in Samarian Hills 6 km. SE of Jenin. Sherds indicate occupation in Iron Age, Byzantine Period, Middle Ages and Ottoman Period. Remains of a structure with a niche alongside it and a carved stone door; apparently a holy Moslem tomb.

Kh. Tannura *154:171*

Byzantine ruin in Samarian Hills 10 km. SE of Qalqilya. Remains of structures whose walls are preserved to height of 3 m., outline of main street and side streets still perceivable; plastered water pool.

Kh. Tarafein *170:155*

Settlement ruin 10 km. N of Ramallah. Many remains of structures, foundations, mosaic stones and terraces. Occupied in Early Bronze Age, Persian, Roman and Byzantine Periods and Middle Ages.

Kh. et Taratir *131:125*

Settlement ruin in Judean Foothills 5 km. E of Qiryat Mal'akhi. Sherds indicate occupation in Roman Period and Middle Ages.

Kh. Tawas *146:099*

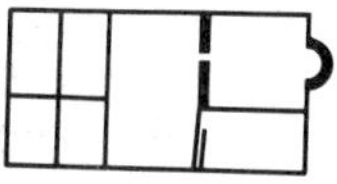

Settlement ruin in Judean Hills 15 km. SW of Hebron. Agricultural installations. Sherds indicate occupation in Iron Age, Roman-Byzantine Period and Middle Ages.

Kh. et Tayyiba *153:107*

Tel 7 km. NW of Hebron. One theory claims this is site of city Beth-le-aphrah (Micah 1:10). Remains from Middle Bronze Age, Iron Age, Byzantine Period and Middle Ages. Near tel is a ruin, well — Bir et Tayyiba, many cisterns and rock-cuttings from later periods.

Kh. Tell el Fari'a (Samaria) *182:188*

Tel in Samarian Hills at Wadi Far'a ascent (Naḥal Tirẓa) 5 km. SW of Tubas. Believed to be site of ancient city of Tirzah. Its king was one of the "31" who fought against Joshua (Josh. 12:24). Capital of Kingdom of Israel during reign of Jeroboam I (son of Nebat; 928-907 BCE). Its beauty is mentioned in Song of Songs (6:4). During Talmud period was called Tir'an in Aramaic. Excavations have uncovered occupational levels from Neolithic and Chalcolithic Periods; structures, wall and gate from Middle Bronze Age, remains from Late Bronze Age and Iron Age.

Kh. Tell el Fukhar *185:181*

Ruin of khan in Samarian Hills 10 km. S of Tubas. Sherds indicate occupation in Byzantine and early Arab Periods.

Kh. eth Thawm *202:253*

Ruin by a spring on NW shore of Lake Kinneret near Kare Deshe. Remains of later structures built over early Arab remains.

Kh. Tibna *160:157*

Settlement ruin 15 km. NW of Ramallah, near Deir Nidham. Believed to be site of Timnah, Timnath-serah or Timnath-heres — in Joshua's allotment (Josh. 19:50) and where he died and was buried. Also mentioned in first book of Maccabees. Sherds indicate occupation in Middle Bronze Age, Iron Age, Persian, Hellenistic, Roman and Byzantine Periods, and Middle Ages (from which there are still remains).

Kh. Tililya *169:135*

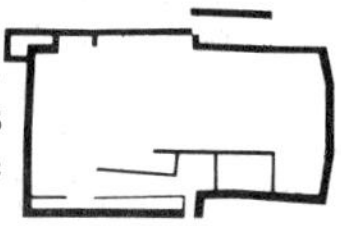

Settlement ruin NW of Jerusalem 1 km. S of Beit Ḥanina. Remains of fortress or way-station from Roman Period. The rectangular structure (70x37 m.) has towers and is divided into rooms. Sherds and other remains indicate occupation in Iron Age, Roman and Byzantine Periods.

Kh. et Tuwani *164:091*

Arab village on border of Judean Hills 13 km. SE of Hebron.

Kh. el 'Umdan *146:127*

Byzantine ruin in Judean Foothills 1 km. S of *moshav* Yish'i. Two stone pillars from an olive oil press were found here.

Kh. Umm el 'Amad *154:094*

Ruin in Hebron Hills 11 km. SW of Hebron. Remains of Byzantine church, columns, other architectural fragments, pedestals and capitals. Near church are caves, cisterns and remains of houses. A tel nearby was occupied in Iron Age, Hellenistic and Roman-Byzantine Periods.

Kh. Umm el Baqar *130:104*

Large ruin in Lakhish region 8 km. SE of Qiryat Gat. Foundations of large structure. Scattered over the area are sherds from Late Bronze Age through Byzantine Period.

Kh. Umm Beteine *138:076*

Ruin from Roman-Byzantine Period 7 km. NE of Be'er Sheva'. Remains of buildings. To the N, on banks of a small stream, are wells and cisterns.

Kh. Umm el Butm *178:203*

Remains of structure from Middle Ages or from Ottoman Period in Samaria 3.5 km. S of Jenin. Built on ruins of settlement occupied in Iron Age, Hellenistic, Persian, Byzantine, Middle Ages and Ottoman Periods.

Kh. Umm Butma *196:183*

Low structure from Byzantine Period built of undressed stone, in Samaria 15 km. SE of Tubas.

Kh. Umm Dimna *143:086*

Ruin in Hebron Hills 20 km. NE of Be'er Sheva'. Remains of structure with courtyard and cistern. Apparently from Roman Period.

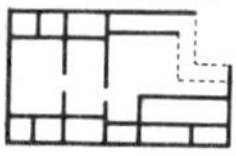

Kh. Umm Jarfan *131:045*

Ruin in Negev 13 km. W of Yeroḥam. Building remains and terraces. Nearby is Kh. Abu Ḥubeira *131:045*. Byzantine sherds found.

Kh. Umm Jina; Kh. Umm Jimal *145:128*

Ruin 4 km. W of Bet Shemesh. Remains of houses, streets and burial caves. Sherds found from Roman-Byzantine and Arab Periods.

o **Kh. Umm en Naml** *176:204*

Arab village in Samarian Hills 4 km. SW of Jenin.

Kh. Umm el Qal'a *161:124*

Settlement ruin in Judean Hills 7 km. W of Bethlehem. Remnants of rectangular hewn stone fortress and other remains including columned buildings. Remains indicate occupation from Iron Age until Middle Ages.

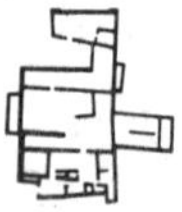

Kh. Umm el Qita' *165:120*

Settlement ruins in Samaria 9 km. W of Shekhem. Sherds indicate occupation in Iron Age I B, Persian and Byzantine Period. A few well-preserved structures remain.

Kh. Umm er Riḥan *163:210*

Settlement ruin from Byzantine Period 3 km. SW of Umm el Faḥm. Houses and side streets are well preserved. Remains of an olive oil press and flour mills were found. Nearby are mausoleum ruins containing sarcophagi.

o **Kh. Umm Salamuna** *165:116*

Arab village 6 km. SW of Bethlehem. Pop.: 150.

Kh. Umm es Su'ud *196:219*

Antiquities site in Yizre'el Valley 7 km. N of Bet She'an. Low tel with ruins of rough basalt stones. Alongside are remains of large stone wall. To the N, 300 m. from tel, is another ruin, apparently of a Roman estate. Sherds indicate occupation in Persian, Roman, Byzantine and Arab Periods.

Kh. Umm et Tala' *163:116*

Settlement ruins 10 km. SW of Bethlehem. Remains of wall and towers from Iron Age and remains of road-fortress from Roman Period.

Kh. Umm Zuweitina *171:109*

Settlement remains in Judean Desert, 13 km. NE of Hebron on E bank of Naḥal 'Arugot. Tumuli scattered over area, as well as remains of rectangular and round structures. Occupied in Chalcolithic Period, Early Bronze Age, Iron Age and from Hellenistic Period until Middle Ages.

Kh. el 'Urma *180:172*

Tel 9 km. SE of Shekhem. Believed to be site of Arumah, city in Hills of Ephraim, where Abimelech stayed before he ascended to Shekhem (Judg. 9:41 ff.). Tel has remains of fortified structure, a wall and glacis. Sherds indicate occupation in Middle Bronze Age, Iron Age, Roman and early Arab Periods.

Kh. 'Uskur *163:176*

Settlement ruin in Samarian Hills near el Funduq village. Remains of structures and ancient building stones re-used in fences and terraces. Sherds indicate occupation from Byzantine until Ottoman Periods. NE of ruin is sheikh's tomb. Persian and Hellenistic sherds found nearby.

Kh. el 'Uyun *212:236*

Tel in Golan 1.5 km. SE of Mevo Ḥamma. Occupied in Middle Bronze Age, Iron Age, Byzantine and Ottoman Periods. The now-abandoned Arab village was built on tel. According to one theory, site of 'Iyon, town in Roman-Byzantine Period.

o Kh. Wadi ed Dabi' *181:206*

Arab village in Samaria 3 km. E of Jenin.

o Kh. Wadiḥ *150:101*

Arab village in Judean Hills 10 km. W of Hebron.

Kh. el Waziyya *168:259*

Settlement ruin from Roman and Byzantine Periods in Galilee 10 km. E of Acre. Area is scattered with large building stones, column fragments, roof tiles and mosaic stones.

Kh. el Wureidat → Ḥurbat Weradim

Kh. el Yahud → Battir

Kh. Yahuda *178:188*

Moslem holy site in Samarian Hills 8 km. NE of Shekhem, alongside Talluza village.

Kh. Yamma → Yamma

Kh. Yaubak *151:180*

Settlement ruin in W Samarian Hills 10 km. S of Tulkarm. Remains of foundations, coarse white mosaic floor and rock-cut steps. Occupied in Early Bronze Age, Iron Age, Persian and Byzantine Periods and Middle Ages.

Kh. Zalafa *144:201*

Settlement ruin from Roman-Byzantine Period, within kibbutz Giv'at Ḥayyim, 10 km. NE of Netanya. Sherds and mosaic stones scattered over 4 adjacent hills.

Kh. Za'tara *179:203*

Settlement ruins in Samarian Hills 4 km. SE of Jenin. Sherds indicate occupation in Middle Bronze Age, Iron Age and Persian Period. Remains of rhomboidal structure.

o **Kh. Zeita** *162:107*

Arab village 4 km. N of Hebron.

Kh. Zeitun er Rama (Kh. Jul) *187:259*

Settlement ruin in Galilee adjacent to Ḥananya junction. Built-in steps ascending to summit of hill. Sherds indicate occupation in Iron Age, Persian and Hasmonean Periods.

Kh. Zuḥeiliqa *114:094*

Tel in Negev 3 km. NE of Netivot. Occupied in Middle Bronze Age, Iron Age and later. On surface are building fragments from Byzantine Period scattered around.

∴ **Khushniyya** *226:267*

Abandoned Circassian village on Golan Heights 10 km. W of Qaẓrin. Within village is tel of ancient settlement from Roman-Byzantine Period upon which a khan was built in Ottoman Period. On SW and W parts of tel are many ancient building walls, one of which has a decorated gate. The lower half of a statue of a man dressed in a toga was found here.

o **Kifl Ḥarith** *165:169*

Arab village 17 km. SW of Shekhem. Pop.: 1,100. Perhaps site of Timnath-heres, where Joshua, son of Nun, was buried (Judg. 2:9). The village has tombs purported to be those of Joshua (en Nabi Yusha), his father Nun, and Caleb son of Jephunneh (en Nabi Kifl).

Kinneret (Lake) → Lake Kinneret

● **Kinneret** *(moshava)* *203:236*

Farming village on SW shore of Lake Kinneret 4 km. NW of Ẓemaḥ junction. Founded 1909. Area: 5,000 d. Pop.: 220. **Kinneret Courtyard** Within village are a few buildings enclosed in a courtyard. This was the site of the original Kinneret farm, "workshop" of the kibbutz movement and focus of an important stage in the history of settlement in Ereẓ Israel and of the Labour movement. Established 1908 by the Palestine Office of the Zionist Organization. Here men like A.D. Gordon, Yiẓḥak Tabenkin, Ben Ẓion Yisre'eli and others lived and worked. **Sennabris** The Kinneret Courtyard was built on the ruins of ancient Sennabris, mentioned in writings of Josephus Flavius as a fortified city in days of Jewish Revolt against Rome. **Gan Raḥel** (see entry) Cemetery of ancient city of Beth-yerah is to the W.

★ **Kinneret** *(qevuẓa)* *203:235*

Collective settlement on SW shore of Lake Kinneret between *moshava* Kinneret and Deganya. Organized in Kinneret Courtyard and established in 1913 on a nearby hill to the S. From here a number of pioneer groups set out to establish their settlements in Yizre'el Valley. Here too the kibbutz movement, Iḥud HaQevuẓot VeHaKibbutzim, was established in 1929. During the years of the Arab Disturbances and before establishment of the State it served as a *peluggot sade* (field companies) and Palmaḥ base. Area: 7,500 d. Pop.: 750. A burial cave was uncovered within the settlement grounds from Early Bronze Age; it contained a variety of pottery and jewellery. To the E, on shore of Lake Kinneret, is a cemetery where the leaders and philosophers of Israel's Labour movement are buried: Berl Katznelson, Nachman Syrkin, Moshe Hess, the poetess Raḥel, Dov Ber Borochov and Avraham Harzfeld.

Kipros *191:138*

Remains of Hasmonean fortress 3 km. SW of Jericho. Named after Herod's mother who expanded the fortress and built a palace inside. Foundations of a round tower and other remains from Hasmonean

Period; remains of a bathhouse, aqueduct, 4 reservoirs, columns and capitals from Herodian Period.

Kis Faluja → Peluggot

★ **Kishor** *175:263*

Kibbutz in Upper Galilee 5 km. S of Ma'alot. Founded 1976 as *naḥal* outpost. Received civilian status in 1979.

Kislot; Kislot Tavor → Iksal

○ **Kisra** *178:263*

Druze village in Galilee 7 km. SE of Ma'alot. Kisra is an ancient name (mentioned in list of cities conquered by Ramesses II in 14th c. BCE). Also inhabited in Roman Period. Resettled about 300 years ago. Pop.: 1,500.

★ **Kissufim** *092:087*

Kibbutz in Negev 10 km. NE of Khan Yunis. Founded 1951. Area: 6,000 d. Pop.: 350. Local museum, named after 'Ami Shaul, houses a collection of prehistoric objects. Also exhibits from Hellenistic, Roman and Byzantine Periods.

Kokhav → Kokhav Michael

● **Kokhav HaShaḥar** *183:150*

Community settlement in Samarian Hills 15 km. NW of Jericho. Established 1975 as *naḥal* outpost. Received civilian status in 1980. To NE is Wadi Samiya reserve with spring — 'Ein el 'Auja.

Kokhav HaYarden (Belvoir) *199:222*

Ruins of Crusader castle Belvoir (fair view) on 500 m. high hill with panoramic view of part of Jordan Valley, 10 km. N of Bet She'an. The castle was built between 1138 and 1140 on ruins of a Persian and Byzantine village. One theory claims this was one of the sites where beacons were kindled to announce the new moon. Another theory claims it to be site of Kokhava, a town during Roman-Byzantine Period. The name Kokhav or Kokhava was used to designate a place's location on high places. In 1168 Hospitaller Knights purchased the property and enlarged the fortress. In 1189, after a siege that lasted 18 months, Saladin captured the castle. In 1220, after rumours of a new Crusade, the Moslems wrecked Belvoir. Its remnants are of basalt stone, measuring 140x100 m. with 4 towers and deep moats on 3 sides. Three statues, now at the Rockefeller Museum in Jerusalem, were uncovered in the castle chapel. Until War of Independence there was an Arab village here called Kaukab el Hawa (star of the winds) which was abandoned during the war. The site was excavated and restored and established as a national park.

● **Kokhav Michael** *118:115*

Moshav on Coastal Plain 3 km. S of Giv'ati junction. Named after English philanthropist Michael Sobell (Shuval). Founded 1950 on lands of abandoned village Kaukaba — one of the 3 Arab villages that cut off road to Negev during War of Independence. Pop.: 460. *Moshav* has memorial to soldiers of Giv'ati Brigade who lifted siege of the road to the Negev.

Korazim *(Matt. 11:21)* *203:257*

Ruins of ancient settlement and synagogue in Galilee, NW of Lake Kinneret. Important Jewish town during Second Temple days and Roman-Byzantine Period. The New Testament relates that Jesus cursed Korazim and Capernaum because their inhabitants had mocked him. Travellers relate in their journals that even at end of

Middle Ages a Jewish community existed here. Excavations uncovered a black basalt 3rd-4th c. synagogue, similar to that of Capernaum, with carved decorations, Jewish symbols and inscriptions in Aramaic and Hebrew. Erected in the form of a basilica measuring 24x17 m., it has 2 rows of columns along its length and one row along its width. Most interesting feature is the Seat of Moses, a single block of basalt carved in the shape of a chair where the scribe may have sat while reading the Law. The back of the chair is decorated with a rosette and on the front is a Judaeo-Aramaic inscription naming a certain Judah, son of Ishmael, as builder of the synagogue's colonnade and staircase. Remains of temporary settlement from a later period were also found.

▲ Kufakha; Kofakha *118:098*

Settlement ruin in Negev 9 km. NE of Netivot, near Tel Mifsaḥ. Remains of structures, cisterns and Moslem cemetery. Finds indicate occupation from Roman-Byzantine Period until Middle Ages.

o Kufeir *182:197*

Arab village (pop.: 150) in Samarian Hills 8 km. N of Tubas. Name means little village. A decorated, stone, 1st c. sarcophagus was found here.

o Kufeirat *169:205*

Arab village (pop.: 600) in Samarian Hills 9 km. W of Jenin. Name means small villages.

o Kur *159:182*

Arab village (pop.: 350) in Samarian Hills 10 km. SE of Tulkarm.

▲ Kureiz el Wawi *229:257; 228:258*

Dolmen field on Golan Heights 6 km. N of Ramat Magshimim.

Kurnub → Mamshit

∴ Kursi ▲ *211:248*

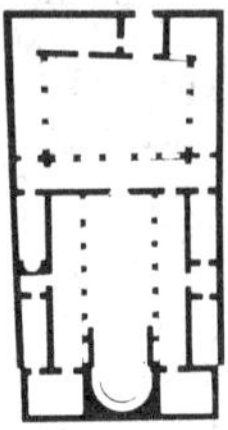

Abandoned village with remnants of a Byzantine monastery on E shore of Lake Kinneret 5 km. N of 'En Gev. A Syrian military position up to Six-Day War, it is believed to be site of ancient town of Kursi where a pagan temple stood, according to the Talmud. Christian tradition associates this site with Jesus' miracle of the swine. (Here Jesus healed a man possessed by devils and changed them into a herd of swine who then rushed into Lake Kinneret and drowned.) Excavations uncovered remains of large monastery, surrounded by a wall that has Greek inscriptions from 585 CE. Along shore are remains of an ancient boat anchorage.

L

★ **Lahav** *137:088*

Kibbutz 5 km. NE of Be'er Sheva'. Founded 1952. Initially its economy was based on pasture and unirrigated crops, but in 1966 when water was discovered in area, it switched to irrigated crops. Area: 33,000 d. of which 13,500 are pasture lands. Pop.: 400. Museum for archaeology and Bedouin folklore. **Tel Halif (Khuweilifa)** NW of kibbutz is ancient tel supposed to be site of Biblical city Ziklag. During Israelite conquest it was included in Judah's tribal allotment (Josh. 15:31) and in Simeon's within that of Judah (Josh. 19:5). David, who was fleeing from Saul, received Ziklag from Achish, King of Gath, and dwelled there (I Sam. 27:6). It was here that he learned of the death of Saul and Jonathan (II Sam. 1:1). Ziklag was one of cities resettled after the return from Babylonian Exile (Neh. 11:28).

★ **Lahavot HaBashan** *210:283*

Kibbutz in Ḥula Valley at foot of Golan Heights, 10 km. SE of Qiryat Shemona. Founded 1945 by members of Lahavot (Youth Aliyah from Germany and Poland and local graduates of HaShomer HaẒa'ir). Hence the name. (HaBashan is the Biblical name of Golan.) Attacked during War of Independence by Syrians who continued to harass the kibbutz until Six-Day War. Area: 14,500 d. Pop.: several hundred. Within kibbutz area is a dolmen field and a boundary stone, with inscription from Hellenistic Period.

★ **Lahavot Ḥaviva** *151:200*

Kibbutz between Samaria and the Sharon Plain 8 km. SE of Ḥadera. Named after Ḥaviva (Emma) Reik who, on a secret mission to Europe in WWII, was captured and killed by the Nazis. Founded 1949. Area: 3,800 d. Pop.: 250.

Lake Kinneret *(Josh. 12:3)*

Sweet water lake in N Jordan Valley known as Sea of Galilee and associated with the miracles of Jesus. Boundaries: E — Golan Heights, W — Heights of Lower Galilee, N — Ḥula Valley and S — Jordan Valley. Major sources: Jordan River, streams from the hills and rainfall. Has been called by many names: Sea of Galilee, Sea of Tiberias, Sea of Ginnesar and others. Its surface height is approximately 210 m. below sea level. Length — 21 km., average width — 12 km., area — 170 sq. km. and capacity — 4 billion cub. m. Along its generally narrow shores are 3 fertile valleys: Biq'at Ginnesar in NW, Biq'at Bet Ẓayda (Buteiḥa) in NE and Jordan Valley in S. During Israelite conquest it was included in Naphtali tribal allotment and during Second Temple Period its shores were lined with many Jewish villages: Tiberias, Migdal, Susita, Bet Yeraḥ, Kefar Naḥum. The lake and many adjacent sites are holy to Christians. With renewed Jewish settlement in 19th c. settlement sprang up on shores of the Kinneret and there was also an attempt to settle the E shore of the lake. After War of Independence, the entire lake was included within Israel. However, the Syrians controlled commanding points over the NE shore and harassed fishermen and nearby settlements. The entire area was captured by Israel Defence Forces in Six-Day War, and today the Kinneret is a popular recreation and swimming spot.

• Lakhish *(Josh. 10:3)* *135:107*

Archaeological site and *moshav* on border of Judean Hills and Foothills 10 km. SE of Qiryat Gat. Named after ancient city of Lakhish, which has been identified at an adjacent tel. Founded as *nahal* outpost in 1955, and became a civilian settlement in 1956. Pop.: 320. **Tel Lakhish** Large tel of fortified city which dominated the road from the Philistine coast (S Coastal Plain) and S Judean Foothills to Judean Hills, Jerusalem and Hebron. Excavation finds indicate earliest habitation in 4th c. BCE. During entire Bronze Age it was a fortified city. Mentioned as a royal city in Tell el 'Amarna letters and in Bible (Josh. 10:3). Joshua captured Lakhish (Josh. 10:31) and it was included in Judah tribal allotment (Josh. 15:39). After division of Kingdoms of Judah and Israel, Rehoboam fortified it along with other cities in the S, apparently against an Egyptian threat (II Chron. 11:9). Lakhish was taken by Sennacherib, King of Assyria, in 701 BCE (II Kings 18:13-17). He commemorated the event by depicting his victories and recording the spoils on a relief that he erected in his palace at Nineveh. The city was restored and refortified at end of First Temple Period as ascertained by the contemporary Lakhish Letters found in the tel. It was again destroyed, this time by Nebuchadnezzar, King of Babylon, during his first campaign in 598 BCE (II Kings 24:10) and in his second campaign (II Kings 25:1). Although resettled after Babylonian Exile (Neh. 11:30), it did not achieve its past glory. The settlement diminished in Hellenistic Period and in Roman Period was removed to an adjacent site (Kh. Duweir *136:107*). **Excavations** The old and new digs in the tel and its surroundings uncovered an Early Bronze Age cemetery; Middle Bronze Age fosse and glacis; Late Bronze Age temple; Iron Age gateway and double walled fortifications; large building called the Residency and a Solar Shrine from Persian Period. The most famous finds are the Lakhish Letters, 21 ostraca inscribed with ink in a paleo-Hebraic script. The letters deal with local administrative matters and contemporary events. The ostraca are important epigraphic and historic documents of the end of First Temple Period, just before the destruction. Other finds include pottery, inscriptions and jar-handle seals, one of them having the inscription "(Belonging) to Gedaliah Royal Steward," apparently referring to Gedaliah son of Ahikam (II Kings 25:22).

Lapidot *177:266*

Industrial village 3 km. SE of Ma'alot-Tarshiḥa.

∴ Latrun *148:138*

Monastery, ruins of abandoned village and police fort near Latrun junction at S fringe of Ayyalon Valley. There are two theories about origin of the name: one claims it is a distortion of name of Crusader castle that once stood here,

Le Toron des Chevaliers — the tower of the knights; the other claims it is a distortion of name it was called by Christian pilgrims, Castrum Boni Latronis — the home of the good thief (*latro*). According to Christian tradition the good thief crucified with Jesus and promised by him a place in heaven, came from here. E of the junction is the Cistercian Abbey of the Trappist Order, built in 1890. The monks observe a vow of silence. They engage in viniculture and production and sale of wine. At hill summit S of monastery are ruins of abandoned Arab village of Latrun, built on site of the Crusader castle. N of the junction is a British Mandate Tegart police fort. To NW 3 km. from the junction is Canada Park, opened in 1976. It contains: vineyards, almond orchards, ancient fig trees, ruins of ancient settlement of Emmaus and other antiquities and recreation facilities. **History** Latrun is located on a junction where the road from the foothills divides into two approaches to Jerusalem — one through Ma'ale Bet Ḥoron and the other through Sha'ar HaGay.

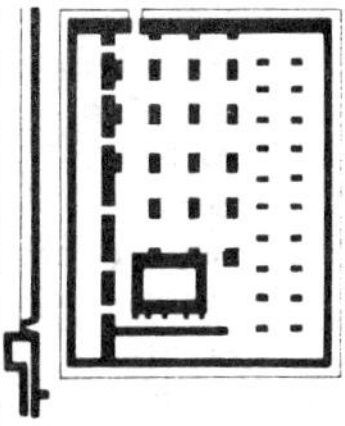

Therefore, it was always considered a key point for conquest and control of Jerusalem and it was an object of many battles in various periods. During Israelite conquest, Joshua defeated the Amorite kings in adjacent Ayyalon Valley (Josh. 10-11). In 166 BCE Judah Maccabee defeated Greek general Gorgias in this area. During Roman Period a number of Legions encamped here. In the 7th c. the Arab armies established a large military camp near Emmaus. The Crusaders built a castle here to protect the road to Jerusalem. In WWI the British captured Latrun and opened the way for the capture of the Holy City. Prisoner-of-war camps for German and Italian prisoners were set up here by the British during WWII. Two of these camps later served as internment camps for Jewish underground fighters apprehended by the British before the establishment of the State. On Black Saturday in 1946 most of Palestine's Jewish leaders were arrested and interned here. At outbreak of War of Independence, the Jordanian Arab Legion occupied the police fort and the military positions, thus blocking the road to Jerusalem. All Israeli attempts at a takeover to break the blockade failed and resulted in heavy casualties. The siege of Jerusalem was lifted only after an alternative S route was found — the "Burma Road". The Armistice Agreement signed at the end of War of Independence contained a clause that provided for free passage for citizens of Israel on the Sha'ar HaGay-Latrun-Ramla road, but the Jordanians never honoured this clause. On the first night of Six-Day War, the Israeli Defence Forces took the police fort and the Latrun corridor and the road from Latrun to Jerusalem was opened.

Latrun Monastery → Emmaus, Latrun

★ Lavi *191:243*

Kibbutz 10 km. W of Tiberias, off road to Nazareth. Named after a Jewish town from Roman-Byzantine Period whose name was retained in that of Arab village of Lubya. Founded 1948, and in 1949 moved to present site on lands of abandoned village of Lubya. During the Disturbances of 1936-1939 and War of Independence, the village served as a base for Arab gangs. Area of kibbutz: 12,000 d. Pop.: 650. N of kibbutz is educational institute Hodayot (see entry).

● Liman *161:274*

Moshav on coast 5 km. N of Nahariyya. Named after American senator, Herbert Lehman. Founded 1949 by demobilized Israeli soldiers on lands of abandoned village, Akhziv; initially called Ẓahal. Area: 2,400 d. Pop.: 300. Within *moshav* is nature reserve with tulips.

Li On *144:120*

Rural centre for settlement in 'Adullam region, 2 km. S of HaEla junction. Name based on that of a Jewish philanthropist. Regional school.

● Livnim *196:252*

Moshav under construction in Galilee, 4 km. NW of Ginnosar. Named after large white trees planted in area.

■ Lod (Lydda) *(I Chron. 8:12)* *140:150*

City on border of Judean Foothills and central Coastal Plain, with a rich history. Area: 9,200 d. Pop.: 37,000, of whom 4,500 are Moslems. N of Lod is Ben-Gurion International Airport. **History** First mentioned in City Lists of Egyptian King Thutmose III (15th c. BCE) as Rathan. Mentioned in Bible as being built by Elpaal one of sons of Benjamin. According to Talmudic source, it was fortified in the days of Joshua, son of Nun. After Babylonian Exile it was settled by tribe of Benjamin. A Jewish city during

Persian Period, it became an important centre in Hasmonean Period. After destruction of Second Temple, it was seat of small Sanhedrin and site of large *yeshiva* headed by Rabbi Eliezer b. Hyrcanus, and staffed by Rabbi Tarfon, Rabbi Aqiva, Rabbi Yehuda and many other sages. During Roman Period most rulers harassed Jewish inhabitants. After Bar Kokhba revolt the Emperor Hadrian settled many pagans here; during reign of Emperor Septimius Severus (193-211) the city was called Diospolis (city of god) and the Jews enjoyed a measure of tolerance. It seems that the local Jews participated in revolt against Gallus Caesar (Flavius Claudius Constantius who ruled Rome's E provinces, 351-354) and were punished when revolt failed. During Byzantine Period it was called Georgiopolis after St. George, who, according to Christian tradition, was buried here. After Arab conquest the city served as capital of province el Filastin, until Ramla was built (8th c.). The Crusaders once again gave the city a Christian character and restored its Christian name — St. George. Rabbi Benjamin of Tudela mentions the name San George. When he visited, he found only one Jew here. In 1191 it was captured by Saladin and apparently the Jewish community then revived. Although the Mongol invaders destroyed Lod in 1271, Estori HaParḥi found a Jewish community here in 14th c. During Ottoman Period it was a small Moslem town with a few Christian inhabitants. During British Mandate it was a district centre and railway junction. Until Disturbances of 1936, there were a few Jewish inhabitants. It was captured from Arabs during War of Independence together with Ramla in operation "Dani". **Antiquities** Excavations at the local cattle market uncovered remains indicating habitation in Late Stone Age, Chalcolithic Period and Early Bronze Age. At another site, sherds were found indicating occupation from Middle Bronze Age until Second Temple Period. Other finds from later periods: 2 ancient mosques — one built on ruins of Byzantine and Crusader church; near the second mosque an inscription was found from 666 (Hegira) or 1268 CE; bathhouse and khan from Middle Ages; ancient sheikh's tomb and a church built partially on remains of 12th c. Crusader church and in whose basement is tomb of St. George.

Lod Bridge *140:152*

Bridge over Naḥal Ayyalon, N of Lod on road to Ben-Gurion Airport. In Arabic known as Jisr Baybars or Jisr Jindas. The foundations are from a 13th c. Mamluk bridge, built apparently on a more ancient bridge from Roman or Byzantine Period. Arabic inscription on bridge states that it was built at the command of Sultan Baybars. Above inscription is a relief of 2 lions — the sultan's emblem. Stones taken from Crusader church in Lod were used to build the bridge.

★ Loḥame HaGeta'ot *159:263*

Kibbutz near Galilee shore 4 km. N of Acre. Founded 1949 by partisans and ghetto fighters from Poland and Lithuania. Area: 3,500 d. Pop.: 400. Kibbutz has Ghetto Fighters' House — a museum commemorating those who perished in the Holocaust and a Holocaust research institute in memory of Yitzḥak Katznelson, writer and poet killed by the Nazis; a youth educational centre in memory of Jewish educator Janusz Korczak, also killed in Holocaust. **Aqueduct** Within kibbutz is a segment of a 19th c. Turkish aqueduct used to pipe water from Kabri springs to Acre. Near aqueduct is a large open air theatre used for central memorial assemblies on Holocaust Remembrance Day.

★ Lotan (Yahel "B") *157:935*

Kibbutz under construction in the 'Arava off Elat road, 12 km. N of Yotvata. Named after one of the sons of Seir (Gen. 56:20).

★ **Lotem** ❀ ⚘ ⚘ ✓ *183:254*

Kibbutz in Galilee on Mt. Ḥillazon, 7 km. SW of Ḥananya junction. Named after one of local wild shrubs (*cistus*). Founded 1978. Pop.: 80.

○ **(El) Lubban** *153:160*

Arab village (pop.: 500) in Samarian Hills 10 km. SE of Rosh Ha'Ayin, N of Rantis village. Sometimes called el Lubban Rantis, to distinguish it from el Lubban Sharqiyya, off Ramallah-Shekhem road. Identified with Bet Lavan — a settlement from Second Temple Period mentioned in the Mishnah (Men. 8:6).

○ **(El) Lubban Sharqiyya** *172:164*

Arab village (pop.: 850) midway between Ramallah and Shekhem. Believed to be site of Biblical city Lebonah (Judg. 21:19). From here the road begins to wind. Near village, at beginning of ascent, are ruins of roadside inn, Khan el Lubban.

● **Luzit** ✓ *139:121*

Moshav in Lakhish region, 5 km. W of HaEla junction. Area has an abundance of almond trees hence name of *moshav* (*luz* = almond). Founded 1955 during "ship to settlement" programme. Pop.: 320. **Caves of Luzit** Near *moshav* *139:120* are rock-cut caves, bell-shaped and containing niches. Also found was a fragment of an Arabic inscription.

Lynch Strait → **HaLashon**

Ma'agan ● ▥ ❤ ⋏ ⋏ 206:234

Kibbutz on S shore of Lake Kinneret 1 km. E of Zemaḥ junction. Founded 1949. Until the kibbutz moved to its permanent site it was located in an abandoned army camp. Area: 2,200 d. Pop.: 300. Kibbutz has Bet HaZanhan (paratrooper's house) in memory of Perez Goldstein, a paratrooper sent on a mission to Europe during WWII. He was caught and executed by Nazis. Alongside kibbutz is Ma'agan campsite.

Ma'aganit HaMelaḥ ⋏ 198:131

Tiny peninsula in N Dead Sea. Called Rujm el Bakhr in Arabic (*rujm* = conical hill; *bakhr* = near the sea). Remains of Israelite fortress. Bathing beach and restaurant.

Ma'agan Mikha'el ❀ ⅋ ● ▥ ❤ ⌁ ⌬ ✳ ⌂ ● 142:217

Kibbutz on Karmel coast 4 km. SW of Zikhron Ya'aqov. Named after Mikha'el Pollak, a director of PICA, on whose land the kibbutz was established. Founded 1949. Area: 4,000 d. Pop.: 1,000. Alongside kibbutz is Naḥal Tanninim nature reserve and field school, including underwater archaeological museum.

Ma'agan Zemaḥ → Zemaḥ

Ma'agar Bet Netofa (Eshkol Lake) 174:242

Artificial lake on W side of Biq'at Bet Netofa, 9 km. NW of Nazareth. Capacity: 6 million cub. m. Part of National Water Carrier network. At this point the open water canals terminate, and from here on the water is carried S in a tunnel and through pipes. Nearby is an observation point near Bir el Maksur and Tel Ḥannaton.

Ma'agar Kefar Barukh (HaQishon Lake) 170:227

Artificial storage lake in Yizre'el Valley 8 km. NW of 'Afula. Collects rain and flood waters from Naḥal Qishon drainage basin. Capacity: 10 million cub. m. Used also for fish breeding and irrigation.

Ma'agar Shiqma 104:112

Storage dam 9 km. S of Ashqelon in bed of Naḥal Shiqma. Stores and directs flood waters to subsoil to enrich groundwater reserves. Capacity: 4 million cub. m. SW of kibbutz is an artificial lake for Naḥal Shiqma flood waters.

Ma'agar Yeroḥam 140:045

Water reservoir for storing flood waters 2 km. W of Yeroḥam. Capacity: 0.8 million cub. m. Used for irrigation.

Ma'agar Zalmon 189:251

Water reservoir, part of National Water Carrier project, in Lower Galilee. Capacity: 0.8 million cub. m. Water is brought to reservoir in open canal and passes through 'Eilabun tunnel on way to Bet Netofa Valley.

Ma'agar Zohar *121:112*

Artificial storage lake in Lakhish region 7 km. W of Qiryat Gat. Part of Yarqon–Negev water project. Area: 1,200 d., with capacity of 7 million cub. m. Derives its name from *moshav* Zohar, S of reservoir.

Ma'agorat Ashlon (Ḥarabat Abu Tureifa) *155:051*

Ancient site in Negev Hills 3 km. E of Dimona. Remains of rectangular tower (4x8 m.) in ascent of Naḥal Mamshit; stone wall along 200 m. of stream bed, apparently remains of aqueduct, 6 pools and cisterns enclosed by remains of rough stone wall. Sherds indicate ruins of agricultural settlement from Roman and Byzantine Periods.

Ma'agorat Yitma (Ḥarabat Abu Ithnein) *132:050*

Settlement remains in Negev 5 km. NE of Mash'abbe Sade. Rock-cut Byzantine cistern and steps leading down into water chamber.

Ma'ale Adummim *(Josh. 18:17)*

Ascent on Jerusalem–Jericho road (from *181:134* to *184:136*). Mentioned in Bible as part of Benjamin tribal allotment. Limestone hills in area have reddish colour. In Arabic called Tal'at ed Damm (ascent of blood). Arab legend claims soil became red from blood of wayfarers killed by robbers. At summit of ascent are ruins of Khan el Ḥatruri. Alleged site of Inn of the Good Samaritan, mentioned in New Testament (see Khan el Ḥatruri). Above the khan are remains of a Crusader fortress (known as Ċastrum Dumi, Maldoim or Rouge Cisterne) built on ruins of a Roman fort. Became a town in September 1982.

Ma'ale Adummim "A" *181:134*

Civilian outpost at edge of Judean Desert 10 km. E of Jerusalem. Established 1976. Joined to Ma'ale Adummim in 1982.

Ma'ale Afor

Ascent in Negev Hills on Miẓpe Ramon–Elat road, 8 km. SE of Miẓpe Ramon.

Ma'ale Alummot

Ascent in Lower Galilee between the Kinneret and Alummot (from *203:235* to *201:235*).

Ma'ale 'Ammi'az

Ascent from 'Arava to Negev Hills, W of Mt. Sedom (extends from *182:053* to *180:055*).

Ma'ale 'Aqof

Ascent in Negev Hills 18 km. NW of Yotvata. Links a track through Biq'at 'Uvda with one through Naḥal Girzi (from *142:932* to *141:933*).

Ma'ale 'Aqrabbim *(Num. 34:4)*

Ascent in Negev Hills 20 km. SE of Dimona, SW of HaMakhtesh HaQatan. Section of old road from Be'er Sheva' to Elat through Mamshit–Ma'ale Aqrabbim–Ḥazeva. Name mentioned in Bible (Num. 34:4; Josh. 15:3; Judg. 1:36). Scholars, however, believe it to be in land of Moab, E of Dead Sea. A passage through the ascent was cleared by Engineering Corps of the Israel Defence Forces in 1950.

Ma'ale 'Arod

Ascent in Negev 20 km. SW of Miẓpe Ramon. Bridge between Naḥal 'Arod and track passing along length of Makhtesh Ramon (from *117:988* to *116:990*).

Ma'ale 'Arugot

Ascent in Judean Desert near 'En Gedi; passes through Naḥal 'Arugot and connects Dead Sea shore with mountain track leading W.

Ma'ale Avraham

Ascent in SE of HaMakhtesh HaGadol *142:033.* Access to site by front-wheel drive vehicle only. Blown up by paratroopers and named after Avraham Krinitzi, former mayor of Ramat Gan.

Ma'ale Berekh

Ascent in Elat Hills, 15 km. SW of Yotvata. Connects Biq'at Sayyarim with Har Berekh (from *140:911* to *142:913*).

Ma'ale Bet Ḥoron

(Josh. 10:10)

One of the important passes from Judean Foothills to Judean Hills. Section of Latrun-Ramallah road, between Beit 'Ur et Taḥta and Beit 'Ur el Fauqa (Upper and Lower Bet Ḥoron). A battlefield during Israelite conquest, Hasmonean Period (I Macc. 3:24) and during Six-Day War.

Ma'ale Deqalim

Ascent in Negev Hills 15 km. E of Mizpe Ramon. Part of track connecting Naḥal Naqarot with 'En Saharonim in Makhtesh Ramon (from *145:001* to *143:001*). Part of ancient route Gaza–'Avedat–Petra.

Ma'ale Deragot

Ascent on border of Judean Hills and Negev Hills (from *157:079* to *158:081*). Section of ancient route from Judean Hills to Negev Hills. Ascent is well paved, with retaining walls forming flat steps, hence name (*deragot* = steps).

Ma'ale Doron

Ascent in Samarian Hills 8 km. SE of Tubas (from *195:193* to *192:194*). Named after two Israeli officers who died in 1970 while on a reconnaissance flight over Jordan Valley.

Ma'ale Efrayim

188:164

Urban centre on border of Jordan Valley and Samarian Hills, 13 km. SW of Adam Bridge. Established 1978. Urban centre for settlements in Biq'at Peẓa'el. Pop.: 200. Field school.

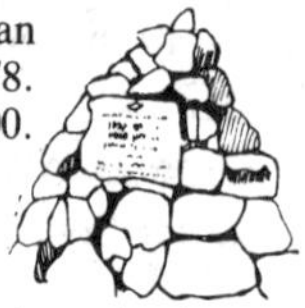

Ma'ale Elat

An ascent beginning 8 km. W of Elat, on Elat–Ras en Naqb road, where road passes through Naḥal Shelomo (from *138:888* to *141:885*).

Ma'ale Elisha'

Ascent on border of Jordan Valley and Lower Galilee. Begins on Bet She'an–Ẓemaḥ road, 3 km. S of kibbutz Gesher (*201:222*) and ends at Kokhav HaYarden (*199:202*). Named after Elisha' Soltz, who was chairman of Bet She'an Valley local council.

Ma'ale Elot

Ascent in Galilee between Yavne'el and Menaḥemya, linking Biq'at Yavne'el with Jordan Valley (from *202:231* to *199:233*). S of ascent is Mizpe Elot nature reserve. To the E is sheikh's tomb.

Ma'ale Enmar

Ascent in Negev Hills between Biq'at Ardon and Mt. Enmar which is at NE corner of Makhtesh Ramon (from *150:007* to *151:010*). Part of ancient route from 'Avedat to Petra.

● **Ma'ale Gamla** *215:255*

Moshav on Golan Heights 3 km. E of Biq'at Bet Ẓayda (Buteiḥa) near Naḥal Daliyyot on ascent leading to Gamla, hence its name. Founded 1976.

Ma'ale Gedud

Ascent in Negev 5 km. SE of Dimona. Links Mishor Rotem and Hare Ef'e (from *158:049* to *157:050*).

Ma'ale Gerofit

Ascent in 'Arava 50 km. N of Elat (from *157:933* to *155:936*). At summit is an observation point.

Ma'ale Gid'on

Ascent on SW Mt. Ḥermon, on way to Mt. Dov (from *211:296* to *218:303*). Named after Gid'on Bendel, a high-ranking officer who died in an accident here.

★ **Ma'ale Gilboa'** *189:209*

Kibbutz in Bet She'an Valley 8 km. W of Bet She'an. Started as *naḥal* outpost in 1962 by Bene 'Aqiva group, and became a civilian settlement in 1968. Area: 7,200 d. Pop.: 100. Near kibbutz is an observation point — Mizpe Gilboa'.

Ma'ale Ha'Aẓma'ut

Ascent on Be'er Sheva'–Mizpe Ramon–Elat road; descends from Mizpe Ramon to Makhtesh Ramon; 3 km. long (from *131:002* to *133:003*). Constructed in 1953 by the army Engineering Corps.

★ **Ma'ale HaḤamisha** *160:136*

Collective settlement 10 km. NW of Jerusalem, alongside Qiryat 'Anavim. Named after 5 of its members who were killed here during Disturbances in 1938. Founded 1938 by Polish immigrants. During War of Independence served as base for HaPorzim battalion of Palmaḥ's Har'el Brigade. In vicinity of Ma'ale HaḤamisha there was heavy fighting for Radar and Qastel military posts in an attempt to clear the road to Jerusalem. Area: 6,000 d. of which 5,000 are in the Judean Foothills. Pop.: 400. Memorial to Holocaust victims.

Ma'ale HaMeshar

Ascent in Negev Hills on Mizpe Ramon–Elat road, 18 km. SE of Mizpe Ramon; 4 km. long (from *144:988* to *144:991*).

Ma'ale HaPeradot

Ascent in Judean Desert, along a section of Naḥal Ḥever (from *183:092* to *182:092*). Constructed in 1955 by Israel Defence Forces unit in order to transport supplies by mule to archaeological expedition at Naḥal Ḥever caves.

Ma'ale HaẒe'irim

Track to Mt. Meron (Upper Galilee) beginning from Sasa–Ma'alot road *186:269*; 7 km. long with observation point at its summit. Constructed in 1961 by JNF and named after organization of young Jews from England and Ireland, as recognition for their contribution to development projects in Israel.

Ma'ale HaẒiẓ

Footpath ascent in Judean Desert from 'En Gedi spring to summit of ridge (from *186:097* to *185:097*). From summit is an ancient way to Teqoa' which linked 'En Gedi to Jerusalem during First and Second Temple Periods.

Ma'ale Isiyyim

Ascent in Judean Desert 3 km. SW of 'En Gedi (from *184:096* to *183:095*). Named after Essene (*isiyyim*) sect who lived in region during Second Temple Period. The ascent was constructed by Romans during Bar Kokhba revolt in order to besiege the rebels who hid in the caves of nearby Naḥal Ḥever.

Ma'ale Loẓ

Ascent in Negev Hills 25 km. SW of Mizpe Ramon. Links Naḥal Loẓ with Meẓuqe Loẓ (from *111:986* to *115:985*).

Ma'ale Maḥmal (Naqb el Maḥamla)

Ascent in Negev Hills 15 km. NE of Miẓpe Ramon, adjacent to N corner of Makhtesh Ramon. Part of ancient 'Avedat–Petra route (from *143:010* to *142:012*).

Ma'ale Milḥan

Ascent on border of 'Arava and central Negev, 15 km. SW of Yotvata. Part of track between Naḥal Timna' and Naḥal Milḥan (from *148:913* to *146:913*).

Ma'ale Mishmar

Ascent in Judean Desert 8 km. N of Masada. Links track through Naḥal Mishmar with upper track to Hebron Hills (from *182:087* to *181:089*).

Ma'ale Namer

Ascent in Judean Desert 7 km. NW of Masada. Links Namer spring (in Naḥal Ẓe'elim) and Mt. Namer. The Romans brought water via this ascent to their camps which besieged Masada.

Ma'ale Noaḥ

Ascent in Negev Hills 20 km. NE of Miẓpe Ramon. Links Naḥal Teref track with one through NE corner of Makhtesh Ramon (from *145:010* to *146:012*). Road passable with front-wheel drive vehicles.

Ma'ale Nurit

Ascent in NW corner of Gilboa' Hills from region of Tel Yizre'el to Kh. Mazrim — ruins of abandoned village of el Mazar — (from *181:218* to *184:214*).

Ma'ale Palmaḥ

Ascent in Naḥal Ḥatira *155:038*, passable by foot only. Surrounds large waterfall. First tracked in 1944 by a Palmaḥ detachment on a trip to Negev.

Ma'ale Paran

Ascent in Negev Hills, section of Be'er Sheva'–Miẓpe Ramon–Elat road crossing Naḥal Paran (from *146:970* to *145:970*).

Ma'ale Raḥaf

Ascent in Judean Desert 3 km. S of Masada. Links Naḥal Raḥaf with upper mountain tracks (from *184:077* to *184:076*).

Ma'ale Ramon

Ascent in Negev Hills 9 km. SW of Miẓpe Ramon. Ascent track that passes along length of Makhtesh Ramon and then ascends along its N wall (from *124:998* to *124:999*).

Ma'ale Roded

Ascent in 'Arava 6 km. NW of Elat. Passes through Naḥal Roded (from *140:890* to *139:891*).

Ma'ale Roma'im
Ascent on ancient Roman road to Jerusalem. Starts at Moẓa *166:133* and is partly congruent with road from Moẓa through Jerusalem Forest.

Ma'ale Saggi
Ascent in Negev Hills 31 km. S of Miẓpe Ramon. Section of track from Naḥal Saggi to Mt. Saggi (from *115:969* to *115:973*).

Ma'ale Shay
First section of road that branches off Jordan Valley road to el Buqei'a in Samarian Hills (from *201:192* to *198:187*). Constructed by Israel Defence Forces Engineering Corps and named after Yeshayahu Weisman, killed at the Suez Canal.

Ma'ale Shelomo
Ascent on Mt. Ḥermon, from Naḥal Si'on to Mt. Dov (from *222:303* to *221:303*). Named after an Israeli officer, Shelomo Cohen, killed nearby.

Ma'ale Shomeron
Civilian outpost in Samarian Hills 13 km. E of Qalqilya. Established 1979.

Ma'ale Tamar
Ascent on Sedom–Dimona road from 'Arava to Negev Hills (from *176:046* to *174:047*).

Ma'ale Timna'
Ascent in Elat Hills 20 km. N of Elat. On ascent a track passes from the 'Arava into the Negev Hills (from *143:905* to *142:906*).

Ma'ale Yair
Steep ascent in Judean Desert from region of Meẓad Ḥatrurim *179:070* to region of 'En Boqeq *184:069*. Named after Yair Peled, Israeli officer who discovered the pass. (He was murdered by Bedouin in 1959.) Only vehicles with front-wheel drive can descend via this route.

Ma'ale Yamin
Ascent in Negev Hills 10 km. E of HaMakhtesh HaGadol *157:037*. Ancient road through Naḥal Ḥatira passed along ascent.

Ma'ale Ye'elim
Steep ascent in Judean Desert from Dead Sea shore along length of Naḥal Ye'elim.

Ma'ale Yesha'
Ascent in Galilee 10 km. S of Qiryat Shemona. Starts N of Koaḥ junction and is 5 km. long; ends at Meẓudat Yesha'.

Ma'ale Ẓafir (Ma'ale 'Aqrabbim HaRomi)
Ascent in Negev Hills 20 km. SE of Dimona, 4 km. W of Ma'ale 'Aqrabbim (from *160:036* to *161:035*). Constructed in Roman Period. Along its length are hundreds of rock-hewn steps and remains of three Roman fortresses.

Ma'ale Ẓe'elim
Ascent in Judean Desert 4 km. N of Masada. Passes through Naḥal Ẓe'elim and links Dead Sea shore with upper mountain tracks (from *183:084* to *182:086*).

Ma'ale Ẓenifim
Ascent in Negev Hills linking Mishor Faran and Naḥal Ẓenifim (from *134:945* to *134:944*).

Ma'ale Ẓin

Ascent in Negev Hills 4 km. SE of Sede Boqer. Section of ancient route, Darb es Sultan, which passes through Biq'at Ẓin (from *131:030* to *132:028*).

★ **Ma'ale Ẓivia** *181:255*

Kibbutz in Galilee 5 km. SE of Karmi'el. Named after Zivia Lubetkin, one of leaders of Warsaw ghetto uprising. Established 1979.

Ma'ale Ẓurim

Ascent 15 km. S of Mt. Sedom. Forms a pass from 'Arava to Har Ẓurim in Negev Hills (from *180:046* to *179:047*).

Ma'alot-Tarshiḥa *176:269*

Jewish development town (Ma'alot) and Arab village (Tarshiḥa) united in one local council, in Upper Galilee 20 km. E of Nahariyya. **Ma'alot** Initially an immigrant town founded in 1957, its name derives from nearby Arab village of Mi'ilya. Pop.: 4,000. Economy based on industry and services. In 1974 a squad of Arab terrorists penetrated a school building in the town holding school children hostage. Before being overcome by an Israeli army force they killed 18 and wounded 70 of the 100 pupils, who were using the school building as a hostel. **Tarshiha** Large Arab village built on ruins of ancient Jewish settlement. Local tradition claims the village is named after holy Moslem recluse, Shiḥa, who, while sitting on summit of adjacent hill, was "taken to heaven." (*Tar Shiḥa* means Shiḥa disappeared.) Fierce battles between Christians and Moslems were fought here during Crusader Period. During War of Independence served as central base for Kaukji's Liberation Army until the Israel Defence Forces took the village. Pop.: 2,500, 74% Christian, the rest Moslem. In the village there is a monastery, a number of churches and 3 mosques.

★ **Ma'anit** *153:207*

Kibbutz on NW border of Samarian Hills 4 km. S of 'Iron junction. Founded by immigrants from Volhynia and Czechoslovakia who, in 1935, settled in Karkur. In 1942 they moved to present site, near remains of ancient Jewish settlement of Narbata. During War of Independence the kibbutz was under siege. Area: 4,600 d. Pop.: 500. **Narbata** On hill NE of kibbutz are remains of settlement from Roman–Byzantine Period. Apparently site of Narbata, the neighbouring district of Caesarea. At beginning of Jewish Revolt against Rome, the Jews of Caesarea fled to Narbata, but were pursued by Romans who destroyed the city and neighbouring villages. During Roman-Byzantine Period it was rebuilt. Rock-cut tomb containing stone sarcophagi and small tel with sherds indicating Iron Age occupation. Also many flint tools were found in area.

• **Ma'as** *139:163*

Moshav in Sharon in S Petaḥ Tiqwa. Formed 1952 by amalgamation of 2 *moshavim*: Kefar HaYovel, founded 1934 to commemorate 50 years of Bilu *aliyah*, and BeHadraga, founded 1935. Area: 8,700 d. Pop.: 440.

★ **Ma'barot** *141:196*

Kibbutz in 'Emeq Ḥefer 5 km. N of Sharon junction. Located near a bridge crossing Naḥal Alexander, hence its name (*ma'barot* = crossings). Founded 1933 by HaShomer HaZa'ir groups from Poland, Rumania, Bulgaria and Hungary. Area: 3,200 d. Pop.: 670. **Prehistoric remains** Within kibbutz burial caves and other remains of a prehistoric settlement have been found. These are in the local museum.

Mabbu'im *117:095*

Rural centre in Negev 5 km. NE of HaGaddi junction. Name from Biblical passage (Isa. 35:7), "the burning sand shall become a pool, and the thirsty ground *springs* of water." Founded 1958. Pop.: 200. Provides services for Eshkol, Nir Moshe, Nir 'Aqiva, Pa'ame Tashaz, Qelaḥim, Sede Ẓevi and Talme Bilu.

Madama *171:176*

Small Arab village (pop.: 450) in Samarian Hills 5 km. SW of Shekhem.

Ma'galim *111:089*

Rural centre in Negev 3 km. SW of HaGaddi junction. Name from Biblical passage "the *tracks* of thy chariot drip with fatness." (Ps. 65:12). Pop.: 90. The centre provides services for neighbouring settlements of Sharsheret, Giv'olim, Melilot and Shibbolim.

Magdi'el → Hod HaSharon

Magen *095:078*

Kibbutz in Negev with Byzantine church ruin 3 km. N of Magen junction. Founded 1949 by Rumanian HaShomer HaẒa'ir group on War of Independence battle site — Sheikh Nuran military outpost. Area: 8,500 d. Pop.: 300. **Sheikh Nuran** Within kibbutz is tomb of Bedouin sheikh and around it ruins of Byzantine settlement and church. On account of unusual features like crosses inlaid in the floor, experts believe it was used by Bedouin converted to Christianity. Site believed to be that of Bethul or Bethuel, a city in Simeon tribal allotment (Josh. 19:4; I Chron. 4:30). Mentioned as Bitylion in Madaba map. Remains of structures, wine presses, columns and capitals.

Magen Sha'ul *179:214*

Moshav in Yizre'el Valley 10 km. S of 'Afula. Named for King Saul who died on nearby Mt. Gilboa'. Founded 1976.

Maggal *153:199*

Kibbutz in Samarian Hills 8 km. N of Tulkarm. Name derives from *naḥal* emblem — sickle (*maggal*) and sword. At first a *naḥal* outpost peopled by a scout group in 1953 and called Military Outpost "86" (so called in War of Independence). Since 1954 it has been permanent civilian settlement. Area: 3,000 d. Pop.: 350. Centre called Bet No'am in memory of kibbutz members who died in Israel's wars.

Maghar *188:255*

Arab village in Galilee 4 km. S of Ḥananya junction, on S slopes of Mt. Ḥazon. Name means caves. Perhaps site of ancient priestly city of Ma'ariya. Since 1956 it has had a local town council. Pop.: 8,500: 54% Druze, 33% Christian and 13% Moslem. Village has 2 churches, a Druze *khilwa* (prayer house) and a mosque.

(El) Maghar *129:138*

Ancient settlement remains on hill among ruins of abandoned Arab village of el Maghar, 2 km. N of Gedera. According to sherds site was occupied in Chalcolithic Period and Bronze Age. Many Hellenistic and Roman tombs in area.

Magharat et Tabun → Me'arot Karmel

Magharat Tur eṣ Ṣafa *154:110*

Large underground cave in Judean Hills 3 km. NE of Tarqumiya. Contains prehistoric remains.

Magharat el Wad → Me'arot Karmel

Magharat el Watwat *147:156*

Cave off Ben Shemen–Rosh Ha'Ayin road, 7 km. E of Ben-Gurion Airport. Name means cave of the bat. Prehistoric remains were found here. Nearby in bed of adjacent stream (a tributary of Naḥal Ayyalon) are remains of a Roman way and alongside it, following almost an identical course, are remnants of another ancient way.

○ **Maghar Shab'a** *212:296*

Arab village on SE slopes of Mt. Ḥermon, 2.5 km. NE of kibbutz Dan. Hewn burial tombs. An ancient road was discovered at lower part of village — apparently a secondary road to Banyas–Zur road. Nearby, Roman milestones were found, one with an inscription from Hadrian's day (beginning of 1st c.).

(El) Maghtas *202:138*

Site of Jesus' Baptism and Christian holy place on W bank of Jordan River, 8 km. SE of Jericho and 4 km. S of Allenby Bridge. In 5th c. a Byzantine church was erected here. Object of Christian pilgrimages for immersion in the Jordan. Greek Orthodox, Coptic, Armenian, Rumanian, Franciscan, Syrian and Ethiopian churches in the area commemorate the Baptism. Most are located across river in Jordan. The Greek Monastery of St. John is known in Arabic as Qaṣr el Yahud, castle of the Jews, since tradition associates el Maghtas as the place where Joshua led the Children of Israel into the Promised Land.

● **Magshimim** *140:161*

Moshav in Sharon 3 km. S of Petaḥ Tiqwa. Founded 1949 by demobilized soldiers. Area: 2,500 d. Pop.: 400. Memorial to its members who died in Yom Kippur War.

★ **Maḥanayim** *(Gen. 32:2) 203:266*

Kibbutz in Galilee 3 km. NE of Rosh Pinna. Named after Biblical Mahanaim. Lands for the settlement were purchased in 1892. During War of Independence the kibbutz was in front line facing the Syrians. In 1952 when kibbutz movement split, some members left Maḥanayim. Area: 5,000 d. Pop.: 400. Within kibbutz is grave of Michael Ḥelpern, Second Aliyah pioneer who became a legendary figure. S of kibbutz is a small airfield.

Maḥane Yisra'el *142:157*

In past, an immigrant transit camp NE of Ben-Gurion Airport. Established 1949 on site of British army camp. Named after Yisra'el Sheḥori, Haganah commander, killed nearby. Later an immigrant housing complex was built here, but over the years the population dwindled.

● **Maḥseya** *150:128*

Moshav on border of Judean Hills and 2 km. E of Bet Shemesh. Mahseiah is a personal name in Bible (Jer. 32:12). Founded 1950 on lands of abandoned village, Deir Aban, by immigrants from Yemen and Morocco. The population changed over the years and original settlers were replaced by immigrants from Cochin. Area: 1,500 d. Pop.: 220.

Majami' **(Ghadir en Naḥas)** *215:264*

Small fort on Golan Heights 2.5 km. SW of Qazrin. Elliptical wall surrounding square structure with several rooms. Sherds found on site from Roman Period. Small spring and pools nearby. Arab village near fort. Along road to Qaẓrin and on banks of Naḥal Zawitan are enclosures, stone mounds and remains of Megalithic structures.

○ **(El) Majd** *145:098*

Arab village in Judean Hills 13 km. SW of Hebron. Pop.: 500. Built on ruins of ancient settlement. Burial caves and cisterns. Sherds indicate Byzantine, Medieval and Ottoman occupation.

Majdal Bani Fadil *184:165*

Arab village (pop.: 650) in Samarian Hills 5 km. S of ʻAqraba village. Memorial to 3 soldiers who fell here in 1969 while on a chase after terrorists.

Majdal esh Shams *222:297*

Druze town on Golan Heights on SE slopes of Mt. Ḥermon, 1,150 m. above sea level. Name means tower of the sun. Pop.: 3,000. The road to Hermon ski slope runs through town. **Ancient remains** The N part of the town is built on ruins of 2nd-3rd c. settlement. Foundations and fragments of ancient structures near burial caves, known by the locals as Maqbarat el Yahud (Jewish graves). S of town is small nature reserve (270 d.).

Majd el Kurum *173:258*

Arab village in Galilee in Biqʻat Bet HaKerem 3 km. NW of Karmi'el. Site of Bet Kerem, a Jewish settlement mentioned in the Talmud. Pop.: 5,400.

(El) Makhruq *198:170*

Settlement ruins in Jordan Valley near road junction of Jericho–Bet She'an road and Shekhem–Damiya Bridge route. Name means the blazing one. Remains of large settlement and brick wall from Early Bronze Age; round and square tower of unhewn stones from Iron Age and rock-cut and plastered canal.

Makhtesh Ramon

The largest crater in the country which is actually a valley in form of a crater, in Negev Hills near Mizpe Ramon. Valley lies NE to SW. Length: 35 km. Width: 8 km. Depth: 500 m. Hebrew name originates from the Arabic Wadi Ruman. In Arabic *ruman* means Romans, and it was apparently named thus because a Roman track once passed through here. Many quarries in crater. Gypsum and clay soil.

(El) Makr *163:260*

Arab village in Galilee 5 km. E of Acre. Founded more than 500 years ago by Lebanese Christians on ruins of Byzantine settlement. Pop.: 3,200, mostly Moslem, some Christians. **Remains of ancient settlement** Within village are many tombs from Roman and Byzantine Periods. S of village is a low tel; sherds and other remains indicate occupation in Roman, Byzantine and Arab Periods.

Malkiyya *198:278*

Kibbutz near Lebanese border off the N road, 6 km. W of Koaḥ junction. Name of ancient origin (of a priestly family who left Jerusalem after destruction of Second Temple and settled here) which was retained in that of abandoned Arab village upon whose lands the kibbutz was established. Founded 1949 by demobilized Palmaḥ soldiers who fought here during War of Independence. Area: 16,000 d. Pop.: 100. Memorial to fallen in Israel's wars.

(El) Mallaḥa *142:214*

Archaeological site W of Binyamina, 1 km. W of Bet Ḥananya. Building foundations, quarries and columbarium from Roman Period.

Maʻlul *172:233*

Ruins of abandoned village on border of Yizreʻel Valley 2 km. N of Migdal HaʻEmeq. Built on ruins of ancient settlement which some claim to be site of Biblical Nahalal, a city in allotment of Zebulun (Josh. 21:35). Known as Mahalul during Roman–Byzantine Period.

Mamshit (Kurnub) 156:048

Just north of HaMakhtesh HaGadol 5 km. SE of Dimona are ruins of ancient Mamshit, a Nabatean commercial centre which appears in the 6th c. Madaba map under the name of Mampsis. The spot called Kurnub by the Arabs, was where the ancient roads from Jerusalem and from Gaza converged en route to Elat. The Nabateans, an Aramaic-speaking people of Arabian stock who practiced a form of Greek paganism, founded Mamshit in the Hellenistic era. Later, in the Roman Period, a bathhouse and ramparts were added. In the Byzantine age, two churches were built which to this day are the most beautiful buildings on the site. Most of the ruins in the 40 d. site date from the late Nabatean Period, when Romans and Byzantine Christians occupied the city. It was destroyed during Arab conquest in 7th c. A police fort was built here during British Mandate Period. Excavations have uncovered remains of city wall, its towers and gates, palaces, houses, a tower fortress, water reservoir and bathhouse, remains of the 2 Byzantine churches with mosaic floors, hoards of coins, jewellery, utensils and other objects. Outside city walls a caravanserai and Nabatean tombs were found. In adjacent stream bed an almost complete network of dams for containing flood waters has been preserved from Byzantine Period.

Manof (Segev "C") 172:251

Industrial village under construction in Galilee, 8 km. NE of Shefar'am.

○ **(El) Manshiyya** 172:206

Small Arab village in Samarian Hills 6 km. W of Jenin.

(El) Manshiyya 219:250

Ruins of Jewish settlement from Roman–Byzantine Period on S Golan Heights 12 km. NE of 'En Gev. Located under barrel vaulted cliff wall enclosing a spring. Foundations of a synagogue. Ancient stones were used in buildings of abandoned Arab village.

○ **Manshiyyat ez Zabda** 169:235

Arab village (pop.: 200) 20 km. W of Nazareth, near *moshav* Bet She'arim.

● **Ma'or** 151:203

Moshav on border of Sharon and Samarian Hills 5 km. SE of Pardes Ḥanna. Founded 1953 in framework of "from city to settlement" movement. Pop.: 240.

Ma'oz Bridge 204:211

Destroyed bridge on Jordan River near kibbutz Ma'oz Ḥayyim. In Arabic: Jisr (*gesher*) Sheikh Ḥusein. One of important fords of Jordan River. Judah Maccabee crossed the river here in his campaign to save the Jewish villages in Transjordan. In 63 CE Pompey passed here with his army en route to Bet She'an. The Moslem armies invaded via here and conquered the country in 638, and Saladin crossed here in 1183. On the "night of the bridges" (June 1946) the Haganah demolished the bridge. It was rebuilt but again demolished by Israel Defence Forces at beginning of War of Independence.

★ **Ma'oz Ḥayyim** 201:211

Kibbutz 5 km. E of Bet She'an. Name after Ḥayyim Sturman, Haganah leader who, together with 2 friends, was killed by Arabs in vicinity in 1938. Founded 1937 as one of "stockade and watchtower" settlements. Area: 10,000 d. Pop.: several hundred. **Ancient remains** Excavations uncovered remains of synagogues with mosaic floor (the designs include a seven-branched *menorah*) which existed from end of 5th to 7th c. About 2 km. E of kibbutz is the Sheikh Ḥusein Bridge across Jordan River, also called Ma'oz Bridge.

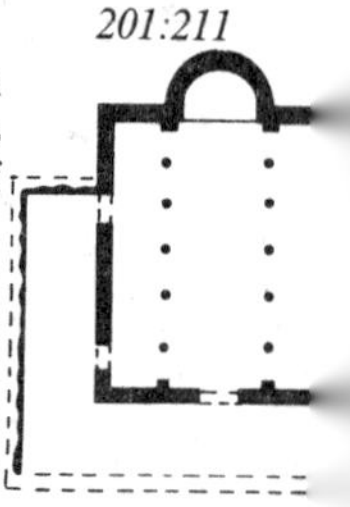

Ma'oz Ẓiyyon → Mevasseret Ẓiyyon

Mappal Devora *212:272*

Waterfall on Golan Heights, in bed of Naḥal Gilbon (Wadi Devora) which empties into Jordan River, 4 km. N of Benot Ya'aqov Bridge. Height: 41.5 m. Included in Gilbon nature reserve.

Mappal Gamla *220:258*

Waterfall on Golan Heights, in N tributary of Naḥal Daliyyot, 6 km. NE of *moshav* Ma'ale Gamla. Height: 51 m. (highest waterfall in territory under Israel's supervision). Its waters collect in a pool 15x20 m. At descent of stream is another waterfall, 20 m. high.

Mappal Gilbon *211:271*

Waterfall on Golan Heights, in bed of Naḥal Gilbon (Wadi Devora), which empties into Jordan River 4 km. N of Benot Ya'aqov Bridge. Height: 42 m. Has water all year round and in rainy season the quantity is doubled. Included in Gilbon nature reserve.

Mappal HaBanyas → Banyas

Mappal Naḥal 'Iyyon (HaTannur) *204:297*

Waterfall in Galilee near Metulla. Also called HaTannur because its shape is like an Arab oven (*tabun*). Called Nequbta Divyon in Talmud. Height: 15 m. Receives its water from Naḥal 'Iyyon. Dry in summer. Included in Naḥal 'Iyyon nature reserve.

Maqura *151:227*

Ruin of fortified enclosure on Mt. Karmel 10 km. SE of 'Atlit. Mound of stones 6 m. high, remains of 3 walls, structures and a tower. Finds indicate Iron Age occupation. It was possibly a fortified cattle or sheep ranch. During Disturbances of 1936-1939 the ranch houses served as a base for Arab gangs. Today it is a private ranch. Pop.: 40.

○ **Marda** *168:168*

Arab village (pop.: 800) 15 km. SW of Shekhem.

● **Margaliyyot** *201:291*

Moshav near Lebanese border 3 km. W of Qiryat Shemona. Named after Haim Margolis-Kalveryski, an ICA administrator in Galilee from 1900. Founded 1951 on lands of abandoned village of Hunin. Area: 1,000 d. Margaliyyot forest S of *moshav* is a nature reserve (380 d.) with remains of an ancient Mediterranean forest.

Mar Ilyas *170:126*

Greek monastery on Jerusalem–Bethlehem road SW of Ramat Raḥel. Built in 6th c., destroyed by earthquake and restored apparently in 14th c. According to Christian tradition, named after prophet Elijah who stopped here during his flight to Be'er Sheva' desert. Near monastery is an ancient well. Opposite monastery, across the road, is a stone bench which was set up by Mrs. Holman Hunt, for her husband who would sit and paint on this spot.

Mar'it → Ḥawwat Shiqmim

○ **Marja** *154:196*

Arab village (pop.: 400) in Samarian Hills 5 km. N of Tulkarm.

Mar Jiryes → St. George Monastery (Deir Mar Jiryes)

Marj Man → Biq'at Man

○ **Marj Na'ja** *200:176*

Arab village in Jordan Valley 3 km. NE of Argaman.

Marj Sanur → Biq'at Sanur

Mar Saba

181:123

Greek Orthodox monastery in Judean Desert, built on hillside of Naḥal Qidron, 12 km. E of Bethlehem. Founded in 5th c. by the monk Saba and called after him (*mar* means holy). Mar Saba, inhabited by close to a dozen monks today, has been the biggest Judean Desert monastery for 1,500 years. The monastery consists of many structures which seem to be piled on top of each other, and is enclosed by a fortress-like wall. The entrance is through a narrow opening in the W. Within monastery: main church with marble floor and many paintings, Church of the Cave which is the oldest church and contains a few Byzantine paintings, and a large burial cave containing hundreds of skulls of monks slaughtered by Persians and Arabs. To the N is a network of stairs descending to Naḥal Qidron and a spring in stream bed. Next to spring is an ancient cave where Saba lived before he established the monastery. In the walls of the ravine are many caves that were used during various periods as retreats for monks who were accustomed to congregate solely for Sunday prayers. Only men can enter the compound. Women can look into the compound from the 17th c. watch-tower called the Women's Tower. The skeleton of St. Sabas lies in a glass coffin draped in green silk in the main cathedral. The monastery has had a bloody history. It was destroyed in 614 by Persians and in 788 by Saracens. Rebuilt by Crusaders, it sustained repeated attacks by Bedouin. In the 19th c. the Russian church helped in reconstructing the walls and watch-towers.

Martyrs' Forest (Ya'ar HaQedoshim)

153:133

Large planted forest in Jerusalem Hills 4 km. S of Sha'ar HaGay, in memory of Holocaust victims. Planted by JNF. In centre of forest is Martyrs' Cave, prayer and communion room.

Masada (Meẓada)

183:080

Remains of large fortress from Second Temple Period in Judean Desert, 17 km. S of 'En Gedi and 2 km. from W shore of Dead Sea. Site of the most dramatic and symbolic act in Jewish history, where rebels chose mass suicide rather than submit to Roman capture. Built on summit of steep cliff 450 m. above level of Dead Sea, occupying area of 80 d. It appears this is the site of Stronghold of En-gedi, where David ascended after meeting King Saul in desert of En-gedi (I Sam. 23:29). According to Josephus Flavius, the fortress was built by Jonathan, the Hasmonean, as a refuge in time of need. Herod continued to build and fortify it until it was one of the strongest fortresses in Judea. During Jewish Revolt against Rome, it was taken by the rebels. After fall of Jerusalem the remaining zealots under leadership of Eleazar b. Jair gathered at Masada. For 3 years they held out against a siege by Roman armies under command of Flavius Silva. When the defenders realized that all hope was lost they burned the fortress and then committed suicide, 960 men, women and children (on 1st day of Passover, 73 CE). During Byzantine Period the ruins of Masada served as a monk's retreat; they also built a small church here. During Crusader Period it was inhabited; however, with succeeding generations the place was forgotten and its identity lost. **Discovery of Masada** In 1842 Masada was rediscovered by an English painter called Tipping, who was illustrating an English edition of Josephus Flavius *The Jewish War*. In 1848 an American expedition visited Masada and in 1851 it was followed by a French one. In 1932 a German expedition began digging on the site. Masada became a symbol of courage for the emerging modern Jewish state and in the early years it was a pilgrimage site for youth movements and Haganah members. The ascent was from the E, the Dead Sea side, up the Snake Path, mentioned by Josephus

Flavius. In 1949, at end of War of Independence, the Israel flag was hoisted on Masada's summit; in 1954 the Snake Path was repaired and in 1955 renovated by the Israel Defence Forces Engineering Corps in preparation for a renewal of excavations here. The site was inspected and explored by Shemaryahu Guttman and in 1963 full-scale excavations began under the supervision of professor Yigael Yadin, assisted by volunteers from all over the world. In 1970, the road leading to foot of mountain on the W side was opened and in the following year a cable car, descending most of the slope, was constructed.

Restoration and finds Remains of the wall, its towers and gates; the triple-tiered Northern Palace, other palaces, bathhouse, living quarters, storerooms, synagogue and a water storage system. Finds include pottery, weapons, coins, scroll fragments and ostraca. Among the ostraca, eleven were remarkable in that they were inscribed with a single name or nickname. Perhaps these were the "lots" cast by the Masada defenders in order to determine which one of a group of ten would kill his companions and then himself (as described by Josephus Flavius). Surrounding the mountain are remains of 8 Roman army camps, an assault ramp on the W and remains of 2 parallel aqueducts in the NW. There is a **youth hostel** at the foot of Masada; on the E side is a local museum, and cable-car station. Three km. NE of Masada, on shore of Dead Sea, is a small airfield named after I. Bar Yehuda, former minister of transport.

○ Mas'ada — *220:293*

Druze village on Golan Heights, near Mas'ada junction. An important road junction: Quneitra–Banyas–Majdal Shams–Wasit. Pop.: 700. Village has central high school for Druze youth on Golan Heights. E of village is Birkat Ram and alongside it a restaurant and observation point. S of village is Ya'ar Odem nature reserve.

○ Masḥa — *155:168*

Arab village (pop.: 450) in Samarian Hills 9 km. E of Rosh Ha'Ayin. A group of settlers called Ma'arav Shomeron lived in the nearby police fort in 1977 before they settled at Elqana.

★ Mash'abbe Sade — *129:045*

Kibbutz in Negev 25 km. S of Be'er Sheva'. Named after General Yizḥaq Sade, one of the founders of the Palmaḥ. Started as kibbutz Mash'abbim in 1947 on lands of Ḥaluẓa *117:056*. During War of Independence, kibbutz was under siege, and in 1949 it moved to its present site. Area: 9,000 d. Pop.: 370.

Mashaikh Sa'adiyya — *165:238*

Bedouin settlement (pop.: 200) near Basmat Tab'un in Galilee, 3 km. NE of Qiryat Tiv'on.

● Mash'en — *114:118*

Moshav on Coastal Plain 4 km. E of Ashqelon. Name based on passage from Isaiah (3:1) "...the Lord of hosts is taking away...*stay* and staff..." Founded 1950 on lands of abandoned village of Majdal. Area: 3,800 d. Pop.: 780.

Mash-had — *180:238*

Arab village in Galilee 5 km. NE of Nazareth. Pop.: 2,800. **Tel Gath-hepher** Near village is tel believed to be site of Gath-hepher, a city in Zebulun tribal allotment (Josh. 19:13) and birthplace of prophet Jonah (II Kings 14:25). Tel contains cisterns and wells. Sherds indicate occupation in Early Bronze Age, Middle Bronze Age, Iron Age and Byzantine Period. Local mosque is called en Nabi Yunis and, according to Arab tradition, was built on family tomb of prophet Jonah. Two Aramaic inscriptions were found here.

Mash-had et Teir → Har HaBetarim

Mashmia' Shalom *129:130*

A rural settlement which existed in Judean Foothills 5 km. NE of Qiryat Mal'akhi. Founded 1949 on lands of abandoned village of Masmiyya, from which the symbolic Hebrew name (proclaim peace) was derived. Today it is part of *moshav* Bene Re'em.

• **Maslul** *110:081*

Moshav in Negev 4 km. W of Ofaqim. Name derived from Biblical passage "And a *highway* shall be there" (Isa. 35:8). Established 1950. Area: 8,000 d. Pop.: 270.

(El) Maṣqara *194:153*

Ruins of fortress in Jordan Valley 10 km. N of Jericho off Bet She'an road. Fortress enclosure measures 20x30 m. Alongside is part of an aqueduct and other remains which indicate occupation in Byzantine and Arab Periods.

Massad *190:250*

Observation point in Lower Galilee on Har HaQoẓ 2 km. E of 'Eilabun. Established 1980.

★ **Massada** *206:232*

Collective settlement in Jordan Valley 4 km. S of Lake Kinneret. Founded 1937 in framework of "stockade and tower" settlement programme. During War of Independence it was evacuated before being destroyed by Syrians. It was rebuilt after the war. Area: 4,200 d. Pop.: several hundred.

• **Massu'a** *196:167*

Moshav shittufi in Jordan Valley off Jericho–Bet She'an road, 3 km. S of el Makhruq junction. Origin of name: on adjacent Keren Sartaba it was a practice during Second Temple Period to light bonfires when the new moon appeared and on festivals in order to announce the event (*massu'a* = beacon). Founded originally as a *nahal* outpost in 1969 by Bene 'Aqiva group. Area: 6,600 d. Pop.: several hundred.

• **Massu'ot Yiẓḥaq** *120:123*

Moshav shittufi on Coastal Plain 7 km. SW of Qiryat Mal'akhi. Named after late Chief Rabbi of Israel, Rabbi Isaac Halevi Herzog. Started as a kibbutz in 1949 by members of kibbutz Massu'ot Yiẓḥaq in Gush 'Eẓyon, after they were returned from Jordanian captivity. Since 1952 it has been a *moshav shittufi*. Area: 6,000 d. Pop.: 450. **Remains of church** Within *moshav* a mosaic floor and marble slabs inscribed with crosses — probably remains of a Byzantine church — were uncovered.

Mas'udiyyin el 'Azazma *133:067*

Central settlement of Bedouin tribe of 'Azazma, 4 km. S of Be'er Sheva'.

• **Matta'** *155:124*

Moshav in Judean Hills 8 km. SE of Bet Shemesh. Founded 1950 on lands of abandoned village of 'Allar. Pop.: 270. **'En Matta'** (spring) is W of *moshav*, and nearby are ruins of a Crusader farm.

• **Mattitiyahu** *153:148*

Moshav shittufi in Judean Foothills 15 km. E of Ramla, adjacent to Arab village Midya. According to one theory this is site of Modi'in, and thus named after Mattitiyahu the Hasmonean. Established 1980.

● **Mavqi'im** *109:114*

Moshav shittufi on Coastal Plain 5 km. S of Ashqelon. Named Mavqi'im (breached) as it was in this area that Israeli forces breached Egyptian lines in the War of Independence. Originally founded as a collective settlement (*qevuẓa*) in 1949 on abandoned village lands of Barbara, and called Barbarit. Since 1954 it has been a *moshav shittufi*. Area: 3,500 d. Pop.: 150.

★ **Ma'yan Barukh** *207:293*

Kibbutz N of Ḥula Valley near Lebanese border 5 km. NE of Qiryat Shemona. Named after Baruch (Bernard) Gordon, S African Zionist leader. Founded 1947 on abandoned village lands of Sanbariyya by group of S African immigrants (WWII veterans), Palmaḥ veterans, and HaBonim group from USA. Area: 2,500 d. Pop.: several hundred. Local museum of prehistoric objects found in Ḥula Valley.

Ma'yan Ḥarod *183:218*

Spring and recreation park in Yizre'el Valley at foot of Mt. Gilboa'. The spring is 'En Ḥarod mentioned in the Bible as site where Gideon camped before his battle with the Midianites (Judg. 7:1). Nearby there were battles between Crusaders and Moslems, and later, between Mamluks and Mongols. The early pioneers of the *kibbutzim* 'En Ḥarod, Bet HaShitta and Daverat set up temporary camps here before moving to their permanent sites. The spring gushes from a rock-cut cave with ancient walls of a rock-cut pool. Alongside are the graves of Yehoshua Hankin, "redeemer" of the Yizre'el Valley, and his wife Olga. Youth hostel, Gilboa' field school, swimming pool and campsite. Nearby is memorial to soldiers of the Yizre'el Valley who fell in Israel's wars.

★ **Ma'yan Ẓevi** *144:219*

Kibbutz on Karmel coast 2 km. W of Zikhron Ya'aqov. Named after Zevi (Henri) Frank, a director of ICA, on whose lands the kibbutz was established in 1938 in area of Kabara swamps as a "stockade and tower" settlement. Area: 4,500 d. Pop.: 700. Nature museum.

∴ **(El) Mazar** *185:214*

Abandoned village NW of Mt. Gilboa' 15 km. S of Nurit. Built on ruins of ancient settlement from Mesolithic, Persian, Hasmonean, Byzantine and Arab Periods. Perhaps site of Biblical Meroz, mentioned in Song of Deborah (Judg. 5:23).

○ **Mazari' en Nubani** *165:161*

Arab village (pop.: 850) in Samarian Hills 17 km. NW of Ramallah.

Mazkeret Batya *134:140*

Farming village (*moshava)* on Coastal Plain 4 km. SE of Bilu junction. Founded 1883 by Russian pioneers. The original village was founded through aid of Baron de Rothschild and named after his mother. Later renamed 'Ekron after the Biblical city which was located in area. Later still it reverted to original name. Area: 7,600 d. Pop.: 2,700.

● **Maẓliaḥ** *137:146*

Moshav in Judean Foothills 2 km. S of Ramla. Established 1950 by Karaite immigrants from Egypt. Named after Sahl ben Maẓliaḥ, a 10th c. Karaite leader from Jerusalem who published a proclamation calling for *'aliyah* from the diaspora to Jerusalem. Area: 2,000 d. Pop.: 650. Near *moshav* is tiny reserve (3 d.), only one in country with exposed chalk rocks from Oligocene age.

● **Mazor** *142:162*

Moshav on Coastal Plain 3 km. SE of Petaḥ Tiqwa. Name based on sound of name of abandoned village el Muzeiria'. Founded 1949. Area: 2,300 d. Pop.: 360. Memorial to fallen in Israel's wars.

Roman mausoleum To SE is 3rd c. Roman mausoleum — one of the few buildings west of the Jordan which has remained intact up to its 2nd storey. Probably because it was for a long time used as a Moslem shrine — Maqam en Nabi Yeḥya. Nearby Byzantine building remains and a mosaic floor were found.

o **Mazra'a** *159:265*

Arab village on Galilee coast 2 km. S of Nahariyya. Name means agricultural farm. Founded more than 200 years ago. Pop.: 1,700, mostly Moslem, some Christian. Within village are remains of Roman and Medieval settlements, part of Kabri-Acre aqueduct built 1814 in days of Suleiman Pasha, and remains of another aqueduct built in 18th c. during reign of Aḥmad el Jazzar Pasha.

o **(El) Mazra'a el Qibliyya** *164:151*

Arab village 8 km. NW of Ramallah. Name means the southern farm. Pop.: 1,000.

o **(El) Mazra'a esh Sharqiyya** *175:156*

Arab village 13 km. NE of Ramallah, N of Ba'al Ḥaẓor. Name means the eastern farm. Pop.: 2,000.

∴ **Mazra'at Kanaf** *214:253*

Abandoned village on Golan Heights 3 km. NE of Ramot. Remains of small Jewish settlement from Roman-Byzantine Period, a synagogue, gate lintel and Aramaic inscription. Park and observation point overlooking the Kinneret.

∴ **Mazra'at Nab** *224:249*

Ruins of abandoned village on Golan Heights 5 km. NE of *moshav* Eli 'Al. Believed to be site of Jewish settlement in Susita district.

∴ **Mazra'at Quneitra** *223:255*

Abandoned village on Golan Heights 6 km. NW of Ramat Magshimim. Partly built on ruins of ancient Roman-Byzantine settlement. Remains of houses roofed with slabs of basalt, foundations, columns and ancient building stones which were re-used in village houses.

★ **Maẓẓuva** *165:274*

Kibbutz in Galilee 1 km. SE of Ḥanita junction. Named after town of Pi Maẓẓuva mentioned in Talmud which has been identified with nearby Kh. Ma'ṣub. Founded 1940. Area: 3,000 d. Pop.: 450. Kibbutz has collection of local archaeological finds. Within kibbutz and its environs are remains of Byzantine settlement and church.

● **Me 'Ammi** *164:212*

Moshav shittufi in Samarian Hills 2 km. S of Umm el Faḥm. Named thus because of its similarity in sound to the American city of Miami, whose citizens contributed towards the establishment of this *moshav*. Founded as a *naḥal* outpost in 1963. Until 1967 it was a frontier settlement; since 1969 it has been a permanent civilian settlement. Area: 3,500 d. Pop.: 70. Memorial to Yiẓḥaq Neufeld, commander of the *naḥal* outpost who fell in 1966.

Me'arat Amira (Magharat el Amira) *199:252*

Prehistoric cave in Naḥal 'Ammud 3 km. NW of Ginnosar. Remains of prehistoric occupation were found here and at the Cave of Skulls, at ascent of Naḥal 'Ammud.

Me'arat Avshalom → Me'arat Soreq

Me'arat Eliyyahu ♟ *147:248*

Cave in NW Mt. Karmel, named after Elijah the Prophet, who according to an ancient tradition, slept here on his way to fight the prophets of Ba'al. It is a traditional pilgrimage site visited during Hebrew month of Av. Some believe that a visit to the cave will cure illness and alleviate pain. The cave is also holy to Christians, who believe Jesus' parents hid here after they returned from Egypt. In W and E walls are memorial inscriptions in Greek, Latin and Hebrew from 5th and 6th c. The grotto's interior is richly decorated in Byzantine style.

Me'arat Eẓba' (Magharat Abu Uṣba) *147:235*

Cave in Mt. Karmel on S cliff of Naḥal Oren, 2 km. E of 'Atlit interchange. Its shape is long, like a finger (*eẓba'*). Remains of prehistoric man have been found here.

Me'arat Gamal → Me'arot Karmel

Me'arat Ge'ula *150:244*

Cave within city of Haifa by Naḥal Gibborim on NE slopes of Mt. Karmel. Most of it has been destroyed by quarrying. Excavations in the remaining part uncovered utensils of more than 42,000 years old, as well as many bones of a variety of game animals.

Me'arat Gulgolet (Magharat ez Zuttiyya) *196:253*

Prehistoric cave in ascent of Naḥal 'Ammud 6 km. NW of Ginnosar. The skull (*gulgolet*) of the Galilean prehistoric man was found here and fauna remains from various prehistoric periods.

Me'arat HaEma (Me'arat Ḥever HaDeromit) *181:093*

Cave in Judean Desert called Cave of Horror, 6 km. SW of 'En Gedi, in S cliff wall of Naḥal Ḥever. Excavations revealed 40 skeletons of men, women and children, coins and pottery believed to date from Bar Kokhba rebellion, remains of clothing, food and papyri fragments written in Hebrew and Aramaic. The cave apparently served as a refuge for Jewish fugitives, besieged by the Romans, until they died of starvation and thirst.

Me'arat HaGedi → Me'arot Karmel

Me'arat HaIggerot (Me'arot Ḥever HaẒefonit) *182:093*

Cave in Judean Desert called Cave of Letters, 5 km. SW of En Gedi, in N cliff wall of Naḥal Ḥever. This is one of the caves that served as a refuge for Bar Kokhba rebels. Finds include skeletons of men, women and children and many wrapped objects (as if the occupants were ready to flee from the cave). The most important find was 15 letters from Simeon bar Kosiba (Kokhba) to the leaders of the revolt in the En Gedi region. Other letters found deal with administrative matters.

Me'arat HaMakhpela → Hebron

Me'arat HaMatmon *181:088*

Cave in Naḥal Mishmar in Judean Desert, called Cave of the Treasure, 8 km. NW of Masada. The mouth of the cave is 50 m. below the cliff top and access is only possible by rope ladder. Excavations uncovered a cache of 429 metal vessels (mostly copper) from Chalcolithic Period, some Iron Age sherds, tools, clothes, pottery, glass, papyri fragments and ostraca in Hebrew and Greek from Bar Kokhba Period.

Me'arat HaNaḥal → Me'arot Karmel

Me'arat HaNetifim → Me'arat Soreq

Me'arat HaQemaḥ *184:055*

Cave SW of Dead Sea, called Flour Cave, 5 km. NW of Sedom. Length:

70 m. Lower entrance is in Naḥal Peraẓim and upper entrance in Mishor ‘Ami‘az. Its walls are made up of soft and powdery white marl, hence its name (*qemaḥ* = flour).

Me‘arat HaTe'omim *151:125*

Large cave and nature reserve in Judean Hills, called Cave of the Twins, 4 km. SE of Bet Shemesh, within Naḥal HaMe‘ara which descends beyond Bar Giyyora. Name is derived from popular legend about a barren woman who bathed in the waters which collected in the cave, and later gave birth to twins.

Me‘arat Kevara *144:218*

Prehistoric cave in S Mt. Karmel 2 km. S of Zikhron Ya‘aqov. Excavations uncovered a large collection of flint and bone artifacts dating from Upper and Middle Paleolithic Periods. The finds from this cave have resulted in a classification called the Kevara Culture. S of the cave *143:217* are the remains of a Byzantine church with mosaic floor.

Me‘arat Khureitun *173:117*

Large branching cave in Judean Desert in Naḥal Khureitun, S of Herodium. The largest cave discovered in Israel: its total length is 4 km. The cave and the stream are named after a 4th c. Greek monk and founder of a number of monasteries, who, in his last years, became a recluse and died in this cave. Prehistoric remains have been found here and in Magharat Umm Qal‘a, Magharat Umm Qetafa and Magharat Umm en Naqus.

Me‘arat Mitla (Kh. Masilya) *147:238*

Cave at outlet of Naḥal Mitla 2.5 km. S of Tirat Karmel. Preliminary examinations have revealed occupational levels from Lower and Middle Paleolithic Periods.

Me‘arat Naḥal Namer *168:276*

Stalactite cave near Lebanese border 7 km. E of Rosh HaNiqra, in Naḥal Namer. The cave has a number of rooms, some naturally formed and others bear signs of rock-cutting. Sherds from Chalcolithic Period, Early Bronze Age and Middle Bronze Age.

Me‘arat Oren *148:235*

Cave in Mt. Karmel at entrance to Naḥal Oren, 2 km. E of ‘Atlit interchange. In the cave and just outside it remains of prehistoric man from the Middle and Upper Paleolithic Periods were found.

Me‘arat Ornit *150:240*

Cave in Naḥal Gallim 2 km. E of Tirat Karmel. Excavations uncovered occupational levels from Middle Paleolithic Period and from Chalcolithic Period onwards.

Me‘arat Qedumim *178:232*

Cave in Har Qedumim 2 km. S of Nazareth where remains of Ereẓ Israel prehistoric man from Lower Paleolithic Period were found.

Me‘arat Qeshet *169:276*

Destroyed stalactite cave in Galilee 9 km. E of Rosh HaNiqra, between Adamit and Ḥanita. Only the entrance arch (*qeshet*) to the cave is left.

Me‘arat Raqqefet *157:229*

The only prehistoric cave discovered in E slope of Mt. Karmel, in Naḥal Raqqefet 4 km. SW of Yoqne‘am junction. Excavations uncovered remains from a number of prehistoric epochs, starting from Upper Paleolithic.

Me'arat Sedom *187:055*

Cave in Mt. Sedom 2 km. NE of Sedom. The cave has a tall chimneylike ceiling. Also known as Cave of Lot's Wife because of a formation reminiscent of a pillar of salt which stands above it.

Me'arat Sefunim *148:238*

Cave with prehistoric remains from Upper Paleolithic Period in Naḥal Sefunim on Mt. Karmel, 2 km. SE of kibbutz HaḤoterim.

Me'arat Shimshon *153:130*

Cave in Judean Hills on N bank of Naḥal Soreq, 2 km. SE of Shimshon junction. Popular legend claims this to be one of the caves in which Samson took refuge from the Philistines. Rock-cut steps lead up to it.

Me'arat Soreq *152:129*

Stalactite cave in Judean Hills between Bet Shemesh and Nes Harim. Part of Avshalom nature reserve, named after Avshalom Shoham who fell in the Suez Canal region. Financial aid from his parents enabled the authorities to prepare the cave for visitors. It is the largest and most beautiful stalactite cave discovered in Israel. Area: 60 d. It was discovered by chance in 1968 during quarry blasting. Opened to the public in 1977. The cave has many types of stalactites and stalagmites.

Me'arat Tannur → Me'arot Karmel

Me'arot 'Adullam (Kh. Sheikh Madhkur) *150:117*

Group of caves in Tel 'Adullam 10 km. NE of Bet Guvrin. Occupied in ancient times; some theories identify them with the cave in which David hid from Saul.

Me'arot Arbel *197:248*

Caves in cliffs of Naḥal Arbel in Galilee, 5 km. NW of Tiberias. During Herod's reign they served as hide-outs of Jewish Zealots. Herod's soldiers succeeded in overcoming them by penetrating caves from above with ropes and cages. Caves fortified in days of Dahir el 'Amr. (See Arbel.)

Me'arot Bareqet (Kh. el Bira) *146:158*

Settlement remains 7 km. NE of Ben-Gurion Airport, near *moshav* Bareqet. Rock-cut cisterns and tombs, remains of a Roman-Byzantine tower and other structures.

Me'arot Bet Guvrin *141:112*

About 3,000 caves in Bet Guvrin region in Judean Foothills. Some of largest caves in the country. Most were created by quarrying building stones for limestone industry, apparently during Roman Period. Near Tel Maresha there are about 200 more Hellenistic Period caves, used for burial, water storage, wine and olive presses. Two of them are rock-cut burial caves with burial niches. (See Bet Guvrin.)

Me'arot Ḥever → Me'arat HaEma; Me'arat HaIggerot

Me'arot Karmel *147:230*

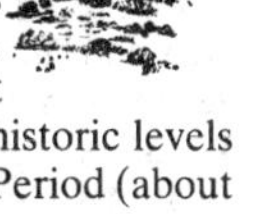

Group of prehistoric caves in Naḥal Me'arot (Arabic: Wadi el Maghara) in Mt. Karmel, 5 km. S of 'Atlit interchange. The 4 major caves, located on S bank of the stream, are Me'arat Tannur (Magharat et Tabun), Me'arat HaGamal, Me'arat HaNaḥal (Magharat el Wad) and Me'arat HaGedi. The caves were discovered by chance in 1928 and were first excavated from 1929-1934 and again from 1967-1971. Prehistoric levels were uncovered revealing artifacts from Lower Paleolithic Period (about 150,000 years ago). The caves are part of a nature reserve.

Me'arot Luzit *139:120*

Group of caves in 'Adullam region 1 km. S of *moshav* Luzit. Most are bell shaped, like those at Bet Guvrin, some bear signs of rock-cutting and others are columbaria caves. Nearby are remains of structures, fences and cisterns indicating occupation from Hasmonean Period to Middle Ages.

Me'arot Yonim *170:258*

Caves in Galilee near Acre-Safed road 4 km. E of Aḥihud junction. In the caves and on the step in front of them, prehistoric remains were discovered.

Mediterranean Sea (Yam HaTikhon) *(Josh. 15:47)*

Large sea W of Ereẓ Israel. Occupies the cavity between continents of Europe and Africa and borders on continent of Asia, hence its name. In ancient days it was known by many names: HaYam HaGadol, Yam Pelishti, HaYam HaAḥaron and others. It stretches from Israel to Gibraltar over 3,900 km. Maximum width: 1,300 km.; area: 2,500,000 sq. km.; maximum depth: 4.5 km. Length of coastline within Israel's jurisdiction is 220 km.

★ Mefallesim *108:101*

Kibbutz on Coastal Plain 3 km. W of Gevim junction. Founded 1949. Area: 11,300 d. Pop.: 450.

● Megadim *146:237*

Moshav on Karmel coast 2 km. from 'Atlit interchange. Founded 1949. Area: 2,000 d. Pop.: 450.

★ Megiddo *(Josh. 12:21)* *167:220*

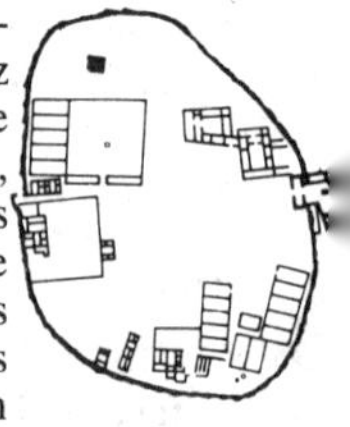

Kibbutz in Yizre'el Valley near Megiddo junction and tel of Megiddo. Considered the Armageddon of the New Testament with a history stretching back 6,000 years. Kibbutz founded 1949. Area: 3,700 d. Pop.: 380. **Tel Megiddo** One km. NE of kibbutz *167:221* is tel of ancient city of Megiddo, renowned in antiquity. It was a fortified city due to its strategic location on a junction of the *via maris*. The immediate area has been a battlefield between kingdoms and countries from ancient to present times. Its beginnings were in the 4th millennium BCE; it was first mentioned in an Egyptian document at time of Pharaoh Thutmose III (15th c. BCE) describing the latter's battle with the Canaanite kings. In a later document, describing the campaign of Amenḥotep II, Megiddo is mentioned as an Egyptian base, and it is again mentioned in the Tell el 'Amarna letters of the 14th c. BCE and in documents from 13th c. BCE. The king of Megiddo was one of the 31 kings defeated by Joshua (Josh. 12:21). However, the city itself did not become part of the tribal allotments until King David's day. During Solomon's reign it was an important city in one of his 12 administrative districts (I Kings 4:12) and a fortified chariot city (I Kings 9:15-19). After division of kingdom it remained an important city in kingdom of Israel. During reign of Rehoboam, it was captured and destroyed by Shishak I, king of Egypt (920 BCE). Rebuilt by Kings Omri and Ahab. During revolt of Jehu, Ahaziah was killed in Megiddo while fleeing from Jehu. It was again destroyed in 815 BCE by Hazael, king of Aram. Later it was restored and enjoyed a period of prosperity during reign of Jeroboam II. In 722 BCE Megiddo was taken by Tiglath–pileser III, king of Assyria, and made capital of an Assyrian province. King Josiah of Judah was killed at Megiddo in a battle with Pharaoh Neco (II Kings 23:29). After destruction of First Temple, it was rebuilt and apparently became capital of a Persian province. However, it could not be restored to its former greatness. During Hellenistic Period it was abandoned, and nearby, the new centre of Othnai, called Legio during the Roman Period, was established. In 1918 a decisive battle was fought near Megiddo between British and Turkish armies. General Allenby received the title of Lord of Megiddo for his victory here. The most recent battle at Megiddo was during War of Independence, when the Israel Defence Forces routed Kaukji's Liberation Army. **Excavations, finds and restoration** Excavations began before WWI and continued between 1924 and 1939 and again from 1960 to 1967. Twenty strata were uncovered — the earliest from 4000 BCE. Major finds: remains of walls, palaces and temples from Early and Middle Bronze Ages; palaces, utensils and jewellery from Late Bronze Age; a hidden path to a spring, remains of a wall, gate, stables and dwellings from period of King Solomon; a water system from Ahab's reign; remains of structure, granaries, seal with inscription "Shema, servant of Jeroboam" and other seals from the days of the Monarchy; and remains from later periods.

● **Meḥola** *198:196*

Moshav shittufi in Jordan Valley 6 km. S of Tirat Ẓevi. Named after Biblical city Abel-meholah (mentioned in Judg. 7:22 and I Kings 19:16). Founded as a *naḥal* outpost in 1969. Civilian status since 1960. Area: 4,000 d. Pop.: several hundred.

■ **Me'ir Shefeya** *148:221*

Youth village and agricultural school on S Mt. Karmel 3 km. NE of Zikhron Ya'aqov. Name originates from Shefeya — the Arabic name of the site, and Me'ir — after Mayer Amschel Rothschild. Founded originally as a farming village (*moshava*) in 1892 on land purchased by Baron de Rothschild; in 1904 it became a home and educational institute for orphans of Kishinev pogroms. In 1917 when Jews of Tel Aviv and Jaffa were expelled by the Turks, the Herẓliyya high school was transferred to Shefeya. After WWI a youth village was set up here, at first, in 1923, only for boys, but from 1924 also for girls (H.N. Bialik wrote a poem "To the girls of Shefeya" in 1926). In 1925 it was given over to the Hadassah organization and after 1948 it became an agricultural school. It was taken over by the government in 1958. Pop.: 550 students and staff. Shefeya has an old established and still-performing mandolin orchestra. In the Shefeya wood Haganah members trained in pre-State years.

○ **Meisar (Kh. esh Sheikh Meisar, Kh. Meisar)** *154:205*

Arab village in Samarian Hills N of kibbutz Meẓer, 4 km. SE of 'Iron junction. Pop.: 650.

○ **Meithalun** *175:194*

Arab village in Samarian Hills 14 km. N of Shekhem. Pop.: 2,300.

● **Mekhora** *190:174*

Moshav in Samarian Hills 8 km. NW of Qeren Sartaba. Founded as a *naḥal* outpost in 1973.

● **Mele'a** *172:218*

Moshav in Yizre'el Valley 4 km. SE of Megiddo junction. Name taken from Biblical passage, "You shall not sew your vineyard with two kinds of seed lest the *whole yield* be forfeited to the sanctuary..." (Deut. 22:9). Founded 1956 as part of the operation "from ship to settlement". Area: 5,000 d. Pop.: 310.

● **Melilot** *111:088*

Moshav in Negev between Netivot and Ofaqim 4 km. SW of HaGaddi junction. Name means ripe ears of corn and is taken from the passage "You may pluck the *ears* with your hand" (Deut. 23:25). Founded 1953. Area: 4,000 d. Pop.: 350.

Menaḥemya 202:230

Rural settlement (with local council) in Jordan Valley 5 km. SW of Zemaḥ. Named after Menaḥem, father of Sir Herbert Samuel, first British high commissioner of Palestine. Started as a farming village (*moshava*) in 1902 called Milḥamiyya, after Arab name of site. It was the first Jewish settlement in Jordan Valley. In its early years it was subjected to attacks by local Bedouin. Area: 12,000 d. Pop.: 710.

★ **Menara** *201:289*

Kibbutz near Lebanese border 2 km. E of Qiryat Shemona. Founded 1943. During War of Independence it was isolated and besieged and only relieved after heavy fighting. During 1969 and 1970 it sustained infiltrator attacks from across the border. Area: 3,700 d. Pop.: several hundred. Near kibbutz is Mt. Shenan *200:291* with a tomb purported to be that of Rabbi Ashi.

● **Menuḥa** *129:118*

Moshav in Lakhish region 5 km. N of Qiryat Gat. Name taken from Biblical passage "Blessed be the Lord who has given *rest* to his people Israel..." (I Kings 8:56). Founded 1953. Area: 4,500 d. Pop.: 540.

● **Me'ona** *174:268*

Moshav in Galilee 2 km. W of Ma'alot. Name means dwelling place. Founded 1949. Area: 650 d. Pop.: 270.

● **Me'or Modi'im** *149:149*

Moshav shittufi in Judean Foothills 10 km. E of Lod. Named after Modi'im — the ancient town and birthplace of the Maccabees which was located nearby. Established in 1964 as a religious *naḥal* outpost called Mevo Modi'im. *Moshav shittufi* set up by religious immigrants from the USA. Area: 2,800 d. Pop.: 80. Finds include remains of mosaics and agricultural installations which were part of a Byzantine monastery.

★ **Merḥavya** (kibbutz) *179:223*

Kibbutz in Yizre'el Valley 2 km. E of 'Afula at foot of Giv'at HaMore, near *moshav* Merḥavya. First settled by members of Oppenheimer's cooperative established 1911 and dissolved 1918. Later various work groups attempted to take over, but without success. In 1929 the present kibbutz was founded by members of HaShomer HaẒa'ir from Galicia. Area: 8,000 d. Pop.: 660. Kibbutz has editorial offices of Sifriyyat HaPo'alim Publishing Co. and HaShomer HaẒa'ir archives. **Remains of Crusader fortress** The kibbutz is located on site of the Crusader fortress La Fève (Arabic: el Fula). In 1183 a battle was fought here between Moslems and Crusaders, and in 1799 Napoleon's army and the Turks fought here. Remains of fortress and moat.

● **Merḥavya** *(moshav)* *179:224*

Moshav in Yizre'el Valley 2 km. E of 'Afula, at foot of Giv'at HaMore. Founded 1922 at site of farming village (*moshava*) established by private farmers who purchased the land in 1910. Area: 7,400 d. Pop.: 260.

Meqorot HaYarqon → Rosh Ha'Ayin

○ **Mereish** *150:097*

Small Arab village 12 km. SW of Hebron. Pop.: 350.

Merkaz Shapira *122:122*

Regional centre for settlements of Shafir regional council on Coastal Plain 5 km. SW of Qiryat Mal'akhi. Named after the late minister Moshe Ḥayyim Shapira. Administrative, medical and educational facilities and *yeshiva* high school, Or 'Eẓyon.

★ Merom Golan *222:281*

Kibbutz on Golan Heights 5 km. W of Quneitra. Founded 1967; moved to present site in 1972. Area: 4,500 d. Pop.: several hundred.

● Meron *192:266*

Moshav in Galilee at foot of Mt. Meron. Traditional site of a Lag Ba'Omer celebration each spring in honour of Talmudic sage, Rabbi Simeon b. Yoḥai, who hid here for 12 years after being sentenced to death by the Romans. *Moshav* founded 1949. Area: 1,800 d. Pop.: 400. **Ancient Meron**, S of *moshav*, *191:265*, is site of important city during Roman-Byzantine Period. Residence of a priestly clan and of Rabbi Simeon b. Yoḥai, the great 2nd c. sage and author of the Zohar. Consequently, Meron became a Kabbalist centre. Tombs of Rabbi Simeon b. Yoḥai and his son Eliezer, Rabbi Yiẓḥaq Nafḥa and Rabbi Johanan HaSandelar. In mountainside are Roman-Byzantine burial caves, one of which is supposed to be that of Hillel and another of Shammai. Remains of 3rd c. synagogue and ancient settlement. Excavations near synagogue have uncovered remains of houses and workshops, a pool and ritual bath. Finds indicate occupation from Hellenistic until Roman Period, and from early Arab Period until Middle Ages. **Rashbi festivity** Every year on Lag Ba'Omer a huge festivity is held at tomb of Rabbi Simeon b. Yoḥai (Rashbi). According to tradition, he died on Lag Ba'Omer.

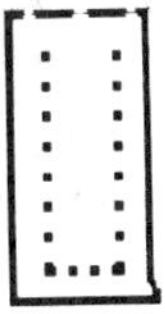

● Meshar *126:136*

Moshav on Coastal Plain 2 km. W of Gedera. Name means flat land. Founded 1950 by demobilized soldiers of Polish origin on lands of abandoned village, Bash-shit. Area: 2,500 d. Pop.: 260.

● Mesillat Ẓiyyon *151:134*

Moshav on border of Judean Hills and Foothills 2 km. SW of Sha'ar HaGay. Founded 1950 by Yemenite immigrants, who were eventually replaced by immigrants from Cochin. Area: 1,000 d. Pop.: 280.

★ Mesillot *194:212*

Kibbutz 2 km. W of Bet She'an. Founded 1938 as "stockade and tower" settlement by Polish and Bulgarian immigrants. Area: 7,800 d. Pop.: 650.

● Metav *178:216*

Moshav in Yizre'el Valley 7 km. S of 'Afula. Name based on Biblical passage "... gave them a possession in the land ... in the *best* of the land" (Gen. 47:11). Founded 1954. Area: 4,500 d. Pop.: 520.

Metulla *204:298*

Village at tip of "finger of the Galilee," on the Lebanese border. Name based on Arabic name of Druze village Umtulla, meaning overlooking the area. Founded 1896 by pioneers from Russia, on lands purchased by Baron de Rothschild. Druze tenant farmers were forcibly evicted by Turkish authorities and for many years harassed the village. In 1920, after Tel Ḥay battle, it was evacuated. However, the residents returned shortly afterwards and up to War of Independence the farmers lived harmoniously with their Lebanese neighbours across the border. After the war, most of Metulla's lands in 'Emeq 'Iyyon (Marj 'Ayun) fell outside the borders of Israel. Following Six-Day War, it was often attacked by terrorists from across the border. Area: 2,000 d. Pop.: several hundred. In 1977 a border crossing, called the Good Fence, near Metulla, was opened between the Lebanese Christian villages in S Lebanon and Israel. Nearby is Naḥal 'Iyyon nature reserve which includes the waterfalls of HaTaḥana and the large Tannur.

⚓ Mevasseret Ẓiyyon ✿

Settlement with local council 8 km. W of Jerusalem on both sides of main road to Tel Aviv. Incorporates 2 older settlements — Ma'oz Ẓiyyon and Mevasseret Yerushalayim, the latter located S of the main road — *163:133* — and founded in 1951. Name commemorates War of Independence battles which took place nearby (the Qastel). Mevasseret Yerushalayim situated N of main road — *165:134* — was founded in 1956. Name from Biblical passage "Get you up to a high mountain, *O Zion, herald of good tidings*; lift up your voice with strength, O Jerusalem, herald of good tidings" (Isa. 40:9). The joint settlement has a population of 6,000 (3,500 in Ma'oz Ẓiyyon and 2,500 in Mevasseret Yerushalayim).

● Mevo Betar ‖●❣L *160:125*

Moshav shittufi in Judean Hills 10 km. SW of Jerusalem. Named after ancient city of Beththter which was located nearby. Founded 1950. Because of its proximity to the border before Six-Day War, it was often object of infiltrator attacks; 6 members were killed in a border incident against nearby Arab village Ḥusan (25 September 1956). Cultivated area: 3,500 d. Pop.: 200. Within *moshav* are remains of a Roman track.

★ Mevo Ḥamma ✿‖●❣■'❣▬✳ *211:237*

Kibbutz on Golan Heights 8 km. NE of Zemaḥ junction. Name based on that of nearby springs of el Ḥamma (Ḥammat Gader). Founded 1968, and initially located at el Ḥamma. In 1969 moved to present site which had previously been a Syrian military post called 'Imrat 'Iz ed Din. Pop.: several hundred.

● Mevo Ḥoron ✿‖■' ❣ *153:141*

Moshav shittufi on edge of Ayyalon Valley 5 km. NE of Latrun junction. Located on track leading to Ma'ale Bet Ḥoron, hence its name. Founded 1969 by *naḥal* group. Moved to present site in 1974. Area: 19,300 d. Pop.: several hundred.

Mevo Modi'im → Me'or Modi'im

⚑ Mevo'ot *124:126*

Inter-rural centre for Be'er Toviyya and Kefar Warburg.

▰ Mevo'ot Yam *138:201*

Nautical and fishing school 10 km. N of Netanya, next to *moshav* Mikhmoret. Name from Biblical passage "and say to Tyre, who dwells at the *entrance to the sea*..." (Ezek. 27:3). Situated near a small bay called by the Arabs Minat Abu Zabura (see Mikhmoret). Founded 1951. Pop.: 700 students and staff.

⋏ Meẓad Abbirim *177:272*

Remains of Crusader fort in Galilee 4 km. N of Ma'alot, near Arab village of Fassuta.

⋏ Meẓad 'Aqrabbim *166:038*

Remains of Nabatean watch-tower, near Ma'ale 'Aqrabbim. Built to guard the ancient road which passed by here.

⋏ Meẓad 'Arugot *186:096*

Ruins of Roman-Byzantine fort in Naḥal 'Arugot, N of kibbutz 'En Gedi. Remains of 2 rooms and courtyard. Apparently served as living quarters and guard station.

Meẓad ‘Ateret *209:267*

Remains of Crusader fort Chastelet (the little castle) near Jordan River 1 km. S of Benot Ya‘aqov Bridge. Built on ruins of settlement from Early Bronze Age and Roman Period. Built to protect the Jordan ford. Destroyed by Saladin.

Meẓad Boqeq (Qaṣr Umm Baghiq) *184:067*

Remains of Roman-Byzantine fortress on W shore of Dead Sea on high hill at entrance to Naḥal Boqeq. Remains of aqueduct joining adjacent spring — ‘En Boqeq — with fortress. Near shore are remains of a quay and next to it 2 pools with steps inside. Excavations uncovered pottery, bronze objects and coins from Hasmonean Period. Sherds found date from Roman, Byzantine and Arab Periods.

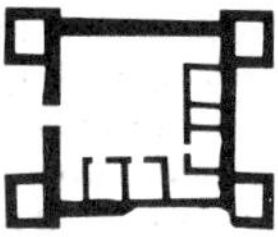

Meẓad Eflal (Rujm Shi‘b el Tur; Rujm Qandul) *114:115*

Remains of small fort 4 km. NE of Bet Guvrin. Situated on a spot that commands the area. The fort was square and alongside it were pools, columns and a wine press. Sherds found date from Roman Period.

Meẓad Giv‘at Barnea‘ (temporary name) *107:005*

Remains of square Israelite fort in Negev Hills 23 km. NW of Miẓpe Ramon. Remains of structures were found containing Iron Age sherds. Built in days of kingdom of Judah, apparently to secure a nearby route which was a branch of the ancient Way of the Atharim. On SE slope of hill are 2 open cisterns, typical of that period, and at foot of hill are remains of a large Byzantine farm.

Meẓad Gozal (Umm Zughal) *186:060*

Ruins of ancient fort on Dead Sea shore at N edge of Mt. Sedom. Apparently built by Edomites and captured during reign of King David. Name originates from the Arabic Umm Zughal. Room foundations around a central courtyard.

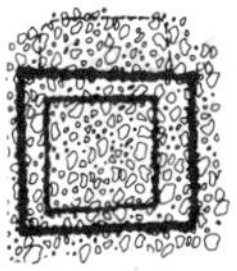

Meẓad Ḥakhlil (Kh. Ḥauran) *144:117*

Remains of Israelite fort in ‘Adullam region 1 km. S of *moshav* Ẓafririm. Built during time of the Monarchy and flourished during Persian and Hasmonean Periods. Remains of walls, foundations, caves and cisterns. Nearby is a Roman-Byzantine columbarium and Arab tomb.

Meẓad Har Boqer *123:031*

Remains of Israelite fort from days of kings of Judah on Mt. Boqer in the Negev Hills 8 km. W of Sede Boqer. Polygonal shape with uneven sides. At centre is large courtyard encompassed by large and small rooms.

Meẓad Ḥashavyahu *120:145*

Remains of fortress on Coastal Plain 3 km. S of kibbutz Palmaḥim. Built apparently during reign of King Josiah and also inhabited after Babylonian Exile. An ostracon with Hebrew inscription erroneously read as "Hashavyahu ben Ya..." (instead of "Hoshayahu ben Ya...") was found here.

Meẓad Ḥashmonay *167:134*

Remains of watch-tower W of Jerusalem near Moẓa, at foot of Ma‘ale Roma'im. One of a series of forts built in days of Ḥasmoneans to protect major roads. Seems to have been destroyed in 2nd half of 1st c. BCE.

Meẓad Ḥasidim → Qumeran

ᴧ Meẓad Ḥatrurim *178:070*

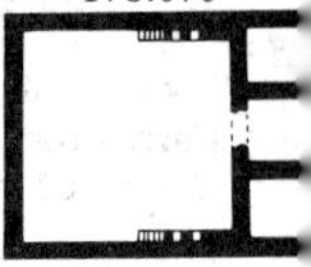

Remains of Roman fort in Judean Desert 12 km. SW of Masada. Belonged to Roman border defences — *Limes Palestinae*. Built to protect the road from Rosh Zohar to Dead Sea. Remains of wall and towers, decorated gate and cistern.

ᴧ Meẓad HaYarqon (Tell el Kudadi) *129:169*

Remains of Israelite fort N of Yarqon River outlet, near Reading power station. Built in 10th c. BCE in days of David or Solomon, to prevent infiltration from the sea. Repaired at a later date but destroyed in 8th c. BCE, apparently by Tiglath-pileser III, the Assyrian king. Excavations uncovered remains of ancient track which apparently led from the fort to a ford over the Yarqon. Nearby is a marble column with a Hebrew and English inscription describing how the British forded the Yarqon in WWI.

ᴧ Meẓad Ma'ale Ẓin *132:029*

Remains of fort in Negev Hills at Ma'ale Ẓin 3 km. SE of Sede Boqer. Built at end of Byzantine Period to protect ancient route from Gaza to Petra. Square in shape, it had 2 towers flanking a gate built of hewn stones.

ᴧ Meẓad Maḥmal *143:010*

Ruins of fort in Negev Hills at summit of Ma'ale Maḥmal off Roman road from 'Avedat to Petra. Remains of square stone-hewn structure still extant to a height of 1.5 m. A water pool built of large stones lies 300 m. to the N. Sherds and Roman and Nabatean glass fragments have been found here.

ᴧ Meẓad Mazzal *180:043*

Remains of fort on border of 'Arava and Negev Hills near 'Arava junction. Rectangular in shape, it contained 2 rooms and was enclosed by a thick wall. Remains include several courses of thick stones with wood trunks between them. Sherds indicate that the fort was built in Iron Age and also used during Hellenistic Period.

ᴧ Meẓad Moḥila (Qasr el Mahalla) *141:004*

Remains of Nabatean guard post in Negev Hills in Makhtesh Ramon, off ancient route from Gaza to 'Avedat and Petra.

ᴧ Meẓad Naḥal Boqer (temporary name) *128:038*

Remains of hilltop Israelite fort in Negev Hills 3 km. NW of Sede Boqer. Square in shape, it was enclosed by a casemate wall. At foot of hill and extending to the opposite hill, are remains of a contemporary settlement.

ᴧ Meẓad Neqarot (Qasr es Siq) *151:999*

Remains of ancient fort in Negev Hills 20 km. SW of Mizpe Ramon off Nabatean Gaza-Petra road. Mound of stones and vaulted cistern.

ᴧ Meẓad Qarḥa (Kh. Qarhata) *178:270*

Ruins of fortress, apparently Crusader, in Galilee 1 km. N of Ma'alot. Near fortress are rock-cut tombs, wine presses and cisterns.

ᴧ Meẓad Qaẓra (Kh. Qaṣra) *158:996*

Remains of Nabatean guard post in Negev Hills 10 km. NW of Ẓofar. Built to guard ancient route from Ḥaluza via 'Avedat to Petra.

ᴧ Meẓad Rahav *180:276*

Remains of Crusader fort in Galilee near *moshav* Shetula.

Meẓad Raḥel (Qaṣr 'Ein Kharuf) *167:004*

Remains of ancient fort in 'Arava 7 km. SW of 'En Yahav. Sherds from Iron Age, Nabatean, Hellenistic, Roman and Byzantine Periods.

Meẓad Sayif *164:031*

Remains of Roman fort in Ẓin Desert 5 km. S of Ma'ale 'Aqrabbim.

Meẓad Seraya *163:210*

Remains of ancient fort in Samarian Hills 3 km. S of Umm el Faḥm.

Meẓad Sorer (Qaṣr es Sir; Kh. es Sir) *148:054*

Ruins of fort in Negev Hills 5 km. NW of Dimona. Remains of fortified rectangular building with towers and an internal courtyard. Alongside is a man-made vaulted pool with steps descending to floor level. Byzantine sherds have been found here.

Meẓad Tamar (Qaṣr el Juheiniyya) *173:048*

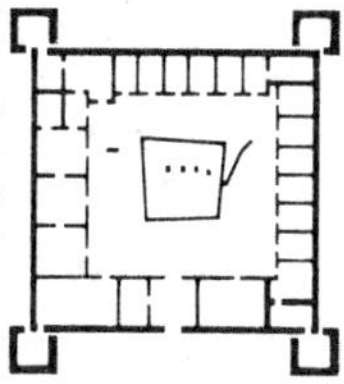

Remains of Roman fort in Negev Hills 20 km. E of Dimona. One of the forts in the *Limes Palestinae* border defences. Built in 3rd c. on site of Tamar, mentioned in Ezek. 47:19. Perhaps this was site of Nabatean city, Tamara. It is mentioned in the Onomasticon of Eusebius and appears on the Madaba map. The fort measures 36 by 38 m. with corner towers which were built at a later date. Its walls have been preserved to a height of 4 to 5 m. A central courtyard is surrounded by rooms abutting the fort walls and contains a pool. Outside, next to the W wall, is a second pool. E of the fort is a small ruin. In Naḥal Ẓafit, W of the fort is a dam, 25 m. long and 3 m. wide, which creates a reservoir with a capacity of 6,000 cub. m. N of dam are low burial mounds with uninscribed tombstones.

Meẓad Yarqe'am *154:038*

Remains of Byzantine fort in Negev Hills E of Makhtesh HaGadol alongside 'En Yarqe'am. Situated at junction of two routes: one descending to Mamshit along Naḥal Mamshit, and the other descending from Meẓad Yeroḥam crossing the Makhtesh HaGadol. A 1 m. high wall is all that remains of the fort which had 2 separate wings.

Meẓad Yeroḥam (Qaṣr Rikhma) *140:044*

Remains of fort among ruins of large ancient settlement in Negev Hills 2 km. W of Yeroḥam. Apparently a Nabatean, Roman and Byzantine way-station off ancient route from 'Avedat to Mamshit. Excavations uncovered town streets and remains of structures whose roofs were made of stone slabs. Other finds include pottery, candles, jar fragments, building remains, coins, 2 ostraca with Greek inscriptions inscribed in ink and finds from late 2nd c. and from 5th and 6th c. At S corner of fort are remains of a wall with towers 2.5 m. apart, and to the SE is a cemetery with stone slab tombs.

Meẓad Ẓafir *160:037*

Remains of Roman fort in Negev Hills 3 km. W of Ma'ale 'Aqrabbim.

Meẓad Zohar (Qaṣr ez Zuweira) *183:062*

Remains of rock cliff Roman-Byzantine way-station in Naḥal Zohar, SW of Dead Sea. Intended to secure ancient route from Be'er Sheva' via Dead Sea to Hills of Moab. Rock-cut cisterns for collecting and storing rain-water. S of the station is a rock-cut dwelling cave.

Meẓad Ẓurim *179:048*

Remains of hilltop Roman-Byzantine fort SW of Dead Sea 3 km. N of 'Arava junction. Built to protect ancient route from Be'er Sheva' via 'Arava to Elat.

★ **Meẓer** 154:205

Kibbutz in Samaria 7 km. SE of Pardes Ḥanna. *Meẓer* means boundary; named after adjacent Arab village of Meisar. Founded 1953. Area: 2,400 d. Pop.: 360. **Antiquities** Among remains discovered within kibbutz are remnants of Chalcolithic and Early Bronze Age agricultural settlement, large building and burial caves from Roman and Byzantine Periods and a recent mosque.

Meẓudat Gadin → Yeḥi'am

Meẓudat HaYehudim (Qaṣr el Yahud) 165:133

Ruins of antiquities alongside Moẓa Bridge off Jerusalem–Sha'ar HaGay road. N of bridge is a domed structure of dressed stone, apparently remains of a small Byzantine monastery. Alongside are remains of Crusader fortress wall, and S of bridge are remains of a Roman army camp.

Meẓudat Naḥal Sirpad 111:007

Fortress from time of kings of Judah in Negev Hills 20 km. NW of Miẓpe Ramon. Elliptical in shape with rooms around a square central courtyard; 1.5 m. high remains of walls. On hill slopes are remains of open cisterns.

Meẓudat Nimrod → Qal'at Nimrud

Meẓudat Pattish (Qal'at Futeis) 115:079

Remains of dominating Ottoman fortress in Negev 2 km. SE of Ofaqim. Named after ancient settlement in the area (Ḥurbat Pattish, *114:081*). There is a large cave beneath ruins of the fortress.

Meẓudat Yesha' (Meẓudat Koaḥ) 202:280

Tegart police fort in Galilee 2 km. NW of Koaḥ junction on Rosh Pinna–Metulla road. Name based on that of abandoned village, Nabi Yusha', where, according to Arab tradition, Joshua, son of Nun, is buried. At end of British Mandate, the fort, which dominates the Ḥula Valley, was turned over to the Arabs. Three attempts by the Israel Defence Forces to capture the fort cost 28 lives (*koaḥ* — 28 in gematria). A memorial was erected near fort. **Naḥal Qadesh** Near fort is a nature reserve of 1,500 d.

Meẓudat Yoav 120:117

Tegart police fort on Coastal Plain 2 km. E of Giv'ati junction, 3 km. S of kibbutz Negba. Its previous name was 'Iraq Suweidan, and was scene of fierce fighting during War of Independence: the attack on Negba, battle for the junction outpost *118:118*, relief of the besieged Negev, encirclement of Faluja pocket and the battle to take the fort itself. Named after Yiẓḥaq Dubnow whose undercover name in the Haganah was Yoav and who was commander of Negba; he fell in battle. **Ancient remains** Near fort are remains of Roman mosaic floor and rock-cut vaulted tomb.

Meẓuqe On

Nature reserve on Golan slopes SE of Kinneret. Area: 3,700 d. Has highest cliff on Golan Heights and variety of plants.

Meẓuqe Ramim 202:290

Cliff on Mt. Ramim in Galilee W of Qiryat Shemona. Part of nature reserve of 250 d.

● **Midrakh 'Oz** 165:222

Moshav in Yizre'el Valley 4 km. NW of Megiddo junction. Name from

Song of Deborah: "*March* on, my soul, with *might*!" (Judg. 5:21). Founded 1952. Area: 2,200 d. Pop.: 500.

■ **Midreshet Ben-Gurion** *129:029*

Educational and research centre in Negev Hills 3 km. S of Sede Boqer. Founded 1964 through initiative of David Ben-Gurion. Regional school, field school, desert research institute and Ben-Gurion's library. Memorial to David and Paula Ben-Gurion, who are buried here.

■ **Midreshet Ruppin** *142:194*

Seminary in Sharon 3 km. N of Sharon junction. Named after Arthur Ruppin (1876-1943), head of Palestine Office and director of Zionist Executive Colonization Department from 1921. Founded 1949. Area: 700 d. Pop.: 600 students and staff. Offers courses in agriculture, administration and industry. Biological institute with collection of tropical butterflies.

Midreshet Sede Boqer → Midreshet Ben-Gurion

o **(El) Midya** *150:149*

Arab village (pop.: 200) 12 km. E of Lod. Believed to be site of Modi'in, birthplace of the Maccabees, whose name has been preserved in village name. The tel has a structure from Ottoman Period, extensive network of tunnels and a sheikh's tomb. Sherds indicate occupation in Early Bronze Age, Iron Age, Persian, Roman, Byzantine, Middle Ages and Ottoman Periods.

Mifraẓ Elat (Gulf of Elat)

The NE gulf of the Red Sea. Named after Elat which is located at its N end. On its W shore is Sinai Peninsula; on the E shore most of the area is in Saudi Arabia and a small part (region of 'Àqaba) in Kingdom of Jordan. At its S end are the Straits of Tiran with the 2 islands that form the strait: Tiran and Senappir. Length: 175 km.; maximum width: 14 km. Serves as important transport artery between Israel and the Far East.

◆ **Migda** *115:085*

Farm in Negev 4 km. N of Ofaqim. Founded 1957.

Migdal *197:249*

Agricultural settlement W of Lake Kinneret at S corner of Biq'at Ginnesar. Same name as ancient city located here, and whose name had been preserved in the Arab name of Majdal. In 1909 it was established as a farm on land originally purchased by a German Catholic order who had attempted to settle in Biq'at Ginnesar, but was abandoned because of the prevalence of malaria. In 1920 private farms were set up, with mainly citrus and banana groves. In 1921 a work camp was located at Migdal for workers on the Tiberias–Rosh Pinna road. Here the Joseph Trumpeldor Labour Battalion was established. Migdal now has an area of 3,700 d. and population of 730 (approx. 200 families). **Ancient Migdal** Large city during Second Temple Period. Also known as: Magdala, Magdala Nunaya (*nun* means fish in Aramaic), Magdala Tarikheai (in Greek: Magdala of the fish salters), and Magdala Ẓaba'aya (Aramaic: Magdala of the dyers). Birthplace of Mary Magdalene, a "loose" woman who became a disciple of Jesus and has been sanctified in Christian tradition. During the Jewish Revolt against Rome a large battle was fought in the area. However, after destruction of Second Temple Jewish Migdal continued to exist. Excavations uncovered parts of paved roads, remains of a villa with swimming pool, public building, water system and a structure thought to be a 1st c. synagogue.

Migdal Afeq *146:165*

Remains of ancient settlement among ruins of abandoned village E of Petaḥ Tiqwa, 2 km. S of Rosh Ha'Ayin. Named after Biblical city of Aphek that has been identified with adjacent Tel Afeq (Antipatris). At the close of Second Temple Period, during Jewish Revolt against Rome, Jewish rebels at Afeq attempted to delay Roman forces ascending from Caesarea to Jerusalem. Remains of Byzantine church and Crusader fortress of Mirabel, which was built on ruins of an older fortress. Mirabel was destroyed by Saladin. On an adjacent hill is a rock-cut, Jewish-type tomb from Second Temple Period. Sherds indicate occupation in Hasmonean Period till Middle Ages. In 19th c. an Arab village developed here called Majdal eṣ Ṣadiq after Sheikh Ṣadiq el Jam'ini who controlled the area. This is source of the Hebrew name Migdal Ẓedeq. Its other name, Majdal Yaba, may have resulted from the proximity to Jaffa and to differentiate this site from others of similar name. The village was abandoned during War of Independence.

Migdal Ha'Emeq *172:231*

Urban settlement on edge of Yizre'el Valley 6 km. SW of Nazareth. Named after abandoned village, Mujeidil. Started as a *moshav* in 1953 by immigrants from China. Area: 4,000 d. Pop.: 14,000.

Migdal 'Oz *163:116*

Kibbutz in Judean Hills 3 km. SE of 'Eẓyon Bloc. In place of Migdal 'Eder, a settlement founded in 1927 and destroyed in Riots of 1929. Migdal 'Oz was founded in 1977 by a Bene 'Aqiva group. Area: 5,000 d.

Migdal Tefen *176:265*

Industrial centre in Tefen region in Upper Galilee 4 km. S of Ma'alot-Tarshiḥa. Established 1980.

Mi'ilya *174:269*

Arab village in Galilee 3 km. NW of Ma'alot. Pop.: 1,700, mostly Christians. **Crusader fortress** Within village are ruins of 12th c. Crusader fortress Castellum Regis or Chastiau dou Rei (king's castle). First occupied by Crusader king and later by one noble family after another. Purchased in 1220 by Teutonic knights, and in 1265 by Mamluk Sultan Baybars.

Mikhmannim *181:257*

Settlement under construction in Lower Galilee on Mt. Kammon 3 km. SW of Shezor.

Mikhmoret *138:201*

Moshav near mouth of Naḥal Alexander 9 km. N of Netanya. Founded 1945 by demobilized soldiers from British army, and initially based on fishing. Over the years *moshav* developed holiday resort industry. Area: 600 d. Pop.: 1,100. To S is Naḥal Alexander nature reserve. Alongside *moshav* is the nautical school, Mevo'ot Yam. **Minat Abu Zabura** Remains of old port, called Minat Abu Zabura in Arabic. Sherds and other remains indicate occupation from Late Bronze Age to Roman-Byzantine Period. During much of its history it was a fishing village.

Minheret 'Eilabun → National Water Carrier

Minheret Menashe → National Water Carrier

Minheret Shimeron → National Water Carrier

■ Miqwe Yisra'el 129:159

Agricultural school SE of Tel Aviv off Ḥolon junction–HaShiv'a junction road. First modern Jewish agricultural settlement, it was founded in 1870 at the initiative of Charles Netter, local representative of Alliance Israelite Universelle. Name taken from Jer. 14:8; 17:13. Plaked important role in Palestine's agricultural development. Pop.: 1,000 students and staff. Area: 3,300 d. Experimental station, botanical garden, and wine cellar — the first established in the country. Charles Netter is buried in grounds. Memorial room to graduates who fell in Israel's wars.

(El) Mird → Hureqanya

○ Mirka 172:200

Arab village (pop.: 150) in Samarian Hills 9 km. SW of Jenin.

★ Misgav 'Am 201:294

Kibbutz 4 km. NW of Qiryat Shemona, near Lebanese border. Founded 1945 by Palmaḥ members. During War of Independence it was a key outpost on Lebanese border. In the spring of 1980 it sustained an Arab terrorist attack in which two people were killed. Area: 6,500 d. Pop.: several hundred. **Naḥal Misgav** NE of kibbutz is a nature reserve (1,300 d.), with spring, 'En Misgav, and Ḥurbat Noḥa containing Bronze Age remains.

● Misgav Dov 125:136

Moshav 3 km. W of Gedera, 1 km. SE of Bene Darom junction. Named after Dov Gruner, Irgun member, caught and hanged by British in 1947. Area: 2,200 d. Pop.: 220.

Mishlat Ma'aḥaz 131:102

Battle site in War of Independence in S Judean Foothills, 11 km. S of Qiryat Gat. Outpost on hill (Kh. el Maqhaz) controls route from Judean Foothills to Negev. Bitterly contested by Israeli and Egyptian armies and changed hands several times. **Ancient remains** Recently discovered remains of large settlement from Early Bronze Age, including utensils imported from Egypt.

Mishlav 146:190

Rural centre in Sharon. Shared by following settlements: Be'erotayim, Burgeta, Ḥanni'el, Nizzane 'Oz, Tenuvot, Yanov, Ge'ullim and Ẓur Moshe.

● Mishmar Ayyalon 145:142

Moshav in Judean Foothills 8 km. SW of Ramla, overlooking Ayyalon Valley, hence its name. Founded 1949 on land of abandoned village of Qurayyat el Qubab. Pop.: 240, According to various sources believed to be site of Medieval Qiryat Qubab. Not yet excavated.

★ Mishmar Dawid 140:136

Kibbutz in Judean Foothills 2 km. NW of Naḥshon junction. Named after Col. David Marcus (Mickey Stone), Jewish officer in US army who volunteered for service in the Israel Defence Forces during War of Independence and was appointed commander of Jerusalem front. He was killed accidentally near Abu Ghosh. Founded 1949. Area: 6,700 d. Pop.: 200. **Memorial of Heroism** Near kibbutz is memorial commemorating construction of road to Jerusalem during War of Independence.

★ **Mishmar Ha'Emeq** *165:224*

Kibbutz in Yizre'el Valley 6 km. NW of Megiddo junction. Founded 1926 by Polish HaShomer HaZa'ir group. Educational centre of HaShomer HaZa'ir movement in Israel. In pre-State years it served as Palmaḥ base and Haganah training courses were held in the woods nearby. During War of Independence it was attacked by Kaukji's Liberation Army — an attack which, although repulsed, incurred heavy losses. Area: 11,700 d. Pop.: 870. **Ancient remains** Within kibbutz are remains of building and olive press from Roman-Byzantine Period and a Roman milestone. Nearby a cemetery from Hellenistic Period was discovered. **Ghabiyya, el Ghaba** Below village of el Ghaba, *163:223*, Chalcolithic and Early Bronze flint implements and numerous sherds were found. Nearby, alongside stream bed, are remains of Middle Bronze Age settlement.

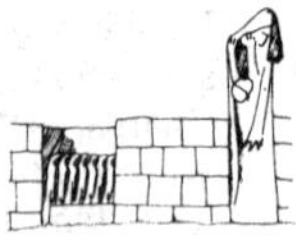

★ **Mishmar HaNegev** *123:085*

Kibbutz at N approach to Negev 4 km. N of HaNasi junction. Founded 1946 together with 10 other settlements by member of No'ar Borochov and HaMaḥanot Ha'Olim. Area: 20,000 d. Pop.: 620. Regional museum.

★ **Mishmar HaSharon** *141:195*

Kibbutz in 'Emeq Ḥefer 6 km. N of Sharon junction. Founded 1933 by Mishmar and Gordonia "B" groups from Poland who initially resided at Yavne'el (1925) and later in Herzliyya. Area: 3,150 d. Pop.: 450.

Mishmar HaShelosha → Yavne'el

● **Mishmar HaShiv'a** *133:157*

Moshav on Coastal Plain near HaShiv'a junction. Named after the 7 (*hashiv'a*) Haganah supernumerary policemen killed at entrance to Yazur village (today Azor) during War of Independence. Founded 1949 by demobilized soldiers. Area: 1,600 d. Pop.: 470. Memorial to *moshav* members who fell in Israel's wars. SW of *moshav* alongside HaShiv'a junction are remains of Turkish fortress. Opposite *moshav* entrance are ruins of JNF House which existed during War of Independence. Next to it is a memorial to soldiers who died defending this post.

● **Mishmar HaYarden** *206:268*

Moshav in Galilee 3 km. W of Benot Ya'aqov Bridge. Named after veteran farming village (*moshava*) located on adjacent banks of Jordan River (which is today within kibbutz Gadot). The village was founded in 1890 in place of the farm Shoshanat HaYarden, established 1884 and later abandoned. During War of Independence it was captured by Syrians, many of defenders were killed and others taken prisoner. In terms of the Armistice Agreement it was returned to Israel and in 1949 a *moshav* was established, 2 km. SW of the original village. Area: 3,000 d. Pop.: 230.

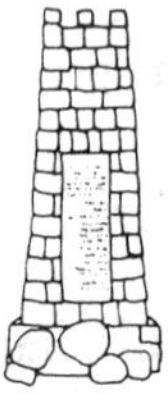

★ **Mishmarot** *148:210*

Kibbutz in N Sharon 2 km. N of Pardes Ḥanna. Founded 1933. During pre-State years served as base for Haganah field companies and Palmaḥ, transit camp for "illegal" immigrants and a weapons manufacturing workshop. Area: 3,800 d. Pop.: 250.

● **Mishmeret** *142:181*

Moshav in Sharon 5 km. N of Kefar Sava. Founded 1946. Area: 2,500 d. Pop.: 330.

Mishor Adummim *182:134*

Industrial complex, work camp and a future settlement on border of

Judean Desert 13 km. E of Jerusalem on road to Jericho. Established 1975. Ruins of a Byzantine church nearby. Pop.: several hundred.

Misilya *177:199*

Arab village in Samarian Hills 9 km. S of Jenin.

Mitḥam Lawiyya *214:250*

Early Bronze Age enclosure on Golan Heights 2 km. SE of *moshav* Ramot. Three walls are still extant to 5 m. in height and area covers more than 1 km. in length and 300 m. in width. At E corner of enclosure are remains of small Mamluk and Ottoman settlement.

Mitḥam esh Sha'baniyya *226:258*

Ancient enclosure on Golan Heights 8 km. N of Ramat Magshimim. Stone wall encompasses an area 300 m. long and more than 100 m. wide. Along sides of the wall are small elliptical rooms. Within enclosure are 15 dolmens and around it a large dolmen field which extends to the dolmen fields of Rujm el Hiri and Rekhes HaDolmanim. Early Bronze Age sherds and Upper Paleolithic and Mesolithic flint implements have been found in and around the enclosure.

Mitḥam Yiẓḥaqi (temporary name) * *219:265*

Enclosure of ancient settlement on Golan Heights 5 km. SE of Qaẓrin. Remains of walls and cube-like structure which possibly served as living quarters. Sherds indicate occupation from Early Bronze Age. Discovered in 1968 by Yiẓḥaqi Gal. View of Lake Kinneret.

Mivḥor *128:114*

Seed farm in Lakhish region 1 km. N of Qiryat Gat. Founded 1955. Area: 3,500 d. Produces seeds for vegetables, summer and winter grain crops, and grass for pasture.

Mivsam **(Na'aran)** → **Niran**

Mivtaḥim *093:072*

Moshav in Negev 5 km. SW of Magen junction. Name taken from Biblical passage "My people will abide in a peaceful habitation, in *secure* dwellings..." (Isa. 32:18). Founded as a kibbutz in 1947. Attacked in War of Independence and evacuated. *Moshav* founded in 1950. Area: 3,800 d. Pop.: 440. Memorial to soldiers of 128th regiment killed in War of Independence. **Kh. Rabiya** Many scattered architectural fragments and sherds indicating occupation from Byzantine Period until Middle Ages.

Miẓpa *197:243*

Moshav 3 km. W of Tiberias, off Tiberias-Nazareth road. Overlooking (*miẓpa*) Lake Kinneret, hence its name. Founded 1908 by Second Aliyah pioneers from Russia. Area: 8,000 d. Pop.: 40.

Miẓpe Bol'an * *223:300*

Observation point on top of Mt. Ḥermon overlooking Golan Heights. Height 1,800 m. Circular structures were found in area.

Miẓpe 'En Gedi * *186:097*

Observation point in Judean Desert on cliff above 'En Gedi, overlooking Dead Sea and oases along its shores.

Miẓpe Gadot * *210:269*

Observation point on Golan Heights 1 km. NE of Benot Ya'aqov Bridge, opposite kibbutz Gadot. There was a Syrian military post here which was captured in Six-Day War. Memorial.

Miẓpe Golani * — *212:291*

Memorial on Golan Heights 3 km. N of Kefar Szold. In past, there was a fortified Syrian post here called Tell Fakhr which was taken in Six-Day War by Golani Brigade after a bitter battle. Memorial to 23 soldiers of Baraq regiment and Golani scouts killed in the battle. View of Ḥula Valley.

Miẓpe HaOn * — *211:237*

Observation point on Golan Heights on cliff SE of Lake Kinneret. In past it was a Syrian fortified post called ʻAmrat ʻAz ed Din (house of ʻAz ed Din). Included in Meẓuqe HaOn nature reserve. View over Lake Kinneret and settlements on its SE shore.

Miẓpe HaShelosha — *193:211*

Look-out tower 4 km. W of Bet She'an, near kibbutz Nir Dawid. Built during Disturbances of 1936-1939 to protect local field workers. Named after 3 watchmen killed by Arabs in 1939 while on their way to the tower.

Miẓpe Hod * — *184:261*

Observation point on border of Upper and Lower Galilee 5 km. NW of Ḥananya junction, near er Rama village. View of Lake Kinneret and hills of Lower Galilee.

Miẓpe Kinneret * — *204:236*

Observation point SW of Lake Kinneret above Kinneret village. View of the lake, Jordan Valley and hills of Gilʻad and Golan.

Miẓpe Pe'er * — *201:286*

Observation point in Galilee 3 km. S of Qiryat Shemona. View of Mt. Ḥermon, Golan Heights, Ḥula Valley and hills of Upper Galilee.

Miẓpe Pundaq * — *160:270*

Observation point on Galilee coast near Pundaq Rosh HaNiqra. View of Galilee and coast up to Haifa Bay and Mt. Karmel.

Miẓpe Ramon ▲ — *131:002*

Development town in Negev Hills on NW edge of Makhtesh Ramon. Overlooks Makhtesh Ramon, hence its name. Started as work camp for labourers at Makhtesh Ramon industries in 1954. Developed when the road, which runs alongside the camp, to Elat was paved. When the alternative ʻArava road to Elat was opened, the Makhtesh industries closed down. Following the Camp David Agreement much of the Negev, particularly around Miẓpe Ramon, is being developed anew. Area: 12,000 d. Pop.: 2,600. Three km. NW of town, a modern observatory was established in 1971. **Prehistoric and other remains** SW of town, *130:001*, on edge of the Makhtesh is a prehistoric site where Chalcolithic flint implements were found. Another prehistoric site was discovered on a track leading down to Makhtesh. Here Paleolithic flint implements were found. On ridge above the crater are remains of a Nabatean settlement.

Miẓpe Ramta * — *214:299*

Observation point on Ketef Si'on (shoulder) on Mt. Ḥermon. Height: 1,194 m. above sea level. View of Ḥula Valley and S Lebanon.

Miẓpe Sayyarim → Biqʻat Sayyarim

★ **Miẓpe Shalem** * — *188:108*

Kibbutz in Judean Desert 13 km. N of ʻEn Gedi between mouths of Naḥal Ḥaẓeẓon and Naḥal Darga. Named after Dr. Nathan Shalem, a Judean Desert scholar. Founded as *naḥal* outpost in 1970. Received civilian status in 1976. Area: 200 d. First located at summit of cliff, *187:111*; moved to present site in 1980. W of kibbutz is **Murabba'at caves** and other caves used as dwellings in Bar Kokhba Period. Cemetery and remains of cultic altars. **Naḥal Darga** N of kibbutz is Naḥal Darga, a popular site for hikers. Nearby is **'Enot Qane** nature reserve. At former site of kibbutz, on cliff top is a **field school** for cliff climbing operated by kibbutz 'En Gedi.

Mizpe Sheloshet HaYammim * *184:175*

Observation point in Samarian Hills 10 km. SE of Shekhem near Beit Furik. Height: 866 m. above sea level. View of the Dead Sea, Mediterranean Sea and Lake Kinneret.

Mizpe Shivta (Kh. el Musheirifa) *112:036*

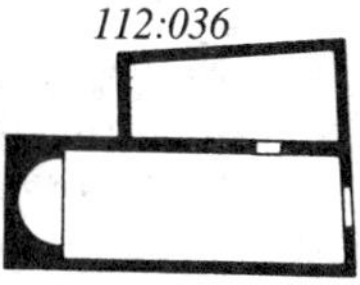

Remains of ancient fort in Negev off Mash'abbim junction–Nizzana road near Mishlat Shivta. Similar in shape to Iron Age forts. Sherds indicate later occupation in Roman Period. Flint implements were found in area.

Mizpe Ya'ar Balfour * *176:221*

Observation point in Galilee 4 km. SW of Nazareth. View of Yizre'el Valley hills of Lower Galilee and Karmel.

Mizpe Yammim * *193:261*

Mount and observation point on border of Upper and Lower Galilee near *moshav* Amirim. View of Mediterranean in W and Lake Kinneret in E, hence its name (*yammim* = seas). Remains of Iron Age fort.

Mizpe Yeriḥo *187:135*

Civilian outpost off Jerusalem–Jericho road 3 km. E of Ma'ale Adummim. Established 1978.

★ **Mizra'** *177:228*

Kibbutz in Yizre'el Valley 4 km. N of 'Afula. Name same as that of local ancient settlement mentioned in Medieval maps. Founded 1923 by pioneers from Galicia. Until "Black Saturday" the Palmaḥ headquarters were located here. Area: 8,200 d. Pop.: 720.

Modi'im (Modi'in) *149:148*

Site of rock-cut tombs in Judean Foothills 10 km. E of Lod. Traditionally believed to be site of tombs of the Maccabees: Mattathias and his sons Eleazar, John, Jonathan and Judah. The 5th son, Simeon HaNasi, erected a tombstone for his father and brothers. Joseph b. Mattathias mentions this tombstone and it is also mentioned in the 4th c. letters of Eusebius. Arabs called the site Qubur el Yahud (graves of the Jews). During Hanukkah festival school children and youth movements meet here — a custom inaugurated in 1910 by pupils of Herzliyya high school in Tel Aviv. Members of Maccabee sport organization hold a torch-lighting ceremony at Modi'im every year on Hanukkah; the torch is relayed by runners to the home of Israel's president in Jerusalem. Two km. to E is a small Arab village, Midya; believed to be location of Modi'im birthplace of the Maccabees.

● **Moledet (Bene Berit)** *192:221*

Moshav shittufi in Galilee 5 km. N of Bet HaShitta. Named after Bene Berit order in USA; Moledet is name of the founder organization, immigrants from Germany. Founded 1937 as a "stockade and tower" settlement. Area: 10,000 d. Pop.: 510.

Montfort * *171:272*

Ruins of what was the most impressive Crusader fortress in the Galilee above Naḥal Keziv, 6 km. NW of Ma'alot. Built by Crusaders in middle of 12th c. Protected by steep cliffs on three sides and by a moat. Name means the strong hill. In 1229 it was sold by Frankish Crusaders to the German Teutonic Order of St. Mary, who changed its name to Starkenberg (strong hill). Destroyed by Saladin in 1187 and rebuilt by Hospitaller knights in 1229. Taken by Moslems again in 1271. Arabic name is Qal'at el Qurein (Qurein fortress) after Naḥal Qurein which is Arabic name for Naḥal Keziv. The fortress was mainly in Gothic style and included a single gate, knights' quarters, halls, chapel and an 18 m. high tower built of large dressed stones. At foot of fortress on slope towards Naḥal Keziv are remains of another Crusader structure — the main building of a farmstead. In the stream bed are remains of a dam from where water was taken to the fortress.

★ Morag *082:080*

Kibbutz in Gaza Strip 3 km. S of Khan Yunis. *Morag* means threshing sledge. Established 1972 as *naḥal* outpost; received civilian status 1978.

★ Moran *187:258*

Kibbutz in Galilee 2 km. SW of Ḥananya junction. Named after the shrub viburnum (*moran*) which grows in the surrounding woods. Founded 1977.

Mt. Addir *185:270*

Mountain in Galilee off the N road W of kibbutz Sasa. Height: 1,006 m. above sea level. Remains of Iron Age settlement on summit.

Mt. Aggas (Gebel Sumaq) *215:300*

Offshoot on Ḥermon shoulder, adjacent to Lebanese border. Remains of ancient border settlement (called the Lost City), including houses built of hard hewn limestone (3-4 courses). Each house had 3 rooms, cisterns, a courtyard and an installation probably used for squeezing juices from fruits. The Roman road from Banyas to Lebanon passed nearby.

Mt. Alexander (Ras Iskandar) *165:213*

Mountain E of 'Emeq 'Iron near Umm el Faḥm. Height: 518 m. Called Ras Iskandar in Arabic after Sheikh Iskander whose tomb is on summit of mountain. One theory holds that Iskander refers to Alexander Yannai, who conquered the area during his reign.

Mt. Avital (Tell Abu en Nida) *224:279*

Inactive volcano on Golan Heights 3 km. SW of Quneitra. Height: 1,204 m. The Hebrew name (father of the dew) is based on translation of Arabic name. On its summit is a Moslem shrine — tomb of Sheikh Abu en Nida. Included in Mt. Avital nature reserve.

Mt. Bental (Tell el Gharam) *223:281*

Inactive volcano on Golan Heights 3 km. W of Quneitra. Height: 1,171 m. above sea level. Included in Mt. Avital nature reserve.

Mt. Carmel → Mt. Karmel

Mt. 'Eval *(Deut. 11:29) 175:182*

Mountain N of Shekhem. Height: 940 m. above sea level. Known in Bible as the mountain of the curse as opposed to Mt. Gerizim, S of Shekhem, which is known as the mountain of the blessing. In fact, 19th c. travellers noted that while trees swathed Mt. Gerizim, Mt. 'Eval was rocky and barren. Also called Jebel 'Askar after the village of that name at foot of mountain. Ancient tombs from various periods of occupation of Shekhem were found at foot of mountain. (See also el Qal'a.)

Mt. Gerizim *(Deut. 11:29)* *175:178*

Mountain S of Shekhem. Height: 881 m. above sea level. Known in Bible as mountain of the blessing as opposed to Mt. ‘Eval, N of Shekhem, known as mountain of the curse. Called Jebel et Tur in Arabic, a version of the Aramaic *tura brikha* (mountain of the blessing). According to Samaritan belief this is the holy Mt. Moriah, to which Samaritans make pilgrimage and sacrifice the paschal lamb. They called the mountain Beth-el, the house of God, the place to which God directed Abraham after he left Ur of the Chaldees. During days of Alexander the Great, the Samaritans built their temple on this mountain, and it served as their spiritual and cult centre. During Hellenistic Period a pagan shrine in honour of Zeus was created here; remains were discovered on N offshoot of mountain, known in Arabic as Tell er Ras. Steps led from the bottom of the mountain up to the shrine; their remains can still be seen today near the police fort. In 125 BCE the Samaritan temple was destroyed by John Hyrcanus, the Hasmonean. In Byzantine Period an octagonal Christian church was built here; it was fortified with a wall during the Samaritan revolt in 6th c. and destroyed in 8th c. Near the church ruins is a mosque-cum-tomb called Sheikh Ghanam. Named after Ghanam Ibn ‘Ali, senior minister of Saladin. Some believe this to be tomb of Ḥamor, father of Shekhem. The Samaritans continue their cultic practices on Mt. Gerizim to this very day. The paschal sacrifice is now performed in a fenced in field with a long trench in the middle which serves as an altar; 2 additional trenches serve as ovens. Nearby is the Samaritan synagogue and a new Samaritan neighbourhood.

Mt. Giyyora *157:128*

Mountain W of Jerusalem above Naḥal Soreq, near *moshav* Bar Giyyora. Height: 725 m. above sea level. Named after Simeon Bar Giyyora, one of leaders of Jewish Revolt against Rome. Called Jebel Sheikh Marzuq in Arabic after the sheikh whose tomb is on the mountain. Included in Naḥal Soreq nature reserve.

Mt. Ḥermon * *(Deut. 3:8)* *226:302*

The highest mountain in the country. In N, on border of Israel, Lebanon and Syria. Mentioned in Bible as northernmost border of conquests of Moses and Joshua. Called Jebel esh Sheikh (mountain of the old one) because its snowcapped summit is reminiscent of an old man's pate. Its pinnacle, outside Israel's control, is 2,814 m. above sea level. Since the Six-Day War the W and S offshoots have been under Israel's control including Ketef Ḥermon, Har Betarim, Har Kaḥal and Mt. Dov. The highest of the offshoots is 2,224 m. above sea level. At outbreak of Yom Kippur War a number of Israeli army outposts on Mt. Ḥermon were taken by the Syrian army, but they were later recaptured along with nearby Syrian outposts after bitter fighting. Most of Mt. Ḥermon has been declared a nature reserve. Recreation and winter sport facilities, including a ski slope, run by members of Newe Ativ, at foot of the mountain.

Mt. Ḥermonit *224:287*

Mountain in Golan off Mas‘ada–Quneitra road. Height: 1,211 m. above sea level. Called Tell esh Sheikha (mountain of the old woman). Supposedly the mate of Mt. Ḥermon, called Jebel esh Sheikh in Arabic (mountain of the old man). At foot of the mountain heavy battles were fought during Yom Kippur War.

Mt. Herzl → Jerusalem

Mt. Karmel * *(I Kings 18:19, 20)*

A range of mountains between Yizre‘el Valley in NE and Coastal Plain in W. Length: 25 km. Its summit is 546 m. above sea level. Scattered over the range are many settlements, Jewish, Druze and Arab, ancient sites and prehistoric caves. Holy place for Jews, Christians, and Druze. It is largely covered with woods and a large portion is a nature reserve.

Mt. Kena'an *198:266*

Mountain near Safed in Upper Galilee. Height: 936 m. above sea level.

Mt. Meron *190:267*

Range of mountains in Upper Galilee 8 km. NW of Safed. Its summit is 1,208 m. above sea level — the highest peak in Israel until the Six-Day War. Called Jarmaq in Arabic. S of summit are remains of Jewish settlement called Zarmiq (distortion of Arabic name) founded in 1837 by Israel Bak from Safed. It was later destroyed. Part of the mountain is a nature reserve. On slope is a field school, and below Mt. Meron, to the E, is the tomb of Talmudic sage, Rabbi Simeon b. Yoḥai where every year the *hillula* (Lag Ba'Omer festivity) is held.

Mt. of Olives → Jerusalem

Mt. Ora *164:129*

Mountain in W Jerusalem above the 'En Kerem Hadassah Medical Centre. Height: 850 m. above sea level. At summit is a house of prayer which is a combined church, synagogue and mosque. Built during British Mandate by an English woman, Miss Cary, who wanted to establish a spiritual centre for the 3 faiths. Later it became a guest house and during War of Independence served as base for Arab gangs until captured by a company of Gadna commanders from Jerusalem serving in the Israel Defence Forces. Today it is an institute for girls called Ma'ale under the Ministry of Social Welfare. In 1950 *moshav* Ora was established at foot of the mountain, and since then it has been called Mt. Ora.

Mt. Scopus → Jerusalem

Mt. Sedom *186:056*

Mountain on W shore of Dead Sea, measuring 10 km. from N to S; width: 3 km; height: 234 m. below sea level. It consists of cap rock (marls, etc.) and salts easily penetrated by rainwater which seeps through the mountain, creating many stalactite and stalagmite caves, and in some parts vertical funnels. The most well known caves in the area are Me'arat Sedom (Me'arat Eshet Lot), Me'arat Col. Tuluq and Me'arat Arubotayim.

Mt. Tabor *(Josh. 19:22)* *187:233*

Dome shaped mountain in Galilee in heart of Yizre'el Valley where Deborah and Barak led the armies of Israel. Also the traditional site of the Transfiguration of Jesus. Height: 588 m. above sea level. Commands surrounding area and routes alongside it, and was therefore considered strategically important in ancient times. In various periods it was a battleground (Ramesses II, Israelites vs. Midianites, Deborah's wars, Alexander, son of Aristobulus II, and Gabinius and others). The mountain was occupied during First Temple Period (the city of Tabor was given to the Levites). A fort was built here during Second Temple Period, and even after the destruction of the Temple a Jewish community continued to exist here. During Byzantine and Crusader Periods several monasteries were built here but were destroyed during Arab conquest. In their place a large fort was built in 1213 which was destroyed in 1263 by the Mamluks. According to Christian tradition the Transfiguration of Jesus took place on the mountain. Jesus appeared miraculously to his disciples in the company of Moses and Elijah. Mt. Tabor is thus also known as the Mt. of the Transfiguration. Today a Franciscan church stands here, built in 1921 on ruins of a 4th c. basilica. A mosaic of the Transfiguration decorates the apse. Alongside the church are remains of Roman fortifications, wall fragments, a Crusader tower and a Franciscan monastery with Crusader gate. Nearby is the Greek Orthodox Church of Elias (Elijah). At summit is a nature reserve.

Mt. Zion → Jerusalem

Moẓa (Taḥtit) ● *(Josh. 18:26) 165:133*

Rural settlement 5 km. W of Jerusalem alongside Moẓa bridge on Jerusalem–Tel Aviv highway. Named after city in Benjamin tribal allotment. During Second Temple Period it was known for its willow branches. According to Josephus, Vespasian established a settlement for demobilized Roman soldiers called Qoloniya (*The Jewish War* 7, 6, 6). Jewish settlement in modern period began in 1860 when a hostel was established by Jerusalemites for Jewish pilgrims to Jerusalem. In 1894 a village (*moshava*) was set up based on farming and a tile factory. In the 1929 Riots it was attacked by neighbouring Arabs, seven Moẓa residents were murdered and much property destroyed, after which the village was temporarily abandoned. Today it has 40 resident families and is a sort of rural suburb of Jerusalem.

Moẓa 'Illit *164:133*

Rural residential quarter, 6 km. W of Jerusalem, off Jerusalem–Tel Aviv highway. Founded as agricultural settlement in 1933 at foot of Mt. Qastel. During War of Independence it was evacuated for a while because of fighting in the vicinity. Area: 200 d. Pop.: 540. **Arza** Convalescent home near Moẓa 'Illit, founded 1923 and named erroneously for the cedar (*erez*) tree which Herzl planted here in 1898. (Actually he planted a juniper and not a cedar tree.) It was cut down by Arabs during 1929 Riots; only a stump remains. Alongside it are cedar trees planted by presidents of Israel.

Mu'askar el 'Arub *163:114*

Refugee camp 12 km. SW of Bethlehem, 3 km. SE of Kefar 'Eẓyon. Pop.: 3,700. S of village are the abundant springs of 'Ein el 'Arub which supply water to 'Emeq HaBerakha and Gush 'Eẓyon. In past its waters were piped via aqueduct to Bethlehem and Jerusalem. A 5th c. inscription was found on the aqueduct prohibiting the sowing or growing of crops within 5 m. of the aqueduct. Nearby is an extensive tunnel cave, where coins from Bar Kokhba Period were discovered.

o **Mu'awiya** ✓ *159:215*

Arab village on border of Samarian Hills and Ramat Menashe 9 km. SW of Megiddo junction. Named after Sheikh Mu'awi, whose tomb is in village. Pop.: 1,000.

o **(El) Mu'azi** *091:092*

Village and refugee camp in Gaza Strip 3 km. E of Deir el Balaḥ. Pop.: 8,200.

o **(El) Mughayyir** (near Jenin) *186:203*

Arab village (pop.: 450) in Samarian Hills 8 km. SE of Jenin.

o **(El) Mughayyir** (near Ramallah) *183:158*

Arab village (pop.: 450) in Samarian Hills 7 km. NE of Ba'al Ḥaẓor.

Mukhayyam Fari'a *182:188*

Arab refugee camp in Samarian Hills 3 km. SW of Tubas. Pop.: 2,500.

Mukhayyam Qalandiya *171:141*

Arab refugee camp N of Jerusalem, near Jerusalem airport, 5 km. S of

Ramallah. Named after adjacent Arab village of Qalandiya. Pop.: 2,700.

o **Mukhmas** 176:142

Arab village (pop.: 850) on border of Judean Hills and Desert 10 km. NE of Jerusalem. Built on remains of ancient settlement and the ancient building stones have been re-used in village houses. Sherds indicate occupation in Iron Age, Roman and Byzantine Periods. **Michmash** Believed to be site of Biblical city of Michmash. During Israelite conquest it was included in Benjamin tribal allotment (Isa. 10:28). The Philistines camped at Michmash while Saul and his army camped at Geba, before one of the decisive battles between the two armies (I Sam. 13:5). Jonathan, son of Saul, and his men surprised the Philistines after having stealthily traversed the Michmash pass and attacked their camp (I Sam. 14). After Babylonian Exile many Benjaminites returned to Michmash (Ezek. 2:27). Jonathan the Hasmonean settled in Michmash after he defeated Bacchides (I Maccabees 9:73). During Roman Period Michmash was known for its superior wheat. Mentioned as a large village in Onomasticon of Eusebius. In WWI Turkish forces fortified themselves here until they retreated under pressure from the British.

(El) Muntar 220:251

Remains of tower, apparently Roman-Byzantine, on summit of hill Giv'at Natur on Golan Heights 14 km. NE of 'En Gev. Many tumuli and dolmen fields below hill.

o **(El) Muqeibila** 178:213

Arab village in Yizre'el Valley 6 km. N of Jenin. Named after Moslem shrine located in village. Founded over 160 years ago by villagers of Birqin. Pop.: 1,100, mostly Moslem, some Christians. Ancient well and other Roman-Byzantine remains.

o **(El) Musheirifa** 165:218

Arab village near Ḥadera-'Afula road 4.5 km. SW of Megiddo junction. Founded over 90 years ago by Umm el Faḥm villagers. Pop.: 1,200.

o **Muṣmuṣ** 164:216

Arab village in 'Emeq 'Iron 5 km. SW of Megiddo. Situated alongside a narrow pass through which the British attacked and captured Megiddo in WWI. Pop.: 1,500.

o **(El) Muwaraq** 147:104

Arab village (pop.: 150) in Judean Hills 13 km. W of Hebron.

Muẓẓve HaBerekh 198:192

Formerly a network of Jordanian fortifications on one of Jordan River fords, 5 km. S of Meḥola. The fortifications were given the nickname *berekh* (knee) by Israeli soldiers owing to the knee-shaped bends in road which passes through these military positions. Captured by the Israel Defence Forces in Six-Day War.

N

◆ **Na'ama** (Ḥula Valley) *206:287*

Farm 3 km. SE of Qiryat Shemona. Name originates from nearby Arab village, en Na'ima. Established 1940. Formerly served as temporary camp for kibbutz settlers in the area. Today it belongs to kibbutz Misgav 'Am.

★ **Na'an** *136:143*

Kibbutz in Judean Foothills 4 km. E of Reḥovot. Name originates from abandoned village of Ni'ana. Perhaps site of Biblical Naamah. Founded 1930; it was the first kibbutz set up by HaNo'ar Ha'Oved graduates. In pre-State years it was a Palmaḥ base and had a Haganah workshop for manufacturing weapons. Area: 7,800 d. Pop.: 1,200. **Ni'ana (Naamah)** SE of kibbutz are ruins of abandoned village, Ni'ana. Alongside is tel of ancient settlement, possibly site of Naamah, a city in tribal allotment of Judah (Josh. 15:41) and also known during Second Temple Period. A few capitals were found in the village; one bears a Greek inscription "God is one". Jewish symbols were found on other remains. Nearby are remnants of large cemetery from Hyksos Period (17th c. BCE).

∴ **Na'aran** (Golan Heights) *214:270*

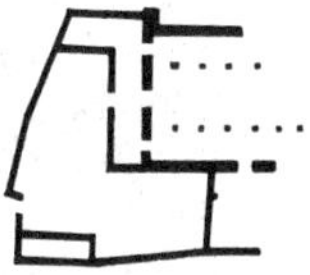

Abandoned village ruin, with settlement remains from Byzantine Period, on Golan Heights, 6 km. NE of Benot Ya'aqov Bridge. Houses roofed with basalt slabs have been preserved in the abandoned village. A Greek inscription was found on one of the stones. To the S are remains of an ancient track.

Na'aran (Jordan Valley) *(I Chron. 7:28)* *190:144*

Ancient site 5 km. NW of Jericho. Identified with Naarah or Naarath (Josh. 16:7), also called Naaran (I Chron. 7:28). During Second Temple Period and after destruction of the Temple it was a Jewish city and counterpart to pagan Jericho. Called Shelomi during Hasmonean Period after queen of Judea, Salome Alexandra (Shelomẓiyyon). Discovered by chance in 1918 after an artillery shell exploded here. Remains of 6th c. synagogue with mosaic floor, a section of which has been moved to Rockefeller Museum. However, a beautiful mosaic of two gazelles facing each other against a background of flowers is still in situ. From synagogue there is a good view of a Byzantine aqueduct crossing the wadi.

(En) Nabi Bulus → Beit Jimal

Nabi Daniyal *164:121*

Moslem holy site in Judean Hills 6 km. SW of Bethlehem. According to Arab tradition, it is the tomb of the prophet Daniel. The War of Independence battle, between the last convoy returning from 'Eẓyon Bloc and the Arabs barricading the road to Bethlehem, was named after this site.

Nabi Huda *211:291*

Tomb holy to Moslems and 'Alawites in Ḥula Valley 2 km. N of Kefar Szold. According to Arab tradition it is the tomb of Judah, son of Jacob. Alongside are domed buildings and terebinth trees. Remains of structures and sherds from Roman till Arab Period.

Nabi Lawin *167:192*

Settlement ruins in Samarian Hills 15 km. NW of Shekhem. Building remains indicate occupation from Iron Age until Ottoman Period. In centre of ruin is sheikh's tomb.

(En) Nabi Musa *191:133*

Holy Moslem site in Judean Desert 1 km. S of Jerusalem-Jericho road, 20 km. E of Jerusalem. Mosque with tomb inside. According to Moslem tradition, the tomb is that of Moses — Nabi Musa. Mosque built in 1269 by Mamluk Sultan Baybars; its compound is surrounded by a wall with a single gate facing W. The minaret was built in 1500. Till 1947, every spring Moslems celebrated the week-long Nabi Musa festival here, coinciding with the Jewish Passover as both commemorate the Exodus from Egypt. The festival opened with a procession of believers from the El Aqṣa mosque in Jerusalem. Nearby is a cemetery for the Bedouin tribes of the region. Also in the vicinity is tomb of Sitna 'Aiesha, the prophet Moḥammed's beloved concubine.

Nabi Rubin (Coastal Plain) *125:148*

Holy Moslem tomb near mouth of Naḥal Soreq, E of kibbutz Palmaḥim. Arab tradition believes this to be tomb of Reuben, son of Jacob. Site of popular Moslem festivities up till 1948.

Nabi Rubin (Samarian Hills) *186:199*

Holy Moslem tomb 10 km. S of Jenin, near village of Raba. Traditionally believed by some Arabs to be tomb of Reuven, son of Jacob.

Nabi Sabalan *182:268*

Holy Moslem and Druze mountain site in Galilee 6 km. E of Ma'alot-Tarshiḥa. Arab tradition claims this is tomb of Zebulun, son of Jacob.

o **Nabi Ṣaliḥ** (Samaria) *161:158*

Arab village (pop.: 200) 15 km. NW of Ramallah. Holy Moslem tomb. Alongside village is Tegart police fort.

o **(En) Nabi Ṣamwil** *167:137*

Supposed tomb of Prophet Samuel in Arab village 6 km. NW of Jerusalem. Located on high mountain (912 m. above sea level) off ancient road from Judean Foothills to Jerusalem. One theory claims this is site of Mizpeh, where Samuel judged and where he announced the kingship of Saul (I Sam. 7:6; 10:24, 25). An ancient Christian tradition mentioned in 5th c. Byzantine writings designates it as burial place of Samuel. In days of Justinian a large church was built above the tomb within an enclosure. The Crusaders believed this to be site of Shiloh and therefore called their new church here The Holy Church of Samuel from Shiloh. They named the mountain Montjoie (mountain of joy) because it was from this spot that pilgrims coming from the foothills had their first sight of Jerusalem. Jews also accepted the tradition that Samuel was buried here and therefore assumed that this was location of Ramah, where Samuel was buried according to the Biblical account. Jewish travellers from the Middle Ages onwards mention this site and relate how it was customary for Jews to visit it in pilgrimage. At the close of the 19th c. a group of Jews attempted to settle here but without success. In 1917 the ridge was a battleground between British and Turkish armies and only after the British gained control of the ridge, did the way to Jerusalem lie open to them. In War of Independence the site was an important Jordanian outpost from where their artillery bombarded Jewish Jerusalem. All attempts to take the position failed until its capture in Six-Day War by the Har'el armoured brigade. **Archaeological site** Within village is a building with a turret housing the tomb attributed to Samuel; the building is used as a mosque. Underneath are remains of a Crusader church. Encompassing the village are remains of a wall and other Iron Age and Second Temple Period remains. To the S are remnants of a Paleolithic settlement and, on the mountainous slopes, a large Neolithic settlement.

Nabi Shu'eib *193:245*

Druze holy site in Galilee 7 km. NW of Tiberias, at foot of Qarne Ḥittim. Druze believe this to be tomb of their prophet Shu'eib (Jethro — father-in-law of Moses). The shrine is decorated with colourful carpets. An annual festival is held here in the spring; it is a spontaneous celebration, not a religious ritual. Campfires are lit and races are held.

Nabi Ya'furi *222:294*

Druze holy site on Golan Heights N of Birkat Ram. According to tradition it is tomb of Druze holy man — Ya'furi. An annual religious ceremony of release from vows is held here in summer.

Nabi Yaqin *165:101*

Holy Moslem tomb on border of Judean Desert 5 km. SE of Hebron alongside Bani Na'im village. Local tradition claims this is the spot from where Abraham viewed the destruction of Sodom and Gomorrah. Remains of a 10th c. structure, apparently built over burial cave. Sherds from Byzantine Period and Middle Ages.

Nablus → Shekhem

● **Naḥala** *130:118*

Moshav in Lakhish region 5 km. N of Qiryat Gat. Founded 1953. Area: 1,300 d. Pop.: 400.

● **Nahalal** *(Josh. 19:15)* *169:233*

Moshav in Yizre'el Valley 7 km. SE of Qiryat Tiv'on; Moshe Dayan grew up here. Named after Biblical city in Zebulun tribal allotment. Called Mahalol in Byzantine Period, a name that was retained in that of adjacent Arab village, Ma'lul. Founded 1921, it was the first *moshav* in the country. Pop.: 1,200. Area: 8,700 d. Seminary for school and kindergarten teachers, and a girls' agricultural training farm.

Naḥal Alexander

Stream whose source is in Samarian Hills 10 km. SE of Tulkarm; enters Mediterranean Sea S of Mikhmoret. Named after Hasmonean Alexander Yannai, who conquered the Sharon area and annexed it to his kingdom. Called Wadi el Ḥawarith in Arabic (Arabic name for 'Emeq Ḥefer). Last stretch of the stream has water all year round; included within nature reserve of 700 d.

* **Naḥal 'Ammud**

Perennial stream in Galilee. Source in Ramat Dalton *194:269*, flows S; mouth in Lake Kinneret, N of kibbutz Ginnosar. Entire length flows through nature reserve. Name derives from tall rock pillar (*'ammud*) standing in its bed. Two prehistoric caves, Me'arat Amira and Me'arat Gulgolet, were discovered in stream bed.

Naḥal 'Amram

Small seasonal watercourse in Elat Hills 10 km. N of Elat. Banks of the stream are full of caves in which copper was mined during Roman and Byzantine Periods. In stream bed are many remains and sherds from Iron Age, Roman and Byzantine Periods and much evidence in the area of copper mining.

Naḥala'ot — *163:226*

Orchard in Yizre'el Valley 4 km. SE of Yoqne'am junction. Established 1954. The owners of the orchard do not live on the farm and it is cultivated by a company.

Naḥal 'Arugot

Seasonal watercourse in Judean Desert. Source is 10 km. S of Bethlehem *169:115* and flows SE to Dead Sea, entering it N of 'En Gedi. An ancient route from Bethlehem to 'En Gedi passed through its bed. On N bank of stream, 3 km. NW of 'En Gedi *184:097*, are ruins of ancient settlement: square and rectangular Roman–Byzantine structures built of undressed stones.

Naḥalat Yehuda — *132:153*

Urban settlement on Coastal Plain 2 km. N of Rishon LeZiyyon. Named after Judah Leib Pinsker (1821-1891), one of leaders of Ḥoveve Ziyyon. Established as a farming village (*moshava*) in 1914. Area: 4,200 d. Pop.: 2,400.

Naḥal Avnon — *146:044*

Stream in Negev Hills E of Yeroḥam. Alongside are ruins of Middle Bronze Age settlement. Remains of some 50 structures scattered over 3 hills.

Naḥal Ayyalon

Seasonal watercourse, source in Judean Hills (S of Ramallah), traverses Judean Foothills in Ayyalon Valley and joins Yarqon River N of Tel Aviv. Called Muṣrara in Arabic (heaps of stones).

Naḥal 'Azmon — *178:254*

Naḥal outpost in Galilee on Giv'at Qered, 4 km. S of Karmi'el. Established 1979.

Naḥal Be'er Sheva'

Seasonal watercourse in S Judean Hills, traverses N Negev from E to W and joins Naḥal Besor SW of Ẓe'elim. Passes through Be'er Sheva', hence its name. Arabic name is Wadi es Saba'.

Naḥal Bet Ha'Emeq

Spring in Galilee, flows from foot of Mt. Shezor and empties into Mediterranean Sea near Shave Ẓiyyon. Section between Jatt and Naḥal Kishor is part of nature reserve (2,500 d.) with large concentration of Jerusalem pine trees and irises.

Naḥal Beẓet (Wadi Karkara)

Seasonal watercourse in Galilee with source near Adamit *171:275*. Flows W and enters Mediterranean S of Rosh HaNiqra. Part of stream is within Naḥal Beẓet nature reserve. Along its bed are remains of an ancient aqueduct made up of an open canal and clay pipes.

Naḥal Boqeq

Seasonal watercourse with source in Negev Hills SE of 'Arad. Flows from W to E and empties into Dead Sea near Meẓad Boqeq.

Naḥal Daliyya

Seasonal watercourse with source in Ramat Menashe near kibbutz

Daliyya. Flows W and empties into Mediterranean S of Dor coast. There are a number of springs in the stream bed. Along its length are remains of ancient aqueducts and ruins of flour mills. Close to its mouth the stream has water all year round. Its Arabic name is Wadi Dufaila or Nahr et Tantura.

Naḥal Daliyyot *

Stream in Golan Heights with source SW of Mt. Peres *227:259*; it descends in a deep bed SW towards Lake Kinneret. Many waterfalls including the highest in the country, 55 m. high, *220:258*. Before emptying into Kinneret, it joins Naḥal Yehuda in Biq'at Bet Ẓayda (Buteiḥa).

Naḥal Dan

Perennial stream, and one of the 3 major sources of Jordan River. Source at Tel Dan *211:295*; joins Naḥal Ḥermon (Naḥal Banyas) near Sede Neḥemya. Its waters were a point of contention between Syria and Israel until Six-Day War.

Naḥal Darga

Seasonal watercourse in Judean Desert with source in SE Jerusalem. Flows SE and empties into Dead Sea 3 km. from Miẓpe Shalem. The cliff caves located above last section of the stream contained scrolls, documents, pottery, wood and metal implements and other finds from period of Bar Kokhba revolt.

Naḥal Dawid

Seasonal watercourse in Judean Desert with source 8 km. NE of kibbutz 'En Gedi. It empties into Dead Sea 2 km. NE of kibbutz. At ascent of stream bed a burial cave was discovered which seems to have been used by residents of 'En Gedi during Hasmonean epoch. At its descent, about 1 km. from shore, is 'En Dawid, a gushing spring and small waterfall; part of 'En Gedi nature reserve.

Naḥal Dishon

Seasonal watercourse in Galilee with source at foot of Mt. Meron. From here the stream bed turns NE and then SE. Emerges in Ḥula Valley and empties into Kinneret near Ḥulata. Its last section has water all year round. Middle section is included in Naḥal Dishon nature reserve.

Naḥal El 'Al

Nature reserve on Golan Heights stretching from *moshav* Eli 'Al to Avne Etan. Area: 2,100 d. A stream passes through reserve forming several waterfalls, among them HaMappal HaLavan *220:247*. Height: 20 m.

Naḥal Eshḥar *178:254*

Naḥal outpost in Galilee 3 km. S of Karmi'el. Named after the buckthorn (*eshḥar*) shrubs prevalent in the area. Established 1979.

Naḥal Ga'aton

Stream in Galilee with source near Me'ona; flows W. Last section passes through main street of Nahariyya and empties into Mediterranean. Has water all year round.

Naḥal Gadid *074:082*

Naḥal outpost in Gaza Strip 6 km. N of Rafah. Name symbolic (*gedida* means date harvesting). Established 1979.

Naḥal Gerar

Seasonal watercourse with source in S Judean Foothills, near kibbutz Lahav. Flows W and empties into Naḥal Besor near kibbutz Re'im. Middle section, between Tel Sheva' and Tel Haror, has some springs.

Here too there are a number of Chalcolithic and Middle Bronze Age sites.

Naḥal Geshur → Geshur

Naḥal Gilbon (Wadi Dabbura)

Stream in Golan Heights with source near Or Tal *222:277* and flows SW to Jordan River, 2 km. SE of Ḥulata. **Nature reserve** At lower end, past a deep channel, the stream forms two large waterfalls, Mappal Devora and Mappal Gilbon; included within a nature reserve of 1,500 d.

Naḥal Gishron

Seasonal watercourse in Elat Hills with source 7 km. W of Elat *138:887*; flows S to Wadi Taba. Writings and drawings were discovered on banks of stream bed which was blocked at one point by a large boulder. Under the boulder a narrow passage developed reminiscent in shape of a bridge. (*Gishron* = small bridge.)

Naḥal Giv'at Adumma (Mevo Shilo) *184:159*

Naḥal outpost in Samarian Hills SE of 'Emeq Shilo, on one of routes ascending from Jordan Valley to the hills. Established 1976.

Naḥal Ha'Arava

Seasonal watercourse in 'Arava on Israel–Jordan border, with source in 'En Yahav region; flows N and empties into Dead Sea. Streams from Mt. Edom and Negev Hills flow into it and drain into Dead Sea.

Naḥal HaBesor *(I Sam. 30:9)*

Seasonal watercourse with source in Negev Hills near Sede Boqer; flows NW through Naḥal Negev and enters Mediterranean Sea S of Gaza. On its course it is joined by many streams and tributaries descending from S Judean Hills and Negev Hills. Mentioned in Bible. Arabic name is Wadi 'Aza (Naḥal 'Aza) and Wadi esh Shallala (Naḥal HaMappalim). **Nature reserve** Part of Naḥal HaBesor is included in nature reserve of 6,400 d. which is 5 km. N of Ẓe'elim.

Naḥal Ḥadera

Stream with source in Samarian Hills; flows W and empties into Mediterranean N of Ḥadera. Most of it is a seasonal watercourse but the last section has water all year round.

Naḥal HaEla (Wadi Zakariyya)

Seasonal watercourse with source in HaEla Valley. Made up of several streams descending from Judean Hills. Its course runs NW, traverses Judean Foothills and S Coastal Plain joining Naḥal Lakhish SE of Ashdod.

Naḥal Ḥamdal (Wadi Ḥandhal)

Nature reserve on slope of Golan 3 km. S of kibbutz Gonen. Area: 1,500 d. Naḥal Ḥamdal and Naḥal Parash, which pass through here, form several small waterfalls during rainy season.

Naḥal HaRo'a

Seasonal watercourse in Negev Hills with source in Ḥatira Hills SW of Makhtesh HaGadol, moving N of Sede Boqer where it joins Naḥal Boqer. Along its bed are a number of ancient sites: a Roman fort *137:036*, 3 pools and rock-cut canals *135:033*, and a large structure *134:034*. Sherds indicate occupation in Nabatean and Roman–Byzantine Periods.

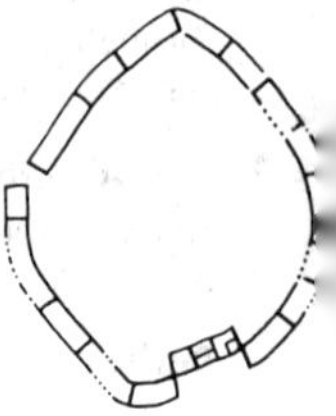

Naḥal Ḥaṣbani → Naḥal Senir

Naḥal Ḥaẓeẓon ⛰

Seasonal watercourse in Judean Desert which empties into Dead Sea S of Mizpe Shalem. Remains of 3 large enclosures and a plastered pool were found in its bed *175:108*. Finds indicate occupation in Iron Age, and from Roman until Arab Periods. Along wadi bed are additional contemporary remains.

Naḥal Ḥaẓor

Seasonal watercourse in Galilee with source in Ramat Dalton. First flows NE and then SE, emptying into the Jordan River near Ḥulata. In mid-course is a canyon with several caves; included in a nature reserve of 1,100 d. **'Alma Cave** *188:271*, has a large opening branching out into wide tunnels containing stalagmites and stalactites.

Naḥal Ḥemdat (Naḥal Yaboq) *200:184*

Naḥal outpost in N Jordan Valley 4 km. E of Ro'i. Named after one of S.Y. Agnon's fictional heroes. Established 1979.

Naḥal Ḥermon (Naḥal Banyas)

Perennial stream and one of major sources of Jordan River. Source on slopes of Mt. Ḥermon *218:296*. Joins Naḥal Dan near Sede Neḥemya.

Naḥal Ḥever

Seasonal watercourse in Judean Desert with source in S Judean Hills 8 km. SE of Hebron. Descends E and empties into Dead Sea 5 km. S of 'En Gedi. Lower section passes between high cliffs dotted with caves used as refuges by rebels during the Revolt against Rome and during Bar Kokhba revolt (see Me'arot Ḥever).

Naḥal Ḥomesh (Ma'ale Naḥal) *168:190*

Naḥal outpost in Samarian Hills 10 km. NW of Shekhem. Established 1979. Name derives from adjacent Arab village, el Fandaqumiya which was site of Pentacomia — a group of five Byzantine villages (*ḥamesh* = five).

Naḥal 'Iron → Biq'at 'Iron

Naḥal 'Iyyon *

Perennial stream and nature reserve in Galilee with source in Biq'at 'Iyyon (Marjayoun) in Lebanon. Flows S emptying into Ḥula Valley. In its ravine are a number of waterfalls: HaTannur, HaTaḥana and HaEshed.

Naḥal Keziv ⛰

Stream in Galilee with source on W slope of Mt. Meron *184:264*. Flowing W it emerges on Galilee shore, near Tel Akhziv. Middle section has water all year round. It is part of a nature reserve of 9,000 d. with varied vegetation, ancient flour mills and Crusader ruins (among them Montfort fortress).

Naḥal La'ana ⛰

Seasonal watercourse in Negev Hills with source at foot of Ramat Matred, 15 km. SW of Sede Boqer. Descends NW and joins Naḥal Resisim and Naḥal Nizzana *104:021*. **Remains of ancient settlement** In region of the first tributaries (between *111:015* and *119:012*) are remains of rural settlements from Hellenistic, Nabatean, Roman and Byzantine Periods. Sherds indicate earlier habitation in Early Bronze, Middle Bronze and Iron Ages.

Naḥal Lakhish

Seasonal watercourse with source in Judean Hills 10 km. W of Hebron *105:106*. Flowing W it passes alongside Tel Lakhish and then turns NW, emptying into Mediterranean S of Ashdod port.

Naḥal Lavan

Seasonal watercourse in Negev Hills with source N of Mt. Lavan 10 km. SW of Sede Boqer. Descends NW and joins Naḥal Nizzana *092:040*. A number of ancient sites are located in stream bed and alongside it. **Remains of ancient settlement** In stream bed, *117:026*, are ruins of 2 buildings, a natural cave and animal pens. Sherds indicate occupation in Persian and Hellenistic Periods. Nearby, on summit of hill, *113:029*, are remains of watch-tower built of large undressed stones. Sherds indicate Iron Age habitation. Alongside, *114:029*, are remains of a building with 2 rooms and an animal pen amid settlement ruins and sherds from Hellenistic, Roman and Byzantine Periods. On summit of another hill is a two-roomed building which has been repaired by Bedouin. Sherds found here are from Byzantine Period. Nearby is a square building with hewn stones occupied in Roman–Byzantine Period according to sherds.

Naḥal Malkishua‘ *189:205*

Naḥal outpost of religious settlers in Gilboa‘ on Mt. Malkishua‘. Named after Malchishua, son of Saul, killed together with his father and brother Jonathan in battle with Philistines. Established 1976. **Ancient remains** S of settlement, *190:204*, are rock-cut wine press, remains of square tower built of large limestones, and sherds from Byzantine Period.

Naḥal Marwa *177:251*

Naḥal outpost in Galilee 1 km. S of Sakhnin. Name means sage (plant), a herb used for medicine and seasoning. Established 1979.

Naḥal Me‘arot → Me‘arot Karmel

Naḥal Meron

Seasonal watercourse in Galilee with source in E slope of Mt. Meron *190:265*. Flows E and enters Naḥal ‘Ammud 2 km. NW of Safed.

Naḥal Meshushim

Stream on Golan Heights with source in area of ‘En Ziwan. Flows SW to Naḥal Eitan where it forms a waterfall and pool (Berekhat HaMeḥushim). In Biq‘at Bet Ẓayda it joins Naḥal Yehudiyya, emerges with Zekhiyya River and empties into Lake Kinneret.

Naḥal Mishmar (Wadi Maḥraṣ)

Seasonal watercourse in Judean Desert with source at *176:091*; flows E emptying into Dead Sea 7 km. N of Masada. Caves in the ravine contained remains from Chalcolithic Period and time of Revolt against Rome and Bar Kokhba revolt (see Me‘arat HaMatmon).

Naḥal Na‘aman

Perennial stream in Haifa Bay with source at springs of Afeq *160:250*. Flows N and emerges S of Acre.

Naḥal Na‘aran → Yitav

Naḥal Neẓarim *094:098*

Naḥal outpost in Gaza Strip 4 km. SW of Gaza. Named after adjacent Arab village Nuṣeirat. Established 1972 alongside Tell el ‘Ajjul.

Naḥal Oren

Stream on Mt. Karmel with source between villages of ‘Isfiya and Daliyyat el Karmil. Emerges N of ‘Atlit. Near its exit from the mountains, *147:235*, remains of prehistoric settlement were discovered. (See Me‘arat Oren.)

Naḥal ‘Orevim

Stream on Golan Heights with source at *220:283*; flows W emptying into Naḥal Qalil in Ḥula Valley alongside kibbutz Lehavot HaBashan. Its descent is steep with many waterfalls. At its lower end, 1 km. E of Lehavot HaBashan, is a nature reserve of 1,000 d.

★ Naḥal ʻOz *102:098*

Kibbutz 5 km. SE of Gaza. Founded as first *nahal* outpost in 1951 and called Naḥla'im "A". Became a civilian settlement in 1953. Until Six-Day War it was on the front line and suffered attacks from infiltrators and Egyptian army in Gaza Strip. Area: 14,000 d. Pop.: 340. Nearby is Assaf Forest, planted in memory of those who fell in Sinai Campaign.

Naḥal Paran (Wadi el Jirafi)

Seasonal watercourse (the largest in Israel) in Negev Hills. Source in Paran Desert *123:948*; flows NE and empties into Naḥal Ha'Arava. Its wide bed accommodated ancient routes from Egypt to the 'Arava and the Dead Sea.

Naḥal Peraẓim (Nakhabir el Baghl)

Seasonal watercourse in S Dead Sea with source at Mishor 'Ami'az *182:055*. Flows N and empties into Dead Sea 2 km. E of Newe Zohar.

Naḥal Poleg (Wadi Faliq)

Perennial stream in Sharon with source N of kibbutz Ramat HaKovesh *143:180*. Flows NW and empties into Mediterranean near Udim. Its last section has water all year round and is part of Naḥal Poleg nature reserve.

Naḥal Qidron (Wadi en Nar) *(II Sam. 15:23)*

Seasonal watercourse in Judean Desert, mentioned in Bible and other ancient sources. Name in Arabic means stream of fire (because of the local hot climate). Source in E Jerusalem, from where it descends SE to Mar Saba monastery and then veers E emptying into Dead Sea 3 km. S of 'Ein Fashkha. The slope of Naḥal Qidron within Jerusalem (called Valley of Jehoshaphat between Mount of Olives and Temple Mount) have been used as burial sites from time immemorial. Near Jerusalem the river bed has always been used for refuse disposal and sewage. The banks are steep and have many caves and crevices, some of which were formerly used as refuges for fugitives, rebels and hermits — especially monks in Byzantine Period. The descent to Dead Sea is very steep and in the rainy season several waterfalls are created near the mouth.

Naḥal Qishon

Stream with source at bottom of Samarian Hills in Jenin region. General direction of flow is NW. It is a seasonal watercourse in its E section and perennial in its last section. Traverses Yizre'el Valley and empties into Mediterranean at Haifa Bay adjacent to Qishon port.

Naḥal Raqqad (Wadi Ruqad)

The largest stream on Golan Heights. Source at foot of Mt. Ḥermon *227:292*. Flows S along length of the Golan Heights, emptying into the Yarmouk 9 km. E of Mevo Ḥamma. The N section is a seasonal watercourse and S section is a perennial stream.

Naḥal Resisim

Seasonal watercourse in Negev Hills with source at foot of Mt. Resisim 18 km. SW of Sede Boqer. Enters Naḥal Niẓẓana 8 km. to W. Here settlement ruins from Middle Bronze Age are scattered over 3 hills *107:021*. Remains of another settlement from same period are located to the E alongside Be'er Resisim *109:020*.

Naḥal Rimmonim (Kokhav HaShaḥar "B") *182:149*

Naḥal outpost in SE Samarian Hills off Ramallah-Jericho road. Established 1977.

Naḥal Sa'ar **(Nahr es Sa'ar)**

Stream on Golan Heights included in nature reserve. Source at 'Ein es Sa'ar on slopes of Mt. Ḥermon, NE of Majdal Shams *224:296*. Flows S and then W until it enters Naḥal Ḥermon. Its W course is steep and along it are a number of ancient flour mills and a few waterfalls, the highest being Mappal Resisim (23 m.).

Naḥal Samakh **(Wadi es Samak)** *

Watercourse on Golan Heights that empties into Lake Kinneret N of 'En Gev, alongside abandoned village of Kursi. Named after sound of Arabic name which means stream of fish. Lower part of the watercourse in perennial.

Naḥal Senir **(Nahr el Ḥaṣbani)**

Perennial stream, one of 3 major sources of Jordan River, with its source in Lebanon. Flows S and joins the other 2 sources of Jordan River by Sede Neḥemya.

Naḥal Sharakh

Spring in Galilee with source N of Netu'a. Joins Naḥal Bezet 2 km. E of Adamit *172:275*. Upper part is in a nature reserve of 1,240 d. of dense woods.

Naḥal Shelaḥ

Nahal outpost in Jordan Valley 3 km. SE of Meḥola. Named after local desert plant with spear-like leaves (*shelaḥ* = spear). Established 1979.

Naḥal Shelomo **(Wadi el Maṣri)**

Seasonal watercourse in Elat Hills with source S of 'En Netafim *139:888*. Flows S and empties into Gulf of Elat 4 km. SW of Elat.

Naḥal Shillo **(Wadi Deir Ballut)**

Seasonal watercourse in Samarian Hills with source 10 km. NE of Ramallah *173:155*. Joins Yarqon River 3 km. N of Petaḥ Tiqwa. In ancient times a route from Coastal Plain to Mt. Efrayim passed through this stream bed.

Naḥal Shiqma **(Wadi el Ḥasi)**

Seasonal watercourse on Coastal Plain with source in S Judean Foothills, E of kibbutz Devira. Flows NW and empties into Mediterranean 10 km. SW of Ashqelon.

Naḥal Shuaḥ

Nature reserve with stream bed on slopes of Golan Heights 3 km. NE of Yesud HaMa'ala. Area: 1,100 d. Naḥal Shuaḥ flows through the reserve along the foot of Mt. Avital, and then SW emptying into the Jordan River.

Naḥal Si'on *214:297*

Nahal outpost on slopes of Ḥermon 4 km. N of Banyas. Established 1979.

Naḥal Si'on **(Wadi el 'Asal)**

Seasonal watercourse with source on slopes of Mt. Ḥermon *220:304*. Flows S and joins Naḥal Ḥermon E of She'ar Yashuv. Arabic name means stream of honey.

Naḥal Soreq **(Wadi eṣ Ṣarar)**

Seasonal watercourse with source in Judean Hills S of Jerusalem. On its way W it traverses Judean Foothills and Coastal Plain and empties into Mediterranean at kibbutz Palmaḥim. The Valley of Sorek is mentioned in Bible (Judg. 16:4); Arabic name means stream of pebbles.

Naḥal Soreq (railway station) *138:135*

Railway station on Jerusalem–Lod line, in Naḥal Soreq, 5 km. W of Naḥshon junction. In WWI the Turks laid railway tracks to the Negev and Sinai from this railway junction. During British Mandate many army camps were located in this area.

Naḥal Tanninim (Nahr ez Zarqa)

Stream with source in Ramat Menashe; flows SW and empties into Mediterranean 2 km. S of kibbutz Ma'agan Mikha'el. Its last section has a perennial flow of water. According to various accounts, there were in the past many crocodiles in the stream, hence its name (*tannin* = crocodile). Arabic name means the blue stream. In past a dam was built here to create a large lake alongside which a flour mill was built. The aqueduct to Caesarea began S of the dam. Over the years the lake became a swamp, known as swamps of Kabara. Adjacent to mouth of stream is Naḥal Tanninim nature reserve.

Naḥal Tavor (Wadi el Bira)

Stream in Galilee with source in Nazareth Hills. Flows SE emptying into Jordan River, 3 km. S of Naharayim Bridge. Part of stream is included within Naḥal Tavor nature reserve. Last section of stream has perennial water flow. **Ruins of ancient settlement** Next to stream bed on hill with steep incline, *197:225*, are ancient settlement ruins: remains of walls, flint implements and sherds indicating continuous occupation from Early Bronze Age until Iron Age.

Naḥal Tirẓa → 'Ein el Fari'a

Naḥal Tut

Seasonal watercourse in Ramat Menashe with source near *moshav* Elyaqim, *156:225*. Flows SW and, near Bat Shelomo *150:142*, joins Naḥal Daliyya and empties into Mediterranean. A section of Zikhron Ya'aqov–Yoqne'am road passes through stream bed.

Naḥal Yardinnon

Perennial stream that descends from Golan Heights to Ḥula Valley and passes between *kibbutzim* Shamir and Lahavot HaBashan. Before Six-Day War the upper part of the stream was controlled by the Syrians who tried to divert its waters from Jewish settlements.

Naḥal Yavne'el

Seasonal watercourse in Galilee with source in Biq'at Yavne'el, *195:240*. Flows SE and empties into Jordan River W of Deganya "B".

Naḥal Yeḥi'am

Stream in Galilee with source S of Ma'alot–Tarshiḥa. Near *moshav* 'Amqa it joins Naḥal Bet Ha'Emeq. Arabic name is Wadi Majnuna (the crazy stream) because of its winding course. Near Yeḥi'am the stream is part of a nature reserve (1,270 d.) of dense woods. Ruins of Gadin fortress located here.

Naḥal Yehudiyya

Watercourse on Golan Heights with source 10 km. S of Quncitra *226:270*. Flows SW, joins Naḥal Meshushim in Bet Ẓayda Valley, and flows into Nahr Zakiyya, which empties into Lake Kinneret.

Naḥal Yiẓhar

Stream in Galilee with source N of Deir el Asad, and joins Naḥal Yasaf 2 km. E of Shamerat. Partly within nature reserve of 11,000 d.

Naḥal Ẓalmon *184:254*

Nahal outpost in Galilee 6 km. SW of Ḥananya junction. Established 1976. Future plan is for an industrial kibbutz.

Naḥal Ẓari *193:149*

Naḥal outpost in Jordan Valley 10 km. N of Jericho. Name means a type of perfume made from tree sap and used in ancient times for medicinal and religious purposes. Established 1979.

Naḥal Zawitan *

Stream on Golan Heights with source at 'En Ziwan, 7 km. S of Quneitra. Flows SW in a deep channel, forming several waterfalls during rainy season. Joins Naḥal Meshushim *213:259*. Nearby is Berekhat HaMeshushim.

Naḥal Ẓofar

Seasonal watercourse in 'Arava with source at *159:985*. Flows NE entering Naḥal 'Arava near Ẓofar.

Naḥal Zohar (stream)

Seasonal watercourse SW of Dead Sea with source on Zohar ridge, SE of 'Arad. Flows SE and joins with Naḥal Ḥalamish near Meẓad Zohar. Empties into Dead Sea near Newe Zohar.

Naḥal Zohar (settlement) *147:090*

Naḥal outpost 18 km. S of Hebron off Hebron–Be'er Sheva' road, near Arab village edh Dhahiriyya. Established 1978 in a British police fort, which was used by Arab Legion during Jordanian rule.

● **Naḥam** *150:130*

Moshav in Judean Hills 1 km. S of Naḥshon junction. Naham is mentioned in Bible as related to tribe of Judah (I Chron. 4:19). Founded 1950. Area: 1,200 d. Pop.: 420.

Naharayim Bridge *203:226*

Demolished bridge over Jordan River 10 km. S of Ẓemaḥ junction, alongside kibbutz Gesher. Called Jisr el Majami' (the joining bridge) in Arabic, because near the bridge the Yarmouk and Jordan Rivers join one another. This too is meaning of Hebrew name. An important by-way in all periods. During War of Independence the Jordanians took adjacent power station and consequently the Haganah forces blew up the bridge. **Khan el Jisr** Alongside bridge are remains of a khan from early Arab Period. Nearby, sherds were found from the Chalcolithic Period.

■ **Nahariyya** *158:267*

City on Galilee coast 8 km. N of Acre. Name derived from Naḥal Ga'aton which traverses the city. (In Hebrew *nahar* = stream; Arabic name is en Nahr.) Founded as a farming village (*moshava*) in 1934 by German immigrants. During WWII a seaside resort industry started and has assumed a continuously growing part of its economy ever since. During War of Independence it was isolated in the fighting and its sole contact with the rest of the country was maintained by sea using small boats. After the war the town grew and industry began to develop. In 1962 it received municipal status. Area: 10,500 d. Pop.: 30,000. **Remains** from various periods have been uncovered within the city. Near the shore, *159:268*, ruins of a Middle Bronze Age temple were found and on an adjacent hill are remains of a Late Bronze Age and Iron Age settlement. At Dhahr el Mazra'a *159:267* are remnants of a cemetery, used from Second Temple Period till Byzantine Period. At Dhahrat el Ḥumeima or Kh. 'Eitayyim *160:268*, within Giv'at Katznelson quarter, are remains of an Iron Age settlement, Roman tombs and aqueduct, church, mosaic fragments and workshop remnants from the Byzantine Period.

○ **Naḥf** *179:260*

Arab village in Galilee 3 km. NW of Karmi'el. Pop.: 3,800. Remains of a workshop furnace from Byzantine Period.

NAHARIYYA

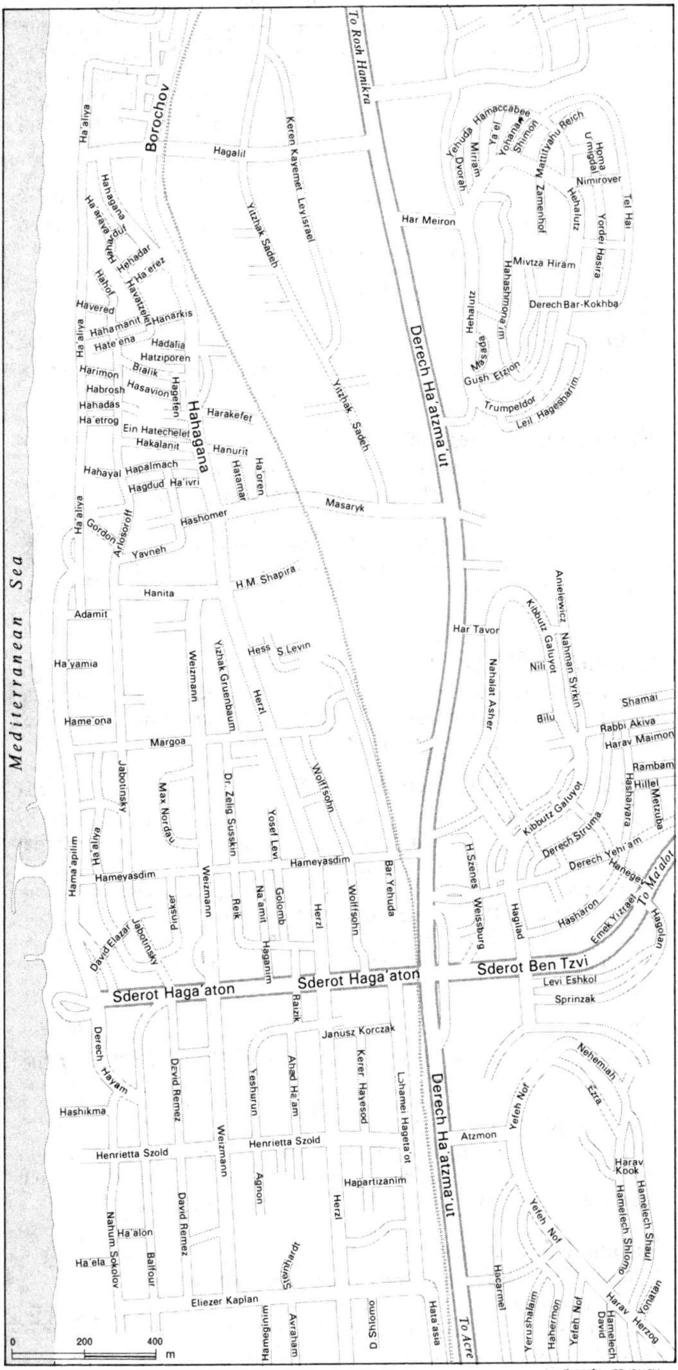
To Rosh Hanikra
Borochov
Ha'aliya
Hagalil
Keren Kayemet Leyisrael
Yehuda Hamaccabee
Dvorah
Miriam
Ya'el
Yohanan
Shimon
Mattityahu
Reich
U'migdal
Homa
Nimirover
Tel Hai
Yordei Hasira
Zamenhof
Hehalutz
Har Meiron
Yitzhak Sadeh
Hahagana
Ha'arava
Hahaduf
Hehadar
Ha'erez
Havatzelet
Hahof
Havered
Hahamanit
Hanarkis
Hate'ena
Hadalia
Hatziporen
Bialik
Harimon
Habrosh
Hasavion
Hagefen
Hahadas
Ha'etrog
Harakefet
Ein Hatechelet
Hakalanit
Hanurit
Hatamar
Ha'oren
Hahayal
Hapalmach
Hagdud Ha'ivri
Hashomer
Masaryk
Gordon
Arlosoroff
Yavneh
Mivtza Hiram
Hahashmona'im
Derech Bar-Kokhba
Masada
Gush Etzion
Trumpeldor
Leil Hagesharim
Derech Ha'atzma'ut
Mediterranean Sea
H.M. Shapira
Hanita
Adamit
Ha'yamia
Hame'ona
Weizmann
Yizhak Gruenbaum
Hess
S. Levin
Herzl
Margoa
Har Tavor
Anielewicz
Kibbutz Galuyot
Nahman Syrkin
Nili
Nahalat Asher
Bilu
Shamai
Rabbi Akiva
Harav Maimon
Rambam
Hillel
Metzuba
Hashayara
Derech Siruma
Derech Yehi'am
Hanegev
To Ma'alot
Jabotinsky
Max Nordau
Dr. Zelig Susskin
Yosef Levi
Wolffsohn
Hama'apilim
Hameyasdim
Pinsker
Bar Yehuda
H. Szenes
Weissburg
Hagilad
Hasharon
Emek Yizrael
Hagolan
Reik
Na'amit
Golomb
Haganim
David Elazar
Sderot Haga'aton
Sderot Ben Tzvi
Levi Eshkol
Sprinzak
Raziel
Janusz Korczak
Derech Hayam
David Remez
Yeshurun
Ahad Ha'am
Keren Hayesod
Lohamei Hageta'ot
Nehemiah
Ezra
Yefeh Nof
Hashikma
Atzmon
Henrietta Szold
Agnon
Hapartizanim
Harav Kook
Hamelech Shaul
Hamelech Shlomo
Nahum Sokolov
Ha'alon
Balfour
Ha'ela
Eliezer Kaplan
Hacarmel
Yerushalaim
Hahermon
Harav Herzog
Yonatan
Hamelech David
Hamegînim
Avraham
Shlomo
Hata'asia
To Acre
0
200
400
m

o Naḥḥalin *161:121*

Arab village in Judean Hills 2 km. N of 'Eẓyon Bloc. Pop.: 1,100. Arab infiltrators used the village as a base prior to 1956 Sinai Campaign and thus in 1954 the Israel Defence Forces executed a retaliatory raid on the village. **Ancient ruins** Village is built on ruins of a Medieval settlement. To the W *160:121* is Kh. el Kabra with remains of rectangular structures made of hewn stones. Finds indicate occupation from Iron Age until Middle Ages. Site of Nehelam mentioned in Bible (Jer. 29:31).

Naḥli'eli Island *159:275*

Island 2 km. S of Rosh HaNiqra, 1 km. off Mediterranean shore. Named after the wagtails (*naḥli'eli*) that nest here.

Nahr el Ḥaṣbani → Naḥal Senir

Nahr el Majrasa *211:253*

Mouth of Naḥal Daliyyot in Biq'at Bet Ẓayda (Buteiḥa) on NE shore of Lake Kinneret. Woods, orchards and thick foliage.

★ Naḥsholim *143:224*

Kibbutz on Karmel coast 4 km. N of Zikhron Ya'aqov interchange. Founded 1948 on lands of abandoned village, Tantura. Area: 4,500 d. Pop.: 350. Within kibbutz is a ruined building which housed a glass factory established by Baron de Rothschild in 1891 for bottle production for Zikhron Ya'aqov winery. It was closed down after a few years.

★ Naḥshon *145:137*

Kibbutz in Judean Foothills 3 km. W of Latrun. Named after Naḥshon operation to relieve siege of Jerusalem in War of Independence. Founded 1950. Area: 8,000 d. Pop.: 340.

★ Naḥshonim *145:163*

Kibbutz on border of Judean Foothills and central Coastal Plain, 3 km. S of Rosh Ha'Ayin. Founded 1949 on lands of abandoned village, Majdal Ṣadiq, by the first group of immigrants from Egypt after War of Independence. Area: 4,700 d. Pop.: 240. **Ancient remains** Within kibbutz are Late Bronze Age rock-cut tombs which were still in use in Iron Age and Persian Period. Other finds include rock-cut pools, fragments of a white mosaic, buildings and other Roman and Byzantine finds.

Najidat *185:246*

Bedouin settlement in Galilee 5 km. NW of Golani junction. Pop.: 1,100.

o (En) Naqura *169:185*

Arab village (pop.: 600) in Samarian Hills 7 km. NW of Shekhem. Within village is a rock-hewn tunnel leading to a water source from where a stream flows N to Sebastiya.

National Water Carrier

Network for transporting water from N part of country, with its abundant water sources, to the more arid regions of the S and Negev. It has been in operation since 1964. Water is pumped from Lake Kinneret through Ma'agar Ẓalmon, Minheret Eilabun and Bet Netofa canal to Agame Eshkol (Ma'agar Bet Netofa), through Minheret Shimeron and Minheret Menashe to Rosh Ha'Ayin, near Petaḥ Tiqwa. From here water is distributed through subsidiary pipelines to S regions and N Negev.

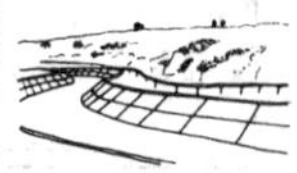

NAZARETH

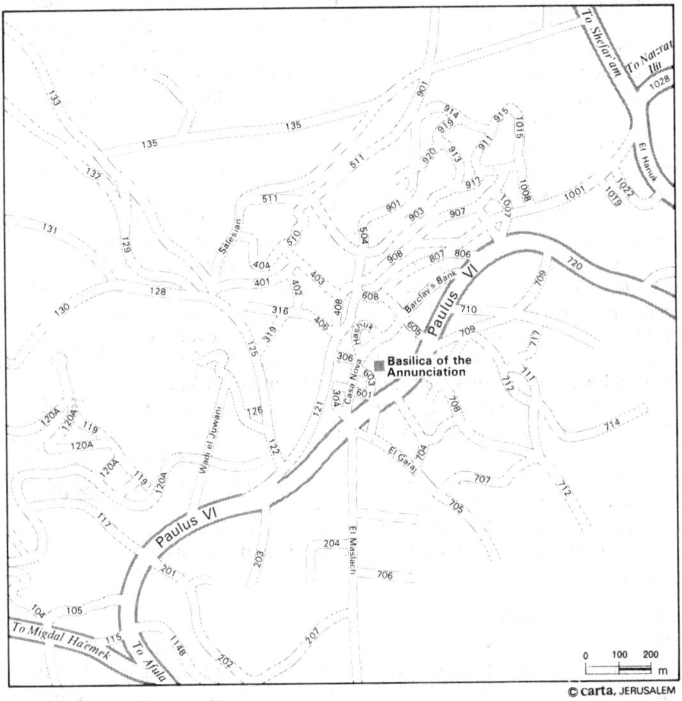

★ **Natur** *220:250*

Kibbutz on Golan Heights 4 km. W of Khisfin. Established 1980. Same name as adjacent hill. Area: 2,700 d. Pop.: several tens.

○ **Na'ura** *187:224*

Arab village in Galilee 10 km. E of 'Afula. Name means a large wheel operated by water power. Established more than 500 years ago by the Zu'abiyya tribe. Pop.: 700. **Remains** Within village is a low tel which one theory claims to be site of Anaharath, city in Issachar tribal allotment (Josh. 19:19). According to another theory it is the site of Ne'uran mentioned in Talmud. Finds from tel include flint implements, remains from Iron Age and Persian Period, building and sarcophagi from Roman and Byzantine Periods and remains from Arab Period.

□ **Nazareth (En Naṣira)** *(Matt. 2:23)*

Arab city in Galilee with many churches and monasteries where Jesus grew to manhood (Jesus of Nazareth). Area: 6,000 d. Pop.: 38,000. **History** Archaeological evidence indicates that site was occupied in Early Bronze Age. First mentioned as a Jewish city in New Testament. Even after the destruction of Second Temple it continued to be a Jewish city. Mentioned in liturgical poems of Eleazar Kallir (from sometimes between 2nd and 4th century). Also mentioned by traveller Antoninus Placentinus (570). Jews of Nazareth, together with those of Tiberias, aided the Persians in their war against the Byzantines (614), but after the Byzantine victory, the Jews were slaughtered and Jewish Nazareth was apparently destroyed. After the Moslem conquest the town became Arab. In 1099 it was taken by the Crusader Tancred and became a Christian town. In 1263 it was again captured by the Arabs who completely destroyed it. It remained desolate until 1620 when the Druze ruler Fakhr ed Din allowed the Franciscans to settle here and build churches and monasteries. The Bedouin ruler Dahir el 'Amr made it capital of Lower Galilee. During WWI it was headquarters of Turkish army in Palestine and during British Mandate it was a district capital. During War of Independence it was the centre of Kaukji's Arab Liberation Army until captured by the Israel Defence Forces. **Sites** The Basilica of the Annunciation is built on the traditional spot where the angel announced to Mary that she would give birth to a son. A Byzantine church was built here in the 4th c. but it was destroyed by Persians in 615. The Crusaders built a Romanesque church on its ruins but this too was destroyed by Moslems. It was restored in the 18th c. when the Ottoman Turks allowed Spanish pilgrims to build a small church called Casa Nova. Napoleon stayed here when he visited Nazareth in 1799. The Catholics then built a magnificent new structure in 1955 — the Basilica of the Annunciation. The basilica is a blend of modern architectural styles and preserves a Medieval structure. It is decorated with works of art from all over the world. Just over a km. N of the basilica is the Greek Orthodox church with a well, called the Fountain of Mary, where the angel Gabriel appeared before the Virgin. The Russian Orthodox, Maronites, Syrians, Copts, Armenians and Protestants also have churches in Nazareth. The Nova Hospice serves Christian pilgrims. In the bazaar area are remains of a 6th c. synagogue consisting of 80 stones, some of which are inscribed and stuccoed, as well as column bases. There are also rock-cut tombs, caves, and cisterns in the area.

Nazareth Ridge

Range of hills S of Nazareth covering an area of 12 km. in length and 3 km. in width extending from NE to SW. The average height is 400 m. above sea level. On S part, overlooking Yizre'el Valley, is Mt. Qedumim, known as the Mount of the Precipice or Saltus Domini (Leap of the Lord) where, according to Christian tradition, Jesus jumped while escaping his pursuers (Luke 4:28-30). In one of the local caves (el Qafze — Cave of the Ancients) remains of the Paleolithic Palestinian man were found. They included part of a female skull and the jaw and forehead of a man. In the lowest stratum there were remains of 7 individuals. Early man lived in these hills between 100,000 and 500,000 years ago.

■ Naẓerat 'Illit — *180:234*

City alongside Nazareth in Galilee. Founded as development town in 1957. Area: 18,000 d. Pop.: 24,000.

o (En) Nazla el Gharbiyya — *158:200*

Arab village (pop.: 300) in Samarian Hills 13 km. N of Tulkarm.

o (En) Nazla esh Sharqiyya — *160:202*

Arab village (pop.: 550) in Samarian Hills 12 km. NE of Tulkarm.

o Nazlat Abu Nar — *157:201*

Arab village in Samarian Hills 11 km. NE of Tulkarm.

o Nazlat 'Isa — *155:202*

Arab village (pop.: 660) in Samarian Hills 11 km. N of Tulkarm.

o Nazlat Zeid — *166:207*

Arab village (pop.: 280) in Samarian Hills 11 km. W of Jenin. Named after Sheikh Zeid whose tomb is in village.

o (En) Nazla el Wusta — *159:201*

Arab village (pop.: 180) in Samarian Hills 12 km. NE of Tulkarm, alongside en Nazla esh Sharqiyya.

★ **Negba** 120:118

Kibbutz on Coastal Plain 12 km. E of Ashqelon. Name means to the Negev. Founded 1939 as a "stockade and tower" settlement by Polish immigrants. At the time it was the southernmost Jewish settlement in the country. During War of Independence it was almost destroyed by repeated attacks from the Egyptian army, but the settlers withstood them and did not abandon the kibbutz. Egyptians were then repulsed by the Israel Defence Forces. Area: 12,600 d. Pop.: 500. Near Negba is a military cemetery and memorial to those who died in the fighting.

Negev *(Num. 13:29)*

Largest and southernmost region in the country (*negev* means south). Its shape is that of an upside-down triangle with its base across the waist of the country and its apex in Elat. Boundaries: in N — S Coastal Plain, Judean Foothills, Hills and Desert; in E — 'Arava; in SW — N Sinai along El 'Arish–Elat line. Its major sub-regions from N to S are N Negev, Negev Hills, central Negev and Elat Hills. The region has sparse precipitation which decreases to the S. All its streams are seasonal watercourses and relatively few areas can be cultivated. Its hills have a number of quarries. Important for its geographical position between Asia and Africa, between the Mediterranean and Red Seas and a pivot between Israel and Egypt, Saudi Arabia and Transjordan. **History** Two international routes passed through the Negev since the earliest recorded history: the *via maris* in the W, and King's Highway in the E. A large number of archaeological finds indicate that the Negev was occupied in all historical periods. During Israelite conquest it was included in Simeon tribal allotment. However, it was King David who succeeded in extending Israelite dominion over the whole of the Negev. King Solomon set up copper mining works here and developed the port of Elath. After the division of the kingdom into Israel and Judah, the Negev gradually slipped out of the control of the Kingdom of Judah. In 7th c. BCE the Edomites gained control over S Judean Hills creating a buffer zone between Judah and the Negev. The Nabateans expelled the Edomites and established, in Edom and the Negev, a kingdom with its capital at Petra. At beginning of 2nd c. the Nabatean kingdom was annexed by the Romans (*Provincia Arabia*) and in 4th c. the Negev constituted the 3rd portion (*Palaestina Tertia*) of the Roman province of Palestine. In Byzantine times the Negev developed considerably and only after the Persian invasion, early 7th c., did the Negev's importance begin to wane. This continued throughout the Crusader Period and its subsequent wars. Interest in the Negev was revived at end of 19th c. when Jewish settlement was renewed in Palestine. Attempts at settling the Negev were made by Jews in 1882 but Turkish and then British objections caused their failure. It was only in 1939 that the first Jewish settlement, Negba, was established. In 1943, 3 observation outposts were set up: Gevulot, Revivim and Bet Eshel. In 1946, 11 new settlements were established in one day. During War of Independence fierce battles were fought for control of the Negev which was cut off from the rest of the country. The Negev was liberated in a number of military actions, particularly in the N around Be'er Sheva' and in the S at port of Elat.

● **Neḥalim** 142:163

Moshav on Coastal Plain 3 km. S of Petaḥ Tiqwa. Founded 1948 by members of *moshav* Neḥalim in Ḥula Valley and Newe Ya'aqov in N Jerusalem who were evacuated during War of Independence. Area: 2,400 d. Pop.: 1,000.

Nehar HaYarden → Jordan River

Nehora 121:114

Rural centre in Lakhish region 4 km. W of Peluggot junction. Founded 1955 as service centre for settlements in the area: Zohar, Nogah, Nir Ḥen, 'Oẓem and Shaḥar. Pop.: 200. Elementary and high school, clinic, library and Bet Devora — rest home for writers named after the authoress Devora Baron.

Neḥusha 144:114

Forest watch-tower in Judean Hills 5 km. E of Bet Guvrin. Name derives from abandoned village, Deir Nakhas, perhaps site of Irnahash in Judah tribal allotment (I Chron. 4:12). Initially established as a *moshav shittufi* in 1955.

Nein **(Na'im)** 183:226

Arab village in Yizre'el Valley at foot of Giv'at HaMore, 5 km. NE of 'Afula. Pop.: 600. **Na'im** Built on ruins of ancient settlement, it is possibly the city of Na'im from Second Temple Period. Mentioned in Talmud and New Testament. According to Christian tradition it was here that Jesus performed the miracle of reviving the dead youth. Mentioned in Onomasticon of Eusebius. An Italian traveller attests to the existence of Jewish community here in 18th c. Franciscan church built on ruins of Crusader church. Cisterns and rock-cut tombs. Sherds indicate occupation from Roman Period.

Ne'ot Golan 215:243

Moshav shittufi on Golan Heights 6 km. E of 'En Gev. Founded 1968 on lands of abandoned village of Fiq and moved to present site in 1972. Area: 4,500 d.

Ne'ot HaKikar 185:038

Moshav 8 km. SE of 'Arava junction. Founded 1959 as experimental farm; became a *moshav* in 1972. Area: 630 d. Pop.: several hundred.

Ne'ot Mordekhay 206:285

Kibbutz in Ḥula Valley 6 km. SE of Qiryat Shemona. Named after Argentinian Zionist, Mordecai Rozovsky. Founded 1946 by Czechoslovakian and Austrian immigrants. Area: 4,500 d.

Nes 'Ammim 161:263

Village of Christian sect in Galilee 4 km. NE of Acre. Established 1963 with the aim of bringing together Jews and Christians. Pop.: 50.

Nes Harim 155:128

Moshav in Judean Hills 7 km. E of Bet Shemesh. Name derived from passage in Bible "...when a signal (*nes*) is raised on the mountains (*harim*), look!" (Isa. 18:3). Founded 1950 by Kurdish immigrants on lands of abandoned village, Deir el Hawa. Area: 500 d. Pop.: 450.

Nesher 155:241

Urban settlement in Haifa Bay 6 km. SE of Haifa. Founded as Nesher quarter in 1925 to house workers of Nesher cement factory. Area: 14,000 d. Pop.: 13,000.

Nes Ẓiyyona 129:149

Urban settlement (with local council) on Coastal Plain between Rishon LeẒiyyon and Reḥovot. Began 1883 when Reuben Lehrer, a Russian Zionist, obtained an orchard in Wadi Khunein (meaning stream of roses). Later additional plots were purchased, some by Michael Helpern (1860-1919), a visionary and fighter, who named the settlement Nes Ẓiyyona from the Biblical passage, "Raise a *standard toward Zion*, flee for safety, stay not" (Jer. 4:6). It later became a farming village (*moshava*). Area: 16,000 d. Pop.:

NETANYA

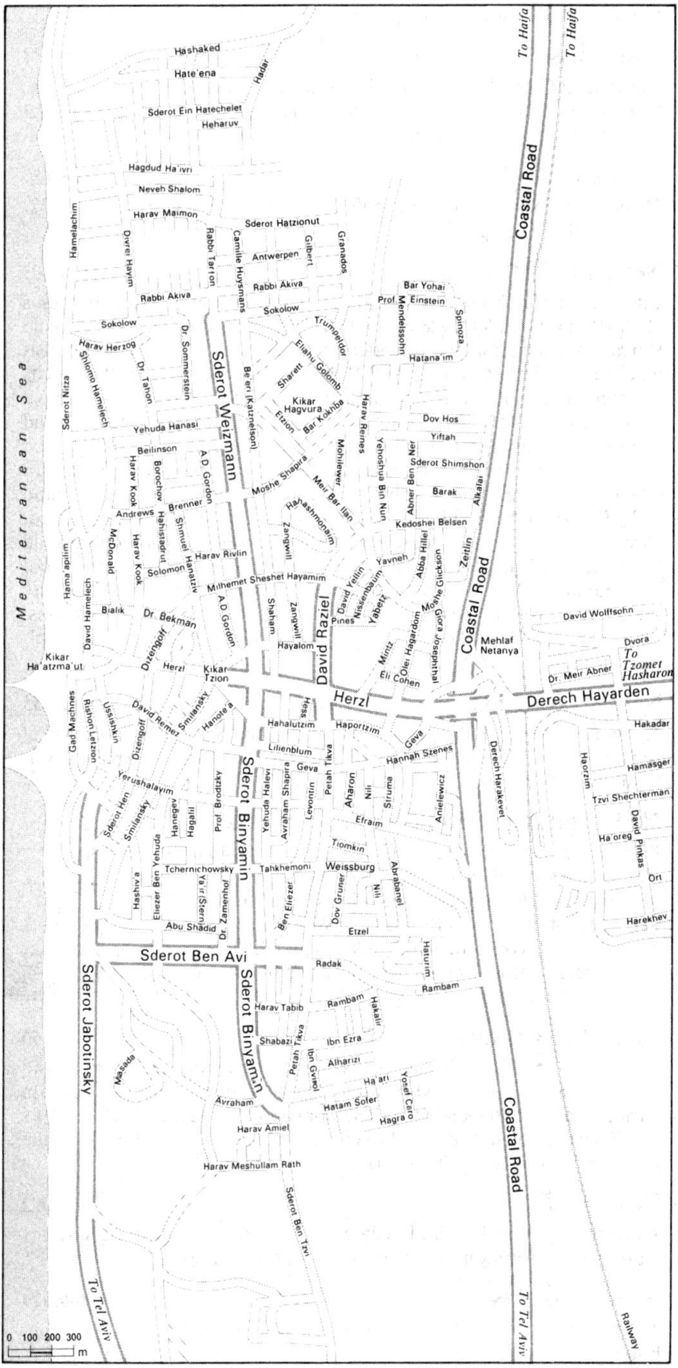

© carta, JERUSALEM

14,000. A centre for biological research is located here. **Sarafand el Kharab** On hill of local cemetery, within Yad Eliezer quarter, are remains of Roman Period settlement.

◆ **Neta'** *128:134*

Orchard on Coastal Plain 5 km. SW of Gedera, adjacent to Bene 'Ayish. Established 1952 by a society whose members work for agricultural institutions. Area: 1,800 d.

● **Neta'im** *128:150*

Moshav on Coastal Plain 4 km. SW of Rishon LeẒiyyon. Founded 1932. Area: 1,100 d. Pop.: 200.

■ **Netanya** *136:193*

City on Sharon coast named after US philanthropist Nathan Straus (1848-1931). Founded 1928 by youth of veteran farming villages of Bene Binyamin association and intended as agricultural village. Due to crisis in citrus marketing during WWII Netanya turned to developing its diamond and holiday resort industries. In 1948 received municipal status. Area: 30,000 d. Pop.: 100,000. **Ancient remains** On seashore and at entrance to city *135:190*, a number of prehistoric sites were discovered containing flint implements from Mesolithic and Neolithic Periods. In city centre, Iron Age remains and a Roman aqueduct were found *192:137*. Along rock cliffs on seashore a Roman road was uncovered. Roman and Byzantine rock-cut tombs and caves are scattered around Netanya. **Kh. Umm Khalid** To the S a Crusader fortress was discovered. **Kh. Ḥannuna** Within area of Shikun Darom on steep hill *137:189* are remains of a Roman-Byzantine settlement containing building remains, fragments of mosaic floor and wine press. Many scattered flint tools were found on nearby flat hill.

● **Netiv HaGedud** *192:155*

Moshav in Jordan Valley 15 km. N of Jericho. Name based on that of Jewish Legion (HaGedud Ha'Ivri) who camped in this area in WWI. Founded 1976.

★ **Netiv HaLamed He** *148:121*

Kibbutz on border of Judean Hills and Foothills 4 km. E of HaEla junction. Named in memory of the "35" (*lamed he* in gematria) Haganah soldiers who set out to re-enforce defenders of the 'Eẓyon Bloc during War of Independence. They were discovered, surrounded and killed by Arabs after a fierce battle. Founded 1949 by demobilized Palmaḥ soldiers. Area: 4,500 d. Pop.: 330.

● **Netiv HaShayyara** *163:266*

Moshav 4 km. SE of Nahariyya. Named in memory of a supply and re-enforcement convoy who attempted to relieve siege of Yeḥi'am during War of Independence. The convoy was attacked and 47 of its fighters were killed. Memorial to convoy is located 2 km. to N, near the junction. Founded 1950. Area: 2,100 d. Pop.: 340.

Netivot *111:092*

Town in Negev 30 km. S of Ashqelon. Founded as regional centre for immigrant absorption in 1956. Area: 6,000 d. Pop.: 7,100.

● **Netu'a** *180:274*

Moshav alongside Lebanese border 9 km. NW of Ḥiram junction. Founded 1966.

■ **Ne'urim** *137:198*

Youth village 5 km. N of Netanya, alongside *moshav* Bet Yannai. During War of Independence it was a temporary shelter for Ben Shemen evacuees. Since 1953 it is affiliated to Hadassah organization and Youth Aliyah and has a vocational high school, regional elementary school, community centre and runs varied annual courses. Area: 200 d. Pop.: 1,400 students (half live-in in dormitories).

● **Nevatim** *138:070*

Moshav 8 km. E of Be'er Sheva' on road to Dimona. Founded 1949 at kibbutz Nevatim before moving to present site as part of programme to set up settlements in Negev after Yom Kippur in 1946. During War of Independence it was besieged but held out with aid of supplies dropped from the air. Pop.: 450.

■ **Newe 'Ammi'el** *163:234*

Vocational school in Yizre'el Valley 3 km. SE of Qiryat Tiv'on, near *moshav* Sede Ya'aqov. Named after Rabbi Moshe Avigdor Amiel (1883-1946), from 1936 chief rabbi of Tel Aviv. Curriculum includes aeroplane mechanics and catering.

● **Newe Ativ** *219:296*

Moshav shittufi on Golan Heights 8 km. E of Banyas. Named after 4 soldiers who died on Golan (acronym in Hebrew of Avraham, Toviyya, Yair, Binyamin). Established 1969. The original settlement was disbanded and in its place the present *moshav* was founded in 1971 by demobilized soldiers. *Moshav* operates ski facilities on Mt. Ḥermon.

Newe Efrayim *138:159*

Urban settlement 4 km. NW of Ben-Gurion Airport. Named after Efrayim (Fred) Monosson, US Zionist. Founded 1953 by El 'Al workers. Area: 650 d. Pop.: 1,900.

★ **Newe Etan** *200:211*

Kibbutz 3 km. E of Bet She'an. Name based on Biblical passage "Behold, like a lion coming up from the jungle of the Jordan against a *strong sheepfold*" (Jer. 49:19). Founded 1938 by members of 'Aqiva movement from Poland in framework of "stockade and tower" settlements. Area: 7,000 d. (aside from pasture lands on Golan Heights). Pop.: several hundred.

■ **Newe Hadassa** *138:184*

Educational institute in Sharon near Tel Yiẓhaq. Founded 1949 by Yesodot educational organization of HaNo'ar HaẒiyoni. Area: 400 d. Farm and workshops.

● **Newe Ilan** *158:135*

Moshav shittufi in Judean Hills 3 km. W of Abu Ghosh. The area has many pine trees planted by JNF in the area, hence its name (*ilan* = tree). Initially set up as a kibbutz by French immigrants, former members of the *maquis*, a WWII anti-Nazi underground resistance movement. Kibbutz disbanded and from 1954 to 1967 it was an educational institute. In 1971 an American-Israeli group settled here and established a rural, industrial, educational settlement.

Newe Mikha'el *151:120*

Regional centre on E fringe of Judean Hills 3 km. S of 'Eẓyona junction. Named after US Zionist Michael Weiss. Founded 1958. Services settlements of Avi'ezer, Adderet and Rogelit in 'Adullam region.

● **Newe Mivtaḥ** *125:134*

Moshav on Coastal Plain 3 km. SW of Gedera. Founded 1950. Area: 2,000 d. Pop.: 200.

Newe Shalom *148:136*

Beginnings of international cooperative settlement in Judean Foothills alongside kibbutz Naḥshon. Planned as farming and craft settlement for people of all faiths and nationalities. Founded 1969 and based on an idea proposed by a Dominican monk of Jewish extraction. Name derives from Biblical passage "My people will abide in a *peaceful habitation*" (Isa. 32:18).

★ **Newe Ur** *202:221*

Kibbutz in Jordan Valley 4 km. S of Gesher. Founded 1949. Name taken from Ur of the Chaldees, birthplace of the patriarch Abraham. Area: 3,900 d. Pop.: several hundred.

Newe Ya'ar *167:234*

Experimental agricultural station in Yizre'el Valley opposite Bet She'arim. Established 1954 on lands of former German colony Waldheim, hence its name. It was here that a superior strain of wheat called Newe Ya'ar was developed.

★ **Newe Yam** *143:232*

Kibbutz on Karmel coast 2 km. SW of 'Atlit. Founded 1939 by Gordonia group of "illegal" immigrants from Poland. Area: 3,000 d. Pop.: 200.

● **Newe Yamin** *144:175*

Moshav in Sharon 1 km. SE of Kefar Sava. Name based on sound of Arab name, en Nabi Yamin, of an ancient tomb in the area. Founded 1949 by Greek immigrants. Area: 3,300 d. Pop.: 560. Near *moshav* on Qalqilya road are 2 adjacent Moslem tomb structures. Arab tradition claims that en Nabi Yamin is the tomb of Benjamin, son of Jacob. Remains of Byzantine settlement nearby.

● **Newe Yaraq** *143:170*

Moshav in Sharon 5 km. NW of Petaḥ Tiqwa. Founded 1951. Area: 2,800 d. Pop.: 420.

Newe Zohar *185:061*

Regional centre, health and holiday resort on Dead Sea shore near 'En Gedi–Sedom–'Arad junction. Contains offices of Tamar local council, hot baths (Ḥamme Zohar), guest house, youth hostel, small museum, Bet HaYozer, with boat of Molineux, the Dead Sea explorer, Meẓad Zohar observation point and campsite.

● **Neẓer Ḥazzani** *085:088*

Moshav in Gaza Strip 5 km. N of Khan Yunis. Named after the late Mikha'el Ḥazzani, former minister of Social Welfare. Established 1973 as *naḥal* outpost, Qatif. Received civilian status 1977. Area: 60 d. Pop.: 120.

★ **Neẓer Sereni** *134:148*

Kibbutz on Coastal Plain, 3 km. E of Nes Ẓiyyona. Named after Enzo Sereni (1905-1944), one of the parachutists sent by Jews of Palestine into occupied Europe during WWII. He was captured by the Germans in N Italy and shot. Founded 1948 by survivors of Nazi concentration camps. Area: 6,000 d. Pop.: 650. **The Schepoon agricultural school** Alongside kibbutz are remains of a German Templer agricultural school and courtyard (established by Ludwig Schneller at end of 19th c.). This was General Allenby's headquarters during WWI.

○ **Ni'lin** *152:150*

Arab village 12 km. E of Lod. Pop.: 1,250.

∴ **Nimrin** *190:245*

Abandoned village in Galilee 3 km. NE of Golani junction. Built on ancient settlement ruins, apparently town of Nemerim from Second

Temple Period (mentioned in ancient liturgical poem for Hanukkah festival). After destruction of Temple it was called Kefar Nimra and mentioned in Talmud. Ancient synagogue remains and other remnants from Roman–Byzantine Period.

Nimrod Fortress → Qal'at Nimrud

★ **Nir'am** *110:103*

Kibbutz in Negev 2 km. W of Sederot. Founded 1943 by members of Gordonia group from Bessarabia. During War of Independence served as important base for defence of besieged Negev. Area: 20,000 d. Pop.: 330. Nearby is nature reserve (245 d.) surrounded by coarse-sand ridge. Has typical local flora mixed with desert vegetation.

★ **Niran** *193:152*

Kibbutz in Jordan Valley 10 km. N of Jericho, near remains of 5th-6th c. synagogue. Established 1975. First settlers housed at kibbutz Gilgal; later moved to abandoned Jordanian army camp on N shore of Dead Sea. In 1977 moved to present site. Area: 300 d.

● **Nir 'Aqiva** *116:097*

Moshav shittufi in Negev 6 km. NE of Netivot junction. Named after Akiva Jacob Ettinger (1872-1945), director of agricultural settlement department of Jewish Agency. Founded 1953. Area: 1,000 d. Pop.: 180.

● **Nir Banim** *127:119*

Moshav in Lakhish region 7 km. S of Mal'akhi junction. Established 1954 by *moshav* youth from Nahalal, Kefar Vitkin, Kefar Yeḥezqel, Ḥerut, and Be'er Toviyya. Hence its name (*banim* = sons). Area: 3,500 d. Pop.: 350.

★ **Nir Dawid (Tel 'Amal)** *193:212*

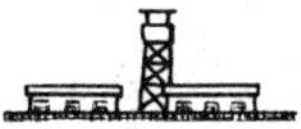

Kibbutz 3 km. W of Bet She'an. Named after David Wolffsohn (1856-1914), 2nd president of World Zionist Organization. Founded 1936 as first of the "stockade and tower" settlements and called Tel 'Amal. Area: 7,800 d. Pop.: 700. **Tel** Within kibbutz, excavations have uncovered remains of Iron Age structures including a weavers' and dyers' workshop. Settlement destroyed during campaign of Shishak. An impoverished settlement continued to eke out its existence here until the 8th c. BCE.

★ **Nir Eliyyahu** *145:178*

Kibbutz in Sharon 4 km. NE of Kefar Sava. Named after Eliyahu Golomb (1893-1945), Haganah leader. Established 1950. Area: 3,600 d. Pop.: 330.

● **Nir 'Eẓyon** *149:233*

Moshav shittufi on Mt. Karmel 4 km. SE of 'Atlit interchange. Named in memory of Kefar 'Eẓyon, destroyed during War of Independence. Established 1950 by survivors from Kefar 'Eẓyon. Area: 3,000 d. Pop.: 270.

● **Nir Gallim** *120:137*

Moshav shittufi on Coastal Plain, at N entrance to Ashdod. Name means field of the waves. Founded in 1949 by Bene 'Aqiva group. Area: 3,500 d. Pop.: 510. **Mevo Ashdod reserve** NE of *moshav* is a nature reserve (870 d.) with concentration of white acacia trees.

● **Nir Ḥen** *123:113*

Moshav in Lakhish region 5 km. W of Qiryat Gat. Named in memory of "58" (*ḥen* in gematria) El 'Al passengers shot down over Bulgaria in 1955. Founded 1956. Area: 5,200 d. Pop.: 270.

★ **Nirim** *092:082*

Kibbutz in Negev 5 km. NW of Ma'on junction. Founded 1946, one of 11 settlements established in one day in Negev. Founded by Nir group of HaShomer HaẒa'ir. Although besieged and badly damaged by Egyptian army during War of Independence it was not abandoned. After the war the settlers relocated to present site. Area: 22,000 d. Pop.: 350. One km. SE of kibbutz are ruins of Ma'on.

● **Nir Moshe** *114:098*

Moshav in Negev 4 km. SE of Sederot. Named after Moshe Smilansky (1874-1953), Hebrew writer, farmer and public figure. Founded 1953. Area: 2,000 d. Pop.: 250.

★ **Nir 'Oz** *093:080*

Kibbutz in Negev 5 km. NW of Magen junction. Founded as *naḥal* outpost in 1955; became civilian settlement in 1957. Border settlement up to Six-Day War. Area: 20,000 d. Pop.: 300.

● **Nir Yaffe** *173:219*

Moshav in Yizre'el Valley 5 km. E of Megiddo junction. Named after M. Jaffe, S African Jewish philanthropist. Founded 1956. Area: 5,000 d. Pop.: 280.

● **Nir Yisra'el** *115:122*

Moshav on Coastal Plain 6 km. E of Ashqelon. Named after an industrialist and philanthropist. Founded 1949. Area: 4,000 d. Pop.: 270.

★ **Nir Yiẓḥaq** *088:072*

Kibbutz in Negev 13 km. SW of Ma'on junction. Named after Yiẓḥak Sadeh (1890-1952), one of founders of Palmaḥ. Established 1949 on former site of kibbutz Nirim by HaShomer HaẒa'ir members. Area: 5,000 d. Pop.: 450.

● **Nir Ẓevi** *136:151*

Moshav in Judean Foothills 2 km. NW of Ramla. Named after Baron Hirsch (1831-1896) (Hirsch = Ẓevi). Founded 1954 by Argentinian immigrants and first called Kefar Argentina. Area: 2,500 d. Pop.: 680.

○ **Niṣf Jubeil** *170:187*

Arab village (pop.: 220) in Samarian Hills 2 km. E of Sabastiya.

◆ **Niva** *117:112*

Farm on Coastal Plain 6 km. S of Giv'ati junction, off road to Sederot. Established 1954 and owned by Amir company.

● **Niẓẓana** *094:033*

Moshav in Negev Hills 2 km. NW of ancient site 'Auja el Ḥafir. Established 1980.

Niẓẓana ('Auja el Ḥafir) *096:031*

Site of ancient settlement alongside wells and road junction, on border of Negev and Sinai. From Niẓẓana routes branch out to Sinai and Egypt, to Negev and Judean Hills and to Elat and Rafah. Flint tools and sherds indicate occupation already in Late Stone Age. It was a road station in Hellenistic, Nabatean and Roman Periods, a fortified city in Byzantine Period, an impoverished village during Arab Period and finally abandoned. During WWI it was a German–Turkish base from where attacks were made on the Suez Canal. During British Mandate it was a desert border post and regional centre. Captured by Israel Defence Forces in the War of Independence, it was, according to Armistice

Agreement, included in demilitarized zone between Israel and Egypt. Meeting place of Israel–Egypt Mixed Armistice Commission between 1949 and 1956. Remains of fort, churches, Byzantine houses, cemetery with Hellenistic, Nabatean, and Arab grave-stones from 5th, 6th and 7th c. Excavations uncovered 6th and 7th c. documents written on papyrus which mention the name Nessana.

● **Niẓẓane ‘Oz** — *150:190*

Moshav on border of Sharon and Samarian Hills, 3 km. W of Tulkarm. Founded as *naḥal* outpost in 1951. Area: 3,000 d. Pop.: 360. Adjacent to *moshav* is memorial to Ḥativa "5", the unit that captured the area in Six-Day War.

★ **Niẓẓanim** *(qevuẓa)* — *115:125*

Collective settlement on Coastal Plain 7 km. NE of Ashqelon. Founded 1943. During War of Independence 37 members of the collective were killed, the settlement captured and its defenders taken prisoner. After a few months it was retaken by Israel Defence Forces and in 1951 the repatriated prisoners-of-war re-established the collective on present site. Area: 5,000 d. Pop.: 300. **Remains** To the W *112:125* are remains of settlement from Persian Period. Remains of Roman-Byzantine church, coloured mosaic and tomb. Flint implements found from Mesolithic and Neolithic Periods.

■ **Niẓẓanim** (youth village) — *115:127*

Youth village and educational institute on Coastal Plain N of *qevuẓat* Niẓẓanim. Founded 1949 on original site of kibbutz Niẓẓanim (destroyed during War of Independence and re-established 3 km. to the S). Area: 2,000 d. Pop.: 370, students and staff. Courses offered in agriculture, agricultural mechanization and seamanship. SW of youth village is a nature reserve (7,650 d.) including coarse-sand dunes, coastal flora and Naḥal Evtaḥ.

● **No‘am** — *130:108*

Moshav in Lakhish region 6 km. S of Qiryat Gat. Founded 1955. Area: 4,000 d. Pop.: 520. **Kh. Sakariya** Within *moshav* is Moslem holy tomb with 14th c. inscription and remains of an ancient khan. To the W Byzantine sherds were found.

Nofekh — *142:161*

Rural settlement in Sharon 4 km. SE of Petaḥ Tiqwa. Name means an emerald, one of the stones in the breastpiece of judgment (Ex. 28:18). Founded 1949 on lands of abandoned village of Rantiyya as a settlement for stone masons. Pop.: 210.

● **Nogah** — *121:114*

Moshav in Lakhish region 7 km. W of Qiryat Gat. Founded 1955. Area: 3,600 d. Pop.: 550.

● **Nordiyya** — *140:191*

Moshav shittufi in Sharon 1 km. SW of Sharon junction. Named after Max Nordau (1849-1923), Zionist leader. Founded 1948 by Irgun and Betar members who served in British army. Area: 2,200 d. Pop.: 300.

◆ **Notera** — *210:278*

Farm in Ḥula Valley 3 km. S of kibbutz Gonen. Name based on Biblical passage "they made me *keeper* of the vineyards" (Song 1:6). First a *naḥal* outpost, it later became a kibbutz.

● **Nov** — *224:248*

Moshav on Golan Heights 3 km. SW of Ramat Magshimim. Named after ancient Jewish town mentioned in Talmud which was near Susita.

Established 1972 and moved to present site in 1973. Pop.: several hundred. Area: 4,000 d. Torah study institute. **Ancient Nob** Within abandoned village Mazra'at Nab is a tel with remains of ancient building stones, columns, capitals and a pool from Roman–Byzantine Period. **Nature reserve** To the SE, near the road, is a small nature reserve (20 d.) with many swamp irises — a flower which is almost extinct in rest of country.

o Nuba *153:112*

Arab village in Judean Hills 10 km. NW of Hebron. Pop.: 1,200.

o Nu'eima *193:144*

Arab village with refugee camp alongside it in Jordan Valley, 4 km. NW of Jericho. Pop.: 500.

∴ Nukheila *211:296*

Ruins of abandoned village in Galilee 2 km. N of kibbutz Dan. Alongside it is a former Syrian military post, which was involved in a border incident over use of water from Naḥal Dan.

Nurit *183:216*

Gadna camp at NW corner of Mt. Gilboa', 2 km. S of Ma'yan Ḥarod. Named after both abandoned village Nuris and Hebrew name for ranunculus — a flower common in the area.

Nur esh Shams *155:191*

Refugee camp in Samaria 3 km. E of Tulkarm. Pop.: 2,500. During British Mandate there was a prison here and inmates worked at nearby stone quarries.

Nuṣeirat *092:095*

Arab refugee camp in Gaza Strip 5 km. NE of Deir el Balaḥ.

O

Odem 222:290

Moshav shittufi on Golan, 4 km. S of Mas'ada junction. Established 1975 on site of abandoned Syrian army camp. **Mt. Odem** (1,187 m. above sea level), 1 km. W of *moshav, 220:289.* The Hebrew name, as the Arabic one Tell el Aḥmar, means the red mountain because of its distinctive red colouring. To the N is the Odem forest nature reserve.

Ofaqim 113:080

Town in Besor region in Negev 24 km. W of Be'er Sheva'. Name means horizons owing to wide open vistas in the area. Founded 1955. Attained its own municipality in 1958. Area: 4,400 d. Pop.: 12,000. **Ruins** Within town are remains of Turkish fortress, Byzantine grain silos and other antiquities which have not yet been studied. Possibly site of Futeis.

'Ofer 148:225

Moshav on Mt. Karmel 7 km. N of Zikhron Ya'aqov. Name translated from name of abandoned Arab village 'Ein Ghazal meaning a baby gazelle. Founded 1950 by Indian immigrants in framework of "city to settlement" programme. Pop.: 250.

'Ofra *(Josh. 18:23)* 174:151

Community settlement on border of Judean and Samarian Hills 7 km. NE of Ramallah. Same name as Biblical city in Benjamin tribal allotment. Identified with adjacent village et Taiyiba. First Gush Emunim settlement. Established 1975 in abandoned Jordanian army camp. In 1977 it became a permanent settlement. Youth hostel and field school.

Ohad 096:072

Moshav in Negev Eshkol region 18 km. SE of Rafah. Biblical name, one of sons of Simeon (Gen. 46:10). Founded 1969. Pop.: 200. Remains of Roman settlement within *moshav.*

Oholo 204:236

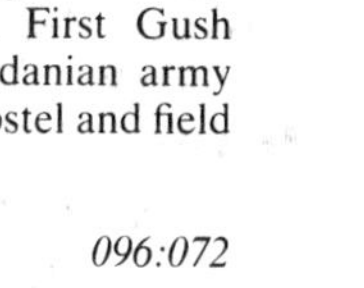

Educational institute and college on shore of Lake Kinneret, between Deganya "A" and Kinneret *(moshava)*, on site of ancient city of Beth-yerah. Named in memory of Berl Katznelson who pitched his tent (*oholo*) here when he was a member of Kinneret *(qevuẓa)*. Founded 1951. Seminar and training college for nursery school and school teachers. College has live-in dormitories. (See Bet Yeraḥ.)

'Olesh 148:193

Moshav 8 km. E of Sharon junction. Named for indigenous chicory plant. Founded 1949 by Rumanian immigrants. Area: 2,900 d. Pop.: 330.

Oman 173:218

Rural centre 5 km. E of Megiddo junction for settlements of Ta'anakh region: Mele'a, Gadish and Nir Yafe. Founded 1958.

'Omer 135:075

Urban settlement 6 km. NE of Be'er Sheva' on road to Hebron. Founded as *moshav shittufi* in 1949 by group of demobilized soldiers. Over the years the population, nature and name of the settlement changed many times: 1951 — Elata Cooperative, 1953 — ‘Omer, 1962 — Qevuzat Tomer, 1964 — ‘Omer residential quarter and from 1974 — local council. Area: 12,000 d. Pop.: 2,600.

Omez *149:197*

Moshav in Sharon 6.5 km. NW of Tulkarm. Name is Hebrew acronym for Irgun Mityashvim Zeva'i (military settlers organization). Founded 1949 by demobilized soldiers. Pop.: 200.

Ora *164:129*

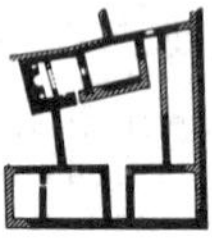

Moshav 2 km. W of Qiryat Yovel neighbourhood in Jerusalem. Named after nearby Arab village, Jura. Founded 1950. Area: 3,500 d. Pop.: 350. **Spring and antiquities** Near *moshav* is spring, ‘En Sarig, formerly ‘Ein Jadida, and nearby is a ruin with remains of church and mosaic floor.

Oranim *161:235*

Educational centre 12 km. W of Qiryat Tiv‘on. Surrounded by pine woods (*oranim*). Founded 1951. Includes training college for nursery, primary and high school teachers, linked to Haifa University. Botanical garden and small zoo.

Or ‘Aqiva *142:212*

Development town off Haifa–Tel Aviv road 2 km. E of ancient Caesarea. Named after Rabbi ‘Aqiva, one of 10 Jewish martyrs tortured and executed by Romans at Caesarea. Founded 1951 to house Qesari *ma‘bara* (immigrant transit camp) dwellers of Caesarea. Area: 2,600 d. Pop.: 7,000.

Or HaNer *112:107*

Kibbutz in N Negev 3.5 km. N of Sederot. Origin of name from Talmud (Sanh. 4:32 b), "and the light of a candle (*or haner*) at Beror Ḥayil, showed that a feast (was being celebrated) there." This was a secret code referring to a circumcision ceremony, forbidden by Roman Emperor Hadrian (117-138 CE). Established 1955. Pop.: 330.

Oron *151:036*

Phosphate plant in Negev, S of Makhtesh Ḥatira (HaMakhtesh HaGadol). Name originates from Greek word *phos* meaning light (*or* in Hebrew). Established 1954 to provide employment for residents of Dimona and Yeroḥam.

Orot *125:128*

Moshav in Negev 1 km. NW of Qiryat Mal'akhi. Name derived from Bible (Isa. 26:19): *tal orot* = dew of light. Founded 1952 by immigrant members of Ikar Ha‘Oved movement from USA. Area: 2,200 d. Pop.: 300.

Or Tal *221:277*

Kibbutz on Golan Heights 3 km. SW of kibbutz ‘En Ziwan. Established 1978. Pop.: tens.

Or Yehuda *136:159*

Development town 7 km. SE of Tel Aviv. Named after Rabbi Yehuda Alkalai, a protagonist of the Return to Zion ideal. Founded 1950. Today it has a local council (5,800 d.) and includes Mesubbim village, which was established on abandoned lands of Kheiriya village. Pop.: 20,000. Memorial to 2 Jews hanged in Iraq. **Ono** Tel of ancient Ono on site of former ‘Ana village. City inhabited in days of Ezra and Nehemiah by returning exiles. Important town during Second Temple and Roman Periods. Flourished in 3rd c. CE but probably destroyed in 7th c. CE.

‘Ozem *121:116*

Moshav in Lakhish region 6 km. NW of Qiryat Gat. Founded 1955. Area: 2,200 d. Pop.: 680.

P

Pa'ame Tashaz *121:094*

Moshav in Negev 10 km. E of Netivot. Named after operation in which 11 settlements were established in Negev in one night in October 1946. Founded 1953. Area: 1,500 d. Pop.: 280.

Palmaḥim *122:149*

Kibbutz on Mediterranean shore 10 km. SW of Rishon LeẒiyyon. Founded 1949 by scout youths and demobilized Palmaḥ soldiers. Area: 3,300 d. Pop.: 370. S of kibbutz are ruins of the port of ancient Jabneh.

Paran *164:975*

Moshav in 'Arava 33 km. S of 'En Yahav. Name from nearby Naḥal Paran. Founded 1971. Area: 1,200 d. Pop.: a few hundred.

Pardes Ḥanna-Karkur *148:208*

Amalgamation of 2 adjacent settlements in Sharon 6 km. NE of Ḥadera. Joint local council established 1969. Area: 17,000 d. Pop.: 16,000. **Pardes Ḥanna** Founded as a farming village (*moshava*) in 1929 and named after wife of Nathan Mayer Rothschild. After 1948 a large *ma'bara* (transit camp for new immigrants) existed in the village. Eventually most of inhabitants were resettled. Suburbs of Pardes Ḥanna include: Meged, Newe Asher (named after Selig Brodetsky, 1888-1954, mathematician and British Zionist leader) and Tel Ẓevi (named after Ẓevi Henri Frank, a director of ICA). Remains of Byzantine settlement. **Karkur** Initially a farming village, it adopted the Arabic place name, the origin of which is unknown. Lands were purchased in 1913, and when water was discovered in 1922, it became a permanent settlement. Over the years it absorbed the adjacent settlements of Newe Efrayim and Tel Shalom. **Tel Shalom** Remains of large structure on summit of hill *148:208*, built of large hewn stones. Perhaps remains of Roman mausoleum. **Nature reserve** Small nature reserve of Tabor oak trees. Cemetery of Kh. Ẓerqes, a Circassian village established in 1860's and abandoned after residents were stricken by malaria.

Pardesya *141:190*

Rural settlement 3 km. S of Sharon junction. Named for plentiful orchards (*pardes*) in the area. Founded 1942 by Yemenite immigrants. Area: 1,000 d. Pop.: 950.

Park HaSharon

Nature reserve in Sharon, between Mikhmoret and Jisr ez Zarqa. Area: 2,200 d. Coastal cliffs, coarse-sanded hills, and a natural wood of carob and *pistacia lentiscus* trees — the only one of its kind in the coastal area.

Parod *191:260*

Kibbutz in Galilee off Acre–Safed road, 2 km. E of Ḥananya junction. Same name as Jewish settlement from Byzantine Period. (It was retained in name of abandoned village, Farradiyya.) Founded 1949 by immigrants from Hungary and Transylvania. Initially called Gardosh, after the group leader who died in the Holocaust. Area: 3,500 d. Pop.: 300. **Eshed Taḥanot** Three ancient water-powered flour mills. W of kibbutz *189:260*, is an **experimental station** which belongs to Ministry of Agriculture. Nearby are ruins of Kafr ʻInan, site of Kefar Ḥananya from Byzantine Period.

Parod ʻIllit → Amirim

• **Pattish** *108:081*

Moshav in Negev 6 km. W of Ofaqim. Named after ancient Pattish, identified with site of adjacent Kh. Futeis (see Ḥurbat Pattish). Founded 1950. Area: 5,000 d. Pop.: 630.

• **Pedaya** *139:140*

Moshav in Judean Hills 7 km. S of Ramla. Named after Pedaiah, father of Zebidah, mother of King Jehoiakim (II Kings 23:36). Founded 1951. Area: 1,600 d. Pop.: 450.

• **Peduyyim** *112:081*

Moshav in Negev 2 km. N of Ofaqim. Name originates from passage, "And the *ransomed* of the Lord shall return" (Isa. 35:10). Founded 1950 by Yemenite immigrants and initially called ʻImara "A". Area: 4,000 d. Pop.: 300.

★ **Pelekh** *172:259*

Kibbutz under construction in Tefen region in Upper Galilee 4 km. NW of Majd el Kurum. Name means spindle.

Peluggot *126:115*

Road junction in Judean Foothills NW of Qiryat Gat. Named after Arab village Faluja, destroyed in War of Independence. Village used as base by invading Egyptian army, while it was encircled by Israel Defence Forces in the area known as Faluja Pocket.

• **Peqiʻin HaḤadasha** *180:265*

Moshav in Galilee 5 km. SE of Ma'alot–Tarshiḥa, NW of ancient Peqiʻin (Buqeiʻa). Founded 1955. Pop.: 260. Near *moshav* is tomb attributed to Rabbi Oshaiah of Tirya (4th c. CE). In stream bed is spring called ʻEin Tirya. **Ḥurbat Gis** Within *moshav* are ruins of ancient settlement that was located at summit and at foot of hill called Kh. Jus in Arabic. Sherds indicate occupation in Iron Age; however, some remains on summit are from a later period.

• **Perazon** *179:216*

Moshav in Yizreʻel Valley 8 km. S of ʻAfula. Name taken from Song of Deborah: "The *peasantry* ceased in Israel..." (Judg. 5:7). Founded 1953. Area: 2,200 d. Pop.: 500.

Perfume Route → Derekh HaBesamim

■ **Petaḥ Tiqwa** *145:166*

City on Coastal Plain 10 km. E of Tel Aviv. Name originates from passage "And there I will give her her vineyards, and make the Valley of Achor a *door of hope...*" (Hos. 2:15). Founded 1878 by religious Jews from Jerusalem on swamp land near sources of Yarqon River. Land was purchased from the share-croppers' village of Mulabbis. It was the first modern Jewish farming village (*moshava*) and was therefore known as the "mother of the *moshavot*". Due to malaria and local Bedouin attacks, the founders were forced to move to nearby Yehud until the swamps had been drained. From the outset it served as a depot for Jewish labourers, and thus became an important station for pioneers of the 2nd ʻAliyah and members of the labour movement. It was here that the foundations were laid for HaPoʻel HaẒaʻir and Aḥdut HaʻAvoda political parties.

PETAḤ TIQWA

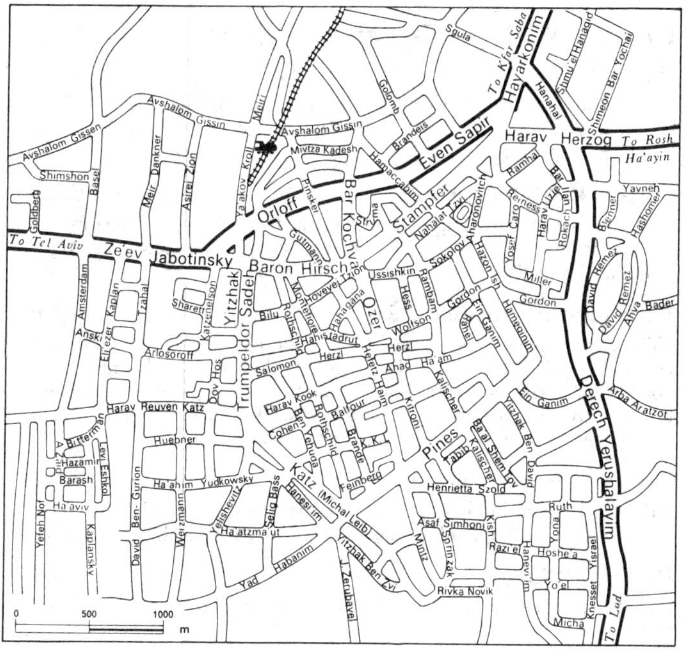

© carta, JERUSALEM

During WWI Petaḥ Tiqwa was on the front line of the fighting and the settlers suffered as a result. In the 1921 Riots it was the target of many attacks by Arab gangs. However, in same year, it received status of local council and in 1937, municipality status. Over the years it expanded and absorbed adjoining settlements of Kefar Gannim, Baptist Village, Qiryat Arye, Qiryat Matalon, Gat Rimmon, 'Amishav, She'areha, Maḥane Yehuda, Kefar Avraham and Kafr Fajja. Area: 38,000 d. Pop.: 115,000. At entrance to city is a monument in honour of Baron de Rothschild who supported the village in its early days. Memorial to those who fell in 1921 Riots and a memorial centre to those who died in Israel's wars. **Kefar Avraham** Formerly a religious *moshav*, it was founded in 1932. Over the years it lost its agricultural character and became a quarter of Petaḥ Tiqwa. Two *yeshivot*: Torah U'Melakha and Naḥalat Dawid.

• Petaḥya *139:141*

Moshav in Judean Hills 6 km. S of Ramla. The name is a personal name in Bible — Pethahiah (I Chron. 24:16). Founded 1951 in framework of "ship to settlement" movement. Area: 9,500 d. Pop.: 460.

• Peẓa'el *192:161*

Moshav in Jordan Valley 10 km. SW of Adam Bridge (Damiya). Named after ancient city Phasaelis (see Kh. Faṣayil). Founded 1970 and located at Ma'ale Efrayim till 1975. Area: 3,000 d. Pop.: 80. **Statue to Biq'a fighters** Two km. NW of *moshav*, off Biq'a road, is a statue commemorating soldiers who fell here during Six-Day War and War of Attrition. Concrete structure, iron statue, made from war materials, and inscription of names of fallen.

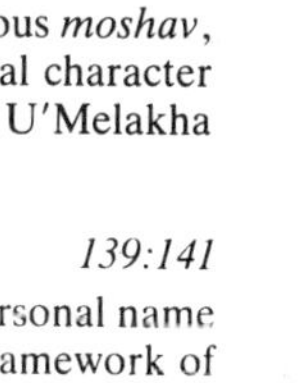

Pigeon Islet *141:218*

Three small islands 400 m. from shore, opposite Ma'agan Mikha'el.

Named thus owing to the many pigeons who nest here. Ancient remains on S of island.

Pilgrims' Way → Derekh HaḤogegim

Pirḥe Aviv *169:249*

Observation point in Lower Galilee 5 km. NE of Shefar'am. *Aviv* is acronym for name Abraham Jacob Brawer, a geographer and educator in Israel. Established 1980.

● Porat *145:187*

Moshav 7 km. SE of Sharon junction near Kefar Ya'beẓ. Name means fruitful, from Jacob's blessing in Genesis (49:22). Founded 1950. Area: 2,800 d. Pop.: 850.

Poriyya (Kefar 'Avoda) *201:236*

Village in Galilee 4 km. NW of Ẓemaḥ junction. In 1912 it was established as a fruit farm by a group of American Zionists, but abandoned during WWI. In 1940 a group from nearby kibbutz Alummot temporarily settled here and in 1949 a work village was established nearby by Yemenite immigrants. Pop.: 180.

Poriyya (Newe 'Oved) ▲ *200:238*

Urban settlement in Galilee 5 km. S of Tiberias. Founded 1949. Pop.: 750. To the N is Poriyya hospital — medical centre for Lower Galilee.

Poriyya 'Illit *201:237*

Urban settlement in Galilee 6 km. S of Tiberias. Founded 1955. Pop.: 800.

Q

○ **Qabalan** *177:167*

Arab village in Samarian Hills 13 km. S of Shekhem. Pop.: 2,000.

○ **Qabatiya** *176:201*

Arab village in Samarian Hills 5 km. S of Jenin. Pop.: 6,000. Within village is tel of ancient settlement with cisterns and ancient tombstones nearby. There is a cemetery for Iraqi soldiers who died in battle for Jenin during War of Independence. Three km. NW of the village, near the junction of Jenin–Shekhem road, is a memorial to Israeli soldiers from a tank unit who died in the Dotan Valley battle during Six-Day War.

⋀ **Qabr ʻUbayan** *173:109*

Byzantine settlement ruins in Judean Desert 14 km. NE of Hebron, above Wadi ʻUbayan.

★ **Qaddarim** *193:257*

Kibbutz in Galilee 5 km. SE of Hananya junction. Nearby is site of ancient village of Hananya dating from Byzantine and Roman times which was renowned for its excellent potters (*qaddar* = potter). Hence the name of the kibbutz and the hill to the N. Founded 1980. Pop.: 60.

⊾ **Qadima** ⋀ ✿ ● *142:188*

Settlement 5 km. S of Sharon junction. Founded 1933 by Yehoshua Hankin (1864-1945) for settling German immigrants. Area: 9,000 d. Pop.: 4,000. **Manzura** Flint implements were discovered here indicating occupation in Paleolithic and Mesolithic Periods.

○ **Qaffin** *158:204*

Arab village in Samarian Hills 8 km. E of ʻIron junction. Pop.: 2,500.

⋀ **(El) Qalʻa** *176:181*

Ruins of Byzantine fortress on E summit of Mt. ʻEval 1 km. NE of Shekhem. Square structure 30x30 m. with long rooms around central courtyard.

○ **Qalandya** ⋀ *169:141*

Arab village 8 km. N of Jerusalem, near Jerusalem airport. Pop.: 800. Ancient remains including Byzantine bathhouse were discovered here. A Roman villa has recently been excavated near the village.

⌐ **Qalansuwa** ⋀ ⁝ ● ◆ *148:187*

Arab village in Sharon 5 km. SW of Tulkarm. Name is Turkish and means piace with tower. Founded more than 300 years ago on a more ancient settlement. During Disturbances of 1936-1939 it served as base for Arab gangs and in War of Independence it was a base for Iraqi army. By Armistice Agreement it fell within territory of Israel. Pop.: 6,500. **Calansue** Within village are remains of Crusader tower and church.

Qalʻat el Burak → **Berekhot Shelomo**

Qal'at Futeis → Meẓudat Pattish

Qal'at Hunin → Ḥurbat Meẓudat Hunin

Qal'at el Ḥuṣn → Susita

Qal'at Ibn Ma'n → Arbel

Qal'at Jiddin → Yeḥi'am

Qal'at Nimrud **(Meẓudat Nimrod)** * *217:295*

Ruins of large fortress on S slopes of Mt. Ḥermon, 2 km. NE of Banyas. Erected by Crusaders between 1130 and 1140. Taking advantage of mountain's natural features, it was built long and narrow — 450x60 m. Arab legend attributes building of fortress to Nimrod, the mighty hunter. Also called Qal'at eṣ Ṣubeiba by the Arabs. In 1164 it fell to Nureddin. In 1219 the sultan of Damascus destroyed the fortress to prevent it from falling into Crusader hands. Between 1228 and 1230 it was rebuilt by 'Othman, nephew of Saladin, and additional building was carried out by Sultan Baybars. After fall of Crusader Kingdom, the fortress lost its importance and was later abandoned. Remains of its towers and walls can be seen today. Moslem wall paintings were discovered in the keep, at the eastern edge of the castle. Fortress can be approached from western side, where a rock-cut moat protects the ramparts.

Qal'at el Qurein → Montfort

Qal'at Ras el 'Ein → Afeq **(Rosh Ha'Ayin)**

Qal'at eṣ Ṣubeiba → Qal'at Nimrud

∴ **Qalla'** *219:288*

Abandoned village on Golan Heights 5 km. SW of Mas'ada junction. Also called er Ruheila after Bedouin tribe resident in this area in 19th c. Part of village was a Syrian military post. Scene of fierce fighting during Six-Day War. Within village are a number of memorials to Israeli soldiers.

Qalmaniyya *142:178*

Regional centre and educational institute in Sharon 3 km. N of Kefar Sava. Formerly a private farm founded in 1927.

□ **Qalqilya** *146:176*

Arab town on border of Sharon and Samarian Hills 3 km. E of Kefar Sava. Site of ancient settlement. Road station during Roman Period called Calceailea. During WWI a number of Jewish families expelled from Tel Aviv settled here. The Armistice Agreement left Qalqilya in the Kingdom of Jordan. It was a base for terrorist attacks on Israel during 50's and 60's, and as a result suffered a number of reprisal attacks by the Israel Defence Forces. During Six Day War some of the municipality buildings were blown-up, and have since been rebuilt. Pop.: 9,000. Within Qalqilya some flint implements were found indicating prehistoric habitation here.

Qalya (beach) *197:131*

Bathing beach on N shore of Dead Sea. Before War of Independence there was a hotel here. The name is a Hebrew acronym that translates as "Dead Sea comes to life".

★ **Qalya** (kibbutz) *194:128*

Kibbutz near NW shore of Dead Sea near Ḥurvot Qumeran. Name is Hebrew acronym that translates "Dead Sea comes to life". Name also appears in Talmud as name of a plant found in area of Dead Sea (Eruvin 3:28). *Naḥal* outpost in 1968 in abandoned Jordanian army camp by old

Qalya (the site of the hotel before the War of Independence). In 1974 it became a permanent civilian settlement and kibbutz and moved to present site. At first called Almog (after Yehuda Almog, former head of the regional council) and later the name changed back to Qalya. Area: 2,000 d.

Qanat Musa *188:148*

Remains of Roman aqueduct in Jordan Valley 10 km. NE of Jericho. Part of aqueduct carried water from 'Ein el 'Auja to Jericho. Nearby, *188:147*, are remains of Roman structure.

Qaqun *149:195*

Ruins of abandoned village in Sharon 13 km. E of Netanya. Built on ruins of ancient settlement which was inhabited during Roman Period. In 1170 Benjamin of Tudela founded a Jewish town here. A castle was built during Crusader Period and called Caco; its remains are still evident. Mamluk Sultan Baybars captured Qaqun in 1260's and enlarged the castle in 1266. In 1799 a battle between Napoleon's army and Turkish army was fought nearby. In pre-State years Arab gangs used the village as a base. Captured by Israel Defence Forces during War of Independence after battle with Iraqi army.

Qarantal → Deir el Quruntul

Qarawet Bani Ḥasan (Qarawa et Taḥta) *159:170*

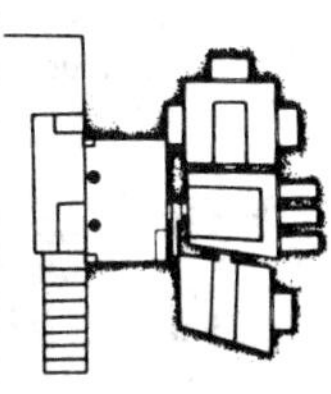

Arab village (pop.: 700) in Samarian Hills, 15 km. SE of Qalqilya. Apparently one of 2 towns of Qeruḥayim and Qerutayim inhabited during Roman-Byzantine and Mamluk Periods. Within village are many remains: wine presses, ancient watch-towers, cisterns, burial cave — Deir ed Darb (wayside monastery) and quarries. **Qaṣr Abu Jaliya** S of village, *159:169*,is a well-preserved watch-tower built of large hewn stones. According to its style it was probably built during Herod's reign.

Qarawet Bani Zaid (Qarawa el Fauqa) *162:162*

Arab village (pop.: 700) in Samarian Hills 12 km. W of Ma'ale Levona. Apparently one of the 2 adjacent towns of Qeruḥayim and Qerutayim, inhabited during Roman–Byzantine and Mamluk Periods. (See Qarawet Bani Ḥasan.)

Qarne Ḥittim (Tel Qarne Ḥittim) *193:244*

Tel of ancient settlement in Galilee, 6 km. W of Tiberias, near where Crusaders were decisively beaten by Moslems. Located in mouth of dormant volcano at height of 326 m. above sea level. It was a strategic strong point on ancient *via maris*. One theory claims it is site of Madon, a Canaanite city kingdom (Josh. 11:1) identified with city of Shemesh-edom, mentioned in lists of cities conquered by Thutmose III (1468 BCE). Remains of fort and wall. Sherds indicate occupation from Early Bronze Age until Hellenistic Period. In 1187 CE the famous Battle of Hattin, where Saladin and his Moslem army defeated the Crusaders, took place nearby. On the tel is a memorial erected by a Protestant sect —the Church of God's Prophecy.

Qarne Ramon *

Group of basalt hills in SW Makhtesh Ramon *118:993*. There are large concentrations of hexagon-shaped basalt — remains of early volcanic activity.

Qarne Shomeron (temporary name) *159:175*

Civilian outpost in Samarian Hills 12 km. E of Qalqilya, near 'Azzun. The terrain is reminiscent of a horn (*qeren*) shape, hence its name.

○ **Qaryut** *177:164*

Arab village in Samarian Hills 2 km. N of ruins of Shillo. Pop.: 1,000.

Qaṣr Bardawil *219:247*

Remains of Early Bronze Age enclosure on Golan Heights 2 km. E of *moshav* Eli ‘Al. Name is corruption of Baldwin, first Crusader king of Jerusalem, and means Baldwin's fortress. Apparently the true source of the name is Qaṣr Bardil (fortress of the reed). Remains of wall surrounded by moat and remnants of many structures. Sherds indicate occupation in Early and Middle Bronze Ages, Iron Age, Roman and Ottoman Periods.

Qaṣr Bint esh Sheikh *156:184*

Ruins of Byzantine mausoleum in Samarian Hills 7 km. SE of Tulkarm. Ruins of many mausoleums nearby built of hewn stones; some are well preserved.

Qaṣr ed Dawla *180:191*

Area of stone heaps from Byzantine Period in Samarian Hills 4 km. W of Tubas.

Qaṣr Faqqus *154:216*

Roman–Byzantine settlement ruins in Ramat Menashe, S of Giv‘at Nili. Remains of several structures. Alongside it is Ḥurbat Gedishim *155:216*, with structural remains and stone heaps. Iron Age sherds were found here.

Qaṣr el Feid Wa'al Muntar *160:210*
(Kh. Muḥammad eṣ Ṣaliḥ)

Ruins of fort on summit of hill at S approaches to Naḥal ‘Iron, between ‘Ar‘ara and Barta‘a. On slope of hill, at fixed intervals, are remains of 8 watch-towers. The architectural style and few sherds found here indicate that this was part of a Canaanite and Israelite defence network of Yizre‘el Valley and N part of the country.

Qaṣr el Khan → Khan el Aḥmar

Qaṣr Maḥrun *174:202*

Settlement ruins in Samarian Hills 6 km. SE of Jenin. Remains of structure and burial cave. Sherds indicate occupation in Early Bronze Age and late Byzantine Period.

Qaṣr er Rubai‘ *191:121*

Ruins of Roman fortress near W shore of Dead Sea, 2.5 km. S of ‘Enot Ẓuqim (‘Ein Fashkha). The fortress is rectangular (30x40 m.) with a smaller structure attached to it. Its walls are built of undressed stone and its corners and lintels of dressed stone.

Qaṣr el Yahud *201:138*

Greek Orthodox monastery in Jordan Valley on bank of Jordan River, 10 km. SE of Jericho. Name means castle of the Jews. According to local tradition this is the site where the Israelites forded the Jordan on their way to conquering Canaan. According to Christian tradition, it was here that John the Baptist baptized Jesus in the Jordan. The monastery, called Deir Mar Johanna (the monastery of St. John), was built on ruins of a Byzantine monastery. Alongside it are other Byzantine remains as well as a fortress and church from Crusader Period (see el Maghtas).

(El) Qastel *163:133*

Hill and settlement ruin 6 km. W of Jerusalem S of Har'el interchange. Height: 750 m. above sea level. Dominates the route from Judean Foothills to Jerusalem. Identified with Mount Ephron mentioned in Book of Joshua (15:9) on border between tribal allocations of Benjamin and Judah. During Roman Period a fortress was built on hill summit, and later replaced by Crusader fortress — Castellum Belveer. The Arab village of el Qastel was built on ruins of ancient fortresses and its name, and that of the hill, was derived from the word *castellum*. During War of Independence it was a base for Arab gangs who blockaded the road to Jerusalem. The village changed hands several times during the battles for this strategic hill, and was finally taken by the Haganah. After the war, a *ma'bara* (new immigrant transit camp) was set up at the Qastel; this later became a permanent settlement called Ma'oz Ẓiyyon. On hill summit are the ruins of the Arab village and Crusader fortress. On the slopes are remains of a Paleolithic settlement.

Qastina "B" → **'Arugot**

○ **Qatanna** *160:137*

Arab village in Judean Hills 1 km. N of Ma'ale HaḤamisha. Pop.: 1,600. Burial caves containing ossuaries were found in village. Site was apparently occupied in Iron Age.

● **Qatif** *084:087*

Moshav in Gaza Strip 5 km. W of Deir el Balaḥ. Name derives from nearby Tell el Qatifa. Founded as *naḥal* outpost in 1973, and became permanent civilian settlement in 1977.

■ **Qaẓrin** *216:266*

New city in Golan Heights 8 km. SE of Benot Ya'aqov Bridge, near site of ancient synagogue. Apparently a Jewish settlement in Roman–Byzantine Period, called Qisrin or Qesareyon — names which were retained in that of abandoned village, Qaẓrin. First started in 1974 and the first settlers moved in in 1977. **Remains** Excavations within abandoned village in 1971 uncovered remains of early 3rd c. synagogue, with a magnificent entrance of ornamented lintel and doorposts, fragments of walls, auxiliary rooms vaulted with basalt slabs, cistern, columns, pedestals, capitals, Aramaic inscriptions and *menorah* reliefs in stone.

Qedesh (Yizre'el Valley) → **Tell Abu Qudeis**

Qedesh (Upper Galilee) → **Tel Qedesh**

Qedesh Naftali → **Ḥurbat Qedesh**

Qedma *128:123*

Youth village in Lakhish region 4 km. SE of Qiryat Mal'akhi founded in 1979. Formerly a kibbutz which was founded in 1946 as one of the 11 settlements simultaneously established in one night with the express purpose of developing the Dead Sea–'Arava region. *Qedma* means eastward. The kibbutz was disbanded in 1962.

Qedumim (temporary name) *165:179*

Civilian outpost in Samarian Hills 10 km. W of Shekhem. Established 1977.

● **Qelaḥim** *119:095*

Moshav in Negev 8 km. NW of Netivot junction. Name means stalks. Founded 1954. Area: 4,700 d. Pop.: 300.

Qeren *203:277*

Regional centre under construction in Galilee, 2 km. SE of Ramot Naftali. Near summit of Qeren Naftali, hence its name.

Qeren Karmel (Deir el Muḥraqa) *158:231*

S summit of Mt. Karmel 2 km. NW of Yoqne'am junction. Height: 482 m. above sea level. At summit is a Carmelite monastery built in 1886 on ruins of earlier church. A statue in its courtyard depicts Elijah in his confrontation with the prophets of Baal. Ancient tradition designates this as the spot where Elijah contested the prophets of Baal (I Kings 18). The Arabs call the site el Muḥraqa (site of the fire) to commemorate the fire of the Lord that consumed Elijah's offering. The summit provides a view of Yizre'el and Zevulun Valleys and Ramat Menashe.

Qeren Naftali *202:277*

Summit in Hills of Naftali 3 km. SW of Koaḥ junction. Height: 510 m. above sea level. At summit are ruins of Byzantine building with lintel and Greek inscription. Observation point overlooking Ḥula Valley.

Qeren Sartaba → Sartaba

Qesareya → Caesarea

Qesari → Caesarea

● **Qeshet** *226:265*

Moshav shittufi on Golan Heights 6 km. NW of Har Peres. *Qeshet* means a bow and is a translation of the Arab name Quneitra, where the first settlers were located in 1974. When Quneitra was returned to Syrians, the settlers moved to an abandoned Syrian camp near Khushniyya. N of *moshav* at er Ramthaniyya, an unsuccessful attempt at Jewish settlement, called Golan BaBashan, was made in 1886.

★ **Qetura** *155:931*

Kibbutz in 'Arava 10 km. N of Yotvata. Named after Mt. Qetura, N of kibbutz. Keturah was second wife of Abraham (Gen. 25:1). Founded as *naḥal* outpost in 1971 and became a civilian settlement in 1973. Area: 900 d. Pop.: several hundred.

Qever Rabbi Meir Ba'al HaNes → Tiberias

Qever Raḥel → Rachel's Tomb

Qever Shemu'el HaNavi → Nabi Ṣamwil

Qever Yehoshua' Ḥankin → Ma'yan Ḥarod

Qever Yitro (Jethro) → Nabi Shu'eib

Qever Yosef → Balata

★ **Qevuẓat Yavne** *123:136*

Collective settlement on Coastal Plain 5 km. E of Ashdod. Named after ancient Jabneh which was the Jewish spiritual centre after destruction of Second Temple. Established 1929 by German immigrants near Petaḥ Tiqwa and later moved to present site in 1941. During War of Independence, because it was in front battle line against Egyptian army, it suffered casualties and property damage. Area: 5,900 d. Pop.: 950.

Qeẓi'ot *098:032*

Abandoned settlement in Negev 2 km. E of Nizzana, alongside old Israel–Egypt border. At first a *naḥal* outpost, established 1953, it is now a Gadna camp.

○ **Qibya** *151:153*

Arab village 10 km. E of Ben-Gurion Airport. Pop.: 950. Object of Israeli retaliatory raid in 1953. Ancient rock-cut pool within village.

● **Qidron** *130:136*

Moshav in Judean Foothills 2 km. E of Gedera. Same name as ancient city mentioned in I Maccabees and partly retained in name of abandoned village, Qatra. Perhaps site of Biblical city Gederah (Josh. 15:36). Founded 1949. Area: 4,000 d. Pop.: 660. Burial cave with niches containing clay oil lamps, and sherds from Iron Age and Persian Period were found within area of *moshav*.

○ **Qira** *166:169*

Arab village in Samarian Hills 15 km. SW of Shekhem. Pop.: 260. Holy Moslem tomb of Sheikh Naṣir.

★ **Qiryat 'Anavim** *161:135*

Collective settlement 10 km. W of Jerusalem near village of Abu Ghosh. Name based on name of former Arab village, Qaryat el 'Inab. Founded 1920 by pioneers from the Ukraine. In its time, it was the pioneer Jewish settlement in the hill region around Jerusalem. During War of Independence it served as a base for Har'el Brigade of the Palmaḥ which attempted to relieve the siege of Jerusalem. Area: 4,600 d. Pop.: 380. For a number of years, a group of Finnish Protestants, whose symbol is the cross and the star of David, have lived and worked in the kibbutz.

Qiryat Arba' → Hebron

■ **Qiryat Ata** *160:246*

City in Zevulun Valley 14 km. E of Haifa. Established through amalgamation of 2 urban settlements, Kefar Ata and Qiryat Binyamin in 1965. Area: 14,500 d. Pop.: 30,000. **Kefar Ata** Previously an independent town which was founded as a farming village (*moshava*) in 1925. First called Kefar 'Ata after Arab village called Kufritta from which lands were purchased for the village. However, it was destroyed during Arab Riots of 1929. Renewed in 1934, it developed into an industrial centre and in 1935 the Ata textile plant was set up here. (*Ata* is a Hebrew acronym for "textiles produced in our country".) During War of Independence it was on front line of the fighting. Remains of a building, a mosaic, tombs, foundations and sherds from Roman and Arab Periods. **Qiryat Binyamin** Previously an independent town, it was founded as a farming village (*moshava*) in 1938 and named after Baron Edmond (Binyamin) James de Rothschild. Over the years it amalgamated with adjacent districts of Qiryat Naḥum, Shekhunat HaTemanim, Qiryat Shtand and Qiryat Prostig. **Tell el 'Idham** Within city is a tel of an ancient settlement which is now overgrown in a pine wood. Sherds indicate occupation in Iron Age and Persian Period.

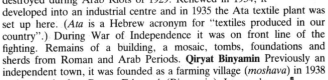

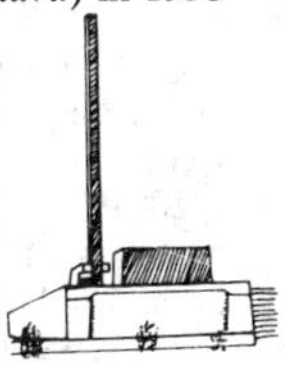

Qiryat Ben-Gurion → Jerusalem, HaQirya

■ **Qiryat Bialik** *158:248*

City in Zevulun Valley off Haifa–Acre road. Named after poet Ḥayyim Naḥman Bialik (1873-1934). Founded as residential quarter by German immigrants in 1934. Over the years it absorbed the adjacent suburbs of 'En Na'aman, Ẓir Shalom and Sabiniya. Area: 5,500 d. Pop.: 27,000.

Qiryat 'Eqron *(Josh. 13:3) 133:140*

Development town on Coastal Plain 2 km. S of Reḥovot. Based on name of Philistine city of Ekron. Perhaps the ancient name was retained in that of abandoned village of 'Aqir, on whose lands the town was established in 1948. At first it was a district of Reḥovot but later became an independent settlement called Kefar 'Eqron. Area: 2,100 d. Pop.: 4,400.

■ Qiryat Gat ✽ *(I Sam. 6:17)* *128:112*

City in Judean Foothills 20 km. SE of Ashqelon. Named after ancient Philistine city of Gath, home of Goliath, which is believed to have been located in the area. Founded as immigrant town in 1954 in the area known as the Faluja Pocket during War of Independence. Urban centre of Lakhish region. Area: 7,500 d. Pop.: 22,000.

Qiryat Ḥaroshet ✽ *(Judg. 4:2)* *160:233*

Settlement in Yizre'el Valley 3 km. SW of Qiryat Tiv'on. Named after Biblical city of Harosheth "of the Gentiles" (Judg. 4:2) believed to have been located in the area. Founded 1935 on private lands as a workers' suburb. Area: 900 d. Pop.: 240.

Qiryat Ḥayyim *157:247*

Suburb of Haifa in Zevulun Valley near Haifa–Acre road. Named after Chaim Arlosoroff, head of political department of Jewish Agency and killed in Tel Aviv in 1933. From the time it was founded in 1933 until it merged with Haifa in 1950, it was an independent labourers' village. Pop.: 30,000. Largest suburb in Zevulun Valley.

Qiryat Mal'akhi ✽ *126:126*

Development town in Judean Foothills 10 km. SE of Ashdod. Named after US city Los Angeles. (Los Angeles: angels — Hebrew: *mal'akhim.*) Founded 1951 on site of large *ma'bara* (transit camp for immigrants). Area: 3,000 d. Pop.: 11,000.

Qiryat Motzkin ✽ *157:248*

City in Zevulun Valley N of Qiryat Ḥayyim. Named after Zionist leader Leo Motzkin (1867-1933) and founded 1934. During War of Independence a large Arab arms convoy en route to Haifa was destroyed near Qiryat Motzkin. Area: 4,000 d. Pop.: 25,000.

Qiryat Ono ✽ *(I Chron. 8:12)* *137:163*

Urban settlement with local council status on central Coastal Plain, E of Ramat Gan. Named after Biblical town which was located in the area. Founded 1939. Area: 3,500 d. Pop.: 24,000.

■ Qiryat Shemona ✽ *203:290*

City in NW corner of Ḥula Valley off Rosh Pinna–Metulla road, near Lebanese border. Named after Joseph Trumpeldor (1880-1920) and his 7 comrades (*shemona* = eight) killed in defence of nearby Tel Ḥay in 1920. Formerly, in 1949, a *ma'bara* (transit camp for immigrants) set up on lands of abandoned village of Khaliṣa. Because of its proximity to Lebanese border, the city has suffered repeatedly from terrorist attacks. Area: 10,000 d. Pop.: 16,000.

Qiryat Telz-Stone ✽ *159:134*

Residential quarter with orthodox inhabitants in Judean Hills 1 km. W of Abu Ghosh. Origin of name: Telz — after city in NW Lithuania which housed a famous *yeshiva* which was destroyed in Holocaust and reestablished in USA in 1941; and Stone — after Colonel David (Mickey Stone) Marcus, West Point graduate and commander of Jerusalem front during War of Independence; accidentally killed in the area. Founded 1975.

Qiryat Tiv'on 162:236

Urban settlement with local council status on border of Yizre'el and Zevulun Valleys 15 km. SE of Haifa. Named after city of Tiv'on from Roman Period, apparently located on site of adjacent kibbutz Allonim. Qiryat Tiv'on was established in 1958 through an amalgamation of the 3 settlements of Qiryat 'Amal, Tiv'on and Elro'i. Area: 7,800 d. Pop.: 11,000. **Elro'i** Farming village (*moshava*) founded 1935 by Kurdish immigrants. **Qiryat 'Amal** A workers' residential quarter founded 1937. **Tiv'on** Residential quarter founded 1947. **Remains** Within town are rock-cut tombs from Roman and Byzantine Periods, some containing clay sarcophagi.

Qiryat Yam 156:250

City in Zevulun Valley N of Qiryat Ḥayyim, on seashore. Founded 1946. First settlers were demobilized soldiers of WWII Jewish Brigade and other units. After War of Independence it was a housing estate for new immigrants. Received its own municipality in 1976. Area: 4,700 d. Pop.: 27,000.

Qiryat Ye'arim *(Josh. 9:17)* 160:135

Youth village and educational institute N of Abu Ghosh. Named after Biblical city of Kiriath-jearim, located in vicinity. Founded 1952 by virtue of contributions by Swiss Jews. Pop.: 200 students and 60 staff.

Qishon Police Station (Jalama) 159:237

Police station on border of Lower Galilee and Yizre'el Valley near Ha'Amaqim road branch. Name means small hill. Excavations uncovered remains of glass industry from 13th c. BCE.

Qomemiyyut 124:118

Moshav on Coastal Plain 6 km. NW of Qiryat Gat. Name based on Biblical passage "and may you walk *erect*" (Lev. 26:13). Founded 1950 by demobilized soldiers from a religious company that fought in area during War of Independence. *Moshav* members who are extremely observant, are assisted by a Druze family to carry out essential farming tasks on sabbath and festivals. Area: 5,000 d. Pop.: 330.

Qoranit 174:249

Industrial village in Galilee 2 km. NW of Yodefat. Name *qoranit* means thyme (*za'atar* in Arabic) owing to the abundance of this herb in the area. Established 1978.

Qubbat Qar'a * 217:258

Dolmen field on Golan Heights between Naḥal Yehudiyya and Naḥal Daliyyot, 4 km. NE of *moshav* Ma'ale Gamla. The dolmens are meticulously built and their capstones have been preserved. Some of them cover long corridors. Site also contains structural remains. View of Lake Kinneret, Bet Zayda Valley and central Golan.

(El) Qubeiba (Judean Hills) 163:138

Arab village in Judean Hills 4 km. NE of Ma'ale HaḤamisha. Pop.: 700. Site of Crusader settlement called Mahomaria Lapetita in Spanish. The Frankish name was Parva Mahomaria. Both names are translations of the Arabic Qubeiba, which means little dome. According to a late Christian tradition, the site was identified with the New Testament Emmaus. Remains of Crusader fortress and church, built over ruins of Byzantine one which was in turn erected over ruins of an ancient room, believed to be house of Cleopas who saw the risen Jesus in Emmaus. What remains of traditional house of Cleopas is enclosed in glass. Qubeiba is also the location of an ancient Samaritan synagogue.

Qubur Bani Isra'il (Judean Hills) *175:138*

Remains of 5 Megalithic structures 6 km. NE of Jerusalem, 1 km. N of Hizma village. Local tradition claims these to be ancient Jewish tombs, hence the name (tombs of the children of Israel). However, there is no evidence as to the purpose and dating of these structures.

Qubur Bani Isra'il (Golan Heights) *223:249*

Ruins of abandoned village on Golan Heights within *moshav* Avne Etan, 1 km. W of Nov. Near village is a cemetery which, according to the local inhabitants, belonged to the Israelites; hence its name (tombs of the children of Israel). In order to obliterate the name Israel, the Syrians changed the village name to es Ṣufeira (the bright one). Enclosures, dolmens and tumuli scattered over a large area.

Qubur el Walaida *101:032*

Settlement remains on banks of Naḥal Rut 3 km. E of Qeẓi'ot. Remnants of 2 round ovens and sherds, indicating occupation in Late Bronze Age. About 500 m. W of ruins is a perennial water source.

Qumeran (Meẓad Ḥasidim) *194:128*

Remains of settlement from days of Second Temple, where the Dead Sea Scrolls were discovered. Located near NW shore of Dead Sea. Two Bedouin shepherds accidentally came across a clay jar in a cave that contained the world famous parchment scrolls. Some consider Qumeran to be the site of the Biblical city of Salt (Josh. 15:22). It was destroyed by Babylonians and resettled by Essene sect who came here in 2nd c. BCE. This small sect functioned as an ascetic cooperative community, rejected established Temple rituals, and, among other activities, engaged in writing and copying holy manuscripts. Some experts consider the Essenes to be the forerunners of Christianity. During the Revolt against Rome some Essenes joined the insurgents. When the Roman army approached Qumeran in 68 CE, the inhabitants hid their holy writings in the caves of Naḥal Qumeran to the W. Some of these writings were discovered in 1947 and have been named the Dead Sea Scrolls. Coins show the place was again inhabited in 132-135 by Bar Kokhba's fighters, before being deserted forever. The ruined settlement was excavated and restored and one can now see remains of a tower, interconnected buildings, assembly hall, scriptorium, refectory, water reservoirs, ritual baths, storerooms and pottery workshop. W of the settlement, outside the fence, is an extensive cemetery. The Qumeran caves contained many manuscripts including First and Second Isaiah Scrolls (7 m. long), Thanksgiving Psalms, Pesher Habakkuk, Manual of Discipline and the War Scroll. Most of the scrolls are now located in the Israel Museum and some are on display in the Shrine of the Book, of which the Isaiah Scrolls make up the centre piece. A carbon-dating test shows the scrolls date from the 1st c.

(El) Qurein *103:067*

Prehistoric site in Negev 2 km. SW of Ẓe'elim. Neolithic finds include flint tools, arrowheads, flaked blades and scrapers.

Quṣabiyya *160:218*

Settlement ruins in Ramat Menashe 8 km. W of Megiddo junction. Sherds indicate occupation chiefly in Middle Bronze Age, but also in Iron Age, Byzantine Period and Middle Ages.

(El) Quṣayyiba *219:253*

Ruins of abandoned village on Golan Heights 5 km. S of Gamla. Built on settlement ruins from Roman–Byzantine Period. Also inhabited during Middle Ages. Nearby are tumuli, cists and prehistoric enclosures.

○ **Quṣin** **(Quṣin es Sahl)** ⛫ *167:182*

Arab village in Samarian Hills 7 km. W of Shekhem. Pop.: 520. Site of Qazeh mentioned in Samarian Ostraca; also known during Middle Ages. Remains of tower, ancient cistern and wine press. Sherds indicate occupation in Iron Age, Persian Period, Byzantine Period, Middle Ages and Ottoman Period.

○ **Quṣra** *181:165*

Arab village in Samarian Hills, 15 km. SE of Shekhem. Pop.: 1,200. Foundations of ancient structures.

⛫ **(El) Quṣur** *151:106*

Remains of square Byzantine fort 9 km. SW of Hebron. Probably built to guard meeting point of the 2 streams below it, and also the way to Kh. el Fari'a.

R

Ra'ananna *138:176*

Urban settlement in Sharon near Tel Aviv–Haifa and Kefar Sava–Herzliyya road junctions. Founded as a farming village (*moshava*) in 1921 by a group of American Jews. In 1936 received local council status. Area: 16,000 d. Pop.: 23,000. The Kefar Batya college is located here.

Raba *186:199*

Arab village in Samarian Hills 8 km. N of Tubas. Pop.: 1,000. Near village is a Moslem holy shrine called en Nabi Raba.

Rabud *151:093*

Arab village (pop.: 320) in Judean Hills 12 km. SW of Hebron. **Kh. Rabud (Debir)** NE of village is a tel with remains of double wall, built of hewn stones, in addition to other structures. Sherds indicate occupation from Early Bronze Age to Iron Age and during Hellenistic Period. Around tel sherds were found belonging to Hellenistic, Roman and Byzantine Periods. Site of Biblical Debir (Josh. 15:15).

Rachel's Tomb *(Gen. 35:19)* *169:125*

Holy tomb at N entrance to Bethlehem. Ancient tradition designates site as burial place of the matriarch Rachel: "So Rachel died and she was buried on the way to Ephrath (that is Bethlehem)" (Gen. 35:19). Other sources locate the tomb N of Jerusalem (I Sam. 10:2 and Jer. 31:14). Perhaps the place called Qubat Rahil (the dome of Rachel) by the Arabs is the burial site near Bethlehem. It is also mentioned in New Testament (Matthew 2:16-18). Descriptions of Rachel's tomb have been recorded by pious travellers since the 4th c. The structure changed over the generations. It has been described as a pyramid of stones, according to Bishop Arculfus at end of 7th c.; as a structure of 12 stones (laid by 11 sons of Jacob, with the 12th stone laid by Jacob himself) covered with a dome, according to el Adrisi in 1154; and as a dome supported by 4 columns according to Rabbi Moses Basola in 1522. In 1623 Muhammad Pasha, Governor of Jerusalem, built a new structure over the tomb and gave the site to the Jewish community. Since then Jews have made pilgrimages to the grave, particularly on the 14th of the Hebrew month of Heshvan, traditional anniversary of Rachel's death; during intermediate festival days of Passover; on 33rd day of the counting of the Omer; and during the month of Elul. In 1841 the tomb structure was renovated with the funding of Sir Moses Montefiore. After War of Independence, during Jordanian occupation of 1948 to 1967, Jews were not allowed to visit the tomb. After Six-Day War it was renovated and reopened to visitors.

Rafah (Rafiah) *078:079*

Arab town in S Gaza Strip; site of ancient and important city on *via maris* and on border between Erez Israel and Egypt. Today it is a regional centre and has a population of 11,000, some of them refugees. **History** Mentioned many times in ancient Egyptian and Assyrian documents. Site of clashes between armies coming or going between Egypt and Erez Israel. Alexander Yannai conquered city and annexed it to Hasmonean kingdom; Pompey granted it autonomy; during Byzantine Period it was a bishopric, but in 634 it was captured by the Arabs.

After the Arab conquest a large Jewish community developed here and flourished in 9th and 10th c. Although impoverished by internal conflicts and by wars between Moslems and Crusaders in 11th and early 12th c., it flourished again in latter part of 12th c. However, it was again destroyed in 13th c. and has been a backwater ever since. In 1917 Rafah was captured by British and served as their base to attack Gaza. During British Mandate it was more of an army camp than a town. In War of Independence the Israel Defence Forces advanced to outskirts of city. In Sinai Campaign and Six-Day War Israeli armoured units, after bitter fighting, broke through here to N Sinai. **Antiquities** At Tel Rafaḥ *075:081*, remains of a defensive wall and Greek temple were uncovered. At nearby Kh. Rafaḥ foundations of brick buildings, an ancient cemetery and other remains were found. On the seashore is a 2nd tel with ruins of Rafiaḥ Yam. **Deqel Avshalom** Near Rafah, *077:075*, is site where Avshalom Feinberg, Nili member, was killed in WWI while trying to cross the Turkish front line and establish contact with the British. He was buried in the sand and from the dates he had in his pocket a palm tree grew. Based on evidence obtained from local Bedouin after Six-Day War, searchers found his remains under a lone palm tree. Remains were reinterred in Jerusalem and a new palm was planted in place of the original.

o **Rafat** (near Ramallah) *168:142*

Arab village (pop.: 500) 3 km. S of Ramallah, E of Jerusalem airport. Believed to be site of Biblical Irpeel, a city in Benjamin tribal allotment. W of the village are rock-cut burial caves. Sherds from Byzantine Period were found here.

o **Rafat** (Samarian Hills) *154:164*

Arab village (pop.: 400) in Samarian Hills 15 km. E of Petaḥ Tiqwa. Located on summit of hill on ancient settlement ruins. Finds include building remains with stone and mosaic floors, cisterns and tombs. Sherds indicate occupation in Iron Age, Byzantine Period, Middle Ages and Ottoman Period.

o **Rafat** (near Sammu') *155:088*

Arab village (pop.: 350) in Judean Hills 1 km. S of Sammu' (Eshtemoa'). Built on ancient settlement ruins. Ancient building stones have been re-used in village houses. Sherds from Byzantine Period and Middle Ages.

o **Rafida** *171:119*

Arab village (pop.: 250) in Judean Hills, 4 km. SE of Bethlehem.

o **Rafidiya** *172:181*

Arab village W of Shekhem. Pop.: 1,200. Built on Crusader settlement ruins. Remains of building walls, foundations and a tower.

o **(Er) Ram** *(Ramah: Josh. 18:25) 172:140*

Arab village 7 km. N of Jerusalem off Jerusalem-Ramallah road. Pop.: 900. Believed to be site of **Biblical Ramah**, a city in Benjamin tribal allotment where Samuel sat in judgment (I Sam. 7:17). From Ramah the voice of "Rachel weeping for her children" was heard (Jer. 31:15). Resettled after Babylonian Exile (Ezra 2:26, Neh. 11:33). Within village, 3 ossuaries with Hebrew inscriptions were found. To the S are remains of ancient buildings, cisterns and quarries.

o **(Er) Rama** *166:195*

Arab village (pop.: 350) in Samarian Hills 15 km. NE of Tulkarm. **Kh. er Rama** NE of village, *167:195*, are settlement ruins from Persian and Byzantine Periods and Middle Ages. Remains of stone structures. S of ruin sherds were found from Middle Bronze Age and Iron Age.

(Er) Rama; (Er) Rami *184:260*

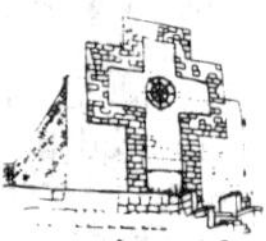

Arab settlement in Galilee 6 km. E of Karmi'el, with a local council since 1954. Pop.: 4,300, two-thirds Christian, a quarter Druze and rest Moslem. Present-day village built alongside ruins of ancient Jewish settlement, not yet identified. According to one theory, this is site of Ramah included in Naphtali tribal allotment (Josh. 19:36). Finds include an Aramaic inscription in Hebrew characters, remains of bathhouse and church from 6th c., remains of columns and bases and 2 burial caves. Sherds indicate occupation during Roman Period.

Ramallah *169:145*

Arab city in Judean Hills 13 km. N of Jerusalem. Extends over several hills with an altitude of 872 m. above sea level. An important road junction in ancient times and in present — roads from Jerusalem to Shekhem, from Judean Foothills through Ma'ale Bet Horon and from Ramallah to Jericho and Jordan Valley, all meet here. Pop.: 12,200, mostly Christian. Ramallah's E neighbour, the Arab town of el Bira, is mainly Moslem. On one of Ramallah's hills the British Mandatory authorities built a central broadcasting station for Palestine in 1936; today it is used by Kol Yisrael as a relay station. A number of prehistoric sites and Bronze Age tombs have been found in and around the city. According to one theory Ramallah is site of Biblical city of Ramah (Ramathaim-zophim), where the prophet Samuel was born, resided and was buried (I Sam. 1:1; 1:19; 25:1), where Saul was anointed King (I Sam. 10:1) and where David hid from Saul (I Sam. 19:18). **Ras et Tahuna** Within city *170:146* is a tel which was inhabited in Chalcolithic, Early and Middle Bronze Ages, Iron Age, Persian and Arab Periods. Believed to be site of Zemaraim, included in Benjamin tribal allotment and located on Mt. Zemaraim (Josh. 18:22).

Ramat Dawid *169:231*

Kibbutz in Yizre'el Valley 3 km. W of Migdal Ha'Emeq. Named after David Lloyd George, British prime minister at time of Balfour Declaration. Founded 1926 by pioneers from Poland, Russia and Bessarabia. In 1931 settlers moved from nearby Nahalal to present location. Area: 6,000 d. Pop.: 400.

Ramat Ef'al *134:161*

Residential quarter on Coastal Plain 1 km. S of Tel HaShomer junction. Included within regional council of Ono. Named after kibbutz Ef'al established here in 1946 and disbanded in 1952. Name is Hebrew acronym for Association of Hebrew National Workers — a US Jewish workers organization that assisted in founding the kibbutz. Pop.: 2,200. **Ef'al** Within district is the central seminar of HaKibbutz HaMe'uhad established in 1953. It too retains name of former kibbutz.

Ramat Gan

City on Coastal Plain NE of Tel Aviv. Founded as garden suburb in 1921. In 1923 declared a *moshav* and from 1926 had local council status. Its agricultural character was maintained until 1933. From then on it expanded, absorbing adjacent quarters and settlements and in 1950 attained municipal status. **Principal quarters:** Nahalat Gannim, Tel Binyamin, Ramat Yizhaq, Newe Yehoshua', Tel Gannim, Qiryat Borochov, Ramat Hen, Shekhunat HaGefen, Shekhunat Hillel, Ramat Amidar, Shekhunat Rassco, Kefar HaMakabiyya. National Park and Safari Park. **Principal institutions:** Bar Ilan University, Bet Zevi School for Drama and Film, College of Textiles, national stadium, Sheba Hospital, Bet 'Imanu'el municipal museum, Bet HaEzrah cultural centre. **Historical sites** Archaeological survey uncovered a rock-cut burial cave, cistern and remains of a mosaic. Sherds indicate occupation in Bronze Age and

RAMAT HASHARON

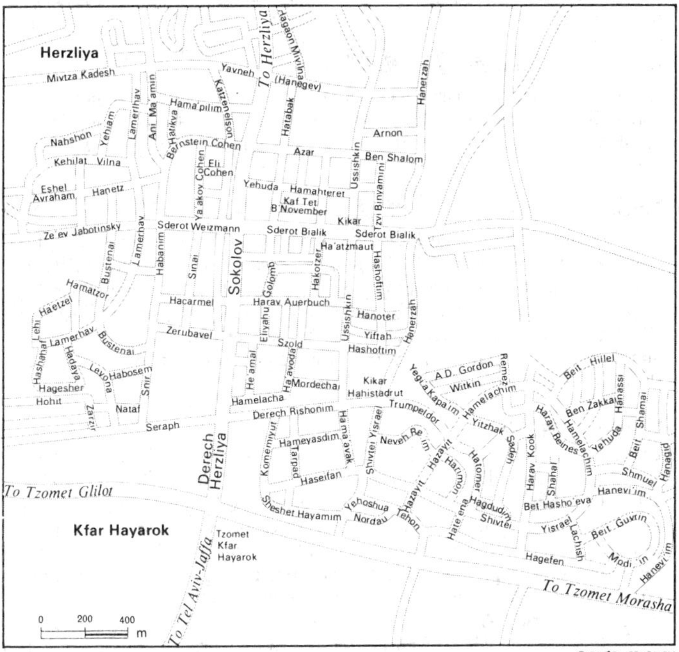

© carta, JERUSALEM

Roman Period. Near Yarqon river is a monument to commemorate General Hill's crossing of the river in WWI.

Ramat Hadar → Hod HaSharon

Ramat Hadassah — 164:237

Youth 'Aliyah school and boarding school in Qiryat Tiv'on. Named after Hadassah organization; founded 1948. Pop.: 400 pupils and staff.

Ramat HaGolan → Golan Heights

★ Ramat HaKovesh — 144:180

Kibbutz in Sharon 5 km. N of Kefar Sava. Named after founding group HaKovesh from Poland. Founded 1932. Attacked several times during Disturbances of 1936-1939. One of bases of Haganah field companies (*peluggot sade*). During WWII it was a training camp for Jewish parachutists sent on missions into occupied Europe. In 1943 there was a clash between settlers and British troops when the latter searched the kibbutz for arms and "illegal" immigrants. Palmaḥ base on front line during War of Independence, it was target of infiltrator attacks until Six-Day War. Area: 4,500 d. Pop.: 680.

Ramat HaNadiv — 145:218

Burial site of Baron Edmond (Binyamin) James de Rothschild, known as HaNadiv (the generous), and his wife Adelaide ('Ada). Built on S offshoot of Mt. Karmel, between Zikhron Ya'aqov and Binyamina amid settlements established through his financial aid. The grave is surrounded by a beautifully landscaped park. On a stone tablet is a list of names of all settlements established and supported by him. Adjacent to park is a picnic site.

Ramat HaSharon — 135:172

Urban settlement in Sharon 2 km. S of Herẓliyya. Founded as *moshav* in

1923. Since 1948 it has had its own local council. Over the years it has developed to become a mixed rural-urban community. Area: 19,000 d. Pop.: 28,000.

★ Ramat HaShofet *159:224*

Kibbutz in Ramat Menashe 6 km. S of Yoqne'am junction. Named after Judge Julian Mack, US Zionist leader. Founded 1941 by members of HaShomer HaẒa'ir from Poland and Lithuania. Area: 6,750 d. Pop.: 680.

● Ramat Magshimim *226:250*

Moshav shittufi on Golan Heights 7 km. NE of *moshav* Eli 'Al. Same name as founding group — Magshimim — who were graduates of Bene 'Aqiva. Founded 1968 and temporarily located in abandoned village of Fiq. In 1972 moved to permanent location near abandoned village of Khisfin. As a result of Separation of Forces Agreement between Israel and Syria in 1974, part of *moshav*'s farming land was lost. Area: 4,500 d. Pop.: several hundred.

Ramat Menashe

Elevated hill plateau in N. Bounded by Karmel in NW, Yizre'el Valley in E, Samarian Hills in SE and Sharon in W. Average height of hills: 250-400 m. High precipitation rate. Traversed by 2 streams from N and S — Naḥal Yoqne'am and Naḥal 'Iron, which serve as major thoroughfares from centre of country to Yizre'el Valley and N. Sherds and other remains found on plateau indicate Early Bronze Age habitation. During Israelite conquest it was included in allotment of half-tribe of Manasseh, hence its name. A well-populated and flourishing area at time of Israelite kingdom. The Hasmoneans annexed it to Judea and once again it flourished during Roman Period. After 7th c. Arab conquest it was impoverished and eventually became wasteland. Jewish settlement was renewed in late 19th c. when village of Bat Shelomo was set up in 1889. More settlements followed in the 1930's and after 1948. The National Water Carrier passes through Menashe Hills, through a 6.5 km. rock-cut tunnel called Minheret Menashe.

Ramat Pinkas *134:160*

Urban settlement on Coastal Plain SE of Mesubbim junction. Named after David Ẓevi Pinkas (1895-1952), a Mizraḥi leader and a former minister of transport. Founded 1952 to settle new immigrants. Pop.: 790.

★ Ramat Raḥel *171:127*

Kibbutz in S Jerusalem. Located on a rise from where Rachel's Tomb, on road to Bethlehem, is visible: hence its name. Founded 1926 by Jerusalem branch of Joseph Trumpeldor's Gedud Ha'Avoda. Attacked and destroyed by Arab gangs in 1929 Riots. Rebuilt in 1930, it once again suffered Arab attacks in Disturbances of 1936-1939. During War of Independence it was a front line post between Israeli, Egyptian and Jordanian forces. It changed hands several times until finally attackers were repelled. In course of the fighting the kibbutz was completely destroyed and most of its members left. Reestablished after the war. Because of its proximity to Jordanian border, it was continuously harassed by the Jordanians. In 1956 an archaeological conference was held here and participants were fired upon from across the border; 4 were killed and 17 wounded. Since Six-Day War the kibbutz has developed. Area: 4,000 d. Pop.: 130. **Antiquities** Archaeological excavations were carried out within kibbutz, near the old road from Jerusalem to Bethlehem. Finds include remains of fortress dating to Kingdom of Judah which were destroyed at the same time as First Temple and rebuilt after Babylonian Exile, remains of Byzantine monastery and church and remains of Arab Period settlement. Popularly believed to be site of Biblical Beth-haccerem. Prehistoric remains have also been found within kibbutz.

Ramat Razi'el *157:131*

Moshav in Judean Hills 7 km. E of Shimshon junction. Named after David Raziel (1910-1941), Irgun commander who died on a mission for the British in Iraq. Founded 1948. Area: 1,000 d. Pop.: 210.

Ramat Yishay *166:234*

Rural-urban settlement off Haifa-Nazareth road 4 km. E of Qiryat Tiv'on. Named after Yishay Adler, teacher, communal leader and philanthropist. Founded 1925 by Polish immigrants and called after the Arab name of the site, Jeida. Local council since 1958. Area: 2,200 d. Pop.: 920.

Ramat Yoḥanan *162:244*

Kibbutz in Zevulun Valley 2 km. SE of Qiryat Ata. Named after Jan (Yoḥanan in Hebrew) Smuts, former prime minister of South Africa and champion of Zionism. Founded 1932. During War of Independence its members participated, together with those of neighbouring settlements, in fighting against Arab and Druze forces. Area: 9,200 d. Pop.: 650.

Ramat Ẓevi *189:221*

Moshav in Galilee 4 km. N of 'En Ḥarod. Named after Henry (Ẓevi) Monsky (1890-1947), president of B'nei B'rith in USA. Founded 1942 and first called Tamra, after neighbouring Arab village. Area: 7,800 d. Pop.: 200.

Ramin *164:187*

Arab village in Samarian Hills 12 km. NW of Shekhem. Located on summit of high wall, on ruins of ancient settlement. Sherds found indicate occupation in Iron Age, Persian, Roman, Byzantine, Medieval and Ottoman Periods.

Ramla (Er Ramla) *138:148*

City on border of Judean Foothills and Coastal Plain, on junction of major N-S and E-W arteries. Name is Arabic and means sand (a reference to the sand dunes on which town was built). Area: 10,000 d. Pop.: 37,500 of whom 5,300 are Arabs. **History** Founded 717 in days of Umayyad Caliph Suleiman Ibn 'Abd el Malik, the only city in Palestine founded by Arabs. It replaced Christian Lod as the centre of Moslem authority. In 9th c. it was a large and beautiful city, renowned for its markets and mosques. At that time it was populated by Arabs, Persians and Samaritans. In 10th c. it was the largest city and capital of Palestine. By then it had a Jewish and Karaite community. The non-Arab communities suffered badly during the Bedouin revolt against Egyptian rule (1024-1029). Ramla was severely damaged in earthquakes of 1033 and 1067. Captured by Seljuks in 1071, and again taken by Crusaders in early 12th c. and became a military and commercial centre. No Jews lived in the city during this period. After continuous attacks Ramla fell to Mamluk Sultan Baybars who destroyed it. In 14th c. it was once again a large and capital city, and a Jewish community took up residence and continued to exist here until middle of 17th c. Ramla declined and became impoverished as the central authority weakened. Napoleon spent a short while here during his campaign in the Holy Land. In the 19th c. it was an important station for Christian pilgrims. Ramla once again hosted a Jewish community at end of 19th c. when new Jewish villages were being set up, but it ceased to exist during WWI. It revived for a short time subsequently until Disturbances of 1936-1939. At outbreak of War of Independence Ramla was base for hostile Arab forces and effectively blocked the way to

Jerusalem. Captured by the Israel Defence Forces in operation "Dani" (July 1948) after most of the Arab inhabitants abandoned city. After the war it became an immigrant development town and in 1949 received municipal status. **White Mosque** (el Jami'a el Abyad) — remains of mosque built by founder of city, Caliph Suleiman. Alongside it is **Mosque of the Forty** — a square tower built by the Mamluks in 1318 and named after the forty companions of Muḥammad. The 6-storey, 30 m. high tower had been designed as a minaret for an adjacent 8th c. mosque. Some say Napoleon directed his assault on Jaffa from this tower. **The Great Mosque** (el Jami'a el Kabir) — formerly the 12th c. Crusader Cathedral of St. John. **The Vaulted Pools** (in centre of town) — an underground water cistern which is one of the 2 underground water cisterns built in 9th c. in days of Haroun er Rashid, for storing water which was apparently brought by aqueduct from Gezer spring; the other cistern is alongside the square tower. **Qabr en Nagi Salih**,near White Mosque, is site of Moslem religious spring festivities. **Hospice of St. Nicodemus** — owned by Franciscan Order, served as Napoleon's staff headquarters in 1799. Recent excavations in Ramla have uncovered a **coloured mosaic pavement**, with an Arabic inscription and a drawing of stars, fruits, flowers, star of David and other elements. Within city is a British WWI military cemetery and a memorial to soldiers who fell in Israel's wars.

o Rammun *178:148*

Arab village in Judean Hills 9 km. NE of Ramallah. Pop.: 1,200. Believed to be site of "rock of Rimmon", to which Benjaminites fled after incident with "concubine in Gibeah" (Judg. 20:45-47).

• Ram-On *174:215*

Moshav in Yizre'el Valley 8 km. SE of Megiddo. Named after Ram-On Paldi, *naḥal* soldier killed in an encounter with infiltrators. Founded 1960. Area: 6,500 d. Pop.: 330.

• Ramot *212:250*

Moshav on Golan Heights 7 km. N of 'En Gev. Located on height (*rama*) between Naḥal Kanaf and Naḥal Samakh. Founded 1969 by demobilized *naḥal* youth within abandoned village of Sequfiyya. In 1973 moved to present site. Area: 10,000 d. Pop.: several hundred.

Ramot HaShavim *139:174*

Rural settlement in Sharon 1 km. S of Ra'ananna junction. Founded 1933 by German immigrants. Name *HaShavim* means the returnees, and signified those who "returned" from the diaspora in Germany. Area: 2,000 d. Pop.: 550.

• Ramot Me'ir *136:142*

Moshav in Judean Foothills 4 km. SE of Reḥovot. Named after Dr. Me'ir Rozov, Zionist leader from USA. Founded 1949 by demobilized soldiers; disbanded 15 years later. Reestablished in 1969 by N African immigrants. Area: 1,300 d. Pop.: 240.

⭑ Ramot Menashe *155:222*

Kibbutz in Ramat Menashe 10 km. NE of Zikhron Ya'aqov. Founded 1948 by Polish immigrants, ghetto fighters and Holocaust survivors. Area: 12,000 d. Pop.: 550.

• Ramot Naftali *202:278*

Moshav in Galilee 10 km. S of Qiryat Shemona. In Naftali region, hence its name. Founded 1945 by Wingate group of demobilized soldiers who served in British army in WWII. During War of Independence it was besieged and attacked several times by large Arab forces; defenders repelled all attacks. Area:

3,000 d. Two km. N of *moshav* is Tel Qedesh, and 1 km. to NE is Meẓudat Yesha'.

∴ (Er) Ramthaniyya *225:269*

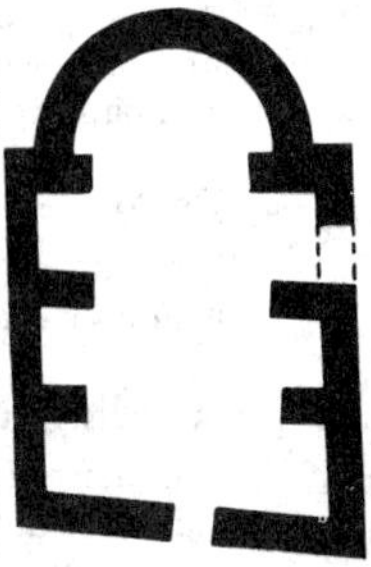

Abandoned village in Golan Heights 10 km. NE of Qaẓrin. Built on ruins of Byzantine settlement, remains of which have been incorporated in village buildings. Remains of small church which was later used as living quarters and large vaulted building (apparently a monastery) with stones decorated with crosses, date palms and Greek inscriptions. Mentioned as Rumsaniya in 19th c. sources, most probably because of Christian remains (*rum* in Arabic means Romans). In 1886 a group of Jews from Safed attempted settlement here called Bene Yehuda and Golan BaBashan. But the plan was subsequently abandoned owing to opposition from Turkish authorities. Those who had already moved to the site left.

● Rannen *112:083*

Moshav in Negev 2 km. N of Ofaqim. Name Biblical from passage "it shall blossom abundantly, and rejoice with joy and *singing*" (Isa. 35:2). Founded 1950 by Yemenite immigrants. In 1952 original settlers were replaced by Karaite immigrants from Egypt. Area: 1,200 d. Pop.: 450. **Tel** Within *moshav*, on S bank of Naḥal Pattish *112:084*, is tel of ancient settlement. Sherds indicate habitation from Iron Age through Hellenistic Period.

○ Rantis *152:159*

Arab village in Samarian Hills 12 km. NE of Ben-Gurion Airport. Pop.: 900. Built on ruins of Iron Age, Persian, Roman and Byzantine settlement. Perhaps site of Ramata mentioned in I Macc. 11:34. Tomb of Sheikh Barhum.

(Er) Ras → Beit Jala

○ (Er) Ras (in Samarian Hills) *156:184*

Arab village (pop.: 250) 7 km. SE of Tulkarm. Situated on summit of hill (hence its name — *ras* means head) on ruins of ancient settlement. Finds include sherds from Byzantine Period, Middle Ages and Ottoman Period.

(Er) Ras (in Judean Foothills) *150:148*

Tel 2 km. SE of Me'or Modi'im. Area: 30 d. Sherds indicate occupation in Early Bronze Age, Iron Age, Persian and Ottoman Periods. Sheikh's tomb at summit of hill by sacred tree. Network of tunnels and cisterns.

Ras Abu Balat *160:185*

Settlement ruins in Samarian Hills 9 km. SE of Tulkarm. Remains of hewn-stone structure. Inhabited in Iron Age and again in Byzantine Period. Identified with Sefar mentioned in Samarian Ostraca.

Ras el Ḥamama *180:099*

Settlement ruins in Judean Desert 7 km. W of 'En Gedi. Remains of round structure enclosed in square wall on hill summit. Sherds indicate occupation in Iron Age and Roman Period. To the N is **Rujm el Ḥamama** *182:099*. Remains of square structure divided in two alongside courtyard. Sherds indicate Iron Age occupation.

○ Ras Karkar *159:150*

Arab village (pop.: 400) 10 km. NW of Ramallah.

Ras Qurunṭul *190:142*

Remains of Dagon (Dok) Hasmonean fortress on Mt. Qurunṭul 4 km.

NW of Jericho. Remains of walls, aqueduct and a water system of 9 cisterns.

Ras esh Shiqaf *181:100*

Ruin in Judean Desert 4 km. W of Mizpe Qedem. Remains of a round structure within a square one with corner towers. Sherds indicate occupation in Iron Age and early Roman Period.

★ **Ravid** *193:250*

Kibbutz in Galilee 6 km. W of kibbutz Ginnosar on coast of Lake Kinneret. Same name as nearby mount.

Reading Bridge *129:167*

Wooden bridge on Yarqon River in N Tel Aviv, near Reading power station. Built in 1938 by Palestine Electric Corporation and at first called Wauchope Bridge after British High Commissioner, Sir Arthur Wauchope (1931-1938). Later called after Lord Reading (1860-1935), British Zionist and chairman of Palestine Electric Corporation.

Red Sea (Yam Suf) *(Josh. 24:6)*

Narrow, elongated sea which divides continents of Africa and Asia. In the Bible called Yam Suf (Reed Sea). At its N end it divides into 2 gulfs that encompass the Sinai Peninsula: Gulf of Elat and Gulf of Suez (which terminates in Suez Canal). Its length from straits of Bab el Mandeb in the S until Port Said in the N is 2,200 km. An important sea lane between Europe and the Far East and Australia. Vital sea link for Israel. On eve of Six-Day War the Egyptians closed the Gulf of Elat and during Yom Kippur War the Arabs threatened to close the straits of Bab el Mandeb.

★ **Regavim** *153:214*

Kibbutz in Ramat Menashe 3 km. E of Giv'at 'Ada. Founded 1948 on site of abandoned village Buteimat by immigrant youth from N Africa and Italy, and immigrants from Cyprus internment camps. Later moved to permanent site on lands of Qannir village. Area: 10,000 d. Pop.: 420.

● **Regba** *159:264*

Moshav shittufi on Galilee coast 3 km. S of Nahariyya. Founded 1946 by demobilized soldiers who served with British army in WWII. Area: 2,600 d. Pop.: 450.

● **Reḥan** *162:208*

Moshav in Samarian Hills 5 km. SW of *moshav* Me 'Ammi. Began as *naḥal* outpost in 1977; received civilian status in 1979. **Reḥan forest nature reserve** is nearby. Observation point.

● **Reḥov** *196:205*

Moshav 4 km. S of Bet She'an near ancient synagogue (see below). Name derives from ancient Rehob. Founded 1951. Area: 2,000 d. **Tel Reḥov** NE of *moshav*, *197:207*, is tel of ancient settlement identified with Biblical Rehob. Adjacent is ruin of Moslem holy shrine called Sheikh er Riḥab (apparently a distortion of name Reḥov). Rehob is mentioned in ancient Egyptian texts and in Onomasticon of Eusebius. Ruins of buildings and what was probably a fortress. Also remains of a Moslem shrine between the trees. Sherds found from Byzantine and Arab Periods. **Remains of synagogue** Near tel, *196:207*, remains of a 6th or 7th c. synagogue have recently been uncovered. Its roof was supported by columns and it had a mosaic floor with a Hebrew-Aramaic inscription dealing with laws of fruits in sabbatical year. Also fragments of other Hebrew inscriptions.

REHOVOT

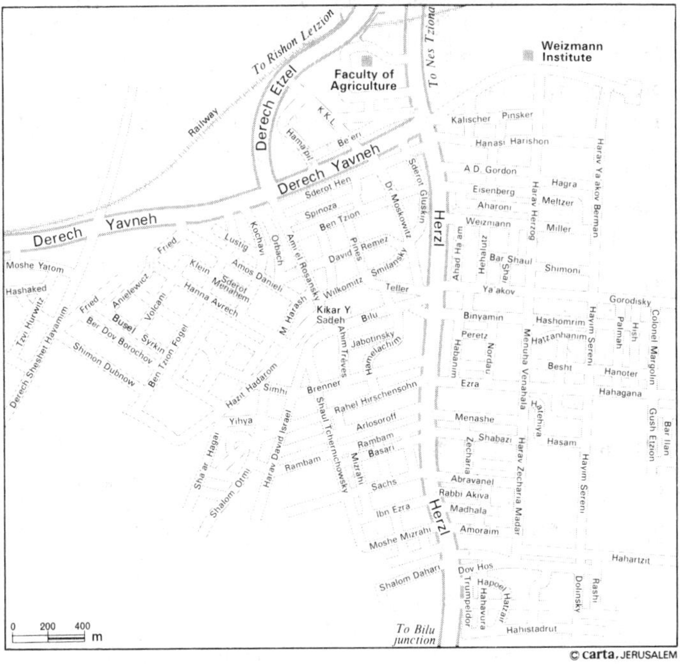

■ **Reḥovot** *(Gen. 26:22)*

City on Coastal Plain 20 km. S of Tel Aviv. Name from Biblical passage: "so he called its name Rehoboth, saying 'For now the Lord has made room for us and we shall be fruitful in the land'" (Gen. 26:22). Founded as a farming village (*moshava*) in 1890 by Menuḥa WeNaḥala association from Poland. Ovor years it became a citrus growing centre, and at the time of the Second 'Aliyah it was social and cultural centre. It was here that Hebrew with Sephardi pronunciation was first taught. Dr. Chaim Weizmann, Israel's first president, built his home here in 1936. Municipal status in 1950. Area: 23,000 d. Pop.: 58,000. Principal quarters: Kefar Gevirol, *129:144*, named after poet Rabbi Solomon Ibn Gabirol and founded 1949 by immigrants from Yemen and Iraq; Sha'arayim; Marmorek; Zarnuqa; Kefar HaNagid and Ramat Aharon. Within Reḥovot is the Weizmann Institute (see entry), Faculty of Agriculture of Hebrew University and Yad Chaim Weizmann.

★ **Re'im** *098:088*

Kibbutz in Negev adjacent to Gaza Strip 8 km. N of Ma'on junction. Founded 1949 by scouts from the Palmaḥ. Called Re'im (companions) in memory of members who died in War of Independence. Also a translation of name of nearby Tell Jamma' (in Arabic *jamma'* means friends). Area: 14,000 d. Pop.: 300.

o **(Er) Reina** *179:236*

Arab village 2 km. N of Nazareth. Rebuilt in 1927 after it was destroyed by an earthquake. Pop.: 5,000, 70% Moslems, rest Christians. According to one theory, this is site of city of Abel, from which water was carried to Sepphoris (Zippori). Remains of Roman aqueduct, pool and rock-cut tombs

Rekhasim *159:239*

Urban settlement in Zevulun Valley 5 km. NW of Qiryat Tiv'on. Built on 4 ridges (*rekhasim*), hence its name. Founded 1952. Area: 3,000 d. Pop.: 3,000.

Rekhes HaDolmenim *224:257*

Dolmen ridge on Golan Heights 7 km. N of Ramat Magshimim. Spread out in an arc W of Rujm el Ḥiri (from *224:257* to *223:256*). Large concentrations of dolmens and tumuli.

Reshafim *195:209*

Kibbutz 2 km. SW of Bet She'an. Named after neighbouring Arab village el Ashrafiyya. Founded 1948 during War of Independence, by HaShomer HaẒa'ir members from Poland and Rumania, after capture of Bet She'an. Area: 6,400 d. Pop.: 570.

Retamim *120:051*

Kibbutz under construction in Negev Hills 3 km. W of Revivim. Named after desert broom plant (*rotem*).

Revadim *133:131*

Kibbutz in Judean Foothills 5 km. SE of Gedera. Founded 1948 on lands of abandoned village of el Kheima. Started by members of the destroyed kibbutz Revadim of the 'Eẓyon Bloc after their return from Jordanian captivity. Area: 8,200 d. Pop.: 300.

Revivim *123:050*

Kibbutz in Negev 25 km. S of Be'er Sheva'. Name originates from passage "Thou waterest its furrows abundantly, settling its ridges, softening it with *showers*, and blessing its growth." (Ps. 65:10). One of 3 observation outposts (Revivim, Bet Eshel and Gevulot) established in Negev in 1943 to explore settlement potential. When founded it was the southernmost Jewish settlement in the country. Besieged during War of Independence. After being abandoned during the war, the kibbutz was relocated in 1950 at present site. At the old site, next to the kibbutz, is an observation point. Pop.: 660.

Rewaḥa *124:117*

Moshav in Judean Foothills 4 km. NW of Peluggot junction. Founded 1953 as part of "city to settlement" programme. Area: 3,800 d. Pop.: 580.

Rewaya *195:206*

Moshav 6 km. SW of Bet She'an. Abundant water sources, one called 'En Rewaya. Founded 1952. Area: 2,000 d.

(Er) Riḥaniyya *195:272*

Circassian village in Galilee 8 km. N of Safed. Founded 1873 by Moslem immigrants from Russian Caucasus. Pop.: 500. SE of the village are ancient tombs, cisterns and stone heaps.

(Er) Riḥiyya *157:097*

Arab village in Judean Hills 7 km. S of Hebron. Pop.: 680.

Rinnatya *143:162*

Moshav in Judean Foothills 5 km. SE of Petaḥ Tiqwa. Name originates from abandoned village of Rantiyya on whose land *moshav* was established in 1948. Area: 2,000 d. Pop.: 460. Remains of rock-cut wine cellars. Mentioned in Byzantine sources.

■ Rishon LeẒiyyon

City on Coastal Plain 8 km. S of Tel Aviv. Name from Biblical passage "I *first* have declared it to *Zion*" (Isa. 41:27). Set up as a farming village (*moshava*) in 1882 by 10 pioneers. Baron de Rothschild came to its aid after considerable difficulties in the early years, and through his initiative the village took to viticulture and wine making. The first Hebrew kindergarten and Hebrew cultural centre in the country were set up here in 1898. Naphtali Herẓ Imber wrote the words of HaTiqwa (later the national anthem) in Rishon LeẒiyyon. Here, too, the idea of a national flag was born and the Jewish National Fund inaugurated. Rishon residents played an important role in the Nili organization during WWI. After the war the population numbered 1,200, and on eve of statehood totalled 8,000. Municipal status in 1950. Area: 44,000 d. Pop.: 85,000. Principal suburbs: Gane Yehudit, Ramat Eliyyahu, Shikun Gordon and Shikun HaMizraḥ. Sites: Rishon LeẒiyyon wine cellars (Carmel Oriental) established 1889; Bet HaPeqidut — formerly Baron de Rothschild's administrative centre in Palestine.

RISHON LEẒIYYON

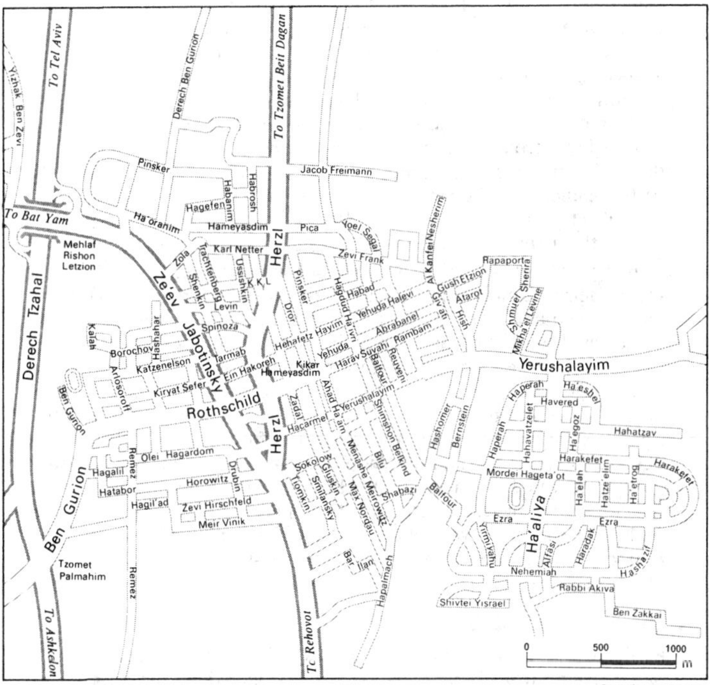

• Rishpon *133:178*

Moshav in Sharon 2 km. N of Herẓliyya. Named after ancient city of Rishpon which was located in the area (see Tel Arshaf). Founded 1936. Area: 3,000 d. Pop.: 480.

• Rogelit *150:120*

Moshav in Judean Hills 9 km. S of Bet Shemesh. Name means a creeping vine. Founded 1958. Pop.: 320. Remains of a Byzantine church with mosaic floor.

Rogem Be'er Yeroḥam *141:044*

Ruined structure in Negev alongside Yeroḥam junction. Remains appear to be part of a corner tower built of unhewn stones. Sherds indicate Iron Age occupation.

● Ro'i *196:183*

Moshav in Samarian Hills 3 km. N of *moshav* Beqa'ot. Name from Biblical verse "The Lord is my *shepherd*, I shall not want (Ps. 23:1). Established 1976 as *naḥal* outpost; civilian status in 1978.

Rosh Ha'Ayin *145:165*

Urban settlement alongside sources of Yarqon River, 4 km. E of Petaḥ Tiqwa. Name is a translation of the Arabic Ras el 'Ein (head of the spring). Initially a transit camp for new immigrants (*ma'bara*) which was set up in an abandoned British army camp that was later used by Arab gangs and the Iraqi army at beginning of War of Independence. Area: 12,000 d. Pop.: 12,500. **Sources of the Yarqon** to the E near Tel Afeq. In 1934 a pipeline was laid from Rosh Ha'Ayin to Jerusalem (65 km.) to increase water supply to the holy city. In 1955 the Yarqon–Negev pipeline (100 km.) was completed and in 1964 was incorporated in National Water Carrier network.

Rosh HaNiqra *160:277*

Cliff on cape of Galilee coast on Israel's border with Lebanon. Below the cliff are crevices and tunnels carved out by water erosion and incessant pounding of waves against the limestone. Name derives from Arabic Ras en Naqura (head of the crevices). This is beginning of the Ladder of Tyre which was always an important natural thoroughfare from Acre to Tyre. Via this route Alexander the Great in 333 BCE and Antiochus in 167 BCE entered Palestine. The British penetrated Lebanon this way in WWI (1918) and in WWII (1942). The road from Haifa to Beirut passed along this route and during the British Mandate a police station and customs checkpoint were set up at Rosh HaNiqra. After Lebanon was taken in WWII, the Haifa–Beirut railway line was laid through the heart of the cliff in a man-made tunnel. At beginning of War of Independence a Palmaḥ unit demolished railway bridge, and police station and customs house were taken by Lebanese army but were evacuated after Armistice Agreement. After War of Independence it became a tourist attraction and is part of Sulam Ẓur nature reserve. Crevices in cliff have been safely fitted for receiving visitors and a cable car affords easy access. Scenic observation point, restaurant, shops, and picnic site. **Kh. et Tabayiq** A partly excavated tel near Rosh HaNiqra where remains of a wall, structures and ancient tombs have been uncovered. According to flint tools and sherds it was inhabited from Chalcolithic until Byzantine Period. Nature reserve extends along coast from Akhziv to Rosh HaNiqra (area: 230 d.), with several inlets and small shallow pools.

Rosh Pinna *200:263*

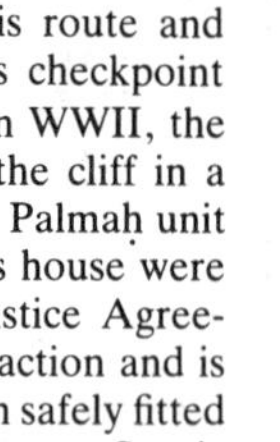

Settlement with local council status in Galilee 4 km. E of Safed. Name from Biblical passage "the stone which the builders rejected has become *the head of the corner.*" (Ps. 118:22). The land was bought in 1875 from Arab village of Ja'una by residents from Safed. Some tried to settle but left after a few years. In 1882 Rumanian pioneers purchased two-thirds of the land and the other third was bought by Russian pioneer families. Turkish authorities prohibited new houses so the settlers were forced to live in the Arab houses of Ja'una. However, Baron de Rothschild came to the aid of this first Jewish agricultural settlement in Galilee. During WWI the settlers suffered an epidemic of pestilence, a locust plague and Turkish harassment. In 1920 Joseph Trumpeldor and his companions set out from Rosh Pinna to defend Tel Ḥay. During British Mandate it was the first centre for Jewish settlement police and an operational base for a Betar collective, whose member, Shelomo Ben-Yosef, was tried and hanged by the British for a retaliatory attack on an Arab bus in 1938. It was also a centre for smuggling Jewish "illegal" immigrants from Syria and an operational base for settling 'Amir, Ne'ot Mordekhay and Biriyya. After War of Independence new immigrants from Arab countries settled here and the settlers abandoned lands of Ja'una (now included within Rosh Pinna). Area: 15,000 d. Pop.: 1,000. Burial caves.

Rosh Zohar (Ras ez Zuweira) — *172:071*

Mountain peak on Zohar ridge on border of Judean Desert and Negev Hills 4 km. SE of 'Arad. Height: 552 m. above sea level. During British Mandate it was a desert police station; destroyed in Disturbances of 1936-1939. Memorial to Pinḥas Sela (Steinberg), an activist in Negev development who was killed in 1951.

★ Rosh Ẓurim — *162:119*

Kibbutz in 'Eẓyon Bloc, 8 km. SW of Bethlehem. Name originates from Biblical passage "For from the *top of the mountains* I see him" (Num. 23:9). Founded 1969. Area: 7,100 d. Pop.: several hundred. Rosh Ẓurim is built on Kh. 'Abid, ruins of a Byzantine Period settlement.

★ Ruḥama — *122:100*

Kibbutz on border of Coastal Plain and Negev. Name from Biblical passage "And I will have *mercy* upon her that had *not obtained mercy*" (Hos. 2:23). Established on lands of previous Jewish settlement, built apparently on site of place called Jammama in Arabic. In 1913 it was attacked twice by Arabs and during WWI completely destroyed. Resettled 1920 by a group of labourers, but they were forced to leave during Arab Riots of 1929. Members of the group returned in 1932, but were again forced to abandon site during the Disturbances of 1936-1939. In 1944 the present kibbutz was established by a HaShomer HaẒa'ir group from Poland and Rumania. Served as training camp for Palmaḥ and Haganah. In 1946 the British army and police searched kibbutz for arms and caches. During War of Independence used as a central base by Negev Brigade. Area: 26,500 d. Pop.: 650. Near kibbutz are two nature reserves. To the E is Ruḥama Badlands Reserve (300 d.) and to W is Ruḥama Hills Reserve (600 d.) with southernmost coarse-sand ridge in country.

○ Rujeib — *177:177*

Arab village 4 km. SE of Shekhem. Pop.: 850. Rock-cut cisterns, caves and tombs from Roman and Byzantine Periods.

Rujm Abu Ḥashaba — *163:141*

Remains of square fort in N Judean Hills 7 km. SW of Ramallah. Dressed stone structure with 6 rooms and a corner tower. Sherds from Persian, Roman and Byzantine Periods.

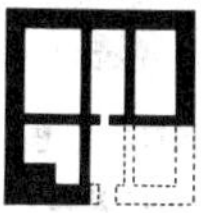

Rujm Abu Hilal — *153:100*

Ruin in Judean Hills 8 km. SW of Hebron. Hewn stone walls of square structure — perhaps a fortified tower, and sherds from Hasmonean, Roman and Byzantine Periods.

Rujm Abu Muḥeir — *189:162*

Remains of round tower on border of Samarian Hills and Jordan Valley, off Peẓa'el-Ma'ale Efrayim road. Diameter of 19 m. with walls preserved to a height of 3 m. Sherds indicate it was built at beginning of Iron Age.

Rujm Barakat — *162:091*

Ruin in Judean Hills 6 km. SE of Yatta village. Remains of Byzantine church, column fragments, pools and other structures.

Rujm el Barara → Ḥurbat Barir

Rujm ed Deir *157:095*

Ruin of fort in Judean Hills 6 km. N of Sammu'. Remains of a wall encompass hill upon which ruined fort is located. Sherds indicate occupation in Roman and Byzantine Periods.

Rujm Fiq *218:244*

Hilltop ruin on Golan Heights 2.5 km. NE of Afiq. Remains of small hewn stone walls. Apparently remnants of fort from Roman-Byzantine Period. Sherds from Early Bronze Age have been found here. Remains of additional enclosures to the N.

Rujm el Ḥamri *160:089*

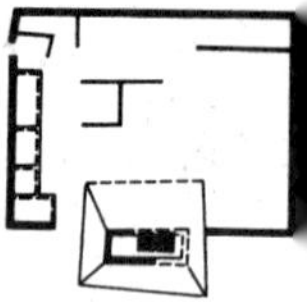

Ruin of a Roman-Byzantine fort on border of Judean Hills and Desert 4 km. E of Sammu' (Eshtemoa'). Rectangular in shape with central courtyard lined with rooms. Walls are preserved to a height of 6 courses. Nearby are burial caves, rock-cut cisterns and other remains. Sherds indicate occupation in Iron Age, Roman and Byzantine Periods.

Rujm el Hiri (Galgal Refa'im) *225:257*

Unique ancient site in heart of dolmen fields on Golan Heights 7 km. N of Ramat Magshimim. Includes 4 huge concentric walls of round stones. In the inner space is a heap of stones, 20 m. in diameter and 8 m. high. The first wall, partly preserved, is attached to the heap and the second wall encompasses the first. It too is partly preserved. The third wall is almost completely preserved. The fourth (outermost) wall measures 156 m. in diameter. Between the concentric walls are smaller radial walls built of large undressed stones and some courses have been preserved. Its origins are not known; some claim it was a cultic site; another theory is that it was an astronomical observatory, not unlike Stonehenge. The tendency (according to nearby finds) is to date it to the Early Bronze Age.

Rujm en Naqa (near 'En Gedi) *179:102*

Ruin of ancient fort adjacent to abandoned Jordanian police station on summit of hill in Judean Desert. Occupied in Iron Age, Hellenistic and Roman Periods.

Rujm en Naqa (near Teqoa') *171:113*

Remains of 2 Roman camps on border of Judean Hills and Desert 3 km. S of Teqoa'. The walls have been preserved in some places to a height of 1 m. Nearby, and along the road to Teqoa', are remains of various contemporary structures.

Rujm el Qaṣr *166:109*

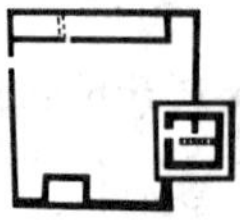

Remains of square Byzantine fortress on border of Judean Hills and Desert 8 km. NE of Hebron. Its walls have been preserved to a considerable height. Iron Age sherds also found here.

Rujm es Sabbit *163.117*

Tel in Judean Hills 2 km. E of Kefar 'Eẓyon. On summit is a stone heap. Sherds from Middle Bronze Age, Iron Age and Byzantine Period.

∴ Rujm el Yaquṣa *219:241*

Abandoned village on Golan Heights, 3 km. E of Afiq. Built on ruins of Roman–Byzantine settlement which was inhabited till Ottoman Period. Old building stones have been re-used in village houses.

Rujm Zaki (Rujm Zeiki) *217:246*

Hilltop ruin overlooking Lake Kinneret on Golan Heights, 2.5 km. W of Eli 'Al. Remains of large structure (apparently a Roman border station), column fragments, capitals and an olive press. Sherds indicate occupation in Roman, Byzantine, Medieval and Ottoman Periods. Nearby are sections of a paved Roman road.

Rumet Heib *179:242*

Bedouin settlement 8 km. N of Nazareth. Established 1971 for members of 'Arab el Heib tribe. Pop.: 500.

o Rummana (Lower Galilee) *179:243*

Arab village 10 km. N of Nazareth. Pop.: 300. Site of Biblical Levite city Dimnah (Josh. 21:35), and Byzantine settlement called Rimmon or Ruma. Remains of structures, cisterns and caves.

o Rummana (Samarian Hills) *169:214*

Arab village on border of Samarian Hills and Yizre'el Valley 6 km. S of Megiddo junction. Pop.: 1,200. Believed to be site of Gath-rimmon, Canaanite city mentioned as Gat Rimmonima in Tell el 'Amarna letters.

S

★ **Sa'ad** *105:098*

Kibbutz in Negev 7 km. NW of Netivot. Founded 1947 by 'Alumim group of Bene 'Aqiva. During War of Independence, it was on front line and badly hit by Egyptian attacks. After war kibbutz moved to present site, slightly E of previous site. Area: 12,000 d. Pop.: 730.

★ **Sa'ar** *160:270*

Kibbutz on Galilee coast 2 km. N of Nahariyya. Founded 1948 by HaShomer HaẒa'ir group. Initially intended as a fishing village. Area: 3,000 d. Pop.: 350. **Antiquities** Large collection of underwater archaeological finds. Within kibbutz are many ancient rock-cut tombs, one with incised flowers.

o **Sabastiya** *168:186*

Arab village in Samarian Hills 8 km. NW of Shekhem. Name derives from Greek name for ancient city of Shomeron, whose ruins are adjacent to the village. Pop.: 1,300. (See Shomeron.)

■ **Safed** **(Ẓefat)** *196:263*

City associated with Jewish mysticism in Galilee at ascent of Mt. Kena'an, at a height of 845-900 m. above sea level. Origin of name is not known. Perhaps from the Hebrew root *ẓafa* (observe, watch) since the city is a natural lookout over its surroundings. Popular lore explains the name as an acronym for the Hebrew *ẓevi* (gazelle), *pe'er* (magnificence), *tiferet* (glory). Its beginnings were apparently in Second Temple Period and throughout its history played an important role in the country, its people and religion. One of 4 sacred cities of Judaism (Jerusalem, Hebron, Tiberias and Safed), and city of mystery and Kabbala. Served intermittently in the past as capital of Galilee. Today it is a city of 14,500 inhabitants. **History** First mentioned in writings of Joseph b. Mattathias as one of cities of Galilee which he fortified in preparation for Jewish Revolt against Rome.

After destruction of Second Temple the priestly clans of Yaqim and Pashḥur resided here. During Roman–Byzantine Period, many *Tannaim* and *Amoraim* lived here. It was one of high points where beacons were lit to announce the new moon and festivals. In fact there is no real evidence regarding the early history of Safed, until it was taken by the Crusaders. In 1140 the Crusaders built a castle here which was sold to the Templars in 1168. According to Benjamin of Tudela, who visited the city in 1170, no Jews resided here. In 1180 it was captured by Saladin but in 1240 the entire Galilee was ceded to the Crusaders by a peace treaty and the castle was returned to the Templars. In 1266 the Mamluk Sultan Baybars captured Safed. In the early 13th c. (according to account by Judah Al-Ḥarizi of his visit in 1216), a Jewish community existed here and reports attest to the existence of a Jewish and Samaritan community in 14th c. Then Safed was capital of a *mamlakha* — a province — which included the Galilee and Lebanon. After Jewish expulsion from Spain

SAFED

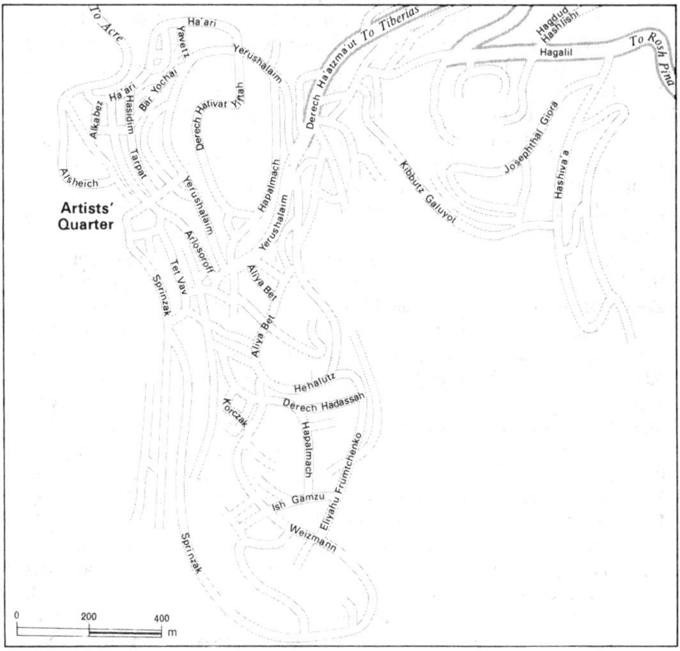

(1492) many exiled Jews settled in Safed and after the Ottoman conquest (1516) many of the emigres who fled to Turkey also came and settled here. In 16th c. Safed became a Jewish financial and religious centre which attracted many pilgrims from Europe and N Africa. Many Kabbalists too were drawn to Safed and it eventually became a Kabbalistic centre. (The tomb of Simeon bar Yoḥai, 2nd c. *Tanna*, is located in neighbouring Meron. Bar Yoḥai is believed by Kabbalists to be the author of the Zohar, the primary Kabbalistic text.) Great rabbis and scholars resided in the city at this time: Rabbi Joseph Caro (1488-1575), author of "Shulḥan Arukh" resided in neighbouring village of Biriyya; Solomon b. Moses HaLevi Alkabeẓ (ca. 1505-1584), composer of Sabbath hymn "Lekha Dodi"; and Kabbalist Rabbi Isaac b. Solomon Luria (HaAri, 1534-1572). In 1577 the Ashkenazi brothers established a printing press in Safed, the first in the Near East. At beginning of 17th c. there were internal power struggles between local rulers causing economic and spiritual decline in Safed which continued into the 18th c. There was a slight revival in late 18th and early 19th c., with the arrival of Ḥasidim of the Ba'al Shem Tov (1778) and disciples of Elijah Gaon of Vilna (1810). But the Jewish community soon declined as a result of epidemics, earthquakes and wars: 1812-1814 there was an epidemic in which Jews fled the city; in the 1830's there were wars between Druze and Arabs and a revolt against Ibrahim Pasha; in 1837 an earthquake completely destroyed the city and 5,000 people were killed (4,000 of whom were Jews). Only in the second half of 19th c., with strengthening of central authority, did Jews resettle in Safed. The community was augmented when new Jewish villages were established in Galilee in late 19th c. However, after WWI, when a large area of Upper Galilee was excluded from Palestine, the economic importance of the city and its Jewish population declined until the end of British Mandate. At outbreak of War of Independence Safed had a mixed population numbering 2,000 Jews and 12,000 Arabs. With the outbreak of war, the

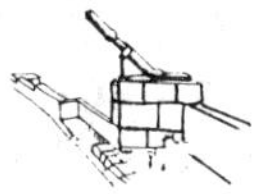

Arabs took over the citadel and police station, and besieged the Jewish quarter. The citadel was taken and siege lifted by a Palmaḥ battalion which was rushed to Safed. Within a few days the Palmaḥ was victorious and all Arab residents fled. **Government House** Governor's residence during Turkish Period; used by government offices during British Mandate. Now a community centre named after Wolffsohn. **Jewish cemetery** Old cemetery in W part of city, on hill slope. Burial site of Joseph Caro, HaAri and many other scholars and pious men. One tomb is purported to be that of the prophet Hosea. **Synagogue: Aboab** — named after Isaac Aboab I (end of 14th c.) rabbinic author who probably lived in Spain. Synagogue contains an ancient Torah scroll claimed to have belonged to Aboab and brought to Safed by Jews expelled from Spain. The 2 **HaAri synagogues, Ashkenazi and Sephardi**, the latter of which is oldest synagogue in Safed. Synagogue of **Yose Benea or Rabbi Yose HaBanai** — containing his 3rd c. tomb. This synagogue contains the Torah Scroll that is taken every year on Lag Ba'Omer in special procession to Meron. Synagogue of **Rabbi Moses Alshekh. Meẓuda** Ruins of ancient citadel on hill summit commanding a view of city and its environs. This was site of a Jewish fort during Revolt against Rome. Crusaders built castle here in 12th c. During War of Independence the Arabs took possession of it and only after its capture by the Jews could Israeli troops capture Safed. **Museums: Glicenstein Museum** — near citadel contains collection of works by Glicenstein. **Printing Museum** in Artists' Colony. **Caves:** Burial caves from Middle and Late Bronze Age containing many sherds and weapons. **Cave of Shem and Eber** Ancient burial cave near bridge. Tradition holds that Patriarch Jacob transmitted to his son Joseph the secrets of the Torah which he received from Shem and Eber. Arab legend claims it was here that Jacob was foretold of the fate of Joseph. **Artists' Colony** in old city has studios, permanent exhibits, galleries and residences of many artists.

o Ṣaffa *155:146*

Arab village in Samarian Hills 13 km. W of Ramallah. Pop.: 1,200.

o Saffarin *160:185*

Arab village (pop.: 500) in Samarian Hills 10 km. SE of Tulkarm.

St. George's Monastery (Deir Mar Jiryes) *189:139*

Greek Orthodox monastery in Judean Desert, built on mountain side of Wadi Qilt ravine, 5 km. W of Jericho. Believed to stand on site of 4th c. synagogue founded by John of Coziba in 5th c., extended and enlarged in days of Georgius of Coziba at end of 6th and beginning of 7th c. Rebuilt by Crusaders following Persian destruction. Constructed on three levels: upper — church and cave (Elijah's cave, according to Christian tradition); middle — main building and 3 churches named after John and Georgius of Coziba and the Virgin Mary. The lower level contains arched storerooms and monks' tombs. E of monastery on mountain slope are cave niches to which the monks retreat during the week, returning to the monastery for prayers on Saturday night and Sunday. Chapel contains numerous icons and frescoes.

St. Theodosius' Monastery *176:125*

Greek Orthodox monastery on border of Judean Hills and Desert, off Bethlehem–Abu Dis road, 7 km. NE of Bethlehem. Named after Greek monk Theodosius, who found refuge here in 2nd half of 5th c. The original monastery was destroyed at time of Arab conquest and Persian invasion. Rebuilt during Crusader Period but again destroyed by Arabs. Present structure built between 1914 and 1952. In courtyard of monastery is a small cave — Theodosius' retreat and where he was buried together with his mother and sister. According to legend the three Magi stopped in this grotto when they came to Bethlehem to see the newborn Jesus. The monastery also contains mosaic pavements of older churches, column fragments and remains of underground water canals. The Arabs call it Deir Dosi and Deir Ibn 'Ubeid. The nearby Arab village is called 'Ubeidiyya.

o **Sajur** ✓ *182:260*

Druze village in Galilee 5 km. NE of Karmi'el. Site of town of Shezor from Roman Period. Pop.: 1,300. Ancient tombs purported to be those of Rabbi Simeon Shezori and Rabbi Simeon b. Eliezer. In Middle Ages it was customary for Jewish pilgrims to visit the graves. SE of the village is *moshav* Shezor.

Sakhnin (**Siḥnin**) ✓ *177:252*

Urban Arab settlement in Galilee 6 km. S of Karmi'el. Pop.: 13,000 (90% Moslem, 10% Christian). **Siḥnin (Siḥni)** Village built on ruins of Jewish city Siḥni, or Siḥnin from Roman–Byzantine Period. Situated in a very fertile valley (Biq'at Sakhnin). Residence of renowned sages whose tombs were visited by Jewish pilgrims in Middle Ages. One tomb is a dome-covered structure purported to be that of Rabbi Joshua of Siḥnin, called by the Arabs en Nabi es Siddiq. Remains of Roman mausoleum and Byzantine burial cave. Ancient building stones have been re-used in village houses. One stone has Greek inscription.

o **Salfit** *167:165*

Arab village (pop.: 3,200) 20 km. N of Ramallah.

o **Salim** (Yizre'el Valley) *168:216*

Arab village 4 km. SE of Megiddo junction. Established by youth of neighbouring villages. Pop.: 350.

o **Salim** (Samarian Hills) *181:179*

Arab village 6 km. E of Shekhem. Pop.: 1,100. Believed to be "Shalem, a city of Shechem" to which Jacob came (Gen. 33:18). Samaritan tradition claims there was a Samaritan community here until 8th c.

● **Sal'it** *154:183*

Moshav shittufi in Samarian Hills 8 km. S of Tulkarm. Established 1978 as *naḥal* outpost. Civilian status 1979.

★ **Samar** *150:916*

Kibbutz in 'Arava 10 km. SE of Yotvata. Established 1976.

Samarian Hills *(I Kings 16:24)*

Large hilly region in centre of country. Bounded in N by Yizre'el Valley, in NW by Biq'at Naḥal 'Iron, in W by Sharon, in S by Judean Hills and in E by Jordan Valley. Inhabited since ancient times. Its capital Shekhem is mentioned in Tell el 'Amarna letters. After Israelite conquest it fell to tribe of Ephraim. After division of Solomon's kingdom, it was heart of Kingdom of Israel. In 887 BCE King Omri built city of Shomeron as capital of his kingdom which persisted till its destruction in 721 by Sargon II, King of Assyria, who deported large numbers of its population replacing them with people from other lands. These newcomers eventually developed a separate national entity — the Samaritans. Today, inhabited mainly by Arabs; since Six-Day War it has been under Israeli control.

o **(Es) Sammu'** *(Eshtemoa: Josh. 21:14)* *156:089*

Arab village in Judean Hills 23 km. S of Hebron. Ancient synagogue ruin. Site of Biblical city of Eshtemoa, a Levite city in Judah tribal allotment. Mentioned as a large Jewish village in Onomasticon of Eusebius as late as 4th c. CE. Also mentioned in manuscript of Jerusalem Talmud discovered in Cairo Genizah. Present village has population of

3,800. In 1966 an Israeli force raided village which had been used as a terrorist base. **Eshtemoa'** Within village are many Mishnaic and Talmudic remains. Remnants of synagogue (alongside a later mosque) that probably existed from 4th c. CE to end of Byzantine Period. Mosaic pavement flanked by 4 pillars. Synagogue measures 13 x 21 m. Portion of western wall rises to height of 8.5 m. In a room alongside the synagogue a treasure of silver jewellery and ingots was discovered. Believed to date from period of Kingdom of David. May have been presents that King David sent residents of the town after the defeat of the Amalekites (I Sam 30:28).

Sanabir — *212:267*

Abandoned village on Golan Heights 4 km. E of Benot Ya'aqov Bridge. Built on ruins of ancient settlement from Roman–Byzantine Period. Ancient building stones which have been re-used in village houses, arches of dressed stones, column fragments and carved capitals (including one with pomegranate reliefs).

Ṣandala — *180:214*

Arab village in Yizre'el Valley at foot of Mt. Gilboa' 4 km. SW of 'En Ḥarod. Founded more than 110 years ago by residents of neighbouring village of 'Arana. Pop.: 670.

Sanniriya — *154:170*

Arab village in Samarian Hills 10 km. SE of Qalqilya. Pop.: 900. The village mosque was built in 15th c. on ruins of Crusader fortress. Within mosque is a cave where human skulls and skeletons are preserved. Arab tradition claims these are remains of Moslem soldiers, killed in battle with Crusaders.

Sanur — *173:195*

Arab village in Samarian Hills 12 km. SW of Jenin. Pop.: 2,000. Within village are rock tombs, ancient cisterns and caves. Sherds from Arab and Mamluk Periods.

Sapir — *167:002*

Regional centre for settlements of Paran, Ẓofar, Ḥaẓeva and 'En Yahav. Located in 'Arava 8 km. SW of *moshav* 'En Yahav.

Sarid — *(Josh. 19:12) 171:229*

Kibbutz in Yizre'el Valley 2 km. SW of Migdal Ha'Emeq. Same name as Biblical city of Sarid included in tribal allotment of Zebulun and identified with Tell Shaddud. Founded 1926 by pioneers from Russia, Czechoslovakia and Poland. In pre-State years it was a Palmaḥ and Haganah base. Area: 7,200 d. Pop.: 750. **Tell Shaddud** Within kibbutz is tel of ancient Sarid, *172:229.* Sherds indicate occupation from Late Bronze Age until Arab Period, particularly during Iron Age (period of Judges and the Unified Kingdom). During Roman Period a road led through here from Legio to Ẓippori. Some of the milestones have been found within kibbutz. E of tel are remains of a settlement from Early Bronze Age.

Sarona — *194:236*

Moshav in Galilee 5 km. NE of Kefar Tavor. Named after ancient town whose name has been preserved in that of adjacent ruin, Kh. Sarona. Began as workers' farm in 1913, but abandoned during WWI. Resettled in 1938 by A.D. Gordon organization. Area: 7,000 d. Pop.: 230.

Ṣarra — *168:179*

Arab village 6 km. W of Shekhem. Pop.: 750. Site of Samaritan community in Middle Ages.

Sar Shalom *176:273*

Look-out point in Galilee 4 km. N of Ma'alot–Tarshiḥa. Same name as nearby mount. Name of Biblical origin, from Isa. 9:6 (*sar shalom* = prince of peace). Established 1979.

o Ṣarta *158:167*

Arab village in Samarian Hills 15 km. SE of Qalqilya. Pop.: 750.

Sartaba (Alexandrion) *194:167*

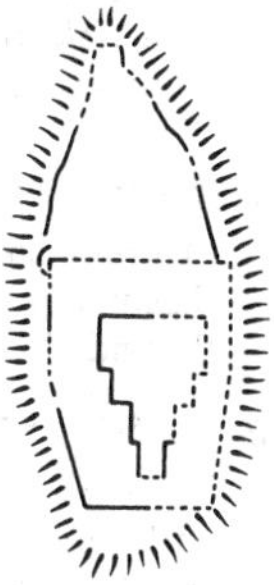

Cone-shaped hill overlooking Jordan Valley 6 km. W of Adam Bridge (Damiya). Height: 377 m. above sea level. At summit is Alexandrion fortress built by King Alexander Yannai (ca. 126-76 BCE) or by Queen Salome Alexandra (Shelomẓiyyon HaMalka) in 90 BCE. Also called Sartaba. The fortress was destroyed by Gabinius (1st c. BCE Roman governor) but then rebuilt. Here Queen Salome Alexandra (139-67 BCE) kept her treasures, Herod imprisoned his wife Mariamne I, and his two sons, Alexander and Aristobulus, met their death here. During Second Temple Period this was probably a signal mount where fires were lit to announce a festival and new moon. Fortress destroyed around 70 CE. Remains of fortress, aqueduct and plastered pools.

★ Sasa *187:270*

Kibbutz in Galilee off N road near Ḥiram junction. Named after ancient city which was located here; its name was preserved in name of Arab village Sa'sa'. Established 1949 on lands of abandoned village used as base by Arab forces during War of Independence. Initial settlers were members of HaShomer HaẒa'ir. Area: 16,200 d. Pop.: several hundred. **Pa'ar Cave reserve** Half a km. NW of kibbutz is spout-shaped cave within a grove. Area: 14 d. **Ancient Sasa** Site occupied from Second Temple Period. According to documents it was a Jewish pilgrimage site in the Middle Ages traditionally believed to be gravesite of the sages Rabbi Sisi and his sons. Roman finds within kibbutz: burial caves, cisterns, pool, building stones, column fragments and remains of synagogue. Remains of fortress from days of Dahir el 'Amr. Sherds indicate occupation in earlier periods as well.

∴ Ṣataf *162:131*

Site with springs, remains of antiquities and ruins of abandoned village in Judean Hills 5 km. W of Jerusalem, off the road leading from 'En Kerem to Bar Giyyora. Large hewn stone buildings from Roman Period; two springs: 'Ein el Balad and 'Ein Bakura ('Ein Sharqiyya); tunnel, ponds and Roman reservoirs and irrigation channels. **St. John in the Desert Monastery** On opposite mountain, E of road is the 12th c. Franciscan monastery of St. John in the Desert. According to Christian tradition, John the Baptist spent his youth here and prepared for his mission. Grotto with spring 'Ein el Ḥabis (spring of the prophet).

Savyon *138:162*

Urban settlement on Coastal Plain 2 km. SW of Petaḥ Tiqwa. Named after *savyon* (ragwort) flower common to region. Established 1954 to provide housing for S African immigrants. Pop.: 2,350. One of the first houses built by Petaḥ Tiqwa residents who moved temporarily to escape a malaria epidemic still exists in Savyon.

o (Es) Sawiya *174:165*

Arab village 15 km. S of Shekhem. Pop.: 900.

Sea of Galilee → Lake Kinneret

Sebaste → Shomeron

★ **Sede Boqer** *130:031*

Kibbutz in Negev Hills 40 km. S of Be'er Sheva'. Name originates from Arabic name of adjacent mountain, Shajarat el Baqqar. In 1953, Sede Boqer became David Ben-Gurion's permanent residence after he ceased his political activity until he died. Area: 1,300 d. Pop.: 220. Home and library of Ben-Gurion. In 1964, Midreshet Sede Boqer was established next to his house. Nearby are graves of David and Paula Ben-Gurion overlooking the Ẕin Wilderness. Prehistoric drawings were found on stones nearby. Sede Boqer is now a world-renowned centre for desert research: the Jacob Blaustein Institute of Ben-Gurion University of the Negev is located here.

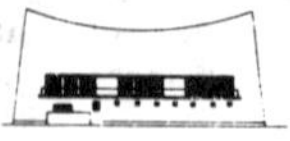

● **Sede Dawid** *119:109*

Moshav in Lakhish region, 8 km. SW of Qiryat Gat. Named after Zalman David Levontin (1856-1940) founder of Rishon LeẔiyyon. Founded 1955. Area: 2,200 d. Pop.: 480.

● **Sede Eli'ezer** *203:272*

Moshav in Galilee W of Yesod HaMa'ala. Named after Robert (Eli'ezer) Philippe de Rothschild (1880-1946). Founded 1952. Area: 3,000 d. Pop.: 330.

★ **Sede Eliyyahu** *199:206*

Kibbutz 6 km. S of Bet She'an. Named after Rabbi Elijah Gutmacher, German Zionist rabbi. Founded 1939 as a "stockade and tower" settlement by a Youth 'Aliyah group from Germany on lands belonging to the German Templer sect. Area: 4,700 d. Pop.: several hundred.

● **Sedei Ḥemed** *145:174*

Moshav in Sharon 1 km. SE of Kefar Sava. Name taken from Biblical passage "...for the *pleasant fields*, for the fruitful vine" (Isa. 32:12). Founded 1952 in framework of "city to settlement" programme. Area: 1,500 d. Pop.: 280.

● **Sede Ilan** *190:240*

Moshav in Galilee 3 km. S of Golani junction. Name derives from neighbouring veteran village (*moshava*) of Ilaniyya. Founded 1949. Area: 5,700 d. Pop.: 230.

● **Sedei Terumot** *196:205*

Moshav 6 km. S of Bet She'an at foot of Mt. Gilboa'. Name originates from David's lament over death of Jonathan "Ye mountains of Gilboa, let there be no dew or rain upon you, nor *upsurging of the deep*!" (II Sam. 1:21). Founded 1951. Area: 3,000 d. Pop.: several hundred. **Tel Terumot** Ancient tel within *moshav* with sherds indicate occupation in Iron Age, Persian, Hellenistic and Roman Periods. **Hurbat Shamrit** S of *moshav* is settlement ruin from Byzantine Period. Sherds also indicate earlier habitation in Persian Period.

● **Sede Moshe** *131:113*

Moshav in Lakhish region 2 km. E of Qiryat Gat. Named after Baron Maurice (Moshe) de Hirsch (1831-1896). Founded 1956 as part of "city to settlement" programme. Area: 5,000 d. Pop.: 300.

★ **Sede Naḥum** *195:214*

Kibbutz 2 km. NW of Bet She'an. Named after Naḥum Sokolow (1859-1936), president of World Zionist Organization from 1931 till 1935. Founded 1937 as a "stockade and tower" settlement by Sade group of Miqwe Yisra'el graduates and immigrants from Poland, Austria and Germany. Area: 10,000 d. Pop.: 300. **Byzantine mosaic floor** Remains of a Byzantine monastery from 5th and 6th c. were uncovered within kibbutz with a mosaic church floor — one of the most beautiful found thus far in the country.

★ **Sede Neḥemya** *208:288*

Kibbutz in Ḥula Valley 5 km. E of Qiryat Shemona. Named after Nehemiah de Lieme (1882-1940), Dutch Zionist. Founded 1940 by immigrants from Holland, Austria, Czechoslovakia and N Africa. Area: 3,500 d. Pop.: 360.

● **Sede Nizzan** *094:071*

Moshav in Negev 5 km. SW of Magen junction. Named after Jewish philanthropist Blumfield. Founded 1973 by immigrants from English-speaking countries. Area: 3,000 d. Pop.: 240.

Sederot *111:103*

Town in Negev 14 km. S of Ashqelon. Named in honour of Jewish National Fund's activity of planting avenues (*sederot*) of trees. Originated as immigrant camp in 1951. Area: 5,500 d. Pop.: 9,000.

● **Sede 'Uzziyahu** *119:129*

Moshav on Coastal Plain 5 km. SE of Ashdod. Named after King Uzziah, of whom it is written "...and he built cities in the territory of Ashdod and elsewhere among the Philistines" (II Chron. 26:6). Established 1950. Pop.: 870.

● **Sede Warburg** *141:179*

Moshav in Sharon 2 km. N of Kefar Sava. Named after Otto Warburg (1859-1938), president of World Zionist Organization from 1911 to 1920. Founded 1938 by German immigrants. Area: 3,000 d. Pop.: 370.

● **Sede Ya'aqov** *163:233*

Moshav in Yizre'el Valley 2 km. SE of Qiryat Tiv'on. Named after Rabbi Isaac Jacob Reines (1839-1915) founder and leader of Mizraḥi movement. Founded 1927. Area: 6,000 d. Pop.: 550.

● **Sede Yiẓḥaq** *149:201*

Moshav on border of Sharon and Samarian Hills 7 km. SE of E Ḥadera junction. Named after Yiẓḥak Sadeh (1890-1952), one of the founders of Palmaḥ and a Haganah leader. Founded 1952. Area: 2,200 d. Pop.: 250.

★ **Sede Yo'av** *119:117*

Kibbutz on border of Judean Foothills and S Coastal Plain, 2 km. SE of Giv'ati junction. Named after Yo'av — the underground alias of Yiẓḥaq Dubno, commander of kibbutz Negba during War of Independence, who died in the war. Founded 1956. Area: 6,000 d. Pop.: 150.

● **Sede Ẓevi** *122:095*

Moshav in Negev 4 km. W of Bet Qama junction. Named after Ẓevi Hirschfeld, early settler in Ruḥama before WWI. Founded 1953 as part of "city to settlement" programme. Area: 4,000 d. Pop.: 330.

Sedom *(Gen. 13:10)* *187:053*

Dead Sea Works S of Dead Sea, 13 km. NE of 'Arava junction. Same name as Biblical Sodom, destroyed together with Gomorrah, and, according to one theory, was located in the area. Founded as the Palestine Potash Co. by Moshe Novomeysky (1873-1961), to exploit minerals of Dead Sea (potash, bromide, etc.). In 1930 the first plant was established at Qalya, on N shore of Dead Sea. In 1934 the second plant was set up at Sedom. During War of Independence the N premises had to be evacuated, and was subsequently destroyed by the Arabs. The workers were taken to the S plant, which was also isolated and besieged until relieved by Israel Defence Forces.

In 1953 the Be'er Sheva'–Sedom road was completed and in 1954 the Dead Sea Works re-opened. In 1964 the road from Sedom to Elat through the 'Arava was completed, facilitating a comfortable route to export Dead Sea minerals to Far East.

● **Sedot Mikha** *142:125*

Moshav in Judean Foothills 7 km. SW of Bet Shemesh. Named after Hebrew writer Micha Josef Berdyczewski (Bin-Gorion, 1865-1921). Founded 1955 in context of "ship to settlement" programme. Area: 1,200 d. Pop.: 340.

★ **Sedot Yam** *140:211*

Kibbutz on Mediterranean shore 5 km. N of Ḥadera. Founded 1940 by HaNo'ar Ha'Oved group who were initially engaged mainly in fishing. During pre-State years, kibbutz served as a port for "illegal" immigrants. Area: 4,700 d. Pop.: 800. Cultural centre named after Hannah Szenes (1921-1944), kibbutz member and parachutist who, on WWII mission in Hungary, was arrested by Germans and executed. N of kibbutz are ruins of Caesarea.

Segavyon Island *158:272*

Island 1.5 km. from Akhziv shore. Named after Segavyon, head of Akhziv synagogue during lifetime of Rabban Gamaliel II of Yavne (1st c. CE).

Segev *174:252*

Rural settlement in Galilee 8 km. SE of Aḥihud junction. Founded as *naḥal* outpost in 1953; received civilian status in 1957. Pop.: 220.

● **Segula** *129:113*

Moshav in Lakhish region 6 km. N of Qiryat Gat. Founded 1953 as part of "city to settlement" programme. Area: 4,600 d. Pop.: 300.

○ **Ṣeida** *161:199*

Arab village in Samarian Hills 12 km. NE of Tulkarm. Pop.: 1,000.

○ **Seifa** *100:106*

Arab village (pop.: 650) in Gaza Strip 5 km. N of Gaza, near Jabaliya village.

Sejera, (Esh) Shajara → Ilaniyya

Sela' Andromeda

Rock in Mediterranean off Jaffa shore. According to Greek mythology Andromeda was placed on this rock by her father King Cepheus in order to placate the sea monster (Poseidon). Perseus saw her, fell in love with her and saved her from the monster. (See Jaffa.)

★ **Senir** *213:293*

Kibbutz in Ḥula Valley 2 km. E of kibbutz Dan. Named after Naḥal Senir (Ḥaṣbani), one of the 3 major sources of Jordan River. Founded as *naḥal* outpost in 1967; received civilian status in 1968. Initially called Kefar Sharett after Moshe Sharett (1894-1965), second prime minister of Israel. As a young kibbutz it suffered terrorist harassment from across the border. Area: 3,600 d.

Senir Bridge *207:292*

Bridge in Ḥula Valley over Naḥal Senir (Ḥaṣbani), where the Qiryat Shemona–Banyas road crosses the river.

∴ **Sequfiyya (Sukufiyya)** *215:245*

Abandoned village on Golan Heights 4 km. NE of 'En Gev, within *moshav* Giv'at Yo'av. Built on ruins of 2nd-4th c. Jewish town. Burial caves, mosque, columns and capitals. Sherds indicate occupation in Roman-Byzantine Period.

Sha'ab **(Sha'av)** *173:254*

Arab village in Galilee 8 km. SE of Aḥihud junction. Site of Jewish town of Sha'av from Roman-Byzantine Period. Pop.: 2,500. Remains of structures, cisterns and ancient tombs. Sherds indicate occupation in Middle Bronze Age, Late Bronze Age, Iron Age and from Hellenistic until Arab Period.

Sha'al *217:280*

Moshav shittufi on Golan Heights 6 km. E of Gonen. Founded 1976.

Sha'alvim *(Josh. 19:42) 148:142*

Kibbutz in Ayyalon Valley 4 km. N of Latrun junction. Named after ancient city of Shaalabbin located on site of abandoned village of Salbit. Founded 1951. Border settlement until Six-Day War, opposite the Latrun enclave. Area: 25,000 d. Pop.: 550. *Yeshiva* high school, *hesder yeshiva* (*yeshiva* students serving in Israel Defence Forces), and rabbinical school. **Tel Sha'alvim (Salbit)** The city of Sha'alvim (Shaalabbin) has been identified with abandoned village of Salbit, S of kibbutz, *148:141*. Sherds indicate occupation in Middle Bronze Age, Iron Age, Roman and Byzantine Periods. During Israelite conquest it was included in Dan tribal allotment, and in King Solomon's reign it was within his 2nd district (I Kings 4:9). During Roman and Byzantine Periods it was a Samaritan village. Excavations have uncovered remains of a Samaritan synagogue and inscriptions. The synagogue's mosaic floor has been removed to the Dept. of Antiquities.

Sha'anan *126:110*

Farm in Judean Hills 4 km. S of Peluggot junction. Established 1955 and owned by Yiẓur U'Pittuaḥ company.

Sha'are Avraham *130:130*

Youth village and educational institute on Coastal Plain 1 km. E of Re'em junction. Named after its donor, Abraham Greenwald of England. Founded 1958. Pop.: 120 pupils and staff.

Sha'ar Efrayim *150:188*

Moshav on border of Sharon and Samarian Hills 3 km. SW of Tulkarm. In ancient times this region was part of Ephraim's tribal allotment, hence its name. Founded 1953. Area: 2,500 d. Pop.: 550.

Sha'ar Ha'Amaqim *160:236*

Kibbutz on border of Zevulun and Yizre'el Valleys 1 km. NE of Qiryat Tiv'on. Founded 1935 by HaShomer HaẒa'ir group from Rumania and Yugoslavia. Area: 7,250 d. Pop.: 610. Nearby are ancient remains, possibly of the city of Geva' of the Parashim, from Second Temple Period. **Sha'ar Ha'Amaqim forest** Nature reserve with remains of large ancient forest. Area: 2,800 d. Tabor oaks.

Sha'ar HaGay *152:135*

Gorge opening that serves as gateway from Judean Foothills to Jerusalem Hills, hence its name (gateway of the valley). Called Bab el Wad in Arabic. Throughout history a major route from Judean Foothills to Jerusalem has passed through this natural gateway. In the War of Independence fierce battles raged here. At the beginning of the war the Arabs attacked supply convoys to Jerusalem; Haganah and Palmaḥ units succeeded in gaining control of the E section of the road, but the W part (Latrun road) remained in Arab hands. In order to bypass this section, the "Burma Road" was forged and later the "Heroes Road" was paved. After Six-Day War the Latrun road was reopened, and is now part of the main highway from Jerusalem to Tel Aviv. Remains of the Roman road have been found at Sha'ar HaGay. N of the gorge opening is a ruin of a watch-tower and to the S a khan ruin — both from Ottoman Period. To the E is an abandoned British police station from Mandatory times. From Sha'ar HaGay E, scattered along the road, are remains of armoured cars, relics of the convoy battles of the War of Independence.

★ **Sha'ar HaGolan** *206:232*

Kibbutz in Jordan Valley 2 km. SE of Zemaḥ junction. Name means gateway to the Golan. Founded 1937 as a "stockade and tower" settlement by members of 'En HaQore group from Poland and Czechoslovakia. In pre-State years served as base for *peluggot sade* (field companies) and transit station for Jewish "illegal" immigrants from Syria. During War of Independence evacuated and then destroyed by Syrian army. Recaptured 3 days later, and rebuilt after the war. But it was intermittently shelled and mined after War of Independence and during War of Attrition (1968-1970). Area: 3,000 d. Pop.: several hundred. **Neolithic remains** The first signs of a complex of Neolithic cultures in Near East were found near the kibbutz fish ponds. Named Yarmoukian Culture, after nearby Yarmouk River, its people were engaged in agriculture, sheep raising, fishing and hunting. Many varied flint implements were found along with mainly female figurines of stone or clay, mixed with quartz grit. Apparently evidence of a fertility cult. Most finds are displayed in kibbutz museum.

Sha'ar Menashe *151:206*

Malben institute (old age home) on border of Ramat Menashe 3 km. SE of Pardes Ḥanna. Established 1949 in former British army camp.

∴ **Shabba** *220:259*

Abandoned village on Golan Heights 8 km. SE of Qaẓrin. Alongside is small tel dating apparently from Roman-Byzantine Period. Ancient vaulted structure with paving stones. Area has many dolmens.

○ **Shabtin** *154:153*

Arab village (pop.: 200) on border of Samarian Hills and Judean Hills, 7 km. NE of Me'or Modi'im. Sheikh's tomb. To the S are Roman-Byzantine ruins.

● **Shadmot Devora** *191:233*

Moshav in Galilee NE of Kefar Tavor. Named after Devora (Dorothy), wife of James Armand de Rothschild (1878-1957), and after the prophetess Deborah who gathered the Israelites in this region to fight the Canaanites. Founded 1939. Area: 7,800 d. Pop.: 230.

● **Shafir** *(Micah 1:11) 124:123*

Moshav in Judean Foothills 4 km. SW of Qiryat Mal'akhi. Named after Biblical city of Saphir whose name was retained in that of neighbouring abandoned villages Sawafir esh Sharqiyya, Sawafir esh Shamaliyya and Sawafir el Gharbiyya. Founded 1949. Area: 3,000 d. Pop.: 200. Ancient remains within abandoned village.

Shaḥaf Island *159:275*

Island 1 km. off N shore, opposite Misrafot junction, near Naḥli'eli Island. Named for gulls that nest here.

● **Shaḥar** *124:114*

Moshav in Lakhish region 4 km. W of Qiryat Gat. Founded 1955. Pop.: 450.

Shajarat el Arba'in → Ḥureshat HaAreba'im

Shajarat el ‘Ashara → Ḥureshat Tal

Shajarat el Kalb → Ḥureshat Ya‘ala

Shalhavit *132:086*

Community settlement in NE Negev 6 km. SW of Lahav. Named for Jerusalem sage plant prevalent in area. Established 1980.

● **Shalwa** *128:108*

Moshav in Judean Foothills 4 km. S of Qiryat Gat. Name taken from Biblical passage "*Peace* be within your walls, and security within your towers" (Ps. 122:7). Founded 1952. Area: 5,000 d. Pop.: 580.

★ **Shamerat** *159:260*

Kibbutz on Galilee coast, near el Bahja Persian garden. Name derives from Hebrew root *shamar* — to guard. Founded 1948 by HaShomer HaẒa‘ir group from Rumania and Czechoslovakia. Area: 5,000 d. Pop.: 380.

★ **Shamir** *211:285*

Kibbutz in Ḥula Valley 9 km. SE of Qiryat Shemona. Founded 1944 by HaShomer HaẒa‘ir group from Rumania. During War of Independence it was attacked by Syrian army. Pop.: 500. **Finds** Border stones with 3rd c. Greek inscriptions and dolmens. Regional archaeological collection.

○ **Sharafat** *168:128*

Arab village SW of Jerusalem, alongside Beit Ṣafafa.

Sharon *(Isa. 33:9)*

Region on W central coast bounded in N by Mt. Karmel and Karmel shore (along Naḥal Tanninim), in NE by Ramat Menashe, in E by Samarian Hills, in S by central Coastal Plain (along Yarqon River) and in W by the Mediterranean Sea. Length: 60 km., width: 14 to 20 km. Archaeological investigation indicates habitation in area from Chalcolithic Period. Traversed in ancient days by *via maris*. Mentioned in ancient Egyptian documents. King of Lasharon was one of 31 kings defeated by Joshua (Josh. 12:18). The Bible extols the region for its fecundity, its forests and its beauty (Isa. 33:9; 35:2; Song 2:1). After division of kingdom it was included in Kingdom of Israel. After conquest by Tiglath-pileser III (732 BCE) it became an Assyrian province. Destroyed by Shalmaneser IV in 722 BCE. After conquest by Alexander the Great the region was Hellenized. Annexed to Hasmonean kingdom in reign of Alexander Yannai, but reverted to Hellenism when Caesarea became its capital during Roman Period. The Arab conquest brought a decline: tracts of land were flooded and turned into deadly swamps and the impoverished population dwindled. With the expulsion of the Crusaders, the region was intentionally turned into a wasteland in order to prevent invaders from the sea establishing a foothold. It remained desolate until beginning of Jewish settlement in late 19th c. (1878 — founding of Petaḥ Tiqwa).

● **Sharsheret** *112:090*

Moshav in Negev 2 km. S of Netivot. Founded 1951. Area: 6,500 d. Pop.: 550.

Shatta *190:217*

Prison in Yizre‘el Valley 2 km. SW of kibbutz Bet HaShitta. Prison housed in British-built Tegart police fort. Name taken from that of former Arab village, Shatta, which was located on lands of present Bet HaShitta.

Shave Shomeron *167:185*

Civilian outpost in Samarian Hills 10 km. NW of Shekhem, off the Shekhem–Tulkarm road. Established 1977.

▙ **Shave Ẓiyyon** *158:265*

Moshav shittufi on Galilee coast 2 km. S of Nahariyya. Founded 1938 by German immigrants as a "stockade and tower" settlement. Over the years a residential quarter sprang up near the *moshav* called Shekhunat Ḥof. In 1949 the two settlements joined. Area: 1,800 d. Pop.: 600. **Nature reserve** Along the coast to S of Nahariyya. Area: 170 d. **Ancient remains** N of Shave Ẓiyyon, above mouth of Naḥal Bet Ha'Emeq, are remains of ancient settlement alongside a small natural bay. Sherds indicate it was inhabited during 7th and 6th c. BCE, then abandoned and reoccupied in Hellenistic Period. Mainly occupied during Roman and Byzantine Periods (from 2nd c. BCE to 6th c. CE), and called Neakom (new settlement). Excavations have uncovered a Phoenician pottery coffin containing a face, Phoenician cemetery and altars and remnants of Byzantine church — one of the oldest churches found in the country. An inscription found in the church dates from 320-330 CE. Roman bathhouse from 2nd and 3rd centuries.

● **She'ar Yashuv** *210:292*

Moshav in Ḥula Valley, 7 km. E of Qiryat Shemona. Name from Biblical passage: "*A remnant will return*, the remnant of Jacob" (Isa. 10:21). One of the Ussishkin Forts, a series of settlements in Upper Galilee in which members of all Zionist parties could participate. During War of Independence it was attacked by Syrians and then abandoned by settlers. In 1949 it was reinhabited by immigrants from Hungary and Rumania. Up to Six-Day War, it was a frontier settlement frequently harassed by Syrian forces from Tell el 'Azaziyat which lies E of *moshav*. Pop.: several hundred.

Sheba Hospital → Tel HaShomer

● **Shedema** *125:138*

Moshav on Coastal Plain 4 km. NW of Gedera. Name means a field of grain. Founded 1954 on lands of abandoned village of Bash-shit. Area: 1,300 d. Pop.: 160.

▭ **Shefar'am** (**Shafa 'Amr**) *166:245*

Arab city in Galilee 4 km. E of Qiryat Ata. Site of Jewish town in Byzantine Period. Shefar'am has been a city since Ottoman Period. Area: 3,500 d. Pop.: 14,000 (45% Christian, 35% Moslem and 20% Druze). **History** Mentioned in Talmud as city to which Sanhedrin moved from Usha; later it moved to Bet She'arim. The Crusaders fortified it to protect the road from Acre and Nazareth. A Jewish community was reestablished here after Ottoman conquest. In 1761 the Bedouin ruler Dahir el 'Amr made it his residence and changed its name to Shafa 'Amr (the good health of 'Amr). He also encouraged Jews to reside in the city and as a result a small Jewish community persisted here even into the 19th c. The last Jew (Avraham el 'Azari) left in 1920. During War of Independence it was a base for Arab forces in Galilee. Taken by Israel Defence Forces in "Deqel" operation (July 1948). **Remains** of ancient buildings, Roman burial tombs, a cistern and tombs from Byzantine Period; ruins of 2 fortresses from days of Dahir el 'Amr, apparently built on Crusader ruins (es Saraya and el Burj); 17th c. synagogue.

★ **Shefayyim** *133:180*

Kibbutz on Sharon coast 5 km. N of Herzliyya. Name taken from Biblical passage: "I will open rivers on the *bare heights*" (Isa. 41:18). Founded 1935 by members of HeḤaluẓ and HeḤaluẓ HaẒa'ir from Russia, Poland and Latvia. In pre-State years it was a Palmaḥ base and port for "illegal" immigrants. Area: 4,800 d. Pop.: 700. Offices of Ḥof HaSharon regional council located within kibbutz.

Shefela → Judean Foothills

● **Shefer** *191:261*

Moshav in Galilee 3 km. NE of Ḥananya junction. Founded 1950 by demobilized soldiers. Area: 1,000 d. Pop.: 280.

(Esh) Sheikha *196:219*

Settlement ruins in Galilee 4 km. NE of Bet HaShitta. Structural remains on rocky outcrops. Sherds indicate habitation in Early Bronze Age, Iron Age, Persian, Hellenistic and Roman Periods.

o **Sheikh Aḥmad** *095:101*

Arab village in Gaza Strip 2 km. SW of city of Gaza. Sheikh's tomb.

o **Sheikh 'Ajlin** *095:101*

Arab village (pop.: 320) in Gaza Strip on seashore 2 km. SW of Gaza. Sheikh's tomb.

o **(Esh) Sheikh Bureik** *144:231*

Armenian village on Karmel coast 2 km. S of 'Atlit. Established 1926 by Christian Armenians from Jaffa. The only Armenian village within Israel. Pop.: 40. Sheikh's tomb and ruins of ancient settlement.

o **(Esh) Sheikh Dannun** *164:266*

Arab village in Galilee 5 km. SE of Nahariyya. One of 2 villages founded 45 years ago by 2 brothers from Egypt and named after them: Sheikh Daud and Sheikh Dannun. Eventually the villages amalgamated. Pop.: 900. Ancient tombs nearby.

Sheikh Daud → (Esh) Sheikh Dannun

(Esh) Sheikh Ibreik *162:234*

Ancient Moslem holy tomb in Yizre'el Valley S of Qiryat Tiv'on, near Bet She'arim. Attributed to Barak, son of Abinoam, Israelite commander in battle with Jabin, King of Hazor. In Arabic the name means sheikh of the pitcher. Nearby is statue of Alexander Zeid (1886-1938) who settled here with his family and was murdered by Arab gangs in 1938.

Sheikh Khadr *211:250*

Ruins of ancient fortress on E shore of Lake Kinneret 7 km. N of 'En Gev. Remains of double walls of round fortress and several sherds from Middle Bronze Age and Iron Age.

Sheikh Nabhan *095:092*

Settlement ruins in Gaza Strip 4 km. E of el Mughazi refugee camp. Remains of sheikh's tomb built on ruins of church.

Sheikh Qatrawani *168:155*

Tomb of Arab sheikh 10 km. N of Ramallah, between villages of Bir Zeit and 'Attara. Built on ruins of Byzantine church of which columns arranged in 2 rows remain.

Sheikh er Raḥab → Reḥov

(Esh) Sheikh 'Uthman el Khazuri *218:295*

Druze sheikh's tomb on Mt. Ḥermon 1.5 km. SW of *moshav* Newe Ativ. Surrounded by grove of 73 ancient oaks. View of surroundings.

∴ **Sheita** *224:296*

Abandoned village on Golan Heights 3 km. SE of Majdal Shams. Built during Ottoman Period on Byzantine ruins.

∴ **Sheita Judeida** *224:295*

Abandoned Druze village on Golan Heights 2 km. SE of Majdal Shams, near border with Syria.

Shekhaneya ✱ *173:250*

Industrial village in Upper Galilee 2 km. N of Yodefat. Named after one of priestly clans who resided in nearby city of Cabul (Josh. 19:27; I Chron. 24:11).

□ **Shekhem (Nablus)** ✱ *(Gen. 33:18) 174:180*

Arab city in Samarian Hills between Mt. Gerizim and Mt. 'Eval. Site of ancient city continuously occupied from Bronze Age to present-day. District capital; pop.: 80,000, mostly Moslem. (Christian minority and very small Samaritan community.) **History** Shekhem is mentioned in Egyptian writings from 19th j. BCE and in Tell el 'Amarna letters from 14th c. BCE. First mentioned in Bible at time of Patriarchs: Abraham built an altar to the Lord nearby (Gen. 12:6-7), Jacob bought a piece of land outside Shechem and erected an altar (Gen. 33:18-19). Here Dinah, daughter of Jacob was raped and avenged by her brothers Simeon and Levi who destroyed the city (Gen. 34). During Israelite conquest the border between tribal allotments of Ephraim and Manasseh passed through Shechem (Josh. 17:7). It was one of the 6 cities of refuge (Josh. 20:7). The bones of Joseph, brought up from Egypt, were buried here (Josh. 24:32). After division of the Israelite commonwealth, Shechem was residence of Jeroboam and capital of his kingdom (I Kings 12:25). After destruction of Kingdom of Israel, the king of Assyria settled exiled Cuthians in Shechem (II Kings 17:24). In time, they became the Samaritans and made Shechem their political and religious centre. Alexander the Great permitted a Samaritan temple to be built on Mt. Gerizim. In 129 BCE John Hyrcanus seized Shechem and destroyed the temple. In 72 CE Vespasian completely destroyed the old city and built a new city in its stead between Mt. Gerizim and Mt. 'Eval (site of present-day city), calling it Flavia Neapolis (hence Arab name: Nablus). The Mishnah and Talmud also refer to the city as Nipolis or Nipolin. In the Madaba map Shechem is depicted as a walled city. Emperor Hadrian (117-138) built a temple to Jupiter on Mt. Gerizim. Emperor Zeno (474-491) built a church here and Justinian I (527-565) built several churches within the city proper. In 4th c. CE it ranked as an episcopal see. In 636 it was captured by the Arabs. Later Crusaders settled here and built many buildings. In 1259 it was a haven for Jews fleeing Jerusalem fearing a Mongol invasion. Travellers from 16th c. onwards tell of a local Jewish revival. This continued till the beginning of the 20th c. when it declined, only to be renewed after WWI. But the outbreak of Arab Disturbances in 1936 took its toll. The city was destroyed by a violent earthquake in 1927. During the War of Independence Shekhem was a base for Iraqi troops. Taken by the Israel Defence Forces in Six-Day War after battle on outskirts of city. **Ancient remains** Ancient Shechem has been identified with Tell Balata at Shekhem's E outskirts. Excavations have uncovered remains from Chalcolithic till Roman Periods, including city walls, towers and temples, a cuneiform Akkadian inscription and Iron Age seal. Other sites in Shekhem and environs. See **Balata, 'Askar, Mt. Gerizim, Mt. 'Eval.**

Shelomi ✱ *163:275*

Town on Galilee coast 4 km. SE of Rosh HaNiqra, adjacent to Lebanese border. Named after Biblical leader of Asher tribe (Num. 34:27). Founded as immigrant camp in 1949 on lands of abandoned village of el Bassa. Became permanent in 1950. A Byzantine monastic farm was discovered here during excavations in 1977. Area: 1,450 d. Pop.: 2,200.

Shelomo Bridge *206:285*

Bridge over Jordan River in Ḥula Valley near kibbutz Ne'ot Mordekhay. Named after 2 kibbutz members, Shelomo Ben Yehuda and Shelomo Bentov, killed in early days of kibbutz (1946).

★ **Sheluḥot** *195:208*

Kibbutz 3 km. SE of Bet She'an. Founded 1948 during War of Independence by Central European Youth 'Aliyah groups, called Sheluḥot. Area: 7,200 d. Pop.: 500.

Shemurat 'En Gedi → 'En Gedi

Shemurat 'Enot Gibton → Tel Malot

Shemurat 'Enot Qane → Mizpe Shalem, 'Enot Qane

Shemurat Gilbon → Dabbura, Naḥal Gilbon

Shemurat Har Avital → Mt. Avital

Shemurat Har HaTayyasim → Har HaTayyasim

Shemurat Har Meron → Mt. Meron

Shemurat Har Tavor → Mt. Tabor

Shemurat Mizpe Elot → Ma'ale Elot

Shemurat Naḥal 'Iyyon → Metulla, Mappal Naḥal 'Iyyon

Shemurat Naḥal Shiqma → Karmiyya

Shemurat Naḥal Soreq → Har Giyyora

Shemurat Naḥal Tanninim → Berekhat Timsaḥ

Shemurat Rekhes Gevar'am → Gevar'am

Shemurat Tel Dan → Tel Dan

Shemurat Tel Saharon → Tel Saharon

Shemurat Wadi Samiya → Kokhav HaShaḥar

Shemurat Ya'ar Odem → Odem

Shemurat Ya'ar Yahudiyya → Biq'at Bet Zayda, Yahudiyya

● **Shetula** *179:276*

Moshav in Galilee 9 km. NE of Ma'alot, near Lebanese border. Founded 1969. Area: 500 d. Pop.: several hundred.

● **Shetulim** *120:131*

Moshav on Coastal Plain 3 km. SE of Ashdod. Name from Biblical passage "They *are planted* in the house of the Lord, they flourish in the courts of our God" (Ps. 92:13). Founded 1950. Area: 2,500 d. Pop.: 670.

"Sheva' Taḥanot" (seven mills) *132:167*

Ancient site next to Yarqon, N of Tel Gerisa, within municipal area of Tel Aviv. An artificial dam used in past to heighten Yarqon and which operated 3 flour mills. In largest mill 7 pairs of millstones were used, hence its name. (In the other 2 mills, only 2 pairs of millstones were used.) Apparently built during Crusader Period, its remains were well-preserved until War of Independence. Today borders on HaYarqon Park.

Shevut-'Am *142:191*

A former immigrant settlement 1 km. SE of Sharon junction. Name from passage "...I will restore the *fortunes of my people*, Israel and Judah..." (Jer. 30:3). Established 1950. Over the years most residents were absorbed into neighbouring settlements.

Shezaf *107:034*

Former *naḥal* outpost between Negev and Sinai 9 km. NW of Ḥurvot Shivta. Name means jujube, a tree common in hot climates. Established 1956 and abandoned after Sinai Campaign.

● **Shezor** *182:259*

Moshav in Galilee 5 km. NE of Karmi'el. Same name as ancient city of Shezor retained in that of neighbouring Druze village Sajur. Founded as *naḥal* outpost in 1953. Area: 1,000 d. Pop.: 340.

● **Shibbolim** *112:089*

Moshav in Negev 3 km. S of HaGaddi junction. Founded 1952. Area: 4,000 d. Pop.: 400.

● **Shillat** **(Ḥoron "B")** *152:147*

Moshav in Ayyalon Valley 3 km. SE of Me'or Modi'im. Named after abandoned village Kh. Shilta built on ruins of ancient Shilta (now Tel Shillat). Founded 1977. **Military Post "318"** One km. to NE *153:147* is Kh. Kureikur, a military post during War of Independence, which was taken in "Dani" operation and then recaptured by Jordanian Arab Legion.

Shillo **(Shiloh)** *(Josh. 18:1)* *177:162*

Ruins of ancient city of Shiloh, identified with Kh. Seilun in Samarian Hills, 3 km. E of Ma'ale Levona (el Lubban Sharqiyya) on Ramallah–Shekhem road. Religious centre after Israelite conquest (Josh. 18:1). The Benjaminites seized daughters of Shiloh for wives as they came out to dance (Judg. 21:19-23). Apparently destroyed by Philistines after their victory over Israelites at Ebenezer (Jer. 26:6). Later rebuilt (Jer. 41:5), men of Shiloh were among returnees from Babylonian Exile (Neh. 11:5). According to sources, existed during Second Temple, Hellenistic, Roman and Byzantine Periods. Remained desolate during Middle Ages; according to Jewish travellers a mosque, altar remains and the supposed tomb of Eli the priest were located here. Excavations uncovered remains of ancient city and later towns (including two Byzantine church floors). The valley alongside Tel Shillo is called by the Arabs Marj el 'Id (valley of the festival) and Marj el Banat (valley of the daughters). Perhaps these names recall the capture of daughters of Shiloh by the Benjaminites. In the nearby valley are several Moslem holy places associated with the sanctity of Shillo.

Shillo (temporary name) *177:162*

Civilian outpost in Samarian Hills 3 km. E of Ma'ale Levona on Ramallah–Shekhem road. Same name as ancient city of Shillo, identified at nearby tel. Established 1978.

Shimeron → **Tel Shimeron**

Shiqmona → **Haifa**

Shivta **(Subeita, Isbeita)** *114:032*

Ruins of ancient city in Negev S of Be'er Sheva'–Nizzana road, 15 km. to the W of Sede Boqer. Originally it was a Nabatean road station, which was apparently built in the 1st c. BCE; it reached its prime in the

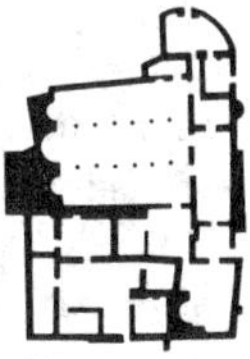

Byzantine Period when it became a transit city for commercial caravans from Egypt northwards, and from the E to Mediterranean shores and Europe. The Nabateans also cultivated extensive farming areas based on a special irrigation system which has been discovered in and around Shivta. In 6th c. it prospered as a result of heavy pilgrim traffic and was about 400 m. by 300 m. in size. After Arab conquest it declined until it was completely abandoned in 12th c. Its building stones remained in situ because of its relative isolation and it was thus better preserved than other ancient Negev cities. Its ruins, restored since 1958, include 3 churches, 1 in the north and 2 in the south. In front of N church is a square and alongside it ruins of a monastery, caravanserai and bathhouse; alongside one of S churches is a 9th c. mosque, streets lined with houses, each with a central courtyard and many with a second storey. Around the city are remains of canals, dams and terraces which were built to utilize rainwater for farming. In nearby fields are mounds of flint stones which were probably cleared to allow a free flow of water along the cultivated slopes. A nearby farm has also been restored.

• Sho'eva 157:133

Moshav in Judean Hills 6 km. E of Sha'ar HaGay. Adjacent to station which pumps water to Jerusalem, hence the name (*sho'eva* = pump). Founded as a work camp in 1950 on abandoned village lands of Saris. Abandoned in 1956, it was later resettled. Area: 3,000 d. Pop.: 270.

• Shomera 177:276

Moshav in Galilee near Lebanese border, 12 km. E of Ḥanita junction. Founded 1949 on lands of Tarbikha. Area: 1,000 d. Pop.: several hundred.

Shomeron (Sabastiya) *(I Kings 16:24)* 168:187

Ruins of ancient city of Samaria in Samarian Hills 8 km. NW of Shekhem, adjacent to Arab village of Sabastiya. Built by Omri, King of Israel, at end of 9th c. BCE and called Shomeron, after Shemer, who owned the land on which it was built. Capital of Kingdom of Israel until its destruction, when its inhabitants were deported and replaced by colonists brought by the Assyrians from many lands (chiefly Cutha and Babylonia). The city became capital of an Assyrian province and apparently later also capital of Babylonia and Persian provinces. During Hellenistic Period it was a gentile city and Hellenistic centre until taken and destroyed by John Hyrcanus, the Hasmonean. King Alexander Yannai rebuilt it and settled it with Jews. The building continued during Roman Period. Emperor Augustus presented it to Herod who then turned it into a magnificent Roman city, calling it Sebaste in honour of the emperor. (Sebastos, meaning magnificent, was the Greek name for Augustus.) However, it was again destroyed during Jewish Revolt against Rome, and remained so until the reign of Emperor Septimus Severus (193-211). It fell into decline during Byzantine Period and in 636 it was again destroyed by Arab conquerors. It stood desolate until Crusader Period when it was rebuilt, becoming a large and important city. After expulsion of Crusaders it was reduced to a small village, similar to the present-day Arab village of Sabastiya. **Excavations and finds** Excavations conducted between 1908 and 1910, and 1931 and 1933, revealed remains of walls, royal palaces, houses and storerooms from time of Kings of Israel; the oldest standing Hellenistic tower; remains of magnificent Herodian palace, hippodrome, theatre and temple; Crusader church, built on ruins of Byzantine structure and converted into a mosque by Arabs; a tomb in the church, which, according to Arab tradition, is that of John the Baptist; and tombs attributed to prophets Elisha and Obadiah. Some also say that St. John's parents — Zachariah and Elizabeth — are buried here as well.

● **Shoqeda** *105:092*
Moshav in Negev 6 km. W of Netivot. Founded 1957. Area: 6,500 d. Pop.: 330.

● **Shoresh** *156:134*
Moshav shittufi in Judean Hills 5 km. SE of Sha'ar HaGay. Named after abandoned neighbouring village of Saris. Founded 1948 on site of War of Independence military outpost by immigrants from E Europe. Initially a kibbutz, it converted to a *moshav shittufi* 4 years later. Area: 7,500 d. Pop.: 200.

Shoshannat Ha'Amaqim *137:196*
Semi-rural town N of Netanya near *moshav* Ḥavazzelet HaSharon. Name from Biblical passage "I am a rose of Sharon, a *lily of the valleys*" (Song 2:1). Composed of 2 neighbourhoods: Shekhunat Rassco, established 1951, pop.: 450, and Shekhunat 'Amidar, established 1956, pop.: 100.

★ **Shoval** *126:091*
Kibbutz on edge of Negev 4 km. SW of Bet Qama junction. Name based on Arabic Kh. ez Zubala, perhaps site of city of Sobila which appears on Madaba map. Established 1946 as part of programme to set up 11 settlements simultaneously in Negev, by group HaShomer HaẒa'ir members. Area: 22,300 d. Pop.: 500. Near kibbutz is Agam Shoval, a rainwater storage dam, and a Bedouin encampment of the el Huzeil tribe.

○ **Shufa** *157:186*
Arab village (pop.: 500) in Samarian Hills 8 km. SE of Tulkarm. Believed to be site of Shiftan mentioned in Samarian Ostraca.

Shu'fat *171:136*
Arab suburb N of Jerusalem. According to one theory, site of Nob, priestly city founded by sons of Eli the priest after destruction of Shiloh. Another theory claims it is site of Ẓofim, located on hill summit from where one could see all of Jerusalem.

Shunat el Maṣna'a, Shunat el Maṣani'a *195:174*
Site of ancient settlement in Samarian Hills 10 km. NE of Adam Bridge (Damiya), near village of Umm Ṣafa. Rows of stones, stone heaps and other Chalcolithic remains. Sherds also indicate Iron Age occupation. In Umm Ṣafa there are remains of Medieval structures and ancient building stones have been re-used in village houses.

○ **Shuqba** *153:154*
Arab village in Judean Foothills 5 km. NE of Me'or Modi'im. Pop.: 900.

● **Shuva** *107:096*
Moshav in Negev E of Sa'ad junction. Name from Biblical passage "*Restore* our fortunes, O Lord, like the watercourses in the Negeb!" (Ps. 126:4). Founded 1950 and divided in 1957; those who left the *moshav* founded *moshav* Zimrat. Area: 4,600 d. Pop.: 460.

○ **Shuweika** *153:193*
Arab village on border of Sharon and Samarian Hills 3 km. N of Tulkarm. Pop.: 2,400. **Kh. Shuweikat er Ras** N of village *153:194* is large tel where sherds discovered indicate continuous occupation from Middle Bronze Age until Middle Ages. Site of Socoh, mentioned in Egyptian documents and Bible as 3rd district in Solomon's kingdom (I Kings 4:10).

○ **(Esh) Shuyukh** *164:109*
Arab village in Judean Hills 7 km. NE of Hebron. Situated 1,000 m. above sea level. Pop.: 1,800.

Sidna 'Ali *132:177*

Arab holy tomb on Herzliyya shore, near Reshef ruins (Apollonia). According to Arab tradition it is burial site of 'Ali son of 'Ulim (descendant of Caliph Omar Ibn el Khattab). 'Ali was killed in battle with Crusaders. Samaritan tradition claims this is tomb of Eli the priest. Khan and turretted building with features from 4 different periods. Formerly an Arab pilgrim site: every year, after the summer, a feast was held here.

● **Sifsufa** *191:268*

Moshav in Galilee 3 km. N of Meron junction. Named after town of Sifsofa mentioned in Talmud. This name was apparently retained in that of adjacent village of Safsaf. Founded 1949. Area: 1,450 d. Pop.: 530. **Ancient synagogue and other remains** Within mosque of abandoned village are remains of an ancient synagogue (entrance arches and doorposts). Within village and its environs are rock-cut tombs attributed to sages of Roman-Byzantine Period. SW of village are a number of dolmens.

o **Si'ir** *163:110*

Arab village in Judean Hills off Bethlehem–Herodium–Hebron road, 4 km. NE of Halhul. Pop.: 4,200. Believed to be site of Zior (mentioned in Josh. 15:54). Within village are ancient remains from Iron, Persian, Byzantine and Middle Ages. Within village and environs are rock-cut burial caves, one attributed to Esau, known as *se'ir* (the hairy one). Sherds indicate occupation from Early Bronze Age.

o **(Es) Sikka** *144:099*

Arab village in Judean Hills 15 km. SW of Hebron, 2 km. S of Beit 'Awwa village.

o **Silat edh Dhahr** *167:191*

Arab village (pop.: 2,200) in Samarian Hills 13 km. NW of Shekhem.

o **Silat el Kharithiyya** *171:212*

Arab village (pop.: 2,700) on border of Yizre'el Valley NW of Jenin.

o **Silwad** *174:154*

Arab village 10 km. NE of Ramallah, at entrance to Wadi el Haramiyya (Nahal HaGannavim). Pop.: 2,600. Built on settlement ruins scattered amongst village houses. Sherds from Mamluk and Ottoman Periods.

o **Silwan** *173:130*

Arab village in SE Jerusalem on offshoot descending S from Dung Gate in area that used to be David's city in the early days of the united Kingdom of Israel. Name taken from Greek name Siloam for Shiloah. In 1884 a Yemenite Jewish neighbourhood was established near the Arab village and called Kefar HaShiloah. The Jewish residents were affected by Arab Riots of 1921 and 1936-1939 and were forced to abandon the neighbourhood. Within village is Berekhat HaShiloah (see Jerusalem).

∴ **(Es) Sindiyana** *150:218*

Abandoned village 4 km. SE of Zikhron Ya'aqov near *moshav* 'Amiqam. Inhabited during Roman and Byzantine Periods. Remains of aqueduct which runs to Caesarea. A Samaritan inscription found in village contains the first part of the "Shema' Yisra'el" prayer.

o **Sinjil** ◇ *175:160*

Arab village in Samarian Hills 16 km. NE of Ramallah. Pop.: 1,900. Site of Crusader settlement named after Count de Toulouse Raymond de

Saint Gilles, hence origin of Arabic name of village. The Crusader estate was built on site of previous Roman settlement. Remains of Crusader fortress and platform measuring 8 by 10 m. Village mosque built on ruins of ancient church.

o **Ṣir** *179:196*

Arab village in Biq'at Sanur 6 km. NW of Tubas. Pop.: 550. Remains of ancient building foundations and rock-cut cisterns. Ancient building stones have been re-used in village houses. Sherds indicate habitation in Byzantine, Medieval and Ottoman Periods.

o **Siris** *177:192*

Arab village in Samarian Hills 12 km. N of Shekhem. Pop.: 1,300. Built on ancient ruins whose stones have been re-used in village houses. Cisterns and caves in the vicinity. Sherds from Byzantine, Medieval and Ottoman Periods.

• **Sitriyya** *135:114*

Moshav on Coastal Plain 3 km. NW of Bilu junction. Founded 1949 by Polish and Rumanian immigrants detained in Cyprus transit camps, on abandoned village lands of Sitriyya. Area: 3,200 d. Pop.: 400.

∴ **Siyar el Khirfan** *211:264*

Abandoned village on Golan Heights 5 km. SE of Benot Ya'aqov Bridge. Built on ancient ruins from Chalcolithic Period and Early Bronze Age. Many dolmens nearby.

Solomon's Pillars ('Ammude Shelomo) * *146:909*

Giant sandstone columns near Timna mines 25 km. N of Elat. Formed by water and wind erosion; has ancient Egyptian inscription. Nearby copper mines were found which were erroneously thought to be those of King Solomon.

Solomon's Pools → Berekhot Shelomo

Strato's Tower → Caesarea

Subeita → Shivta

∴ **(Eṣ) Ṣufeira** *224:250*

Abandoned village on Golan Heights 1 km. W of Nov. Built on Byzantine ruins. Ancient building stones have been re-used in village houses.

o **Sulam (Shunem)** *181:223*

Arab village in Yizre'el Valley at foot of Giv'at HaMore, 4 km. E of 'Afula. Believed to be site of Biblical Shunem. Mentioned many times in the Bible: city in Issachar tribal allotment (Josh. 19:18), residence of Abishag who was brought to serve King David (I Kings 1:3), and Elisha the prophet revived the dead child of the wealthy woman of Shunem (II Kings 4:8 ff.). The Arab village is one of the Zu'abiyya villages, founded more than 800 years ago. Pop.: 970. Within cave in village is Spring of Abishag.

Sulamah Shel Ẓor (Ladder of Sour [Tyre])

Mountain range along Mediterranean coast extending from Rosh HaNiqra in S to Lebanese city of Sour (Tyre) in N. Composed of a series of steps ascending from S to N, hence its name. In ancient days it was traversed by a major Roman road. During British Mandate a railroad ran along foot of the range. **Sulam Ẓor nature reserve** E of Rosh HaNiqra, along Israeli-Lebanese border. Area: 500 d.

Sultan's Way → Derekh HaSultan

∴ Sumaqa *218:284*

Abandoned village on Golan Heights 2 km. NE of Wasit junction. Built on ancient tel; hewn and ornamented stones were found here. Alongside a spring to W of tel, Chalcolithic and Early Bronze Age sherds were found.

(Eṣ) Ṣur *210:264*

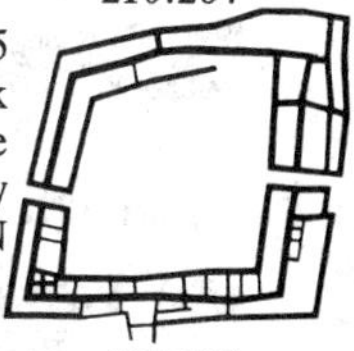

Ancient Early Bronze Age enclosure on Golan Heights, 5 km. SE of Benot Ya'aqov Bridge. Remains of 2 m. thick wall encompasses a square of 8 d. with a tower on W side and gates at N and S. Interior divided into unequal parts by a wall. Around the enclosure are a tumulus, opposite N gate, and some dolmens.

o Ṣur Bahir *173:126*

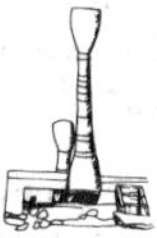

Arab village SE of Jerusalem alongside kibbutz Ramat Raḥel. Site of ancient Ẓar'a. W of village are remains of Jordanian military post (the Bell) taken in Six-Day War. Memorial to those who died in fighting. To the S are traces of Neolithic habitation.

o Surda *169:149*

Arab village (pop.: 450) 4 km. N of Ramallah.

o Ṣurif *156:117*

Arab village in Judean Hills 6 km. W of Kefar 'Eẓyon. Pop.: 3,000. Remains from Roman Period.

∴ Ṣurman (El 'Adnaniya) *228:278*

Abandoned Circassian village on Golan Heights 3 km. SE of Quneitra. Established at end of 19th c. on ancient ruins. Remains of ancient structures, burial caves, Greek inscriptions from Byzantine Period and sheikh's tomb.

Susita *212:243*

Ruins of ancient city at summit of steep hill on E side of Lake Kinneret, overlooking 'En Gev. Started as large Hellenistic city called Hippos (horse) in Greek and Susita in Hebrew. King Alexander Yannai conquered and annexed this area to the Hasmonean kingdom. Pompey made Susita a gentile city and one of the 10 Decapolis cities. Emperor Augustus gave it to Herod; however, when he died it was annexed to the province of Syria. At outbreak of Jewish Revolt against Rome the gentile residents of Susita attacked and slaughtered its Jewish inhabitants. After destruction of Second Temple a number of sages settled here. During Byzantine Period it was seat of bishopric; the number of Jewish residents continued to decline. During Middle Ages it was called Susiyya, a name retained by the Arab village that existed at foot of hill until War of Independence. During the war Susita was a Syrian position; it was taken by the Israel Defence Forces after heavy fighting. **Remains** On hill summit are ruins of Qal'at el Huṣn (fortress of the horses). There are remnants of a thick wall built of large dressed stones. Within the fortress, in the abandoned Arab village and in the area are remains of five Byzantine churches, Jewish sarcophagi, a theatre, columns and two aqueducts which carried water from Naḥal Samakh — a distance of 25 km. On the hill is a **memorial** to Rami Zayit, killed here on Independence Day, 1967.

T

Ta'anakh → Tel Ta'anakh

(Et) Tabkha, (Et) Tabigha (**Tabgha**) *200:293*

Site in N Biq'at Ginnosar on shore of Lake Kinneret. The Arabic names et Tabkha or et Tabigha are distortions of the Greek name Heptapegon meaning (land of) the 7 springs. This too is the meaning of the Hebrew name 'En Sheva'. A Christian holy site, it was here that the miracle of the multiplication of the loaves and fish took place. It appears there was a Jewish community here in Byzantine Period. Of the 7 springs that flowed into the Kinneret only 5 remain today. The **Church of Multiplication** is built on ruins of 4th c. church. A beautiful 5th c. mosaic floor has been preserved from the ancient church, depicting a lake with fowl and flora. Near the springs are remains of a Byzantine flour mill. Another church, **Church of the Primacy**, in honour of St. Peter to whom Jesus gave primacy over the other disciples, was built in 1954 by Franciscans over ruins of an earlier church. Within the church is a rock called Mensa Christi (the table of Jesus). Nearby is Eshed Kinnarot, the giant first pumping station of the National Water Carrier.

o **Taffuḥ** *154:105*

Arab village in Judean Hills 6 km. W of Hebron. Pop.: 1,700. Built partly over ancient ruins with ancient building stones re-used in village houses. Site of Biblical Beth-tappuah, a city in Judah tribal allotment (Josh. 15:53). Sherds found in village indicate occupation in Iron Age, Persian, Roman, Byzantine and Medieval Periods.

Tal-El *167:259*

Observation point in W Galilee 2 km. NE of Aḥihud junction. Established 1980.

o **Talfit** (S Samarian Hills) *177:165*

Arab village 4 km. NE of Ma'ale Levona. Pop.: 850.

o **Talfit** (N Samarian Hills) *182:200*

Small Arab village 8 km. SE of Jenin. Pop.: 220.

Talil *214:238*

Settlement ruins on Golan Heights 3 km. NE of Mevo Ḥamma, on hill summit overlooking Naḥal Mezar (Wadi Mas'ud). Remains of buildings with courtyards, cistern, olive oil press and millstones. Remains indicate habitation in Byzantine and Ottoman Periods. On adjacent hills are rock-cut tombs, some with niches.

o **Tall** *170:178*

Arab village 6 km. SW of Shekhem. Pop.: 1,400. S of village is tomb of Sheikh Ḥamed.

o **Talluza** *177:186*

Arab village in Samarian Hills 7 km. N of Shekhem. Pop.: 3,000. Tomb of en Nabi Harun, traditionally believed by Arabs to be tomb of Moses' brother Aaron. A 4th or 5th c. Jewish inscription was also found on the site. Two km. to E is tomb of en Nabi Huda. Sherds indicate settlement in Iron Age, Byzantine, Medieval and Ottoman Periods. Believed to be site of Tur Lusa, mentioned in Jerusalem Talmud, and in Samaritan literature as Tur Luza.

• **Talme Bilu** — *116:094*

Moshav in Negev 4 km. E of Netivot junction. Named to commemorate 70th anniversary of Bilu settlers. Founded 1953. Pop.: 400.

• **Talme El'azar** — *148:206*

Moshav in Sharon 2 km. S of Pardes Ḥanna. Founded 1952 on PICA lands and named after one of PICA directors. Area: 2,400 d. Pop.: 220.

• **Talme Eliyyahu** — *095:071*

Moshav in Negev 4 km. S of Magen junction. Named after Eliyyahu Krause (1876-1962), a director of Miqwe Israel Agricultural School from 1914. Founded 1970 initially as a *moshav shittufi*. Pop.: 130.

Talme Menashe — *135:150*

Formerly a *moshav* in Judean Foothills, 2 km. NW of Ramla. Founded 1955 and named after Menaché Meerovitch, member of Bilu and one of the founders of Rishon LeẒiyyon. Today it is a neighbourhood of Be'er Ya'aqov.

• **Talme Yafe** — *113:114*

Moshav shittufi on Coastal Plain 5 km. SE of Ashqelon. Named after Leib Jaffe (1876-1948) co-director of Palestine Foundation Fund and killed in 1948 when Arabs bombed Jewish Agency building. Founded as kibbutz in 1950; since 1961 it has been a *moshav shittufi*. Area: 6,500 d. Pop.: 120.

• **Talme Yeḥi'el** — *128:129*

Moshav on Coastal Plain 3 km. N of Qiryat Mal'akhi. Named after Jehiel Tschlenow (1863-1918) Russian Zionist leader. Founded 1949 by Rumanian immigrants on abandoned village lands of Masmiyya. Area: 3,200 d. Pop.: 330.

◆ **Tal-Or** — *102:085*

Farm in Negev 12 km. NW of Ofaqim. Name taken from Biblical passage "for thy dew is a *dew of light*" (Isa. 26:19). Owned by Yizzur U'Pituaḥ company.

• **Tal-Shaḥar** — *140:134*

Moshav on border of Judean Hills and Foothills 2 km. SW of Naḥshon junction. Named after Henry Morgenthau Jr. (1891-1967), US secretary of treasury from 1934 to 1945 and UJA chairman from 1947 to 1950. (Morgenthau = morning dew = *tal-shahar* in Hebrew.) Founded 1948 at height of War of Independence by immigrants from Turkey, Greece and Poland. Area: 4,000 d. Pop.: 450.

○ **Tammun** — *186:187*

Arab village in Samarian Hills 4 km. SE of Tubas. Pop.: 3,000.

○ **Tamra** (Yizre'el Valley) — *188:226*

Arab village 5 km. S of Mt. Tabor. Pop.: 400. Mentioned in documents from Crusader Period. On village slopes are remnants of church with mosaic floor and other Byzantine remains. Within the village itself are ancient burial caves; at least one of them is Jewish — a *menorah* is incised on a lintel.

Tamra (Lower Galilee) — *169:250*

Arab settlement 5 km. N of Shefar'am. Pop.: 8,000. Believed to be site of Jewish Tamra of the Byzantine Period. Building foundations, cisterns, caves and ancient tombs.

Tantura → Dor

● **Ta'oz** *148:134*

Moshav in Judean Foothills 4 km. NW of Shimshon junction. Name taken from Biblical passage "*strong* is thy hand, high thy right hand" (Ps. 89:13). Founded 1950, on abandoned village lands of Beit Susin. Area: 1,500 d. Pop.: 450.

TAP-Line Road → Derekh HaNeft

Tappuaḥ (temporary name) *(Josh. 17:8) 173:170*

Civilian outpost in Samaria 10 km. S of Shekhem. Named after the land of Tappuah, on the border of Manasseh. Established 1978.

Tarabin eṣ Ṣani' *133:062*

Bedouin tribal encampment in Negev 8 km. S of Be'er Sheva'. Pop.: 1,000.

○ **Tarama** *153:098*

Arab village (pop.: 200) in Judean Hills 10 km. SW of Hebron. Built on ancient ruins, whose cisterns and caves were still in use in recent times. Remains indicate habitation in Persian, Herodian and Byzantine Periods.

○ **Tarqumiya** *151:109*

Arab village 10 km. NW of Hebron. Pop.: 2,500. Site of settlement from Roman Period called Tricomias.

Tarshiḥa → Ma'alot-Tarshiḥa

● **Tarum** *148:132*

Moshav in Judean Foothills 3 km. NW of Shimshon junction. Name taken from Biblical passage "strong is thy hand, *high* thy right hand" (Ps. 89:13). Founded 1950. Area: 1,800 d. Pop.: 390.

○ **Tayasir** *187:194*

Arab village in Samarian Hills 4 km. NE of Tubas. Pop.: 600. Built on ancient ruins. Believed to be site of Asher in Manasseh tribal allotment (Josh. 17:7). Remains of Roman mausoleum and milestones, and Roman and Byzantine defensive walls, cisterns and a wine press.

∴ **Taytaba** *194:268*

Abandoned village in Galilee 5 km. NE of Safed near *moshav* Dalton. Two dolmens and ancient tombs were discovered here.

○ **(Et) Tayyiba** (Lower Galilee) *192:223*

Arab village 13 km. E of 'Afula. Believed to be site of Ophrah, birthplace of Gideon (Judg. 6:11). Pop.: 600, of Zu'abiyya clan. Within village are remains of a Crusader fortress and alongside it a Byzantine ruin.

○ **(Et) Tayyiba** (Samarian Hills) *178:151*

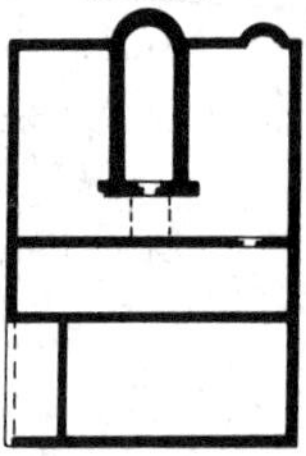

Arab village 10 km. NE of Ramallah. Pop.: 1,500, mostly Christian. Believed to be site of ancient Ophrah, city in Benjamin tribal allotment (I Sam. 13:17). According to Christian tradition, Jesus visited here. There are a number of churches and Christian schools in the village. Remains of Crusader church, built on ruins of Byzantine church, and called el Khadr, a nickname for the prophet Elijah and St. George. On village slopes are ruins of a 12th c. Crusader castle, Baubariya, built on a 5th c. Byzantine structure.

(Et) Tayyiba (Sharon) *151:186*

Arab village at foot of Samarian Hills 6 km. S of Tulkarm. Possibly site of ancient city of Tibta, mentioned in Talmud for its famous inn called Pundeqa De Tibta. More than 300 years ago it was settled by immigrants from Egypt and the Hejaz. It was a provincial city during Ottoman Period, and regional centre during British Mandate. Included within Israel by the Armistice Agreements. Pop.: 14,000. Finds within the village: burial cave from Middle Bronze Age, tel with sherds from Roman Period and many Medieval remains.

● **Te'ashur** *116:086*

Moshav in Negev, 6 km. NE of Ofaqim. Name mentioned in Bible and means a species of tree: "I will put in the wilderness the cypress, the plane and the *pine* (?) together;" (Isa 41:19). (Two of the neighbouring settlements bear the Hebrew names of the cypress and plane.) Founded 1953 as part of "city to settlement" programme. Area: 1,200 d. Pop.: 220.

Tekhelet Island *159:276*

Islet opposite Rosh HaNiqra, 1 km. from shore.

● **Tel 'Adashim** *178:228*

Moshav in Yizre'el Valley 5 km. N of 'Afula. Name derives from that of neighbouring Arab village, Tell el 'Adas. Initially it was set up as a HaShomer (watchmen assoc.) settlement in 1913. In 1921 a group of pioneers from Transylvania resided here and later set up the adjacent *moshav* Kefar Gid'on. Tel 'Adashim has been a *moshav* since 1923. Area: 8,400 d. Pop.: 500.

Tel Afeq (near Rosh Ha'Ayin) *(Josh. 12:18)* *143:168*

Tel of ancient town near sources of Yarqon River, N of Petaḥ Tiqwa. Evidence of Early Bronze Age occupation. Monumental Late Bronze Age structure discovered; apparently a governor's palace. Site of Biblical Aphek. City dominated narrow strip between Yarqon and hills, through which *via maris* passed. From Aphek a route led inland to Shiloh, a religious centre for Israelite tribes. The Philistines gathered near Aphek when they attacked Israelites and destroyed Shiloh. During Hellenistic Period called Pegae (springs), a name retained in that of abandoned Arab village, Fajja. In 20 BCE Herod founded a new city here called Antipatris, after his father Antipater. City was gateway to Judea through which a road linked Caesarea to Jerusalem. Crusaders built castle of Le Toron aux Fontaines Sourdes here. In 17th c. the Turks built a fortified inn over Crusader ruins on summit of a tel (Qal'at Ras el 'Ein); the remains are very impressive.

Tel 'Agol (Tell el 'Ajjul) *185:226*

Tel of ancient settlement in Yizre'el Valley 2.5 km. NE of Giv'at HaMore. One theory identifies site as that of Anaharath, a city in Issachar tribal allotment (Josh. 19:19). Ancient building stones and sherds from Early Bronze Age, Roman Period and Middle Ages.

Tel 'Akko → Acre

Tel 'Alil *164:242*

Ancient settlement mound in Galilee 4 km. SE of Qiryat Ata. Remains of its defensive wall, glacis and a gate can still be seen. Sherds indicate occupation in Iron Age and Persian Period.

★ **Telalim** *128:044*

Kibbutz in Negev 3 km. SE of Mash'abbim junction. Founded 1980. Area: 1,000 d. Pop.: tens.

Tel 'Amal → Nir Dawid

● **Telamim** 119:108

Moshav in Lakhish region 10 km. S of Giv'ati junction. Founded 1950 by immigrants from Djerba (Tunisia). Area: 6,900 d. Pop.: 630.

Tel Anafa (Tell el Aḥdar) *210:286*

Tel of ancient settlement in Ḥula Valley 2 km. NW of Shamir. *Anafa* means a heron; called this owing to the many herons which nest in the area. The name of the ancient town has not been identified. Remains from Early Bronze Age, Persian Period (implements found which indicate existence of a glass and ceramic industry) and Hellenistic Period. The town was destroyed by fire in 30 BCE.

Tel 'Arad *(Josh. 12:14)* *162:076*

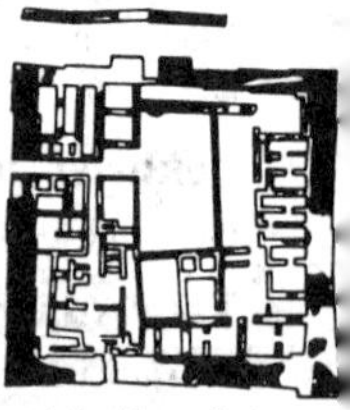

Ancient tel in NE Negev 9 km. NW of modern 'Arad off ancient route from Judean to Negev Hills. Site of ancient Arad. Arad is mentioned in ancient sources and in Bible (Num. 21:1 ff.) where it is related that the king of Arad prevented Israelites from passing through his territory on their way to Canaan. They were consequently forced to detour through the land of Edom and enter Canaan from the E. During Israelite conquest the region was under control of "the descendants of the Kenite", Moses' father-in-law (Judg. 1:16). The fortress of Arad is mentioned in list of cities captured by Egyptian Pharaoh Shishak (ca. 920 BCE). Depicted in 6th c. Madaba map. Travellers in 14th and 17th c. mention the existence of a Jewish community here. **Excavation finds** Tel 'Arad consists of 2 mounds. One is low and extensive with Late Chalcolithic levels (ca. 3400-3200 BCE) and Early Bronze Age II levels (ca. 2900-2700 BCE). Excavations here uncovered a large Early Bronze Age walled city. The other is a relatively high tel from the Iron Age (Israelite Period) with occupation levels from 11th to 6th c. BCE. Excavations here uncovered a fortress with an Israelite temple from 10th c. BCE, destroyed 4 centuries later at time of Kings of Judah. Ostraca were found with Hebrew inscriptions including an official correspondence with royal House of Judah. One letter provides the only direct reference to First Temple that archaeologists have found. The fact that no Middle Bronze and Late Bronze Age remains were found precludes identification with Canaanite Arad which some claim was located at Tel Malḥata (Tell el Milḥ) 12 km. SW of Tel 'Arad. The identification of Tel 'Arad with Israelite Arad (Iron Age) has been confirmed by excavations.

Tel 'Aro'er (Kh. 'Ar'ara) *(I Sam. 30:28)* *148:062*

Tel in Negev 20 km. SE of Be'er Sheva' off road to Dimona. Believed to be site of Biblical city of Aroer in S Judah. Excavations uncovered remains of wall and fort from days of Kingdom of Judah (Iron Age).

Tel Arshaf (Apollonia) *132:178*

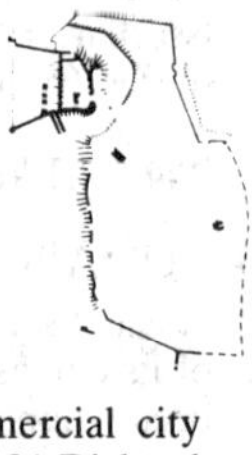

Ruins of ancient port city on Sharon coast 1 km. N of Herẓliyya. Site of Greek city Apollonia (named for Apollo, god of the sun and equivalent to Canaanite deity Reshef) dating from Hellenistic Period. King Alexander Yannai annexed it to Hasmonean kingdom; but during Jewish Revolt against Rome it was destroyed. After it was rebuilt it served as an important station on the coastal road between Egypt and Syria in Roman and Byzantine times. After Arab conquest it was called Arsuf, a distortion of the name Reshef. During Crusader Period it was a fortified, commercial city called Arsur (a corruption of Arsuf). In battle of Arsur in 1191 Richard the Lion-Heart defeated Saladin. In 1265 it was captured by Mamluk Sultan Baybars and completely destroyed along with other coastal cities.

Finds include statues, coins and inscriptions from Hellenistic, Roman, Byzantine, Crusader and Early Mamluk Periods. Remains of port city, fortress and city walls from Crusader Period.

Tel 'Artal (Tell esh Sheikh Daud) *202:207*

Tel 7 km. SE of Bet She'an, next to Jordan River and dominating one of its fords. Remains of walled fortress were found on tel summit. Sherds indicate occupation in Chalcolithic, Early Bronze, Late Bronze, Iron, Roman, Byzantine, Arab and Medieval Periods. Nearby at el Qad *203:207* remains of Byzantine and Arab structures and coins were found.

Tel 'Avdon (Kh. 'Abda) *(Josh. 21:30) 165:272*

Tel of ancient settlement in Galilee 7 km. NE of Nahariyya, 1.5 km. W of *moshav* 'Avdon. Site of Abdon, Levite city in Asher tribal allotment. Remains of defensive walls, wine presses, cisterns and sherds indicate occupation in Iron Age, Persian, Hellenistic, Byzantine, Arab and Crusader Periods. At foot of tel, adjacent to Naḥal Keziv, is a Paleolithic and Mesolithic site. Many Stone Age flint implements were found in area.

Tel Avel Bet Ma'akha → Avel Bet Ma'akha

Tel Aviv

City on Mediterranean shore — the economic and social centre of the country, and the largest metropolitan area. First all-Jewish city established in modern Israel. Municipally joined with city of Jaffa and officially named Tel Aviv–Jaffa. Founded 1908 as a Jewish residential neighbourhood near Jaffa and called Aḥuzat Bayit. Its name was changed to Tel Aviv in 1910 by inspiration of Naḥum Sokolow's Hebrew translation of Herzl's *Altneuland*, which he called Tel Aviv: (*alt* = old, *tel* = old ruin; *neuland* = new land, *aviv* = spring). The words also appear in the Bible (Ezek. 3:15). The neighbourhood expanded and in 1909 the cornerstone was laid for Herẓliyya High School (Gymnasium), which would develop over the years and become a vital focus for the city and the whole *Yishuv* (Jewish community in Palestine in pre-State years). But Tel Aviv's development was halted with the outbreak of WWI, when foreign nationals were forced to leave the country and those who remained were harassed by the Turks. In 1917 the Turkish authorities expelled all residents from Tel Aviv and they were scattered in various places throughout the country. Only after the British conquered Palestine could they return; Tel Aviv then developed with giant strides. In the wake of the 1921 Arab Riots, Tel Aviv separated from Jaffa and became an independent city. Its population suffered attacks by Arabs of Jaffa in 1929 Riots and again during 1936-1939 Disturbances. In 1936 a port was opened in Tel Aviv thus ending the *Yishuv*'s dependence on the Arab-controlled port of Jaffa. But it was superseded in 1966 by the deep water port at Ashdod. The city grew and expanded during WWII and in the pre-State years of struggle and "illegal" immigration Tel Aviv was *de facto* capital of the emerging state. At outbreak of War of Independence its residents were harassed by hostile Arab forces based in Jaffa and its neighbouring villages. When the Arab armies staged their invasion, Tel Aviv was bombed several times from the air. On the 5th of Iyar 5708 (14 May 1948), the State of Israel was proclaimed in Tel Aviv. It was the provisional capital, and the *knesset* (parliament) and government offices were located here until 1949. In 1950 Jaffa was once again joined to Tel Aviv (see Jaffa). Area: 50,000 d. Pop.: 350,000, including 7,500 non-Jews. Tel Aviv is first and foremost Israel's **economic centre** and headquarters of most of its industry, commerce and finance; it is a major tourist centre and has many hotels and vacation facilities. It is also an important **social and political centre** and is headquarters of political parties, youth movements, national organizations, trade unions, most of the daily newspa-

TEL AVIV

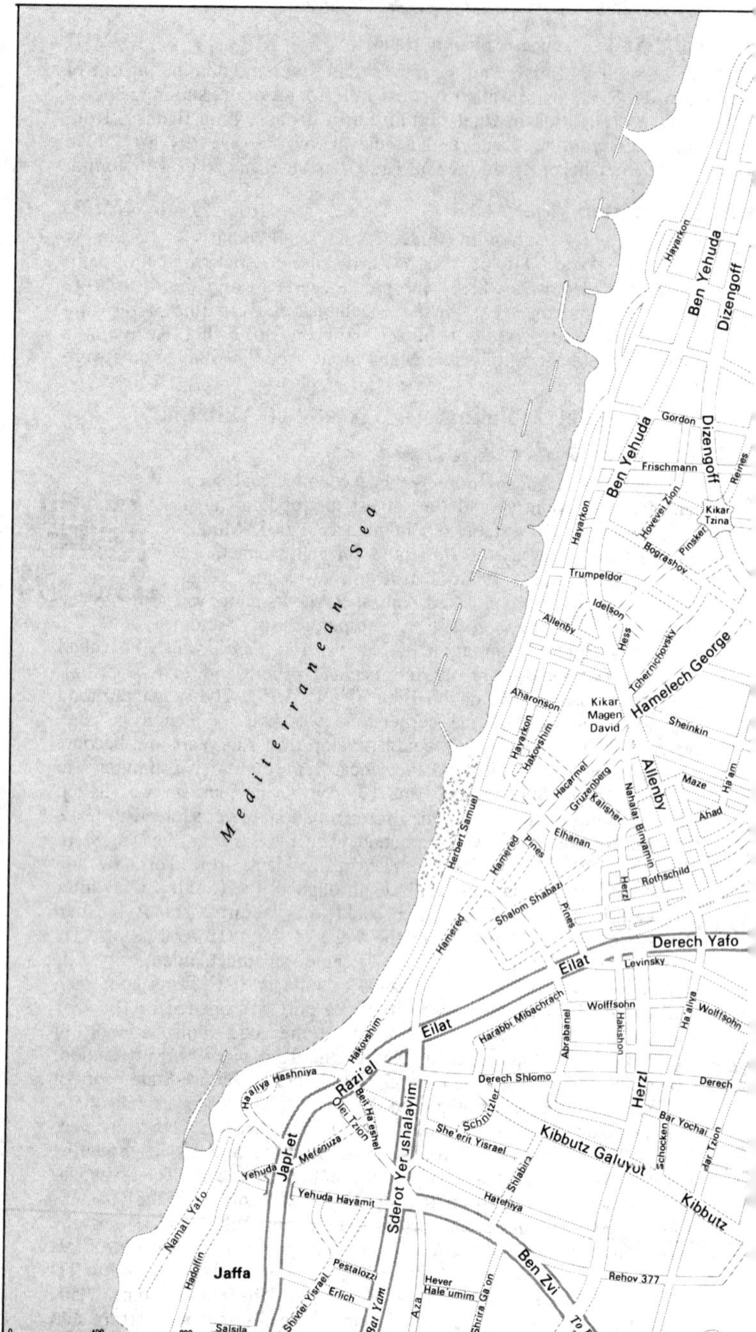
Mediterranean Sea
Hayarkon
Ben Yehuda
Dizengoff
Gordon
Frischmann
Reines
Kikar Tzina
Hovevei Zion
Pinsker
Bograshov
Trumpeldor
Idelson
Allenby
Hess
Tchernichovsky
Hamelech George
Aharonson
Kikar Magen David
Sheinkin
Hakovshim
Hacarmel
Gruzenberg
Kalisher
Nahalat Binyamin
Maze
Ha'am
Ahad
Herbert Samuel
Elhanan
Hamered
Pines
Rothschild
Herzl
Shalom Shabazi
Derech Yafo
Eilat
Levinsky
Wolffsohn
Ha'aliya
Harabbi Mibachrach
Abrabanel
Hakishon
Derech Shlomo
Derech
Ha'aliya Hashniya
Razi'el
Beit Ha'eshel
Olei Tzion
Schnitzler
She'erit Yisrael
Kibbutz Galuyot
Bar Yochai
Schocken
Har Tzion
Melanuza
Yehuda
Japhet
Sderot Yerushalayim
Yehuda Hayamit
Hatehiya
Shiabira
Kibbutz
Namal Yafo
Hadolfin
Jaffa
Pestalozzi
Erlich
Shivtei Yisrael
Ben Zvi
Rehov 377
Hever Hale'umim
Aza
Shrira Ga'on
To Bat Yam
To Ramla
Salsila
0
400
800
m

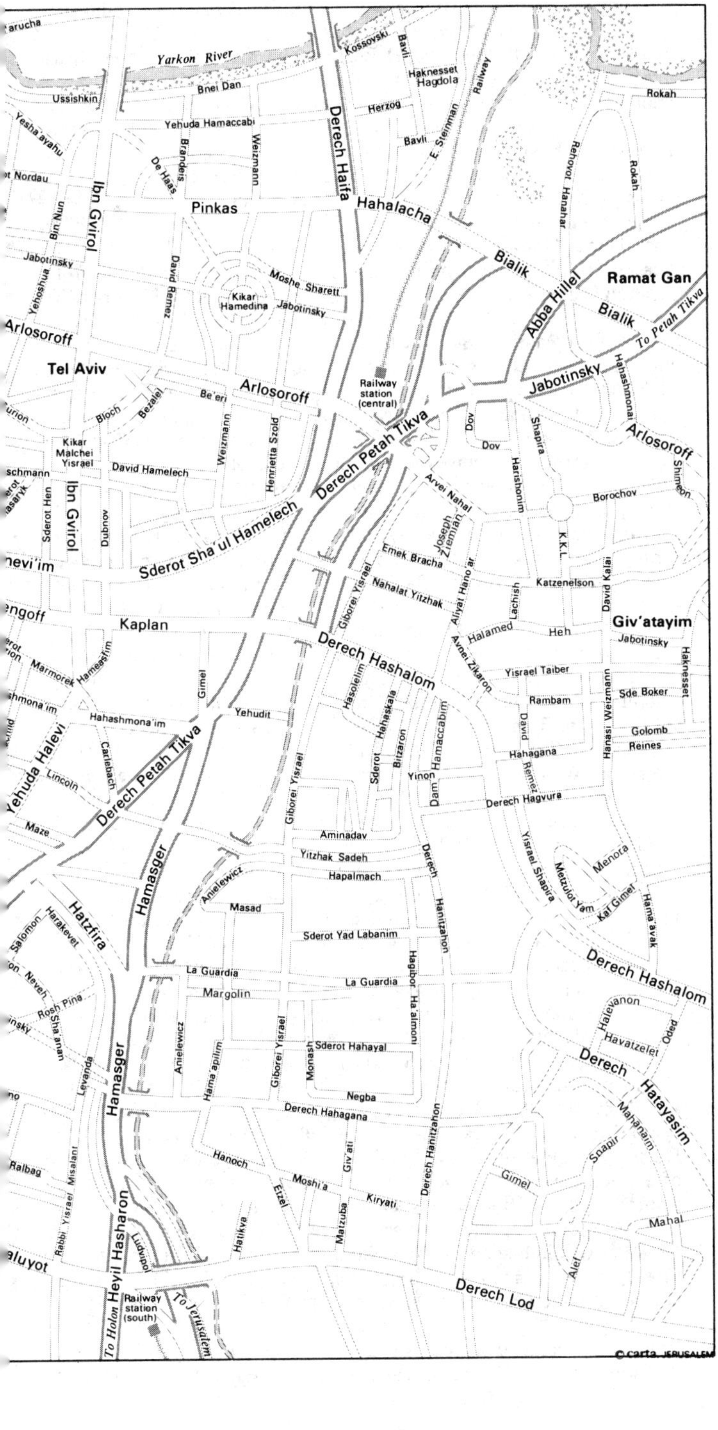
Yarkon River
Ussishkin
Bnei Dan
Kossovski
Bavli
Haknesset Hagdola
Railway
Rokah
Herzog
Yehuda Hamaccabi
Yesha'ayahu
Brandeis
Weizmann
Derech Haifa
E. Steinman
Rehovot Hanahar
De Haas
Nordau
Ibn Gvirol
Pinkas
Hahalacha
Bin Nun
Jabotinsky
David Remez
Moshe Sharett
Bialik
Ramat Gan
Kikar Hamedina
Abba Hillel
Yehoshua
Arlosoroff
To Petah Tikva
Tel Aviv
Railway station (central)
Hashmonai
Bloch
Bezalel
Be'eri
Henrietta Szold
Derech Petah Tikva
Dov
Shapira
Kikar Malchei Yisrael
David Hamelech
Harishonim
Shimeon
Sderot Hen
Dubnov
Sderot Sha'ul Hamelech
Arvei Nahal
Borochov
Joseph Ziemian
K.K.L.
Emek Bracha
Giborei Yisrael
Nahalat Yitzhak
Aliyat Hano'ar
Lachish
Katzenelson
David Kalai
Kaplan
Halamed
Heh
Giv'atayim
Derech Hashalom
Avnei Zikaron
Marmorek
Hame'asfim
Gimel
Hasolelim
Hahaskala
Yisrael Taiber
Sde Boker
Haknesset
Hahashmona'im
Yehudit
Rambam
Hanasi Weizmann
Golomb
Reines
Hahagana
Carlebach
Bitzaron
Yehuda Halevi
Lincoln
Sderot
Yinon
Dam Hamaccabim
Derech Hagvura
Maze
Aminadav
Yisrael Shapira
Menora
Hamasger
Yitzhak Sadeh
Hapalmach
Metzulot Yam
Kaf Gimel
Hama'avak
Hatzfira
Anielewicz
Masad
Derech Hanitzahon
Salomon
Harakevet
Sderot Yad Labanim
La Guardia
Neveh
Rosh Pina
Sha'anan
Margolin
Hagibor Ha'almoni
Halevanon
Havatzelet
Oded
Monash
Sderot Hahayal
Derech Hatayasim
Levanda
Hama'apilim
Negba
Derech Hahagana
Mahanaim
Snapir
Misalant
Hanoch
Giv'ati
Ralbag
Moshi'a
Kiryati
Gimel
Rabbi Yisrael
Etzel
Hatikva
Matzuba
Mahal
Heyil Hasharon
Ludvipol
Alef
Derech Lod
Railway station (south)
To Holon
To Jerusalem
©carta JERUSALEM

pers and Hebrew journals, branches of government offices and the foreign embassies. As a **cultural and art centre**, Tel Aviv is the home of the University of Tel Aviv, the Institute for Science and Research, most of the country's theatres, Israel Philharmonic Orchestra, Israel Opera, many publishing houses, museums, art galleries, libraries and archives, public halls and national sports stadiums. **Political and organizational headquarters:** Farmers' House, B'nei B'rith House, Histadrut centre, Engineers' House, Maccabi House, Teachers' House, Tchernichowsky Writers' House, Sokolow Journalists' House, HaPo'el House, HaPo'el HaMizraḥi House, General Zionists' House, Doctors' House, ZOA House and Hewt House. **Museums:** Bet HaTefuẓot — the Diaspora Museum, Helena Rubinstein Pavilion, Tel Aviv Museum for Art and Sculpture, Archaeological Museum, Museum for History of Tel Aviv–Jaffa, the Israel Defence Forces Museum. HaAreẓ Museum complex (in Ramat Aviv) which includes: museums of glass, numismatics, ceramics, ethnography and folklore, science, technology and alphabet, Bet Neḥushtan with the Timna excavations and the Ramba Museum of Journalism. **Archives:** Aḥad Ha'Am House — library and archive; Bialik House — home of the poet, his library and archive; Liessen House — archives of labour movement; Levanon House — collection of Hebrew press from its inception; Mica Josef House — library and archives of the writer Mica Josef Berdyczewski (Bin Gorion); Jabotinsky Institute — archives of the Revisionist leader and writer, and archives of the underground movement. **Major neighbourhoods:** Afeqa, Biẓẓaron, Daqar, 'Ezra, Florentine, Ganne Ẓahala, Giv'at HaTemarim, Giv'at Herzl, Hadar Yosef, HaQirya, HaTiqwa, Kefar Shalem, Kerem HaTemanim, Lamed Zone, Levana, Manshiyya, Ma'oz Aviv "A", Montefiore, Naḥalat Yiẓḥaq, Ne'ot Afeqa, Newe Avivim, Newe Dan, Newe Sha'anan, Newe Sharett, Nir Aviv, Nir Ḥen, Qiryat Shalom, Qiryat Sha'ul, Ramat Aviv, Ramat Aviv "C", Ramat HaTayyasim, Ramot Ẓahala, Revivim, Shabazi, Shapira, Sheikh Munis, Tel Barukh, Tel Kabbir, Yad Eliyahu, Yafo "C", Yisgav and Ẓahala. **HaQirya** Government and army offices in Tel Aviv. Initially the German colony of Sarona (founded 1870), it became an internment camp for German citizens in Palestine during WWII, and was cleared of its residents after the war. It then became a British army base until taken by Haganah in War of Independence. **Ancient sites** Archaeological excavations in N Tel Aviv on both sides of the Yarqon River have uncovered remains indicating human occupation in Neolithic Period. The digs centred on 2 sites: Tell Jarisha and Tell Qasile, and the finds are now located in the municipal museum of archaeology. **Tel Gerisa (Tell Jarisha)** on border of Tel Aviv and Ramat Gan, near mouth of Naḥal Ayyalon, is named after former nearby Arab village. Excavations uncovered levels from Stone Age through early Iron Age, and include Bronze Age tombs and Hyksos glacis. Believed to be site of Biblical Gath-rimmon, a Levite city in Dan tribal allotment (Josh. 19:45-46). Popularly called Napoleon's Hill owing to erroneous belief that in 1799 Napoleon placed his cannons on this hill when he bombarded Jaffa. During WWI British army camped here. **Tell Qasile** is located on N bank of Yarqon River, off coastal road. Excavations uncovered many levels from Neolithic Period until Mamluk Period. Remains of an Iron Age port were found; perhaps this was the river harbour where wood from Lebanon was unloaded before being transported to Jerusalem for the First Temple during days of King Solomon (II Chron. 2:15), and for the Second Temple (Ezra 3:7). Most remains date from Philistine Period. The 10th c. BCE Philistine city was pre-planned with parallel streets dividing rectangular blocks of buildings. A large hoard of small Philistine objects — scarabs, seals, iron implements, etc. — were found here.

Tel Azenot Tavor (Kh. Umm Jubeil) *(Josh. 19:34) 186:237*

Settlement ruins on hill summit in Galilee 3 km. N of Mt. Tabor, alongside Bet Qeshet. Identified with Aznoth-tabor in Naphtali tribal allotment (Josh. 19:34). Cisterns, network of burial caves and remains of many structures. Flint implements from Paleolithic Period and sherds from Iron Age, Persian Period and from Hasmonean Period until Middle Ages.

Tel 'Azeqa (Kh. Tell Zakariyya) *(Josh. 10:10) 144:123*

Settlement ruins in Shefela off Bet Shemesh–Bet Guvrin road, at E end of HaEla Valley. Site of Azekah, important fortified city presiding over major route from Shefela to Judean mountains. Mentioned in Joshua's wars with the 5 Amorite kings (Josh. 10:10), and in the wars between Israelites and Philistines when David slew Goliath (I Sam. 17:1). Azekah was one of the cities fortified by Rehoboam (II Chron. 11:5-12), and one of the few left at the time of Nebuchadnezzar's conquest (Jer. 34:7). The name also appears in the Lakhish Letters. It was also mentioned as one of the cities reinhabited after the Babylonian Exile (Neh. 11:30). Byzantine town was located next to the tel and also called 'Azeqa. Excavations at the tel have revealed parts of an Israelite city wall and fortress dating back to the period of the Kingdoms of Israel and Judah. The fortress was rectangular and had square corner towers — a fortress plan identical to those uncovered at Qadesh Barnea', Giv'at Sha'ul and Ḥurbat 'Uza.

Tel Barom (Tell el Mabrum) *204:292*

Ancient settlement ruin in Upper Galilee 1 km. S of Tel Ḥay, alongside HaMezudot junction. Remains of a defensive wall, buildings and stone circles. Sherds indicate occupation in Early Bronze Age, Roman, Byzantine and Arab Periods. Nearby is a dolmen field.

Tel Battash (Tell el Batashi) *141:132*

Ancient settlement ruin in Judean Foothills 4 km. S of Naḥshon junction, on W bank of Naḥal Soreq. Identified with Philistine Timnah (Judg. 14:1). Remains of 2 fortification networks apparently from different periods. Excavations in 1979 uncovered remains of fortifications and structures from 8th-7th c. BCE. Pottery jugs inscribed *LaMelekh* "To the King" were found in one of the buildings. On E bank of stream are remains of a Roman road. Sherds from Late Iron Age, Persian and Hellenistic Periods.

Tel Beror (Tell el Mashnaqa) *115:108*

Ancient settlement ruin on Coastal Plain 10 km. S of Giv'ati junction, 1.5 km. NW of kibbutz Beror Ḥayil. Believed to be site of Beror Ḥayil, a Jewish town from end of Second Temple Period and during Byzantine Period. (See Beror Ḥayil.) Sherds and other remains indicate occupation in Roman and Byzantine Periods.

Tel Bet Ha'Emeq (Tell Mimas) *164:263*

Ancient settlement ruin in Upper Galilee 7 km. SE of Nahariyya, 1 km. SE of Bet Ha'Emeq. Remains of structures and alongside tel are cisterns, wine press and tombs. Sherds indicate occupation from Iron Age till Byzantine Period, particularly in Hellenistic Period.

Tel Bet Mirsham (Tell Beit Mirsim) *141:096*

Ancient settlement ruin 20 km. SW of Hebron, alongside village of Beit Mirsim. Excavations uncovered remains of Iron Age walled city built over remains of even older towns from Early Bronze, Middle Bronze and Late Bronze Ages.

Tel Bet She'an → Bet She'an

Tel Bet Shemesh → Bet Shemesh

Tel Burga (Kh. Tell el Bureij) *147:214*

Ancient enclosure in Ramat Menashe 2 km. E of Binyamina. Its embankment encloses an area of some 300 d. Remains indicate habitation mainly in Middle Bronze Age. A smaller settlement in SE corner of enclosure existed for a longer period — until the Iron Age.

Tel Burna (Tell el Birnat) *138:115*

Ancient settlement ruin in Judean Foothills 3 km. NE of Bet Guvrin. Remains on summit of square defensive walls built of large roughly hewn stones. Early Iron Age sherds. Some identify the ruin as Biblical Libnah, captured by Joshua (Josh. 10:29-30) and given to Levites (Josh. 21:13).

Tel Dan (Tell el Qadi) *(Judg. 18:29) 211:294*

Tel, 20 m. high, in N alongside sources of Jordan River, 1 km. N of kibbutz Dan. Site of ancient city of Leshem (Josh. 19:47), also called Laish. Called Dan after its capture by tribe of Dan (Judg. 18:27-29). During First Temple Period it was the cult centre of tribes of the N. Here Micah set up his graven image (Judg. 18:30-31) and, after the division of the Kingdom, Jeroboam, son of Nebat, set up one of the two calves of gold (I Kings 12:28-29). Site destroyed by Ben-Hadad, King of Damascus in 9th c. BCE. Excavations uncovered levels from Bronze Age and Iron Age with remains of a ritual site, rampart, magnificent tomb, city gate complex (same design as in Megiddo, Ḥazor and Gezer) and ancient building stones. Excavations in 1979 uncovered an arched brick wall 3-4 m. high from Middle Bronze Age. The tel was used as a military outpost during War of Independence, and today, the tel, the springs below and surrounding area are part of Tel Dan nature reserve.

Tel Dotan *(Gen. 37:17) 172:202*

Ancient settlement ruins in Dotan Valley in Samaria 10 km. SW of Jenin. The Biblical Valley of Dothan is first mentioned in story of Joseph being sold into slavery. Dothan is mentioned as one of cities captured by Thutmose III (1504-1450 BCE), King of Egypt. Also mentioned in Book of Judith. Excavations indicate that the earliest occupation was in Chalcolithic Period. At end of Early Bronze Age it was a large fortified city, and there are remains of a defensive wall and several structures from Middle Bronze Age. Four Iron Age levels were uncovered. It was apparently abandoned at end of Iron Age, but re-occupied in Hellenistic Period. The majority of remains date from Roman Period.

Tel Dove *203:210*

Ancient hill settlement in Bet She'an Valley 1 km. E of Ma'oz Ḥayyim. Sherds from Chalcolithic Period, Early Bronze Age, and Roman and Byzantine Periods.

Tel Dover (Tell ed Duweir) *209:232*

Ancient settlement in Jordan Valley 5 km. SE of Zemaḥ junction. In its time it controlled the road junction from which the route to Damascus branched off along bed of Yarmouk River. Occupied in Middle Bronze Age, Iron Age, Persian, Hasmonean, Roman and Byzantine Periods. Remains of acropolis on tel summit surrounded by a Byzantine wall. Used as military outpost on Israel–Syrian border and called Giv'at Golani.

Tel Eder (Kh. 'Ein Ḥaur) *167:276*

Ancient hill site in Upper Galilee 1 km. E of Ḥanita. Name means maple — a common tree in the area. Stone mounds, foundations and sherds indicate habitation in Early Bronze Age and Middle Bronze Age.

Tel 'Efroni *199:212*

Small tel E of Bet She'an. Remains of Byzantine structures and Roman sherds.

Tel 'Eli (Kh. esh Sheikh 'Ali) *202:234*

Ancient settlement in Jordan Valley 1.5 km. W of Deganya "B". Excavations uncovered Neolithic, Chalcolithic and Early Bronze Age remains. Inhabited again later in Byzantine and early Arab Periods.

Tel 'Erani (Tell Sheikh el 'Areini) *129:113*

Large settlement ruins made up of 2 tels in Judean Foothills 1 km. E of Qiryat Gat, and spread out over several hundred dunams. One of the tels is broad and low with Chalcolithic remains and remnants of walls and buildings which contained tools imported from Egypt. (Among them was a sherd inscribed with the name of one of the first pharaohs — Na'armer.) The other taller tel has remains from beginning of Iron Age until Hasmonean Period. The tel was erroneously identified with Philistine Gath and was therefore known for a while as Tel Gath. However, its true identity has not yet been established.

Tel Eshtori (Tell el Maliḥ) *199:211*

Ancient settlement in Bet She'an Valley NW of Newe Etan. Sherds and other remains from Late Bronze Age, Iron Age, Persian and Roman Periods.

Tel Esur (Tell el Asawir) *152:209*

Ancient settlement at entrance to Naḥal 'Iron, alongside 'Iron junction — major crossroad in ancient times. Believed by some to be site of Yaḥam, mentioned in a 15th c. BCE Egyptian document. Another theory identifies it as site of Arubboth, residence of prefect of King Solomon's 3rd district (I Kings 4:10). Sherds indicate occupation in Early Bronze, Middle Bronze and Iron Ages as well as Hellenistic and Roman Periods. Nearby tombs date from Chalcolithic, Early Bronze and Middle Bronze Ages.

Tel 'Eton *143:099*

Prominent tel on natural hill between Judean Hills and Foothills, 5 km. S of Amaẓya. Believed to be site of Biblical Etham within tribal allotment of Simeon (I Chron. 4:32). Sherds indicate occupation in Bronze Age, Iron Age and Persian Period. Remains of outer and inner defensive walls and glacis. On tel summit are remains of structures and stone heaps. Many rock-cut cisterns and caves, house foundations and towers have been excavated nearby, along with a large necropolis with tombs from Late Bronze Age, Early Iron Age (including Philistine graves), Hellenistic, Roman and Byzantine Periods.

Tel Gamma (Tell Jamma) *097:088*

Large tel in NW Negev 8 km. N of Ma'on junction. Believed to be site of Yarza, mentioned in ancient Egyptian documents. Finds from Early Bronze Age, Late Bronze Age, Persian, Roman and Byzantine Periods: a typically Assyrian-built large brick structure, Late Bronze Age pool, an iron smelting furnace from Iron Age, a grain silo from Persian Period, and 2 large Byzantine buildings and tombs.

Tel Gem'a (Tell el Jama'in) *202:201*

Ancient settlement in Bet She'an Valley 2.5 km. SE of Tirat Ẓevi. Sherds indicate habitation from Chalcolithic Period till Iron Age. Remains also found from Byzantine and Arab Periods.

Tel Gerisa → Tel Aviv

Tel Gezer → Gezer

Tel Gishron *128:118*

Remains of ancient settlement 5 km. N of Qiryat Gat, alongside abandoned village of Juseir, within *moshav* Menuḥa. Sherds from Middle Bronze Age, Roman, Byzantine and Arab Periods.

Tel Gittim (Ras Abu Ḥumeid) *139:145*

Ancient settlement ruin in Judean Foothills 3 km. SE of Ramla. In its upper part, 12 occupational levels have been uncovered and in the lower part, 10 more dating from Iron Age till late Arab Period. On tel summit is tomb of Sheikh Abu Ḥumeid, hence the Arabic name of the tel.

Tel Goded (Tell el Judeida) *141:115*

Ancient settlement ruins in Judean Foothills 2.5 km. NE of Bet Guvrin. One theory claims this is site of Moresheth-gath, birthplace of Prophet Micah (Micah 1:14); another that it is site of Libnah, captured by Joshua and given to descendants of Aaron (Josh. 21:13). Remains of fortifications and a Roman structure. Sherds indicate continuous occupation in Bronze Age, Iron Age and Roman Period.

Tel Ḥalif (Tell Khuweilifa) *137:087*

Ancient settlement ruin in Negev, alongside kibbutz Lahav. According to one theory this is site of Biblical Ziklag, originally within tribal allotment of Judah (Josh. 15:31) but given over to Simeon (Josh. 19:5). It appears, though, to have remained a Philistine city; David resided here when he fled from Saul (I Sam. 27:2-6). After Babylonian Exile it was resettled (Neh. 11:28). Sherds indicate occupation in Chalcolithic, Early Bronze, Late Bronze and Iron Ages as well as Persian, Hellenistic, Roman, Byzantine and Medieval Periods. Remains of fortifications and glacis from Late Bronze Age, burial cave and sarcophagi from Roman Period.

Tel Ḥanan *155:242*

Neighbourhood within urban settlement of Nesher in Zevulun Valley 5 km. SE of Haifa. Named after Ḥanan Zelinger, a Haganah member killed in area. Founded 1948.

Tel HaNappaḥ *208:289*

Low tel in Hula Valley 5 km. E of Qiryat Shemona and 2 km. S of kibbutz HaGosherim. Most sherds found date from early Arab Period and Middle Ages.

Tel Ḥannaton (Tell Badawiyya) *174:243*

Large tel at SW corner of Bet Netofa Valley 8 km. SE of Shefar'am. Believed to be site of Hannathon mentioned in ancient Egyptian documents. Identified with city of Siḥin dating from Second Temple Period and Byzantine Period. Residence of *Tannaim, Amoraim* and priestly clan of Jeshebeab. Remains of ancient structures; sherds indicate occupation from Early Bronze Age to Middle Ages.

Tel Ḥarashim (Kh. et Tuleil) *181:263*

Ancient settlement in Galilee 1 km. S of Peqi'in. Located on high peak overlooking Naḥal Peqi'in. Excavations uncovered olive oil press, workshop for bronze working, cave used in Middle Bronze Age and remains of Iron Age structure.

Tel Ḥarasim *134:128*

Ancient settlement in Judean Foothills 1.5 km. N of Kefar Menaḥem. Located on hill above a confluence of streams. Sherds from Middle Bronze Age, Late Bronze Age, Iron Age, Hellenistic, Roman and Byzantine Periods.

Tel Ḥaraz **(Tell Abu Ḥaraza)** *119:142*

Small tel prominent on a gravel hill near sea in Yavne sand dunes, 6 km. N of Ashdod. Many sherds, mostly from end of Iron Age.

Tel Haror **(Tell Abu Hareira)** *112:087*

Large tel in Negev alongside Naḥal Gerar, 4 km. S of HaGaddi junction. According to one theory this was site of Biblical city of Gerar, associated with wanderings of patriarchs (Gen. 20:1; 26:1, 26) and named Siatos Geraritikos on 6th c. Madaba map. Sherds indicate occupation from Bronze Age onwards. At tel summit is tomb attributed to Sheikh Abu Hareira, pupil of Muḥammad, and revered by Bedouin, hence Arabic name of site.

Tel HaShomer *136:162*

Situated in SE Ramat Gan, alongside Kefar Azar, it was formerly a small settlement established in 1934 by the Litwinsky family and called Tel Litwinsky. During WWII a British army camp was built here and in War of Independence it was a military hospital; later it became a government hospital and was called Tel HaShomer. The name has now been changed to Sheba, in memory of its late director.

Tel Ḥasi **(Tell el Ḥasi)** *124:106*

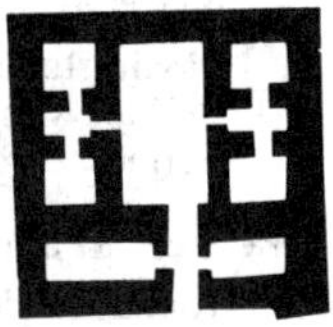

Ancient settlement on bank of Naḥal Shiqma (Wadi el Ḥasi), 7 km. SW of Qiryat Gat. Believed to be site of Biblical Eglon, mentioned in Joshua's battles (Josh. 10:3; 12:12) and included in Judah tribal allotment (Josh. 15:18). Excavations at end of 19th c. uncovered Early Bronze Age to Byzantine levels. Major finds include a tablet with a letter written in cuneiform script from 14th c. BCE and a sherd of bowl incised with a Canaanite inscription *bl'* (בלע) apparently from 14th c. BCE. Recent excavations uncovered remains of an Iron Age fortified city, traces of pre-Early Bronze Age settlement and remains from Hellenistic and Persian times.

Tel Ḥay *204:293*

Memorial site in Galilee 2 km. N of Qiryat Shemona, alongside Kefar Gil'adi. Named after the Arab name of site, Kh. Talḥa. The lands were purchased in 1893 by Baron de Rothschild and were first settled in 1905. In 1918 a group from HaShomer and HaRo'e movements settled here. In early 1920 Arab bands attacked Jewish settlements in area. Joseph Trumpeldor together with a small group were sent to help defend Tel Ḥay, but on 11 Adar 5680 (1 March 1920) Trumpeldor and seven of his comrades fell in battle. Their courageous stand at Tel Ḥay became a symbol for the *Yishuv* (Jews of Palestine) and was influential in having the area included within British Mandatory territory rather than the French Mandatory territory of Syria. Today it is part of Kefar Gil'adi and includes a restoration of the Tel Ḥay compound, permanent exhibition of settlement and defence history of Upper Galilee; a memorial to Tel Ḥay defenders (statue of the roaring lion), cemetery where Trumpeldor and his comrades are buried, youth hostel, and a recently discovered burial cave from Roman Period. Every year on 11 Adar a memorial service is held here.

Tel Ḥazirim *152:217*

Tall steep tel in Ramat Menashe 6 km. SE of Zikhron Ya'aqov. Many remains of ancient structures. Sherds indicate continuous occupation from Early Bronze Age till Arab Period.

Tel Ḥaẓor *(Josh. 19:36) 203:269*

Largest ancient tel in the Holy Land (40 m. in height, 600 m. in length and 200 m. in width), in Upper Galilee, 6 km. N of Rosh Pinna. Site

of ancient Hazor, one of the largest and most important cities in ancient Ereẓ Israel. Located on a branch of *via maris*. Mentioned in Egyptian documents from 19th c. BCE and in Tell el 'Amarna letters from 14th c. BCE. During Israelite conquest, Jabin, King of Hazor, headed a league of Canaanite cities against Joshua (Josh. 11:1 ff.). During period of Judges, Deborah and Barak fought here against Sisera, army commander of Jabin, King of Hazor (Judg. 4:1 ff.). King Solomon fortified the city (I Kings 9:15). However, during reign of Pekah, King of Israel, Hazor and other Galilean cities were destroyed by Tiglath-pileser III, King of Assyria, and its inhabitants exiled (732 BCE; II Kings 15:29). Mentioned in Book of Maccabees, in context of Jonathan's campaign against Demetrius (I Macc. 11:67). Ḥazor consists of 2 separate areas: a lofty tel covering an area of 120 d. (Upper City), and to the N a large enclosure covering some 700 d. (Lower City) and encompassed by huge rampart of beaten earth and deep fosse. Excavations in 1938, 1955 and 1960's uncovered 23 strata in the Upper City. Among finds are Middle Bronze Age cemetery, Late Bronze Age temple, casemate wall and gate complex, underground water system quarried during reign of King Ahab and can be reached by descending 123 steps, Late Iron Age fortress and remains from Persian and Hellenistic Periods.

Tel Ḥuga (Tell el Bart'a) *200:214*

Settlement ruins in Jordan Valley 4 km. NE of Bet She'an. Covers about 200 d. alongside a spring called 'En Ḥuga. Foundations of undressed and basalt stones, stone implements and sherds. Occupied in Neolithic Period, Middle Bronze Age, Early Iron Age and Byzantine and Arab Periods.

Tel 'Ira (Kh. el Gharra) *148:071*

Ruins in Negev 11 km. SE of Shoqet junction. Remains of large structures, encompassed by casemate wall and glacis. Sherds indicate occupation in Middle Bronze Age, mainly in Iron Age, Persian, Hellenistic, Roman and Byzantine Periods.

Tel 'Irit (Tell Wadi ez Zeit) *107:100*

One of a pair of mounds on Coastal Plain, 3 km. NE of Sa'ad junction. The other is Tel Mefalsim (Tell er Rasm). Sherds indicate occupation mainly in Iron Age and later in Roman and Byzantine Periods.

Tel Karpas (Tell el Karantina) *202:208*

Tel in Bet She'an Valley 1 km. N of Kefar Ruppin W of Tel 'Artal. Occupied during transition from Early Bronze Age to Middle Bronze Age, and from Iron Age till Byzantine Period.

Tel Kefar Qarnayim (Tell Abu Faraj) *199:203*

Small mound in Bet She'an Valley NW of Tirat Ẓevi. Sheikh's tomb and rock-cut caves. To S is a 4th c. synagogue with mosaic floor depicting a *menorah* and *shofar*. Sherds indicate occupation at end of Early Bronze Age until Iron Age, and Byzantine and early Arab Periods. At foot of tel is a spring.

Tel Kelekh (Tell Umm Kalkha) *133:098*

Ancient settlement ruin in Judean Foothills 7 km. NE of Bet Qama. Remains of Byzantine structures and cave. SE of tel sherds were found dating from Chalcolithic Period.

Tel Kinnerot (Kh. el 'Ureima) *201:253*

Ancient settlement ruin on NW shore of Lake Kinneret. Apparently site of Chinnereth, a fortified city in Naphtali tribal allotment (Josh. 19:35), which was situated on a branch of an ancient highway. Also mentioned in ancient Egyptian documents. Excavations uncovered fragment of stele of Pharaoh Thutmose III (1504-1450 BCE), a broken iron knife and a copper fragment. Sherds indicate occupation from beginning of Early Bronze Age until end of Iron Age.

Tel Kison **(Tell Keisan)** *164:253*

Ancient settlement ruin in Zevulun Valley 4 km. S of Aḥihud junction. Believed to be site of Achshaph, an important Canaanite city mentioned in ancient Egyptian documents. Its king was one of the 31 who fought against Joshua (Josh. 12:20). After the Israelite conquest it was included in Asher tribal allotment (Josh. 19:25). Excavations uncovered 2 Iron Age levels, one from the Persian Period and remains of buildings and church from Roman-Byzantine Period.

Tel Kittan **(Tell Musa)** *204:221*

Large mound in Jordan Valley 12 km. NE of Bet She'an, 2 km. E of Newe Or. Excavations uncovered remains dating from Chalcolithic Period till Iron Age which include a Chalcolithic room, structures, floors, pottery and a warrior's tomb from Early Bronze Age, temple from Middle Bronze Age, and a cultic high place from Late Bronze Age.

(Et) Tell (near Ramallah) *175:148*

Ruins of ancient settlement 5 km. E of Ramallah. Believed to be site of Biblical Ai. Digs uncovered many Early Bronze Age remains including a wall and temple; Late Bronze Age and Early Iron Age remains as well.

Tell Abu Hawam *152:245*

Site of ancient settlement in Zevulun Valley near Naḥal Qishon within grounds of the oil refineries. The tel itself is no longer visible but excavations have revealed 5 occupation levels from Late Bronze Age until Roman Period. Remains of defensive wall, fortresses and houses from various times, Bronze Age cemetery and many other finds, such as pottery, metal implements, graven images, jewellery, etc.

Tell Abu Mudawwar *218:247*

Ruins of ancient hill settlement on Golan Heights overlooking Naḥal El 'Al, 3 km. NW of *moshav* Eli 'Al. Remains of square structures and stone enclosures on hilltop, and tombs below. Sherds indicate habitation in Middle Bronze Age, Byzantine and Ottoman Periods.

Tell Abu Qudeis *(Kedesh: Josh. 12:22)* *170:218*

Ancient settlement ruins in Yizre'el Valley 3 km. SE of Megiddo junction. Site of Kedesh in Yizre'el Valley, whose king was among the 31 kings whom Joshua fought. After Israelite conquest it became a Levite city within the tribal allotment of Issachar.

Tell Abu ez Zeitun *225:248*

Abandoned village built over ancient ruins on Golan Heights, 2 km. SW of Ramat Magshimim. Scant building remains and an ancient wine press. Occupied in Byzantine, early Arab and Medieval Periods.

Tell el Aḥmar (Golan Heights) → **Odem**

Tell el Aḥmar (Upper Galilee) *214:295*

Ancient cemetery 1 km. W of Banyas which belonged to city of Banyas in Roman and Byzantine Periods. Many burial caves with sarcophagi, columns and dressed stones. Up to Six-Day War it was a Syrian military outpost, overlooking a canal dug by the Syrians to divert the Jordan waters.

Tell el 'Alya *199:200*

Small mound in Bet She'an Valley 2 km. S of Tirat Ẓevi, adjacent to Tel Shalem. Sherds from Early Bronze Age.

Tell Bazzariya *166:190*

Ruins of ancient, unidentified settlement alongside village of Bazzariya in Samarian Hills, off Shekhem–Jenin road. Sherds indicate occupation in Early Bronze Age and Iron Age.

Tell el Beida *197:198*

Arab village (pop.: 200) in Jordan Valley 3 km. NE of Meḥola.

Tell 'Ein el Ḥariri *226:258*

Settlement mound from Roman and Byzantine Periods. Remains of walls, and on W slope, a cemetery. Sherds from Late Bronze Age and Iron Age found nearby.

Tell Faras → Har Peres

Tell el Fari'a (Negev) → **Tel Sharuḥen**

Tell el Ful (near Gedera) *132:136*

Small mound in Judean Foothills 2 km. E of Gedera on N bank of Naḥal Soreq. Inhabited during Middle Bronze Age, Late Bronze Age, Hellenistic, Roman and early Arab Periods. Used today as a cemetery by local Arabs.

Tell Ghazza *124:150*

Large mound on Coastal Plain 2 km. NE of Palmaḥim, next to mouth of Naḥal Soreq. Sherds indicate occupation from Iron Age to Arab Period.

Tell Ḥamma *197:197*

Large mound in Jordan Valley 2 km. NW of Meḥola. Site is identified with Ḥammat, mentioned in stele of Pharaoh Seti I (1318-1304 BCE) found at Bet She'an. Sherds indicate continuous occupation from Early Bronze Age until Ottoman Period. Fragment of a jug was found on the site with Hebrew inscription, "Le Aḥav".

Tell el Ḥashash *130:131*

Remains of ancient settlement in Judean Foothills 1 km. NE of Re'em junction, alongside Revadim. Sherds from Chalcolithic, Roman and Byzantine Periods.

Tell el Ḥilu (Tell Abu Sifri) *197:192*

Small mound in Jordan Valley 4 km. S of Meḥola. Believed by some to be site of Abel-meholah, city in Issachar tribal allotment and included in 5th district during Solomon's reign (I Kings 4:12). Birthplace of Prophet Elisha (I Kings 19:16). Sherds indicate continuous occupation from Early Bronze Age to Middle Ages.

Tell Ḥisa *202:207*

Small mound in Bet She'an Valley N of Kefar Ruppin. Sherds found from Middle Bronze Age and some nearby from Chalcolithic Period.

Tell Jaljul (Ghalghala) *196:139*

Ruins of Roman fortress 3 km. E of Jericho. Sherds, glass fragments and mosaics from Roman, Byzantine and Arab Periods. In immediate surroundings are additional remains of forts, aqueducts and buildings from Roman and Byzantine Periods. Claimed by some to be site of Gilgal where Israelites camped after crossing the Jordan (Josh. 4:19).

Tell el Judeida → Tel Goded

Tell Kharazat *139:168*

Recently discovered ancient settlement ruin on Coastal Plain between Petaḥ Tiqwa and the Yarqon, 2 km. NW of Segula junction. Today situated within a citrus grove alongside an ancient road junction. Sherds found indicate occupation in Middle Bronze Age, Late Iron Age, Persian, Byzantine and Arab Periods.

Tell el Magharbi *101:088*

Large mound in Negev 4 km. S of Be'eri and on right bank of Naḥal Gerar. Remains of defensive wall and possibly of a fosse. Sherds and other remains indicate occupation in Chalcolithic, Middle Bronze Age, Late Bronze Age, Iron Age, Persian, Roman and Byzantine Periods.

Tell el Maḥalḥil *192:133*

Ruins in Judean Desert off Jerusalem–Jericho road, 1 km. N of en Nabi Musa. Several round enclosures with remains of rooms which were attached to their perimeters. Apparently inhabited during Chalcolithic Period and Iron Age.

Tell Maryam *175:141*

Ancient settlement ruin 8 km. NE of Jerusalem, SW of Mikhmash (Mukhmas). Believed to be site of Beth-aven, city on N border of Benjamin tribal allotment (Josh. 18:12). Remains of square Byzantine fortress and remains from Iron Age.

Tell el Maṣalla *168:205*

Heap of undressed stones on peak of Samarian Hills 10 km. SW of Jenin, measuring 6 m. in diameter and 2.5 m. in height. Sherds found here indicate occupation in Early Bronze, Middle Bronze and Iron Ages.

Tell el Mazar (central Jordan Valley) *201:224*

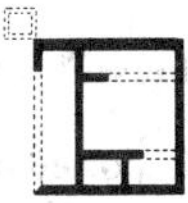

Remains of ancient settlement 1 km. SW of kibbutz Gesher. Flint implements found here indicate prehistoric habitation; other remains bear witness to Early Bronze and Middle Bronze Age occupation.

Tell el Mazar (lower Jordan Valley) *195:171*

Site of ancient settlement near junction of Jericho–Bet She'an and Shekhem–Adam Bridge roads. On hill are remains of Crusader round tower and fortress. Sherds indicate occupation in Chalcolithic, Early Bronze and Iron Ages.

Tell Mimas → Tel Bet Ha'Emeq

Tell Miska *187:182*

Ancient settlement ruins in Samarian Hills 10 km. SE of Tubas. Remains of defensive walls, buildings bearing conflagration marks and remains from Byzantine Period. Sherds indicate occupation in Early Bronze, Late Bronze and Iron Ages till Arab Period.

Tell el Muḥaffar *170:205*

Stepped tel in Samarian Hills 7 km. SW of Jenin. Building stones and sherds found here indicate habitation in Early Bronze Age and later from Iron Age till Byzantine Period.

Tell el Mukharkhash → Tel Rekhesh

Tell en Naṣba (Tel Miẓpa) *170:143*

Tel of ancient city in Judean Hills 3 km. N of Jerusalem airport. One theory claims it to be site of Mizpeh, city in Benjamin tribal allotment (Josh. 18:26), regular haunt of Prophet Samuel (I Sam. 7:5-16); residence of Gedaliah, governor appointed by Nebuchadnezzar, King of Babylon, after destruction of First Temple, and site of his murder (II Kings 25:25; Jer. 41:11). Excavations uncovered remains of city walls, towers, structures, tombs and utensils dating from Iron Age and post-Babylonian Exile. In one of the tombs a seal was discovered with inscription "of Jezaniah servant of the King". The Bible records that among the ministers of Zedekiah was a certain Jezaniah who fled from Jerusalem on the eve of the destruction and later pledged allegiance to Gedaliah (II Kings 25:23-24; Jer. 40:8-9).

Tell Qasile → Tel Aviv

Tell el Qauqa (El Qawqa') *152:138*

Settlement remains in Judean Hills 5 km. E of Latrun junction. Ruins are scattered at foot of hill offshoot, over area of 5 d. At its summit is a heap of unhewn stones, 10 m. in diameter and 3 m. high. Remains indicate occupation from Middle Bronze Age until end of Iron Age.

Tell Qila → Kh. Qila

Tell Rafaḥ → Rafah

Tell er Ras (Samarian Hills) *176:174*

Ancient site 7 km. S of Shekhem, W of 'Awarta. Cisterns, building remains, ruins of either a mosque or a Samaritan synagogue and a tomb ascribed to Eleazar, son of high priest Aaron. Sherds and other remains indicate habitation in Iron Age, Byzantine and from early Arab until Ottoman Periods.

Tell er Riḥ → Tel Mashav

Tell er Ruqeish *086:092*

Settlement ruins on Mediterranean shore in Gaza Strip 2 km. W of Deir el Balaḥ. Excavations uncovered 6 levels dating from Iron Age till Persian Period. Alongside tel, *085:091*, is a contemporary cemetery with signs of cremation burials and, nearby, burial objects which were imported from Cyprus were found.

Tell es Samak → Haifa

Tell es Saqi *228:252*

Basalt hill on Golan Heights 3 km. NE of Ramat Magshimim. To W are remains of Byzantine and Ottoman structures. Nearby are a number of dolmens and tumuli.

Tell Shaddud → Sarid

o **Tell esh Shamsiyya** *198:198*

Arab village in Jordan Valley 1.5 km. N of Meḥola. Pop.: 200.

Tell esh Shaqf (Jordan Valley) → **Tel Sheqafim**

Tell esh Shaqf (Judean Foothills) → **Tel Sheqef**

Tell Sheikh Abu Faraj (Ed Dumeiri) *143:207*

Ancient settlement ruins in Sharon 2 km. N of Ḥadera. Evidence of prehistoric occupation and sherds from Iron Age, Roman, Byzantine and early Arab Periods.

Tell esh Sheikh Dhiyab *190:161*

Ancient settlement ruins in Jordan Valley 1 km. W of *moshav* Peẓa'el. Building foundations on tel, and nearby is a pool with remains of an aqueduct. Sherds indicate occupation in Early Bronze Age, Middle Bronze Age, Iron Age, Roman, Byzantine and Arab Periods. Alongside tel is a modern Arab cemetery.

Tell esh Sheikh Ḥasan *188:215*

Ancient settlement ruins in Yizre'el Valley 2.5 km. S of Tel Yosef. Sherds indicate continuous occupation from Early Bronze Age until

Iron Age. Half a km. to S are remains of a Roman settlement. Kibbutz Tel Yosef was located here in its early years.

Tell esh Sheikh Muḥammad → Tel Saharon

Tell esh Sheikh Ṣaliḥ *200:213*

Tel alongside a spring 4 km. NE of Bet She'an. Sherds indicate occupation in Bronze Age, Iron Age, Byzantine and Arab Periods. Near spring Early Bronze Age sherds were found, and 200 m. to E of tel flint implements and sherds were discovered dating from Neolithic, Chalcolithic and Iron Age times.

Tell eṣ Ṣimadi *196:170*

Prominent mound in Jordan Valley 3.5 km. NW of Massu'a. According to one theory it is site of Jokmeam, city in Ephraim tribal allotment (I Chron. 6:68) and included in 5th district during Solomon's reign (I Kings 4:12). Inhabited from Early Bronze Age through Iron Age. At foot of tel are ruins of large Roman–Byzantine settlement which also existed in Middle Ages.

Tell eth Thuraya *210:233*

Ancient settlement ruin adjacent to SE shore of Lake Kinneret, 2 km. SE of Tel Qaẓir. Commands the ancient route to Golan Heights from S part of Lake Kinneret. Sherds indicate occupation in Middle Bronze Age, Late Bronze Age and Iron Age. Remains of defensive walls, towers and large structures.

Tell et Turmus (Ḥula Valley) *210:290*

Small mound 7 km. E of Qiryat Shemona next to She'ar Yashuv. Excavations uncovered levels from Chalcolithic Period, Early Bronze Age and Hellenistic Period.

Tell 'Ubeidiyya *202:231*

Mound in Jordan Valley 3 km. SW of Deganya "A" adjacent to W bank of Jordan. One theory claims site to be city of Yanoam, mentioned in Tell el 'Amarna letters. NW of tel is a prehistoric site where human and animal remains dating from the Lower Pleistocene Epoch were found. These are the earliest remains discovered in Israel and among the earliest in the world. Excavations uncovered a human settlement which existed in a tropical climate (before the geological rift created the Jordan Valley). Its population subsisted on a vegetarian diet and meat from hunting. In these early archaeological levels, fragments of a human skull and teeth were found, also fossilized bones of elephants, hippopotami, giraffes, gazelles, horses and many other smaller animals; a large assortment of flint tools — choppers, handaxes and picks — were also found.

Tell el Wawiyat *178:244*

Mound of ancient settlement in Galilee alongside Rummana. The village was unfortified and occupied chiefly in Bronze and Iron Ages.

Tell ez Zanbaqiyya el Gharbi → Tel Zan HaMa'aravi

Tell ez Zanbaqiyya esh Sharqi → Tel Zan HaMizraḥi

Tel Maḥoz (Tell Abu es Sultan) *125:147*

Large mound on Coastal Plain 3 km. SE of Palmaḥim. According to one theory it is site of Makhaz mentioned in Egyptian documents. Sherds indicate continuous occupation from Early Bronze Age until beginning of Iron Age; re-occupied in Roman and Byzantine Periods.

Tel Malḥata (Tell el Milḥ) *152:069*

Large mound in Negev 18 km. W of 'Arad. According to one theory it is site of ancient Arad, mentioned in Bible in connection with the

Israelites' unsuccessful attempt to enter Canaan from the S (Num. 21:1). Another theory claims it to be site of Hormah, also mentioned in the same context (Deut. 1:44). It was a fortified city in Roman and Byzantine times but sherds found here indicate occupation from Chalcolithic, Early Bronze, Late Bronze and Iron Ages. Recent excavations uncovered remains of Roman-Byzantine fortress, living quarters, farm houses and a tower.

Tel Malot (Tel Gibton, Tell el Malat) *137:140*

Ancient settlement mound on border of Judean Foothills and Coastal Plain. Remains indicate its earliest inhabitants lived here during the Chalcolithic Period; it was then inhabited during most historical periods from Early Bronze Age till Byzantine Period. At foot of tel is a spring and it is part of 'Enot Gibton nature reserve.

Tel Manoaḥ (Tell Uṣeifir) *116:078*

Ancient settlement mound on natural hill in Negev 2.5 km. SE of Ofaqim. Inhabited from Iron Age until Hellenistic Period. Remains of fortifications indicate its importance in the area.

Tel Maresha (Tell Ṣandaḥanna) *(Josh. 15:44)* *140:111*

Ancient settlement mound in Judean Foothills 2 km. S of Bet Guvrin. Site of Biblical Mareshah, city in Judah tribal allotment. It was one of cities fortified by Rehoboam to protect the road from Lakhish to Jerusalem. Later, in the 3rd c. BCE it was a Hellenistic centre with a predominantly Edomite population, besides some Sidonites and Greeks. Served as Edomite capital. It was captured by John Hyrcanus and possibly destroyed by him. Rebuilt and again destroyed in 40 BCE, this time by the Parthians. Re-occupied in Byzantine Period. Remains of 3rd c. synagogue and 5th-6th c. mosaic church floor. The church of St. Anne (mother of Mary) dates from Crusader Period. On and around tel are remains of city streets and buildings, burial caves, olive oil presses, rock-cut caves, columbarium (tiers of niches) caves and reservoirs.

Tel Marwa *172:269*

Hill in Galilee 3 km. W of Ma'alot–Tarshiḥa, between two tributaries of Naḥal Ga'aton. Included in nature reserve (1,100 d.).

Tel Mashav (Tell er Riḥ) *200:269*

Mound of unidentified ancient settlement in Galilee 7 km. NE of Safed.

Tel Mashosh *146:068*

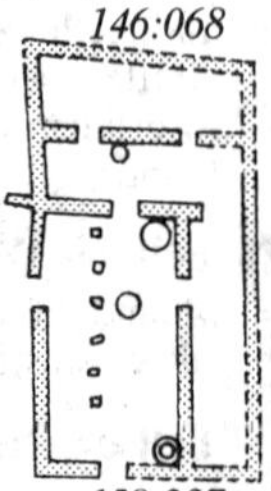

Mound in Negev 17 km. E of Be'er Sheva' near important ancient road junction. Sherds and other remains indicate occupation in Bronze and Iron Ages and from Roman–Byzantine Period till Arab conquest. Excavations uncovered remains of Middle Bronze Age road fort, a group of Iron Age structures and a fortress from time of Kings of Judah. Much pottery and ostraca, and remains of Byzantine church and monastery were also found.

Tel Me'ammer (Tell el 'Amr) *159:237*

Ancient settlement mound in Galilee near Ha'Amaqim junction. Also known as Tel Geba Shemen. Believed to be site of city of Geba Shemen, mentioned in City Lists of Thutmose III. The glacis of an ancient settlement is clearly visible on the tel. Early Bronze Age tombs and Iron Age sherds.

Tel Megadim (Tell Qar'a) *146:237*

Ancient settlement ruins on Karmel shore 2 km. N of 'Atlit. Site of Phoenician city of Qarta, which was possibly the Phoenician name for 'Atlit. According to one theory it is site of Kartah, a Levite city in Zebulun tribal allotment (Josh. 21:34). Site mentioned by a Bordeaux pilgrim (ca. 330 CE) as Mutatio Certha. Excavations uncovered various levels. Finds include remnants of a walled Phoenician city, pottery and metalware fragments including Cypriot pottery ("milk bowl" type), two levels from Persian Period, remains of walls of a building from Roman–Byzantine Period which was apparently the caravanserai listed by the Bordeaux pilgrim.

Tel Megiddo → Megiddo

Tel Mevorakh *143:215*

Small mound on S bank of Naḥal Tanninim 2.5 km. NW of Binyamina. Excavations uncovered remains of a Middle Bronze Age fortress encircled by a rampart, a sanctuary and cultic objects from Late Bronze Age as well as a Late Bronze Age scarab bearing name of Pharaoh Thutmose III; a large Iron Age structure with 4 enclosures surrounded by a broad thick-walled courtyard (probably a public building, administrative centre or storehouse); remains of large structure encircled by casemate wall from Persian Period; and a Roman mausoleum with several marble sarcophagi (2 are on display at the Rockefeller Museum). S of tel is a Roman aqueduct which leads from Naḥal Tanninim to Caesarea.

Tel Midegge *197:210*

Ancient settlement mound 2 km. S of Bet She'an, alongside 'En HaNaẓiv fish ponds. Excavations uncovered remains of large 6th c. building containing much pottery and a sherd of an oil lamp with a Samaritan inscription.

Tel Midrash (Tell el Madrasa) *202:211*

Small mound in Bet She'an Valley alongside Ma'oz Ḥayyim. Occupied time and again at intervals during Early, Middle and Late Bronze and Iron Ages and Roman Period.

Tel Mikhal (Tell el Qantur) *131:174*

Ancient settlement mound on Mediterranean shore S of Herẓliyya. Excavations uncovered a post-Babylonian Exile sanctuary and below it an Iron Age occupation level. Sherds from tel and surroundings indicate occupation during Second Temple, Hellenistic and Roman Periods.

Tel Milḥa (Tell el Muleiḥa) *128:096*

Ancient settlement mound in Judean Foothills 2 km. NE of Qama junction. Covers some 8 d. on bank of Naḥal Shiqma, alongside railway tracks. Sherds indicate continuous occupation from Middle Bronze Age till Middle Ages.

Tel Miqne (Kh. el Muqanna') *135:132*

Ruin of ancient settlement in Judean Foothills 7 km. SW of Naḥshon junction. Believed to be site of Ekron, one of 5 Philistine cities (Josh. 13:3) and allotted to tribe of Judah (Josh. 15:11, 45-41) although presumed to be in tribal allotment of Dan (Josh. 19:43). Ekron was also a Jewish city during Second Temple Period and is mentioned as such in 4th c. CE Onomasticon of Eusebius. Remains of defensive walls, structures and column fragments. Sherds and other fragments indicate a large Iron Age settlement here and a smaller one during Byzantine and Arab times.

Tel Mond *143:184*

Agricultural settlement in Sharon 7 km. N of Kefar Sava. Named after Sir Alfred Mond (1868-1930), later Lord Melchett, the British Zionist leader. Founded as a farming village in 1929 on private land, today it has a local council and includes Kefar Sieff (named after British Sieff family) and Ya'aqov suburbs. Area: 8,000 d.; pop.: 3,200. Nearby is Tel Mond youth prison.

Tel Mor (Tell Murra, Tell el Khaidar) *117:136*

Tel of ancient settlement N of Ashdod alongside mouth of Naḥal Lakhish, off the ancient *via maris.* Excavations indicate earliest occupation in Middle Bronze Age, flourishing in Late Bronze Age, and then declining in Iron Age. During reign of Uzziah (769-733) a fortress was built here. Settlement was destroyed in 8th c. BCE; it was re-inhabited in Hellenistic Period and continuously occupied till Byzantine Period.

Tel Na'ama (Tell en Na'ima) *205:288*

Ancient settlement ruin in Ḥula Valley 3 km. SE of Qiryat Shemona. Sherds and other remains indicate occupation in Early Bronze, Late Bronze and Iron Ages and again from Hellenistic till Middle Ages. Sheikh's tomb.

Tel Nagila (Tell en Najila) *127:101*

Ancient settlement ruin in Judean Foothills 7 km. N of Qama junction. Believed to be site of Gath, one of the 5 Philistine cities (Josh. 13:3). Another theory claims it to be site of Eglon, mentioned in connection with Joshua's wars (Josh. 10:3; 12:12). Sherds indicate continuous occupation from Chalcolithic until Roman Periods. Excavation levels of Early Bronze, Middle Bronze and Iron Ages, containing remains of private houses and public structures. The city's cemetery was discovered alongside the tel.

Tel Naḥal (Tell en Nahl) *156:245*

Ancient settlement ruin in Zevulun Valley 3 km. W of Qiryat Ata. Late Bronze, Iron, Byzantine and early Arab sherds and other remains.

Tel Nimrod *202:210*

A pair of mounds 5 km. SE of Bet She'an. The larger of the two has remains of defensive walls and caves. Sherds indicate habitation in Early and Middle Bronze Ages, and from Iron until Middle Ages.

Tel Nissa (Tell el Manshiyya) *198:210*

Tel of ancient settlement 2 km. SE of Bet She'an, alongside Newe Etan. Inhabited in Late Bronze and Iron Ages and again after Babylonian Exile until Middle Ages, as evidenced by remains.

Tel Par (Tell el Far) *160:241*

Ancient settlement ruin in Zevulun Valley 3 km. S of Qiryat Ata. Possibly site of ancient Beten included in tribal allotment of Asher (Josh. 19:25). Its name has been preserved in that of adjacent Arab village, Ibtin. Sherds indicate it was continuously inhabited from Early Bronze until Byzantine times.

Tel Parur (Kh. Fureir) *159:226*

Byzantine ruin 3 km. SW of Yoqne'am and next to 'En Ha'Emeq. Rock-cut burial niches.

Tel Peḥa (Tell el Basha, Tell el Ḥamir) *202:209*

Small tel 6 km. SE of Bet She'an, S of Ma'oz Ḥayyim. Sherds found from Roman and early Arab Periods. On road leading S to Tel 'Artal is a Roman milestone.

Tel Poleg *135:185*

Ancient site on Sharon coast on left bank of Naḥal Poleg, N of kibbutz Yaqum. Inhabited during Middle Bronze Age, Iron Age, Persian and Hellenistic Periods. Nearby is an ancient tunnel, apparently Roman, which was used as a rain-water drain.

Tel Poran **(Tell el Farani)** *113:124*

Ancient settlement mound on Coastal Plain 5 km. NE of Ashqelon. Covers a broad area and its E part is embanked to a height of 10 m. Sherds indicate occupation in Early Bronze Age and Late Bronze Age until Byzantine Period. A survey here uncovered a 5 m. thick brick wall, which encompassed the settlement in the Early Bronze Age.

Tel Qashish **(Tell el Qasis)** *160:292*

Ancient settlement mound on W edge of Yizre'el Valley 3 km. N of Yoqne'am junction. Sherds from Chalcolithic through Hellenistic Periods.

Tel Qataf **(Tell el Qitaf Makab)** *202:207*

Large mound in Bet She'an Valley next to Kefar Ruppin, and adjacent to a Jordan River ford. Sherds indicate it was continuously inhabited from Early Bronze Age until early Arab Period, interrupted only in the Middle Bronze Age.

★ **Tel Qaẓir** *208:234*

Kibbutz on SE shore of Lake Kinneret, 4 km. E of Ẓemaḥ junction. Named after Arabic name for site, Tell el Qaṣr. Overlooks routes along Kinneret shore and the Yarmouk ford. Battlefield between British and Turks during WWI. British border post during WWII and Syrian post during War of Independence. Kibbutz founded 1949. Area: 2,900 d. Pop.: 220.

Tel Qedesh *(II Kings 15:29)* *200:279*

Ancient mound on Lebanese border, 4 km. W of Koaḥ junction. Site of ancient Kedesh in Upper Galilee (as distinguished from Ḥurbat Qedesh which is site of Kedesh-naphtali). The name has been preserved in that of the now-abandoned village of Qadis. Kedesh was originally a Canaanite city; it was mentioned in Egyptian inscriptions and in "topographical lists" of cities conquered by Egyptian kings. During Israelite conquest it was included in tribal allotment of Naphtali. Conquered by Assyrian king, Tiglath-pileser III in 734 BCE. During Second Temple Period it was a gentile city. It flourished during the Middle Ages when it was repopulated with Jews and, according to various accounts, it survived into the 17th c. A Medieval tradition has it that the prophetess Deborah, Barak, son of Abinoam, Heber the Kenite and his wife Jael were all buried at Kedesh (which was erroneously thought to be Kedesh-naphtali). Excavations uncovered 5 occupation levels: upper level — early Arab Period (8th-10th c. CE) remains; 2nd level — remains of 3rd and 4th c. structures; 3rd level — remains from Persian Period; 4th and 5th levels — remains from Iron Age. Finds include ossuaries and remnants of a Roman sun god temple.

Tel Qeriyyot **(Kh. el Qaryatein)** *161:084*

Tel of ancient settlement in Judean Hills 8 km. SE of Sammu' (Eshtemoa'). According to one theory this is site of Kerioth-hezron, city in tribal allotment of Judah (Josh. 15:25). Another claims it was home town of Judas Iscariot. Local caves were used as dwellings and have entrances built of dressed stones.

Tel Qeshet **(Tell el Quneitra)** *127:105*

Ancient settlement mound in Judean Foothills 2 km. SW of *moshav* Aḥuzzam. Arabic name means bridge of arches (*qeshet* = arch) and hence its Hebrew name. Sherds indicate habitation from Early Bronze Age until early Arab Period. Scene of heavy fighting during War of Independence between Israeli and Egyptian forces.

Tel Qidda *173:269*

Hill in Galilee 3 km. N of Ma'alot–Tarshiḥa and within nature reserve of 1,100 d.

Tel Qiri *161:227*

Ancient settlement mound on W edge of Yizre'el Valley within kibbutz HaZore'a. Excavations prove it was inhabited during Chalcolithic, Early Bronze and Middle Bronze Ages, and again from Iron Age until the reign of Herod. Major finds are remains of a fortress and 2 structures which contained many Iron Age utensils, and remains of Persian and Roman structures.

Tel Qishyon (El Khirba) *187:229*

Group of low mounds in Galilee 3 km. S of Mt. Tabor. Sherds from Chalcolithic, Bronze, Iron, and Hellenistic times.

Tel Raqqat → Tiberias

Tel Regev (Tell el Harbaj) *158:240*

Ancient settlement mound in Zevulun Valley 2 km. NE of Yagur. Believed to be site of Achshaph, important Canaanite city mentioned in ancient Egyptian documents. Its king was one of the 31 who fought against Joshua (Josh. 12:20). After Israelite conquest it was included in tribal allotment of Asher (Josh. 19:25). Sherds and other remains from Early Bronze, Late Bronze, Iron, Persian and Arab Periods. In 1750 it was fortified at the command of the Bedouin ruler, Dahir el 'Amr, to protect his capital, Acre.

Tel Reḥov → Reḥov

Tel Rekhesh (Tell el Mukharkhash) *194:228*

Ancient settlement mound in Galilee 7 km. SE of Mt. Tabor and within Naḥal Tabor nature reserve. Sherds from Chalcolithic Period and from Early Bronze Age until early Arab Period. Nearby are burial caves, a ruin and cisterns.

Tel Ridan (Tell er Ridan) *082:088*

Ancient settlement mound on Mediterranean coast in Gaza Strip, 2 km. W of Naḥal Qatif. Excavations uncovered Middle Bronze Age remains including tombs, a furnace and pottery workshop.

Tel Ro'e (Tell er Ru'yan) *199:204*

Ancient settlement mound in Bet She'an Valley E of Sede Eliyyahu. Sherds from Bronze Age, Iron Age, Persian, Roman and early Arab Periods. A Roman milestone found here dates from reign of Emperor Caracalla.

Tel Rosh (Kh. Tell er Ruweisi) *181:271*

Ancient hilltop mound in Galilee 5 km. E of Ma'alot–Tarshiḥa. Extends over 35 d. Traces of a stone wall were found. Sherds indicate continuous occupation from Early Bronze Age until early Arab Period, chiefly in Early Bronze Age and Middle Bronze Age. Sheikh's tomb at summit.

Tel Saharon (Tell esh Sheikh Muḥammad) *201:206*

Mound on banks of Jordan River 7 km. SE of Bet She'an. Remains of ancient structures and an abandoned mosque. Sherds indicate occupation in Bronze Age, Iron Age, Byzantine and Arab Periods. Alongside is the Tel Saharon nature reserve.

Tel Selawim (Tell el Firr) *188:216*

Ancient settlement mound in Yizre'el Valley 2.5 km. SE of Tel Yosef. Sherds indicate habitation in following periods: Early Bronze, Late Bronze, Iron, Persian, Roman, Byzantine and early Arab.

Tel Seluqiyya *219:265*

Ancient settlement mound on Golan Heights 3.5 km. SE of Qaẓrin.

Remains of Early Bronze defensive wall and foundations. Below tel are springs, some of them hot. Paleolithic and Mesolithic flint tools found nearby.

Tel Sha'ar (Tell Abu Babein) *181:275*

Ancient mound on summit of steep hill in Galilee, 1 km. NE of Netu'a. Remains of a building and what was possibly a gate. Iron Age sherds.

Tel Shalem (Tell er Radgha) *199:200*

Large mound in Bet She'an Valley 2 km. S of Tirat Ẓevi. Sherds indicate it was inhabited in Bronze Age, beginning of Iron Age, Persian, Hellenistic, Roman and Byzantine Periods. Believed to be site of Samarian city of Shalem. (The tomb of Sheikh Shalem on tel summit seems to support this theory.) Its Arabic name means the tel of mud; this is associated with the episode when the Arabs attempted to invade the country in 638, and the Byzantine residents of the town, in order to stop them, opened the irrigation dams and the Arab cavalry got bogged down in mud. This battle became known to Arabs as er Radgha (the day of mud).

Tel Shamat (Tell esh Shamdin) *203:224*

Ancient settlement mound in Jordan Valley between kibbutz Gesher and Jordan River. Remains of walls and buildings on tel slopes are still perceptible. In the SE corner are remains of a wall or glacis. Sherds indicate almost continuous occupation from Neolithic Period through early Arab Period.

Tel Sharuḥen (Tell el Fari'a in the Negev) *(Josh. 19:6)* *101:077*

Ancient settlement mound 4 km. SE of Ma'on junction within Naḥal Besor nature reserve. Believed to be site of Sharuhen, ancient Canaanite city and Hyksos administrative centre of the S in the 16th c. BCE. It was densely populated by Philistines. Appears as Sharuham in ancient Egyptian documents. After Israelite conquest it was given to tribe of Simeon although located within Judah's tribal allotment. Excavations uncovered remains of fortifications and structures from Middle Bronze Age, Late Bronze Age, Iron Age, Hellenistic and Roman Periods. Among the many finds were: Egyptian artifacts, cooking utensils, pottery fragments, Hebrew seals and sarcophagi. Philistine burial caves contained bones in earthenware pitchers.

Tel Sheqafim (Tell esh Shaqf) *198:203*

Ancient settlement mound in Bet She'an Valley 1.5 km. E of Tirat Ẓevi. Remains from Persian and Hellenistic Periods.

Tel Sheqef (Tell esh Shaqf) *123:107*

Small mound in Judean Foothills 10 km. SW of Peluggot junction. Sherds indicate continuous occupation from Iron Age through Byzantine Period.

Tel Shera' (Tell esh Shari'a) *119:089*

Large mound in Negev 8 km. SE of Netivot junction. Prominent on a gravel hill on N bank of Naḥal Gerar; area: 20 d. Believed to be site of Biblical Ziklag, which fell within Judah's tribal allotment (Josh. 15:31) but was given to tribe of Simeon (Josh. 19:5). It apparently remained in Philistine hands, and here David resided with the Philistines when he fled from Saul (I Sam. 27:2-6). Resettled after Babylonian Exile (Neh. 11:28). Sherds indicate occupation from Chalcolithic till Arab Periods. Excavations uncovered Middle Bronze Age settlement remains, 8 Late Bronze Age occupation levels, several 4-roomed houses (perhaps palace from days of Kings of Judah) and a magnificent Iron Age structure. Other finds are dug-out granaries from Persian Period and a large Roman structure. During Byzantine Period a large settlement existed around the tel covering an area of 400 d. At summit of tel is an Arab *maqam* (holy shrine) with a Moslem cemetery.

Tel Sheva‘ *137:073*

Permanent Bedouin settlement in Negev 5 km. E of Be'er Sheva‘. Established 1969 by Ministry of Housing. Pop.: 100.

Tel Shillat **(Kh. Shilta)** *152:147*

Ruins of abandoned village built over ancient settlement in Judean Foothills, 3 km. SE of *moshav* Mevo Modi‘im. Sherds indicate Iron Age, Roman, Byzantine, Medieval and Ottoman occupation.

Tel Shimeron **(Kh. Sammuniyya)** *(Josh. 19:15) 170:234*

Ancient settlement mound between Lower Galilee and Yizre‘el Valley 3 km. NE of Bet She‘arim. Believed to be site of Biblical Shimron also known as Shama‘nu, Shim‘on and Shamkhuna in Egyptian Execration texts and Tell el ‘Amarna letters. Its king was one of the 31 kings defeated by Joshua (Josh. 12:20). After Israelite conquest it was included in Zebulun tribal allotment (Josh. 19:15). During Second Temple Period the town was called Shim‘onia and, during Roman and Byzantine Periods, Simonia or Simonias. Nearby Joseph b. Mattathias fought a battle against the Romans. Sherds indicate occupation during Bronze Age. Nearby at Kh. Sammuniyya remains were found from Hellenistic, Roman and Byzantine Periods, including remnants of a synagogue.

Tel Shoqeq **(Tell esh Shamdin)** *193:211*

Ancient settlement mound in Bet She'an Valley 1 km. S of Nir Dawid. Construction remains, sarcophagi fragments and parts of defensive walls. Sherds indicate occupation in Chalcolithic, Bronze, Hellenistic and early Arab Periods.

Tel Shoqet **(Tell es Saqati)** *141:080*

Ancient settlement mound in Negev 12 km. NE of Be'er Sheva‘, alongside Shoqet junction. Sherds indicate occupation in Chalcolithic Period and again from Iron Age until Roman Period.

Tel Shura **(Kh. esh Shura)** *204:264*

Low mound in Galilee 3 km. E of Rosh Pinna. Elliptical in shape it measures 100 by 200 m. Site of Roman and Byzantine settlement. On SW offshoot of tel are remains of square structure, believed to be a synagogue, dating from Roman–Byzantine Period till Mamluk conquest.

Tel Shush **(Tell Abu Shusha)** *163:224*

Ancient settlement mound at W end of Yizre‘el Valley N of Mishmar Ha‘Emeq. Remains of many structures, Byzantine olive oil press and burial cave. Sherds indicate occupation from Chalcolithic until early Arab Periods.

Tel Siḥan **(Tell Siḥan)** *105:095*

Small mound in NW Negev 3 km. S of Sa‘ad junction. Remains of ancient structures. Sherds indicate occupation in Roman and Byzantine Periods. Byzantine remains are scattered nearby along Naḥal Shuva, one of Naḥal Besor's tributaries.

Tel Ta‘anakh *(Josh. 12:21) 170:217*

Ancient settlement mound in Yizre‘el Valley off Jenin–Megiddo road. Site of ancient city of Taanach, mentioned in ancient Egyptian lists and documents. Its king was among the 31 who fought Joshua; the prophetess Deborah mentions it in her song (Judg. 5:19); and it was included in King Solomon's 5th administrative district (I Kings 4:12). No longer heard of after destruction of First Temple. Early excavations uncovered an archive of 12 Akkadian cuneiform tablets from 15th c. BCE. Later excavations uncovered remains of Early Bronze Age stone walls and large fortifications, a Middle Bronze Age glacis and an Iron Age underground water system.

Tel Tanninim *141:216*

Ancient settlement mound on Mediterranean shore, alongside mouth of Naḥal Tanninim. Occupied from Hellenistic till Byzantine Periods. Remains of large structure and a pool from which a low aqueduct leads to Caesarea. W of village is a Roman cemetery with rock-cut tombs, sarcophagi fragments and statues. W of the high aqueduct are remains of an agricultural settlement. Milestones found near shore indicate the presence of a Roman road. To the S is a Neolithic prehistoric site.

Tel Temes *195:213*

Ruin with remains of a Roman villa 1 km. NW of Bet She'an.

Tel Te'omim (Tell eth Thaum) *196:205*

Ancient settlement mound in Bet She'an Valley between Sede Terumot and Sede Eliyyahu. Occupied from Early Bronze Age until Persian Period and again in Roman and Byzantine Periods. A bulldozer accidentally uncovered several occupation levels including walls destroyed by fire.

Tel Ya'af (Tell el Qaṣab) *202:264*

Ancient settlement mound in Galilee 1 km. E of Rosh Pinna. Construction fragments which are perhaps remains of city walls. Sherds indicate occupation in Middle Bronze, Late Bronze and Iron Ages.

Tel Yarmut (Kh. el Yarmuk) *(Josh. 10:3) 147:124*

Large mound in Judean Foothills 5 km. S of Bet Shemesh. Identified as Biblical city of Jarmuth whose king was one of the 5 Amorite kings defeated by Joshua (Josh. 10:3-27). Resettled by exiles returning from Babylon (Neh. 11:29). Mentioned in Onomasticon of Eusebius. Tel covers an area of 250 d. and has remains of stone defensive wall as well as traces of an Early Bronze Age fosse. The NE section of the tel has remains of a settlement inhabited from Iron Age to Byzantine Period.

Tel Yasur *126:130*

Mound on Coastal Plain 4 km. W of Re'em junction. Remains from Iron Age, Persian, Roman, Byzantine and Arab Periods.

Tel Yeshua' (Tell Sa'wa) *(Neh. 11:26) 149:076*

Ancient settlement mound in N Negev 9 km. SE of Shoqet junction off road to 'Arad. Site of Jeshua, one of the cities where the exiles settled after their return from Babylon. Ruins of a Roman–Byzantine fort with a round tower dating from the reign of Herod. According to sherds found nearby it was inhabited also in Chalcolithic Period, Bronze and Iron Ages.

Tel Yisaskhar (Tulul esh Sheikh Ṣaliḥ, Kh. Zab'a) *200:217*

Small mound in Jordan Valley 6 km. NE of Bet She'an and SW of Bet Yosef. Traces of a stone wall. On S slope soil erosion has bared remains of another stone wall and an occupation level destroyed by fire. Sherds indicate occupation from Early Bronze until Iron Ages and later in Roman and Byzantine Periods.

Tel Yishma'el (Tell Isma'il) *202:217*

Two adjoining mounds in Jordan Valley 8 km. NE of Bet She'an and E of Tel Yosef. On the higher tel (Tel Yishma'el "A") Roman and Byzantine sherds were found. On the lower and broader tel (Tel

Yishma'el "B") sherds were found from Chalcolithic Period, Early Bronze Age, Iron Age, Byzantine and early Arab Periods.

★ Tel Yiẓḥaq — *137:184*

Kibbutz in Sharon 3 km. SE of Poleg interchange. Named after Yiẓḥak Steiger, leader of HaNo'ar HaẒiyyoni (Zionist Youth movement) in Galicia. Founded 1938 by immigrants from Galicia and S America. Area: 2,700 d. Pop.: 580. The kibbutz has a museum and memorial, **Masua**, for members of HaNo'ar HaẒiyyoni who died in the Holocaust; **Bet Gadi**, in memory of Gad Manela, killed while on a chase after terrorist infiltrators in Jordan Valley; **Bet Rishonim**, in memory of kibbutz founders and the archives of the HaNo'ar HaẒiyyoni movement. Alongside kibbutz is a Youth 'Aliyah school, **Newe Hadassah.**

Tel Yona (Tell Yunis) — *125:156*

Ancient settlement mound on Mediterranean shore S of Bat Yam. Remains of Byzantine structure and Roman, Byzantine and Medieval sherds. The name is associated with the Biblical prophet, Jonah.

★ Tel Yosef — *188:218*

Kibbutz in Yizre'el Valley alongside 'En Ḥarod. Founded 1921 by members of the Gedud Ha'Avoda (Labour Legion) and named after Joseph Trumpeldor. During 1936-1939 Arab Riots it served as base for nearby "stockade and tower" settlements, and as Palmaḥ and Haganah base before founding of State. Area: 15,000 d. Pop.: 520. **Bet Trumpeldor** Museum and archives of Gedud Ha'Avoda, Third 'Aliyah, and kibbutz movement.

Tel Yuvla — *194:220*

Ancient settlement mound in Lower Galilee 4 km. NE of Bet HaShitta. Sherds indicate occupation from Late Bronze Age until Middle Ages.

Tel Ẓaf — *202:201*

Ancient settlement mound on hill in Bet She'an Valley 2 km. SE of Tirat Ẓevi. Sherds indicate occupation in Chalcolithic Period and perhaps even earlier, in Neolithic Period.

Tel Ẓafit (Tell eṣ Ṣafi) — *135:123*

Ancient settlement mound in Judean Foothills 4 km. S of Kefar Menaḥem, off an ancient route from Coastal Plain to Judean Hills along Naḥal HaEla. Situated on hilltop with white limestone cliffs. According to one theory this is site of Biblical Libnah which fell in tribal allotment of Judah (Josh. 21:13). During Roman and Byzantine Periods a city called Saphitha, mentioned in the 6th c. Madaba map, was located alongside the tel. During Crusader Period a fortress was built on N part of the tel and called Blanchegarde (White Citadel); it was destroyed in 1191 by Saladin. On S part of tel are remains of the Byzantine church of St. George. The ruins of a *maqam* — holy shrine — of Sheikh Muḥammad and other more recent buildings were built over the ruins of the tel.

Tel Zahara (Tell Zahra el Kabir) — *192:213*

Ancient settlement mound in Yizre'el Valley 1 km. N of kibbutz Nir Dawid. Ruins of Roman and Byzantine structures and fragments of coloured mosaics.

Tel Zan HaMa'aravi (Tell ez Zanbaqiyya el Gharbi) — *201:223*

Ancient settlement mound in Jordan Valley alongside Newe Or and W of Tel Zan HaMizraḥi. Sherds and other remains indicate occupation in Early Bronze Age, Middle Bronze Age, Iron Age and from Hasmonean Period until Middle Ages.

Tel Zan HaMizraḥi (Tell ez Zanbaqiyya esh Sharqi) *202:223*

Ancient settlement mound in Jordan Valley 2 km. N of Newe Or. On summit and slopes are remains of structures and paving with basalt stones. Sherds indicate occupation in Early Bronze Age, Middle Bronze Age, Iron Age, Roman and Byzantine Periods. In old maps the site is recorded as Tell Abu el Jimal.

Tel Zayit (Tell Zeita) *133:115*

Small mound 6 km. NE of Qiryat Gat. Sherds indicate occupation chiefly in Late Iron Age and again from Hasmonean Period until Middle Ages.

Tel Ze'evim (Kh. el Mugheir) *154:206*

Ancient settlement mound 10 km. E of Ḥadera. Sherds and other remains indicate that it was inhabited intermittently from Middle Bronze Age until the Middle Ages.

Tel Ẓefi *150:215*

Ancient settlement mound 5 km. E of Binyamina and S of *moshav* Avi'el. According to one theory, site of city of Djefti, mentioned in City Lists of Thutmose III. Sherds indicate occupation in Chalcolithic Period, Bronze Age and later periods. Remains of structures and rock-cut tombs.

Tel Ẓemed (Tell esh Sheikh Ṣamad) *199:202*

Ancient settlement mound in Bet She'an Valley 1.5 km. SW of Newe Etan. Occupied in Bronze Age, Iron Age, Byzantine and Arab Periods. Remains of sheikh's tomb.

Tel Zeton (Tell Abu Zeitun) *134:167*

Small mound within Bene Beraq alongside the bridge over Yarqon River. Apparently site of ancient fortress. S of tel is a broad step upon which sherds were found from Iron Age, Persian and Hellenistic Periods.

Tel Zif *(Josh. 15:24)* *163:098*

Mound in Judean Desert 6 km. SE of Hebron. Remains of defensive walls. Sherds indicate occupation in Iron Age, Persian Period and from Hellenistic Period until Middle Ages. Possibly site of Biblical city of Ziph. **Ḥurbat Zif (Kh. Abu Ḥammam)** Settlement ruins nearby with cisterns, burial caves, pools and many structures. According to sherds found it was inhabited in Byzantine Period and Middle Ages.

Tel Zivda (Tell ez Zibda) *159:248*

Ancient settlement mound in Zevulun Valley 1 km. E of Qiryat Bialik. Continuously inhabited from Late Bronze Age until Hasmonean Period.

Tel Ẓofan *173:181*

Ancient settlement mound in Samarian Hills 2 km. NE of Shekhem. Commands W entrance of Biq'at Shekhem. Comprised of 2 parts: one a low, broad section with remains of Early Bronze Age city, and a high area containing remains of an Iron Age settlement. Sherds indicate occupation in Early and Late Bronze Age, Iron Age and from Persian until Byzantine Period.

Tel Ẓur *140:188*

Neighbourhood of Even Yehuda. Formerly a *moshav* which was founded in 1932.

Temanun Islet *143:231*

Islet opposite kibbutz Newe Yam, 300 m. from shore. Name means octopus.

● Tenuvot *146:190*

Moshav 6 km. E of Sharon junction S of Netanya–Tulkarm road. Founded 1952 by Yemenite immigrants. Area: 1,700 d. Pop.: 590. Within *moshav* are ruins of a Roman–Byzantine settlement, Tel Shevaḥ (Kh. Ṣubeiḥ).

○ Teqoa' *(II Chron. 11:6) 170:116*

Arab village 7 km. S of Bethlehem off Beit Sahur–Ḥalḥul road. Pop.: 1,500. Site of Biblical city of Tekoa, birthplace of Ira son of Ikkesh, one of David's commanders (II Sam. 23:26), and of Prophet Amos (Amos 1:1). One of the cities fortified by Rehoboam. After Babylonian Exile residents of Tekoa aided in building the walls of Jerusalem (Neh. 3:5). The city is mentioned in Hasmonean war descriptions of Jewish Revolt against Rome and in Bar Kokhba documents. Also mentioned in Onomasticon of Eusebius, Madaba map and Crusader sources. Within village are remains of buildings, a church, water channels and column fragments.

Teqoa' *171:117*

Civilian outpost on outskirts of Judean Desert 2 km. SW of Herodium. Same name as that of Biblical city of Tekoa, whose name has been preserved in that of adjacent Arab village..Founded as *naḥal* outpost in 1970; civilian status since 1977.

● Tequma *110:095*

Moshav on Coastal Plain 3 km. NW of Netivot junction. Founded 1949. Pop.: 270. Area: 7,500 d. SW of *moshav*, *109:094*, is a major reservoir of the Yarqon–Negev water carrier.

Teradyon *175:252*

Regional centre under construction in Galilee, 7 km. SW of Karmi'el. Named after the Tannaite rabbi, Hananiah b. Teradyon, who settled in nearby Sakhnin.

Teveẓ → Tubas

○ Ti'annik *170:213*

Arab village on fringe of Yizre'el Valley off Jenin–Megiddo road. Pop.: 300. Origin of name: from ancient city of Taanach identified with adjacent tel.

■ Tiberias *(Rakkath: Josh. 19:35)*

City on shore of Lake Kinneret which has played an important role in the history of the area and Jewish people for over 2,000 years. One of 4 Jewish holy cities (together with Jerusalem, Hebron and Safed). Today a holiday resort and centre for surrounding area. Area: 14,000 d. Pop.: 30,000. **History** Founded between 17 and 22 CE by Herod Antipas on ruins of Rakkath, a city in Naphtali tribal allotment. Named after Roman emperor Tiberius and fortified in anticipation of Jewish Revolt against Rome, but surrendered without a fight and was therefore not destroyed. Important spiritual centre during Mishnah and Talmud Periods (Roman and Byzantine Periods). The Sanhedrin moved here from Zippori (Sepphoris) and it was seat of a major academy of Jewish learning which contributed to the compilation of the Jerusalem Talmud. During this period it expanded S until it joined with the adjacent city of Ḥammat. In mid-4th c. it hosted a Samaritan community and in 5th c. its population was augmented by a number of Christians. During Persian invasion (614) the Jews of Tiberias aided the Christian residents in their struggle against Byzantium. In 628 the Byzantines returned, conquered the country and slaughtered Jews, particularly those of Tiberias. Most important Christian centre after Jerusalem on eve of Arab conquest. Capital of

TIBERIAS

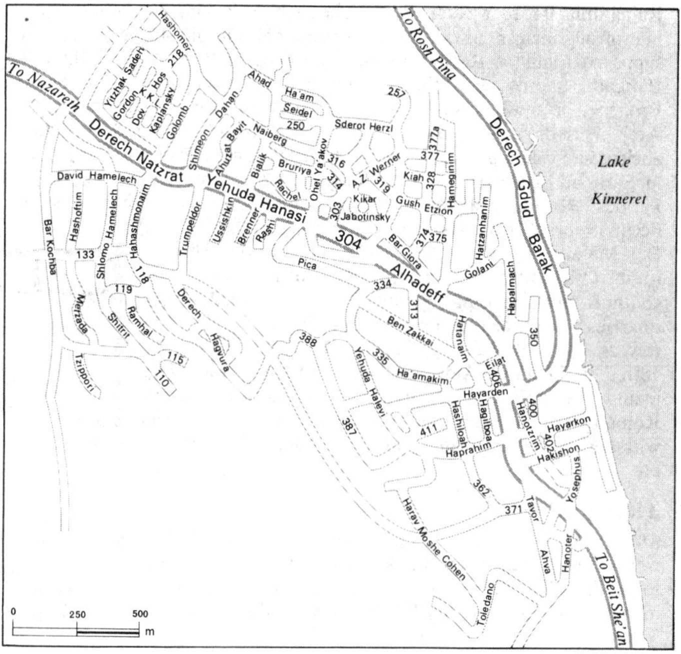

Galilee and important Jewish centre after Arab conquest (636). Between 8th and 11th c. it was an episcopal see for Greeks and Syrian Jacobites. Seat of scholars and poets and masoretes (compilers of Hebrew Bible vocalization). Taken in 1099 by Crusaders and destroyed in 1187 after great battle between Moslems and Crusaders. Popular city for Christians during Crusader Period since Christians believed Jesus lived here. Remained desolate until 1560 when Sultan Suleiman I (the Magnificent) granted Tiberias and its environs to Don Joseph Nasi who rebuilt it and planned it as an independent Jewish city. He was thwarted in his attempt by hostile Arabs and Turks. The Bedouin sheikh, Dahir el 'Amr, who conquered the Galilee in 1740, rebuilt Tiberias and the city walls and its Jewish community began to grow. In 1777 a group of Hasidic Jews from Europe settled here. It was hit by a severe earthquake in 1837. When Jewish settlement escalated throughout the country at the turn of the century, Tiberias benefited too, and by 1917 Tiberias had a Jewish majority. But disaster soon struck: in 1934 it was struck by a heavy flood, and again during the 1936-1939 Disturbances the Jews of Tiberias were attacked by their Arab neighbours. In War of Independence, Tiberias was the first mixed Jewish–Arab city to establish a Jewish local authority. There are many sites of significance and interest in Tiberias and environs: Ḥamme Teverya (Tiberias Hot Springs), a Crusader church, tombs of famous sages, remains of ancient walls and structures etc. **Ḥamme Teverya** Two km. to S are the hot springs famous in ancient times for their therapeutic properties and are still used today. **Crusader church of St. Peter** Crusader church on Kinneret restored by Franciscans in 19th and 20th c. The apse is shaped like the keel of a boat, perhaps intended to commemorate St. Peter who was a fisherman here when he met Jesus. **Tomb of Rabbi Meir Ba'al HaNes** White domed building, near hot springs, houses tomb of Rabbi Meir Ba'al HaNes. Every year on 14 Iyar a popular festival is held here. **Tomb of**

Maimonides (Rambam) Maimonides died in 1206 in Egypt and was buried in Tiberias. Near his tomb (in lower city) are supposed tombs of Rabbi Johanan b. Zakkai, Rabbi Eliezer b. Hyrcanus and other sages. Site of pilgrimages, festivities and a memorial. On hill slope, *199:243*, is supposed tomb of Rabbi 'Aqiva. **Tel Raqqat** *199:245* Site of Biblical Rakkath. Sherds and other remains indicate occupation from Early Bronze Age until Persian Period and later in Roman, Byzantine and Arab Periods. **'En Qozer** Ancient site, *198:245*, alongside another ancient site called in Arabic Sidrat el Bustan. Sherds indicate occupation in Early and Late Bronze Age, Early Iron Age, Roman and Byzantine Periods. **Hurbat Bet Ma'on** Ruins within Tiberias. Sherds indicate occupation in Bronze Age and Iron Age. Perhaps site of Bet Ma'on, city from Second Temple Period. Sheikh's tomb. Other sites of interest: remains of a tower and the southern city gate, long aqueduct (Berenice's canal), caves, quarries and other remains from Roman Period; Crusader towers and walls built by Tancred (1100) and repaired in 18th c. by Dahir el 'Amr and later by Ibrahim Pasha. Digs in and around the city have uncovered an ancient cemetery, Roman bath, mosaic floor, remains of 5th c. synagogue with central hall and side rooms, sarcophagi, inscriptions, etc.

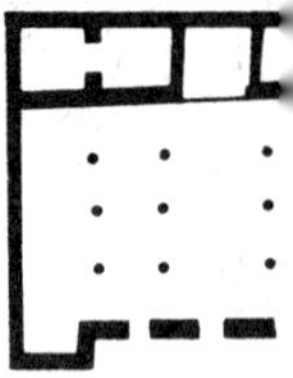

● **Tidhar** *115:087*

Moshav in Negev 7 km. N of Ofaqim. Named after plane tree mentioned in passage "I will set in the desert the cypress, the *plane* and the pine together" (Isa. 41:19). The cypress (*berosh*) and pine (*te'ashur*) are names of neighbouring settlements. Founded 1953. Area: 1,000 d. Pop.: 370.

● **Tifraḥ** *119:082*

Moshav in N Negev 3 km. W of HaNasi junction. Name taken from passage "the desert shall rejoice and *blossom*" (Isa. 35:1). Founded 1949. Area: 5,000 d. Pop.: 450.

● **Timmorim** *127:124*

Moshav shittufi on Coastal Plain 1 km. S of Mal'akhi junction. Name means a decoration or carving in shape of palm leaf or palm trunk. Mentioned in Bible in I Kings 6:29; II Chron. 3:5. Founded 1954. Area: 5,300 d. Pop.: 300.

Timna' *(Gen. 36:40) 147:907*

Copper mine in 'Arava, 25 km. N of Elat. A mining company began operating on site of ancient copper mines in 1955 and adopted the Biblical name Timnah which was the name of an Edomite chief. Shut down in 1976 because of fall in copper price, but was re-opened in 1980. **Ancient mines** W of new mines are the ancient ones, popularly known as "King Solomon's Mines". However, archaeological finds indicate that the mines were Egyptian, and were operated chiefly in Late Bronze Age and Iron Age. Surveys have uncovered mining tools, smelting and casting installations within a fortified camp, (*144:909*), slag heaps, storerooms and remains of what was apparently a major town (Ḥurbat Timna' *144:909*). Remains of a small fort, *145:909*, and 2 sanctuaries to the goddess of the earth and the mines — Hathor, were also found alongside King Solomon's Pillars *145:908*. The sanctuaries contained Egyptian implements and inscriptions from 12th-11th c. BCE.

○ **(Et) Tira** (Judean Hills) *161:141*

Arab village (pop.: 500) 9 km. SW of Ramallah.

○ **(Et) Tira** (Sharon) *145:182*

Arab village 7 km. N of Kefar Sava. Mentioned by a 15th c. Arab geographer. Resettled about 200 years ago by residents from Shekhem area. During Disturbances of 1936-1939 and in War of Independence it was used as a base by Arab gangs. By Israel–Jordan Armistice Agreement it was included within boundaries of Israel. Pop.: 10,000.

Tir'an (Tur'an) *185:242*

Arab village in Galilee 3.5 km. W of Golani junction. Pop.: 4,500, mostly Moslem, some Christian. Remains of defensive wall, ancient building stones, caves, cisterns, rock tombs and sherds from Roman Period.

Tirat Karmel *147:240*

Town (with local council) 6 km. S of Haifa. Founded 1949 on site of abandoned village of Tira. Its former inhabitants had harassed Jewish transport during the 1936-1939 Disturbances and at outbreak of War of Independence. The Arab village itself was built on ruins of an ancient settlement. Area of present settlement: 2,900 d. Pop.: 18,000. Within town are remains of Roman aqueduct and burial cave, remains of Crusader fort, St. Jean de Tira, and a mosque built on Byzantine foundations.

Tirat Shalom *129:146*

Farming suburb within Nes Ẓiyyona. Founded 1931 by Yemenite immigrants and named after the 17th c. Yemenite poet Shalem Shabazi.

Tirat Ya'el *190:261*

Private farm off Acre–Safed road alongside *moshav* Shefer. Founded 1952.

Tirat Yehuda *145:158*

Moshav 3 km. NE of Ben-Gurion Airport. Founded 1949 by Hungarian immigrants on abandoned village of et Tira. Area: 2,500 d. Pop.: 440. Abandoned village of et Tira 1.5 km. to the SW is located on site of ancient settlement. Remains were found from Iron Age, Persian, Hellenistic and Byzantine Periods and ruins of caravanserai from Mamluk Period.

Tirat Ẓevi *200:203*

Kibbutz 3 km. S of Bet She'an. Named after Rabbi Ẓevi Kalischer, harbinger of Zionism. Founded 1937 as a "stockade and tower" settlement by immigrants from Poland and Germany. Attacked in its first year by Arab bands and by Kaukji's forces during War of Independence.

Area: 8,000 d. Pop.: several hundred. Fragments of a Roman road and milestone were found within the kibbutz as well as a mosaic floor and sherds from Roman Period. Nearby, at foot of Tel Kefar Qarnayim, remains of a 4th c. synagogue and Early Bronze dug-out tomb were discovered as well as Middle Bronze and Hellenistic remains.

Tirosh *139:128*

Moshav in Lakhish region 10 km. E of Re'em junction. Name means new wine. Founded 1955. Pop.: 520.

Tiv'on → Qiryat Tiv'on

Toḥelet *136:156*

Rural settlement on Coastal Plain 2.5 km. SE of Bet Dagan junction. Name means hope. Founded 1951 on abandoned village lands of Safiriya. Pop.: 310.

Tomer *191:158*

Moshav in Jordan Valley off Jericho–Adam Bridge road, 3 km. S of Peẓa'el.

Trappist Monastery → Emmaus, Latrun

o **Tuba** ⁂ *206:263*

Bedouin village in Galilee 6 km. SW of Benot Ya'aqov Bridge, alongside Kefar HaNasi. Name means clay brick used for building houses. Founded 400 years ago by Bedouin from Homs district in Syria. Pop.: 1,600, mainly Bedouin of the el Heib tribe and some Christians. The villagers aided the Israel Defence Forces during War of Independence and its youth serve in the army.

o **Tubas** *184:191*

Arab village in Samarian Hills 12 km. NE of Shekhem. Believed to be site of Biblical city of Thebez (Judg. 9:50 ff.). Pop.: 5,300, mostly Moslem and some Christian. Military cemetery for Jordanian soldiers who fell in region during Six-Day War.

□ **Tulkarm** *152:190*

Arab city between Samarian Hills and Sharon 16 km. E of Netanya. The name originates from a distortion of the Aramaic *tur karma* (mountain of vines). Inhabited since Roman times. Mentioned in Samaritan writings as centre for Samaritan towns. Used as a base by Arab gangs during 1936-1939 Disturbances and by Iraqi forces during War of Independence. Taken by the Israel Defence Forces during Six-Day War. Pop.: 10,000, mostly Moslem and some Christians. Agricultural school founded in 1930 and financed from estate of Jewish philanthropist, Kadoori, and named after him. Within city and its environs, tombs from Early Bronze Age and various remains from Roman Period were discovered: building foundations, cisterns, wine presses, rock-cut tombs, a mausoleum and a stone altar with Greek inscription.

o **Tura el Gharbiyya** *164:208*

Small Arab village in Samarian Hills 14 km. W of Jenin.

o **Turmus 'Ayya** *177:160*

Arab village in Samarian Hills 4 km. SE of Ma'ale Levona. Pop.: 1,600. Greek inscribed lintels and Roman sarcophagi have been found here.

Tushiyya *106:093*

Rural centre in Negev 5 km. NW of Netivot. Name means wisdom. Founded 1958. Pop.: 300. Services neighbouring settlements: Zimrat, Kefar Maymon, Shuva, Shoqeda.

Tuval *173:259*

Industrial village in Galilee 6 km. NW of Karmi'el. Named after the Biblical Tubal-cain, "he was the forger of all instruments of bronze and iron" (Gen. 4:22).

Tuwayyil edh Dhiyab *197:185*

Ancient site in Samarian Hills SE of Tubas. Remains of a single structure, apparently from Hellenistic Period.

(Et) Tuweiri *162.269*

Ruin in Galilee 2 km. E of Nahariyya, in fields of kibbutz Kabri. Remains from Roman and Byzantine Periods. A fragment of a grille with Greek inscription — apparently remnant of a synagogue or church — was found here.

U

(El) 'Ubeidiyya — 177:125

Bedouin village on fringe of Judean Desert 9 km. E of Bethlehem. Pop.: 1,400. Tomb of Sheikh Ḥalifa. Near village is St. Theodosius' monastery (see separate entry). Name from Ibn Abeid — Arabic for son of the servant, since the Bedouin who live here are supposedly the offspring of Greek guards and servants who protected the nearby monasteries during the Byzantine Period.

Udala — 176:173

Small Arab village in Samaria 6 km. S of Shekhem. Pop.: 400. According to Jewish and Samaritan traditions, the graves of high priest Eleazar and his son Phinehas are located here.

Udim — 135:185

Moshav in Sharon 5 km. S of Netanya. The name from passage in Zech. 3:2, "a brand plucked from the fire," commemorates its founders, survivors of the Holocaust. Founded 1947. Pop.: 400. Nearby are remains of an Israelite fort. Signs of an ancient settlement were also found near the artificial breach cut through the gravel ridge W of *moshav* to Naḥal Poleg.

'Ulam ('Aulam) — 197:230

Ruins of abandoned village in Galilee 4 km. S of Yavne'el. Built on ruins of ancient settlement, perhaps the Ulam mentioned in Talmud and Onomasticon of Eusebius. Building foundations and stones from Roman Period and part of an ancient olive oil press was found nearby. Village was resettled early in 19th c. by Moslem emigrants from Algeria.

Umm 'Allas — 151:112

Arab village 10 km. NW of Hebron. Pop.: 500.

Umm 'Asla (Mughar Abu 'Asla) — 176:122

Arab village on border of Judean Desert 8 km. E of Bethlehem.

Umm Buteine (Umm Betina) — 138:076

Seat of Bedouin court of Negev 7 km. NE of Be'er Sheva'. Built in 1955.

Umm el Faḥm — 164:213

Arab city above 'Iron Valley (Wadi 'Ara) E of Ḥadera–'Afula road. Name means mother of the coals, which hints at former occupation of inhabitants. Traditionally believed to have been founded 500 years ago by settlers from Bet Guvrin area. In time it expanded beyond the valley. During 1936-1939 Disturbances it served as a base for armed bands of Arab terrorists who fought against British and Jews. A large military operation in 1939 destroyed the bands. In 1948 village was controlled by Iraqi army and then by Jordanians. By Armistice Agreement it was included within Israel. Pop.: 18,000, all Moslem. City has 4 mosques. 'Ein Ibrahim and Kh. el Biyar are satellite towns of Umm el Faḥm.

Umm el Ghanam — 187:231

Bedouin village at foot of Mt. Tabor. Name means mother of flocks. Inhabitants are from the Sa'aide and Shibli tribes. Pop.: 400.

Umm Hajarein *169:274*

Ruins of a town 8 km. E of Rosh HaNiqra junction. Remains of houses, defensive walls, workshops, wine presses, mills and cemetery. Sherds indicate habitation from Hasmonean Period until Middle Ages. Nearby is Kh. Qarqara.

Umm Khalid *137:192*

Remains of Roger the Lombard's Crusader fortress built on a more ancient site, now situated within city limits of Netanya. Finds include mosaic floor, remains of olive oil press, defensive walls, column fragments, 2 cisterns and a large collection of flint implements. Inhabited in Mesolithic Period and from Roman–Byzantine times till Middle Ages.

Umm Khashaba (Ḥazzan) *220:258*

Ruins of Roman–Byzantine settlement on Golan Heights 8 km. SE of Qaẓrin. Abandoned Arab village, Shabba was built on its ruins. Many dolmens with interconnecting walls.

Umm Nukheila *102:090*

Byzantine ruin in Negev 3 km. S of Be'eri. One of many ruins spaced out over half km. interval along Naḥal Gerar, which probably served as farm units. Remains of Byzantine church.

Umm el Qanatir *219:250*

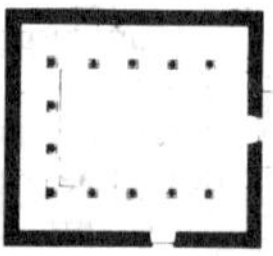

Abandoned Arab village on Golan Heights 15 km. SE of Qaẓrin. Spring in village called 'Ein es Sufeira. Name of village means mother of arches, referring to arched structure built over spring. Believed to be site of town of Qamattirya mentioned in Talmud. Remains of synagogue from Roman and Byzantine Periods.

Umm el Qatan *194:184*

Settlement ruins in Samaria 13 km. SE of Tubas. Remains of buildings from Iron Age, Byzantine Period and Middle Ages.

Umm el Qutuf *156:208*

Arab village in Samaria 7 km. E of Pardes Ḥanna at entrance to 'Iron Valley (Wadi 'Ara). Name means mother of scholars. Founded 50 years ago by inhabitants of neighbouring village, Barta'a, on ruins of Crusader fortress. Pop.: 300.

Umm er Rukab *194:181*

Remains of solitary Iron Age structure built of unhewn stones, in Samaria 14 km. SE of Tubas.

Umm Ṣafa *165:157*

Arab village 12 km. N of Ramallah. Pop.: 200. Several ancient structures and in some village houses ancient building stones have been re-used. Sherds found from Byzantine, Medieval and Ottoman Periods. **Umm Ṣafa forest** located 2 km. to W is made up of remains of an ancient forest as well as more recent flora. Area: 800 d. Principal trees: pine, artubus and oak. Noted for rare plant growth of shrubs and flowers and large variety of birds. Several springs.

Umm Tabun *110:105*

Ruins 1.5 km. NW of Sederot. Remains of what seems to have been a 2nd c. Roman villa, with mosaic of crosses composed of small flowers. Many man-made cisterns in area.

Umm et Tut *182:204*

Arab village in Samaria 6 km. SE of Jenin. Name means mother of the berries. Pop.: 100.

Umm el 'Umdan *200:198*

Four Roman milestones, one with Roman inscription, alongside Jordan Valley road 1 km. N of Meḥola.

Uri'el *129:135*

Village for the blind in Gedera. Established by Malben in 1949, it had a straw products factory. Today it is one of the neighbourhoods of Gedera.

○ **'Urif** *171:174*

Arab village (pop.: 650) in Samarian Hills 8 km. SW of Shekhem.

★ **Urim** *104:079*

Collective settlement (*qevuẓa*) in Negev 9 km. W of Ofaqim. *Urim* means source of light and the name refers symbolically to the spark in the "darkness" during Mandatory times when land purchases were restricted. Founded 1946 (11 Tishri 5707) as part of settlement scheme for 11 pioneer groups in the Negev. First located further S near Gevulot, but in 1948 moved to present site. Pop.: 600.

○ **'Uṣarin** *179:170*

Arab village (pop.: 350) 10 km. S of Shekhem.

★ **Usha** *161:244*

Collective settlement (*qevuẓa*) in Zevulun Valley near Qiryat Ata. Name derives from ancient city of Usha, whose name is identified with nearby Kh. Husha. Founded 1937 as "stockade and tower" settlement. During War of Independence Usha and neighbouring Ramat Yoḥanan were attacked by Druze regiment of "Liberation Army". Pop.: 400. **Ancient Usha,** *163:244*, 3 km. from modern village on site of abandoned village of Kh. Husha. Ruins of fortified city from Roman and Byzantine Periods. Seat of Sanhedrin after suppression of Bar Kokhba revolt. After abrogation of Hadrian's restrictive decrees, sages convened synod and promulgated the Usha Taqqanot (regulations). Among the sages of Usha were Rabbi Judah b. Ilai and Rabbi Yose b. Ḥalafta. Hebrew seal found here from 8th c. BCE.

∴ **'Uyun Ḥamud** *217:254*

Abandoned village on Golan Heights 5 km. NE of Ramot. Built over Byzantine ruins which were reinhabited in Ottoman Period. Ancient building stones had been re-used in village houses. W of village are groups of dolmens.

● **'Uza** *127:111*

Moshav S of Qiryat Gat, off road to Be'er Sheva'. Name taken from passage "Summon thy might, O God; show thy *strength*, O God, thou who hast wrought for us" (Ps. 68:28). Founded 1950 in an area known as the Faluja Pocket during War of Independence. (An Egyptian brigade was encircled here forming an enemy pocket.) Area: 6,800 d. Pop.: 760.

○ **'Uzeir** *181:244*

Arab village in Galilee 8 km. NW of Golani junction. Pop.: 830. Believed to be site of Kefar 'Uzi'el, residence of the priestly clan of Abijah, after destruction of Second Temple.

W

Wadi el Fari'a

Perennial watercourse in E Samaria. Empties into Jordan River 7 km. S of Adam Bridge, *199:161*. One theory posits this to be the Brook of Cherith where Elijah hid from Ahab.

o **Wadi Fukin** *160:124*

Arab village S of Mevo Betar, 10 km. W of Bethlehem. During War of Independence it was taken by the Israel Defence Forces, but was returned to Jordan under Armistice Agreement.

Wadi Ḥamam *196:248*

Bedouin settlement in Naḥal Arbel 7 km. NW of Tiberias. Name means pigeon's stream. Established 1948. Pop.: 1,200.

Wadi el Ḥaramiyya

Narrow pass in Samarian Hills 15 km. N of Ramallah, between villages of 'Ein Sinya *172:153* and Sinjil *175:160*. Name means robber's stream. In the past it was used as a hideout by highwaymen. Off the road are remains of a Crusader watch-tower and a British Mandatory police fort.

Wadi el Qilt *

Watercourse in Judean Desert. Originates alongside Beit Ḥanina, N of Jerusalem, and empties into Jordan River 10 km. SE of Jericho, *202:137*. Fed by a few springs, the larger ones being 'Ein Fara, 'Ein Fawwar and 'Ein Qilt. An aqueduct runs along the watercourse and irrigates the Jericho region. In the river bed are many caves which were used by hermits through the ages. Clinging to the cliffs overlooking the ravine are the monasteries of St. George, 'Ein Fara, and Deir el Banat.

Wadi Samiya → Kokhav HaShaḥar

Wadi eṣ Ṣarar → Naḥal Soreq

Wadi esh Shallala → Naḥal Besor

Wadi Ẓafa → Naḥal Yehudiyya

Wardon *129:118*

Rural centre 5 km. N of Qiryat Gat. First called Menuḥa but in 1965 changed to Wardon after Julius Rosenwald, US Jewish leader and philanthropist. Provides services to neighbouring settlements of Segula, Menuḥa, Naḥla.

∴ **Wasit** *218:283*

Abandoned village on Golan 8 km. W of Quneitra. Name means middle. One time headquarters of Bedouin tribe el Fadl and residence of its chief sheikh. Abandoned in Six-Day War. Alongside village is a pile of capitals and granite stones brought here from other sites.

Way of Shur → Derekh Shur

Way of the Arabah → Derekh Ha'Arava

Way of the Atharim → Derekh HaAtarim

Way of the Hauranites → Derekh HaḤoranim

Way of the Land of the Philistines → Derekh Ereẓ Pelishtim

Way of the Mountain → Derekh HaHar

■ **Weizmann Institute** ▙ *131:146*

Scientific institute in Reḥovot. Founded in 1934 by the Sieff family from London in memory of their son Daniel and originally called the Daniel Sieff Research Institute. In 1944, to celebrate the 70th birthday of Dr. Chaim Weizmann, the first major building of the enlarged institute was planned. It became the Weizmann Institute of Science in 1949 and today it is a vast scientific complex of international repute in the fields of natural and life sciences. The institute is part of **Yad Chaim Weizmann**, a memorial to Dr. Weizmann, and site of his grave.

■ **Weradim** *137:181*

Educational institute 10 km. S of Netanya, alongside *moshav* Bene Ẓiyyon. Founded 1955, it belongs to Kibbutz HaArẓi–HaShomer Ḥa Ẓa'ir movement.

Wered HaGalil ◆ ⋏ ⓝ *202:257*

Community settlement in Upper Galilee 13 km. N of Tiberias off Tiberias–Rosh Pinna road. Established 1980. Nearby is privately owned horse ranch, established 1961, restaurant and guest house.

Wered Yeriḥo (Miẓpe Yeriḥo "B") *190:135*

Community settlement in Judean Desert off Jerusalem–Jericho road 2 km. NW of en Nabi Musa. Established 1979.

■ **Wingate Institute** *135:186*

Institute of higher learning in physical education, on Sharon coast 8 km. S of Netanya. Named after Charles Orde Wingate, well known British soldier and friend of Zionism killed in Burma during WWII. Founded 1955. The school offers courses for sports instructors and boarding facilities.

Y

• **Ya'ad** *173:253*

Industrial *moshav shittufi* in Galilee 8 km. SW of Karmi'el. Founded 1974 by group of professionals. Pop.: 90.

Ya'af *147:186*

Rural centre in Sharon 10 km. SE of Netanya. Established 1968, it services the settlements 'Azri'el, Kefar Ya'beẓ and Porat.

• **Ya'ara** *167:274*

Moshav in Galilee 8 km. SE of Rosh HaNiqra. Name derives from word *ya'ar* (forest) owing to the many forests nearby. Founded 1950. Pop.: 350.

Ya'ar Ḥadera → Berekhat Ya'ar

Ya'ar HaQedoshim → Martyrs' Forest

Ya'ar Herẓl → Herẓl Forest

Ya'ar Odem (Forest)

Large nature reserve on Golan Heights, stretching 11 km. from Mas'ada to kibbutz El Rom. Typical mediterranean flora. A group of pits in the reserve (with diameters of between 30 to 200 m.) were formed by volcanic action as a result of gas explosion but without lava.

Ya'arot HaKarmel *151:236*

Rest home, formerly a farm, off Bet Oren–'Atlit road. Founded 1934. During 1936-1939 Disturbances it was attacked several times by Arab gangs. Served as Haganah training base before establishment of State.

YA'AROT HAKARMEL

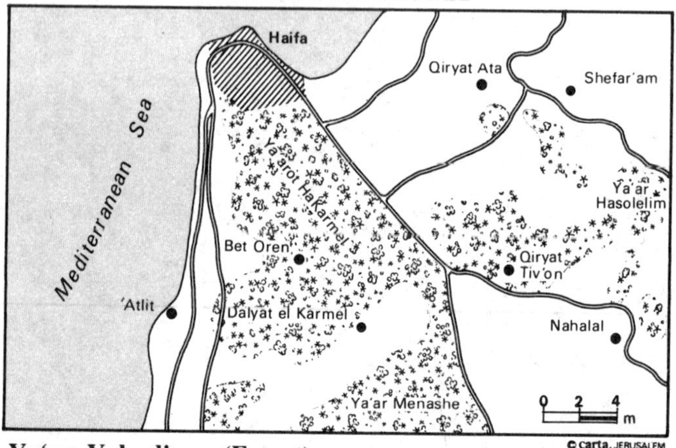

Ya'ar Yahudiyya (Forest).

Large nature reserve on Golan Heights, stretching from Giv'at Bazaq to Biq'at Bet Ẓayda. Area: 66,000 d. Tabor oaks, local plum trees and Atlantic terebinths.

○ **Ya'bad** *166:205*

Arab village in Samarian Hills 15 km. W of Jenin. During 1936-1939 Disturbances Arab gangs used it as a base camp. Pop.: 5,000. Ancient ruins alongside village.

○ **Yabrud** *173:154*

Arab village (pop.: 300) 9 km. NE of Ramallah off road leading to Shekhem. Built on settlement ruins from Iron Age, Persian Period and from Roman Period until Middle Ages. Discovered within village: wine presses, an ancient altar ("high place") strewn with stone pieces obviously used as counters for a game, ancient building stones and other remains. To the N are ruins of a Crusader fortress, Burj Bardawil (see entry).

■ **Yad Binyamin** *133:134*

Religious educational centre in Judean Foothills 4 km. SE of Gedera. Founded 1962 and named after Rabbi Benjamin Minz. Area: 400 d. Pop.: 350.

★ **Yad Mordekhay** *108:111*

Kibbutz on Coastal Plain 10 km. S of Ashqelon, off road to Gaza. Named after Mordecai Anielewicz, commander of Warsaw Ghetto revolt during WWII. Founded 1943 on lands of Ḥarbiyya by HaShomer HaẒa'ir group from Poland. During War of Independence its settlers halted advance of Egyptian army in 5 days of bitter fighting. However, they had to abandon kibbutz and it was only retaken a half year later. Area: 5,000 d. Pop.: 600. Remains of its shelled water tower was left as it was after the fighting in order to commemorate the heroic stand of the kibbutz. Park in memory of the fallen, statue of Mordecai Anielewicz (erected in 1951 by sculptor Nathan Rapaport), model of 1948 battle site and museum of Holocaust and ghetto resistance and military history of Negev. **Remains** On hill to W of kibbutz, *108:110*, a 1st and 2nd c. tomb was uncovered. Flint implements and coins from Hellenistic to Ottoman Periods were found in vicinity.

★ **Yad Ḥanna** *150:192*

Kibbutz between Samarian Hills and Sharon Plain 2 km. NW of Tulkarm. Named after Ḥanna Szenes sent by Haganah on mission to Hungary during WWII. She was captured and executed by the Nazis in 1944. Founded 1950 within military outpost "61", a battle site during War of Independence. When Mapam split in 1953, the kibbutz split too and some members left and founded a new kibbutz nearby called Yad Ḥanna Szenes (disbanded 1972). Pop.: 120. Area: 2,600 d.

● **Yad HaShemona** *159:135*

Moshav shittufi in Judean Hills 3 km. W of Abu Ghosh. Named after 8 (*shemona*) Jews held by Nazis in Finland during the Holocaust. Residents are Finnish Christians who immigrated in 1971. Pop.: 30.

Yad Kennedy *162:128*

Memorial on hill summit 825 m. above sea level in Jerusalem Hills near *moshav* 'Aminadav. Inaugurated 1966 in memory of US President John F. Kennedy who was assassinated in 1963. The 7 m. high round structure gives the impression of a tree stump. It has 51 columns symbolizing the 50 states and capitol of USA. Inside is a bust of Kennedy and around the interior are the 51 official seals.

● **Yad Natan** *122:117*

Moshav in Judean Foothills 6 km. NW of Peluggot junction. Named after Otto (Nathan) Komoly, Hungarian Zionist leader, killed in 1945. Founded 1953 on abandoned village lands of Beit 'Affa, which served as Egyptian military post opposite Negba during War of Independence. Pop.: 230. Area: 4,000 d.

● **Yad Rambam** *140:145*

Moshav in Judean Foothills 5 km. SE of Ramla. Founded 1955 by Moroccan Jews from Fez and named after the Rambam (Maimonides) to commemorate the 750th anniversary of his death. Area: 3,000 d. Pop.: 630.

Yad Weizmann → Weizmann Institute

Ya'el *179:216*

Rural centre 6 km. S of 'Afula. Named after Jael, wife of Heber the Kenite (Judg. 4:17 ff.). Services neighbouring settlements of Avital, Metav and Perazon.

Yafa **(Yafit en Naṣra)** *176:232*

Arab village 1 km. SW of Nazareth. Pop.: 6,000, 69% Moslems, rest Christian. **Yafia'** Site of ancient city of Japhia mentioned in Bible and in ancient Egyptian documents. During Jewish Revolt against Rome it was a large village fortified by Joseph b. Mattathias and destroyed by the Romans. Within Arab village is tel of ancient Japhia. Near village church are remains of a 4th c. synagogue with a mosaic floor depicting Israelite tribal symbols. In the church is a lintel incised with seven-branched candelabrum (*menorah*).

● **Yafit** *194:163*

Moshav in Jordan Valley 3 km. S of Qeren Sartaba. Named after Colonel Yossi Yaffe, active in capture of Old City of Jerusalem during Six-Day War and killed in training. Founded 1979.

● **Yagel** *138:155*

Moshav 2 km. W of Ben-Gurion Airport. Name taken from Biblical passage "When the Lord restores the fortunes of his people, Jacob shall *rejoice*" (Ps. 14:7). Founded 1950. Area: 1,300 d. Pop.: 370. **Giv'at Dani** (Kh. es Sibtari) Within *moshav* is large Byzantine ruin. War of Independence battle site of operation "Dani", hence Hebrew name.

★ **Yagur** *157:238*

Kibbutz in Haifa Bay at foot of E slopes of the Karmel, 12 km. SE of Haifa. Name derives from neighbouring Arab village of Yajur. Founded 1922 and in 1933 joined by group of Polish immigrants becoming (for a time) the largest kibbutz in the country. Served as important Haganah and Palmaḥ base and hideout for "illegal" immigrants. On "Black Saturday" (29 June 1946) British forces searched the kibbutz and uncovered the central Haganah arms cache. Area: 10,000 d. Pop.. 1,200.

★ **Yahel** *162:943*

Kibbutz in 'Arava 70 km. N of Elat. Name means "will pitch a tent" (Isa. 13:20). Founded 1976 by group from Progressive Judaism movement.

∴ **Yahudiyya** *216:260*

Abandoned village built on ancient Jewish settlement ruins on Golan Heights, 10 km. NE of mouth of Jordan River. In order to disguise its Jewish origins the Syrians called it Ya'arbiyya. Within village are remains of a walled Roman and Byzantine settlement. According to one opinion, this is site of Sogane, one of cities fortified by Joseph b. Mattathias in preparation for the Jewish Revolt against Rome. Five or six courses of the wall have been preserved and there are remains of a tower and vaulted adjoining rooms. Remains of contemporary synagogue, columns and capitals were also found as well as Stone Age flint implements. To the W is the Yahudiyya forest reserve with Tabor oaks, jujubes and other trees.

● **Yakhini** *111:099*

Moshav in Negev 4 km. S of Sederot. Named after a member of Simeon tribe who settled in this region. Founded 1950. Pop.: 600. Area: 4,000 d.

∴ **Yalu** *152:138*

Ruins of abandoned village 2 km. NW of Sha'ar HaGay, within Canada Park in Ayyalon Valley. Site of ancient city of Ajalon (Josh. 19:42). Remains indicate it was continuously inhabited from Early Bronze Age until Ottoman Period. Remains of Crusader fortress, stone mound (Tell el Qauqa) and Roman water system.

Yam HaGalil → Lake Kinneret

Yam HaMelaḥ → Dead Sea

Yam HaTikhon → Mediterranean Sea

○ **Yamma (Yaḥam)** *153:197*

Arab village in Samarian Hills 6 km. N of Tulkarm. Pop.: 900. Believed to be site of Yaḥam, a city on ancient route from Egypt to the Fertile Crescent. Mentioned in account of Thutmose III's campaign on his way to Megiddo (15th c. BCE).

Yam Suf → Red Sea

○ **(El) Yamun** *171:210*

Arab village in Samarian Hills 7 km. NW of Jenin. Pop.: 4,500.

○ **Yanuaḥ** *173:265*

Druze village in Galilee 4 km. SW of Ma'alot. Believed to be site of Janoah, mentioned in Bible (II Kings 15:29) and Talmud. Pop.: 1,500. Village has holy tomb called Sit Shamsa (the lady Shamsa).

○ **Yanun** *183:172*

Arab village (pop.: 80) 12 km. SE of Shekhem. Inhabitants are Moslem from Bosnia who immigrated in 1878. On E hill is tomb of en Nabi Nun. According to Arab tradition, tomb of Nun, father of Joshua.

● **Yanuv** *145:190*

Moshav 5 km. SE of Sharon junction. Founded 1950 by Tunisian immigrants on lands of the landlord Nabulsi. Area: 2,000 d. Pop.: 500.

★ **Yaqum** *135:184*

Kibbutz in Sharon 10 km. N of Herzliyya. Founded 1947 on lands of ez Zababida, next to swamps of Wadi Faliq (Naḥal Poleg). Before 1948 a secret Haganah industrial workshop was run at the kibbutz. Area: 3,000 d. Pop.: 450. **Antiquities** N of kibbutz is the Naḥal Poleg reserve with a Roman gate located at the point where the stream cuts through the gravel ridge. Alongside it are remains of Canaanite fort.

∴ **(El) Yaquṣa** *218:240*

Abandoned village on Golan Heights 10 km. E of 'En Gev. The Battle of the Yarmouk was fought near here in 636, between Moslems and Byzantines. It ended with a Moslem victory which opened the way for the Arab conquest. Tradition has it that the village was built to commemorate the victory.

Yarden → Jordan River

• Yardena 203:219

Moshav in Jordan Valley 10 km. NE of Bet She'an. Located alongside Jordan River, hence its name. Founded 1952 by Kurdish immigrants as part of movement from "city to settlement". During War of Attrition (1967-1970) it was often the object of terrorist attacks from across the border with Jordan. Area: 3,200 d. Pop.: several hundred.

• Yarḥiv *147:173*

Moshav between Samarian Hills and Sharon Plain 4 km. S of Qalqilya. Name taken from Biblical passage "When the Lord your God *enlarges* your territory" (Deut. 12:20). Founded 1949 by demobilized Israeli soldiers, members of a group called Simḥa. The *moshav* was formerly called Simḥa. Until Six-Day War was right on Jordan border. Area: 2,100 d. Pop.: 530.

Yarmouk River

Largest river in Transjordan. Originates in the Bashan, flows along a narrow gorge which divides the Golan and Gil'ad Mts. and empties into Jordan River S of Lake Kinneret. Mentioned in Hebrew sources from Roman Period. In 636 the Arabs defeated a Byzantine force in a battle on the banks of the Yarmouk which lay Palestine open to conquest. After WWI it became the boundary between the British and the French Mandatory territories. In 1935 Pinḥas Rutenberg built the Naharayim power station where the Yarmouk enters the Jordan River. During the War of Independence the Jordanian Legion captured the Naharayim area and the power station ceased to operate. In 1958 the Jordanian government launched a project to divert the waters of the Yarmouk but the project was not completed on account of the Six-Day War. **Yarmukian Culture** Alongside the Yarmouk, near to kibbutz Sha'ar HaGolan, remains of Neolithic habitation were found. Now referred to as the Yarmukian Culture.

• Yarqona *140:172*

Moshav in Sharon 4 km. S of Kefar Sava. Founded 1932. Area: 600 d. Pop.: 140.

Yarqon Bridge *131:167*

Remains of bridge and dam on Yarqon River near Ramat Gan. Its foundations date from the Roman Period. Bridge mentioned in Crusader and Mamluk documents.

Yarqon River *(Josh. 19:46)*

River on Coastal Plain originating in Rosh Ha'Ayin springs and emptying into Mediterranean N of Tel Aviv. Tortuous course (length: 30 km.) and called by Arabs el 'Awja (the twisted one). Many tributaries, important of which are Naḥal Ayyalon (Wadi Muṣrara) and Naḥal Shillo (Wadi Deir Balut). Mentioned in Bible as boundary between tribes of Dan and Ephraim. Along its banks are mounds of ancient settlements: Tell Qasile, Tell el Kudadi, Tell Jarisha, Tell Abu Zeitun and others. During WWI it was a battleground in the fighting between Turks and British. In commemoration 3 memorials were built: one at the river mouth, one near Giv'at Hill, and one close to Ramat Gan stadium. In 1952 the Yarqon–Negev project — a water carrier from the Yarqon to the Negev — was completed. This scheme eventually became part of the National Water Carrier. **Yarqon Park** Near mouth of Yarqon in N Tel Aviv. The large park covers both banks of the river and a new bridge joins the 2 areas.

• Yashresh *136:147*

Moshav in Judean Foothills 3 km. S of Ramla. Name taken from Biblical passage "In days to come Jacob *shall take root*" (Isa. 27:6). Founded 1950. Area: 2,500 d. Pop.: 450

○ **Yaṣid** *176:189*

Arab village (pop.: 800) in Samarian Hills 8 km. N of Shekhem. Site of ancient Yezet mentioned in Samarian Ostraca. Remains of habitation from Iron Age, Persian, Byzantine, Medieval and Ottoman Periods.

○ **Yasuf** *172:168*

Arab village (pop.: 500) 12 km. S of Shekhem. Mentioned in Samaritan Book of Joshua. Believed to be site of a settlement mentioned in Samarian Ostraca. Also recorded in writings of 13th c. Arab geographer. Remains from Roman and Byzantine Periods. Nearby is Tell Abu Zarad.

★ **Yas'ur** *165:256*

Kibbutz 10 km. E of Acre. Name means a type of sea bird — manx shearwater. Founded 1949. Area: 4,400 d. Pop.: 380. **Tel Bira** Within kibbutz is a mound called in Arabic Tell el Bir el Ghurbi. Apparently site of Rehob in Asher tribal allotment (Josh. 19:30). Appears as Birwa in ancient Egyptian sources. Occupied from end of Early Bronze Age until end of Iron Age. At foot of tel a Canaanite–Israelite cemetery and 2 burial caves were uncovered.

● **Yated** *085:068*

Moshav in Besor region 5 km. SE of Kerem Shalom. Established 1980.

○ **Yatma** **(Yitma)** *175:168*

Arab village (pop.: 700) 14 km. S of Shekhem. Believed to be site of Yitma mentioned in Mishnah (Or. 2:5).

□ **Yatta** **(Yutta)** *(Josh. 15:55)* *158:094*

Arab town in Judean Hills 10 km. S of Hebron. Site of Biblical Juttah, a Levite city in tribal allotment of Judah. Mentioned in 4th c. Onomasticon of Eusebius as a sizeable Jewish village. Pop.: 20,000. Tradition has it that the large local clan of el Muḥaimara has Jewish origins, as they are believed to be descendants of Jews from the Chebar region who settled in the town.

Yattir *153:082*

Civilian outpost in Judean Hills 10 km. NW of Tel 'Arad. Established 1979.

Yavne *(II Chron. 26:6)* *126:142*

Town (with local council) on Coastal Plain 8 km. SW of Reḥovot. Site of ancient Jabneh. Established 1949 by immigrants who temporarily moved into houses of abandoned village. Area: 10,800 d. Pop.: 12,000. **Ancient Jabneh** This Biblical city first called Jabneel, then Jabneh, was located in the tribal allotment of Judah. It was a commercial city off the *via maris* with its own port at the mouth of Naḥal Soreq (Yavne Yam). Mentioned during reign of King Uzziah and called Jamnia in Hellenistic Period. During Hasmonean Period it was taken from Greeks and became an important Jewish spiritual centre after destruction of Second Temple. Rabbi Johanan b. Zakkai established his *yeshiva* Kerem DeYavne here. The reconstituted Sanhedrin sat in Jabneh and here too the foundations for the Mishnah were laid. But after the Bar Kokhba revolt, it fell into decline. In 7th c. it was captured by Moslems; ther Crusaders fortified it in the 12th c. and called it Ybellin. Important city in Mamluk Period but reduced to a small village in Ottoman and British Mandate times. During War of Independence it served as base for Arab forces until taken by the Israel Defence Forces. Sites include the tomb of Raban Gamaliel II, called by Arabs Maqam Abu Hureira, name of one of Muḥammad's companions; remains of Crusader fortress and church which was converted into a mosque by the Mamluks.

Yavne'el *(Josh. 19:33)* *198:234*

Rural town with local council in Galilee 10 km. SW of Tiberias. Named after Biblical city in tribal allotment of Naphtali. Founded as a farming village (*moshava*) by ICA in 1901. Apparently site of Kefar Yamma mentioned in the Talmud. It was one of the HaShomer (association of watchmen) centres during the Second 'Aliyah. After the War of Independence it united with the 3 neighbouring settlements of Semadar, founded 1956, Mishmar HaShelosha, founded 1937, and Bet Gan, founded 1903. Total area: 42,000 d. Pop.: 1,500. **Hurbat Yamma** Finds include Early Bronze Age sherds and large Roman settlement.

Yavne Yam → Ḥurbat Yavne Yam

Yavor *167:255*

Seed farm in Galilee S of Acre–Safed road, 2 km. SE of Aḥihud junction. Name means to sort seeds. Founded 1952 and belongs to HaZera' Company.

Yaẓiẓ *137:141*

Moshav in Judean Foothills 7 km. S of Ramla. Name from Biblical passage "In days to come Jacob shall take root, Israel shall *blossom* and put forth shoots" (Isa. 27:6). Founded 1950. Area: 2,000 d. Pop.: 620.

Yedida *160:135*

Boarding school for special education in Jerusalem Hills, between Abu Ghosh and kibbutz Ma'ale HaḤamisha. Named after Jedidah, mother of King Josiah (II Kings 22:1). Founded 1960. Age group of pupils: 9-17; 150 pupils and staff.

Yedideya *140:194*

Moshav 3 km. N of Sharon junction. Founded 1935 with aid of Alexandrian Jews. Named after philosopher, Philo of Alexandria (50-20 BCE): *philon* in Greek means beloved, and *yedideya* in Hebrew means beloved of God. Area: 3,000 d. Pop.: 350.

Yeḥi'am *170:266*

Kibbutz and Crusader fortress in Galilee 12 km. E of Nahariyya. Kibbutz named after Yeḥi'am Weitz who took part in destruction of railway bridge over Naḥal Keziv in "night of bridges" operation and was killed in action. (See Akhziv.) Founded 1946. During War of Independence it came under siege; operation "Ben Ami" (named after its commander) was launched to break the siege but the hapless convoy of 47 soldiers was ambushed and killed. Area: 10,800 d. Pop.: 550. **Gadin fortress** Located within kibbutz (Arab name: Qal'at Jiddin — fortress of the mighty ones). Ruins of 12th c. Crusader fortress built to defend Acre port. Conquered in turn by Saladin and Richard the Lion-Heart. Destroyed during Moslem conquest and lay in ruins when the traveller Burchard visited it in 1283. Partly restored by Bedouin leader Dahir el 'Amr in 18th c. During Disturbances of 1936-1939 it was used as headquarters of Arab gangs. In War of Independence kibbutz members fortified themselves in the ruin until siege was lifted. Flint tools and Hellenistic remains were found in the vicinity.

Yehud *(Josh. 19:45)* *139:159*

Town 5 km. N of Ben-Gurion Airport. Named after Biblical city Jehud. Founded 1948. Area: 4,000 d. Pop.: 10,000. **History** Ancient site of Jehud included in Dan tribal allotment. Arab village of Yahudiyya was built over ancient ruins. According to Arab tradition, the name originates from Judah son of the patriarch Jacob. In 1882, when Petaḥ Tiqwa suffered from an outbreak of malaria, its inhabitants evacuated their homes and moved to this site from 1882-1893, and called it Yehud.

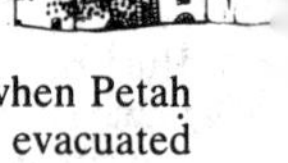

One of the old houses still exists in Savyon. Sherds found within the town from Middle Bronze, Late Iron, Persian and Middle Ages.

Yemin Orde *148:234*

Youth village and religious school on W Karmel alongside 'En Hod. Named after Charles Orde Wingate, British officer and commander of the Special Night Squads of the Haganah during Disturbances of 1936-1939. Founded 1952. Area: 210 d.

Yeroḥam *142:044*

Town in Negev Hills 25 km. S of Be'er Sheva'. Named after ancient city mentioned in list of cities conquered by Shishak, king of Egypt (925 BCE). The ancient name was preserved in the Arabic name Tell Raḥma and Bir Raḥma. In 1951 an immigrant transit camp for Rumanian newcomers was set up here. In 1959 it became a development town and formed its own local council. Pop.: 6,500. **Giv'at Yeroḥam** (*142:045*) Remains from a large settlement that existed here in Nabatean, Roman, Byzantine and Arab Periods. **Be'er Yeroḥam** (Bir Raḥma *141:044*.) According to Arab tradition, this was the well revealed to Hagar after she was sent to the wilderness by Abraham. To the E, *139:044*, is a flood water reservoir.

Yesha' *093:073*

Moshav in Negev 5 km. SW of Magen junction. Name taken from Biblical passage "with mighty *victories* by his right hand" (Ps. 20:6). Founded 1957 after Sinai Campaign by immigrants expelled from Egypt as a result of the war. Area: 2,000 d. Pop.: 200.

Yesodot *137:135*

Moshav shittufi in Judean Foothills 5 km. W of Naḥshon junction. Originally a kibbutz settled in 1946 by refugees of the Holocaust during temporary cease-fire in War of Independence. It was a military outpost until the end of the war and became a *moshav* in 1951. Pop.: 300. Area: 5,800 d. Ancient settlement ruins within *moshav* — Kh. Umm Kalkha.

Yesud HaMa'ala *207:273*

Rural settlement in Ḥula Valley 6 km. N of Benot Ya'aqov Bridge. Name derives from Biblical passage "for on the first day of the first month he *began to go up* from Babylon" (Ezra 7:9). Founded 1883, it was one of the first farming villages in the country. In the early years the settlers suffered much from malaria and Bedouin attacks, and during War of Independence they were often victims of Syrian attacks. Has had its own council since 1950. Area: 12,000 d. Pop.: 1,000.

Yevul *085:066*

Moshav in Besor region 6 km. SE of Kerem Shalom. Established 1980.

Yif'at *172:231*

Kibbutz in Yizre'el Valley alongside Migdal Ha'Emeq. Founded 1952. Area: 11,500 d. Pop.: 800. Kibbutz has museum of ancient agricultural tools. **Antiquities** Roman road with milestone dated 130, rock-cut tomb, and well-preserved 1st-2nd c. mausoleum.

Yiftaḥ *201:281*

Kibbutz in Galilee 9 km. S of Qiryat Shemona. Founded 1948 by members of kibbutz Gevat and Ashdot Ya'aqov from the Palmaḥ Yiftaḥ brigade. Military outpost during War of Independence. Area: 10,400 d. Pop.: several hundred. **Nature reserve** E of kibbutz — Yiftaḥ forest reserve (430 d.).

Yikkon *150:196*

Regional school in Sharon 13 km. E of Netanya.

• Yinnon *129:128*

Moshav in Judean Foothills 2 km. S of Re'em junction. Name derived from passage "his name *shall be continued* as long as the sun" (Ps. 72:17). Founded 1952 on lands of abandoned village of Masmiyya. Pop.: 630. Area: 3,000 d.

Yirka *170:262*

Druze village in Galilee 6 km. NE of Ahihud junction. According to tradition it was named after Husai, the Archite, advisor to King David. Tradition has it that Druze had settled here as early as the 11th c. Pop.: 5,200. Tomb of Nabi es Ṣadiq — attributed to Husai, the Archite, by many Jewish pilgrims who visited the site in the Middle Ages.

★ Yir'on *(Josh. 19:38) 192:275*

Kibbutz in Galilee near Lebanese border. Named after Biblical city of Iron which was in tribal allotment of Naphtali. (The Biblical name also seems to have been preserved in some way in the name Yaroun of the Lebanese village just across the border.) Founded 1949 on abandoned village lands of Ṣalha, by a scout group which served in Palmaḥ Yiftaḥ brigade and fought in this region during War of Independence. Pop.: several hundred. Area: 5,000 d. Flint implements from Paleolithic Period were found within kibbutz.

• Yish'i *146:128*

Moshav 2 km. W of Bet Shemesh. Name taken from Biblical passage "The Lord is my light and my *salvation*" (Ps. 27:1). Founded 1950 by Yemenite immigrants. Area: 1,600 d. Pop.: 570.

Yishuv Isiyyi *189:115*

Remains of settlement, apparently belonging to Essene sect, from Second Temple Period on W shore of Dead Sea, 3 km. N of Mizpe Shalem junction. Excavations uncovered a large structure (20 by 45 m.) containing a hall, 2 independent rooms and another joining room bounded with large stones. Coins minted at the time of Herod, Archelaus and Herod Agrippa I were also found. Half a km. to the N, tombs were discovered which clearly resemble those found at Qumeran.

★ Yitav *190:150*

Kibbutz in Jordan Valley 10 km. NW of Jericho. Yitav is an acronym for Yad Yizḥak Tabenkin (1887-1971), a leader of Aḥdut Ha'Avoda party. Founded as Naḥal Na'aram outpost in 1970. Became a civilian settlement in 1976. Area: 100 d. **Statue to the "54"** One km. to the S is a concrete statue in form of the Hebrew letters "נד", to commemorate the 54 (נ"ד) killed here in 1977 in a helicopter crash during training.

◆ Yizre'am *105:095*

Seed farm in Negev 3 km. NW of Netivot junction. Founded 1954 by HaZera' Company.

★ Yizre'el *(Josh. 19:18) 180:218*

Kibbutz in Yizre'el Valley 6 km. SE of 'Afula. Same name as Biblical city of Jezreel, whose name was preserved in that of abandoned neighbouring village Zar'in. Founded 1948 by demobilized Palmaḥ soldiers. Area: 8,550 d. Pop.: 500. **Ancient Jezreel (Zar'in)** The abandoned village of Zar'in, *181:218*, is built on ruins of Biblical Jezreel, included in tribal allotment of Issachar. Saul camped here before his last battle with the Philistines and here too the incident at Naboth's vineyard involving Ahab, Naboth, Jezebel and the prophet Elijah took place (I Kings 21). Jezreel was destroyed by

Tiglath-pileser III, king of Assyria (722 BCE). It appears to have been reinhabited from the Hellenistic Period till the Middle Ages. (In 1170, the traveller, Benjamin of Tudela, found an impoverished settlement here with one Jewish family.) Finds include: a Roman burial cave, remains of a Byzantine church which was completed by the Crusaders. Sherds found from Iron Age and from Hellenistic Period to Middle Ages.

• **Yodefat** (II Kings 21:19) 175:249

Moshav shittufi in Galilee 13 km. SE of Aḥihud junction. Named after ancient city of Jotbah, ruins of which lie adjacent to the *moshav*. Founded 1960. Initially called Mizpe Yodefat. Pop.: 150. Area: 5,000 d. **Jotbah (Kh. Shifat, Kh. Jifat)** Site of ruins with tel, *176:248*, was location of Jotbah in First Temple Period. (Birthplace of mother of Amon of Judah.) Became known as Yodefat during Second Temple Period when it was fortified by Joseph b. Mattathias, commander of the Galilee during Jewish Revolt against Rome. City heroically withstood a Roman siege for 40 days but was finally taken and destroyed. Resettled during Roman and Byzantine Periods and was residence of priestly family of Miyamin. Sherds from Bronze Age and Early Iron Age. Remains found near tel of Roman buildings, walls, caves, pools and cisterns.

• **Yonatan** 224:260

Moshav shittufi on Golan Heights 7 km. SW of Tel Peres, alongside Tell Farj. Founded 1975 by *naḥal* group. **Ancient ruins** of settlement from Roman and Byzantine Periods include well-preserved buildings.

Yoqne'am (Josh. 12:22) 161:228

Rural settlement between Yizre'el Valley and Mt. Karmel. Named after ancient city of Jokneam identified with adjacent tel. Founded 1935 by German and Dutch immigrants. After War of Independence, an immigrant transit camp was set up in vicinity and later became a development town. (See Yoqne'am 'Illit.) Area: 8,000 d. Pop.: 520. **Tel Yoqne'am** At entrance to Naḥal Yoqne'am, *160:229*, is site of Jokneam — one of the 31 Canaanite cities vanquished by Joshua. Sherds and other remains from Bronze Age, Iron Age and from Byzantine Period to Middle Ages. Excavation finds include: storage jars, an ostracon with a 5 line Aramaic inscription from Persian Period, building remains, rock-cut tombs and pottery from Roman and Byzantine Periods, remains of a large camp from 7th and 8th c., 3 rows of walls from 8th and 9th c., remains of 12th c. Crusader church.

Yoqne'am 'Illit 160:229

Town between Yizre'el Valley and Mt. Karmel, alongside Yoqne'am. Formerly an immigrant transit camp (*ma'bara*) and later a development town. Since 1967 it has had an independent local council. Area: 14,000 d. Pop.: 4,400.

Yosef Bridge 208:287

Bridge over Jordan River in Ḥula Valley near kibbutz 'Amir. Named after 2 kibbutz members (both called Yosef) killed in War of Independence.

• **Yoshiveya** 113:094

Moshav in Negev 3 km. N of Netivot. Named after Josibiah, one of Simeon's descendants in whose tribal allotment this area was included (I Chron. 4:35). Founded 1950 by immigrants from Morocco and Algeria on abandoned village lands of Muḥarraqa. Area: 5,200 d. Pop.: 280.

★ **Yotvata** *(Deut. 10:7) 155:923*

Kibbutz and wildlife reserve in 'Arava 40 km. N of Elat. Named after ancient Jotbathah "and from Gudgodah to Jotbathah, a land with brooks of water" (Deut. 10:7). Founded as a *naḥal* outpost in 1951; became a civilian settlement in 1957. Area: 2,300 d. Pop.: several hundred. **'En Yotvata** *(154:921)* One of largest water sources of the 'Arava. Nearby are ancient settlement ruins and a way-station. Remains of Bronze Age fort, Roman fortress and temple to the goddess Diana. Arabic name is 'Ein Ghadyan, apparently named after an 'Arava plant which in Arabic is called Ghada (*haloxylon persicum*). Mentioned in 13th c. travel books. During British Mandate there was a police post here. The spring waters are also channelled to Elat. **Hay Bar nature reserve** S of 'En Yotvata, *154:918*, is the Ḥay Bar nature reserve (*ḥay bar* meaning wildlife). Established in the 1960's to protect reed and acacia trees indigenous to area. Antelope, deer, ostriches and other animals mentioned in the Bible — all almost extinct in this region — were brought here to breed in their natural habitat.

● **Yuval** *206:294*

Moshav in Galilee 4 km. NE of Qiryat Shemona adjacent to Lebanese border. (*Yuval* = tributary: many of the Jordan's tributaries are near here.) Founded 1952. Area: 2,200 d. Pop.: several hundred.

Z

o (Ez) Zababida *180:199*

Arab village in Samarian Hills 8 km. NE of Jenin. Pop.: 1,600, mostly Christian. (This is the only Christian village in N Samarian Hills.) Remains of Crusader structure called el Baubariyya (meaning bullpen).

• Ẓafririm *145:118*

Moshav in ʻAdullam region, 3 km. S of HaEla junction. Name means morning winds. Founded 1958. Area: 2,300 d. Pop.: 230.

• Ẓafriyya *136:156*

Moshav 4 km. W of Ben-Gurion Airport. Named after abandoned village, Safiriyya, site of Seforya of Byzantine Period. Founded 1949. Area: 2,300 d. Pop.: 360.

Zahrat el Miqtaḥ *173:106*

Ruins of structures in Judean Desert, 13 km. E of Hebron consisting of rectangular buildings, a cistern and a round structure. Sherds indicate occupation in Iron Age and Roman Period.

Zahr er Rujum *155:177*

Square two-storey structure in Samarian Hills 9 km. E of Qalqilya. Built of large dressed stones with 2 standing doorposts. Believed to have been a mausoleum. Nearby are similar ruins.

o Zalafa *167:217*

Arab village 3 km. S of Megiddo junction. Established more than 300 years ago. Pop.: 1,200. Fierce battles were fought in vicinity during War of Independence. Ruins of Roman–Byzantine settlement where sherds, glass fragments and mosaic stones were found.

• Zanoaḥ *(Josh. 15:34) 150:126*

Moshav 3 km. S of Bet Shemesh. Named after Biblical city which has been identified at adjacent Kh. Zanuʻ. Founded 1950. Pop.: 400. **Ancient Zanoah (Kh. Zanuʻ)** S of *moshav* are ruins of ancient settlement which spread over 2 hills. Believed to be site of Zanoah mentioned in Tell el ʻAmarna letters. At the time of the Israelite conquest it fell within the tribal allotment of Judah. In Second Temple Period it was reinhabited (Neh. 3:13) and was renowned for its choice semolina. On one of the hills are remains of structures, cisterns and sherds indicating a flourishing settlement in Iron Age. Sherds found on the second hill from Roman, Byzantine and Arab Periods. To the E is Naḥal HaMeʻara with Meʻarat HaTeʼomim.

• Zarʻit *177:278*

Moshav in Galilee close to Lebanese border. *Zarʻit* means a lark. Name symbolic. Founded 1967. Pop.: several hundred. **Hurbat Zarʻit (Kh. el Mazraʻa)** Within *moshav* are remains of an ancient settlement from Roman and Arab Periods.

Zarnuqa *130:143*

Neighbourhood of Reḥovot. Founded 1948 on abandoned village lands of Zarnuga. A town by the name of Zarnuqi is mentioned in the Talmud.

Zarzir *171:237*

Permanent Bedouin settlement in Yizre'el Valley 9 km. NW of Nazareth. Situated on a hill alongside Ḥurbat Zarzir.

Za'tara *174:120*

Bedouin village and centre of Ta'amre tribe on outskirts of Judean Desert, near Herodium. Name originates from the *za'tar* (thyme) plant. Pop.: 1,300.

Za'ura *216:291*

Abandoned village on Golan Heights 5 km. S of Birkat Ram. Heavy battles raged here during the Six-Day War as the Israeli Defence Force assault route passed by here. Memorial to Major Ami Levtov killed in the fighting.

Zavdi'el *127:118*

Moshav 5 km. NW of Qiryat Gat. Name derives from a passage in Nehemiah (11:14) and means gift of God. Founded 1950 by Yemenite immigrants on lands of abandoned village of Juseir. Area: 3,000 d. Pop.: 450.

Zawata *171:183*

Arab village in Samarian Hills 5 km. NW of Shekhem. Believed to be site of Aza, a city in Kingdom of Israel named on an ostraca found in ruins of adjacent Samaria. Pop.: 600.

Zawiya *154:167*

Arab village in Samarian Hills 8 km. E of Rosh Ha'Ayin. Pop.: 1,300.

(Ez) Zawiya *172:198*

Arab village in Samarian Hills 10 km. SW of Jenin. Pop.: 250. On summit of adjacent hill is a sheikh's tomb and look-out point over surrounding area.

Ẓe'elim *105:068*

Kibbutz in Negev 12 km. SE of Magen junction. *Ẓe'el* is Hebrew for acacia, and the name refers to the many acacia trees in the vicinity. Founded 1947 by youth movement members who later moved to the village of HaḤoresh. In 1949 settled by Holocaust survivors from E Europe. Served as military base during War of Independence. Area: 29,000 d. Pop.: 310.

Zeita *155:199*

Arab village in W Samarian Hills alongside kibbutz Maggal. Pop.: 1,100.

Zeita *167:171*

Arab village in Samarian Hills 12 km. SW of Shekhem, near Jamma'in. Pop.: 600.

Zekharya *144:124*

Moshav off Bet Shemesh–Bet Guvrin road, on fringe of 'Emeq HaEla. Same name as that of abandoned village of Zakariyya. Founded 1950 by Iraqi immigrants. Area: 1,500 d. Pop.: 600. Within village are ancient remains from different periods. A settlement called Bet Zekharya appears in same location on Madaba map.

Ẓelafon *143:134*

Moshav in Judean Foothills 2 km. SE of Naḥshon junction. Named after caper bushes that abound in the region. Founded 1950 by Yemenite immigrants. Area: 2,000 d. Pop.: 560. **Rujm Gizo** Within *moshav* are settlement ruins which, according to sherds, was inhabited in Iron Age and Byzantine Period.

Ẓemaḥ *205:235*

Regional centre at S end of Lake Kinneret, at junction of roads from Jordan Valley, Tiberias and Golan Heights. Named after ancient Ẓemaḥ whose name was retained in that of the abandoned village, Samakh. Regional industrial complex, sports centre and stadium, and memorial to soldiers who died in War of Independence. The town of Ẓemaḥ is mentioned in Talmud as gentile city within boundaries of Susita with a Jewish community. In recent times it was repopulated by Arab immigrants from Morocco (in 19th c.). After the Haifa–Damascus railway line was built in 1905 it became an important junction. Because of its strategic location, it was the scene of heavy fighting between Turks and British during WWI. It became a border and police post during British Mandate. During War of Independence it was taken by the Israel Defence Forces' Golani Brigade, who lost it for a time to the invading Syrian forces.

Zemorot *119:125*

Farm of viticulture and orchards NE of Ashqelon. Founded 1955 by the South American Company for settlement and industry.

Zeraḥya *126:121*

Moshav in Lakhish region 10 km. N of Qiryat Gat. Named after one of descendants of Phinehas, son of Eleazar the priest. Founded 1950 by immigrants from Persia and Morocco. Area: 3,000 d. Pop.: 550.

Ẓerifin *136:151*

Large army camp on Coastal Plain 3 km. NE of Ramla. Named after a Second Temple Period Jewish city which became a Christian city during Byzantine Period. At end of 8th c. it was an Arab village called Ṣarafand el 'Amar (not to be confused with adjacent Ṣarafand el Kharab). During WWI it served as the central British army base for campaigns in the N and E. Volunteers of the Jewish Legion camped here, and it was the Judean Regiment from Ẓerifin that went to the aid of Jaffa Jews attacked by Arab gangs in 1921. During WWII it was a central British army training camp for the Middle East. Upon termination of Mandate it was handed over to the Arabs, but then captured by the Israel Defence Forces. Today too, it is still an army camp. Located at outskirts of the camp are the Asaf HaRofe government hospital, orchards of the Ministry of Agriculture and Jewish Agency stores. Within the camp are remains of Byzantine buildings and tombs.

Zeru'a *114:096*

Moshav in Negev off Sederot–Netivot road. Name derives from Biblical passage "...how you followed me in the wilderness, on a land not *sown*" (Jer. 2:2). Founded 1953 by Moroccan immigrants. Area: 5,000 d. Pop.: 300.

Ẓerufa *145:228*

Moshav on Karmel coast 6 km. S of 'Atlit. Name based on that of abandoned village, Ṣarafand. Founded 1949 by 80 immigrant families from Biskra, Algeria who first settled at 'En Hod. Area: 1,700 d. Pop.: 470.

Zetan *139:153*

Moshav in Judean Foothills 4 km. N of Lod. Area abundant in olive trees (*zetim* = olives). The name is also that of a Benjaminite of the sons of Bilhan (I Chron. 7:10). Founded 1950 by immigrants from Tripolitania and Morocco. Pop.: 500.

Zibda *162:206*

Arab village in Samarian Hills 16 km. W of Jenin. The area is particularly fertile and this is probably the origin of the name, which means butter. Pop.: 500.

Zikhron Ya'aqov *145:220*

Town (with local council) on S reach of Mt. Karmel. Named after Jacob (James), father of Baron Edmond de Rothschild. Founded as a farming village (*moshava*) in 1882 by immigrants from Rumania and first called Zammarin after the adjacent Arab village. The village struggled unsuccessfully for 2 years before coming under the patronage of Baron de Rothschild, who introduced viticulture and built a large wine cellar. Area: 32,000 d. Pop.: 5,000. Zikhron Ya'aqov played a major role in the history of Jewish settlement in the country. In 1902 it hosted a convention of Jewish settlers at which an attempt was made to establish an umbrella organization for the Jews of Palestine. During WWI it was the centre of the Nili spy ring, led by Aaron and Sarah Aaronsohn, residents of Zikhron Ya'aqov. Sites of interest: Bet Aaronsohn — a botanical museum and library with documents concerning the Nili spy ring; Gan Mikha'el — spring and surrounding park off road to Arab village Fureidis, named after Mikha'el Tashabi, local resident who fell in Six-Day War; Bet Remez rest house; Bet Daniel; Ramat HaNadiv — large public park containing mausoleum of Baron Edmond de Rothschild and his wife.

• **Zimrat** *107:096*

Moshav in Negev off Netivot–Sa'ad road. Name taken from Biblical passage "The Lord is my strength and my *song*, and he has become my salvation" (Ex. 15:2). Founded 1957 by Tunisian immigrants. Area: 4,500 d. Pop.: 450.

• **Ẓippori (Sepphoris)** *176:239*

Moshav 4 km. NW of Nazareth near a Crusader fortress atop a hill commanding a fine view of the region. Same name as ancient city of Zippori, distorted in name of abandoned Arab village, Ṣaffuriyya, N of *moshav*. Founded 1949. Area: 2,400 d. Pop.: 180. **History** First mentioned in connection with war fought nearby by Alexander Yannai (103 BCE). In the days of Gabinius it was the centre of the Galilee and seat of a small Sanhedrin. According to Christian tradition it is the birthplace of the Virgin Mary's mother, Anne. It was the heartland of a revolt that erupted after the death of Herod and as a result it was destroyed by Varus. Rebuilt by Herod Antipas who made it his capital; remained capital of the Galilee during reign of Agrippa II. Because its inhabitants did not participate in Jewish Revolt against Rome (66 CE) it was saved from Roman attack. After destruction of Second Temple many Jews from Jerusalem settled here; it was the residence of the Jedaiah priestly clan. Vespasian set up a garrison in the city and Hadrian changed its name to Diocaesarea. Rabbi Judah HaNasi moved the Sanhedrin from Bet She'arim to Ẓippori and resided here for 17 years, where he completed the editing of the Mishnah. He died and was buried here. In 351 it was centre of a revolt against Constantine, who tried to impose Christianity through the apostate Joseph of Tiberias. The revolt was suppressed by Gallus. In 6th c. it was a Christian city, but after Arab conquest Jews returned to live here and during this time it was called Tirẓa. The Crusader Le Sephorie was headquarters for their battles in the Galilee. Christian knights built a large fortress within the city. There is no evidence of a Jewish community here at this time. In 18th c. Dahir el 'Amr made it his administrative capital. During War of Independence the Arab village was used by Arab forces until it was captured in operation "Deqel" (July 1948). **Excavations and finds** In and around abandoned village ruins of Crusader fortress on Roman foundations (rebuilt in days of Dahir el 'Amr), remains of two synagogues, a theatre and water system (which includes aqueducts, reservoirs and a tunnel) from Roman Period, and burial caves.

★ **Ziqim** *104:113*

Kibbutz 8 km. S of Ashqelon. Founded 1949. Area: 8,000 d. Pop.: 250. To the S is Shiqma dam.

Ẓiv'on *189:270*

Observation site in Upper Galilee on Har Qal'an 2 km. E of Ḥiram junction. Established 1980. Named after nearby stream.

● **Ẓofar** *166:989*

Moshav in 'Arava 20 km. S of 'En Yahav. Named after nearby Naḥal Ẓofar. Founded as *naḥal* outpost in 1968; became a civilian settlement in 1975.

● **Ẓofit** *142:178*

Moshav in Sharon 2 km. N of Kefar Sava. Name means a hill overlooking its surroundings. Founded 1933, it expanded after War of Independence. Area: 2,300 d. Pop.: 360.

■ **Ẓofiyya** *125:140*

Institution, refuge for girls, on Coastal Plain 2 km. SW of Yavne. Founded 1955. Administered by Ministry of Social Welfare.

● **Zohar** *121:111*

Moshav in Lakhish region 8 km. SW of Qiryat Gat. Founded 1956 by immigrants from Tunisia and Algeria. Pop.: 300. Nearby is Zohar reservoir.

Ẓoḥar *095:072*

District centre in Besor region servicing settlements of Ohad, Talme Eliyyahu, Sede Niẓẓan, Mivtaḥim, 'Ami'oz and Yesha'. Founded 1973.

★ **Ẓor'a** *(Josh. 19:41) 147:130*

Kibbutz 2 km. NW of Bet Shemesh. Named after Biblical city of Zorah, identified at adjacent Tell Ṣor'a. Established 1948 by Palmaḥ veterans. At first located in abandoned village of Ṣar'a, alongside Tell Ṣor'a. Later joined by HaBonim youth movement groups from S Africa and other English-speaking countries. Area: 8,850 d. Pop.: 630. **Antiquities** Close by, near a spring, *147:130*, is a tel with remains of structures and sherds from Iron Age, Roman and Byzantine Periods. To the SW are 2 mounds where Chalcolithic flint tools and sherds were found. **Tell Ṣor'a** *(148:131)* To the NE is site of Canaanite city mentioned in Tell el 'Amarna letters. At the time of the Israelite conquest it was included within tribal allotment of Dan. Birthplace of Samson (Judg. 13:2). Reoccupied after Babylonian Exile, and once again in Byzantine Period. Alongside tel, on way to Bet Shemesh, is a stone altar known as Manoah's Altar (see Judg. 13:19). In vicinity of village are caves, cisterns, wine presses and tombstones, and a sheikh's tomb which according to Arab tradition is tomb of Samson.

★ **Ẓova** *(II Sam. 23:36) 161:132*

Kibbutz 6 km. W of Jerusalem. Named after the Biblical town of Zobah, a name retained in that of abandoned village of Ẓuba, NE of kibbutz. Founded 1948 by Palmaḥ veterans (of the Har'el Brigade) who fought in the area. Area: 3,500 d. Pop.: 450. Memorial to Palmaḥ war dead. **Ẓuba** NE of kibbutz, on hill summit, are ruins of abandoned village of Ẓuba. Site of Biblical city of Zobah, birthplace of one of King David's mighty men. Crusaders built Belmont fortress here to guard road to Jerusalem. Taken by Saladin in 1187 and partially destroyed in 1191. In 1834 it was used as a hideout by Abu Ghosh and his followers, who rebelled against Egyptian rule. Ibrahim Pasha, ruler of Egypt, captured the town and destroyed the fortress. During 1936-1939 Disturbances the British Mandatory authorities built a small fort here to guard the road. During

War of Independence the village was used as a base by Arab forces who attempted to block road to Jerusalem, until it was taken by the Israel Defence Forces. Within abandoned village are remains of a wall, glacis and gate from the Crusader fortress, wine cellars, cisterns, caves and tombs — some from Roman and Byzantine Periods. On a slope N of the village is a rock platform, with rock-cuttings — apparently used for either agricultural or cultic purposes.

o **Zububa** 171:216

Arab village in Yizre'el Valley 4 km. SE of Megiddo junction. Mentioned in writings of a 13th c. Egyptian traveller. Perhaps the name retains traces of Ba'al Zevuv. Pop.: 650.

Ẓur Hadassah *159:125*

District centre in Judean Hills 10 km. SW of Jerusalem. Named after the Hadassah organization. Pop.: 120.

• **Ẓuri'el** *179:268*

Moshav in Galilee 3 km. E of Ma'alot–Tarshiḥa. Named after Zuriel, son of Abihail (Num. 3:35). Founded 1950 by Moroccan immigrants. Area: 5,000 d.

Ẓurit *174:256*

Community settlement in Lower Galilee 5 km. SW of Karmi'el. Named after sedum plant which flourishes in area. Established 1980.

• **Ẓur Moshe** *142:189*

Moshav 3 km. SE of Sharon junction. Named after Greek Zionist leader, Moshe Kophinas. Founded 1937 as a "stockade and tower" settlement. Area: 2,600 d. Pop.: 440.

• **Ẓur Natan** *151:182*

Moshav shittufi between Sharon and Samarian Hills 8 km. S of Tulkarm. Named after Nathan Simeons, Canadian philanthropist. Founded as *naḥal* outpost in 1966; civilian status — 1967. Area: 6,350 d. Pop.: 150. **Ḥurbat Dardar** SE of *moshav* are remains of Crusader fortress, cisterns and wine presses.